The Importance of Constitutional Rules and Property Rights

Polish Studies in Economics

Edited by Ryszard Kokoszczyński

Volume 13

PETER LANG

Damian Bębnowski

The Importance of Constitutional Rules and Property Rights

The German Economy in 1990–2015

PETER LANG

Bibliographic Information published by the Deutsche Nationalbibliothek
The Deutsche Nationalbibliothek lists this publication in the Deutsche Nationalbibliografie; detailed bibliographic data is available in the internet at http://dnb.d-nb.de.

Library of Congress Cataloging-in-Publication Data
A CIP catalog record for this book has been applied for at the Library of Congress.

This publication was financially supported by the University of Lodz, Poland.

ISSN 2191-8848
ISBN 978-3-631-87753-1 (Print)
E-ISBN 978-3-631-89015-8 (E-PDF)
E-ISBN 978-3-631-89065-3 (EPUB)
DOI 10.3726/b20221

Peter Lang – Berlin · Bern · Bruxelles · New York ·
Oxford · Warszawa · Wien

This publication has been peer reviewed.

www.peterlang.com

Our studies … were propelled by our common hunger for knowledge. / I wandered through this park [at Fürstenried Palace in Munich] over and over again, immersed in all sorts of thoughts. This is where the decisions of those years took shape, and also where I tried to think through and appropriate all of the knowledge imparted to us during the lectures. / … [I drew] on these perspectives.

Cardinal Joseph Ratzinger on his studies and work on his doctorate

TABLE OF CONTENTS

INTRODUCTION

Purpose of the book, reasoning for the topic, chronological framework

The aim of the monograph is to identify, characterize and evaluate the importance of selected formal institutions for the German economy in 1990–2015. The objects of study are: the Basic Law of the Federal Republic of Germany (FRG), i.e. constitutional rules and property rights (property rules). The study deliberately omits the constitutions of the German states[1] and the issue of intellectual property rights, limiting the consideration to the physical (material) aspect of property rights.[2]

An institutional perspective is still a promising approach in economics and other social sciences, including economic history. The gradual penetration of this approach into the mainstream in economics was formerly evidenced primarily by awarding the Nobel Prize in Economic Sciences to institutionalists (Gunnar Myrdal, James M. Buchanan, Ronald H. Coase, Douglass C. North, Oliver Williamson, Elinor Ostrom). In the context of economic history, it should be noted that nowadays, the institutional perspective is an attractive theoretical and methodological alternative to the paradigms[3] dominating in the 20th and 21st centuries, i.e.: historical materialism, the French "Annales" school and the New Economic History (American cliometrics).

Institutional economics has challenged the existing way of studying economic reality, characteristic of orthodox (neoclassical) economics, which is based primarily on the assumption of the decisions' rationality made by individuals and the resulting static perception of economic processes. As an alternative, institutional economics proposes to consider account the complexity and multifaceted nature of the reality under study, e.g. by using descriptive and historical methods in economic research. This work is intended as an attempt to recognize this problem and undertake theoretical and empirical research in setting the theory of institutional economics in a specific space-time, i.e. the German economy in 1990–2015. Thus, it is an economic history study embedded in the theoretical perspective of institutional economics.

---

1 See a representative study of this type: M. Domagała, *Pozycja konstytucyjnoprawna kraju w systemie federalnym RFN na przykładzie Hesji* (Łódź: Wydawnictwo UŁ, 1990).

2 Cf. W. Kasper, M. E. Streit, P. J. Boettke, *Institutional Economics: Property, Competition, Policies* (Cheltenham–Northampton: Edward Elgar, 2012), 202.

3 The term paradigm should be understood – following Thomas S. Kuhn – as a set of model research problems recognized in science, as well as theories, laws, methods, and scientific techniques used to solve them (cf. T. S. Kuhn, *Struktura rewolucji naukowych* (Warszawa: Fundacja Aletheia, 2001), 10, 32–33).

Despite its critical voices, the institutional approach continues to be recognized by theoretical and methodological economists and practitioners of this discipline. A significant interest in this trend can also be seen in other social sciences, e.g.: sociology, political science, law, and history. Therefore, research on institutions is often interdisciplinary in nature, which accounts for its high cognitive value.

The institutional perspective should still be regarded – at least to some extent – as avant-garde and dynamic. A dozen years ago, the differences in defining institutions indicated that the paradigm was still developing and conceptualizing.

Polish economics is dominated by theoretical and methodological studies on institutional economics. There are even comprehensive approaches in the form of handbooks or introductions to the concept.[4] Empirical studies that set this approach in practice, e.g. through *case studies*, are less numerous. The situation is even worse in the field of economic history.

The year 2015 marked a quarter century since German reunification. This presented a unique opportunity to take stock of the German economy's transformation and its co-shaping institutions. The German model of capitalism is based on an economic system, namely the social market economy. In turn, the doctrine of ordoliberalism is its theoretical basis. This concept distinguishes between the economic process and the economic order created by the legal and institutional framework. The state does not interfere directly in the economic process, which takes place within the economic order. It only shapes this order by creating laws and institutions. Thus, it turns out that there is a parallel between ordoliberalism and institutional economics. Institutions – the central concept of the last direction – are historically shaped frameworks in which societies function and political, economic, social, and cultural processes take place.

The choice of the Basic Law and property rights in Germany as the object of study is due to the fact that these institutions form the core of the formal rules' catalog. Moreover, they exhibit a strong relationship with each other. Constitutional rules set the legal and institutional framework for a country's economic system. Property rights are among them. In turn, they are often mainly anchored in constitutions and constitute one of the essential elements of the institutional architecture of the national economy. Therefore, they are among the most frequently studied rules in the field of institutional economics. It should be noted that the criticism of property rights, functioning in a centrally planned economy model,

4 See especially: W. Stankiewicz, *Ekonomika instytucjonalna. Zarys wykładu* (Warszawa: Wydawnictwo AON, 2014); J. Wilkin, *Instytucjonalne i kulturowe podstawy gospodarowania. Humanistyczna perspektywa ekonomii* (Warszawa: WN Scholar, 2016); Z. Staniek, *Ekonomia instytucjonalna. Dlaczego instytucje są ważne* (Warszawa: Wydawnictwo Difin, 2017); B. Borkowska, M. Klimczak, B. Klimczak, *Ekonomia instytucjonalna* (Wrocław: Wydawnictwo UE we Wrocławiu, 2019); K. Bentkowska, *Ekonomia instytucjonalna. Zarys teorii i jej wymiar praktyczny* (Warszawa: Oficyna Wydawnicza SGH, 2020).

was one of the main assumptions of all transition programs in the former Eastern Bloc countries. This was the case, e.g., in the German Democratic Republic (GDR). The new constitutions adopted in these countries or amendments to the existing basic laws played an important role in this regard.[5] Germany in 1990–2015 was an example of a highly developed country where the constitutional guarantee of property rights promoted economic efficiency by creating stable structures of human interaction.[6] The mutual relationship between constitutional and property rules resounds throughout the different parts of this work.

Over the last decades, studies have appeared, mainly English and German language ones, which treat the subject matter.[7] It turns out, however, that they emphasize other issues and do not take into account many of the detailed themes of this book, focus on the influence of selected aspects of the FRG Constitution on the economy, analyze shorter chronological periods, do not organically combine institutions of the Basic Law of the FRG and property rights or the considerations included in them are made from different theoretical and methodological positions than those used in the present economic history study. As a result, this work is

---

5 Cf. K. Metelska-Szaniawska, *Konstytucyjne czynniki reform gospodarczych w krajach postsocjalistycznych. Studium empiryczne* (Warszawa: Wydawnictwa UW, 2008). She omitted the analysis of the former GDR.

6 Cf. M. Zalesko, "Prawa własności filarem rozwoju gospodarczego," *Ekonomia* No. 4 (25) (2013): 92–102.

7 See especially: J. Schumann, ed., *Die Bedeutung der Eigentumsordnung für das Funktionieren einer Volkswirtschaft* (Bad Honnef: Bock und Herchen Verlag, 1991); P. J. Tettinger, "Öffentliche und private Wirtschaft in den neuen Bundesländern," in *Deutsche Wiedervereinigung. Die Rechtseinheit. Arbeitskreis Staats- und Verfassungsrecht*, Vol. II: *Zur Wiederherstellung der inneren Einheit*, Part 2: *Rundfunkrecht – Stasi-Akten – Wiedergutmachung – Öffentliche und Private Wirtschaft*, ed. K. Stern (Köln: Carl Heymanns Verlag KG, 1992), 149–166; J. Heslop, J. Roberto, "Property Rights in the Unified Germany: A Constitutional, Comparative, and International Legal Analysis," *Boston University International Law Journal* 11, No. 2 (1993): 243–298; P. E. Quint, *The Imperfect Union. Constitutional Structures of German Unification* (Princeton: Princeton University Press, 1997); S. Spangenberg, *The Institutionalised Transformation of the East German Economy* (Heidelberg–New York: Physica-Verlag. A Springer-Verlag Company, 1998); H. Brücker, *Privatization in Eastern Germany: A Neo-Institutional Analysis* (London: Frank Cass, German Development Institute, 2005); H.-B. Schäfer, C. Ott, *Lehrbuch der ökonomischen Analyse des Zivilrechts* (Berlin: Springer, 2005), chapters on property rights; Metelska-Szaniawska, *Konstytucyjne czynniki reform gospodarczych*; F. Baur, J. F. Baur, R. Stürner, *Sachenrecht* (München: Verlag C. H. Beck, 2009), 887–910; J. Busche, "Die Privatisierung der volkseigenen Unternehmen der ehemaligen DDR. Der rechtliche und wirtschaftliche Umbruch im Zuge der Wiedervereinigung," in *Staat und Recht in Teilung und Einheit*, eds. J. Krüper, H. Sauer (Tübingen: Mohr Siebeck, 2011), 127–141; J. Schneider, *Einigkeit, Recht und Freiheit. 25 Jahre deutsche Wiedervereinigung (1990–2015). Eine ordnungstheoretische Analyse* (Stuttgart: Franz Steiner Verlag, 2017).

complementary and broadening in relation to such monographs and offers an economic historian's perspective on constitutional and property rules as a whole, as well as shows the channels of relations between them and selected segments of the economy.

The chronological framework of the work covers the years 1990–2015. The opening point of the consideration is the reunification of Germany in 1990. From the economic history point of view, new circumstances occurred then, as well as the systemic transition of the former GDR, and the unification, integration, and convergence of two parts of the country became the challenge. In the light of ordoliberal economics, this date could be referred to as a "historical moment." Following Walter Eucken's proposal, the constitutive principles of economic order (institutions), which had previously been in force only in the FRG. They were extended to new federated states at the moment of German reunification, which created utterly new conditions for their functioning.[8] Therefore, it is not legitimate to speak about continuity in the context of the functioning of the analyzed formal institutions in the FRG and their significance for the economy before 1990 and after that.

The literature offers a variety of publications on the balance sheet of reunification in political, economic, social, and cultural terms. The book adds to these works the problem of the relevance of constitutional rules and property rights for the German economy between 1990 and 2015. References to later years are not made. Firstly, not all source materials were complete when the research was conducted (especially statistical data). Secondly, this kind of treatment would have made the analysis inconsistent. Thirdly, the year of closure marked – according to some researchers – a new period of the German economy's evolution. Although no revolutionary changes in constitutional and property rules were made at that time, in 2015, the German economy entered a phase of confronting challenges arising largely from the immigration crisis, perturbations in the Eurozone, or changes in the general trends of the global economy.[9]

---

8 Cf. P. Pysz, A. Jurczuk, M. Moszyński, "Ordoliberalizm a dynamika społeczno-gospodarcza," *Optimum. Economic Studies* No. 2 (96) (2019): 10.

9 See, e.g.: M. Moszyński, "Ordoliberalism and the Macroeconomic Policy in the Face of the Euro Crisis," *Equilibrium: Quarterly Journal of Economics and Economic Policy* 10, No. 4 (2015): 41–58; M. Moszyński, "Ordoliberalizm a dylematy współczesnej polityki makroekonomicznej," *Biuletyn Polskiego Towarzystwa Ekonomicznego* No. 2 (81) (2018): 45–55; M. Dahl, "Europejski kryzys imigracyjny i jego konsekwencje dla Republiki Federalnej Niemiec – aspekty polityczne, społeczne i gospodarcze," *Studia Polityczne* No. 4 (44) (2016): 241–262; M. Dahl, "Wpływ europejskiego kryzysu imigracyjnego na procesy dezintegracyjne w Unii Europejskiej," *Roczniki Nauk Społecznych* 10 (46), No. 3 (2018): 33–44. Cf. R. Matera, J. Skodlarski, *Gospodarka światowa. Geneza i ewolucja do czasów pandemii* (Warszawa: WN PWN, 2021), 358–384, 403–427. An additional consideration remains that work on the original version of the monograph was completed during the coronavirus pandemic in 2020 and the initial phase of the resulting economic crisis.

The analysis of the institutions of the Basic Law of the FRG and property rights over the course of 25 years is thus part of the "second level" of social analysis by Olivier E. Williamson. It concerns research into the "institutional environment," especially property rights and "positive political theory." Within this level, Williamson additionally indicates the "first-order economizing," i.e. the creation of proper formal institutions by adequate state bodies.[10]

A study of German economic history covering only the last 25 years may be accused of looking too shallowly into the past. However, the quarter-century of economic transition in Germany after reunification deserves a thorough analysis of the course and effects of changes combined with a critical assessment. At the same time, one should be aware of the fact that formal institutions such as the Constitution and property rights are rules that emerged in West Germany already after World War II. The incorporation of the Eastern *Länder* into the FRG in 1990, so far concentrated in the GDR, created new circumstances and conditions for the economic development of the entire unified state. In 2016, Werner Plumpe convincingly stated: "The economic history of Germany following reunification has yet to be written, although numerous drafts exist already and the chorus of contemporaries who have felt called on to pass economic judgment since the early 1990s is almost uncountable."[11] Moreover, the practice of contemporary history helps to understand the present better and, on that basis, to formulate responsible predictions. Thus, the study of economic processes and phenomena after 1989 from an economic history perspective is fully justified.

Main hypothesis and research questions

A detailed study of the source material and the literature enabled the formulation of the main hypothesis and research questions. The main research hypothesis of the work is: *Formal institutions, such as the Basic Law of the FRG and property rights, played a fundamental role in the economic transition in Germany in 1990–2015, setting the frameworks for the process of economic transition of the new federated states and economic unification of the country.*

The following (specific) research questions, corresponding to the themes of subsequent chapters of the work, served to verify the main hypothesis: (1) What theoretical understandings of the category of institutions are found in the social sciences, especially economics and economic history, and how does this result in research on economic transformations? (Chap. 1); (2) What kinds of macroeconomic differences existed in the economic structures of the FRG and the GDR just before German reunification? (Chap. 2); (3) What was the role of the Basic Law

10 O. E. Williamson, "The New Institutional Economics: Taking Stock, Looking Ahead," *Journal of Economic Literature* 38, No. 3 (2000): 597–599.

11 W. Plumpe, *German Economic and Business History in the 19th and 20th Centuries* (London: Palgrave Macmillan, 2016), 276.

of the FRG in the context of the integration of two different economic systems after the GDR joined the FRG? (Chaps. 3–4); (4) To what extent did West German property rights contribute to economic transformations in the former GDR? (Chaps. 5–6).

Previous studies have often dealt with these issues in insufficient detail or in a manner reduced to an economic or legal perspective. Therefore, combining the perspectives of history, economics, law, and other studies, the proposed economic history approach can provide a fresh perspective on seemingly familiar issues, appropriately broadening and deepening the cognitive spectrum.

Sources and literature

The source base of this work consists primarily of normative acts and statistical materials. The first group of documents comes mainly from the resources of the Bundestag and the Federal Ministry of Justice and Consumer Protection of the FRG (the official gazette *Bundesgesetzblatt*), as well as the Council of Ministers of the GDR (the official gazette *Gesetzblatt der Deutschen Demokratischen Republik*). Statistical sources consist especially of materials from the Federal Ministry of Finance, the Federal Ministry of Economic Affairs and Energy, the Federal Ministry of the Interior, the Federal Government Commissioner for the New Federated States, the Federal Statistical Office (FRG), the State Central Administration for Statistics (GDR), as well as source editions, Internet databases, reports of social and economic organizations. The Polish press was complementary.

In the case of normative acts, documents from 1990–2015 were considered the main object of research: constitutions and specific laws with the most important amendments. Regulations, announcements, and corrigenda were also analyzed. In addition, among others, the documentation of the European Union (EU) was used. In justified situations, in order to outline the necessary historical background, reminiscences to the period before 1990 were made, most often to the years 1949–1990, less frequently to the interwar period or the 19th century. It was based on the original versions of each normative act, making most often an addition to the subsequent changes in their content, sometimes limited to the most important or exemplary amendments.

The queries were limited in two ways during the research on normative documents. Firstly, the detailed origins of individual acts and legislative processes were not analyzed. The focus was on the actual state of affairs by examining the final acts of statute law (Latin: *ius civile*). Secondly, the jurisprudence (especially of the Federal Constitutional Court) was deliberately ignored.[12] This represents the most commonly used perspective in the research workshop of (economic)

12 However, this is not a typical approach of legal positivism, which focuses on the analysis of existing legal norms, ignoring their social context (R. Tokarczyk, *Komparatystyka prawnicza* (Warszawa: Wolters Kluwer Polska, 2008), 46).

historians and economists.[13] The analysis of the above group of sources is thus based on the reading of the letter of the law, i.e. the applicable legal rules (norms), and the search for their significance for economic life. This dimension alone, without taking into account the additional one of legal culture, makes it possible to grasp such networks of relationships. In the institutional approach, the study of the statute law (in the form of the constitution, property rules, and legislation related to both institutions) concerns the *de jure* dimension (formal, normative, postulative) of the studied institutions. At the same time, their functioning in the practice of economic life refers to the *de facto* dimension (actual, positive, real).

In terms of statistical material, several observations need to be made. In some places in the study – where necessary – they were indicated. Firstly, it was a major problem during the research to reach complete data for the entire 25-year period. Secondly, data for reunified Germany have been available since 1991. Thirdly, since 2014, the fundamental macroeconomic values for Germany for the period since 1991 have been calculated according to the European System of Accounts (*Europäisches System Volkswirtschaftlicher Gesamtrechnungen*, ESVG 2010).[14] This methodological standard thus covered data for the whole period analyzed in this work. However, it does not always allow for a full comparison of statistical information for 1990–2015 with the earlier period, i.e. the division of Germany into the FRG and the GDR. Fourthly, there are only estimates in some marked cases. Fifthly, data discrepancies can be found in certain materials. This concerns, among

13 Cf. notes on sources in economic history research: L. Beutin, *Einführung in die Wirtschaftsgeschichte* (Köln–Graz: Böhlau Verlag, 1958), 10–49; L. Beutin, H. Kellenbenz, *Grundlagen des Studiums der Wirtschaftsgeschichte* (Köln–Wien: Böhlau Verlag, 1973), 8–50; J. Szpak, *Historia gospodarcza powszechna*, (Warszawa: PWE, 2007), 38–39. One should be aware, however, that this approach differs in many places – though not always – from the methodology of research on (history of) law, including constitutional law. In the latter, the analysis of jurisprudence plays a key role, complementing the study of statute law. The legal academic literature is focused on jurisprudence. For example, Rolf Grawert claims that the case law of the Federal Constitutional Court is the key to understanding the history of German law and constitution (R. Grawert, "Ustawa Zasadnicza w świetle ujętych w niej praw zasadniczych," *Przegląd Sejmowy* No. 6 (95) (2009): 35). From the position of constitutional economics, Stefan Voigt observes that the "lived constitution" consists of a legal act, jurisprudence, and the "constitutional system." The latter is understood as a set of norms, values, and attitudes of elites and the general public (S. Voigt, "Positive Constitutional Economics: A Survey," in *Constitutional Political Economy in a Public Choice Perspective*, ed. Ch. K. Rowley (Drodrecht: Springer, 1997), 20). Cf. also Witold Kula's remarks on the mass character of sources for economic history as opposed to "individual" sources for political history (W. Kula, *Problemy i metody historii gospodarczej* (Warszawa: PWN, 1983), 95–96).

14 *Europäisches System Volkswirtschaftlicher Gesamtrechnungen – ESVG 2010* (Luxemburg: Eurostat, Europäische Kommission, Amt für Veröffentlichungen der Europäischen Union, 2014).

others, publications of the same state bodies published in subsequent years. In more recent reports, data was updated. However, the differences noted do not distort the drawn picture of individual dimensions of the German economy. Sixthly, it is sometimes challenging to find separate data for two parts of Germany, especially as regards the first decades of the 21st century. For some researchers, this is an indirect justification for the progressive unification of the Eastern and Western *Länder*.[15] Seventhly, the FRG and the GDR sources had different methods for compiling data. Methods of calculations in the Eastern Bloc differed from the Western rules.[16] Therefore, attempts were made to reach materials that unified data for both countries. Some methodological differences also exist after reunification, so it is difficult to avoid mistakes when comparing the state of the German economy after 1990 and the FRG's macroeconomic performance before reunification, let alone the GDR.[17] Eighthly, statistics on the GDR are official. One has to be aware of the risk of propaganda and, therefore, false information.[18]

Interdisciplinary literature studies complemented the source analysis. The literature on the subject is vast. German and English language studies from the 1990s dominate in this field. This made it necessary to make an attempt at a constructive selection and ordering of the literature. Selected Polish, English, and German studies were used, mainly in the field of economics, law, history, and sociology. In justified cases, works from other disciplines were also used. Interesting and often lesser-known literature and source materials were provided by research conducted in 2018 in American libraries: the Lehman Social Sciences Library, Columbia University in New York, and the Baker Library, Harvard University in Cambridge.[19] The work was also measurably influenced by two trips in 2020

---

15 See, e.g., M. Moszyński, "Zjednoczenie Niemiec – dwa dekady konwergencji," *Ekonomia i Prawo* 7 (2011): 265. Sometimes in the literature, one can find an accusation that such efforts of state authorities are aimed at concealing objective information about the incomplete convergence of the two parts of Germany.

16 Cf. J. Skodlarski, *Historia gospodarcza* (Warszawa: WN PWN, 2014), 408.

17 C. Schnabel, "Structural Adjustment and Privatization of the East German Economy," in *Economic Aspects of German Unification: National and International Perspectives*, ed. P. J. J. Welfens (Berlin: Springer-Verlag, 1992), 234. With regard to Poland's macroeconomic performance in the late 1980s and early 1990s, similar methodological issues are pointed out by Maciej Bałtowski and Maciej Miszewski (M. Bałtowski, M. Miszewski, *Transformacja gospodarcza w Polsce* (Warszawa: WN PWN, 2006), 214–218).

18 This fact is emphasized by e.g. Hans-Werner Sinn, who raises it in the context of the issue of investments in Eastern Germany after reunification (H.-W. Sinn, "Macroeconomic Aspects of German Unification," in Welfens, *Economic Aspects of German Unification*, 87). See more P. von der Lippe, "The Political Role of Official Statistics in the Former GDR (East Germany)," *Historical Social Research* 24, No. 4 (1999): 3–28.

19 The research was possible thanks to the grant: *Target Grant for Young Researchers and Doctoral Students in 2018* (Ministry of Science and Higher Education of Poland,

to Germany for research internships, during which research was carried out at Fachbereich Wirtschaftswissenschaften, Zweigbibliothek Recht und Wirtschaft, Universitätsbibliothek, Justus-Liebig-Universität in Gieβen,[20] and Jacob-und-Wilhelm-Grimm-Zentrum, Universitätsbibliothek, Humboldt-Universität in Berlin.[21]

The detailed literature is indicated in the relevant sections of the book, so its presence in the *Introduction* has been dispensed with. However, a few remarks should be made. The literature on this problem includes works from disciplines that usually deal with these issues in the present. Although authors examine the changes in reunified Germany from a retrospective perspective, works of a strictly historical character (i.e. written by historians based on their characteristic research methods) are few. Political scientists, lawyers, economists, sociologists, and others are much more likely to comment on this topic, emphasizing political, legal, economic, and socio-cultural processes in turn. This underpinned the need for an interdisciplinary literature search. This corresponds with the fact that history as such and economic history are interdisciplinary. As a result, this study can fill a gap in the so far scarce economic history studies of economic changes in reunified Germany after 1990.

Particular interest was paid to studies with a more extended chronological scope to be able to look at the years 1990–2015 from an appropriate distance, trying at the same time to grasp the dynamics of the analyzed processes in all or most of the discussed period. For this reason, less frequent reference was made to the very rich literature of the 1990s, which *de facto* reported on the course of the former GDR's transition and its integration into the FRG on an ongoing basis, sometimes formulating forecasts for the near future (often diverging).[22]

Research methods

This book has an interdisciplinary character. It is an economic history study combining the theoretical perspective of economics with the research tools

---

Faculty of Economics and Sociology, University of Lodz, Poland). Title of the project under which the research was conducted: *Home and Exile Polish Economic Historiography, 1945–1989: Poland, Great Britain and the United States.* Project code: B1811200001920.02. Decision No. 7066/E-345/M/2018.

20 The internship was awarded within the framework of a partnership program between the University of Lodz and Justus-Liebig-Universität in Gieβen. The stay was supervised by Prof. Matthias Göcke (Professur für Transformations- und Integrationsökonomik, Fachbereich Wirtschaftswissenschaften, Justus-Liebig-Universität in Gieβen).

21 The National Academic Exchange Agency internship was awarded as part of the project: *PROM – International Exchange of Doctoral Students and Academic Staff.*

22 In German economics, the term futurology (*Futurologie*) is sometimes used to describe this type of research.

of an economic historian based on an extensive analysis of source material. Interdisciplinary work on economic history has two dimensions, which result from the specificity of this discipline. Firstly, it is direct interdisciplinarity, i.e. combining the perspectives of history (humanities) and economics (social science). Secondly, it is indirect interdisciplinarity, i.e. drawing on the achievements of other useful disciplines. In the case of this work, references primarily to law and sociology play a key role. Here and there, elements of the history of political and legal thought and a history of social and economic thought are visible.

The primary theoretical reference point is institutional economics, especially the new institutional economics, from which specific understandings of institutions, formal rules, and ways of implementing them have been drawn. Due to the choice of constitutional and property rules, it was essential to rely on other theories to study these institutions' significance for the German economy in 1990–2015. These approaches show strong links with the new institutional economics: constitutional economics, especially its positive current, and property rights theory.[23] These were complemented by occasional references to the findings of other approaches, i.e. economic systems theory, ordoliberal theory, economic analysis of law (law and economics), transition theory or integration theory. Developing in various directions, they do not provide a closed and unambiguous catalog of research methods on the book's issues. It should be noted, therefore, that the mentioned theories were not used autonomously in this study. They are complementary to each other. This is in line with the assumptions of theoretical-methodological pluralism or, as Thomas S. Ulen put it in another context, the "trans-methodological" perspective.[24] Such a research focus is also due to the interdisciplinary nature of this work and economic history as a discipline.

The conducted research within the monograph has a theoretical and empirical dimension. The first one was aimed at setting the necessary analytical and interpretative framework. The concepts of institutions and formal institutions were defined. The main assumptions of constitutional economics and property rights theory were discussed. On this basis, German constitutional rules and property rights as formal institutions were presented. Elements of other economic theories

---

23 Without getting into theoretical and methodological disputes that are side-lined for this book, it is important to point out exemplary insights into the limitations of these theories: M. Buhbe, *Ökonomische Analyse von Eigentumsrechten. Der Beitrag der Economics of Property Rights zur Theorie der Institutionen* (Frankfurt am Main: Peter D. Lang, 1980), 23–28; P. Häberle, "Vielfalt der Property Rights und der verfassungsrechtliche Eigentumsbegriff," in *Ansprüche, Eigentums- und Verfügungsrechte*, ed. M. Neumann (Berlin: Duncker & Humblot, 1984), 65–72; Spangenberg, *The Institutionalised Transformation*, 178–180, 282–291.

24 T. S. Ulen, "Foreword," in M. L. Stearns, T. J. Zywicki, T. J. Miceli, *Law and Economics: Private and Public* (St. Paul: West Academic Publishing, 2018), VII–VIII.

have been presented at appropriate places in the book only to the extent necessary to bring the key issues into focus.

The empirical dimension of the work includes the identification and description of the above formal rules, as well as the analysis of the relationship between the FRG Constitution and property rights, and selected segments of the German economy in 1990–2015. Relevant references were provided by the theories of positive constitutional economics and property rights, as well as by the author's proposals.

Constitutional economics embeds constitutions in various economic contexts. This work is focused on the economic impact of selected provisions of the FRG Constitution during the analyzed period. In doing so, other perspectives offered by constitutional economics, such as the economic effects of political changes in the state or the economic logic of certain provisions of the constitution or legal doctrine, are deliberately omitted.[25] Stefan Voigt notes that the economic history perspective of constitutional studies is more concerned with individual countries. In contrast, (constitutional) economists are interested in a more nomological and comparative approach. On the other hand, he argues that economic history is a good discipline for the study of constitutional (or, more broadly: institutional) change because it sensitizes economists to the precise collection and application of data and warns them against being too detailed or general in the analyses they undertake.[26]

Economic history also has an important place in studying the importance of property rights for the economy. The argumentation in this respect coincides essentially with the position of institutionalists. By adopting a retrospective perspective, economic history reveals the dynamics of the transformation of property rights and its impact on socio-economic reality. This is an alternative to, e.g., the neoclassical approach, which is considered abstract, static, and ahistorical, or the Marxist approach, which is based solely on one general logic of development. The economic theory of property rights provides economic historians with valuable references in this field. Because of their impact on production, investment, trade, resource allocation, or the long-term decisions of economic actors, property rights have played a vital role in the historical process of development.[27]

---

25 Cf., e.g., R. Posner, "The Constitution as an Economic Document," *George Washington Law Review* 56, No. 1 (1987): 4–38.

26 Voigt, "Positive Constitutional Economics," 15–16, 20.

27 Buhbe, *Ökonomische Analyse von Eigentumsrechten*, 12–14; G. D. Libecap, "Property Rights in Economic History: Implications for Research," *Explorations in Economic History* 23 (1986): 227–252; G. D. Libecap, "Property Rights," in *The Oxford Encyclopedia of Economic History*, ed. J. Mokyr, Vol. 4: *Monte di Pietà – Spain* (Oxford: Oxford University Press, 2003), 268–274, constitutional empowerment of property rights and basic literature; D. Bębnowski, R. Matera, "Przegląd regulacji praw własności w Polsce w pierwszych miesiącach niepodległości (listopad 1918 – luty 1919)," in *Społeczny bilans otwarcia polskiej niepodległości w 1918 roku*, eds. T. Głowiński, M. Zawadka (Wrocław: Wydawnictwo GAJT, 2018), 118–121, theoretical prolegomena to the topic.

Thus, the subject matter of this book covers organically with economic history. Firstly, the study presents a retrospective view of the problem from the point of view of the studied space-time. In other words, the work deals with a past and closed (rather than present and open) period in Germany's economic development. Secondly, the methods used in work (especially the critical analysis of historical sources and the historical description integrated with statistical methods) are fundamental in economic history. Thirdly, the approaches that study the analyzed institutions (constitutional economics and property rights theory) show links with economic history. However, institutional economics dominates these theories, strongly emphasizing the role of historical analysis in the study of the institutions' significance for economic development.

Empirical studies of the impact of formal institutions on particular dimensions of the economy have been dominated by a quantitative approach. Authors usually use databases to estimate the quality of specific rules in particular countries and chronological periods. Based on econometric models (accompanied by a number of initial assumptions), they prove the positive or negative correlation between selected packages of institutions (or rather their indicators) and the economy. Despite the existing differences in the results, the conclusions of these studies boil down to a general statement: the higher quality of formal rules in a given group of states, the better the economic performance of these countries.[28] The above findings of economists, although valuable, do not exhaust the subject matter. "Measuring non-measurable phenomena,"[29] i.e. reducing the quality of institutions to conventional estimations, contradicts the idea of multidimensionality of institutional economics' perspective, which consequently takes positions typical of the criticized neoclassical approach, closed in static and abstract models.[30] As a result, this approach should be considered non-exclusive and insufficient.

This study tries to identify, characterize and evaluate the causal links between selected formal institutions and specific aspects of the German economy by outlining the extent of these links. The above premises justify the adoption of a qualitative-quantitative approach. The most important methods characteristic of the research workshop of an economic historian were used, i.e.: external and internal criticism of written historical sources (especially of the texts of German constitutions and

---

28 Example studies are referenced in relevant parts of this work.

29 Pol. *Mierzenie zjawisk niemierzalnych* (A. Czech, S. Czech, "Nowe trendy w ekonomii w perspektywie instytucjonalizmu," in *Instytucje w teorii i praktyce. Przeszłość – teraźniejszość – przyszłość*, eds. H. Pondel, S. Kuźmar (Poznań: Wydawnictwo UE w Poznaniu, 2020), 40).

30 This was one of the conclusions arising from the proceedings of the 3rd Polish scientific conference *Institutions in Theory and Practice. Past – Present – Future*, organized in Poznań on 25–26 September 2019 by Poznań University of Economics and Business in cooperation with Nicolaus Copernicus University in Toruń, Wrocław University of Economics, and the Forum of Institutional Thought (author's private notes).

other normative acts, as well as statistical materials), searching for causal relations in the scope of influence of the constitutional and property rules on selected segments of the German economy in 1990–2015, integrating statistical methods with description. In doing so, different narrative methods were used: theoretical generalizations, retrospective description and analysis of statistical data. Graphical methods allowed the presentation of the study results by tables and annotated figures. Diagrams organize the content discussed. Indicative (statistical) methods illustrate the discussed economic phenomena in Germany in selected years (also those preceding the period 1990–2015). In most cases, indicators of dynamics (e.g. the number of new and liquidated enterprises in Germany in selected years) and structure (e.g. the share of taxes and social contributions in budget revenues in Germany in selected years) are taken into account, less frequently indicators of intensity (e.g. GDP *per capita*). Where justified, statistical (econometric) analysis methods were used to calculate the Pearson correlation coefficient. This mixed approach stems from the belief that qualitative and quantitative perspectives are complementary.[31]

It is clear from the considerations of James M. Buchanan and Gordon Tullock that analysis of institutions only from the standpoint of their economic outcomes is incomplete. The procedures within individual institutions should be studied.[32] Katarzyna Metelska-Szaniawska, performing a critical review of the literature on constitutional economics, points out that most studies focus on the impact of selected aspects of the constitution on economic growth (development) or the links between economic policy (economic reforms) and growth or development. She calls for more attention to the role of constitutional rules in economic policy in the context of economic reforms.[33] The used documents on the constitutional and property rules show the legislative and executive practice of the German state with regard to their adaptation in the economy, especially in the new federated states. It does not mean, however, that these formal institutions were the exclusive influence factors on the presented segments of the economy. It should be remembered about the multidimensional nature of socio-economic processes whose determinants are diverse and not single-factor. However, the research confirmed the fact that the analyzed formal rules had key importance for the described economic changes. A parallel can be seen here to the North's postulate on the study of adaptive efficiency, by which he means the adaptation of entities and societies to the challenges

31 See valuable theoretical and methodological considerations of a practical nature on combining historical (descriptive) and economic (quantitative) methods in historical-economic research: R. Matera, *G8 jako instytucja gospodarki światowej* (Łódź: Wydawnictwo UŁ, 2009), 19–23.

32 J. M. Buchanan, G. Tullock, *The Calculus of Consent. Logical Foundations of Constitutional Democracy* (Indianapolis: Liberty Fund, 1999), *passim*.

33 Metelska-Szaniawska, *Konstytucyjne czynniki reform gospodarczych*, 57–62, 166–168. She undertakes the optics postulated by her.

arising from the dynamics of economic transformations. This includes the creation or modification of adequate institutions.[34]

Book structure

The book is problem-chronological in nature. It consists of an *Introduction*, six chapters corresponding to successive research questions, a *Summary*, a *Bibliography*, a *List of Tables, Figures, and Diagrams*, and an *Index of Names*.

The theoretical Chap. 1 presents the understanding of the category of institutions in selected social sciences. It discusses approaches characteristic of management science, political science, law, and sociology. Most attention was paid to proposals for defining institutions in economics, history, and economic history.

The opening balance of reflections on space-time is made in Chap. 2. The economic structures of the FRG and the GDR in the late 1980s and early 1990s are compared from the point of view of the main sectors and the most representative macroeconomic indicators. The outline of German reunification's political process additionally provides the work context.

The structure of the relevant chapters (3–6) is relatively uniform. The starting point for Chap. 3 is a comprehensive presentation of basic law as a formal institution and the outline of the main assumptions of constitutional economic theory, with particular emphasis on the positive current. The empirical part of the chapter opens with characteristics of the GDR and the FRG Constitutions in the context of the most important systemic aspects. Particular attention is paid to a detailed discussion of the economic and social assumptions of the Basic Law of the FRG. The chapter concludes with a detailed presentation of the process of implementing the West German constitutional rules in the new federated states during the formal reunification of Germany.

Chap. 4 identifies and discusses the characteristic channels of the relationships between the institution of the Basic Law of the FRG and the various dimensions of the German economy after 1990. The theory of positive constitutional economics and some empirical studies were the criteria for selecting these segments. Due to the fact that there are different ways of relating the institution of constitutional rules to particular areas of economic reality in the literature, this list was reduced to selected representative aspects. As far as possible, the analysis was supplemented with the author's proposals. From the point of view of *de jure* institutions showing potential networks of relations between the FRG Constitution and economic transformations, these are: economic order, the basic rights, systemic principles of the state, and systemic objectives related to the economy. In the dimension of *de facto* institutions, an attempt has been made to capture the above relations, taking into account the most important indicators of the quality of German formal institutions,

34 D. C. North, *Institutions, Institutional Change and Economic Performance* (Cambridge–New York: Cambridge University Press, 2009), 80–81.

stability of the political system, economic growth, and fiscal policy. The summary in this part of the work covers the conclusions from Chaps. 3 and 4.

The explanation of the understanding of property rights as a formal institution opens Chap. 5. It characterizes the key assumptions of the theory of property rights. In order to outline the historical and economic context, the problem of property rights in the GDR, regulated according to the Marxist doctrine of law and economics, is discussed. Additionally, the legal basis of this institution in the communist constitutions of East Germany is discussed. A separate section is devoted to a detailed explanation of the process of implementation of the FRG's property rights in the Eastern *Länder* during the period of the formal reunification of the country.

The extensive Chap. 6 provides a detailed analysis of property rights in Germany after 1990 based on its dimensions, indicated by the property rights theory: the degree of completeness of these rights from the perspective of exclusivity and transferability, and the enforcement and protection of property rights involving the role of law, owners and social norms. The second part of the chapter identifies the most important areas of linkage between property rights and the German economy after reunification, with a particular focus on developments in the new federated states. This list is based on suggestions from property rights theory, major empirical studies, and the author's proposals. The legal and institutional framework of property transformations has been approximated, devoting more attention to the processes of privatization and re privatization. The progressive restructuring of the economy in the Eastern *Länder* is characterized, and the challenges for the enterprise sector there are discussed. Problems with adapting the model of employee participation in Eastern Germany are highlighted. The issue of development disproportions between two parts of the country from the point of view of the level of investment was raised. The analysis of property taxation and state spending in 1990–2015 was used to formulate an assessment regarding fiscalism in Germany after reunification. A broader view of the problems with the transition of the Eastern *Länder* and the unification, integration, and convergence of the old and new federated states was provided by a consideration of Germany's economic growth in 1990–2015. It concludes with a summary of Chaps. 5 and 6.

The *Summary* consists of a recapitulation and expansion of the conclusions made in the book, which answer the specific research questions. The main hypothesis has been verified. Research postulates resulting from the topic undertaken were also formulated.

The past tense was used to describe Germany's economic change between 1990 and 2015. Although many legal regulations headed by the Basic Law are still in force in this country today, the subject of interest was a closed chronological period. The study takes into account the legal status in force until December 31, 2015. In addition, some of the normative acts may change in the near or distant future, so the present work would lose its relevance. The same applies to the interpretation of political-legal and economic-social processes. This is the additional function of the caesura closing the consideration.

Wherever possible, extracts from foreign sources or literature were cited in English and in the original. In the main text, only single words or slightly longer expressions, which were specific to the discussed topic, were given the original wording in brackets. Mostly these were German terms. Therefore each quotation is not preceded by a "Ger." abbreviation unless a different language version of the term is cited. Longer and other terms or parts of the text have been placed in footnotes to avoid disturbing the comfort of reading. There were exceptions to this rule only in isolated and justified cases.

The work used two ways of writing the terms "constitution" and "basic law." The lower-case spelling referred to the indefinite constitution as the highest legal act in the state. This was done during the theoretical considerations. The FRG Constitution of 1949 was cited when referring to the Basic Law. The deliberations of German constitutionalism, where the categories of "basic law" and "constitution" are not synonymous, were avoided.[35] In this case, practical considerations, confirmed by the literature, were decisive.

In turn, the FRG and the GDR were used as synonyms for "West Germany" and "East Germany," respectively, during the split period. The following terms were also used interchangeably: "federated state," *Land*, *Länder*. After reunification, "Western (old) *Länder*," "Western (old) federated states," "Western Germany," and "the West" were most frequently distinguished from denoting the former area of the FRG in 1949–1990 without Berlin, and "Eastern (new) *Länder*," "Eastern (new) federated states," "Eastern Germany," "the East," "the former GDR (area)" to denote the area of the former GDR in 1949–1990 without Berlin. The distinctions used do not always coincide with the terminology found in statistical sources, which is noted in the relevant places of the study.

*

This book is a revised and supplemented version of the dissertation entitled *The Importance of Selected Formal Institutions for the German Economy, 1990–2015*,[36] defended with distinction in 2020 at the Faculty of Economics and Sociology, University of Lodz, Poland. I would like to thank my Supervisor and Master, Professor Janusz Skodlarski, for his invaluable support on a substantive and personal level. From the very beginning, Professor Skodlarski has been an enthusiastic supporter of my research. To him, I also owe a broad view of economic history and the enrichment of scientific and didactic perspectives. It is a real honor and obligation for me to belong to the group of Professor students. My thanks for comments and suggestions go to the reviewers of this dissertation: Professor Aldona Podolska-Meducka from the Warsaw School of Economics and Professor Michał Moszyński from the Nicolaus Copernicus University in Toruń. I owe a debt

---

35 This problem is signaled in section 3.5. in this study.

36 Pol. *Znaczenie wybranych instytucji formalnych dla gospodarki Niemiec w latach 1990–2015.*

of gratitude to all the staff, doctoral students, and supporters of the Department of History of Economic Thought and Economic History (presently the Department of History of Economics) at the University of Lodz, headed by Professor Rafał Matera and later by Professor Joanna Dzionek-Kozłowska. Regular, demanding, and constructive seminars have always been a source of inspiration for me. Professor Paul Spicker, *Professor Emeritus* at the Robert Gordon University in Aberdeen (UK), was willing to share with me his critical remarks on the methodology of social science research work. Professor Rafał Kowalczyk from the University of Lodz made substantive comments on some parts of the work. The openness of Professor Matthias Göcke from the Justus-Liebig-Universität in Gieβen made it possible for me to stay at this university and conduct my research. I consulted some of the legal issues raised in the study with Łukasz Płoski. I am grateful to Michał Jacuń for his help in developing the original diagrams for the dissertation. I extend my good thoughts to the staff of the libraries in Poland and abroad in which I conducted searches. The use of the rich collections would be much more difficult without their cordiality. Thanks to Sebastian Antkowicz, who carefully read the typescript and shared his comments. I am grateful to the Peter Lang Publishing House for the fruitful cooperation during the preparation of the book. I would like to address words of thanks to Marzena Plucinski and her family for their hospitality and heartiness during my stay in New York. Finally, I would like to thank my Wife Barbara, Son Jan, Daughter Maria, Parents, Grandparents, other Family members, and Friends. I could always count on them.

Paris–Aubervilliers, July 29, 2022
XIX World Economic History Congress

CHAPTER 1 Category of institution in selected disciplines

1.1. Examples of institutions' conceptualizations in social sciences

The term "institution" finds considerable use in both everyday language and science. Reinhart Koselleck, in his works on historical semantics, repeatedly referred to the etymology.[1] Following this line, it should be noted that the Latin *institutio* means "device, custom, instruction, designation of an heir," while the verb *instituere* – "to place, establish, educate."[2] In the common understanding, this concept is identified with a specific entity, organization, office, grouping. This is related to the intuitive and imprecise use of the term.[3] The situation is more complicated in scientific discourse. The term "institution" is defined differently in various disciplines.[4] This usually results from the subject matter of a particular science.

In management science, an institution is understood as organized things that are composed of people united by a bundle of common goals and having resources used in action.[5] Thus, it can be concluded that an institution is synonymous with an organization in this discipline. Ricky W. Griffin argues that an organization is nothing more than a group of people who undertake coordinated and orderly cooperation to achieve specific goals.[6] For Adam Stabryła, the concept of

1 Cf. R. Koselleck, *Semantyka historyczna* (Poznań: Wydawnictwo Poznańskie, 2001); R. Koselleck, *Dzieje pojęć. Studia z semantyki i pragmatyki języka społeczno-politycznego* (Warszawa: Oficyna Naukowa, 2009).

2 "Instytucja," in W. Kopaliński, *Słownik wyrazów obcych i zwrotów obcojęzycznych* (Warszawa: Wiedza Powszechna, 1990), 232. Interesting etymological considerations regarding the term "institution" were undertaken by Wacław Stankiewicz (W. Stankiewicz, *Ekonomika instytucjonalna. Zarys wykładu* (Warszawa: Wydawnictwo AON, 2014), 47).

3 J. Godłów-Legiędź, "Instytucje i koszty transakcji jako podstawowe pojęcia nowej ekonomii instytucjonalnej," in *Instytucje i transformacja*, ed. J. Godłów-Legiędź (Toruń: Wydawnictwo Adam Marszałek, 2009), 13.

4 T. Gaweł, M. Klimczak, "Pojęcie instytucji w prawie i ekonomii," in *Ład instytucjonalny w gospodarce*, Vol. I, eds. B. Polszakiewicz, J. Boehlke (Toruń: Wydawnictwo UMK, 2005), 73, 77.

5 J. Zieleniewski, *Organizacja i zarządzanie* (Warszawa: PWN, 1979), 279.

6 R. W. Griffin, *Podstawy zarządzania organizacjami* (Warszawa: WN PWN, 2004), 5. Jan Zieleniewski drew attention to another understanding of the term "institution," proposed by Jerzy Kurnal: "organisational wholes of team activities of people, which are subject to consolidation through constant repetition (renewal) of the realization of objectives, become institutions" (Pol. [*C*]*ałości organizacyjne działań zespołowych ludzi, które podlegają utrwaleniu przez stałe powtarzanie (odnawianie)*

organization has two meanings. On the one hand, it is an organized thing (e.g., a team of people, an enterprise), and on the other hand, it is organizing, which is an activity involving the selection and agreement of process elements (people and resources) that work for a common goal.[7]

In political science, institutions are defined as a specific model of behavior that provides stability and predictability in social life. Institutions play a limiting role (they shape the behavior of individuals and groups) and a supporting role (they support the achievement of specific goals by individuals and groups). There are informal institutions (e.g. family, social classes) and formal institutions (e.g. governments, political parties).[8] For Stefan Opara, a political institution is a legally defined organization or function that affects the functioning of the state or is an element of it. He also notes that there is a broader meaning of this term, i.e. permanent principles of the state (e.g. an institution of elections).[9]

In legal science, institutions are sets of legal norms separated into a functional whole. It is a result of the fact that they exhaustively regulate a certain narrow part of social reality.[10] Examples include marriage or property. Włodzimierz Gromski emphasizes that a legal institution is also sometimes understood as a set of actions defined by a set of norms (e.g. an interpellation). According to another meaning, a legal institution is a person or a group of people organized and acting based on legal norms (e.g. a limited liability company).[11]

Sociology offers another understanding of institutions. Barbara Szacka distinguishes two approaches to the term. The first one is new institutionalism, which treats institutions as permanent patterns and rules of human activities, ordering social interactions and defining the framework of games played by

---

realizacji celów, stają się instytucjami (J. Kurnal, *Zarys teorii organizacji i zarządzania* (Warszawa: PWE, 1969), 160. Cited: Zieleniewski, *Organizacja i zarządzanie*, 280)). However, in the management science an institution is most often understood as an organization.

7 A. Stabryła, "Przedmiot i zakres nauki organizacji i zarządzania," in *Organizacja i zarządzanie. Zarys problematyki*, eds. A. Stabryła, J. Trzcieniecki (Warszawa: PWN, 1986), 22. Waclaw Stankiewicz, analyzing the semantic differences between an institution and an organization, proposes treating an organization as a shell, a form in which the rules of an institution occur (Stankiewicz, *Ekonomika instytucjonalna. Zarys wykładu*, 56).

8 P. Ferdinand, "Comparative Politics," in R. Garner, P. Ferdinand, S. Lawson, *Introduction to Politics* (Oxford: Oxford University Press, 2020), 163–164.

9 S. Opara, "Instytucja polityczna," in *Mały słownik politologii*, eds. S. Opara et al. (Toruń: Wydawnictwo Adam Marszałek, 2007), 62.

10 A. Korybski, L. Leszczyński, A. Pieniążek, *Wstęp do prawoznawstwa* (Lublin: Wydawnictwo UMCS, 2007), 109.

11 W. Gromski, "Instytucja prawna," in *Wprowadzenie do nauk prawnych. Leksykon tematyczny*, ed. A. Bator (Warszawa: Lexis Nexis Polska, 2012), 209. Cf. Gaweł, Klimczak, "Pojęcie instytucji," 73–77.

individuals. The second perspective – functionalist – defines an institution as a complex of roles concentrated around activities that aim at satisfying a particular social need.[12]

Norman Goodman notes that social institutions are stable, enduring cultural and structural arrangements designed to solve social problems. These arrangements develop spontaneously or are specifically planned. Social institutions have certain characteristics: (1) a stable set of values, norms, statuses, role rules, social groups, and organizations associated with a particular area of human activity; (2) resistance to change; (3) interdependence (reliance on similar norms, values and serving similar purposes).[13]

Piotr Sztompka links institutions with the concepts of rule (i.e. the external, social frame of reference for individual activity) and social context (i.e. the domain of social life in which people perform socially important functions). Institution involves the integration of rules, whereby they form a specific rule complex. As Sztompka states, every social context has characteristic rules. Such a set of rules is an institution.[14]

At the risk of being somewhat simplistic, it is possible to distinguish two understandings of institutions in social sciences. Firstly, researchers point to institutions as groups of people or organizations. Secondly, institutions are norms, patterns, and frameworks in which people function. What is more, it is clear that the common understanding of this term is similar to the approaches of management and political sciences. An institution is most often identified with an organization.[15]

---

12 B. Szacka, *Wprowadzenie do socjologii* (Warszawa: Oficyna Naukowa, 2008), 136.

13 N. Goodman, *Wstęp do socjologii* (Poznań: Zysk i S-ka, 2001), 55–56, 356. Interestingly, Goodman argues that an example of a social institution is the economy (economic system). It includes the system of producing, distributing, and acquiring goods and services that are necessary for human survival (Goodman, *Wstęp do socjologii*, 55, 249).

14 P. Sztompka, *Socjologia. Analiza społeczeństwa* (Kraków: Wydawnictwo Znak, 2010), 257, 264–265.

15 See additionally the sociological analysis of organizations as institutions: T. Edeling, "Organisationen als Institutionen," in *Neuer Institutionalismus. Zur soziologischen Erklärung von Organisation, Moral und Vertrauen*, eds. A. Maurer, M. Schmid (Frankfurt–New York: Campus Verlag, 2002), 219–235. Cf. the "organizational institutionalism" approach: J. L. Campbell, "Institutional Analysis and the Role of Ideas in Political Economy," in *The Rise of Neoliberalism and Institutional Analysis*, eds. J. L. Campbell, O. K. Pedersen (Princeton–Oxford: Princeton University Press, 2001), 163–165.

1.2. Economic understanding of institutions

1.2.1. Problems with defining institutions

The literature on institutional economics is extremely broad. There is the main distinction between the old and new institutional economics in the history of economic thought. The development of the former was initiated at the turn of the 19th and 20th centuries thanks to the research of, among others, Thorstein Veblen, Wesley C. Mitchell, and John R. Commons. The new institutional economics dates back to the 1930s. Its representatives include: Ronald H. Coase, Armen A. Alchian, Harold Demsetz, Herbert Simon, Oliver E. Williamson, Douglass C. North, James M. Buchanan, Gordon Tullock, and Mancur Olson.[16]

The institution is the central issue addressed by the old and new institutional economics. However, its definition is not unambiguous in both approaches. It

---

16 Among the extremely rich literature treating the main assumptions and theoretical, methodological, and practical aspects of the old and new institutional economics, it is worth mentioning: S. Żurawicki, ed., *Historia myśli ekonomicznej* (Wrocław: Ossolineum, 1979), 227–246, 378–390; M. Rutherford, *Institutions in Economics. The Old and the New Institutionalism* (Cambridge: Cambridge University Press, 1999); M. Blaug, *Teoria ekonomii. Ujęcie retrospektywne* (Warszawa: WN PWN, 2000), 743–746; E. G. Furubotn, R. Richter, *Institutions and Economic Theory. The Contribution of the New Institutional Economics* (Ann Arbor: The Univeristy of Michigan Press, 2008); W. Stankiewicz, *Ekonomika instytucjonalna. Narodziny i rozwój* (Warszawa: Wydawnictwo BBS PWSBiA, 2004); W. Stankiewicz, *Historia myśli ekonomicznej* (Warszawa: PWE, 2007), 220–232, 323–328, 382–389; Stankiewicz, *Ekonomika instytucjonalna. Zarys wykładu*; G. M. Hodgson, *The Evolution of Institutional Economics. Agency, Structure and Darwinism in American Institutionalism* (London–New York: Routledge, 2004); H. Landreth, D. C. Colander, *Historia myśli ekonomicznej* (Warszawa: WN PWN, 2005), 352–375, 415–429 (in addition: J. Godłów-Legiędź, "Aneks do wydania polskiego," in Landreth, Colander, *Historia myśli ekonomicznej*, 564–573); M. Ratajczak, "Instytucjonalizm – wzbogacenie czy alternatywa ekonomii głównego nurtu?," in Polszakiewicz, Boehlke, *Ład instytucjonalny w gospodarce*, 57–72; Gaweł, Klimczak, "Pojęcie instytucji," 77–83; S. Rudolf, ed., *Nowa ekonomia instytucjonalna. Aspekty teoretyczne i praktyczne* (Kielce: Wydawnictwo WSEiA im. prof. Edwarda Lipińskiego w Kielcach, 2005); U. Zagóra-Jonszta, ed., *Dokonania współczesnej myśli ekonomicznej. Ekonomia instytucjonalna – teoria i praktyka* (Katowice: Wydawnictwo Akademii Ekonomicznej w Katowicach, 2006); B. Klimczak, *Wybrane problemy i zastosowania ekonomii instytucjonalnej* (Wrocław: Wydawnictwo AE we Wrocławiu, 2006); S. Rudolf, ed., *Nowa ekonomia instytucjonalna. Teoria i zastosowania* (Kielce: Wydawnictwo WSEiP im. prof. Edwarda Lipińskiego w Kielcach, 2009); S. Rudolf, ed., *Nowa ekonomia instytucjonalna wobec współczesnych problemów gospodarczych* (Kielce: Wydawnictwo WSEPiNM im. prof. Edwarda Lipińskiego w Kielcach, 2014).

seems interesting to chronologically present some variants of this concept, which reflects the evolution of understanding the specificity of institutions in economics.

It turns out that scholars from the old institutional economics differed in their views on the key category of this trend. Veblen (1899), in defining institutions, refers to the sociological and psychological understanding of the concept. He argues that social institutions are dominant ways of thinking that encompass the social conditions and functions of individuals and communities. They are habits of thought and ways of apprehending phenomena. They guide human life. Moreover, they derive from the past and are therefore connected to the realities of the time. Hence, according to Veblen, institutions are not in complete harmony with the conditions of the present.[17]

Mitchell (1910) understands institutions as the psychological arrangements, habits of thought and activities that occur in the social groups under study.[18] He points out that economic rationality must be related to the functioning of social institutions. They are formed by large conceptual systems, which, as a result of evolution, gain independence from their creators and cause objective and unintended consequences.[19]

Commons (1934), proposing his understanding of institutions, refers to the issue of transactions (exchange). He distinguishes three types of them: bargaining, managerial, and rationing. In his view, they combine into a larger unit of economic analysis, which was then referred to as a "Going Concern" (*gutgehendes Geschäft*) in British and American literature. These going concerns, together with the rules of functioning, are institutions. In this sense, an institution can be, e.g., a family, corporation, trade union, business association, or the state.[20]

As already noted, the development and supplementation of the above phase of institutional economics was the new institutional economics. On its basis, attempts were also made to analyze and interpret the concept in question.

Alchian and Demsetz (1972) define a firm (enterprise) as an institution. Moreover, it is a specialized market institution whose purpose is to collect, compare and sell incoming information.[21]

Buchanan (1975), on the other hand, interprets institutions as ways and rules to resolve interpersonal conflicts within certain boundaries. The researcher emphasizes that institutions evolve. However, those that have survived and

---

17 T. Veblen, *Teoria klasy próżniaczej* (Warszawa: PWN, 1971), 171.

18 W. C. Mitchell, "The Rationality of Economic Activity. I," *Journal of Political Economy* 18, No. 2 (1910): 112.

19 W. C. Mitchell, "The Rationality of Economic Activity. II," *Journal of Political Economy* 18, No. 3 (1910): 204.

20 J. R. Commons, *Institutional Economics. Its Place in Political Economy* (New York: The Macmillan Company, 1934), 69.

21 A. A. Alchian, H. Demsetz, "Production, Information Costs, and Economic Organization," *American Economic Review* 62, No. 5 (1972): 791–793.

continue to function are not necessarily judged by the people living within them as the best.[22] A similar understanding of institutions (as rules and frameworks for human activity) is presented by Tullock (1962), co-author – along with J. M. Buchanan – of the classic work on public choice theory, *The Calculus of Consent.*[23]

Williamson (1985), examining the economic institutions of capitalism, stresses the importance of firms, markets, and relational contracting. These are simultaneously the evolutionary product of a series of organizational innovations.[24] Williamson developed the earlier Coase's ideas, the forerunner of the new institutional economics, dealing with issues of firms, transaction costs, and property rights, among others. Coase argues that the study of institutions is central to economics because they affect exchange by, e.g., facilitating it. Such institutions as the firm, market, and law form the institutional structure of the economic system.[25]

The most popular definition of institutions among researchers is presented by North (1990). By this term, he means the rules of the game or constraints created by people, shaping their interactions. They form the structure of incentives for human exchange (political, social, and economic). Institutional changes determine how societies evolve. Thus, they are key to understanding historical change.[26]

Despite the above approaches, which were created by the pioneers and classic representatives of the new institutional economics, also leading contemporary scholars belonging to this trend differ in their formulations of the category in question. For example, Stefan Voigt, referring to Elinor Ostrom, defines institutions as

22 J. M. Buchanan, *The Limits of Liberty. Between Anarchy and Leviathan* (Indianapolis: Liberty Fund, 2000), XVI, 8, 16.

23 J. M. Buchanan, G. Tullock, *The Calculus of Consent. Logical Foundations of Constitutional Democracy* (Indianapolis: Liberty Fund, 1999). More extensively on public choice theory: J. Wilkin, ed., *Teoria wyboru publicznego. Wstęp do ekonomicznej analizy polityki i funkcjonowania sfery publicznej* (Warszawa: WN Scholar, 2005); J. Wilkin, ed., *Teoria wyboru publicznego. Główne nurty i zastosowania* (Warszawa: WN Scholar, 2012).

24 O. E. Williamson, *Ekonomiczne instytucje kapitalizmu. Firmy, rynki, relacje kontraktowe* (Warszawa: WN PWN, 1998), 29.

25 R. H. Coase, *Firma, rynek i prawo* (Warszawa: Oficyna a Wolters Kluwer Business, 2013), 5, 7.

26 D. C. North, *Institutions, Institutional Change and Economic Performance* (Cambridge–New York: Cambridge University Press, 2009), 3. The North's definitions of institutions in some of his other works do not differ substantially (cf. e.g.: D. C. North, "Institutions," *Journal of Economic Perspectives* 5, No. 1 (1991): 97; D. C. North, "Economic Performance Through Time," *The American Economic Review* 84, No. 3 (1994): 360; D. C. North, *Zrozumieć przemiany gospodarcze* (Warszawa: Oficyna a Wolters Kluwer Business, 2014), 51).

"commonly known rules used to structure recurrent interaction situations that are endowed with a sanctioning mechanism."[27]

It can be seen that the category of rules is important in considering the specifics of institutions. In social sciences (e.g. Helmut Leipold), it is pointed out that they may be spontaneous and take the form of unwritten values, norms, institutions, and customs, or they may be conscious, being defined in constitutions, laws, or regulations. In turn, the set of certain rules makes up the concept of order. Within it, rules prescribe certain behaviors or prohibit them. When the behavior of individuals is voluntarily or coercively directed toward rules, their behavioral space becomes restricted. In other words, it becomes "regulated" and "ordered." Therefore, rules select behavior and create their order along with relatively fixed behavior patterns. The set of rules relating to economic behavior shapes the economic order. These are customary (social) or legal rules, creating various complex forms of order, e.g. planning, property, enterprise, price formation, and money supply.[28]

An important aspect of the study of the specificity of institutions is the question of their genesis. The fact is that – regardless of their understanding – they are historically conditioned, often undergoing long-term processes of evolution. Therefore, it is difficult to grasp the genesis of institutions unambiguously. Vernon Smith claims that economic theory cannot fully model or explain the emergence of institutions.[29] On the other hand, Janina Godłów-Legiędź, referring to the example of welfare, treats the genesis of institutions responsible for it as one of the main problems of economics.[30] Daniel Seligson and Anne E. C. McCants argue that institutions are not the rules of the game within which economic growth occurs, but they are its "coevolving sources."[31]

It is not easy to point to the most precise, general, and thus cognitively satisfying definition after analyzing only exemplary approaches to institutions. It is worth referring to the question posed by Wacław Stankiewicz: "Is such definition possible and necessary at all?"[32] He points out that new definitions in the new institutional

27 S. Voigt, "How (Not) to Measure Institutions," *Journal of Institutional Economics* 9, No. 1 (2013): 5. Cf. E. Ostrom, "An Agenda for the Study of Institutions," *Public Choice* 48, No. 1 (1986): 5.

28 H. Leipold, "Gesellschaftstheoretische Fundierung der Wirtschaftssysteme," in *Bundesrepublik Deutschland – DDR. Die Wirtschaftssysteme. Soziale Marktwirtschaft und Soziale Planwirtschaft im Systemvergleich*, ed. H. Hamel (München: Verlag C. H. Beck, 1983), 17–18.

29 V. Smith, *Racjonalność w ekonomii* (Warszawa: Oficyna a Wolters Kluwer Business, 2013), 20.

30 J. Godłów-Legiędź, *Współczesna ekonomia. Ku nowemu paradygmatowi?* (Warszawa: Wydawnictwo C. H. Beck, 2010), 27.

31 D. Seligson, A. E. C. McCants, "Coevolving Institutions and the Paradox of Informal Constraints," *Journal of Institutional Economics* 17, No. 3 (2021): 359–378.

32 Pol. *[C]zy taka definicja jest w ogóle możliwa i potrzebna?* (Stankiewicz, *Ekonomika instytucjonalna. Zarys wykładu*, 49).

economics are created for the needs of detailed studies. Referring simultaneously to Richard R. Nelson and Bhaven N. Sampat, he stresses that these approaches should be in line with a broader definition of an economic institution and an even broader definition of an institution as such.[33] On the other hand, Tomasz Gaweł and Mikołaj Klimczak note that different understandings of institutions within the new institutional economics are associated with a certain pragmatism that stems from the fact that the approach is still developing.[34]

However, it is difficult not to notice that in the above-mentioned understandings of institutions, the keywords are: "habits," "systems," "rules," and "limitations." They are gathered by the category of "framework(s)" in a certain way. Following this line, it is worth making an attempt to present the author's understanding of institutions.

Drawing on North's concept, this book understands institutions as the historically shaped frameworks in which individuals, social groups, and entire societies function, affecting political, economic, social, and cultural transformations. Such an approach – general and as broad as possible – will be the basis for further considerations devoted to the significance of selected formal institutions (constitutional rules and property rights) for the German economy in 1990–2015.

The ambiguous understanding of institutions in institutional economics is reflected, e.g., in the equation of this category with an organization by some of its representatives (e.g. Alchian and Demsetz). However, North makes a clear distinction between these two terms, stating that organizations are groups of individuals united by common goals. He distinguishes between economic organizations (e.g., businesses, unions, cooperatives), political organizations (e.g., political parties, senate, regulatory agencies), and social organizations (e.g., religious associations, clubs).[35] Thus, for North, organizations are a much narrower concept than institutions. He argues that the emergence of certain organizations is determined by the institutional matrix.[36] As can be seen, North's account corresponds to understanding organizations' characteristics in management science.

Given the fact that some institutionalists (e.g. Veblen, Mitchell, North) also understand abstract categories as institutions (e.g. ways of thinking, habits of mind, informal rules), it is reasonable to distinguish institutions from organizations.

---

33 Stankiewicz, *Ekonomika instytucjonalna. Zarys wykładu*, 49. Cf. R. R. Nelson, B. N. Sampat, "Making Sense of Institutions as a Factor Shaping Economic Performance," *Journal of Economic Behavior and Organization* 44, No. 1 (2001): 31–54; R. R. Nelson, "What Enables Rapid Economic Progress: What Are the Needed Institutions?," *Research Policy* 37, No. 1 (2008): 1–11.

34 Gaweł, Klimczak, "Pojęcie instytucji," 80.

35 North, *Zrozumieć przemiany gospodarcze*, 63.

36 North, *Zrozumieć przemiany gospodarcze*, 63. An interesting analysis of the institutional matrix theory was made by Stankiewicz (Stankiewicz, *Ekonomika instytucjonalna. Zarys wykładu*, 62–65).

Therefore, different understandings of these categories are adopted in this work, and the organization – following North's proposal and the definitions from management sciences – is understood here as a group of people integrated by a desire to achieve a specific goal.

The question of what period to consider while examining institutions' structure, functioning, and dynamics also seems relevant. Williamson attempts to outline an analytical chronological framework for specific types of rules: (1) 100 to 1,000 years (informal institutions, customs, traditions, norms, religion); (2) 10 to 100 years (institutional environment, i.e., formal rules, especially property, policy, judiciary, bureaucracy); (3) 1 to 10 years (governance, especially contracts, and transactions); (4) present, continuous (resource allocation, employment, prices and quantities, incentive alignment).[37] Małgorzata Burchard-Dziubińska, referring to the precursors of institutionalism in economics, notes that institutions are accepted at any period. They are a product of the past and sometimes require a longer time to adapt to changed conditions.[38] Tomasz Legiędź argues that the process of institutional change is observable in hindsight because of the slowness, variable pace, ambiguity of institutional change, and the ideological background of the researcher.[39]

Therefore, the chronological framework in institutional research is not of primary importance. Researchers indicate neither relatively long nor short periods. At the risk of some simplification, it can be said that this time should be sufficient, i.e. the structure, functioning, and dynamics of specific institutions can be captured and studied in a particular case study. Thus, it may take a few years to several hundred years or more for particular economies.[40] This is because everything depends on the hypotheses adopted, research problems and questions, theories, methodologies, and research material. In this context, the study of selected institutions'

---

37 O. E. Williamson, "The New Institutional Economics: Taking Stock, Looking Ahead," *Journal of Economic Literature* 38, No. 3 (2000): 597, figure 1.

38 M. Burchard-Dziubińska, "Rola instytucji w kształtowaniu ładu ekonomicznego," in *W poszukiwaniu nowego ładu ekonomicznego*, eds. S. Owsiak, A. Pollok (Warszawa: PTE, 2013), 18.

39 T. Legiędź, "Instytucjonalna teoria przemian gospodarczych – rozwój gospodarczy z perspektywy nowej ekonomii instytucjonalnej," *Ekonomia* No. 4 (21) (2012): 38.

40 In the case of this analytical temporal (chronological) multidimensionality in the study of institutions, it can be seen a parallel to the specific multidimensional conception of time in history by Fernand Braudel, a representative of the 20th-century French "Annales" school of historiography. Braudel distinguishes three terms (durations of time, dimensions, levels, tempos, pace). Short term, involving single events, is characterized by the greatest dynamics of change. Phases of several decades, cycles, conjunctures, periods or epochs are classified as medium term. Finally, long term (French: *longue durée*) refers to a single century, several centuries or millennia. Changes in the last dimension of time are the slowest (F. Braudel, *Gramatyka cywilizacji* (Warszawa: Oficyna Naukowa, 2006), 67–69).

role in Germany's economic transformations in the last quarter of the century is justified.

Interest in the new institutional economics is still growing in Poland. It particularly intensified in the 1990s, during the period of systemic transition. As Godłów-Legiędź stated back in 2008, it is rather an initial stage, both in terms of the new institutional economics' systematization and interpretation, as well as the application of this theory to the analysis of processes taking place in Poland. Among other things, this is hampered by the limited willingness of representatives of economics, sociology, law, or political theory to cooperate.[41] Historians, especially economic historians, should be added to this list.

Referring to the above words, it can be said that studies conducted from the perspective of institutional economics also currently seem to be a scientific challenge. It concerns both the theoretical and practical level, which should be understood as an attempt to apply this approach in reality, e.g. within the framework of a case study and then in a comparative perspective.

1.2.2. Classifications of institutions: Formal institutions

The broad definition of institutions in economics justifies the need to classify them. There are various divisions of this category, the criteria of which are also different. It is worthwhile to outline at least a few of them.

North distinguishes formal and informal institutions. The former include, among others: rules, laws, constitutions, regulations, and property rights. By informal institutions, he means, e.g.: norms of behavior, conventions, voluntary codes of conduct, taboos, customs, and traditions. It is worth noting that the author emphasizes that institutions include both the mentioned formal and informal constraints, as well as the ways of their implementation (imposition) and

---

41 J. Godłów-Legiędź, "Wstęp," in Godłów-Legiędź, *Instytucje i transformacja*, 5–6. Cf. other sample Polish analyses of economic approaches to the term "institution:" Stankiewicz, *Ekonomika instytucjonalna. Narodziny i rozwój*; Stankiewicz, *Ekonomika instytucjonalna. Zarys wykładu*, 47–56; Gaweł, Klimczak, "Pojęcie instytucji," 73–86; Godłów-Legiędź, "Instytucje i koszty transakcji," 11–32; Godłów-Legiędź, *Współczesna ekonomia*, 65–70; D. Kuder, "Pojęcie instytucji w teorii ekonomii," *Nierówności Społeczne a Wzrost Gospodarczy* No. 19 (2011): 84–93. Detailed studies in the field of institutional economics sometimes cite different understandings of the term "institution," but rather in a pragmatic and ad hoc manner. These approaches are often paraphrases of earlier understandings of the classics, especially North. Stankiewicz draws attention to the problem of multiple definitions of institutions in the new institutional economics and the fact that researchers cite successive approaches for the purposes of detailed studies. In his view, they determine the treatment of institutions in particular interpretative contexts, e.g. institutions as transaction costs, property rights, or subordination relations (Stankiewicz, *Ekonomika instytucjonalna. Zarys wykładu*, 49).

enforcement (system of sanctions). Together they form the incentive structures of societies and especially economies.[42] North's classification criterion remains the legal component.[43]

Some researchers try to specify the phenomenon of formal institutions. They are sometimes defined as public rules of behavior and opposed to informal institutions as private rules of behavior. Relating formal institutions to the concept of the tripartite system, it is pointed out that the legislature most often creates them, enforced by the executive and judiciary branches and the apparatus of coercion at the disposal of these authorities.[44] Formal rules are legal systems that shape political and economic relations. They range from state constitutions to the internal regulations of companies or associations. Property rights and contract law play the most crucial role among formal institutions, because they determine the basis of the institutional economic structure of a society. The observance of formal rules takes place both through formal control of power and informal institutions.[45]

Informal rules stem from the broader culture and are less subject to modification than formal institutions. They are more durable than the latter and may affect their effectiveness. Therefore, Williamson embeds informal institutions at the first level of his proposed social analysis, assuming their variability throughout 100 to 1,000 years. Many economic analyses take informal rules as given.[46] Stankiewicz refers to formal institutions as hard institutions because they derive from state law. On the other hand, informal institutions, which he calls soft, are based on custom.[47] Krzysztof Kostro stresses that more attention is paid to formal institutions in the new institutional economics, while the concept of informal rules is limited to customs, traditions, culture or religion. Moreover, these institutions are most often treated as a given, and permanent element of the institutional economic environment and are more often the subject of research in sociology, anthropology, and economic history than in economics.[48]

---

42 North, "Institutions," 97; North, "Economic Performance Through Time," 360; D. C. North, "Pojmowanie zmian ekonomicznych i wzrostu gospodarczego," in *Globalizacja, marginalizacja, rozwój*, ed. G. Kołodko (Warszawa: Wydawnictwo WSPiZ im. Leona Koźmińskiego, 2003), 140.

43 Voigt, "How (Not) to Measure Institutions," 6. There are differences in the interpretation of North's criterion for dividing institutions in the literature.

44 J. Groenewegen, A. Spithoven, A. van den Berg, *Institutional Economics. An Introduction* (New York: Palgrave Macmillan, 2010), 25.

45 Godłów-Legiędź, *Współczesna ekonomia*, 187.

46 Williamson, "The New Institutional Economics," 596–597, figure 1.

47 Stankiewicz, *Ekonomika instytucjonalna. Zarys wykładu*, 52.

48 K. Kostro, "Nieformalne instytucje w życiu gospodarczym," *Studia Ekonomiczne* No. 1–2 (2004): 71–72. In recent years, informal institutions have also received increasing attention in the literature. See, e.g.: S. Pejovich, "The Effects of the Interaction of Formal and Informal Institutions on Social Stability and Economic Development," *Journal of Markets & Morality* 2, No. 2 (1999): 164–181; J. E. Stiglitz, "Formal and Informal Institutions," in *Social Capital. A Multifaceted Perspective,*

Alternative proposals for classifying institutions can be found in the literature. For example, Daron Acemoglu and James A. Robinson created a double division of this category. They first distinguished between economic and political institutions and then divided each of them into "inclusive" and "extractive."[49]

Inclusive economic institutions are those that positively impact the economy. They enable and encourage people to participate in economic activity. They guarantee private property, are supported by the legal system, and have public services that facilitate exchange and contracting. They allow the creation of new businesses and career choices. They support the development of technology and education. In general, these institutions foster economic activity, increase production, and support the economic well-being of a country. Moreover, they create inclusive markets that provide space for free choice of occupation. Significantly, this type of institution requires the state's participation as a guarantor of order, law, private property, contracts, and provider of public services. In contrast, extractive economic institutions are those that, according to the authors, do not have the indicated

---

eds. P. Dasgupta, I. Serageldin (Washington: The World Bank, 2000), 59–68; M. Muczyński, "Znaczenie instytucji nieformalnych w gospodarce rynkowej," in *Ekonomia – polityka – etyka*, Vol. II, ed. A. F. Bocian (Białystok: Wydawnictwo UwB, 2005), 96–103; J. Godłów-Legiędź, T. Legiędź, "Interaction between Formal and Informal Institutions in the Process of Transformation from a Planned to a Market Economy," *Comparative Economic Research. Central and Eastern Europe* 11, No. 1–2 (2008): 105–124; C. R. Williamson, "Informal Institutions Rule: Institutional Arrangements and Economic Performance," *Public Choice* 139 (2009): 371–387; E. Gruszewska, "Transformacja instytucji nieformalnych w Polsce," *Gospodarka Narodowa* 80 (11), No. 3 (247) (2012): 61–83; E. Gruszewska, "Wpływ interakcji instytucji formalnych i nieformalnych na przedsiębiorczość w Polsce," in *Zrozumieć kapitalizm. Podejście ewolucyjno-instytucjonalne*, eds. A. Ząbkowicz, M. Miszewski, P. Chmielnicki, S. Czech (Sosnowiec–Kraków: Forum Myśli Instytucjonalnej, Oficyna Wydawnicza "Humanitas," 2018), 197–215; R. M. Holmes Jr, T. Miller, M. A. Hitt, M. P. Salmador, "The Interrelationships among Informal Institutions, Formal Institutions, and Inward Foreign Direct Investment," *Journal of Management* 39, No. 2 (2013): 531–566; B. Fiedor, "Instytucje formalne i nieformalne w kształtowaniu trwałego rozwoju," *Zeszyty Naukowe Uniwersytetu Szczecińskiego. Studia i Prace Wydziału Nauk Ekonomicznych i Zarządzania* No. 40 (2015), Vol. 2: *Problemy współczesnej ekonomii*: 83–107; M. Godlewska, "Wpływ instytucji formalnych i nieformalnych na działalność innowacyjną polskich przedsiębiorstw sektora MSP," *Nierówności Społeczne a Wzrost Gospodarczy* No. 54 (2018): 289–300.

49 In Polish translations of Acemoglu and Robinson's texts, there are various translations of institutions from their proposed classification. See, e.g.: D. Acemoglu, "Świat, jaki odziedziczą nasze wnuki," in *Gospodarka za 100 lat. Najważniejsi ekonomiści przewidują przyszłość*, ed. I. Palacios-Huerta (Warszawa: Kurhaus, 2014), 41–42; R. Matera, "Studia nad bogactwem i ubóstwem narodów na przełomie mileniów – wkład Darona Acemoglu i Jamesa A. Robinsona," *Ruch Prawniczy, Ekonomiczny i Socjologiczny* 76, No. 1 (2014): 274.

characteristics of inclusive economic institutions. Their name comes from the fact that these institutions aim to exploit a part of society by a particular group. This is done by depriving other groups of property and income.[50]

Political institutions influence the course of politics by determining their incentives and initiatives. Inclusive political institutions are characterized by an optimal degree of centralization and pluralism. They include countries with a clear diffusion of power in society while limiting it. The state is strong, upholds law and order, provides public services, and regulates economic activity. Consequently, this type of political institution fosters inclusive economic institutions. On the other hand, extractive political institutions are characterized by an insufficient degree of centralization or pluralism. In countries where they occur, the distribution of power is limited, and power itself is not limited by anything, making it absolute in nature. The result is the creation of extractive economic institutions.[51]

However, this does not mean that economic growth cannot occur under conditions of extractive institutions (political and/or economic). This is confirmed by the example of the Soviet Union (from the 1920s to 1970s), South Korea (from the 1950s to 1980s), and contemporary China.[52] Acemoglu and Robinson emphasize the strong link between political and economic institutions. Extractive political and economic institutions complement and reinforce each other, as do inclusive institutions. The connections between inclusive and extractive institutions are usually impermanent.[53]

Voigt distinguishes between "internal" and "external" institutions. The former concern rules sanctioned by society, while the latter refer to state sanctions. This corresponds indirectly with the "public" – "private" dichotomy and Max Weber's view of the state, which, according to him, has a monopoly on legitimate physical violence.[54] Voigt developed his classification by distinguishing four types of internal institutions. These are: (1) conventions enforced independently by individuals (e.g., the grammar of a language); (2) ethical rules (e.g., the Decalogue, moral imperatives) to which people commit themselves; (3) customs under informal social control (e.g., etiquette); (4) formal private rules enforced in an organized manner (e.g., trade rules, arbitration courts). In turn, a state law, sanctioned by the state apparatus (e.g., private and criminal law), comprises the external institution.[55]

Parallel to the above typology, Voigt proposes a distinction between *de jure* and *de facto* formal institutions. The former are rules created by the authorities,

---

50 D. Acemoglu, J. A. Robinson, *Dlaczego narody przegrywają. Źródła władzy, pomyślności i ubóstwa* (Poznań: Zysk i S-ka Wydawnictwo, 2014), 85–95.

51 Acemoglu, Robinson, *Dlaczego narody przegrywają*, 95–99.

52 Acemoglu, Robinson, *Dlaczego narody przegrywają*, 108–113.

53 Acemoglu, Robinson, *Dlaczego narody przegrywają*, 97–99.

54 M. Weber, "Polityka jako zawód i powołanie," in M. Weber, *Racjonalność, władza, odczarowanie*, ed. M. Holon (Poznań: Wydawnictwo Poznańskie, 2004), 268.

55 Voigt, "How (Not) to Measure Institutions," 6–8, table 1.

not necessarily observed in reality, while the latter are those enforced by the state apparatus.[56] It is worth noting that these institutions – which can be further defined as formal and actual – refer to respectively to the normative (postulative) and positive (real) dimensions.[57]

Jerzy Małysz presents several different classifications of institutions. He bases them, e.g., on the findings of German researchers. According to him, the division of institutions into formal and informal results from the nature of establishing rules. In the case of formal institutions, the rules are formally written down (e.g. in the constitution and contract), and their function is to facilitate transactions. They are furthermore responsible for controlling or constraining behavior. Informal institutions (e.g., norms, mores, moral attitudes, customs, routines) expand the possibilities for transactions by expanding or modifying the reach of formal rules. They are efficient and circumvent external control. In a period of social stability, attempts to change formal institutions that conflict with informal institutions are difficult. Moreover, informal institutions are characterized by less volatility than formal institutions.[58]

Proximity to the market is a criterion for dividing institutions into external, internal, and neutral. External institutions should be understood as the necessary framework of a free market economy. These include the legal order and the allocation of property rights. Internal institutions are created during the development of the market and adapt to the legal order. They meet the market's needs and evolve into more complex rules. The state creates neutral institutions to serve the economy. An example of this type of institution is standardization, which makes a transaction possible.[59]

---

56 Voigt, "How (Not) to Measure Institutions," 6–8, table 1.

57 Such a classification of institutions is not new in the social sciences. For example, the Polish sociologist in exile Feliks Gross, undertaking in his research, e.g., economic history issues, wrote in 1958: "Similarly, individual rights are the yardstick of political freedom, which are really at the disposal of the individual, and not the constitution of a given state. After all Hitler ruled within the formal framework of the democratic Weimar constitution for some time and the constitution of the Soviet Union is very beautiful in theory but in practice it is a piece of paper without value" (Pol. *Podobnie probierzem wolności politycznej są prawa indywidualne, którymi realnie dysponuje jednostka, a nie konstytucja danego państwa. Hitler rządził wszak przez pewien czas w formalnych ramach demokratycznej konstytucji wejmarskiej* [original spelling], *a konstytucja Związku Sowieckiego jest w teorii bardzo piękna, ale w praktyce stanowi świstek papieru bez wartości* (F. Gross, *Druga rewolucja przemysłowa. Zagadnienia współczesnego socjalizmu* (Paryż: Wydawnictwo Światło, 1958),80)). Cf. J. Lewkowicz, K. Metelska-Szaniawska, "De jure and de facto Institutions – Disentangling the Interrelationships," *The Latin American and Iberian Journal of Law and Economics* 2, No. 2 (2016): 1–26.

58 J. Małysz, "Instytucje a koszty transakcyjne w świetle neoinstytucjonalnej ekonomii," *Ekonomista* No. 3 (2003): 321.

59 Małysz, "Instytucje a koszty transakcyjne," 321–322.

Małysz also points to the division of institutions into fundamental and derivative. The former are created through evolution and long-term accumulation of knowledge. These are, e.g., the common legal sensitivity and ecological awareness of people. These rules constitute the ground for derivative institutions. It is possible to shape them rationally but within the framework of the fundamental institutions, in harmony with them. An example is legal norms.[60] On the basis of the above characteristics, it can be proposed to refer to fundamental institutions as primary while derivative ones as secondary.

Małysz also presents a division of institutions according to the object of study in economics. According to him, institutional economics studies ceremonial institutions, while neo-institutional economics studies instrumental ones.[61]

In summary, citing only sample classifications of institutions confirms the ontological complexity of this category. A large number of proposed divisions is due to different definitions of institutions. Each classification is based on various criteria, which are often unclear or differently understood (e.g. North's criteria for classifying institutions). Therefore, it can be concluded that the divisions presented by researchers are related to the subject of their research and the resulting approach to institutions.

1.3. Concept of institutions in economic history

Historians have always undertaken the study of specific institutions. Despite their different understanding or classification, this issue has been studied in all segments of history (political, economic, social, cultural, etc.).[62] However, historians' rather widespread study of institutions does not mean their precise definition. On the contrary, historians tend not to present their own views on the term. This situation also occurs on the ground of theory and methodology of history.

---

60 Małysz, "Instytucje a koszty transakcyjne," 322, figure 3.

61 Małysz, "Instytucje a koszty transakcyjne," 322, figure 3.

62 Cf. J. Topolski, *Od Achillesa do Béatrice de Planissolles. Zarys historii historiografii* (Warszawa: Oficyna Wydawnicza Rytm, 1998); E. A. Mierzwa, *Historia historiografii*, Vol. 1: *Starożytność–Średniowiecze* (Toruń: Wydawnictwo Adam Marszałek, 2002); E. A. Mierzwa, *Historia historiografii*, Vol. 2: *Renesans–Oświecenie* (Warszawa: Wydawnictwo Neriton, 2007); E. A. Mierzwa, *Historia historiografii. Wiek XIX*, Vol. 3: *Historiografia niemieckojęzyczna* (Piotrków Trybunalski: Naukowe Wydawnictwo Piotrkowskie przy Filii UJK w Kielcach, 2015); A. F. Grabski, *Dzieje historiografii* (Poznań: Wydawnictwo Poznańskie, 2006); A. F. Grabski, *Zarys historii historiografii polskiej* (Poznań: Wydawnictwo Poznańskie, 2006); D. R. Kelley, *Oblicza historii. Badanie przeszłości od Herodota do Herdera* (Warszawa: WN PWN, 2010); D. R. Kelley, *Losy historii. Badanie przeszłości od Herdera do Huizingi* (Warszawa: WN PWN, 2010); D. R. Kelley, *Granice historii. Badanie przeszłości w XX wieku* (Warszawa: WN PWN, 2009); G. G. Iggers, *Historiografia XX wieku. Przegląd kierunków badawczych* (Warszawa: WN PWN, 2010).

There are few studies in the literature in history devoted to theoretical and methodological aspects of institutions. One exception is a study by the Polish researcher Wanda Moszczeńska, published at the end of the 1960s.[63] Analyzing the problem of the subject of historical research, she took up the theme of institutions at the theoretical level. What is interesting, she also referred to them as institutionalized phenomena because institutions are, for her, an exemplification of historical phenomena, understood as a specific type of historical facts, characterized, among others, by their duration, uniqueness, significant temporal and spatial range, large number and variety of interpersonal relations occurring in them, repetition of individual facts or their massiveness. What is more, defining an institution as a historical phenomenon is determined by the broader meaning of the second term. Moszczeńska notes that the term "institution" is often used loosely in history, as in everyday language. However, the institution is always contrasted with the fact understood as an event.[64] As examples, she points to the institution of parliamentarism, nobility, jury courts, credit, private property, monogamous family, priesthood or Church, and educational institutions. Interestingly, she sees the issue of institutions in history more as a manifestation of the changes of the time (the 1960s) in the understanding of the research tasks of this study than an issue concerning the subject of historical research.[65]

Moszczeńska explains: "Historians define the object of their study by the name institution when relations connecting people and relationships of people to things present themselves as something permanent. This is understood in the sense that over the time-space range, which limits the object of study, these relations are the same in some way, or at least analogous. People and things are in the background of interest, the focus shifts from transformations in the relations connecting people and things to the relations, which are considered as a permanently established bond between people."[66] She adds that the goal of institutional research in history

---

63 W. Moszczeńska, *Metodologii historii zarys krytyczny* (Warszawa: PWN, 1968).

64 Moszczeńska understands an event as some type of historical fact, which, among other things, is narrowed in terms of time and space and constitutes a closed whole in terms of the occurring transformations. Although the terms 'institution' and 'event' are not used in history synonymously, the creation of a given institution, as she notes, is described as a momentous, groundbreaking event, etc. (cf. Moszczeńska, *Metodologii historii zarys krytyczny*, 38–39, 41–42).

65 Moszczeńska, *Metodologii historii zarys krytyczny*, 40–42.

66 Pol. *Historycy określają przedmiot swego badania nazwą instytucja wówczas, gdy stosunki łączące między sobą ludzi i stosunek ludzi do rzeczy przedstawiają się jako coś trwałego. Rozumiane to jest w tym sensie, że na przestrzeni zasięgu czasowo-przestrzennego, ograniczającego przedmiot badania, stosunki te są pod jakimś względem takie same, czy przynajmniej analogiczne. Ludzie i rzeczy znajdują się na dalszym planie zainteresowania, punkt ciężkości przesuwa się z przemian w związkach łączących ludzi i rzeczy na same stosunki, które są rozpatrywane jako trwale ustalona więź między ludźmi* (Moszczeńska, *Metodologii historii zarys krytyczny*, 41).

is to "capture what brings states of affairs together, what provides continuity in relationships. This is the case even if the researcher is primarily concerned with tracing the transformations that the institution has undergone over time."[67] In another place, Moszczeńska points out that a historian studying institutions analyses the sequence of transformations occurring in the background of a relatively unchanging system of relations.[68] An important role is also played by studying the genesis of a particular institution's creation.[69] Thus, permanent relations between people and people to things are the object of interest for historians studying institutions.[70]

Economic history is a discipline that develops at the junction of history and economics.[71] Therefore, it is an interdisciplinary study. The interdisciplinarity of study

---

67 Pol. [*U*]*chwycenie tego, co zbliża stany rzeczy, co zapewnia ciągłość stosunków. Tak jest nawet wówczas, gdy badaczowi zależy przede wszystkim na prześledzeniu przemian, jakim instytucja z biegiem czasu podlegała* (Moszczeńska, *Metodologii historii zarys krytyczny*, 41).

68 Moszczeńska, *Metodologii historii zarys krytyczny*, 252.

69 Moszczeńska, *Metodologii historii zarys krytyczny*, 313.

70 Moszczeńska understands the category of things broadly (Moszczeńska, *Metodologii historii zarys krytyczny*, 38–39).

71 From the Polish literature on the relationship between history and economics within economic history, see especially: A. Grodek, "Czego historią jest historia gospodarcza," in *Pamiętnik trzydziestolecia Szkoły Głównej Handlowej w Warszawie 1906–1936* (Warszawa: SGH, 1938), 46–62; J. Rutkowski, *Historia gospodarcza Polski*, Vol. I (Poznań: Księgarnia Akademicka, 1947), 1–6; J. Rutkowski, *Wokół teorii ustroju feudalnego*, ed. J. Topolski (Warszawa: PIW, 1982); O. Lange, *Ekonomia polityczna*, Vol. I: *Zagadnienia ogólne* (Warszawa: PWN, 1959), 85, 149; J. Topolski, "Historia gospodarcza a teoria ekonomii," *Kwartalnik Historyczny* No. 1 (1964): 85–89; F. Bujak, *Wybór pism*, Vol. I (Warszawa: PWN, 1976), 434–448; J. Kuciński, "Miejsce historii gospodarczej w systemie nauk ekonomicznych," *Acta Universitatis Lodziensis. Zeszyty Naukowe Uniwersytetu Łódzkiego. Nauki Ekonomiczne i Socjologiczne* No. 17 (1977): 3–22; W. Kula, *Problemy i metody historii gospodarczej* (Warszawa: PWN, 1983), 82–94; B. Marks, J. Skodlarski, "Uwagi dotyczące nauczania historii gospodarczej na kierunkach ekonomicznych," *Studia Prawno-Ekonomiczne* 52 (1995): 225–228; J. Skodlarski, *Zarys historii gospodarczej Polski* (Warszawa: WN PWN, 2005), 13–22; J. Skodlarski, "O potrzebie rozważań metodologicznych," in *Historia gospodarcza i historia myśli ekonomicznej a teoria ekonomii. Problemy metodologiczne*, ed. J. Skodlarski (Łódź: Wydawnictwo UŁ, 2008), 7–10; J. Skodlarski, "Związki historii gospodarczej z teorią ekonomii," in Skodlarski, *Historia gospodarcza i historia myśli ekonomicznej a teoria ekonomii*, 46–54; R. Matera, "Czy odwrót historii? Rozważania na temat miejsca historii w nauce," in *Z historii myśli ekonomicznej i historii gospodarczej. Księga jubileuszowa prof. dr. hab. Wiesława Piątkowskiego*, ed. J. Skodlarski (Łódź: Wydawnictwo UŁ, 2006), 93–105; R. Matera, "Interdyscyplinarny charakter historii gospodarczej. Perspektywy rozwoju dyscypliny w XXI wieku," in *Rzeczywistość społeczna w badaniach młodych naukowców*, eds. Z. Dziemanko, W. Stach (Poznań: Wydawnictwo

Maiuscula, 2012), 287–306; R. Matera, "Łączenie ekonomii i polityki w badaniach interdyscyplinarnych. Wyzwania dla ekonomisty, politologa i historyka," in *Polityczna kreacja ładu ekonomicznego. Teoria i praktyka*, eds. M. Kalinowski, A. Pieczewski (Łódź: Wydawnictwo UŁ, 2013), 17–34; W. Morawski, "Czego historią jest historia gospodarcza?," in *Przegląd badań nad historią gospodarczą w XXI wieku*, eds. R. Matera, A. Pieczewski (Łódź: Wydawnictwo UŁ, 2011), 15–25; D. Bębnowski, "Czy istnieje przyjaźń między naukami? Polskie spojrzenie na historię gospodarczą, czyli o związkach historii i ekonomii raz jeszcze" (unpublished manuscript). The impressive output of German science in the theoretical and methodological aspects of economic or social history is noteworthy. See, among others: K. Bräuer, *Kritische Studien zur Literatur und Quellenkunde der Wirtschaftsgeschichte* (Leipzig: Verlag von Veit & Comp., 1912); M. Weber, *Wirtschaftsgeschichte* (München–Leipzig: Verlag von Duncker & Humblot, 1923), 1–18; G. von Below, *Probleme der Wirtschaftsgeschichte. Eine Einführung in das Studium der Wirtschaftsgeschichte* (Tübingen: Verlag von J. C. B. Mohr (Paul Siebeck), 1926); J. Kuczynski, *Studien zur Geschichte der Weltwirtschaft* (Berlin: Dietz Verlag, 1952); L. Beutin, *Einführung in die Wirtschaftsgeschichte* (Köln–Graz: Böhlau Verlag, 1958) (see also extended and supplemented edition: L. Beutin, H. Kellenbenz, *Grundlagen des Studiums der Wirtschaftsgeschichte* (Köln–Wien: Böhlau Verlag, 1973)); O. Morf, *Geschichte und Dialektik in der politischen Ökonomie. Zum Verhältnis von Wirtschaftstheorie und Wirtschaftsgeschichte bei Karl Marx* (Frankfurt–Wien: Europäische Verlagsanstalt, Europa Verlag, 1970); K. A. Wittfogel, *Die natürlichen Ursachen der Wirtschaftsgeschichte* (Rotdruck 1970) (reprint of the original edition: Tübingen: Archiv für Sozialwissenschaft und Sozialpolitik, 1932); R. Baumeister, *Die Konzeption der Zukunftsgesellschaft bei Karl Marx, Friedrich Engels und bei neueren westeuropäischen Marxisten – eine ordnungspolitische Analyse* (Köln: Institut für Wirtschaftspolitik an der Universität zu Köln, 1976); H. Radandt et al., eds., *Handbuch Wirtschaftsgeschichte*, Vol. 1 (Berlin: Institut für Wirtschaftsgeschichte der Akademie der Wissenschaften der DDR, VEB Deutscher Verlag der Wissenschaften, 1981), 11–262; K. Kühne, *Geschichtskonzept und Profitrate im Marxismus* (Neuwied: Luchterhand, 1976); H.-U. Wehler, ed., *Geschichte und Ökonomie* (Köln: Athenäum, 1985); T. Kuczynski, ed., *Wirtschaftsgeschichte und Mathematik. Beiträge zur Anwendung mathematischer insbesondere statistischer Methoden in der wirtschafts- und sozialhistorischen Forschung* (Berlin: Akademie-Verlag, 1985); J. Kocka, *Sozialgeschichte. Begriff – Entwicklung – Probleme* (Göttingen: Vandenhoeck & Ruprecht, 1986); J. Kocka, ed., *Sozialgeschichte im internationalen Überblick. Ergebnisse und Tendenzen der Forschung* (Darmstadt: Wissenschaftliche Buchgesellschaft, 1989); M. Hettling et al., eds., *Was ist Gesellschaftsgeschichte? Positionen, Themen, Analysen* (München: Verlag C. H. Beck, 1991); R. Walter, *Einführung in die Wirtschafts- und Sozialgeschichte* (Paderborn: Ferdinand Schöningh, 1994); B. P. Priddat, "Ökonomie und Geschichte. Zur Theorie der Institutionen bei D. C. North," in *Neuorientierungen in der ökonomischen Theorie*, eds. E. K. Seifert, B. P. Priddat (Marburg: Metropolis, 1995), 205–240; T. Pierenkemper, *Unternehmensgeschichte. Eine Einführung in ihre Methoden und Ergebnisse* (Stuttgart: Franz Steiner Verlag, 2000); H. Berghoff, J. Vogel, eds., *Wirtschaftsgeschichte als Kulturgeschichte. Dimensionen eines Perspektivenwechseln* (Frankfurt–New York: Campus Verlag, 2004).

is meant here as an ontological and epistemological reality, which is created by relationships and dependencies occurring between at least two disciplines. These relationships and dependencies affect the formation of a separate study, sometimes aiming at autonomy and independence from other disciplines.[72]

As Witold Kula points out, economic history is a study of the economic aspect of social life in specific cultures and societies. He continues that it studies regularities in social economic activities or in the economic aspect of social activities, as well as social factors of these regularities. It also focuses on the economic aspect of these regularities' results (their results for the social economy).[73] From these two dimensions of economic history arise two perspectives accordingly: micro- and macro-analysis.[74]

Other understandings of this discipline's subject also emphasize the social aspect of economic history research. Jan Szpak points out that economic historians analyze the economic achievements of civilizations in chronological and territorial terms.[75] According to Zbigniew Gazda, this discipline studies the economic past of people and the regularities of development in it.[76] Zdzisław Sirojć, in turn, defines economic history as the study of management in the past, and considers human economic activity throughout history as its subject matter.[77] Thomas Piketty, criticizing the excessive reliance on mathematical models, theoretical speculations, and empirical methods, emphasizes the importance of taking history into account in economic research. He claims that historical experience is the main human source of knowledge about the world.[78] On the other hand, as he notes, representatives of various social sciences cannot leave the study of economic issues only to economists.[79]

In this work, it is assumed that economic history studies the economic reality in a specific space-time together with all elements and relations which compose this reality.[80] Referring to the above-mentioned approaches to economic history, in order to complete them, it may be stated that various institutions are very often subject of economic history research. They are part of concrete economic reality in a certain space-time, together with all the elements and relations which make up this reality. What is more, institutions co-shape this reality.

72 D. Bębnowski, "Czy istnieje przyjaźń między naukami?," 9 (unpublished manuscript).
73 Kula, *Problemy i metody*, 94.
74 Kula, *Problemy i metody*, 195.
75 J. Szpak, *Historia gospodarcza powszechna* (Warszawa: PWE, 2007), 34.
76 Z. Gazda, *Historia gospodarcza*, Vol. 1 (Kielce: WZiA WSP, 1998), 12.
77 Z. Sirojć, "Wprowadzenie," in *Zarys historii gospodarczej. Od czasów najdawniejszych do najnowszych*, ed. Z. Sirojć (Warszawa: WSDG, 2003), 8.
78 T. Piketty, *Kapitał w XXI wieku* (Warszawa: Wydawnictwo Krytyki Politycznej, 2015), 727.
79 Piketty, *Kapitał w XXI wieku*, 727.
80 D. Bębnowski, "Czy istnieje przyjaźń między naukami?," 11 (unpublished manuscript).

Practically, institutions have been the subject of economic history since the beginning of the formation of this study as a separate and sovereign discipline, i.e. since the 18th century.[81] However, the understanding of them varies in economic history. Some approaches narrow the cognitive spectrum to the categories of organizations, which coincides with the proposal of North.[82] John H. Clapham, in his text from 1932, argues that economic history is a branch of general institutional history. It examines the economic aspects of social institutions in the past. Moreover, the emphasis on a quantitative approach determines its methodological distinctiveness. For this reason, Clapham insists that economic history is or should be the most precise branch of history.[83] He adds, however, that a quantitative approach is not always effective for an institutional approach to the object of study.[84]

In turn, North emphasizes the importance of institutions in economics and clarifies that they are a kind of glue connecting the three dimensions of time (past, present, and future) through their incremental evolution. Consequently, as he argues, history largely focuses on institutional evolution. In that sense, the historical performance of economies is understood as a part of a sequential story.[85]

---

81 The origins of economic history as a separate and independent discipline date back to the second half of the 18th century and are associated with the emergence of economics as a separate study. The conventional moment for the formation of these disciplines is 1776, the date of publication of Adam Smith's work entitled *An Inquiry into the Nature and Causes of the Wealth of Nations* (A. Smith, *Badania nad naturą i przyczynami bogactwa narodów*, Vol. 1–2 (Warszawa: WN PWN, 2007)). Thus, he may be regarded as the father of both economics and economic history, understood as disciplines. However, Andrzej Feliks Grabski pointed out there were references to historical argumentation in economic works of the 17th century (Grabski, *Dzieje historiografii*, 573). More on the formation of economic history as a discipline, see: Grabski, *Dzieje historiografii*, 571–584; Kula, *Problemy i metody*, 11–44; Kuciński, "Miejsce historii gospodarczej," 7–10; Topolski, *Od Achillesa do Béatrice de Planissolles*, 104–105; K. Olendzki, "Historiografia dziejów gospodarczych," in *Informator metodologiczny do ćwiczeń z historii gospodarczej*, ed. W. Morawski (Warszawa: SGH, 2000), 55–59; Sirojć, "Wprowadzenie," 11–13.

82 For exemplifications see: Beutin, *Einführung in die Wirtschaftsgeschichte*, 97–103; Beutin, Kellenbenz, *Grundlagen des Studiums der Wirtschaftsgeschichte*, 101–104. It should be noted, however, that a separate place is devoted to the importance of the state and law for the economy in both studies (Beutin, *Einführung in die Wirtschaftsgeschichte*, 76–84; Beutin, Kellenbenz, *Grundlagen des Studiums der Wirtschaftsgeschichte*, 94–98).

83 For comparison, it is worth quoting the position of Tadeusz Łepkowski, who regarded economic history as the least human component of history (T. Łepkowski, *Przeszłość miniona i teraźniejsza* (Warszawa: PIW, 1980), 228).

84 J. H. Clapham, "Economic History as a Discipline," in *The Varieties of History. From Voltaire to the Present*, ed. F. Stern (New York: Meridian Books, 1956), 308.

85 D. C. North, "Institutions," 97. Cf. Priddat, "Ökonomie und Geschichte"; B. P. Priddat, "Historische Methode und moderne Ökonomie. Über das Methodische in der

In Rolf Walter's work, there is the recognition of institutions as a distinct element of structures (social, economic, historical-political or mental) studied from a historical perspective. They are important components of the social and economic system and vehicles of social and economic order or policy. Walter identifies institutions with organizations (e.g., businesses, political parties) and points out that they set the institutional framework for social development. Thus, the institutionalization (*Institutionalisierung*) can be considered a factor that determines and explains contemporary social and economic development. It includes science, treated by some authors as a social institution.[86] It should be added that the above reflections imply the universality of institutions, which, having their roots in the past, make it possible to understand the present and also help to project the future.[87]

Kula highlights the importance of specific aspects of economic reality that are the subject of economic history research. He indicates, among others: enterprises, social structures, and the market.[88] These categories can be described as institutions in light of the definitions cited earlier. Institutions can also be the axial category of comprehensive accounts of economic history. This is the case, e.g., with Rondo Cameron's synthesis of general economic history, which he built around institutions, population, resources, and technology.[89]

The institutional perspective in economics, especially on the ground of new institutional economics, has influenced the development of a distinct approach in economic history research. For example, Hans Frambach considers the specificity of "neoclassical history of economics" (*neoklassiche Geschichte der Ökonomie*).[90] Eirik G. Furubotn and Rudolf Richter distinguish several subfields within the framework of new institutional economics, among which is "New Institutional Economic History."[91] Javier Mejía, tracing the process of changing economic history between 1950 and 2015 (but limiting it to cliometrics[92]), argues that after the cliometric paradigm had broken the dominance, new directions of economic

'Historischen Schule' und das Historische in der 'Neuen Institutionenökonomie'," in Berghoff, Vogel, *Wirtschaftsgeschichte als Kulturgeschichte*, 99–116.

86 Walter, *Einführung in die Wirtschafts- und Sozialgeschichte*, 63–69.

87 In the case of North and Walter, one can see a parallel to the concept of "panhistory," i.e., the omnipresence of history, which includes, among other things, three dimensions of time: past, present, and future. It is a development of the above mentioned concept of Braudel (see D. Bębnowski, "Czy historia jest nauką tylko o przeszłości?," *Transformacje. Pismo Interdyscyplinarne* No. 1–2 (88–89) (2016): 42–43).

88 Kula, *Problemy i metody*, 225–272, 479–581.

89 R. Cameron, L. Neal, *Historia gospodarcza świata. Od paleolitu do czasów najnowszych* (Warszawa: Książka i Wiedza, 2004), 14–17.

90 H. Frambach, *Die neoklassische »Geschichte« der Ökonomie. Bemerkungen zur Standortbestimmung von Douglass C. North's Theorie vom Wandel der Institutionen* (Wuppertal: Bergische Universität Gesamthochschule Wuppertal, 2001).

91 Furubotn, Richter, *Institutions and Economic Theory*, 37.

92 New Economic History, also known as cliometrics or econometric history, emerged as a research direction in the 1950s in the United States. The creators of this

history research emerged in the 1970s. He also mentions "new institutional economic history" among them, drawing on the achievements of cliometrics and new institutional economics. Moreover, Mejía, referring to Avner Greif and Herbert Heaton, draws attention to the contemporary renaissance of the institutional approach in economic history research. It even takes the form of a return to the sources of this study.[93] Therefore, it seems justified to indicate the institutional approach as one of the dominant approaches to economic history in the 20th–21st centuries alongside such paradigms as Marxism (historical materialism), the French Annales school and cliometrics.[94]

Economic history research in Poland also dates back to the 18th century.[95] It also included institutions. A significant output in this area was left by historiography after World War II. Leaving aside the problem of the ideological corset and the resulting Marxist methodology, which was the reference point for the historical research of the time,[96] especially in the field of social and economic history, it must be said that many works from this period are characterized by high reliability and originality of approach. Economic history studies, including research on institutions, continued after 1989. This state of affairs continues to the present day.[97]

---

approach included: Alfred H. Conrad, John R. Meyer, Lance E. Davis, Jonathan R. T. Hughes, Robert W. Fogel, Stanley L. Engerman or North. It assumes the use of economic theory and quantitative methods (especially econometrics) in historical research, especially in the field of economic and social history. See, e.g.: J. Pomorski, *Paradygmat "New Economic History." Studium z teorii rozwoju nauki historycznej* (Lublin: Wydawnictwo UMCS, 1995); C. Diebolt, M. Haupert, eds., *Handbook of Cliometrics* (Berlin–Heidelberg: Springer Reference, 2016).

93 J. Mejía, "The Evolution of Economic History since 1950: From Cliometrics to Cliodynamics," *Tiempo & Economía* 2, No. 2 (2015): 85–88.

94 D. Bębnowski, "Socjologiczny komponent historii gospodarczej. Résumé głównych paradygmatów w XX i XXI w." (unpublished manuscript).

95 More on the development of Polish economic history research: Kula, *Problemy i metody*, 44–52; Olendzki, "Historiografia dziejów gospodarczych," 58–59, 66–68.

96 For Marxist historiography in Poland after 1945 see: Grabski, *Zarys historii historiografii polskiej*, 198–230; R. Stobiecki, *Historia pod nadzorem. Spory o nowy model historii w Polsce (II połowa lat czterdziestych – początek lat pięćdziesiątych)* (Łódź: Wydawnictwo UŁ, 1993); R. Stobiecki, "Między kontynuacją a dyskontynuacją," in *Humanistyka polska w latach 1945–1990*, eds. U. Jakubowska, J. Myśliński (Warszawa: Instytut Badań Literackich PAN, 2006), 127–155; R. Stobiecki, *Historiografia PRL. Ani dobra, ani mądra, ani piękna... ale skomplikowana. Studia i szkice* (Warszawa: Wydawnictwo Trio, 2007); R. Stobiecki, *Historycy polscy wobec wyzwań XX wieku* (Poznań: Wydawnictwo Nauka i Innowacje, 2014); R. Stobiecki, *Historiografia PRL. Zamiast podręcznika* (Łódź: Wydawnictwo UŁ, 2020).

97 Contemporary Polish economic history teams and their achievements have been discussed more than once in the literature. Cf. important studies: E. Kościk, T. Głowiński, eds., *Społeczeństwo i gospodarka w badaniach historycznych – dokonania i perspektywy. W 60-lecie polskich badań statystycznych i gospodarczych na Dolnym*

As Godłów-Legiędź notes, approaches beyond neoclassical theory (thus, beyond mainstream economics) have been recognized in economic research in recent decades. This recognition has extended to institutional economics. This is manifested by the fact that several prominent institutionalists have been awarded the Nobel Prize in Economic Sciences.[98] This current also seems to be increasingly appreciated in economic history studies.[99] In the economic model of economic history research,[100] this is particularly evident.[101]

Śląsku (Wrocław: Wydawnictwo GAJT, 2006); W. Morawski, ed., *Tradycje szkolnictwa ekonomicznego w Polsce po 1945 roku* (Warszawa: Oficyna Wydawnicza SGH, 2007); W. Morawski, *Dzieje gospodarcze Polski* (Warszawa: Wydawnictwo Difin, 2010, 8–9); E. Kościk, "'Wrocławskie Spotkania z Historią Gospodarczą' próbą ożywienia badań historycznych nad gospodarką i społeczeństwem," in Matera, Pieczewski, *Przegląd badań nad historią gospodarczą*, 39–44; J. Chumiński, K. Popiński, "Gospodarka PRL w historiografii polskiej 1989–2010," in Matera, Pieczewski, *Przegląd badań nad historią gospodarczą*, 45–57; D. Grala, "Badania nad dziejami reform gospodarczych w Polsce po roku 1989. Cele, obiekty i metody," in Matera, Pieczewski, *Przegląd badań nad historią gospodarczą*, 59–73; J. Chumiński, K. Popiński, "Dominanty i zaniechania w badaniach PRL – historia gospodarcza po 1989 r.," in *Z Jeleniej Góry do Wrocławia i z powrotem. Wokół historii społecznej i gospodarczej. Tom studiów dedykowany Profesor Elżbiecie Kościk*, ed. T. Głowiński (Wrocław: Wydawnictwo TUM, 2018), 195–216.

98 Godłów-Legiędź, "Wstęp," 4; Godłów-Legiędź, *Współczesna ekonomia*, 39. Among the institutionalists, the winners of the Nobel Prize in Economic Sciences were: Gunnar Myrdal (1974), George Stigler (1982), Buchanan (1986), Coase (1991), North (1993), Williamson and Ostrom (2009) ("All Prizes in Economic Sciences," http://www.nobelprize.org/nobel_prizes/economic-sciences/laureates/ (accessed October 1, 2015)). Cf. S. Czaja, *Blaski i cienie Nagrody Nobla* (Wrocław: Wydawnictwo I-BiS, 2002); L. J. Jasiński, *Nobel z ekonomii. Poglądy laureatów w zarysie* (Warszawa: Wydawnictwo Key Text, 2008).

99 In 1993, the Nobel Prize in Economic Sciences was awarded to North and Fogel "for having renewed research in economic history by applying economic theory and quantitative methods in order to explain economic and institutional change" ("The Sveriges Riksbank Prize in Economic Sciences in Memory of Alfred Nobel 1993," http://www.nobelprize.org/nobel_prizes/economic-sciences/laureates/1993/index.html (accessed October 1, 2015)).

100 Two models of research can be distinguished in economic history. The first, the historical one, is characteristic of researchers who are trained as historians. Their research is dominated by a descriptive and qualitative approach, combined with a strong attachment to direct sources, especially archives. The second model, the economic one, refers to those authors who are trained as economists. Their works emphasize the importance of economic theory, quantitative methods, and the search for relationships between the used statistical data. In this model, the importance of the direct source is reduced. Source information is limited to source editions or data from other studies. Naturally, there are a number of indirect approaches in this regard (see D. Bębnowski, "Czy istnieje przyjaźń między naukami?," 2 (unpublished manuscript)).

101 Cf. valuable reviews and texts: P. Gabrielczak, "Główne nurty w rosyjskiej historii gospodarczej w nowym milenium," in Matera, Pieczewski, *Przegląd badań nad*

1.4. Summary

The understanding of institution in social sciences is diverse. However, it is possible to identify basic common elements within the proposals for defining this category. Firstly, researchers present institutions as groups of people or organizations united by the pursuit of a given goal. Secondly, institutions can be understood as norms or frameworks that set boundaries on how individuals function. The common understanding of the institution, consolidating it with organization, is most often found in management science and political science.

Institutional economics of the 19th–21st centuries has the most significant output of theoretical consideration of institutions. Their understanding clearly evolved from sociological and psychological perspectives to economic or socio-political ones.

Proposals of economic history in defining institutions should be considered in two ways, i.e. in connection with history and humanities, as well as with economics and social sciences. Despite much more limited theoretical literature on the subject, institutions are one of the main objects of study in economic history. Certain streams of this discipline, especially those correlating with institutional economics, combine theoretical and empirical studies of institutions to a greater extent, emphasizing the role of sources. Polish science does not deviate from the above trends in global research.

The very rich theoretical literature shows that the definition of institution is still a fundamental difficulty in the institutional studies of economic transformations. Individual authors adopt a selected view of institutions in an ad hoc manner, which is dictated by the currently undertaken research problem. An additional challenge is to show the causal relationship between institutions and economic

---

historią gospodarczą, 149–159; R. Matera, "Gospodarka światowa w anglosaskiej historii gospodarczej w pierwszej dekadzie trzeciego milenium," in Matera, Pieczewski, *Przegląd badań nad historią gospodarczą*, 177–191; K. Kowalski, "Nowe trendy w historii gospodarczej. 'The Economic History Review' w latach 2001–2009," in Matera, Pieczewski, *Przegląd badań nad historią gospodarczą*, 193–211; A. Pieczewski, "Przegląd publicystyki naukowej amerykańskiego Stowarzyszenia Historii Gospodarczej ('The Economic History Association')," in Matera, Pieczewski, *Przegląd badań nad historią gospodarczą*, 213–224; A. Bukowski, "Przegląd publikacji z historii gospodarczej na łamach 'Explorations in Economic History' w latach 2001–2010," in Matera, Pieczewski, *Przegląd badań nad historią gospodarczą*, 225–234; P. Matera, R. Matera, "Problem światowego bogactwa i ubóstwa jako element badań historii gospodarczej – studia z przełomu mileniów," in Matera, Pieczewski, *Przegląd badań nad historią gospodarczą*, 247–263; J. Dzionek-Kozłowska, "Koncepcja 'path dependence' w historii gospodarczej: przegląd najnowszych publikacji," in Matera, Pieczewski, *Przegląd badań nad historią gospodarczą*, 265–280; R. Matera, "Jak pisać historię gospodarczą – inspiracje z lektury 'Fałszywej ekonomii' Alana Beattiego," in Matera, Pieczewski, *Przegląd badań nad historią gospodarczą*, 281–297.

processes. This involves the still open discussion about the measurability of individual rules and the use of qualitative methods in this regard. These considerations raise concerns about the ambiguity or superficiality of the analysis. Moreover, the above observations apply to both formal and informal rules, and it is not true that these difficulties refer only to informal institutions, which are harder to capture. Also, some detailed studies on the impact of formal rules on socio-economic processes remain unsatisfactory. It should be remembered that the studied economic reality in a specific space-time has a multifaceted character. Institutions are only its components.

CHAPTER 2 Opening balance: Two German economies towards reunification

2.1. Economic structures of the two German states in the late 1980s and early 1990s

Attempts to compare the two German economic structures at the dawn of reunification on the basis of key macroeconomic measures pose serious problems. Some researchers even question the validity of this type of procedure.[1] This is mainly due to methodological differences present in statistical sources before and even after reunification. Moreover, it should be stressed that in the case of East Germany, official statistics may have been influenced by the communist state's propaganda of success.[2] In spite of these reservations, it is worth making an attempt to compare the economic achievements of the FRG and the GDR using statistical data based on a relatively uniform (although not always) methods, although one should be aware that in this case, too, the study will not be free of controversy.[3]

In 1989, the FRG (248,717 km^2) had a population of 62.3 million, of which the labor force was 29.7 million, and the employed population was 27.7 million. Unemployment in West Germany was 7.1 %. In contrast, the labor force consisted of 8.9 million people of the 16.4 million population living in the GDR (108,333 km^2). In accordance with the policy of full employment, East German statistics showed the same level of employed people and thus no unemployment.[4]

Considering the structure of employment, it should be noted that in 1985–1987 the largest percentage of the FRG's citizens worked in industrial manufacturing (32.5 %) and services (27.0 %). The remaining sectors employed, respectively: 14.8 % – trade, 7.5 % – finance and services, 6.7 % – construction, 5.7 % – transport and

---

1 See, e.g., W. R. Smyser, *The Economy of United Germany. Colossus at the Crossroads* (New York: St. Martin's Press, 1992), 3.

2 See *Introduction*, section *Sources and literature* in this work.

3 Noteworthy is a volume of over 800 pages discussing in detail particular aspects of the political and socio-economic systems of the FRG and the GDR. The study contains impressive comparative statistical material: *Materialien zum Bericht zur Lage der Nation im geteilten Deutschland 1987* (Bonn: Bundesministerium für innerdeutsche Beziehungen, 1987). Cross-sectional data for the FRG and the GDR in 1949–1990 concerning social and economic issues is also provided by Erhard Cziomer, using, among others, German materials (E. Cziomer, *Zarys historii Niemiec powojennych 1945–1995* (Warszawa–Kraków: WN PWN, 1997), 329–350, appendix 1–27).

4 G. Sinn, H.-W. Sinn, *Jumpstart: The Economic Unification of Germany* (Cambridge: MIT Press, 1992), 209, appendix A.

communication, 4.6 % – agriculture, 1.1 % – mining. In the same period, selective data for the GDR are as follows: industrial manufacturing – 44.6 %, services (excluding catering and hospitality) – 25.4 %, trade (including catering, hospitality, and financial services) – 11.0 %, transport and communications – 8.2 %, construction – 6.8 %, agriculture – 4.0 %.[5]

In West Germany, the gross average monthly wage (including social contributions paid by employers) in 1989 was DM 3,966 against M 1,322 in the GDR.[6] Within individual economic sectors, the differences were also considerable: DM 3,657 to M 1,324 in industry and manufacturing, DM 2,958 to M 1,310 in construction, DM 2,597 to M 1,242 in agriculture and forestry, DM 2,893 to M 1,168 in trade, DM 3,311 to M 1,436 in transport and communications. In contrast, in the same year, net money income or personal disposable income *per capita* was DM 22,500 per year (DM 1,900 per month) in the FRG[7] and M 10,200 per year (M 850 per month) in the GDR.[8]

Several measures are worth noting from the perspective of industrial production efficiency. In 1988, global output in the FRG reached $479.69 billion, while in the GDR – $64.66 billion, which was $7,838 and $3,879 *per capita*, respectively. The average annual growth of industrial production in 1965–1988 was 2.1 % (1.9 % *per capita*) in the FRG and 4.9 % (5.0 % *per capita*) in the GDR.[9] This was a consequence of the forcible industrialization in communist Germany.

In 1987, the West German economy was one of the most important energy producers in the world (151,416 thousand tons,[10] 13th place), although it imported 218,367 thousand tons of energy (2nd place). The GDR produced a total of 95,931 thousand tons (22nd place) and imported 47,831 thousand tons (13th place).[11]

In 1987, the total land area (*Bodenfläche*) in the FRG was 244,280 km². In turn, the agricultural land area (*landwirtschaftliche Nutzfläche*) consisted of arable land

---

5 M. Smith-Morris, ed., *Welt Wirtschaft in Zahlen* (Düsseldorf: Wirtschaftswoche, The Economist Books, 1991), 196–197, fn. a–b, e–f.

6 Since 1948 the Deutschmark (*Deutsche Mark*, DM) was in use in the FRG, replaced in 2002 by the euro. In 1968–1990 the currency of the GDR was the GDR Mark (*Mark der DDR*), called the mark (M) shortly. At the end of 1989, the average exchange rate of German currencies was: $1 = DM 1.698 = M 1.680 (Smith-Morris, *Welt Wirtschaft in Zahlen*, 176).

7 Such data appear in work by Gerlinde Sinn and Hans-Werner Sinn (Sinn, Sinn, *Jumpstart*, 210, appendix A). Simple calculations indicate that the annual income was DM 22,800 or the monthly income was DM 1,875. The difference is probably due to the rounding of the second figure.

8 Sinn, Sinn, *Jumpstart*, 210, appendix A.

9 Smith-Morris, *Welt Wirtschaft in Zahlen*, 70.

10 In hard coal units (*Steinkohleeinheit*, SKE). 1 kg SKE refers to 7,000 kcal of energy released when 1 kg of hard coal is burned (Smith-Morris, *Welt Wirtschaft in Zahlen*, 82).

11 Smith-Morris, *Welt Wirtschaft in Zahlen*, 84.

(30.6 %), permanent grassland (18.3 %), irrigated parts of agricultural land (4.3 %), and forests and woodlands (3.0 %). The total land area in the GDR was, in turn, 105,240 km^2. Among the agricultural area, 46.9 % was arable land, 28.3 % was forest and woodland, 24.1 % was irrigated parts of agricultural land, and 11.9 % was permanent grassland.[12]

In 1988, agriculture in the FRG employed 3.9 % of the total workforce, while the agricultural sector in the GDR employed 8.6 %. In the West there were 1,303 people per 1 km^2 of agricultural land and 354 in East Germany. Different indicators can illustrate the efficiency of agricultural production in both countries. For example, the level of global agricultural production per 1 person employed in this sector was: $18,589 in the FRG and $7,172 in the GDR.[13] In 1987, an average of 123.0 tractors were used per 10 km^2 of farmland in the West and 26.6 in the East.[14] In 1988, West German agriculture produced 27,131 thousand tons of grain, 5,428 thousand tons of meat, 2,423 thousand tons of vegetables, and 5,399 thousand tons of fruit. In contrast, East German agricultural production included: 9,816 thousand tons of grain, 2,038 thousand tons of meat, 1,265 thousand tons of vegetables, and 1,096 thousand tons of fruit.[15]

The West German state allocated greater financial outlays to investment. In 1989 this amounted to DM 435.6 billion gross and DM 199.6 billion net. In the GDR, investment expenditures reached M 77.1 billion gross and M 43.7 billion net.[16]

From the point of view of public finances, attention should be paid to budget revenues, which amounted to DM 965.5 billion in the FRG in 1988,[17] while in the GDR – M 269.7 billion. The state allocated subsidies to companies (without price subsidies) respectively: DM 75.6 billion (the FRG in 1989) and M 106.8 billion (the GDR in 1988). The proportions in transfers to households were the opposite and amounted to DM 61.8 billion in the FRG (1989) and M 36.3 billion in the GDR (1988). In 1988, West Germany spent DM 173.9 billion on pensions, while the GDR spent M 17.2 billion, with the average pension then being, respectively: DM 1,108 and M 427.[18] As far as the money supply is concerned, it should be noted that in 1989 a total of DM 146.9 billion (DM 2,350 *per capita*) was in circulation in the FRG and M 17.0 billion (M 1,036 *per capita*) in the GDR.[19]

---

12 Smith-Morris, *Welt Wirtschaft in Zahlen*, 54.
13 Smith-Morris, *Welt Wirtschaft in Zahlen*, 56.
14 Smith-Morris, *Welt Wirtschaft in Zahlen*, 58–59.
15 Smith-Morris, *Welt Wirtschaft in Zahlen*, 62.
16 Sinn, Sinn, *Jumpstart*, 214–215, appendix A.
17 *Statistisches Jahrbuch für die Bundesrepublik Deutschland* (hereinafter: SJ BRD), Vol. 1990 (Wiesbaden–Stuttgart: Statistisches Bundesamt, Metzler-Poeschel Verlag, 1990), 442, table 20.2.
18 Sinn, Sinn, *Jumpstart*, 211, appendix A.
19 Sinn, Sinn, *Jumpstart*, 212, appendix A.

The West Germany's advantage also extended to the area of assets and liabilities. In 1989, net fixed assets amounted to DM 6,512.6 billion, while the amount for East Germany is estimated at between M 575.8 billion and M 1,745.0 billion. On the other hand, the FRG's foreign debt was higher than the GDR's and reached DM 426.8 billion (against M 21.2 billion). The indebtedness of the West German companies amounted to DM 1,196.6 billion, while East German enterprises (including the central bank) generated gross debt of M 260.4 billion. The indebtedness of citizens, expressed in terms of the total value of housing loans, was respectively: DM 729.4 billion and M 108.5 billion.[20]

In the area of foreign trade, the FRG had the higher turnover in 1989: DM 641.0 billion in export and DM 506.5 billion in import. The trade balance amounted to DM 134.5 billion. East Germany's export showed a total of M 141.1 billion against the import of M 144.7 billion, which meant a negative balance of M −3.6 billion.[21]

In 1985–1988, the commodity structure of the West German import was dominated by industrial products (31.1 %) and machinery and transport equipment (28.2 %). Other categories of goods were: consumer goods (17.8 %), food (10.6 %), and fuel (9.6 %). The commodity structure of the GDR import was different: 38.0 % – fuels, 34.1 % – machinery and transport equipment, 13.1 % – industrial products, and 5.7 % – consumer goods. From the point of view of export, agricultural products accounted for 1.1 % of the FRG's export, minerals – 0.9 %, food, beverages, tobacco – 4.3 %, textiles and clothing – 5.7 %, and metals – 57.2 %. For the GDR, the part of these measures was as follows: agricultural products – 6.8 % and minerals – 16.7 %.[22]

The geographical structure of the two countries' foreign trade depended on political and economic factors. In 1988, the FRG's trade was dominated, especially by capitalist countries. The most important trading partners included: Austria, Belgium, France, Italy, the Netherlands, Sweden, the United Kingdom, the United States, but also the Soviet Union. The GDR's trade was primarily limited to the Eastern Bloc countries: Bulgaria, Czechoslovakia, Hungary, Poland, and the Soviet Union. Trade with the FRG also played an important role.[23]

As an illustration of social living standards, the savings rate (calculated as a proportion of personal disposable income or net money income) was 13.6 % in the West and 6.3 % in the East in 1989.[24] In the same year, the cost of living index (1970 = 100) was 197.7 in the FRG and 99.5 in the GDR.[25]

20 Sinn, Sinn, *Jumpstart*, 214, appendix A.
21 Sinn, Sinn, *Jumpstart*, 215, appendix A.
22 Smith-Morris, *Welt Wirtschaft in Zahlen*, 162–164.
23 See detailed data on the volume of trade of the FRG and GDR with the listed countries in B. R. Mitchell, *International Historical Statistics. Europe 1750–1988* (New York: M Stockton Press, 1993), 595, 597, table E2.
24 Sinn, Sinn, *Jumpstart*, 215, appendix A.
25 Sinn, Sinn, *Jumpstart*, 214, appendix A.

The consumption structure of both German societies (as a percentage of disposable income) is also characteristic. In 1989, West Germans spent 40.0 % of their income on manufactured goods, 36.8 % on services, and 23.2 % on food and beverages. On the other hand, the GDR citizens spent 45.3 % of their income on manufactured goods, 41.5 % on food and beverages, and only 13.2 % on services.[26]

According to other data, people spent $10,109 *per capita* on consumption in West Germany, of which 21.9 % was spent on food and beverages, 8.6 % on clothing, 20.3 % on energy or housing, 9.0 % on household goods, 3.2 % on health, 15.6 % on transportation or communication, 21.4 % on entertainment and other. Consumption expenditures in the GDR amounted to $6,523 *per capita*. In turn, the individual areas of consumption were spent: 40.7 % – on food and beverages, 12.3 % – on clothing, 2.4 % – on energy or housing, 12.0 % – on household goods, 4.0 % – on health, 2.1 % – on transport without communication, 26.5 % – on entertainment and other.[27]

The different living standards are also illustrated by information regarding household equipment. In 1989, 96 % of households in the FRG and 54 % in the GDR owned cars; 99 % in the FRG and 96 % in the GDR owned televisions (of which color televisions – 95 % in the FRG and 57 % in the GDR); 99 % in the FRG and 17 % in the GDR owned telephones; 81 % in the FRG and 99 % in the GDR owned refrigerators without freezers; 75 % in the FRG and 43 % in the GDR owned freezers with or without refrigerators; and 97 % in the FRG and 99 % in the GDR owned washing machines.[28] In 1980–1988, among the 28,329 thousand housing units in the FRG, there were on average 2.16 persons per 1 of them. In contrast, in the GDR, there were 7,078 thousand housing units and an average of 2.40 persons per 1 of them.[29] There was an average of 35.5 m^2 per 1 person in dwelling in the West and 27.6 m^2 in the East.[30]

An additional illustration of the potential of the two German economies prior to reunification is provided by comprehensive historical and statistical data compiled by Brian R. Mitchell. Details are presented in Table 1.

26 For the FRG, the data include 4-person households with gross incomes from wages and salaries between DM 2,900 and DM 4,400. The data for the GDR is for all households (Sinn, Sinn, *Jumpstart*, 215–216, appendix A, fn. 19).

27 Smith-Morris, *Welt Wirtschaft in Zahlen*, 230, 232, fn. c.

28 For the FRG, the data include 4-person households with incomes from employment between DM 3,000 and DM 4,500. For the GDR, the percentage of households with consumer durables is included (Sinn, Sinn, *Jumpstart*, pp. 215–216, appendix A, fn. 20). Cf. detailed data: Smith-Morris, *Welt Wirtschaft in Zahlen*, 233–235.

29 Smith-Morris, *Welt Wirtschaft in Zahlen*, 240.

30 Sinn, Sinn, *Jumpstart*, 215, appendix A.

Table 1: *Example macroeconomic indicators of the FRG and GDR in selected years 1970–1988*

Indicator	Year, unit, comments	FRG	GDR
Economically active population by employment sector: (1) agriculture, forestry, fishing (2) extractive industry (3) manufacturing (4) construction (5) finances (6) transport and communication (7) services (8) other	FRG: 1970, with West Berlin GDR: 1971, with East Berlin (in thousands of people)	(1) 1,991 (2) 323 (3) 10,264 (4) 2,163 (5) 5,270 (6) 1,443 (7) 5,039 (8) 117	(1) 960 (2) 199 (3) 3,185 (4) 614 (5) 931 (6) 555 (7) 1,772 (8) –
Money wages index in industry	1988 (1975 = 100)	181	145
Area of main cereal, potato, and sugar beet crops: (1) wheat (2) rye (3) barley (4) oat (5) mixed corn and buckwheat (6) potatoes (7) sugar beets	1988 (in thousands of hectares)	(1) 1,743 (2) 378 (3) 1,836 (4) 474 (5) 103 (6) 199 (7) 379	(1) 765 (2) 607 (3) 874 (4) 148 (5) 11 (6) 442 (7) 198
Output of main cereal, potato, and sugar beet crops: (1) wheat (2) rye (3) barley (4) oat (5) mixed corn and buckwheat (6) potatoes (7) sugar beets	1988 (in thousands of tons) GDR: mixed corn without buckwheat	(1) 11,922 (2) 1,579 (3) 9,587 (4) 2,038 (5) 449 (6) 7,434 (7) 18,590	(1) 3,699 (2) 1,785 (3) 3,798 (4) 507 (5) 30 (6) 11,546 (7) 4,625
Output of cows' milk	1988 (in thousands of tones)	23,974	9,204
Butter output	1988 (in thousands of metric tones)	392	306
Meat output	1988 (in thousands of metric tones)	4,969	2,800

Table 1: (*Continued*)

Indicator	**Year, unit, comments**	**FRG**	**GDR**
Landings of fish	1988 (in thousands of metric tons)	209	179
Industrial production index	1988 (1963 = 100)	197	362
Output of natural gas	1988 (in millions of m^3)	15,009	6,396
Output of pig iron	1988 (in thousands of metric tons)	33,016	2,786
Output of crude steel	1988 (in thousands of metric tons)	41,023	8,131
Coal trading: (1) import (2) export	1988 (in thousands of metric tons)	(1) 9,077 (2) 5,806	(1) 7,688 (2) –
Import of iron ore	1988 (in thousands of metric tons)	45,169	2,375
Raw cotton consumption	1988 (in thousands of metric tons)	220	104
Output of cotton yarn	1988 (in thousands of metric tons)	197	152
Output of wool yarn	1987 (in thousands of metric tones)	53	76,9
Output of artificial and synthetic fibres	1987 (in thousands of metric tones)	983	451
Output of sulphuric acid	1988 (in thousands of metric tones)	4,053	799

(*Continued*)

Table 1: (*Continued*)

Indicator	**Year, unit, comments**	**FRG**	**GDR**
Output of motor vehicles: (1) private cars (2) commercial vehicles	1988 (in thousands)	(1) 4,312 (2) 258	(1) 218 (2) 42
Output of beer	1988 (in thousands of hectolitres)	88,166	24,521
Output of electric energy	1988 (in giga Watt hours)	431.16	118.33
External trade aggregate current value: (1) import (2) export	1988 FRG: DM billion GDR: M billion	(1) 440 (2) 568	(1) 87.2 (2) 90.2
Freight traffic on railways	1988 (1) in millions of metric tonnes (2) in billions of ton-kilometres	(1) 310 (2) 61.2	(1) 349 (2) 60.4
Passenger traffic on railways	1988 (1) in millions of passengers (2) in millions of passenger kilometres	(1) 1,121 (2) 41,760	(1) 600 (2) 22,785
Merchant ships registered	1988 Vessels of 60 net tons or over (1) number of ships (2) in thousands of tones	(1) 950 (2) 3,728	(1) 164 (2) 1 314
Inland navigation traffic	1988 (1) in million/ tkm (2) in millions of tones	(1) 52,854 (2) 233	(1) 2,532 (2) 20.3

Table 1: (*Continued*)

Indicator	**Year, unit, comments**	**FRG**	**GDR**
Motor vehicles in use: (1) private cars (2) commercial vehicles	1988 (in thousands)	(1) 28,878 (2) 1,322	(1) 3,764 (2) 389
Commercial aviation	1988 (1) in passenger kilometres (2) in ton-kilometres	(1) 34,097 (2) 3,470	(1) 3,229 (2) 92
Telephone services: (1) telephones in use (2) telephone calls	1988 (1) in thousands (2) in millions	(1) 41,735 (2) 30,419	(1) 3,977 (2) 2,297
Radio and television receiving licences (1) radio (2) TV	1988 (in thousands)	(1) 26,892 (2) 23,742	(1) 6,781 (2) 6,233
Banknote circulation	1988 FRG: total issues (in DM billions) GDR: the GDR State Bank issues (in M millions)	144	15,623
Deposits in savings banks	1988 FRG: in DM billions GDR: in M billions	416	128
Total central government expenditure	1988 FRG: in DM billions, with West Berlin and Saarland GDR: in M billions	278	269

(*Continued*)

Table 1: *(Continued)*

Indicator	**Year, unit, comments**	**FRG**	**GDR**
Children and teachers in schools: (1) pupils in primary schools (2) primary school teachers (3) pupils in secondary schools (4) secondary school teachers (5) teachers in all types of schools	1988 (in thousands)	(1) 3,653 (2) 230 (3) 2,438 (4) 180 (5) –	(1) 1,953 (2) – (3) 40.8 (4) – (5) 167
Students in universities	1988 (in thousands) GDR: including teachers' training colleges	1,105	132

Own calculations and compilation based on Mitchell, *International Historical Statistics*, tables B1, B4, part D; tables C1–C2, C6–C9, D1, D4, D8–D9, D11, D13–D14, D16, D19, D21, D23, D25–D27, E1, F2–F7, F9–F10, G1, G3, G5, I1–I2 (due to the length of the source publication, this footnote is limited to indicating the numbers of specific tables; cf. relevant footnotes in the quoted material).

In 1989, the gross domestic product (GDP) at market prices was DM 2,237 billion in the FRG and M 353.4 billion (346.1 according to other data) in the GDR. GDP per 1 person employed was respectively: DM 80,750 and M 39,700. GDP per 1 person in the workforce was respectively: DM 75,300 and M 39,700. On the other hand, GDP *per capita* was counted respectively: DM 36,300 and M 21,500. West Germany's advantage was also visible in the level of gross income from wages (including employers' social security contributions) and amounted to DM 1,171.5 billion against M 141.2 billion for the GDR.[31]

However, these figures are not entirely comparable. According to unified statistics, West Germany's GDP in 1988 was $1,208.29 billion, while the GDR's figure was $87.62 billion. The level of GDP *per capita* was $19,743 in the FRG and $5,256 in the GDR. In the West, services (58.8 %) and industry (39.7 %, including manufacturing – 33.0 %) had the largest share in GDP output, followed by agriculture (1.5 %). The proportions for East Germany were different: 73.8 % of GDP was produced by the industrial sector (in this respect, the GDR was ranked the 2nd in the world, after Brunei), 13.3 % by services, and 12.9 % by agriculture (data for the net domestic product (NDP) in 1986).[32]

Angus Maddison also presents standardized GDP statistics for the selected years 1950–1991. These are included in Table 2.

31 Sinn, Sinn, *Jumpstart*, 209–210, appendix A; p. 216, fn. 1.

32 The source uses the following conversion rates: $1 = M 3.5; M 2 = DM 1 (Smith-Morris, *Welt Wirtschaft in Zahlen*, 32–33, 36–39, fn. a, d; 40).

Table 2: *GDP of West Germany and East Germany in selected years 1950–1991 (in million 1990 international dollars)*

Year	FRG	GDR
1950	213,942	51,412
1973	814,786	129,969
1990	1,182,261	82,177
1991[a]	1,242,096	85,961

a Post-reunification data for the former West Germany and East Germany.
Source: A. Maddison, *The World Economy*, Vol. 1: *A Millennial Perspective* (Paris: OECD, 2006), 178, table A-d.

The average annual growth rate of real value added between 1980 and 1988 in West Germany was stable at 1.7 % overall. It was 1.7 % in agriculture, 0.9 % in total industry, 4.4 % in manufacturing, and 2.9 % in services. Higher values were achieved by the GDR economy, resulting from forcible industrialization and extensive development. For the same period, the total growth rate was 4.0 % (NDP value), in agriculture – 2.1 %, industry – 3.8 %.[33]

The FRG and the GDR expenditure structures as a proportion of GDP (at market prices) were also characteristic. In West Germany, private consumption (54.5 %) was the largest contributor to GDP, followed by export (32.4 %), investments (20.3 %), government consumption (19.4 %), and import (−26.7 %). The data for the GDR (as part of the NDP in 1985) are incomplete and include private consumption (72.1 %, including net trade), investment (21.5 %), and state consumption (6.4 %).[34]

2.2. Outline of the political process of German reunification in the late 1980s and early 1990s

The term "unification" can be defined as the creation of a state as a result of the merger of at least two states under some conditions in a given historical period. The term "German reunification" will be used here to refer to the connection of the GDR into the FRG in 1990, although from a political-legal point of view, it should be seen as an example of incorporation, i.e. inclusion, annexation, absorption.

Two reunifications stand out in Germany's history. They were multi-faceted processes. The first unification of Germany (*Deutsche Einigung*) took place in the 1860s and was crowned – thanks to the unquestionable role of the Prussian

33 Smith-Morris, *Welt Wirtschaft in Zahlen*, 44–45, 47, fn. b.
34 Smith-Morris, *Welt Wirtschaft in Zahlen*, 48–49, fn. b, e–f.

Prime Minister Otto von Bismarck – with the establishment of the German Empire (German Reich, the Second Reich) on January 18, 1871.[35] The second unification or German reunification (*Deutsche Wiedervereinigung, Deutsche Vereinigung*), also referred to as the restoration of German unity (*Herstellung der Einheit Deutschlands*), consisted of the incorporation of the GDR into the FRG and was one of the stages of the collapse of the communist system in Central and Eastern Europe in 1989–1991, known as the Autumn of Nations.[36]

In a metaphorical way, the Autumn of Nations in Germany had two scenes coinciding with this season, which tied the entire unification process together like a buckle. The starting point was the fall of the Berlin Wall on the night of November 9/10, 1989, and the culmination was the formal reunification of the FRG and GDR less than a year later, on October 3, 1990.[37] The spontaneous dismantling of the Wall by the inhabitants of Berlin was a symbolic symptom of the disintegration of the Eastern Bloc that was taking place at that time,[38]

35 J. E. Rodes, *Germany: a History* (New York: Holt, Rinehart and Winston, 1964), 340–378.

36 A. Burakowski, A. Gubrynowicz, P. Ukielski, *1989 – Jesień Narodów* (Warszawa: Collegium Civitas, ISP PAN, Wydawnictwo Trio, 2009).

37 The literature on German reunification and the transition of the state after 1990 is very rich. Among exclusively Polish studies presenting some aspects of this complex process it is worth mentioning: E. Cziomer, *Polityka zagraniczna Niemiec. Kontynuacja i zmiana po zjednoczeniu ze szczególnym uwzględnieniem polityki europejskiej i transatlantyckiej* (Warszawa: Dom Wydawniczy Elipsa, 2005); M. M. Kosman, *Zjednoczone Niemcy w procesie integracji europejskiej (1990–2002)* (Toruń: Wydawnictwo Adam Marszałek, 2005); T. Jaskułowski, *Pokojowa rewolucja w Niemieckiej Republice Demokratycznej w latach 1989–1990. Geneza – przebieg – efekty* (Wrocław: CSNiE UWr, Oficyna Wydawnicza Atut, 2007); T. Jaskułowski, *Ostatnie miesiące NRD* (Wrocław: CSNiE UWr, Oficyna Wydawnicza Atut, 2010); B. Brocka-Palacz, ed., *Dokąd zmierzają Niemcy. Reformy polityczne, gospodarcze i społeczne* (Warszawa: SGH, 2008); M. A. Stradowski, *Międzynarodowe aspekty zjednoczenia Niemiec* (Toruń: Wydawnictwo Adam Marszałek, 2010); J. Kiwerska, B. Koszel, M. Tomczak, S. Żerko, *Polityka zagraniczna zjednoczonych Niemiec* (Poznań: Instytut Zachodni, 2011); Z. Mazur, H. Orłowski, M. Wagińska-Marzec, *Kultura zjednoczonych Niemiec. Wybrane problemy* (Poznań: Instytut Zachodni, 2013); J. Sawczuk, *Vertragsgemeinschaft 1989/1990. Wzlot i upadek idei konfederacji dwu państw niemieckich* (Poznań: Wydawnictwo WSB w Poznaniu, 2013); Z. Mazur, *Droga Niemiec do zjednoczenia wewnętrznego* (Poznań: Instytut Zachodni, 2015). These works contain extensive bibliographies.

38 The solemnity of this event was reflected in the press of the time. Cf. sample articles in Poland: "Europa bez muru," *Gazeta Wyborcza*, November 10–12, 1989, No. 132, 1; K. Leski, "Oczekuje się od nas, abyśmy dokonali przełomu," *Gazeta Wyborcza*, November 10–12, 1989, No. 132, 1; OS, mm, "NRD. Mur runął," *Gazeta Wyborcza*, November 10–12, 1989, No. 132, 7; J. Reiter, "Karnawał na murze," *Gazeta Wyborcza*, November 13, 1989, No. 133, 1; KL, "Kohl w Polsce – piątek, sobota. Doba przerwy," *Gazeta Wyborcza*, November 13, 1989, No. 133, 3; "Rozmowy

starting with the Round Table talks in Poland between February and April 1989.[39]

While in the political (systemic and legal) dimension, it is sometimes easier to see German reunification as a one-off act (although even this is a simplified interpretation, as political reunification was also a process stretching over time), the economic, social and cultural dimension of reunification is seen in a processual way without much controversy. The symbolic event in October 1990 resulted in a series of consequences of a diverse nature that both the old and the new federated states had to deal with. Thus, in 1990, the full multifaceted reunification of the Eastern and Western *Länder* was only a challenge for the FRG in its new guise. It is no coincidence that the literature uses the terms unification, integration, or convergence in this context, while researchers rather unanimously recognize these processes as unfinished in 2015.[40]

At the risk of relative simplification, it is worth proposing two understandings of the concept of German reunification. A "narrow" understanding would emphasize one (usually political, i.e. the incorporation of the GDR into the FRG) or several dimensions of this phenomenon (e.g. the extension of the West German political and legal system to the GDR). A "broad" understanding would emphasize the multifaceted nature of the phenomenon and include economic, social, and cultural issues in addition to those mentioned above. In this work, the term in question is understood in the broadest possible way because of its double complexity: vertical (i.e. encompassing various fields of reality, especially political (including systemic and legal), economic, social, and cultural) and horizontal (i.e. extending over time). This leads to the conclusion that German reunification in 1990 should be presented in holistic and processual categories rather than monolithic and idiographic ones.

The unification mood, which has been growing since the end of the 1980s, encompassed not only the societies of West Germany and East Germany but also

---

Genschera. Nacjonalizm przezwyciężony," *Gazeta Wyborcza*, November 13, 1989, No. 133, 3; O. Skwiecińska, "Karnawał na murze," *Gazeta Wyborcza*, November 13, 1989, No. 133, 6; K. Leski, "Berliński weekend," *Gazeta Wyborcza*, November 13, 1989, No. 133, 6; M. Kossakowski, "Mur i historia," *Gazeta Wyborcza*, November 13, 1989, No. 133, 6; mk, "Kalendarium wydarzeń w NRD w roku 1989," *Gazeta Wyborcza*, November 13, 1989, No. 133, 6; jj, "RFN – NRD. Najszczęśliwszy naród," *Gazeta Wyborcza*, November 13, 1989, No. 133, 7; jj, OS, "Reakcje światowe," *Gazeta Wyborcza*, November 13, 1989, No. 133, 7; J. Jankowski, "Klucz do Niemiec – klucz do Europy," *Gazeta Wyborcza*, November 15, 1989, No. 135, 6.

39 On the origins and course of the Round Table talks in Poland see A. Dudek, *Historia polityczna Polski 1989–2012* (Kraków: Wydawnictwo Znak, 2013), 15–33.

40 See, e.g., J. Czech-Rogosz, "Gospodarka wschodnich Niemiec w 12 lat po zjednoczeniu – niedokończony proces unifikacji gospodarczej. Wybrane problemy," in *Unifikacja gospodarek europejskich. Szanse i zagrożenia*, eds. A. Manikowski, A. Psyk (Warszawa: WN WZ UW, 2004), 93–102.

local politicians.[41] In spite of various scenarios (often very different from each other), the concept of Helmut Kohl, Chancellor of the FRG,[42] was the most significant because he exerted a decisive influence on the direction and character of the reunification process. On November 28, 1989, during a debate on German unity in the Bundestag, he presented a 10-point program in which he outlined the conditions for German unification and, consequently, the overcoming of the previous division of Europe. This plan was forward-looking but did not yet indicate a specific timeframe.

Firstly, Kohl announced humanitarian aid for East Germans emigrating to the FRG. However, he appealed to the GDR authorities to facilitate such emigration and to support East Germans financially. He also proposed setting up a common fund for this purpose.

Secondly, Chancellor saw the possibility of cooperation between West Germany and East Germany. This was to include the economy, science, technology, culture, environmental protection, and telephone and transport links, including railroads.

Thirdly, fundamental reforms in the GDR were to be a condition of the FRG's assistance. According to the head of the West German government, the changes to the political system should include: amending the constitutional provisions on the opposition; breaking up the monopoly of one party;[43] introducing a new electoral law; organizing free, equal, and secret elections and admitting other political groups to them; introducing the rule of law; abolishing the political criminal law and releasing political prisoners. On the other hand, reforms of the economic system had to address: the transition from a planned to a market economy, opening the GDR to western investments, and creating conditions for private economic initiative. As Kohl stated, the people of the GDR wanted economic freedom, prosperity, and the opportunity to reap the fruits of their labor. Interestingly, Chancellor's postulates about economic reforms also referred to other countries of the Council for Mutual Economic Assistance (COMECON),[44] which, in his opinion, should allow the inflow of the West German capital. Kohl mentioned Poland and Hungary.

---

41 In the case of the GDR, unification moods were preceded by anti-communist sentiment. Here, however, the process of removing the communists from power in East Germany is deliberately omitted. For a synthetic treatment of the problem, see: Cziomer, *Zarys historii Niemiec powojennych*, 244–288.

42 During the period of Germany's division, Kohl served as Chancellor of the FRG three times: 1982–1983, 1983–1987, and 1987–1991.

43 The leadership role in the GDR was played by the Socialist Unity Party of Germany (*Sozialistische Einheitspartei Deutschlands*, SED).

44 The Council for Mutual Economic Assistance (COMECON) functioned between 1949 and 1991. It brought together the countries of the Eastern Bloc under the control of the Soviet Union, coordinating their economic integration (see: G. Burkhardt et al., eds., *Rat für gegensetige Wirtschaftshilfe. Strukturen und Probleme* (Bonn: Ostkolleg der Bundeszentrale für politische Bildung, 1987)); A. Zwass, *The*

Fourthly, Kohl envisaged the strengthening of the network of agreements between West Germany and East Germany in all areas and on all levels. The joint institutions to be established in the future would cover the economy, transport, environmental protection, science, technology, health, and culture.

Fifthly, Chancellor declared his desire for German federalization on the condition that the GDR would have a democratically legitimate government. Kohl saw an opportunity to create new forms of institutional cooperation between the two countries. He pointed to a freely elected joint government committee for permanent consultation and political coordination, joint committees of experts, and a common parliamentary committee. He said that Germany was able to continue its history by drawing on its confederation and federation experience. He acknowledged, however, that the condition for reunification is the will of the people.

Sixthly, Kohl stressed that the process of German reunification must be consistent with European integration, including the Western concept of a lasting and just peace order. In doing so, he referred to his talks with Mikhail Gorbachev, the leader of the Soviet Union in 1985–1991, and raised the importance of respecting the integrity and security of each state and the right of countries to freely choose their political and social system. He also emphasized respect for the principles and norms of international law, especially the right to self-determination of peoples. He also called for the enforcement of human rights and the recognition and cultivation of the cultures of European nations. He pointed out that historical traditions should be referred to, and the division of Europe should be overcome.

Seventhly, according to the West German Chancellor, the attractiveness and influence of the European Community must be strengthened. He stated that it was open to the reforming countries of Central, Eastern, and Southern Europe. He declared that the FRG wanted to help the East German state to open up to these processes by concluding a trade and cooperation agreement that would give the GDR access to the common market. Kohl stated that the FRG could seek various forms of association for the transforming Eastern Bloc countries, which would eventually lead to a reduction of economic and social inequalities in Europe. He stressed that German reunification is also a European issue. Therefore, as he noted earlier, this process should coincide with Europe's integration. In his opinion, it confirms and develops the identity of Europeans. This identity means cultural diversity, freedom, democracy, human rights, and self-determination.

Eighthly, Chancellor expressed his conviction that the foundation of a united Europe should be the continuation of the effects of the Conference on Security and Co-operation in Europe (CSCE).[45] He indicated creating concepts for institutional

---

Council for Mutual Economic Assistance. The Thorny Path from Political to Economic Integration (Armonk–New York: M. E. Sharpe, 1989).

45 The first meeting of the Conference on Security and Co-operation in Europe took place in 1972, culminating in the signing of the CSCE Final Act in 1975. In 1995, the Organization for Security and Co-operation in Europe (OSCE) was established. See more A. Florczak, "Organizacja Bezpieczeństwa i Współpracy w Europie," in

forms of European cooperation as a task for the future, e.g. institutions for coordinating economic cooperation between the East and the West or a common European environmental council.

Ninthly, Kohl supported measures to reduce and control arms, as well as a global ban on chemical weapons. He also expressed approval for the reduction of the nuclear potential to the necessary minimum by the world powers. In this field, he declared to hold appropriate talks with the Warsaw Pact countries.[46]

Tenthly, Chancellor bluntly stated that by implementing the policy outlined in his program, the FRG expects peace in Europe, in which the German people, on the basis of the right to self-determination, will regain their unity. The political goal of his government is – and this was supported by the North Atlantic Treaty Organisation (NATO)[47] – reunification, understood as the restoration of Germany's national unity.[48]

Kohl's program clearly linked the process of German reunification with European integration and abolition of the division of Europe. Chancellor repeated this emphatically in the conclusion of his speech to the Bundestag: "Linking the German question with pan-European development and West-East relations – as I have just explained in ten points – makes possible an organic development which takes account of the interests of all concerned and – this is our goal – paves the way for peaceful and free development in Europe. Only together and in a climate of mutual trust can we peacefully overcome the division of Europe, which is always also the division of Germany. This means that we need prudence, reason, and a sense of proportion on all sides so that the development that has already begun – so hopeful – can continue steadily and peacefully. What could disturb this

Organizacje w stosunkach międzynarodowych. Istota – mechanizmy działania – zasięg, ed. T. Łoś-Nowak (Wrocław: Wydawnictwo UWr, 2004), 138–164.

46 The Warsaw Pact (formally: Treaty of Friendship, Cooperation and Mutual Assistance) was a political and military alliance bringing together the countries of the Eastern Bloc (including East Germany) under the leadership of the Soviet Union. It functioned between 1955 and 1991. See R. Kałużny, "Układ Warszawski 1955–1991," *Zeszyty Naukowe Wyższej Szkoły Oficerskiej Wojsk Lądowych* No. 1 (147) (2008): 190–198.

47 The North Atlantic Treaty Organization (NATO) is an international political and military organization that emerged from a treaty signed on April 4, 1949 in Washington, by the United States and most Western European countries. During the Cold War, it was a counterweight to the Warsaw Pact. The West Germany's accession to NATO took place in 1955. See E. Latoszek, "Pakt Północnoatlantycki jako przykład międzynarodowej organizacji międzynarodowej o charakterze wojskowym," in E. Latoszek, M. Proczek, *Organizacje międzynarodowe. Założenia, cele, działalność* (Warszawa: WSHiFM, Dom Wydawniczy Elipsa, 2001), 484–533.

48 *177. Sitzung. Bonn, Dienstag, den 28. November 1989* (Deutscher Bundestag. Stenografischer Bericht, Plenarprotokoll 11/177, 13510–13514).

process is not reforms but their refusal. It is not freedom that creates instability, but its suppression."[49]

However, while Kohl's 10-point program still took into account the GDR statehood and was rather general (framework), the Chancellor's later actions (from the beginning of 1990) became more and more explicit and unambiguous.[50] On February 5, 1990, a coalition bloc Alliance for Germany (*Allianz für Deutschland*, AfD) was formed in the GDR, inspired by Kohl and consisting of the following East German parties: the Christian Democratic Union of Germany (*Christlich Demokratische Union Deutschlands*, CDU), the German Social Union (*Deutsche Soziale Union*, DSU) and the Democratic Beginning (*Demokratischer Aufbruch*, DA). The bloc's goal was to bring about a monetary, economic, and social union between the FRG and the GDR and, as a consequence, the rapid unification of Germany. Other West German parties also carried out adequate political and financial interference, supporting their sister groups in the GDR. This was possible after the opening of the borders between the German states on November 9, 1989, and the fall of the Berlin Wall. In turn, on February 7, 1990, a meeting of the FRG government established the coordination team German Unity (*Deutsche Einheit*), which included representatives of ministries and experts. Their goal was to work out an accelerated formula for reunification by creating a monetary, economic, and social union and determining the necessary details of reunification's external and internal aspects. Moreover, on March 1, Kohl presented in Bonn to the party chairmen comprising the AfD an election program, in which the accession of the GDR to the FRG under Art. 23 of the Basic Law of the FRG (*Grundgesetz*, GG) was considered the fastest scenario for the restoration of German unity for the first time.[51]

---

49 *Die Verknüpfung der deutsche Frage mit der gesamteuropäischen Entwicklung und den West-Ost-Beziehungen – wie ich sie soeben in zehn Punkten erläuterte – ermöglich eine organische Entwicklung, die den Interessen aller Beteiligten Rechnung trägt und – dies ist unser Ziel – einer friedlichen und freiheitlichen Entwicklung in Europa den Weg bahnt. Nur miteinander und in einem Klima des wechselseitigen Vertrauens können wir die Teilung Europas, die immer auch die Teilung Deutschlands ist, friedlich überwinden. Das heißt, wir brauchen auf allen Seiten Besonnenheit, Vernunft und Augenmaß, damit die jetzt begonnene – so hoffnungsvolle – Entwicklung stetig und friedlich weiterverläuft. Was diesen Prozeß stören könnte, sind nicht Reformen, sondern deren Verweigerung. Nicht Freiheit schafft Instabilität, sondern deren Unterdrückung* (*177. Sitzung. Bonn, Dienstag, den 28. November 1989*, 13513–13514).

50 Suffice it to say that on November 8, 1989, in the Bundestag Kohl showed no faith in the rapid reunification of Germany, while on November 9 he was forced to interrupt his diplomatic visit to Poland, being surprised by the fall of the Berlin Wall (Cziomer, *Zarys historii Niemiec powojennych*, 261–262, 283–284).

51 Cziomer, *Zarys historii Niemiec powojennych*, 285–288.

Many West German politicians painted an optimistic picture of German reunification in front of the public, referring to the post-war "economic miracle." However, such comparisons proved to be unjustified.[52]

In February, the formula for the Two-Plus-Four conferences was crystallized, with the goal of discussing German reunification and having the FRG and the GDR coordinate the process in consultation with the four powers: the United States, the Soviet Union, France, and Great Britain. Four rounds of conferences were held from May 4 to September 12: in Bonn (May 4–5), Berlin (June 22), Paris (July 17), and Moscow (September 12).[53]

The first and last free elections to the East German parliament, the People's Chamber (*Volkskammer der DDR*), held on March 18, were significant. It resulted in the defeat of the communists and a victory for the East German CDU, which was part of the AfD bloc.[54] Generally, the AfD group supported German reunification according to the scenario of Kohl (whom *nomen omen* supported them during the election campaign) and Western countries.[55] The political situation after

---

52 See in more detail: section 3.5. in this work. Although one cannot agree with Michał Moszyński's statement that Kohl devoted only the second point of his program to economic issues, it must be admitted that the political aspects of reunification dominated it. The differences between the "economic miracle" of the FRG and the transition of the former GDR primarily concerned the rate of economic growth, unemployment, and financial transfers (M. Moszyński, "Transformacja systemowa wschodnich Niemiec w perspektywie "cudu gospodarczego" Ludwiga Erharda," in *Ordoliberalizm i społeczna gospodarka rynkowa wobec wyzwań współczesności*, eds. P. Pysz, E. Mączyńska (Warszawa: PTE, 2013), 219–238). No less important for the differences in the development trajectories of the FRG in the 1950s and 1960s and the former GDR were circumstances related to informal institutions. These resulted from the socialist past of post-GDR society (cf. section 6.1.2.3. in this study). Moreover, Wojciech Giza pays attention to external conditions (especially the post-war demand, opening to European markets, Marshall Plan, creation of supply by human capital, importance of demilitarization for investment in the civil sector, migration of the German population to the FRG as a result of border changes), which contributed to the "economic miracle" in the FRG (W. Giza, "Niemiecki 'cud gospodarczy' jako efekt realizacji ordoliberalnej polityki gospodarczej – analiza krytyczna," *Optimum. Studia Ekonomiczne* No. 4 (52) (2011): 107–118).

53 J. Kukułka, *Historia współczesna stosunków międzynarodowych 1945–2000* (Warszawa: WN Scholar, 2003), 387.

54 M. Machnacki, "NRD – chadecja zwycięża," *Gazeta Wyborcza*, March 19, 1990, No. 66 (233), 1; "Wyniki wyborów w NRD," *Gazeta Wyborcza*, March 20, 1990, No. 67 (234), 1; KL, "Polskie nadzieje po zwycięstwie chadecji," *Gazeta Wyborcza*, March 20, 1990, No. 67 (234), 1; J. Reiter, "Co wybrali wschodni Niemcy," *Gazeta Wyborcza*, March 20, 1990, No. 67 (234), 6; M. Mochnacki, "NRD. Zwycięzcy i zwyciężeni," *Gazeta Wyborcza*, March 20, 1990, No. 67 (234), 7.

55 It should not be forgotten that the position of the Soviet Union was also important. Gorbachev, who was implementing a separate reform program in the Eastern Bloc – "restructuring," "transparency" and "acceleration" (*perestroika*, *glasnost* and

the election was conducive to deepening the ties between the two German states. The new and last (first non-communist) Prime Minister of the GDR was Lothar de Maizière of the CDU (April 12 – October 2, 1990), who had previously served as Deputy Prime Minister and Minister for Church Affairs in the last communist government of the GDR under Hans Modrow (November 18, 1989 – April 12, 1990).[56]

The *Treaty Establishing a Monetary, Economic and Social Union Between the Federal Republic of Germany and the German Democratic Republic* was signed on May 18 in Bonn. This 38-article document entered into force on July 1. In terms of monetary union, it regulated, in particular, the following issues: the adoption of a common currency, the Deutschmark, which had previously only been in use in the FRG; the designation of the German Federal Bank (*Deutsche Bundesbank*) as the central bank for issuing currency; and the setting of exchange rates for the East German currency for various social groups and political and economic entities. The provisions of the economic union included, in particular, the introduction of a social market economy model and privatization of state enterprises in the Eastern *Länder*. In turn, within the framework of the social union, it was decided to implement West German solutions, including pensions, health care, accident benefits, unemployment benefits, and changes in labor law.[57]

---

uskorenie) – did not actually oppose the changes taking place in the GDR. For example, on January 30, 1990, he demonstrated to East German Prime Minister Hans Modrow his readiness to allow German reunification (under certain conditions). On February 10, Gorbachev told Kohl that he would accept the results of the GDR elections, which were to be held on March 18. On July 15–17, Kohl visited the Soviet Union, during which, among other things, he received permission to unify the FRG, the GDR, and both parts of Berlin, as well as to gain full and unlimited sovereignty. He negotiated attractive conditions for the withdrawal of Soviet troops from the GDR territory (but at the price of a drastic reduction of the armed forces, i.e. by 45 %). Moreover, Gorbachev accepted the membership of reunified Germany in NATO (Cziomer, *Zarys historii Niemiec powojennych*, 285, 288, 301–303, 306–308).

56 Cziomer, *Zarys historii Niemiec powojennych*, 286–290.

57 *Gesetz zu dem Vertrag vom 18. Mai 1990 über die Schaffung einer Währungs-, Wirtschafts- und Sozialunion zwischen der Bundesrepublik Deutschland und der Deutschen Demokratischen Republik Vom 25. Juni 1990* (hereinafter: Treaty Establishing a Monetary, Economic and Social Union) (*Bundesgesetzblatt* (hereinafter: BGBl.), Part II, 1990, No. 20, 518–568). See the text of the *Treaty Establishing a Monetary, Economic and Social Union between the Federal Republic of Germany and the German Democratic Republic: Gesetz zu dem Vertrag vom 18. Mai 1990*, 537–544. The *Treaty Establishing a Monetary, Economic and Social Union* was accompanied by a protocol ("Gemeinsames Protokoll über Leitsätze," in *Gesetz zu dem Vertrag vom 18. Mai 1990*, 545–546), 9 annexes on the introduction of specific legal regulations in the FRG and the GDR for the purpose of its implementation, as well as on the mutual provision of personal data, the Arbitration Court (*Schiedsgericht*), and the possibility of acquiring property by private investors ("Anlage I–IX," in *Gesetz zu dem Vertrag vom 18. Mai 1990*, 547–566). The document closed with protocol declarations ("Protokollerklärungen," in *Gesetz zu dem Vertrag vom 18. Mai 1990*, 567).

The next step in the progressive reunification process was the *Treaty Preparing and Holding the First All-German Elections to the German Bundestag between the Federal Republic of Germany and the German Democratic Republic*, or the *Election Treaty* (*Wahlvertrag*), of August 3. New electoral districts were organized on the territory of the still existing GDR, and the West German electoral law was introduced.[58]

On August 23, the People's Chamber passed a resolution to bring the country within the scope of the Basic Law of the FRG, according to Art. 23 GG. The new legal status was to take effect on October 3, 1990.[59]

The culminating moment of the deepening unification process was the signing of the *Treaty between the Federal Republic of Germany and the German Democratic Republic on the Establishment of German Unity*, or the *Unification Treaty* (*Einigungsvertrag*), on August 31. This extensive document, consisting of 9 chapters and 45 articles, regulated all aspects of the unified state. Subsequent provisions of the *Unification Treaty* dealt with the following issues:[60] the accession of the GDR to the FRG on October 3, 1990, on the basis of Art. 23 GG (Chap. I), the capital in Berlin and the Day of German Unity on October 3 (Art. 2), extending the legal force of the FRG Constitution to the Eastern *Länder* (Chap. II), legal unification (Chap. III), the introduction of European Community law in Eastern Germany (Art. 10), international treaties and agreements (Chap. IV), public administration and justice (Chap. V), public assets and debts (Chap. VI), labor, welfare, family, women, health and environmental protection (Chap. VII), culture, education, science and sports (Chap. VIII), radio (Art. 36), transitional and final regulations (Chap. IX).[61]

---

58 *Gesetz zu dem Vertrag vom 3. August 1990 zur Vorbereitung und Durchführung der ersten gesamtdeutschen Wahl des Deutschen Bundestages zwischen der Bundesrepublik Deutschland und der Deutschen Demokratischen Republik sowie dem Änderungsvertrag vom 20. August 1990 Vom 29. August 1990* (BGBl., Part II, 1990, No. 31, 813–832). See the text of the *Treaty Preparing and Holding the First All-German Elections to the German Bundestag between the Federal Republic of Germany and the German Democratic Republic*: *Gesetz zu dem Vertrag vom 3. August 1990*, 822–832.

59 *Bekanntmachung des Schreibens der Präsidentin der Volkskammer der Deutschen Demokratischen Republik vom 25. August 1990 und des Beschlusses der Volkskammer vom 23. August 1990 über den Beitritt der Deutschen Demokratischen Republik zum Geltungsbereich des Grundgesetzes der Bundesrepublik Deutschland Vom 19. September* 1990 (BGBl., Part I, 1990, No. 49, 2057–2058).

60 Individual issues are the subject of separate chapters of the *Unification Treaty*. Where justified, the matter of the relevant articles is indicated.

61 *Gesetz zu dem Vertrag vom 31. August 1990 zwischen der Bundesrepublik Deutschland und der Deutschen Demokratischen Republik über die Herstellung der Einheit Deutschlands – Einigungsvertragsgesetz – und der Vereinbarung vom 18. September 1990 Vom 23. September 1990* (hereinafter: Unification Treaty) (BGBl., Part II, 1990, No. 35, pp. 885–1245). See the text of the *Unification Treaty*: *Gesetz zu dem Vertrag vom 31. August 1990*, 889–904. The *Unification Treaty* was accompanied by: (1) a protocol ("Protokoll," in *Gesetz zu dem Vertrag vom 31. August 1990*, 905–906);

The subsequent rounds of the Two-Plus-Four conferences culminated in the *Treaty on the Final Settlement with Respect to Germany* (the *Two-Plus-Four Agreement*), signed in Moscow on September 12. It primarily provided for German reunification within the borders of the FRG and the GDR, considering them as final. Thus Germany renounced any territorial claims to other countries. It was decided to abolish the previous division of Berlin.[62] Germany declared its respect for international peace, renouncing its weapons of mass destruction and reducing the size of its army. The Soviet Union assured the withdrawal of its troops from East Germany, where any other troops were forbidden. The powers also confirmed the sovereignty of a united Germany.[63]

Consequently, on October 1, at the session of the United Nations (UN) General Assembly in New York,[64] the four powers issued a declaration renouncing their

---

(2) 2 extensive annexes (No. 1–2) detailing the implementation of specific legal regulations in the FRG and the GDR for its implementation ("Anlage I–II," in *Gesetz zu dem Vertrag vom 31. August 1990*, 907–1236); (3) the joint statement of the governments of the FRG and the GDR (Annex No. 3) of June 15, 1990, on open property issues ("Anlage III," in *Gesetz zu dem Vertrag vom 31. August 1990*, 1237–1238); (4) the treaty between the FRG and the GDR of September 18, 1990, on the implementation and interpretation of the *Unification Treaty* with specific legal amendments ("Vereinbarung zwischen der Bundesrepublik Deutschland und der Deutschen Demokratischen Republik zur Durchführung und Auslegung des am 31. August 1990 in Berlin unterzeichneten Vertrages zwischen der Bundesrepublik Deutschland und der Deutschen Demokratischen Republik über die Herstellung der Einheit Deutschlands – Einigungsvertrag," in *Gesetz zu dem Vertrag vom 31. August 1990*, 1239–1245).

62 In 1945, Berlin (as well as the rest of Germany) was divided into 4 occupation zones: American, British, French, and Soviet. In 1949, two separate states were created: the FRG and the GDR. The Soviet part of Berlin became the capital of the communist state, while West Berlin remained under Allied control (Bonn was made the capital of the FRG). In 1961, the GDR authorities began to build a wall (the Berlin Wall) separating West Berlin from the territory of East Germany (Cziomer, *Zarys historii Niemiec powojennych*, 44–45, 52–59, 143, 149–150).

63 *Gesetz zu dem Vertrag vom 12. September 1990 über die abschließende Regelung in bezug auf Deutschland Vom 11. Oktober 1990* (BGBl., Part II, 1990, No. 38, 1317–1329). See the text of *Treaty on the Final Settlement with Respect to Germany*: *Gesetz zu dem Vertrag vom 12. September 1990*, 1318–1329.

64 The United Nations (UN) was created as a result of the signing of the UN Charter in San Francisco on June 26, 1945. The primary objectives of the UN are to maintain world peace and security, develop international cooperation, and promote respect for human rights. More extensively see, e.g., M. Proczek, "Organizacja Narodów Zjednoczonych jako międzynarodowa organizacja uniwersalna," in Latoszek, Proczek, *Organizacje międzynarodowe*, 62–98.

rights and responsibilities with regard to Germany. This was to take effect upon reunification.[65]

On October 3, the GDR was incorporated into the FRG. Thus formally, German reunification as the FRG took place. The GDR ceased to exist as a state and a subject of international law.[66]

A month later, on December 2, the first elections for a united parliament were held. They were held on the basis of the treaty of August 3. The coalition of the CDU, CSU (Christian Social Union in Bavaria, *Christlich-Soziale Union in Bayern*), and FDP (Free Democratic Party, *Freie Demokratische Partei*) won 398 of the 662 seats in the Bundestag.[67] Kohl remained Chancellor of the FRG, which showed that his vision of unification of two German states was appreciated by the citizens.[68]

It can be seen from the above that the process of German reunification was carried out according to the vision of the FRG articulated primarily in Kohl's 10-point program. This does not mean, however, that there were no proposals for restoring unity in the GDR. Leaving aside East German projects from the Cold War period, it is worth noting, e.g., the *Reunification Law* of February 21, 1990.[69] This project was abandoned, however, because the reunification process was ultimately dominated by the FRG's policy and the Western powers supporting it.

---

65 *Bekanntmachung einer Erklärung der Außenminister Frankreichs, der Sowjetunion, des Vereinigten Königreichs und der Vereinigten Staaten im Zusammenhang mit dem in Moskau am 12. September 1990 unterzeichneten Vertrag über die abschließende Regelung in bezug auf Deutschland Vom 2. Oktober 1990* (BGBl., Part II, 1990, No. 38, 1331–1332).

66 Ż. Regel, "Nasz sąsiad Niemcy," *Gazeta Wyborcza*, October 3, 1990, No. 230, 1; M. Machnacki, "Nasz sąsiad Niemcy," *Gazeta Wyborcza*, October 3, 1990, No. 230, 1; E. Skalski, "Nasz sąsiad Niemcy," *Gazeta Wyborcza*, October 3, 1990, No. 230, 1; "Listy Mazowiecki – Kohl. Niemcy – dzień pierwszy," *Gazeta Wyborcza*, October 4, 1990, No. 231, 1; K. Żbikowski, "Triumf Kanclerza," *Gazeta Wyborcza*, October 4, 1990, No. 231, 6; Ż. Regel, "Niemcy – dzień pierwszy," *Gazeta Wyborcza*, October 4, 1990, No. 231, 7.

67 *Ergebnisse früherer Bundestagswahlen. Stand: 18. August 2017 Informationen des Bundeswahlleiters* (Wiesbaden: Der Bundeswahlleiter, 2017), 22, table 6.

68 RS, "Niemcy nadal chadeckie," *Gazeta Wyborcza*, December 3, 1990, No. 281, 1; M. Orzechowski, "Kanzler, Kanzler," *Gazeta Wyborcza*, December 4, 1990, No. 282, 4; P. Cegielski, "Po wyborach do Bundestagu. Czas Zielonych się kończy," *Gazeta Wyborcza*, December 4, 1990, No. 282, 5. In reunified Germany Kohl headed the federal government twice more: in 1991–1994 and 1994–1998.

69 K.-H. Christoph, "Das Vereinigungsgesetz der DDR," *Deutsch-Deutsche Rechts-Zeitschrift* No. 8 (1990): 257–261.

2.3. Summary

Even taking into account the differences in area and population, one can see the fundamental differences in the level of economic development of the FRG and the GDR in the late 1980s and early 1990s. The macroeconomic characteristics, illustrating individual aspects of the two countries' economic structures, unequivocally indicate a definite advantage of West Germany. It covered all analyzed sectors: industry, agriculture, public finance, foreign trade, and transport. The FRG's greater economic potential also resulted from its higher level of economic growth. As a consequence of this situation, the standard of living of West German society differed significantly from the existence of the GDR's inhabitants. In turn, the fundamental source of these differences was the other foundations of economic systems: the social market economy in West Germany and the centrally planned economy in East Germany. The main factors that shaped them were constitutional and property rules. This work will discuss particular issues in this regard in subsequent sections.

It is also reasonable to believe that the FRG's economic and institutional predominance had a stronger political and international position than the GDR. This allowed the Bonn government to crystallize the formula for German reunification and impose it on its Eastern neighbor, sinking deeper into political and socioeconomic crises. This issue will be discussed in later sections of the book.

CHAPTER 3 Constitutional rules in the GDR and the FRG: Implementation of West German solutions

3.1. Basic law as a formal institution

Douglass C. North, among distinguished formal institutions, included law, e.g. constitutions.[1] In political and legal sciences, a constitution is most often understood as the highest legal act in the state. Its fundamental character for the political system of a country determines that it is named as a basic law, less frequently as a government law or constitutional charter.[2] From the point of view of economics, a constitution must set the foundations (framework) of the political-legal and socio-economic system of the state.

In constitutional law, several classifications of basic law are indicated. Among others, the following constitutions are distinguished: (1) material and formal; (2) written and unwritten; (3) real, written and fictional; (4) normative, nominal and semantic; (5) complete and incomplete (small); (6) closed, open and diffuse; (7) rigid and flexible. It also separates legal-logical and positive-legal approaches.[3]

It is less common to propose an understanding of the constitution as an institution. In law, e.g., Karl Nickerson Llewellyn (1934) makes such considerations.[4] Ota Weinberger, in turn, presents the constitution from the perspective of institutional positivism.[5] However, such interpretations are rather rare.

A constitutional economy theory also referred to as constitutional political economy, constitutional law and economics, new political economy or constitutional public choice theory, may serve to place the constitution as an institution in an economic perspective. The origins of this approach date back to the 1950s. It

1 Cf. section 1.2.2. in this book. North analyzes the constitution as an example of a (formal) political institution also in his economic history studies (see, e.g., D. C. North, B. R. Weingast, "Constitutions and Commitment: The Evolution of Institutions Governing Public Choice in Seventeenth-Century England," *The Journal of Economic History* 49, No. 4 (1989): 805–806).

2 B. Banaszak, *Porównawcze prawo konstytucyjne współczesnych państw demokratycznych* (Warszawa: Wolters Kluwer Polska, 2007), 45.

3 See more Banaszak, *Porównawcze prawo konstytucyjne*, 46–53.

4 K. N. Llewellyn, "The Constitution as an Institution," *Columbia Law Review* 34, No. 1 (1934): 1–40.

5 O. Weinberger, "Teoria konstytucji w świetle pozytywizmu instytucjonalnego," *Ruch Prawniczy, Ekonomiczny i Socjologiczny* 55, No. 4 (1993): 1–18.

grew out of the theory of public choice, also showing links to the new institutional economics or law and economics.[6] The main representatives of constitutional economics include: James M. Buchanan, Friedrich A. von Hayek, Stefan Voigt.[7]

---

6 K. Metelska-Szaniawska, "Ekonomia konstytucyjna – ekonomia polityczna ładu gospodarczego," in *Teoria wyboru publicznego. Główne nurty i zastosowania*, ed. J. Wilkin (Warszawa: WN Scholar, 2012), 109, 132–134. See the main assumptions of law and economics: H.-B. Schäfer, C. Ott, *Lehrbuch der ökonomischen Analyse des Zivilrechts* (Berlin–Heidelberg: Springer, 2005); R. Cooter, T. Ulen, *Ekonomiczna analiza prawa* (Warszawa: Wydawnictwo C. H. Beck, 2011). The links between constitutional economics and the state theory in the new institutional economics are also apparent (T. Eggertsson, *Economic Behavior and Institutions* (Cambridge: Cambridge University Press, 1995), 59–79, 317–358).

7 See the foundational works of the aforementioned scholars in constitutional economics: J. M. Buchanan, G. Tullock, *The Calculus of Consent. Logical Foundations of Constitutional Democracy* (Indianapolis: Liberty Fund, 1999); F. A. Hayek, *The Law, Legislation and Liberty. A New Statement of the Liberal Principles of Justice and Political Economy* (London–New York: Routledge, 2013). For current theoretical considerations and empirical applications of constitutional economics, see Stefan Voigt's numerous studies. See, e.g., S. Voigt, "Die konstitutionelle Ökonomik als Herausforderung für die Theorie der Wirtschaftspolitik – zugleich eine Skizze zur Weiterentwicklung einer ökonomischen Theorie der Verfassung," in *James Buchanans konstitutionelle Ökonomik*, eds. I. Pies, M. Leschke (Tübingen: Mohr, 1996), 157–183; S. Voigt, "Positive Constitutional Economics: A Survey," in *Constitutional Political Economy in a Public Choice Perspective*, ed. Ch. K. Rowley, (Drodrecht: Springer, 1997), 11–53; S. Voigt, "Das Forschungsprogramm der Positiven Konstitutionenökonomik," in *Unsere Konstitution in gutter Form und Verfassung?*, eds. G. Grözinger, S. Panther (Marburg: Metropolis, 1998), 279–319; S. Voigt, *Explaining Constitutional Change. A Positive Economics Approach* (Cheltenham–Northampton: Edward Elgar, 1999); S. Voigt, "Implicit Constitutional Change – Changing the Meaning of the Constitution without Changing the Text of the Document," *European Journal of Law and Economics* 7, No. 3 (1999): 197–224; S. Voigt, H.-J. Wagener, eds., *Constitutions, Markets and Law. Recent Experiences in Transition Economies* (Cheltenham–Northampton: Edward Elgar, 2002); S. Voigt, "Constitutional Political Economy," in *The Encyclopedia of Public Choice*, eds. C. K. Rowley, F. Schneider (Boston: Springer, 2004), 436–440; L. Blume, J. Müller, S. Voigt, C. Wolf, "The Economic Effects of Constitutions: Replicating – and Extending – Persson and Tabellini," *Public Choice* 139 (2009): 197–225; S. Voigt, "Empirical Constitutional Economics: Onward and Upward?," *Journal of Economic Behavior & Organization* 80, No. 2 (2011): 319–330; S. Voigt, "Positive Constitutional Economics II – a Survey of Recent Developments," *Public Choice* 146 (2011): 205–256; S. Voigt, "Veilonomics: On the Use and Utility of Veils in Constitutional Political Economy," in *Behind a Veil of Ignorance? Power and Uncertainty in Constitutional Design*, eds. L. M. Imbeau, S. Jacob (Heidelberg: Springer, 2015), 9–33; S. Voigt, "Constitutional Economics and the Law," in *The Oxford Handbook of Law and Economics*, Vol. I: *Methodology and Concepts*, ed. Fr. Parisi (New York: Oxford University Press, 2017,

https://books.google.pl/books?hl=en&lr=&id=XTHADgAAQBAJ&oi=fnd&pg=PT243&dq=Constitutional+Economics+and+the+Law&ots=NLgSw2liHU&sig=HMBBpaghe0EWWapD0YhpeG4_qKM&redir_esc=y#v=onepage&q=Constitutional%20Economics%20and%20the%20Law&f=false (accessed May 17, 2022)); S. Voigt, J. Gutmann, "Challenges in Estimating the Effects of Constitutional Design on Public Policy," in *The Oxford Handbook of Public Choice*, Vol. 2, eds. R. D. Congleton, B. Grofman, S. Voigt (New York: Oxford University Press, 2019), 438–450; S. Voigt, *Constitutional Economics. A Primer* (New York: Cambridge University Press, 2020); J. Gutmann, S. Voigt, "Militant Constitutionalism: A Promising Concept to Make Constitutional Backsliding Less Likely?," *Public Choice* (2021), https://link.springer.com/content/pdf/10.1007/s11127-021-00874-1.pdf (accessed May 17, 2022); S. Voigt, "Mind the Gap: Analyzing the Divergence Between Constitutional Text and Constitutional Reality," *International Journal of Constitutional Law* 19, No. 5 (2021): 1778–1809; Ch. Bjørnskov, S. Voigt, M. Khesali, "Unconstitutional States of Emergency" (working paper), Institute of Law and Economics (ILE) Working Paper Series, No. 51 (2021), 1–34; S. Voigt, "Contracting for Catastrophe: Legitimizing Emergency Constitutions by Drawing on Social Contract Theory," *Res Publica* 28 (2022): 149–172; J. Gutmann, S. Voigt, "Quantitative Analysis of Constitutions" (working paper), Institute of Law and Economics (ILE) Working Paper Series, No. 56 (2022), 1–32. See the valuable anthology of works on constitutional economics, including texts by classics of this approach: S. Voigt, ed., *Constitutional Political Economy*, Vol. I–II (Cheltenham–Northampton: An Elgar Reference Collection, 2003). In Poland, the works of Katarzyna Metelska-Szaniawska are of fundamental importance for the dissemination of the theory of constitutional economics and its application in empirical research. See, among others: K. Metelska-Szaniawska, "Ekonomia konstytucyjna – ekonomia polityczna ładu gospodarczego," in *Teoria wyboru publicznego. Wstęp do ekonomicznej analizy polityki i funkcjonowania sfery publicznej*, ed. J. Wilkin (Warszawa: WN Scholar, 2005), 87–110; K. Metelska-Szaniawska, *Konstytucyjne czynniki reform gospodarczych w krajach postsocjalistycznych* (Warszawa: Wydawnictwa UW, 2008); K. Metelska-Szaniawska, "Constitutions and Economic Reforms in Transition: An Empirical Study," *Constitutional Political Economy* 1 (2009): 1–41; K. Metelska-Szaniawska, "Konstytucja w świetle nauk ekonomicznych," *Przegląd Sejmowy* 1 (2010): 49–62; Metelska-Szaniawska, "Ekonomia konstytucyjna," 109–135; J. Fałkowski, K. Metelska-Szaniawska, "Przyczyny ustanawiania i stabilność konstytucji – spojrzenie z perspektywy ekonomicznej," *Gospodarka Narodowa* No. 3 (2015): 79–105; K. Metelska-Szaniawska, *Economic Effects of Post-Socialist Constitutions 25 Years from the Outset of Transition. The Constitutional Political Economy Approach* (Frankfurt am Main: Peter Lang International Academic Publishers, 2016); K. Metelska-Szaniawska, "Post-Socialist Constitutions: The de jure–de facto Gap, Its Effects and Determinants," *Economics of Transition and Institutional Change* 29 (2021): 175–196; K. Metelska-Szaniawska, J. Lewkowicz, "Post-socialist 'illiberal democracies:' Do 'de jure' Constitutional Rights Matter?," *Constitutional Political Economy* 32 (2021): 233–265; K. Metelska-Szaniawska, A. Lewczuk, "Constitutional Overperformance: An Empirical Study of de facto Protection of Rights with No de jure Equivalents," *European Journal of Law and Economics* 53 (2022): 289–317; J. Gutmann, K. Metelska-Szaniawska, S. Voigt, "The Comparative Constitutional Compliance Database" (working paper), Institute of Law and Economics (ILE) Working Paper Series, No. 57 (2022), 1–44.

A much broader community of scholars of this approach includes, e.g., the journal "Constitutional Political Economy" published since 1990.[8]

Based on economic methods, constitutional economics allows the analysis of basic law and its impact on the national economy. The theory's specific understanding of the central category relates to this. For example, the aforementioned Buchanan and Gordon Tullock define a constitution as a predetermined set of rules in which certain actions take place.[9] For Hayek, a constitution is not so much a source of rights in a state but rather "a superstructure erected to secure the maintenance of the law."[10] It builds on the pre-existing legal system while establishing enforcement of that law.[11] Richard A. Posner analyzes basic law as an economic document.[12] Voigt, on the other hand, reviewing the different variants of understanding this category in the social sciences, distinguishes the following approaches: (1) "constitution as a social contract;" (2) "constitutional contract as principal-agent-relationship;" (3) "constitutional contract as precommitment-device;" (4) "constitution as the result of cultural or social evolution;" (5) "constitution as a bundle of (social) conventions." Voigt indicates that some of these perspectives are present in constitutional economics. He presents constitutional rules as the result of certain procedures and constitutional convention, i.e., a "constitutional contract."[13]

The literature points out that understanding basic law in constitutional economics is broader than in legal science. According to this approach, constitutional rules are all metaregulations that define the framework for current political and economic choices.[14] It can be seen here clear connections of the discussed theory with institutional economics. Thus, in the most extreme approach, the mentioned rules are not only a document, such as a basic law but all formal political and economic institutions (referring to the classification of North and Acemoglu and Robinson).[15]

The wide way of defining the constitution allows for distinguishing several meanings of the same term. Katarzyna Metelska-Szaniawska recognizes four variants of this notion on the grounds of constitutional economics, where their common denominator is a certain type of constraint. Thus, a constitution may be: (1) constraints imposed on a person by himself, which serves to achieve specific

8 See *Constitutional Political Economy* 1 (1990) and subsequent issues.
9 Buchanan, Tullock, *The Calculus of Consent*, XVII.
10 Hayek, *The Law, Legislation and Liberty*, 127.
11 Hayek, *The Law, Legislation and Liberty*, 128.
12 R. A. Posner, "The Constitution as an Economic Document," *George Washington Law Review* 56, No. 1 (1987): 4–38.
13 Voigt, "Positive Constitutional Economics," 27–30, 33.
14 See, e.g., Fałkowski, Metelska-Szaniawska, "Przyczyny ustanawiania i stabilność konstytucji," 93, fn. 19.
15 Cf. section 1.2.2. in this work.

goals ("private constitution"); (2) constraints that people impose on themselves in specific social situations (e.g., family, the Church, contracts, statutes of organizations); (3) constraints imposed on politicians; (4) constraints on citizens, the source of which is political power. The last two understandings apply to state constitutions, the focus of constitutional economics.[16]

In this work, however, the concept of the constitution is narrowed down, devoting special attention to the Basic Law of the FRG as a formal institution that is the source of certain constitutional rules. Such an emphasis on the legal act results from the attachment to the source, which is typical for the research workshop of an economic historian.

The scientific literature distinguishes two dimensions (approaches) of constitutional economics. The normative approach tries to indicate in what direction constitutional rules should be developed in order to ensure the efficiency and effectiveness of individual segments of the economy.[17] Positive constitutional economics, on the other hand, analyzes the actual nature and shape of constitutional rules and evaluates their impact on economic change. This approach may use economic history methods, among others.[18]

Voigt characterizes positive constitutional economics in a gradualist manner. He focuses on: (1) the origins of the basic law, (2) its amendments, and (3) the resulting effects (e.g., economic).

Voigt's attention focuses on two steps regarding the enactment of the constitution. Firstly, it is important to present constitutional rules as some outcome. They result from certain procedures. Secondly, factors influencing the constitution-making process should be divided into individual (e.g. preferences, constraints of individuals, norms and values) and collective (e.g. distribution of resources, external influences). Separating the two groups of factors is sometimes not easy, as some of them (e.g. norms and values) can be both individual and collective in nature.[19]

In terms of the modification of the rules once adopted, issues related to "constitutional change" are explained. It may be understood in two ways. The enactment of a fundamental law is sometimes presented as the "total constitutional change," which has a primary and direct character. On the other hand, the amendment of the constitution is connected with the "marginal constitutional change," which is secondary and indirect in relation to the total change. As a consequence,

---

16 Metelska-Szaniawska, "Ekonomia konstytucyjna," 110–111.

17 One of the objections to normative constitutional economics is the formulation of theoretical postulates that ignore the context of a particular country (I. Krastev, R. Peeva, "Invisible Context, Invisible Constraints. The Limits of the Normative Explanation of Constitutional Change," in Voigt, Wagener, *Constitutions, Markets and Law*, 113–128).

18 Metelska-Szaniawska, "Ekonomia konstytucyjna," 111–112.

19 Voigt, "Positive Constitutional Economics," 30–33.

constitutional rules remain potentially unchanged after their enactment, but they determine the permissible ways of their modification. In other words, these rules determine the directions of constitutional change, although they are not determinants. As far as the modification of basic law is concerned, it may take various forms. Voigt lists "explicit change" and "implicit change." While the first one refers to a change in the content of the document of basic law (amendment), the second one refers to changes in its interpretation by the authorities (doctrine and jurisprudence). Voigt adds that a constitutional change may be constitutional ("constitutional constitutional change"), which involves considering the issue of its "formality." However, there is also a possibility of "unconstitutional constitutional change," which is connected with the problem of its "legality." Both classifications overlap, forming a matrix of constitutional change. It is presented in Table 3.

Table 3: *Constitutional change matrix*

Nature of constitutional change	**Constitutional**	**Unconstitutional**
Explicit	*Explicit constitutional constitutional change*[a]	*Explicit unconstitutional constitutional change*
Implicit	*Implicit constitutional constitutional change*	*Implicit unconstitutional constitutional change*

a In order to maintain the precision of the terms cited, the complexity of the notation of the terms was preserved (as is done by the author of the presented matrix), even at the expense of the potential risk of a pleonasm error.
Own compilation based on Voigt, "Positive Constitutional Economics," 34, table 1.

Therefore, constitutional change can proceed in four distinct directions from a theoretical point of view. An explicit or implicit constitutional change can be formal (constitutional) or illegal (unconstitutional).[20] Additional combinations are provided by considering a total and marginal change.

In the final step, Voigt's attention focuses on the effects of the analyzed constitutional rules. These are usually economic in nature.[21]

To sum up, it should be stated that the discussed approach is dominated by an economic perception of the political (social) category, that is, basic law. Specific methodological consequences follow from this. Constitutional economics proposes a set of economic tools to study various dimensions of the constitution, beginning with the process of its creation and enactment, through its provisions and the decision-making mechanisms that it creates, and ending with the consequences

20 Voigt, "Positive Constitutional Economics," 30, 33–41.
21 Voigt, "Positive Constitutional Economics," 30, 41–46.

of its functioning for the economy. However, this is an open set, and the selection of these tools depends on the approach to a given problem proposed by the researcher.

3.2. Review of the GDR constitutions

The drafting of the German Constitution (*Verfassung*) is directly connected with the changes taking place in Germany after World War II.[22] The occupation of German territories by the great powers (the United States, the United Kingdom, France and the Soviet Union), the differences in their economic policies and growing international Cold War tensions were the basis for the creation of two German states in September and October 1949: the FRG and the GDR.

The Constitution of the GDR (*Verfassung der Deutschen Demokratischen Republik*) was adopted on October 7, 1949, in Berlin.[23] In contrast to the neutrality of the Basic Law of the FRG,[24] it strictly defined the features of the social and economic system.[25] Due to the communists consolidating their position in society, the document was

22 The literature on the German occupation in 1945–1949 is broad. Among only Polish more recent synthetic studies it is worth mentioning, among others: J. Kukułka, *Historia współczesna stosunków międzynarodowych 1945–2000* (Warszawa: WN Scholar, 2003), 28–33, 43–47; E. Cziomer, *Historia Niemiec współczesnych 1945–2005* (Warszawa: Wydawnictwo Neriton, 2006), 21–84; J. J. Węc, "Niemcy," in *Wielka historia świata*, Vol. 12: *Od drugiej wojny światowej do XXI wieku*, ed. W. Rojek (Kraków–Warszawa: Oficyna Wydawnicza Fogra, Świat Książki, 2006), 94–108; J. Krasuski, *Historia Niemiec* (Wrocław: Ossolineum, 2008), 485–512; A. Galos, "Najnowsza historia Niemiec od 1945 roku," in W. Czapliński, A. Galos, W. Korta, *Historia Niemiec* (Wrocław: Ossolineum, 2010), 683–714; J. Tyszkiewicz, "Zimna wojna," in J. Tyszkiewicz, E. Czapiewski, *Historia powszechna. Wiek XX* (Warszawa: WN PWN, 2010), 527–533; J. Holzer, *Europa zimnej wojny* (Kraków: Znak, ISP PAN, 2012), 173–196.

23 The first constitutions in the socialist spirit (although still relatively democratic in their meaning with references to the Weimar Constitution of 1919) were adopted by the individual *Länder* in the Soviet occupation zone at the turn of 1946 and 1947 (T. Stammen, "Zur Verfassungsentwicklung," in *DDR. Das politische, wirtschaftliche und soziale System*, eds. H. Rausch, T. Stammen (München: Bayerische Landeszentrale für politische Bildungsarbeit, 1984), 204–205).

24 See section 3.4. in this work.

25 See: S. Mampel, "Die verfassungsrechtlichen und die politischen Grundlagen der DDR-Wirtschaft," in *Materialien zum Bericht zur Lage der Nation im geteilten Deutschland 1987* (Bonn: Bundesministerium für innerdeutsche Beziehungen, 1987), 33–38; H. Hamel, "Die DDR-Wirtschaft auf dem Weg zum 'entwickelten Sozialismus,' " in *Wirtschaftsreformen im Ostblock in den 80er Jahren. Länderstudien: Sowjetunion, DDR, Polen, Rumänien, Tschechoslowakei, Bulgarien, Ungarn*, ed. R. Schlüter (Paderborn: Ferdinand Schöningh, 1988), 57–61; H. Pohl, "Öffentliche und private Wirtschaft," in *Deutsche Wiedervereinigung. Die Rechtseinheit. Arbeitskreis Staats- und Verfassungsrecht*, Vol. II: *Zur Wiederherstellung der inneren Einheit*,

kept fairly democratic in tone. For example, it stated that Germany was a democratic republic (Art. 1, Par. 1) and that state power derived from the people (Art. 3, Par. 1). The Constitution guaranteed a number of civil liberties: equality before the law, personal freedom, inviolability of property, freedom of belief and the right to association (Arts. 6–18). However, this kind of procedure was a mystification, as it was supposed to build public support for the SED politicians. The communist regime gradually took control over all areas of social life.

From an economic point of view, it is important that the GDR Constitution was also democratic in its declarative layer (*de jure* institution), although with a strong social democratic component. Chap. II, devoted to the economic order, stated that it should coincide with the principles of social justice, guaranteeing citizens a decent life. The economy was to serve the nation and its needs and to ensure that its members shared in the production that was adequate to their productivity. To this end, the Constitution guaranteed economic freedom to every citizen (Art. 19). Thus, the private initiative of peasants, merchants and craftsmen was encouraged. They could also develop cooperative activity for this purpose (Art. 20). Employees were guaranteed participation in the activities of production plants through trade unions and work councils (Arts. 14, 17).

The GDR Constitution, however, contained provisions that allowed for state interference in the economy (*de facto* institution). In this way, they exposed the true face of the totalitarian regime, which had adopted a command-and-control model based on the Soviet model. These records referred to such categories as collectivism (nation, society), egalitarianism, social justice, interventionism, statism, and planning. In addition to such references in Art. 19 already cited, it is worth noting that the Constitution explicitly mentions the guarantee of employment and compulsion of labor (Art. 15), central economic planning (Art. 21), or collective land use (Art. 26, Par. 1). Similarly (although with some reservations), issues related to the property were resolved (Arts. 22–25, 27–29).[26]

Leaving aside the amendments to the GDR Constitution, it should be noted that the constitutional principles in East Germany were less stable than in the FRG. In contrast to its Western neighbor, where – despite modifications – one Basic Law was in force throughout the entire post-war period, as many as three legal acts of this type were passed in the GDR.[27]

Part 2: *Rundfunkrecht – Stasi-Akten – Wiedergutmachung – Öffentliche und Private Wirtschaft*, ed. K. Stern (Köln: Carl Heymanns Verlag KG, 1992), 134–135, 142–143.

26 "Gesetz über die Verfassung der Deutschen Demokratischen Republik vom 7. Oktober 1949.," in *Gesetz über die Konstituierung der Provisorischen Volkskammer der Deutschen Demokratischen Republik vom 7. Oktober 1949.* (Gesetzblatt der Deutschen Demokratischen Republik (hereinafter: GBl.-DDR), Part I, 1949, No. 1, 4–16). More on the empowerment of property rights in the GDR Constitutions: section 5.2. in this work.

27 This does not coincide with the view of Bogusław Banaszak, who, from the position of comparative constitutional law, argues that the incompatibility of non-democratic

The new GDR Constitution, which was approved by referendum[28] on April 6, 1968 (this date is considered binding), was promulgated on April 8. It entered into force on the following day. As stated in the preamble, it was a "socialist constitution" (*sozialistische Verfassung*),[29] because it made the political and socio-economic system even more similar to the Soviet model than before. The GDR was defined as a socialist state, created by the working people of towns and villages, led by the working class and its Marxist-Leninist party (Art. 1). In turn, adherence to the Constitution on the basis of universal human values, fraternity, justice, and equality could only be ensured through a socialist society, the power of the people, and their state and law (Art. 86). Although more extensive than before, the provisions for the guarantee of civil rights and liberties (Arts. 19–40), thus became an even greater fiction.

For the economic system, the provisions of Chap. 2, Part I of the Constitution was important. It was stated that the economy of the GDR was based on the socialist model of central planning. All economic and social life areas were subordinated to it (Art. 2, Par. 2; Art. 9). Other provisions referred to property (Art. 2, Par. 2; Art. 9–16). The importance of collectivism was emphasized even more in the provisions concerning towns, municipalities, enterprises, production cooperatives, trade unions, and other associations. They should realize the integrative social function in a socialist state (Arts. 41–46).[30]

On October 7, 1974, a thorough constitutional reform was carried out,[31] hence the new version of the GDR Constitution is indicated as the third such act in the history of East Germany. Although numerous changes were made to the 1968 text, they did not alter its overall tone. Above all, the alliance with the Soviet Union and the Eastern Bloc countries was emphasized even more strongly (Art. 6, Par. 2). Regulations on the economy (including property rights), although corrected (Art. 9, Pars. 1, 3; Art. 44, Par. 3), did not change in their tenor (Arts. 9–16, 41–46).[32]

Accordingly, it must be concluded that constitutional law in the GDR evolved from quasi-democratic to socialist assumptions. In the declarative layer, constitutions contained a guarantee of a number of civil rights and liberties

---

constitutions with reality and their facade (e.g. the Constitution of the People's Republic of Poland of 1952) favored the durability of these legal acts (Banaszak, *Porównawcze prawo konstytucyjne*, 91–92). Cf. theoretical insights on political system stability: section 4.6. in this study.

28 *Gesetz zur Durchführung eines Volksentscheides über die Verfassung der Deutschen Demokratischen Republik vom 28. März 1968* (GBl.-DDR, Part I, 1968, No. 7, 192–195).

29 *Verfassung der Deutschen Demokratischen Republik vom 6. April 1968*, [preamble] (GBl.-DDR, Part I, 1968, No. 8, 203).

30 *Verfassung der Deutschen Demokratischen Republik* (GBl.-DDR, Part I, 1968, No. 8, 199–222).

31 *Gesetz zur Ergänzung und Änderung der Verfassung der Deutschen Demokratischen Republik vom 7. Oktober 1974* (GBl.-DDR, Part I, 1974, No. 47, 425–432).

32 *Verfassung der Deutschen Demokratischen Republik vom 6. April 1968 in der Fassung des Gesetz zur Ergänzung und Änderung der Verfassung der Deutschen Demokratischen Republik vom 7. Oktober 1974* (GBl.-DDR, Part I, 1974, No. 47, 432–456).

(constitutional rules as a *de jure* institution). However, this does not change the fact that throughout the GDR's existence, all areas of political, economic, social, and cultural life were subordinated to the communist regime, embodied in the SED party (constitutional rules as a *de facto* institution).[33]

The East German parliament (the People's Chamber, *Volkskammer der DDR*) was elected by popular vote. It elected the government (*Ministerrat*) and the State Council (*Staatsrat*), which served as the collective head of state. The most important organs of the judiciary also came from the legislature: The Supreme Court (*Oberstes Gericht*) and the Attorney General (*Generalstaatsanwalt*). The executive power in the form of the State Council appointed the National Defense Council (*Nationaler Verteidigungsrat*), which took care of the army. It can be concluded that these components of the system constituted *de jure* institutions. The real power in the state, however, was exercised by the most important party organs of the SED. This dimension of the GDR political system must be considered a *de facto* institution. The Central Committee (*Zentralkomitee*) was a quasi-parliament of the party. It was selected through elections at party congresses, with members approved by the Politburo and Secretariat. The highest executive body of the SED was the Secretariat (*Sekretariat*) headed by the General Secretary (*Generalsekretär*). This function was held successively by Wilhelm Pieck and Otto Grotewohl (commonly, 1946–1950), Walter Ulbricht (1950–1971), Erich Honecker (1971–1989), and Egon Krenz (1989). In turn, the Political Bureau of the SED (*SED-Politbüro*) included party leaders and the highest representatives of the state government. The government implemented the guidelines formulated by the Politburo.[34]

---

33 This was a typical element of the concept of fundamental constitutional rights in communist states (R. R. Ludwikowski, *Prawo konstytucyjne porównawcze* (Toruń TNOiK "Dom Organizatora," 2000), 458–460). More on the successive constitutional changes in the GDR: Stammen, "Zur Verfassungsentwicklung," 204–216. The author distinguishes two stages of this process. The first – anti-fascist and democratic – covered the time when the Constitution of 1949 was in force. There were clear references to the Weimar Constitution. The socialist stage resulted from the legal consequences of the 1968 Constitution. Shortly before German reunification, on March 12, 1990, a draft constitution (eventually not enacted) was created in the GDR, transforming the state in a democratic direction. This was the result of attempts by the last communist government of the GDR, led by Hans Modrow, to carry out political and socio-economic reforms while preserving East Germany's independence and its socialist systemic foundations. The draft constitution was one of the results of the work of the "Round Table" (December 7, 1989 – March 12, 1990), as part of which the government side entered into talks with representatives of the anti-communist opposition (E. Cziomer, *Zarys historii Niemiec powojennych 1945–1995*, (Warszawa–Kraków: WN PWN, 1997), 280–283).

34 See more T. Stammen, "Das zentrale Regierungssystem," in Rausch, Stammen, *DDR*, 255–281.

The economic system of the GDR was based on the model of a centrally planned (command and control) economy.[35] Planning played a key role. The process of creating an economic plan in the GDR is illustrated in Diagram 1.

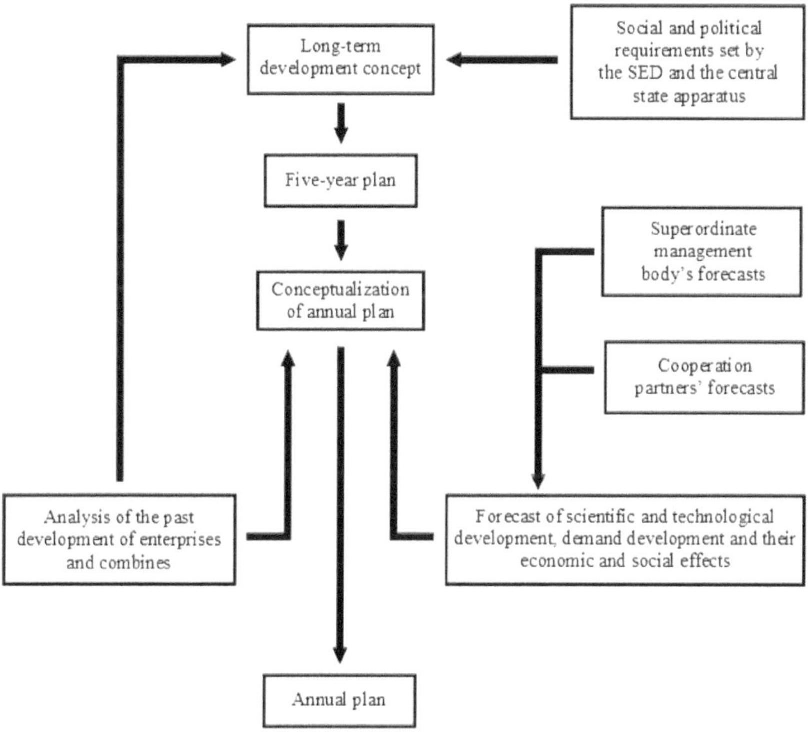

Diagram 1: *Conceptualization and preparing of an economic plan in the GDR*

Source: B. Tietz, *Optionen für Deutschland. Szenarien und Handlungsalternativen für Wirtschaft und Gesellschaft. Ein Handbuch für Entscheidungsträger* (Landsberg/Lech: Verlag Moderne Industrie, 1990), 165, scheme 3.5.

---

35 More on the specifics of a centrally planned economy, see, e.g.: W. Roszkowski, *Gospodraka. Wzrost i upadek systemu nakazowo-rozdzielczego*, WN PWN, Warszawa 2008.
See also a representative work by East German economists explaining the alleged effectiveness of economic planning: *Planung der Volkswirtschaft in der DDR*, ed. H. Steeger, Verlag die Wirtschaft, Berlin 1970.

Each economic plan, drawn up for five-year periods, was the consequence of a socio-economic diagnosis that included, on the one hand, an analysis of the current situation of production enterprises and, on the other hand, forecasts of scientific and technological developments, demand and their effects on the economy and society (the positive dimension). This took place under the strong influence of political bodies, which formulated specific guidelines in this regard. On this basis, a concept of long-term socio-economic development was created (normative dimension), specified in a five-year plan. It consisted of short-term plans covering individual years.

3.3. The Basic Law of the FRG

The Basic Law of the FRG (*Grundgesetz für die Bundesrepublik Deutschland*) was passed in Bonn on May 8, 1949. On May 12, it was approved, with some reservations, by the military governors of the three states occupying the Western *Länder* (the United States, Great Britain, and France). After ratification by the national parliaments (with the exception of Bavaria), it was promulgated on May 23 and entered into force the following day.[36] Between 1951 and 2014, 60 amendments to this legislation were enacted, with as many as 25 between 1990 and 2014. Thus, 41.6 % of all amendments were carried out during the quarter century in question.[37] These calculations allow for the conclusion that German reunification brought challenges not only of a political, economic, social, and cultural nature but also of a constitutional, legal and political nature.

The FRG Constitution defines the principles of the tri-partite division of power and specifies the political principles of a democratic federal republic. A number of civil liberties were also guaranteed.[38] According to the Basic Law, Germany remained a federation (*Bundes*) of federal states (*Länder*). Within a framework of

---

36 *Grundgesetz für die Bundesrepublik Deutschland vom 23. Mai 1949.* (BGBl., Part I, 1949, No. 1, pp. 1–20). Polish translations: L. Janicki, ed., *Ustawa Zasadnicza (Konstytucja) Republiki Federalnej Niemiec z 23 maja 1949 r./Grundgesetz für die Bundesrepublik Deutschland vom 23. Mai 1949* (Poznań: Instytut Zachodni, 2007); "Grundgesetz für die Bundesrepublik Deutschland vom 23. Mai 1949/Ustawa Zasadnicza Republiki Federalnej Niemiec z 23 maja 1949," in J. W. Tkaczyński, *Prawo ustrojowe Niemiec* (Kraków: Wydawnictwo UJ, 2015, 453–562). English translation: *Basic Law for the Federal Republic of Germany*, Federal Ministry of Justice, Federal Office of Justice, https://www.gesetze-im-internet.de/englisch_gg/ (accessed May 18, 2022). Cf. the attempt to model the problem of constitution-making: T. Ginsburg, Z. Elkins, J. Blount, "Does the Process of Constitution-Making Matter?," *Annual Review of Law and Social Science* 5 (2009): 201–223.

37 "Zmiany Ustawy Zasadniczej RFN," in Janicki, *Ustawa Zasadnicza*, 41–55 (compilations for the years 1951–2006); Tkaczyński, *Prawo ustrojowe Niemiec*, 448–452 (compilations for the years 1951–2014).

38 Other features of the FRG Constitution are referred to later. See sections 4.1.–4.4. in this study.

broad autonomy, the individual *Länder* had a parliament (*Landtag*) and a government (*Landesregierung*). Representatives of the *Länder* sat in the upper house of the federal parliament, the Federal Council (*Bundesrat*). The lower house of parliament (*Bundestag*) was elected in elections. This, in turn, appointed the federal government (*Bundesregierung, Bundeskabinett*) headed by the Federal Chancellor (*Bundeskanzler*). The formal head of the state remained the Federal President (*Bundespräsident*), elected by the Federal Assembly (*Bundesversammlung*), i.e. a joint session of the Bundestag and Bundesrat. However, his powers were clearly limited in favor of the Chancellor. One of the functions of parliament was to elect the judges of the Federal Constitutional Court (*Bundesverfassungsgericht*).[39]

3.4. Economic and social components of the Basic Law of the FRG

The legal framework was important for the German economic system.[40] The FRG Constitution, especially its economic and social guidelines, played a fundamental role in this respect.[41] However, the Basic Law did not explicitly define the economic system in Germany. In this context, it has been described as neutral, which means that it only guaranteed the basic freedoms that determined the framework of the German economy's systemic order. The FRG Constitution did not create a specific economic order. It also remained neutral with regard to economic policy. The government could shape a given economic system (order) as long as it respected the individual rights and freedoms of citizens as defined in the Basic Law. In other words, the model of the social market economy was not enshrined in Germany's highest legal act but was derived from it.[42]

---

39 See more D. P. Currie, *The Constitution of the Federal Republic of Germany* (Chicago–London: The University of Chicago Press, 1994), *passim*; Tkaczyński, *Prawo ustrojowe Niemiec, passim.*

40 M. Weilepp, "Das System der rechtlichen Regelungen der Wirtschafts- und Sozialpolitik," in *Elemente der Sozialen Marktwirtschaft. Wirtschaftliche und rechtliche Rahmenbedingungen – Transformationsmöglichkeiten,* eds. K. Fasbender, M. Holthus, E. Thiel (Hamburg: Verlag Weltarchiv GmbH, 1991), 61–76; F. Münzel, "Die Rolle des Rechts in der Deutschen Marktwirtschaft," in Fasbender, Holthus, Thiel, *Elemente der Sozialen Marktwirtschaft*, 103–136.

41 See introductions to German constitutional law: M. Kloepfer, *Verfassungsrecht I. Grundlagen, Staatsorganisationsrecht, Bezüge zum Völker- und Europarecht* (München: C. H. Beck, 2011); Ch. Gröpl, *Staatsrecht I. Staatsgrundlagen, Staatsorganisation, Verfassungsprozess mit Einführung in das juristische Lernen* (München: C. H. Beck, 2018).

42 E. Benda, "Grundgesetz und Wirtschaftsordnung," in *Handbuch Marktwirtschaft*, eds. R. Vaubel, H. D. Barbier (Weinsberg: Neske, 1986), 144–149; R. Scholz, E. Lieser-Triebnigg, "Grundgesetz und Wirtschaftsordnung in der Bundesrepublik Deutschland," in *Materialien zum Bericht zur Lage der Nation im geteilten Deutschland 1987*, 26–32; K. Grimm, *Socjalna gospodarka rynkowa w RFN.*

The main economic and social provisions of the FRG Constitution in force between 1990 and 2015 were as follows: freedom of association and prohibition of measures against labor struggles (Art. 9), freedom of choice of profession and prohibition of forced labor (Art. 12), property rights, inheritance rights and expropriation issues (Art. 14), socialization (Art. 15), maintenance of interference with property in the former GDR (Art. 143),[43] regulation of the merchant fleet (Art. 27), legal and official assistance, disaster relief (Art. 35), division of legislative powers between the Federation and the *Länder*, including in economic matters (Arts. 70–74a), the Federation's own administration in the field of finance, federal waterways and navigation, social insurance institutions, creation of new federal corporations and institutions under public law (Art. 87), generation and application of nuclear energy (Art. 87c), air communication (Art. 87d), rail transport (Art. 87e), conversion of the Federal Railways into a business enterprise (Art. 143a), post and telecommunications (Art. 87 f), conversion of the special trust of the German Federal Post Office into a private enterprise (Art. 143b), purview of the Federal Bank (Art. 88), federal waterways and shipping (Art. 89), federal highways and roads (Art. 90), cooperation of the Federation in the execution of specific tasks by the *Länder* (Arts. 91a–91e), state finances (Arts. 104a–115), purview of the Federal Court of Audit (Art. 114), burdens resulting from World War II (Art. 120), execution of compensation of burdens (costs), purview of the Federal Equalisation of Burdens Office and *Land* Equalisation of Burdens Offices (Art. 120a), law of the Combined Economic Area (Arts. 127, 133), corporations and institutions under public law (Art. 130), legal succession to the assets of the Third Reich (Art. 134), status of assets as a result of territorial changes of the state (Art. 135), debts of the Third Reich, Prussia, the GDR, the *Länder*, municipalities (associations of municipalities) and other corporations and institutions under public law (Art. 135a), financing the *Länder* by the Federation (Art. 143c).[44] Between 1990 and 2015, some of the listed articles were

---

Koncepcja – rozwój – problematyka (Warszawa: Fundacja im. Friedricha Eberta, 1992), 6–7; H. M. Stack, "The 'Colonization' of East Germany?: A Comparative Analysis of German Privatization," *Duke Law Journal* 46 (1997): 1217, fn. 28; *Mitbestimmung – eine gute Sache. Alles über die Mitbestimmung und ihre rechtlichen Grundlagen* (Bonn: Bundesministerium für Arbeit und Soziales, 2018), 78. Hans Willgerodt takes a slightly different view. It follows from his considerations that the fundamental principles and freedoms enshrined precisely in the FRG Constitution prove that it is impossible to speak of its neutrality (H. Willgerodt, "Grundrechte, Grundgesetz und Soziale Marktwirtschaft," in *Lexikon Soziale Marktwirtschaft. Wirtschaftspolitik von A bis Z*, eds. R. H. Hasse, H. Schneider, K. Weigelt (Paderborn: Ferdinand Schöningh, 2002), 247–249). However, this is not the dominant view in the literature. More on the concepts of economic order and the social market economy: section 4.1. in this book.

43 Arts. 14–15, 143 GG are discussed in section 6.1.1.1. in this work.

44 "Pomocnicze zestawienie treści artykułów Ustawy Zasadniczej," in Janicki, *Ustawa Zasadnicza*, 57–64; Arts. 87, 89, 120a, 130, 135a GG.

added to the Constitution or amended. Most of the economic provisions are found in different chapters of the Basic Law.

After a break covering the Third Reich period and the occupation zones' functioning, the FRG Constitution reactivated the capitalist system in 1949, but only in West Germany. The basis of this system was the right to private property guaranteed in Art. 14 GG. However, the property should serve the public good (*Wohl der Allgemeinheit*). It could be expropriated by law and for a certain compensation only in the interest of this good.[45] The same article provided for the right of inheritance.[46]

Art. 9 GG, amended in 1968,[47] guaranteed all Germans the right to form unions and associations. It prohibited the establishment of such associations, whose activities could be illegal under criminal law or could be directed against the constitutional order or "the concept of international understanding" (*Gedanke der Völkerverständigung*).[48] The Basic Law also guaranteed all citizens and professions the right to form associations whose activities were based on the protection and improvement of working conditions and economic realities. Furthermore, it prohibited the taking of measures against labor struggles that were led by these associations.[49]

In Art. 12, the Constitution guaranteed the right to a free choice of profession and place of work and education. Forced labor was prohibited with the exception of public works provided for prisoners.[50]

A separate provision of the Constitution was devoted to the regulation of the organization of the fleet for exchange purposes. Art. 27 GG stated: "All German merchant vessels shall constitute a unitary merchant fleet."[51]

In the event of a natural disaster or other grave situation, Art. 35 GG stipulated that the police of another federated state, the forces and administrative arrangements of other institutions, the Federal Border Police, or the military could be deployed to provide assistance in the territory of that *Land*. If a difficult situation affected several federated states, the federal government could oblige the *Land* authorities to place its police force at the disposal of other *Länder* or support the police force with the Federal Border Police or the army.[52]

Chap. VII of the Constitution (Arts. 70–74a), referred to the division of legislative powers between the Federation and *Länder*, which included economic matters. In this

---

45 Art. 14 GG.
46 Art. 14, Par. 1 GG. More on the empowerment of property in the FRG Constitution: section 6.1.1.1. in this study.
47 *Siebzehntes Gesetz zur Ergänzung des Grundgesetzes Vom 24. Juni 1968*, Par. 1, Pt 1 (BGBl., Part I, 1968, No. 41, 709).
48 Art. 9, Pars. 1–2 GG.
49 Art. 9, Par. 3 GG.
50 Art. 12 GG.
51 *Alle deutschen Kauffahrteischiffe bilden eine einheitliche Handelsflotte* (Art. 27 GG).
52 Art. 35, Pars. 2–3 GG.

respect, a distinction was made between exclusive and concurrent legislation.[53] The first included laws passed only by the central government, while the second covered both the Federation and *Länder*. Certain matters remained the subject of federated states' laws unless the Federation undertook to regulate a matter that was important from the point of view of equal living conditions or legal and economic unity on a statewide scale. Thus German law did not preclude the existence of joint powers of the Federation and *Länder* or their duplication. There was a conflict rule according to which federal law was superior to federated states' law.[54]

Under Art. 73 GG, the exclusive legislation of the Federation included: foreign diplomacy, defense issues, protection of civilians, German citizenship, choice of residence, passport, registration and document issues, immigration, emigration, extradition, currency, money and coinage issues, system of weights and measures, regulation of time, unity of customs and trading area, commerce and navigation treaties, free exchange of goods and payments (including foreign countries), customs and border protection, protection of cultural assets from removal from the country, air and rail transportation, postal services, telecommunications, legal relations of persons in the service of the Federation and federal corporations under public law, legal protection of production, copyright and publishing law, protection against international terrorism,[55] cooperation between the Federation and *Länder* in specific areas (criminal police, "protection of the free democratic basic order, existence and security of the Federation or of a *Land* (protection of the constitution),"[56] protection against threats to foreign interests of the state, international fight against crime), federal statistics, the right to weapons and explosives, care of invalids of war, families of war victims and former prisoners of war, the use of nuclear energy.[57] The individual provisions of the article were amended on the basis of laws from 1954 to 2006.[58] Art. 71 GG stipulated that in the

53 Arts. 70–74a GG.

54 B. Banaszak, *System konstytucyjny Niemiec* (Warszawa: Wydawnictwo Sejmowe, 2005), 78. Cf. Art. 72, Par. 2 GG.

55 Legislative measures related to protection against international terrorism required the consent of the Bundesrat (Art. 73, Par. 1, Pt 9a; Par. 2 GG).

56 *[Z]um Schutze der freiheitlichen demokratischen Grundordnung, des Bestandes und der Sicherheit des Bundes oder eines Landes (Verfassungsschutz)* (Art. 73, Par. 1, Pt 10b GG).

57 Art. 74, Par. 1 GG.

58 *Gesetz zur Ergänzung des Grundgesetzes. Vom 26. März 1954.*, Art. 1, Par. 1 (BGBl., Part I, 1954, No. 6, 45); *Siebzehntes Gesetz zur Ergänzung des Grundgesetzes Vom 24. Juni 1968*, Par. 1, Pt 12 (BGBl., Part I, 1968, No. 41, 711); *Einunddreißigstes Gesetz zur Änderung des Grundgesetzes Vom 28. Juli 1972*, Art. 1, Par. 2 (BGBl., Part I, 1972, No. 76, 1305); *Gesetz zur Änderung des Grundgesetzes Vom 20. Dezember 1993*, Art. 1, Par. 1 (BGBl, Part I, 1993, No. 68, 2089); *Gesetz zur Änderung des Grundgesetzes Vom 30. August 1994*, Art. 1, Par. 1 (BGBl, Part I, 1994, No. 58, 2245); *Gesetz zur Änderung des Grundgesetzes (Artikel 22, 23, 33, 52, 72, 73, 74, 74a, 75, 84, 85, 87c, 91a, 91b, 93,*

above-mentioned matters the *Länder* could pass laws only with the consent of the Federation.[59]

Concurrent legislation remained the subject of Arts. 72 and 74 GG. The first provided that the *Länder* could pass laws unless the Federation exercised in certain cases its legislative competence. In that case, the federated states could enact their laws in the following areas: hunting, environmental and landscape protection, land distribution, spatial and water management, university access, and graduation regulations.[60] These provisions were amended in 1994 and 2006.[61]

Art. 74 GG listed the areas affected by the concurrent legislation. A large part of them was related to the economic sphere. Over the years 1959–2006, they were subject to many amendments[62] hence some areas were temporary. These areas were as follows: civil and criminal law, the court system, court proceedings, the legal profession, notaries, legal advice, civil status matters, association law, residence and settlement law for foreigners, the right to weapons (1972–2006), protection of cultural assets from removal from the country (1949–1994), refugee and expellee issues, social welfare, citizenship at the *Land* level (1949–1994), war damage and compensation, care of invalids of war, families of war victims and former prisoners of war (1949–2006), care of war graves, sector-specific economic law (mining, industry, energy, crafts, production, trade, banking, stock exchanges, private legal insurance), nuclear energy (1959–2006), labor law, organization of enterprises, social insurance, educational assistance and financing of research, expropriation law, transfer of grounds, land, natural resources or means

---

98, 104a, 104b, 105, 107, 109, 125a, 125b, 125c, 143c) Vom 28. August 2006, Art. 1, Par. 6 (BGBl., Part I, 2006, No. 41, 2034–2035).

59 Art. 71 GG.

60 Art. 72 GG.

61 *Gesetz zur Änderung des Grundgesetzes (Artikel 3, 20a, 28, 29, 72, 74, 75, 76, 77, 80, 87, 93, 118a und 125a) Vom 27. Oktober 1994*, Art. 1, Par. 5 (BGBl., Part I, 1994, No. 75, 3146); *Gesetz zur Änderung des Grundgesetzes*, Art. 1, Par. 5 (BGBl., Part I, 2006, No. 41, 2034).

62 *Gesetz zur Ergänzung des Grundgesetzes. Vom 23. Dezember 1959.*, Art. 1, Par. 1 (BGBl., Part I, 1959, No. 56, 813); *Dreizehntes Gesetz zur Änderung des Grundgesetzes Vom 16. Juni 1965*, Art. 1, Pars. 1–2 (BGBl, Part I, 1965, No. 26, 513); *Zweiundzwanzigstes Gesetz zur Änderung des Grundgesetzes Vom 12. Mai 1969*, Art. 1, Par. 1 (BGBl, Part I, 1969, No. 37, 363); *Neundzwanzigstes Gesetz zur Änderung des Grundgesetzes Vom 18. März 1971*, Art. 1 (BGBl., Part I, 1971, No. 23, 207); *Dreißigstes Gesetz zur Änderung des Grundgesetzes (Artikel 74 GG – Umweltschutz) Vom 12. April 1972*, Art. 1, Pars. 1–2 (BGBl, Part I, 1972, No. 31, 593); *Einunddreißigstes Gesetz zur Änderung des Grundgesetzes*, Art. 1, Par. 3 (BGBl., Part I, 1972, No. 76, 1305); *Vierunddreißigstes Gesetz zur Änderung des Grundgesetzes (Artikel 74 Nr. 4a) Vom 23. August 1976*, Art. 1 (BGBl, Part I, 1976, No. 107, 2383); *Gesetz zur Änderung des Grundgesetzes*, Art. 1, Par. 2 (BGBl., Part I, 1993, No. 68, 2089); *Gesetz zur Änderung des Grundgesetzes*, Art. 1, Par. 6 (BGBl., Part I, 1994, No. 75, 3146); *Gesetz zur Änderung des Grundgesetzes*, Art. 1, Par. 7 (BGBl., Part I, 2006, No. 41, 2035).

of production to public property or other forms of public economy, protection against abuse of economic advantage, promotion of agricultural and forestry production, food security, import and export of agricultural and forestry products, fisheries, coastal protection, real estate trade, land law, agricultural leases, housing, settlement and household issues, housing allowance law, homebuilding (including for miners), regulations for protection against human and animal diseases, entitlements to medical professions, regulations relating to medical products, economic security of hospitals and hospital charges (since 1969), food law, maritime, coastal and inland navigation, road traffic, *Länder*'s roads, *Länder*'s railroads (with the exception of mountain railroads), waste management, air pollution control, noise control, state liability (since 1994),[63] fertility, genetics and transplantation regulations (since 1994) and, since 2006, the rights and duties of civil servants and judges in the *Länder*,[64] hunting, environmental and landscape protection, ground distribution, spatial and water management, university and graduation law.[65]

Art. 74a GG complemented these findings. It was added to the Constitution in 1971[66] and concerned concurrent legislation on the emoluments and provisions of persons in the public service. This article was abolished in 2006.[67]

There was also federal framework legislation in Germany between 1949 and 2006. The central authorities had the right to issue "framework laws" (*Rahmenvorschriften*), which defined the directions and limits of the *Länder*'s legislation. As Bogusław Banaszak notes, framework legislation, on the one hand, strengthened the unity and legal system of the state. On the other hand, it was an example of interference of the central government in the autonomy of the *Länder*.[68] It seems that this type of legislation played a special role from the point of view of institutional economics. In the context of a formal institution such as law, these norms determined a narrower but more precise area of the functioning of the economy and society. Under Art. 75 GG, the Federation had the power to enact framework laws in the following areas: the legal relations of persons in the public service of the *Länder*, municipalities and other corporations under public law, the general rules of higher education, hunting, environmental and landscape protection, the division of land, spatial planning, water management, registration and identity cards, and protection of cultural assets from removal from the country.[69]

---

63 Legislative measures related to state liability required the consent of the Bundesrat (Art. 74, Par. 1, Pt 25; Par. 2 GG).

64 Legislative measures related to the rights and duties of civil servants and judges in the *Länder* required the consent of the Bundesrat (Art. 74, Par. 1, Pt 27; Par. 2 GG).

65 Art. 74 GG.

66 *Achtundzwanzigstes Gesetz zur Änderung des Grundgesetzes (Artikel 74a GG) Vom 18. März 1971*, Art. 1, Par. 1 (BGBl., Part I, 1971, No. 23, 206).

67 *Gesetz zur Änderung des Grundgesetzes*, Art. 1, Par. 8 (BGBl., Part I, 2006, No. 41, p. 2035).

68 Banaszak, *System konstytucyjny Niemiec*, 78–79.

69 Art. 75, Par. 1 GG.

Moreover, the framework provisions specified the time within which the *Länder* were obliged to regulate a given issue.[70] This article was amended between 1969 and 1994.[71] However, it was abolished in 2006.[72]

Art. 87 GG indicated the powers of the federal administration concerning foreign policy, state finances, federal waterways and shipping, police, social security institutions, creation of federal authorities of higher, secondary, and basic levels, and new federal corporations and institutions under public law.[73] Individual paragraphs were amended by successive laws from 1972 to 1994.[74]

The laws of 1956–1994, taking into account advances in the economy and technology, added six articles to the Constitution regulating the powers of the federal administration in the following areas: the armed forces, nuclear energy, air, and rail transport, and post and telecommunications.[75] They were amended over the following years. Most of them were concerned with the economic and social spheres.

Art. 87c GG, which deals with nuclear energy, was added to the Constitution in 1959.[76] Its amendment was made in 2006.[77] It referred to Art. 73 GG,[78] which provided for exclusive legislative powers of the federal government in the area of production and use of nuclear energy, construction and use of appropriate facilities, protection against possible danger, and disposal of radioactive substances.[79] Art. 87c GG allowed the *Länder*, with the consent of the Federal Council, to execute laws enacted pursuant to Art. 73 GG.[80]

---

70 Art. 75, Par. 3 GG.

71 *Zweiundzwanzigstes Gesetz zur Änderung des Grundgesetzes*, Art. 1, Par. 2 (BGBl., Part I, 1969, No. 37, 363); *Achtundzwanzigstes Gesetz zur Änderung des Grundgesetzes*, Art. 1, Par. 2 (BGBl., Part I, 1971, No. 23, 206); *Gesetz zur Änderung des Grundgesetzes*, Art. 1, Par. 7 (BGBl., Part I, 1994, No. 75, 3147).

72 *Gesetz zur Änderung des Grundgesetzes*, Art. 1, Par. 8 (BGBl., Part I, 2006, No. 41, 2035).

73 Art. 87 GG.

74 *Einunddreißigstes Gesetz zur Änderung des Grundgesetzes*, Art. 1, Par. 4 (BGBl., Part I, 1972, No. 76, 1305); *Gesetz zur Änderung des Grundgesetzes*, Art. 1, Par. 4 (BGBl, Part I, 1993, No. 68, 2089); *Gesetz zur Änderung des Grundgesetzes*, Art. 1, Par. 3 (BGBl., Part I, 1994, No. 58, 2245); *Gesetz zur Änderung des Grundgesetzes*, Art. 1, Par. 11 (BGBl., Part I, 1994, No. 75, 3147).

75 Arts. 87a–87 f GG.

76 *Gesetz zur Ergänzung des Grundgesetzes*, Art. 1, Par. 2 (BGBl., Part I, 1959, No. 56, 813).

77 *Gesetz zur Änderung des Grundgesetzes*, Art. 1, Par. 11 (BGBl., Part I, 2006, No. 41, 2036).

78 Art. 73 GG was also amended in 2006 (*Gesetz zur Änderung des Grundgesetzes*, Art. 1, Par. 6 (BGBl., Part I, 2006, No. 41, 2034–2035)).

79 Art. 73, Par. 1, Pt 14 GG.

80 Art. 87c GG.

Regulation of air communications was included in Art. 87d GG. It was added in 1961[81] and amended in 1992 and 2009.[82] It stated that air transport was subject to the federal administration. A federal law, with the approval of the Bundesrat, could delegate control of air transport to certain *Länder*.[83]

The railroads remained the subject of Art. 87e GG. It was added to the Constitution in 1993.[84] Under its terms, rail transport was subordinate to the central administration, although there was a statutory possibility to transfer this control to the *Länder*. The German railroads had the status of an economic enterprise in private legal form and were owned by the Federation. The state had a constitutionally guaranteed majority stake in it. Its tasks included the construction of tracks and their operation and maintenance.[85] Particularly noteworthy is Par. 4 of the article. It referred to the respect for the public good, especially in the field of communication, expansion, and maintenance of tracks, as well as the development of appropriate transport offers of the state scope.[86] Par. 5 was indirectly related to this type of responsibility. All regulations regarding the railroad system's status and transformation required the Bundesrat's consent. This included the liquidation, merger or division of a railroad company, the transfer of tracks to other entities, the immobilization of tracks, or the deformation of local passenger transport.[87]

The transformation of the Federal Railways into a business enterprise was dedicated to Art. 143a GG,[88] added to the Constitution in 1993.[89] The German railroad companies operated as part of the Deutsche Bahn Aktiengesellschaft (AG), which was formed in 1994 by the merger of the West and East German railway administrations. The sole shareholder of this joint stock company was the state.[90]

Art. 87 f GG, added to the Basic Law in 1994,[91] deals with postal and telecommunications issues. The state guaranteed these services, but they were carried out

---

81 *Gesetz zur Einfügung eines Artikels über die Luftverkehrsverwaltung in das Grundgesetz (11. Änderung des Grundgesetzes) Vom 6. Februar 1961*, Par. 1 (BGBl., Part I, 1961, No. 7, 65).

82 *Gesetz zur Änderung des Grundgesetzes Vom 14. Juli 1992*, Art. 1 (BGBl., Part I, 1992, No. 33, 1254); *Gesetz zur Änderung des Grundgesetzes (Artikel 87d) Vom 29. Juli 2009* (BGBl., Part I, 2009, No. 48, 2247).

83 Art. 87d GG.

84 *Gesetz zur Änderung des Grundgesetzes*, Art. 1, Par. 5 (BGBl., Part I, 1993, No. 68, 2089).

85 Art. 87e, Pars. 1–3 GG.

86 Art. 87e, Par. 4 GG.

87 Art. 87e, Par. 5 GG.

88 Art. 143a GG.

89 *Gesetz zur Änderung des Grundgesetzes*, Art. 1, Par. 7 (BGBl., Part I, 1993, No. 68, 2089–2090).

90 Cf., e.g., W. Paprocki, "Przemiany europejskich kolei w XXI wieku," *Rynek Kolejowy* No. 2 (2006): 52–53.

91 *Gesetz zur Änderung des Grundgesetzes*, Art. 1, Par. 4 (BGBl., Part I, 1994, No. 58, 2245).

as part of a private economic activity (*privatwirtschaftliche Tätigkeit*). This was carried out by entities that came from the German Federal Post Office's special assets or private companies. All supervisory tasks in this area were carried out by the central administration.[92] The structural transformation in this area was regulated by Art. 143b GG,[93] also added to the Constitution in 1994.[94]

The German central bank remained the subject of Art. 88 GG. Its original form was amended in 1992.[95] in connection with the signing of the Maastricht Treaty on February 7, 1992. According to this article, the Federal Bank had a monetary and emission function. However, its powers could be transferred to the independent European Central Bank, whose most important task was to maintain price stability.[96]

The next two articles of the Constitution dealt with the German road network of various types. Art. 89 GG stipulated that the former waterways of the Third Reich were the property of the FRG. The central administration supervised the federal waterways, as well as sea and inland waterways beyond the borders of a given *Land*. In certain situations, on behalf of the central government, the federated state's administration could manage federal waterways located within the *Land*. A particular federated state could manage waterways involving several *Länder* at the request of these *Länder*.[97] Par. 3 of this article included a dimension of social responsibility for waterway management in Germany. It stipulated that "[i]n the administration, development and new construction of waterways, the requirements of land improvement and of water management shall be assured in agreement with the *Länder*."[98]

In turn, Art. 90 GG concerned federal highways and roads. It also stipulated that the former highways and roads of the Third Reich remained the property of the FRG. Federal highways and long-distance roads were managed by the individual *Länder* or self-governing corporate bodies (*Selbstverwaltungskörperschaften*) on behalf of the central government. If these roads ran through the federated state, it could ask the federal administration to take control of them.[99]

---

92 Art. 87 f GG.

93 Art. 143b GG.

94 *Gesetz zur Änderung des Grundgesetzes*, Art. 1, Par. 5 (BGBl., Part I, 1994, No. 58, 2245).

95 *Gesetz zur Änderung des Grundgesetzes Vom 21. Dezember 1992,* Art. 1, Par. 7 (BGBl., Part I, 1992, No. 58, 2087).

96 Art. 88 GG.

97 Article 89, Pars. 1–2 GG.

98 *Bei der Verwaltung, dem Ausbau und dem Neubau von Wasserstraßen sind die Bedürfnisse der Landeskultur und der Wasserwirtschaft im Einvernehmen mit den Ländern zu wahren* (Art. 89, Par. 3 GG).

99 Art. 90 GG.

A separate Chap. VIIIa GG dealt with joint tasks of the Federation and the *Länder*. It was added in 1969.[100] Art. 91a GG dealt with economic issues. It stipulated that the Federation assisted the federated states in the following tasks: "improvement of regional economic structures" and "improvement of the agrarian structure and coastal preservation."[101] The first task required the Federation to incur half of the expenses in each of the *Länder*, while the second a minimum of the half, which had to be precisely determined for all federated states.[102] The article was amended in 1970 and 2006.[103]

Subsequent articles of Chap. VIIIa GG dealt with joint tasks in the following areas: research and education (Art. 91b GG, added in 1969,[104] amended in 2006 and 2014[105]), information and communication systems (Art. 91c GG, added in 2009[106]), research on federal and *Länder* administration (Art. 91d GG, added in 2009[107]), combating unemployment (Art. 91e GG, added in 2010[108]).

Arts. 104a–115 GG, which make up Chap. X GG, covered issues related to the state finances. Some of them have been added to the Constitution or amended over the years. Basically, these provisions can be divided into two groups. The first (Arts. 104a–108 GG) concerned the division of powers in the area of finance between the Federation and the *Länder*. In turn, the subject of the second set of provisions (Art. 109–115 UZ) remained the budget of the state and the federated states.[109]

---

100 *Einundzwanzigstes Gesetz zur Änderung des Grundegesetzes (Finanzreformgesetz) Vom 12. Mai 1969*, Art. 1, Par. 1 (BGBl., Part I, 1969, No. 37, 359).

101 *Verbesserung der regionalen Wirtschaftsstruktur, ... Verbesserung der Agrarstruktur und des Küstenschutzes* (Art. 91a, Par. 1 GG).

102 Art. 91a UZ.

103 *Siebenundzwanzigstes Gesetz zur Änderung des Grundgesetzes Vom 31. Juli 1970*, Art 1, Par. 2 (BGBl., Part I, 1970, No. 76, 1161); *Gesetz zur Änderung des Grundgesetzes*, Art 1, Par. 12 (BGBl., Part I, 2006, No. 41, 2036).

104 *Einundzwanzigstes Gesetz zur Änderung des Grundegesetzes*, Art. 1, Par. 1 (BGBl., Part I, 1969, No. 37, 359).

105 *Gesetz zur Änderung des Grundgesetzes*, Art. 1, Par. 13 (BGBl., Part I, 2006, No. 41, 2036); *Gesetz zur Änderung des Grundgesetzes (Artikel 91b) Vom 23. Dezember 2014* (BGBl., Part I, 2014, No. 64, 2438).

106 *Gesetz zur Änderung des Grundgesetzes*, Art. 1, Par. 2 (BGBl., Part I, 2009, No. 48, 2248).

107 *Gesetz zur Änderung des Grundgesetzes*, Art. 1, Par. 2 (BGBl., Part I, 2009, No. 48, 2248).

108 *Gesetz zur Änderung des Grundgesetzes (Artikel 91e) Vom 21. Juli 2010* (BGBl., Part I, 2010, No. 38, 944).

109 Cf. Tkaczyński, *Prawo ustrojowe Niemiec*, 195. Tkaczyński makes a slightly different separation of the provisions within Chap. X GG, although he correctly indicates their problematic scopes. However, he includes Art. 109 GG to the first of the mentioned groups. What is more, he wrongly claims that the subject of the second group is only the federal budget.

Art. 104a GG was added to the Basic Law in 1969[110] and amended in 2006.[111] It dealt with the incurring of expenses by the Federation and the *Länder* that resulted from the tasks assigned to them. Costs associated with the performance by the federated states of certain tasks mandated by the Federation were borne by the latter. The article also spoke of the financial responsibility of the *Länder* and the Federation in the event of a breach of Germany's obligations[112].

In 2006, Article 104b GG was added to the Constitution[113] and amended in 2009.[114] Its subject was financial aid provided by the Federation to the federated states. It covered *Länder* and municipal investments that counteracted a disturbance of the "overall economic equilibrium" (*gesamtwirtschaftliches Gleichgewicht*), leveled disparate economic power within the state, or promoted economic growth. Such measures were granted for a limited time, were regularly reviewed, and their value declined in subsequent years. Information on progress in this area was presented to the Bundestag, the Federal Government, and the Bundesrat.[115]

The legislative powers of the Federation related to the state finances were defined by Art. 105 GG. It was amended in 1969 and 2006.[116] The Federation had legislative competence in the area of customs duties and financial monopolies. It exercised competition legislation in the area of specific taxes. The *Länder* had the right to legislate on local consumption and luxury taxes,[117] as long as they were not uniform with taxes regulated by federal laws. In addition, the federated states were allowed to determine the tax rate on acquiring real estate. If a federal law referred to a levy, the revenue from which accrued to the *Länder* or municipalities (associations of municipalities), the consent of the Bundesrat was required.[118]

Tax revenues also remained subject to Art. 106 GG divided them between the Federation, the *Länder*, and the municipalities. It was subject to amendments between 1955 and 2009.[119] The article states that the Federation was entitled to

---

110 *Einundzwanzigstes Gesetz zur Änderung des Grundegesetzes*, Art. 1, Par. 2 (BGBl., Part I, 1969, No. 37, 359–360).

111 *Gesetz zur Änderung des Grundgesetzes*, Art. 1, Par. 16 (BGBl., Part I, 2006, No. 41, 2036).

112 Art. 104a GG.

113 *Gesetz zur Änderung des Grundgesetzes*, Art. 1, Par. 17 (BGBl., Part I, 2006, No. 41, 2036–2037).

114 *Gesetz zur Änderung des Grundgesetzes*, Art. 1, Par. 3 (BGBl., Part I, 2009, No. 48, 2248).

115 Art. 104b GG.

116 *Einundzwanzigstes Gesetz zur Änderung des Grundegesetzes*, Art. 1, Par. 3 (BGBl., Part I, 1969, No. 37, 360); *Gesetz zur Änderung des Grundgesetzes*, Art. 1, Par. 18 (BGBl., Part I, 2006, No. 41, 2037).

117 The luxury tax (*Aufwandsteuer*) refers to a tax on expenses made. There are different translations of the term in the translations of the German Constitution. More on the classification of public tributes in Germany in 1990–2015: sec. 6.2.7.1. in this study.

118 Art. 105 GG.

119 *Gesetz zur Änderung und Ergänzung der Finanzverfassung (Finanzverfassungsgesetz). Vom 23. Dezember 1955.*, Par. 1 (BGBl., Part I, 1955, No. 47, 817–818); *Gesetz zur*

revenues from financial monopolies, customs duties, taxes on consumption, road transport of goods, motor vehicles, transactions of motorized means of transport and capital turnover, insurance tax and bills of exchange, one-off property and compensatory taxes within offsetting charges and supplementary to income and corporate tax, as well as taxes within the scope of the EU.[120] The *Länder* were guaranteed revenues from taxes such as: on property, inheritance, transfer of property values, beer and casino.[121] The "joint taxes" (*Gemeinschaftsteuern*) generated revenues that were due – with certain reservations – to both the Federation and the federated states. These were: income, turnover, and corporate taxes.[122] In turn, municipalities were guaranteed – under specific conditions – a share in revenues from taxes on income, turnover,[123] land, economic activity, consumption, and luxury.[124]

Änderung und Ergänzung des Artikels 106 des Grundgesetzes. Vom 24. Dezember 1956 (BGBl., Part I, 1956, No. 54, 1077); *Einundzwanzigstes Gesetz zur Änderung des Grundegesetzes*, Art. 1, Par. 4 (BGBl., Part I, 1969, No. 37, 360–361); *Gesetz zur Änderung des Grundgesetzes Vom 3. November 1995* (BGBl, Part I, 1995, No. 57, 1492); *Gesetz zur Änderung des Grundgesetzes (Artikel 28 und 106) Vom 20. Oktober 1997*, Art. 1, Par. 2 (BGBl, Part I, 1997, No. 69, 2470); *Gesetz zur Änderung des Grundgesetzes (Artikel 106, 106b, 107, 108) Vom 19 März 2009*, Art. 1, Par. 1 (BGBl., Part I, 2009, No. 16, 606).

120 Art. 106, Par. 1 GG.

121 Art. 106, Par. 2 GG.

122 Art. 106, Pars. 3–4 GG.

123 In the case of income and turnover taxes, the Basic Law referred to the municipalities' share of the revenue (Art. 106, Pars. 5–5a GG).

124 Art. 106, Pars. 5–9 GG. In the case of consumption and luxury taxes, on the basis of *Länder*'s legislation, the proceeds could accrue to associations of municipalities (Art. 106, Par. 6 GG). Helmut Seitz, discussing fiscal federalism in Germany, distinguishes two "sub-systems" within the system of financial equalization. The first (vertical) one concerned the division of tax revenues between the Federation and the *Länder*. The second (horizontal) sub-system concerned the equalization of these revenues per capita between the individual *Länder* (H. Seitz, "Fiscal Policy, Deficits and Politics of Subnational Governments: The Case of the German Laender," *Public Choice* 102, No. 3–4 (2000): 188–190). Cf. R. Wendt, "Der Finanzausgleich im föderalen System der Bundesrepublik Deutschland," in *Handbuch Föderalismus – Föderalismus als demokratische Rechtsordnung und Rechtskultur in Deutschland, Europa und der Welt*, Vol. II: *Probleme, Reformen, Perspektiven des deutschen Föderalismus*, ed. I. Härtel (Berlin–Heidelberg: Springer-Verlag, 2012), 389–423. The need to reform the financial equalization system was highlighted in the work on the second federalism reform of 2009 (see section 3.5. in this book). However, this issue was dominated by the priority challenge of combating the state indebtedness (M. Przybysz, "Pierwsza i druga 'reforma federalizmu' w Republice Federalnej Niemiec – zmiany Ustawy Zasadniczej z 2006 i 2009 r. w odniesieniu do kompetencji prawodawczych i stosunków finansowych Związku i krajów," *Przegląd Prawa Konstytucyjnego* No. 1 (35) (2017): 152).

In Art. 106a GG, the right of the *Länder* to a quota from the Federation's tax revenues for local public passenger transport was guaranteed.[125] The provision was added in 1993.[126]

Art. 106b GG resolved issues related to the participation of the *Länder* in motor vehicle tax revenues.[127] It was added to the German Constitution in 2009.[128]

In turn, Art. 107 GG treated the equalization of finances. It was amended several times between 1953 and 2009.[129] Its provisions concerned the detailed rules for the distribution of *Länder*'s tax revenue, as well as taxes on income, turnover, corporate, salaries and wages, purchase of real estate and others.[130] Significantly, Par. 2 provided for the possibility – by law – to establish "equalisation payments" (*Ausgleichsleistungen*) between the individual federated states and for the Federation to provide "supplementary grants" (*Ergänzungszuweisungen*). These were intended for less developed *Länder* to supplement their financial needs.[131]

The financial administration remained the subject of Art. 108 GG. According to this provision, the federal government administered customs duties, financial monopolies, taxes on consumption, import turnover, motor vehicle, motorized transport and fees within the EU. There was the possibility of establishing intermediate authorities in this area, however, only with the knowledge of the *Länder*. The remaining taxes were subject to the administration of the federated states. As feedback, intermediate authorities in this area were established in consultation with the Federation. In order to improve the quality of the implementation of the tax laws, the possibility of cooperation between federal and *Länder*'s authorities in the administration of taxes was permitted. The administration of taxes owed by municipalities (associations of municipalities) could be delegated to them by the *Länder*.[132] The individual provisions of the article were amended in 1969, 2001, and 2009.[133]

---

125 Art. 106a GG.

126 *Gesetz zur Änderung des Grundgesetzes*, Art. 1, Par. 6 (BGBl., Part I, 1993, No. 68, 2089).

127 Art. 106b GG.

128 *Gesetz zur Änderung des Grundgesetzes*, Art. 1, Par. 2 (BGBl., Part I, 2009, No. 16, 606).

129 *Gesetz zur Änderung des Artikels 107 des Grundgesetzes. Vom 20. April 1953.* (BGBl., Part I, 1953, No. 16, 130); *Zweites Gesetz zur Änderung des Artikels 107 des Grundgesetzes. Vom 25. Dezember 1954.* (BGBl., Part I, 1954, No. 45, 517); *Gesetz zur Änderung und Ergänzung der Finanzverfassung*, Par. 1, Pts. 1–2 (BGBl., Part I, 1955, No. 47, 818); *Einundzwanzigstes Gesetz zur Änderung des Grundegesetzes*, Art. 1, Par. 5 (BGBl., Part I, 1969, No. 37, 361); *Gesetz zur Änderung des Grundgesetzes*, Art. 1, Par. 19 (BGBl, Part I, 2006, No. 41, 2037); *Gesetz zur Änderung des Grundgesetzes*, Art. 1, Par. 3 (BGBl., Part I, 2009, No. 16, 606).

130 Art. 107, Par. 1 GG.

131 Art. 107, Par. 2 GG.

132 Art. 108 GG.

133 *Einundzwanzigstes Gesetz zur Änderung des Grundegesetzes*, Art. 1, Par. 6 (BGBl., Part I, 1969, No. 37, 361); *Gesetz zur Änderung des Grundgesetzes (Artikel 108) Vom*

As already mentioned, Arts. 109–115 GG dealt with detailed issues of the state and *Länder*'s budgets. Art. 109 GG regulated the issues related to the division of the budgets of the Federation and the *Länder* and the principles of budget management. It was amended in the years 1967–2009.[134] The article assumed independence and mutual independence of the federated states and the Federation in terms of budget management, in which they should take into account the requirements of an overall economic equilibrium.[135] Par. 4 stipulated that a federal law could be enacted with the consent of the Bundesrat to specify the principles of budgetary management and long-term economic planning.[136] In order to prevent disturbances in the overall economic equilibrium, the federal law – with the consent of the Federal Council – could introduce provisions regarding the maximum amounts, conditions and order of indebtedness of territorial corporations (*Gebietskörperschaften*) and special-purpose associations (*Zweckverbände*), as well as obligations of the Federation and the *Länder* to maintain interest-free deposits at the Deutsche Bundesbank, the "reserves for economic equalisation" (*Konjunkturausgleichsrücklagen*). The federal government could issue decrees in this regard with the consent of the Bundesrat. However, the Bundestag could demand their repeal.[137] Par. 5, added in 2006, concerning financial regulations resulting from Germany's membership in the EU. It provided for cooperation between the Federation and the *Länder* in maintaining budgetary discipline (*Haushaltsdisziplin*).[138] If the Community imposed sanctions, the Federation bore 65 % of the costs, and the federated states 35 %. Under the latter part, 35 % of the *Länder*'s obligations came from the solidarity contribution of all federated states according to population. The remaining 65 % of the burden

---

26. November 2001 (BGBl., Part I, 2001, No. 61, 3219); *Gesetz zur Änderung des Grundgesetzes*, Art. 1, Par. 4 (BGBl., Part I, 2009, No. 16, 606). More on the allocation of taxation powers between the Federation and the *Länder*, see A. Leisner-Egensperger, "Gesetzgebungs- und Verwaltungskompetenzen von Bund und Ländern im Bereich der Steuern," in Härtel, *Handbuch Föderalismus*, 365–387.

134 *Fünfzehntes Gesetz zur Änderung des Grundgesetzes Vom 8. Juni 1967* (BGBl., Part I, 1967, No. 32, 581); *Zwanzigstes Gesetz zur Änderung des Grundgesetzes Vom 12. Mai 1969*, Art. 1, Par. 1 (BGBl, Part I, 1969, No. 37, 357); *Gesetz zur Änderung des Grundgesetzes*, Art. 1, Par. 20 (BGBl., Part I, 2006, No. 41, 2037); *Gesetz zur Änderung des Grundgesetzes*, Art. 1, Par. 4 (BGBl., Part I, 2009, No. 48, 2248–2249).

135 Art. 109, Pars. 1–2 GG.

136 Art. 109, Par. 3 GG. Since 2009, this provision has operated as Par. 4 (*Gesetz zur Änderung des Grundgesetzes*, Art. 1, Par. 4, Pt. c (BGBl., Part I, 2009, No. 48, 2249)).

137 Art. 109, Par. 4 GG. This paragraph was repealed by the 2009 amendment (*Gesetz zur Änderung des Grundgesetzes*, Art. 1, Par. 4, Pt. d (BGBl., Part I, 2009, No. 48, 2249)).

138 As mentioned in this Art. 109, Par. 5 GG, this followed from Art. 104 of the Maastricht Treaty (Art. 109, Par. 5 GG; "Consolidated Version of the Treaty on the Functioning of the European Union, Art. 126 (former Art. 104 of the Treaty establishing the European Community))," in *Consolidated Versions of the Treaty on European Union and the Treaty on the Functioning of the European Union* (Official Journal of the European Union, 26.10.2012, C 326, 99–102).

was borne by specific *Länder* in an amount corresponding to their degree of contribution to the imposition of burdens.[139] Details on the applicability of Art. 109 GG since 2009 were regulated by Art. 143d GG, added to the FRG Constitution in 2009.[140]

The same amendment also added Art. 109a GG.[141] In the event of a "budgetary emergencies" (*Haushaltsnotlagen*), a federal law (with the consent of the Bundesrat) could establish a Stability Council (*Stabilitätsrat*) and lay down criteria and rules for dealing with such situation, as well as rules for the development and implementation of appropriate recovery programs.[142]

Art. 110 GG indicates the main guidelines for the state budget. It was amended in 1969.[143] It contains basic budgetary principles, such as completeness (Par. 1, partly also Par. 4), balance (Par. 1), annuality (Par. 2)[144] and – indirectly – unity (Par. 4).[145]

The federal government's authority over expenditures made prior to the approval of the following year's budget was governed by Art. 111 GG. These expenditures were related to the maintenance of facilities operating under the law, implementation of projects undertaken by the law, fulfillment of the state obligations, and continuation of construction, supplies, and other services provided for in the previous budget law. If there was a shortage of revenue to meet the mentioned expenditures, the government had the right to mobilize funds in this regard in the form of a credit up to 25 % of the sum of the previous budget.[146]

In accordance with Art. 112 GG, with the approval of the Minister of Finance, it was possible to implement "[e]xpenditures in excess of budgetary

---

139 Art. 109, Par. 5 GG.

140 *Gesetz zur Änderung des Grundgesetzes*, Art. 1, Par. 7 (BGBl., Part I, 2009, No. 48, 2249–2250); Art. 143d GG.

141 *Gesetz zur Änderung des Grundgesetzes*, Art. 1, Par. 5 (BGBl., Part I, 2009, No. 48, 2249).

142 Art. 109a GG.

143 *Zwanzigstes Gesetz zur Änderung des Grundgesetzes*, Art. 1, Par. 2 (BGBl., Part I, 1969, No. 37, 357).

144 Certain exceptions were allowed for the principle of annuality of the FRG budget: "The budget for one or more fiscal years shall be set forth in a law enacted before the beginning of the first year and making separate provision for each year. The law may provide that various parts of the budget apply to different periods of time, divided by fiscal years" (*Der Haushaltsplan wird für ein oder mehrere Rechnungsjahre, nach Jahren getrennt, vor Beginn des ersten Rechnungsjahres durch das Haushaltsgesetz festgestellt. Für Teile des Haushaltsplanes kann vorgesehen werden, daß sie für unterschiedliche Zeiträume, nach Rechnungsjahren getrennt, gelten*) (Art. 110, Par. 2 GG).

145 Art. 110 GG. Cf. S. Owsiak, *Finanse publiczne. Współczesne ujęcia* (Warszawa: WN PWN, 2017), 164–168.

146 Art. 111 GG.

appropriations or for purposes not contemplated by the budget" (*überplanmäßige und außerplanmäßige Ausgaben*). This was done "only in the event of an unforeseen and unavoidable necessity."[147] This regulation was amended in 1969.[148]

Art. 113 GG discussed issues on increasing expenditures and decreasing budget revenues. It, too, was subject to amendment in 1969.[149] Any law regulating revenues and expenditures in this way required the consent of the federal government, which could demand that the Bundestag, under certain conditions, postpone such laws.[150]

Under Art. 114, Par. 1 GG, the Minister of Finance was obliged to report annually on state revenues and expenditures to the Bundestag and Bundesrat. This was a condition for the discharge of the government.[151] Par. 2 of this article outlined the powers of the Federal Court of Audit with respect to this financial report. It was subject to control by the members of the Court, who also checked "whether public finances have been properly and efficiently administered."[152] This body was also obliged to report once a year to the parliament and the Federal Council on its activities.[153] Art. 114 GG was amended in 1969.[154]

A separate place in the FRG Constitution is devoted to borrowing. Art. 115 GG, amended in 1969 and 2009,[155] stated that indebtedness and the assumption of sureties, guarantees, or other warranties that could increase state spending in the future required legislative approval. Until 2009, this included the stipulation that proceeds from borrowing could not exceed the sum of expenditures for investments provided for in the budget law. Exceptions were the "avert a disturbance of the overall economic equilibrium" (*Abwehr einer Störung des gesamtwirtschaftlichen Gleichgewichts*) and the regulations on the "special trust" (*Sondervermögen*) of the Federation.[156] In 2009, Par. 2 was incorporated into Art. 115 GG,[157] clarified the

---

147 [*N*]*ur im Falle eines unvorhergesehenen und unabweisbaren Bedürfnisses* (Art. 112 GG).

148 *Zwanzigstes Gesetz zur Änderung des Grundgesetzes*, Art. 1, Par. 3 (BGBl., Part I, 1969, No. 37, 357).

149 *Zwanzigstes Gesetz zur Änderung des Grundgesetzes*, Art. 1, Par. 4 (BGBl., Part I, 1969, No. 37, 357–358).

150 Art. 113 GG.

151 Art. 114, Par. 1 GG.

152 [*D*]*ie Wirtschaftlichkeit und Ordnungsmäßigkeit der Haushalts- und Wirtschaftsführung* (Art. 114, Par. 2 GG).

153 Art. 114, Par. 2 GG.

154 *Zwanzigstes Gesetz zur Änderung des Grundgesetzes*, Art. 1, Par. 5 (BGBl., Part I, 1969, No. 37, 358).

155 *Zwanzigstes Gesetz zur Änderung des Grundgesetzes*, Art 1, Par. 6 (BGBl., Part I, 1969, No. 37, 358); *Gesetz zur Änderung des Grundgesetzes*, Art. 1, Par. 6 (BGBl., Part I, 2009, No. 48, 2249).

156 *Gesetz zur Änderung des Grundgesetzes*, Art. 1, Par. 6, Pt. a (BGBl., Part I, 2009, No. 48, 2249).

157 *Gesetz zur Änderung des Grundgesetzes*, Art. 1, Par. 6, Pt. b (BGBl., Part I, 2009, No. 48, 2249).

borrowing rules, although it emphasized that the state budget should be balanced without their participation. Among other things, it stated that the share of loans should not be higher than 0.35 % of the nominal value of GDP. Deviations from the upper credit limit were to be booked on a control account (*Kontrollkonto*). The repayment obligation applied to debts above 1.5 % of nominal GDP. These thresholds were to be adjusted to the current economic situation. Details were regulated by law. However, a resolution of the Bundestag was sufficient for natural disasters and emergencies.[158] The applicability of Art. 115 GG since 2009 has been clarified by Art. 143d GG.[159]

Another single economic issue was found in Chap. XI GG. It contained transitional and final provisions.

Art. 120 GG dealt with burdens that resulted from World War II. All burdens resulting from the German occupation and the war were borne by the Federation.[160] The article was amended in 1965 and 1969.[161] The realization of these debts was handled by the central authorities, the *Länder*, the Federal Equalisation of Burdens Office or *Land* Equalisation of Burdens Offices. The latter two institutions were referred to in Article 120a,[162] added to the Constitution in 1952.[163]

Arts. 127 and 133 GG draw attention to the legal aspects of the Combined Economic Area (*Vereinigtes Wirtschaftsgebiet*). This term meant the economically integrated territory of the German state. Originally this term referred to the Bizone, the United Economic Area, i.e. the two occupation zones, British and American, merged on January 1, 1947.[164] After the annexation of the French zone, Bizonia was transformed into Trizonia on April 8, 1949.[165] This laid the groundwork for the creation of West Germany, whose the Basic Law set formal and legal framework. The economic integration of the German state's territory took on renewed significance with German reunification in October 1990. On the basis of the Constitution, the rights and obligations concerning the administration of the Combined Economic Area were vested in the Federation.[166]

---

158 Art. 115 GG.

159 Art. 143d GG.

160 Art. 120 GG.

161 *Vierzehntes Gesetz zur Änderung des Grundgesetzes Vom 30. Juli 1965* (BGBl., Part I, 1965, No. 34, 649); *Vierundzwanzigstes Gesetz zur Änderung des Grundgesetzes Vom 28. Juli 1969* (BGBl., Part I, 1969, No. 68, 985).

162 Art. 120a GG.

163 *Gesetz zur Einfügung eines Artikels 120a in das Grundgesetz. Vom 14. August 1952* (BGBl., Part I, 1952, No. 34, 445).

164 D. Raff, *A History of Germany. From the Medieval Empire to the Present* (Oxford: Berg Publishers, 1988), 344–345.

165 Kukułka, *Historia współczesna stosunków międzynarodowych*, 44.

166 Arts. 127, 133 GG.

The subject of Art. 130 GG remained corporations and institutions under public law. They were subject to the administration of the *Länder* or the supreme authority of the Federation.[167]

Arts. 134–135a GG dealt with the legal succession from the Third Reich and the resulting obligations. The first of these articles expressly stated that the assets of the Nazi Reich were the assets of the FRG. Individual portions of these assets were to be administered by the appointed authorities or by the *Länder* and municipalities (associations of municipalities).[168]

As stipulated in Art. 135 GG, the status of these assets could be altered as a result of changes in the territorial boundaries of the state. Assets belonging to the Third Reich and located outside the FRG belonged, under certain conditions, to the country in which it was located.[169] In exceptional cases, "[i]nsofar as an overriding interest of the Federation or the particular interest of a region requires,"[170] a different regulation could be made by law. Matters of legal succession and distribution of assets should be the subject of agreements between the states concerned and corporations and institutions under public law or (since 1952) of a law.[171] The shares of the Prussian state in private legal companies were subject to the authorities of the Federation.[172]

Art. 135a GG, added to the Constitution in 1957,[173] resolved the issues of FRG's obligations (debts). On the basis of the *Unification Treaty* between the RFG and the GDR of August 31, 1990, the original provision of the Constitution was replaced by a fragment of the *Treaty*.[174] The amended part of the Basic Law allowed for full or partial – under certain conditions – withdrawal by the Federation from the obligations of the Third Reich, Prussia, the GDR, the *Länder*, municipalities (associations of municipalities) and other corporations and institutions under public law.[175]

In 2006, Art. 143c GG was added, which deals with the federal financing of the *Länder*.[176] For the period from January 1, 2007, to December 31, 2019, it provided for annual federal subsidies to the *Länder* as compensation for the withdrawal of the Federation from financing the canceled joint tasks in the construction

---

167 Art. 130 GG.

168 Art. 134 GG.

169 Art. 135, Pars. 1–3 GG.

170 *Sofern ein überwiegendes Interesse des Bundes oder das besondere Interesse eines Gebietes es erfordet* (Art. 135, Par. 4 UZ).

171 Art. 135, Pars. 4–5 GG.

172 Art. 135, Par. 6 GG.

173 *Gesetz zur Einfügung eines Artikels 135a in das Grundgesetz. Vom 22. Oktober 1957.* (BGBl., Part I, 1957, No. 58, 1745).

174 Unification Treaty, Art. 4, Par. 4 (BGBl., Part II, 1990, No. 35, 890).

175 Art. 135a GG.

176 *Gesetz zur Änderung des Grundgesetzes*, Art. 1, Par. 23 (BGBl., Part I, 2006, No. 41, 2037–2038).

and expansion of colleges and university clinics, educational planning, as well as municipal transport infrastructure and social housing. The article sets out the rules for calculating subsidies.[177] This provision of the Constitution was particularly important in the context of equalizing differences in the level of economic development between the Western and Eastern *Länder*.

As a summary of the discussion so far, it is worth referring to the constitutional change matrix proposed by Voigt.[178] In the analyzed years 1990–2015, and even in the long period between 1949 and 2015, the amendments to the FRG Constitution went essentially in two directions. Firstly, there were marginal constitutional changes of an explicit and constitutional nature concerning formal (and, at the same time, legal) amendments to specific provisions of the Basic Law. Those relating to economic life were discussed above. Secondly, these modifications were implicit and constitutional, i.e. they concerned transformations in the interpretation of particular provisions, which resulted primarily from the jurisprudence of the Federal Constitutional Court.[179]

3.5. Implementation of West German constitutional rules in the Eastern *Länder*

The institutional framework for the entire German reunification process was the FRG Constitution. With the accession of the GDR to the West German Basic Law area, East German constitutional rules were rejected in principle. The ensuing legal and constitutional consequences were the starting point for the next stage of reunification in the political, economic, social, and cultural spheres after 1990, which oscillated around the unification and integration of two parts of Germany.[180]

---

177 Art. 143c GG.

178 See section 3.1. in this work.

179 A comprehensive discussion of the evolution of the jurisprudence of the Federal Constitutional Court and its consequences for the FRG in 1949–1989 is carried out by Danuta Janicka (D. Janicka, *Ustawa Zasadnicza w praktyce Republiki Federalnej Niemiec (1949–1989)* (Toruń: WN UMK, 2009)). Anna Tarnowska in her review of the work stresses that the analysis of the changes in constitutional jurisprudence in Germany after reunification requires a separate monographic historical and legal study (A. Tarnowska, "Nota recenzyjna," review of *Ustawa Zasadnicza w praktyce Republiki Federalnej Niemiec (1949–1989)*, by D. Janicka, *Przegląd Prawa Konstytucyjnego* No. 2–3 (2010): 328).

180 Peter E. Quint discusses mainly the political and legal dimension of German reunification on the basis of the FRG Constitution, analyzing in detail, among others, constitutional (system) reforms in the GDR preceding the incorporation of East Germany into the FRG (P. E. Quint, *The Imperfect Union. Constitutional Structures of German Unification* (Princeton: Princeton University Press, 1997)). Georg Brunner draws attention to the fundamental importance of constitutional law for all transforming economies of Central and Eastern Europe (G. Brunner,

The implementation of the FRG constitutional rules in the Eastern *Länder* and the fact that the reunification process was based on them coincided with a discussion on constitutional patriotism (*Verfassungspatriotismus*) in West Germany. Its origins date back to the 1960s and fit into the context of the Germans' search for identity after World War II. The sense of responsibility for Nazism and its crimes, and the post-war disintegration of Germany led to a desire to center society around a category other than the nation. The state, liberal democracy, law, and the constitution were seen as suitable alternatives. Intellectuals such as Dolf Sternberger, Jürgen Seifert, Jürgen Habermas, and Jan-Werner Müller spoke importantly in the debate at various times. Although the discussion around constitutional patriotism continues to this day, its most significant phase came in the 1980s and 1990s, especially through Habermas. Interestingly, this concept did not focus exclusively on Germany. It has infiltrated contemporary political theory, which deals with the problems of antagonized societies, transnational organizations, or the globalized and multicultural world.[181]

Beginning in the 1970s, a number of works appeared in West Germany (though not only) written from the standpoint of economic systems theory, reflecting the high level of interest in the GDR's system and other communist states and addressing the problem of their reform in a democratic and free market direction. The largest number of them was written in the 1980s.[182] In the FRG, there was no

---

"Verfassungsrechtliche Rahmenbedingungen der wirtschaftlichen Transformation," in *Transformationsprozesse in sozialistischen Wirtschaftssystemen. Ursachen, Konzepte, Instrumente*, eds. K.-H. Hartwig, H. J. Thieme (Berlin: Springer-Verlag, 1991), 201–225).

181 See an exemplary synthetic discussion of the concept of constitutional patriotism: J.-W. Müller, *Constitutional Patriotism* (Princeton: Princeton University Press, 2007). Cf. a historical and legal analysis of constitutional identity in Germany in the 19th–21st centuries: M. Polzin, "Constitutional Identity, Unconstitutional Amendments and the Idea of Constituent Power: The Development of the Doctrine of Constitutional Identity in German Constitutional Law," *International Journal of Constitutional Law* 14, No. 2 (2016): 411–438. See also an overview of the debate around German identity after World War II, including constitutional patriotism: J. Jabłkowska, L. Żyliński, eds., *O kondycji Niemiec. Tożsamość niemiecka w debatach intelektualistów po 1945 roku* (Poznań: Wydawnictwo Poznańskie, 2008). Cf. in this context, the fascinating study of the transition of East German historiography after 1945 and then after 1990: A. Fair-Schulz, M. Kessler, eds., *East German Historians Since Reunification. A Discipline Transformed* (New York: SUNY Press, 2017).

182 See examples of works published up to 1990: H.-J. Wagener, ed., *Demokratisierung der Wirtschaft. Möglichkeiten und Grenzen im Kapitalismus* (Frankfurt–New York: Campus Verlag, 1980); H. E. Haase, *Entwicklungstendenzen der DDR-Wirtschaft für die 80er Jahre – Eine Prognose der Probleme* (Berlin: Osteuropa-Instituts an der Freien Universität Berlin, 1980); O. Šik, *Ein Wirtschaftssystem der Zukunft* (Berlin: Springer-Verlag, 1985); *Materialien zum Bericht zur Lage der Nation im geteilten Deutschland 1987*; J. Schumann, ed., *Probleme der Regulierung in den*

shortage of enthusiasts (albeit few and critical) of the GDR's economic system.[183] Nevertheless, the subsequent problems with the transition and integration of the Eastern *Länder* have allowed some scholars to formulate the thesis that reliable research on the actual state of the East German economy has been neglected.[184]

German (but not only) studies from the 1990s analyzed the systemic transition of post-communist countries, including the former GDR, on an ongoing basis. However, it should be noted that especially later literature on transition economics, which undertook a broader comparative analysis of this process in Central and

---

Volkswirtschaften Polens und der Bundesrepublik Deutschland (Bad Honnef: Bock und Herchen Verlag, 1987); M. Haendcke-Hoppe, ed., *Außenwirtschaftssysteme und Außenwirtschaftsreformen sozialistischer Länder. Ein intrasystemarer Vergleich* (Berlin: Duncker & Humblot, 1988); K. Alewell, A. Bohnet, eds., *Leistungswille und Leistungsanreize im Systemvergleich. Wirtschaftswissenschaftliches Symposium anläßlich des 10-jährigen Bestehens der Partnerschaft zwischen den Universitäten Gießen und Łódź. Schloß Rauischholzhausen bei Gießen 12.–17. Juni 1988. Tagungsband* (Gießen: Justus-Liebig-Universität, 1988); Schlüter, *Wirtschaftsreformen im Ostblock in den 80er Jahren*; H. von Berg, *Die Anti-Ökonomie des Sozialismus. Zur Reformfähigkeit parteimonopolistischer Staatswirtschaften* (Würzburg: Creator, 1989); K. Nimtz, G. Fels, eds., *Demokratie und Marktwirtschaft – ein Kuppelprodukt?* (Köln: informedia-Stiftung, Gemeinnützige Stiftung für Gesellschaftswissenschaften und Publizistik, 1989); D. Cassel et al., eds., *Inflation und Schattenwirtschaft im Sozialismus. Bestandaufnahme, Erklärungsansätze und Reformvorschläge für die Volksrepublik Polen* (Hamburg: Steuer- und Wirtschaftsverlag, 1989); T. Miller, ed., *Prager Frühling und Reformpolitik heute. Hintergründe, Entwicklungen und Vergleiche der Reformen in Osteuropa* (München: Olzog Verlag, 1989); H. Timmermann, ed., *Wirtschaftsordnungen im Dialog. Bundesrepublik Deutschland und DDR* (Saarbrücken–Scheidt: Dadder, 1989); K. H. Biedenkopf, *Offene Grenze Offener Markt. Voraussetzungen für die Erneuerung der DDR-Volkswirtschaft* (Wiesbaden: Gabler, Bertelsmann, 1990); J. Bischoff, M. Menard, *Marktwirtschaft und Sozialismus. Der Dritte Weg* (Hamburg: VSA-Verlag, 1990); W. Brus, K. Łaski, *Von Marx zum Markt. Die sozialistischen Länder auf der Suche nach einem neuen Wirtschaftssystem* (Marburg: Metropolis-Verlag, 1990); E. U. Cichy, *Wirtschaftsreform und Ausweichwirtschaft im Sozialismus. Zur Rolle der Ausweichwirtschaft im Reformprozeß sozialistischer Planwirtschaften dargestellt am Beispiel der DDR, Polens und Ungarns* (Hamburg: Verlag Weltarchiv GmbH, 1990); K. Bolz, ed., *Die Wirtschaft der osteuropäischen Ländern an der Wende zu den 90er Jahren* (Hamburg: Verlag Weltarchiv GmbH, 1990); J. Osers, *Zwischen Plan und Markt. Die Suche nach einer humanen Wirtschaft* (Hamburg: Verlag Weltarchiv GmbH, 1990).

183 See, e.g., H. Jung, ed., *Der staatsmonopolistische Kapitalismus. Einführungen in marxistische Analysen aus der DDR, Frankreich und der Sowjetunion* (Frankfurt/Main: Verlag Marxistische Blätter, 1973).

184 See, e.g., E. Tuchtfeldt, "The Transformation of Economic Systems: The Germany Example," in *The Economics of German Unification*, ed. A. G. Ghanssy, W. Schäfer (London–New York: Routledge, 1993), 22–23.

Eastern Europe, usually did not include the former GDR.[185] The distinct development trajectory of the Eastern *Länder* integrating with the old federated states was influenced by the incorporation of the GDR into the FRG. This meant the implementation of West German legal institutions, including property rights.[186] The transition of the new federated states was carried out by the FRG, while other post-communist countries had to undertake it on their own. Apart from the transfer of institutions, the transfer of West German money and "know-how" played an essential role in the Eastern *Länder*. An important dimension was the unification of the currency, which – despite the subsequent costs for the economy of the Eastern *Länder* – is considered necessary. It was impossible to isolate this part of Germany with its own currency. On the other hand, the FRG itself was not prepared for such a version of reunification in such a short time. A sufficiently detailed and strategic plan was not developed, and the implementation of the process itself was more of a sudden and ad hoc action than a coordinated effort.[187]

Concrete arrangements for the implementation of West German constitutional rules in the GDR were made even before the formal German reunification, thus shaping the initial outline of the institutional framework for this process. This was partly related to the enthusiasm of many researchers and politicians in the FRG, who compared the prospect of economic unification of two parts of Germany with the "economic miracle" of the 1950s and 1960s. The resulting belief was that the Eastern *Länder* should immediately (based on a single decision) adopt the West German institutions, constituted in 1949, which set the framework for, among other things, the economic system. Therefore, the FRG's constitutional rules were considered "ready and tested," and the idea that the new federated states should develop their own solutions independently and gradually was abandoned. West Germany, which introduced a model of a social market economy based on ordoliberalism after World War II, was to be used as a parallel in this case.[188]

Because of the FRG's economic and political advantage, it coordinated both the unification process and the transition of the new federated states.[189] Thus,

185 See a representative work from this group of studies, written from an institutional perspective: T. Mickiewicz, *Economics of Institutional Change. Central and Eastern Europe Revisited* (New York: Palgrave Macmillan, 2010).

186 O. Blanchard, R. Dornbusch, P. Krugman, R. Layard, L. Summers, *Reform in Eastern Europe* (Cambridge–London: The MIT Press, 1991), 91–92.

187 M. Myant, F. Fleischer, K. Hornschild, R. Vintrová, K. Zeman, Z. Souček, *Successful Transformations? The Creation of Market Economies in Eastern Germany and the Czech Republic* (Cheltenham–Brookfield: Edward Elgar, 1996), 13–15.

188 M. Moszyński, "Transformacja systemowa wschodnich Niemiec w perspektywie "cudu gospodarczego" Ludwiga Erharda," in *Ordoliberalizm i społeczna gospodarka rynkowa wobec wyzwań współczesności*, eds. P. Pysz, E. Mączyńska (Warszawa: PTE, 2013), 219, 222–223.

189 Cf. W. R. Smyser, *The Economy of United Germany. Colossus at the Crossroads* (New York: St. Martin's Press, 1992), 164–168. See also sections 2.1.–2.2. in this book.

the implementation of West German formal rules ignored the local context and the mentality of the former GDR society. The FRG's authorities abandoned any degree of freedom, flexibility, and institutional innovation. That was the "import" of rules from West Germany, whose structures are sometimes perceived as relatively inflexible and overregulated. The implementation of formal institutions was imposed and then quickly realized by the FRG's authorities, who wanted to take advantage of the current geopolitical situation (the collapse of the Eastern Bloc and the support of the superpowers). As a consequence, difficult political debates and the involvement of the East German elites in developing new strategies or at least modifying the West German model were abandoned.[190] In this context, Moszyński writes about "institutions transplanted" from West Germany, the "transfer of elites, concepts, institutions and resources from West Germany," and the "expansion" or "uncritical copying of the West" (*Erweiterung, Nachbau West*), which was the opposite of the "reconstruction of the East" (*Aufbau Ost*).[191] Elsewhere he uses metaphors: "transplantation of institutional order" or "institutional gift."[192] This, in turn, resulted in a "transition shock," i.e. a kind of "period of disorder" of an economic nature, especially in the new federated states.[193] Other authors use the

---

190 M. Moszyński, "Idee ładu gospodarczego w procesie transformacji systemowej byłej NRD – oczekiwania a rzeczywistość," *Prace Naukowe Uniwersytetu Ekonomicznego we Wrocławiu. Ekonomia* No. 245 (2012), 353–354; Moszyński, "Transformacja systemowa wschodnich Niemiec," 233–234. Cf. C. Offe, *Drogi transformacji. Doświadczenia wschodnioeuropejskie i wschodnioniemieckie* (Warszawa–Kraków: WN PWN, 1999), 229–263. The described references by researchers to the post-war "economic miracle" in the FRG and their search for parallels with the situation of reunified Germany at the beginning of the 1990s can be illustrated by Herbert Giersch's and Holger Schmieding's texts from 1991. While Giersch primarily drew lessons from the post-war reforms, Schmieding presented them as a prescription for the transition economies in Central and Eastern Europe (H. Giersch, "Some General Lessons from West Germany's Postwar Experiences," in *Towards a Market Economy in Central and Eastern Europe*, ed. H. Giersch, (Berlin–Heidelberg: Springer-Verlag, 1991), 1–21; H. Schmieding, "West Germany's Economic Reforms of 1948: The Lessons for Central and Eastern Europe Today," [in:] H. Giersch, *Towards a Market Economy*, 23–53).

191 Pol. *instytucje przeszczepione, transfer elit, koncepcji, instytucji i zasobów z zachodu Niemiec, rozszerzenie, bezkrytyczne kopiowanie Zachodu, odbudowa Wschodu* (M. Moszyński, "Zjednoczenie Niemiec – dwie dekady konwergencji," *Ekonomia i Prawo* 7 (2011): 255; Moszyński, "Idee ładu gospodarczego," 354).

192 Pol. *przeszczep ładu instytucjonalnego, prezent instytucjonalny* (Moszyński, "Idee ładu gospodarczego," 350).

193 Pol. *szok transformacyjny, okres nieładu* (Moszyński, "Idee ładu gospodarczego," 355). Bogumiła Brocka-Palacz sees the short (according to her, only 3–4 months long) period of defining the principles of German reunification as one of the reasons for the unfinished integration process and differences in development between the two parts of Germany. She adds that work on the annual state budget or accession

notions of "adoption" of the social and economic system from the FRG or "incorporation" of the legal system of West Germany.[194] In turn, Hans-Werner Sinn, writing about the implementation of West German rules in the former GDR, refers to the concept of the "Hawaiian solution."[195]

The law literature indicates that German unification and transition processes were swift, consistent, and comprehensive. They were based on the FRG's constitutional order, which was considered to be well established. In this way, the FRG fulfilled the function of an "occupying regime" in relation to the former GDR, incorporating the Eastern *Länder* into its borders and extending its constitutional order to them. This was combined with effective institutional instruments, a well-developed legal reflection, open public debate and considerable economic resources. Consequently, the unification and systemic transition of the new federated states took the form of a transfer. The ready and efficient legal system of the FRG was transferred in its entirety to East Germany based on a relatively low number of transitional regulations.[196]

The specific character of the process of implementation of West German formal institutions and the related introduction of adequate transitional legal regulations makes it possible, following Karol Dobrzeniecki and Marcin Romanowski, to speak of a legal paradigm of the transition period. It should be added that it also included relevant regulations concerning the unification process itself. The introduction of

---

negotiations regarding membership in the EU take much longer. According to her, the belief that only financial support would ensure progress in the convergence of the Eastern and Western *Länder* has proved to be false. In the regulatory sphere, the role of the state was overestimated and market processes were ignored (B. Brocka-Palacz, *Wsparcie rozwoju gospodarki wschodniej części Niemiec – zamierzenia,instrumenty, efekty* (Warszawa: IGŚ SGH, 2008), 25).

194 Myant, Fleischer, Hornschild, Vintrová, Zeman, Souček, *Successful Transformations?*, 14.

195 It involved Hawaii taking over American institutions when it was incorporated into the United States in 1959 (H.-W. Sinn, "Macroeconomic Aspects of German Unification," in *Economic Aspects of German Unification. National and International Perspectives*, ed. P. J. J. Welfens (Berlin–Heidelberg: Springer-Verlag, 1992), 79). Tkaczyński disagrees with the above opinions about the imposition of West German constitutional rules on the GDR. In his opinion, the unity of the state was restored on the basis of consensus. Only afterwards the FRG Constitution's legal force and the entire legal system were extended (Tkaczyński, *Prawo ustrojowe Niemiec*, 149). It is worth noting that in the early 1990s the question of the FRG's role in reforming other Central and Eastern European countries was raised in Germany. See, e.g., B. Thanner, "Wie kann die Bundesrepublik die Reformen in Osteuropa unterstützen?," in *Von der Planwirtschaft zur Marktwirtschaft – Chancen und Risiken für Ost und West*, eds. K. H. Oppenländer, M. Queisser (München: Ifo-Institut für Wirtschaftsforschung, 1990), 321–333.

196 Cf. K. Dobrzeniecki, M. Romanowski, *Reprywatyzacja. Problemy tworzenia i stosowania prawa* (Warszawa: Wydawnictwo UKSW, 2015), 19–20.

transitional regulations for particular areas of law resulted from political factors and the need to guarantee certainty and security of the legal system. Some emergency regulations were more of an obligation of the authorities than their right. Firstly, it was necessary to reactivate the proper functioning of the state and improve the situation of public finances. Secondly, East German institutions were not adequate to the rules of the FRG. Some of them contradicted the West German order, while others could potentially be inconsistent with it in the future. As the authors conclude, "[i]nstitutions, which are based on certain organizational principles, cannot be incorporated into the new system without conflict and violating the basis of its legitimacy, in the sense of justification for the actually existing system of positive law."[197]

Similarly, the literature on new institutional economics indicates that the transition of the East German legal and economic system was a process of rapid adoption and assimilation of an adequate West German system. It was supposedly completed (with some exceptions) when the GDR joined the FRG. The transformation of East German property rights to the Western model had got fundamental importance.[198]

However, a closer economic history analysis shows that the implementation of West German formal institutions in East Germany took longer. Moreover, the subsequent problems with the implementation of the convergence process between the new and old federated states, which had not been completed by 2015 and resulted in a lower level of socio-economic development in the Eastern part of Germany, led to the emergence of political voices in the early 2000s criticizing the excessive initial optimism about the quality of West German rules and the mistakes made during their implementation. The public debate thus focused on the uniqueness of the situation in the Eastern *Länder*, the need to break the hegemony of West German institutions, freedom, and the necessity to look for new regulations of their own. For example, in 2004, the term "third transition for Germany" (*dritte Transformation für Deutschland*) was used in this context.[199]

In the *Treaty Establishing a Monetary, Economic and Social Union,* signed on May 18, 1990, in Bonn, it was agreed that each party to the agreement would base its "basic order" (*Grundordnung*) on such constitutional foundations as a free, democratic, federal, social, and the rule of law state. The parties further undertook to enforce the following types of freedom: contract, business, settlement, choice of residence, choice, and exercise of the profession. It was decided to preserve and support labor and

197 Pol. *Instytucje, które opierają się na określonych zasadach organizacyjnych, nie mogą bezkonfliktowo być wkomponowane w nowy system, bez naruszania podstaw jego legitymizacji, w znaczeniu uzasadnienia dla faktycznie istniejącego systemu prawa pozytywnego* (Dobrzeniecki, Romanowski, *Reprywatyzacja*, 39–40).

198 Cf. H. Brücker, *Privatization in Eastern Germany: A Neo-Institutional Analysis* (London: Frank Cass, German Development Institute, 2005), 124–125.

199 Brocka-Palacz, *Wsparcie rozwoju gospodarki wschodniej części Niemiec*, 24, fn. 18; 25.

business associations and to respect the property of private entities investing in land and means of production.[200] East Germany was obliged to abandon those principles of its socialist state and social order (set out in the GDR Constitution) that were contrary to the norms henceforth adopted.[201] Moreover, the implementation of the monetary, economic, and social union required specific changes in the FRG and the GDR laws, which were regulated by the discussed treaty.[202] One of these changes was the amendment to the GDR Constitution of June 17, which introduced the basic principles of the social market economy, including respect for private property.[203]

The document was ratified in East Germany on June 21.[204] At the same time, a law was passed giving legal force in the GDR to the West German legislation.[205] The FRG parliament passed the relevant law on June 25. It also introduced a number of changes adapting the West German legal system to the conditions that resulted from the conclusion of the union.[206]

As mentioned, the East German parliament decided that the GDR would become a part of the FRG Constitution's scope. In a resolution of August 23, the People's Chamber expressed its readiness to do so, declaring that it would rely on Art. 23 GG in the version from 1949. This provision stipulated that the FRG Constitution would be

200 Treaty Establishing a Monetary, Economic and Social Union, Art. 2, Par. 1 (BGBl., Part II, 1990, No. 20, 537). Cf. "Gemeinsames Protokoll über Leisätze," Part A, Chap. I, Pt 1, in Treaty Establishing a Monetary, Economic and Social Union (BGBl., Part II, 1990, No. 20, 545).

201 Treaty Establishing a Monetary, Economic and Social Union, Art. 2, Par. 2 (BGBl., Part II, 1990, No. 20, 537, 539). Cf. Treaty Establishing a Monetary, Economic and Social Union, Art. 11, Par. 1 (BGBl., Part II, 1990, No. 20, 539); "Gemeinsames Protokoll über Leisätze," Part A, Chap. I, Pt 1, in Treaty Establishing a Monetary, Economic and Social Union, (BGBl., Part II, 1990, No. 20, 545).

202 Treaty Establishing a Monetary, Economic and Social Union, Arts. 3–4; "Anlage I–VIII," in Treaty Establishing a Monetary, Economic and Social Union (BGBl., Part II, 1990, No. 20, 537–538, 547–565).

203 *Gesetz zur Änderung und Ergänzung der Verfassung der Deutschen Demokratischen Republik (Verfassungsgrundsätze) vom 17. Juni 1990* (GBl.-DDR, Part I, 1990, No. 33, 299–300). The last amendment to the GDR Constitution took place on July 22. It entered into force on August 18 (*Verfassungsgesetz über Schulen in freier Trägerschaft vom 22. Juli 1990* (GBl.-DDR, Part I, 1990, No. 52, 1036–1038)).

204 *Gesetz zum Vertrag über die Schaffung einer Währungs-, Wirtschafts- und Sozialunion zwischen der Deutschen Demokratischen Republik und der Bundesrepublik Deutschland vom 18. Mai 1990 (Verfassungsgesetz) vom 21. Juni 1990* (GBl.-DDR, Part I, 1990, No. 34, 331–357).

205 *Gesetz über die Inkraftsetzung von Rechtsvorschriften der Bundesrepublik Deutschland in der Deutschen Demokratischen Republik vom 21. Juni 1990* (GBl.-DDR, Part I, 1990, No. 34, 357–363).

206 Cf. Treaty Establishing a Monetary, Economic and Social Union (BGBl., Part II, 1990, No. 20, 518–536).

valid in the Eastern *Länder* after their incorporation into West Germany.[207] This was to happen on October 3, 1990.[208]

This arrangement was confirmed by the *Unification Treaty* of August 31. It was stated in Chap. 1, Art. 1 that with the accession (*Beitritt*) of the GDR to the FRG on October 3, 1990, on the basis of Art. 23 GG, the Eastern *Länder* (Brandenburg, Mecklenburg-Vorpommern, Saxony, Saxony-Anhalt, Thuringia) would become federated states of the FRG. It was also announced that East Berlin would be merged with West Berlin and that the capital Berlin would be created as a federated state, divided into 23 districts (*Bezirke*).[209] The extension of the FRG Constitution to the Eastern *Länder* meant that specific detailed provisions of the Basic Law had to be amended (e.g. regarding the preamble or the state finances). The *Unification Treaty* introduced the relevant amendments.[210] An analysis of the document shows that the adoption of certain – in this case, West German – constitutional rules was the foundation for the remaining areas of the united German state's functioning.[211]

The ratification of the *Unification Treaty* by the People's Chamber was carried out on September 20, 1990.[212] The Bundestag passed the relevant law on September

---

207 *In anderen Teilen Deutschlands ist es nach deren Beitritt in Kraft zu setzen* (*Grundgesetz für die Bundesrepublik Deutschland*, Art. 23 (BGBl., Part I, 1949, No. 1, 4)). This provision was abolished by Art. 4, Par. 2 of the *Unification Treaty* of August 31, 1990 (Unification Treaty, Art. 4, Par. 2 (BGBl., Part II, 1990, No. 35, 890). By the law of December 21, 1992, Art. 23 was added to the Constitution in a new wording (*Gesetz zur Änderung des Grundgesetzes* (BGBl., Part I, 1992, No. 58, 2086–2087)); Art. 23 GG).

208 *Bekanntmachung des Schreibens der Präsidentin der Volkskammer der Deutschen Demokratischen Republik vom 25. August 1990 und des Beschlusses der Volkskammer vom 23. August 1990 über den Beitritt der Deutschen Demokratischen Republik zum Geltungsbereich des Grundgesetzes der Bundesrepublik Deutschland Vom 19. September 1990* (BGBl., Part I, 1990, No. 49, 2057–2058).

209 Unification Treaty, Arts. 1, 2, Par. 1; Art. 3 (BGBl., Part II, 1990, No. 35, 890). Cf. Treaty Establishing a Monetary, Economic and Social Union, Art. 37 (BGBl., Part II, 1990, No. 20, 544).

210 Cf. Unification Treaty, Arts. 3–7 (BGBl., Part II, 1990, No. 35, 890–892).

211 Cf. Unification Treaty, Arts. 8–45 (BGBl., Part II, 1990, No. 35, 892–904). Heather M. Stack claims that the *Unification Treaty* marked the beginning of the transfer of West German rights to the GDR. This process was supposedly completed when Germany was formally reunified in October 1990 (Stack, "The 'Colonization' of East Germany?," 1216). However, the analysis done in this work shows that it was a more complex and multifaceted evolution. See a detailed discussion of the adaptation of the GDR legal system to the German reunification process: Quint, *The Imperfect Union*, 7–123.

212 *Gesetz zum Vertrag zwischen der Deutschen Demokratischen Republik und der Bundesrepublik Deutschland über die Herstellung der Einheit Deutschlands – Einigungsvertrag – vom 31. August 1990 (Verfassungsgesetz) vom 20. September 1990* (GBl-DDR, Part I, 1990, No. 64, 1627–1986). Cf. *Bekanntmachung über das Inkrafttreten des Vertrages zwischen der Deutschen Demokratischen Republik und der Bundesrepublik*

23. The document also amended some legal regulations in order to adapt the German system to the new circumstances.[213] The formal German reunification took place on October 3, when the GDR joined the FRG, and the legal force of the Basic Law of the FRG was extended to the new federated states.

In its post-reunification rulings, the Federal Constitutional Court stated that it was permissible to introduce legal regulations that departed from the Basic Law in justified cases in the implementation of the FRG constitutional norms in the former GDR. However, these were to be of a purely transitional nature. A time limit was also set for such exceptions, thus establishing a chronological framework for the process of systemic transition: 1992 (for standards on fundamental rights) and 1995 (for other standards). Some exceptions were taken into account in this field, e.g., regarding the admission of former East German judges.[214]

After reunification, one of the fundamental problems was the issue of the FRG Constitution.[215] Art. 146 GG of the 1949 version stipulated that the Basic Law from Bonn would lose its legal force on the day the constitution was freely adopted by the German people came into force.[216] This provision was amended in the *Unification Treaty* of 1990 with the addition that after reunification the same Basic Law would apply to the entire German people, i.e. within the territory of the unified state. However, the amended wording still implied that a new constitution of the FRG could be adopted in the future.[217]

The nuances signaled above were not accidental. German constitutionalism distinguishes between the categories of "constitution" (*Verfassung*) and "basic law"

Deutschland über die Herstellung der Einheit Deutschlands – Einigungsvertrag – vom 29. September 1990 (GBl-DDR, Part I, 1990, No. 65, 1988–1989).

213 Cf. Unification Treaty (BGBl., Part II, 1990, No. 35, 885–888).

214 Dobrzeniecki, Romanowski, *Reprywatyzacja*, 38–39.

215 K. Stern, ed., *Deutsche Wiedervereinigung. Die Rechtseinheit. Arbeitskreis Staats- und Verfassungsrecht*, Vol. I: *Eigentum – Neue Verfassung – Finanzverfassung* (Köln: Carl Heymanns Verlag KG, 1991); K. Stern, ed., Vol. III: *Zur Reform des Grundgesetzes* (Köln: Carl Heymanns Verlag KG, 1993); U.-J. Heuer, G. Riege, eds., *Neues Deutschland. Neue Verfassung?!* (Bonn: Pahl-Rugenstein, 1992); K. H. Goetz, P. J. Cullen, eds., *Constitutional Policy in Unified Germany* (London: Frank Cass, 1995); J. Galster, "Reforma konstytucyjna w zjednoczonych Niemczech," *Przegląd Sejmowy* 4, No. 3 (15) (1996): 58–60.

216 *Dieses Grundgesetz verliert seine Gültigkeit an dem Tage, an dem eine Verfassung in Kraft tritt, die von dem deutschen Volke in freier Entscheidung beschlossen worden ist* (*Grundgesetz für die Bundesrepublik Deutschland*, Art. 146 (BGBl., Part I, 1949, No. 1, 19)).

217 *Dieses Grundgesetz, das nach Vollendung der Einheit und Freiheit Deutschlands für das gesamte deutsche Volk gilt, verliert seine Gültigkeit an dem Tage, an dem eine Verfassung in Kraft tritt, die von dem deutschen Volke in freier Entscheidung beschlossen worden ist* (Unification Treaty, Art. 4, Par. 6 (BGBl., Part II, 1990, No. 35, 891)).

(*Grundgesetz*). While the former constitutes the highest legal act in the state, the status of the latter is lesser and temporary. According to this understanding, the constitution and basic law are not synonymous. It follows that at a certain time – implicitly: after German reunification – a constitution in the full sense had to be adopted.[218]

Shortly after the GDR's incorporation into the FRG, works began to amend the Basic Law accordingly, taking into account the changed circumstances.[219] In 1991, a completely new constitution project was drafted to replace the Basic Law (the "*Kuratorium* draft").[220]

From January 16, 1992, to October 28, 1993, there was a Joint Constitutional Committee consisting of the Bundestag and Bundesrat representatives. Its task was to adapt the Basic Law to the new political circumstances that had arisen as a result of German reunification. Several amendments to the Constitution were passed during and shortly after the Committee's work. Some of these were of key significance in the context of progressing European integration, as manifested by the Maastricht Treaty. However, negative assessments of the constitutional amendments of the early 1990s generally prevailed.[221] On the other hand, as Jan Galster rightly pointed out in 1996, the "[l]ack of flexibility [of the Basic Law] is the result of a relatively stable balance of political forces and the high quality of the original text. The German Constitution's model value is still considered in the constitutional works of many countries. Furthermore, since the constitutional and legal effect of German reunification is not a new constitution, this bodes well for."[222]

The lack of general satisfaction with the work of the Joint Constitutional Committee was also part of the broader context in which the "cooperative federalism model" functioned in Germany, i.e. organic cooperation between the Federation and the federated states, especially in the implementation of common tasks.[223] However, after reunification it turned out that the model of cooperative

---

218 Galster, "Reforma konstytucyjna," 57–58; Kloepfer, *Verfassungsrecht I*, 2–147; Gröpl, *Staatsrecht I*, 29–55.

219 Cf. N. Foster, "The German 'Grundgesetz' After the 1990 Unification Treaty of the Two Germanies," *Netherlands International Law Review* 38, No. 3 (1991): 360–372.

220 Galster, "Reforma konstytucyjna," 59, fn. 18.

221 Galster, "Reforma konstytucyjna," 60–67.

222 Pol. *Brak elastyczności jest wypadkową w miarę stabilnego układu sił politycznych i wysokiej jakości jej pierwotnego tekstu. Walor wzorcowy niemieckiej konstytucji wciąż jeszcze jest uwzględniany w pracach konstytucyjnych wielu państw. I skoro efektem konstytucyjnoprawnym zjednoczenia Niemiec nie jest nowa konstytucja, to dobrze to rokuje* (Galster, "Reforma konstytucyjna," 67).

223 In the literature, cooperative federalism is sometimes defined as a specific formula of cooperation, which is characterized by a strong link between the competencies of all levels of government in both the programming and policy dimensions. State functions are the subject of division between the Federation and the federated states,

federalism under the new conditions resulted in too low socio-economic effectiveness, limited federal policy (due to the strong position of the Bundesrat) and maintained too little autonomy for the *Länder*. This was one of the reasons why the public debate on the necessary constitutional changes continued in the following years.[224]

Two major reforms of Germany's federal system were important in the period in question: August 28, 2006 (entered into force on September 1) and July 29, 2009 (entered into force on August 1). These were the first and second reforms of federalism (*Föderalismusreform I* and *Föderalismusreform II*). They consisted of major amendments to the FRG Constitution, which changed the mutual relations between the Federation and the federated states. This concerned legislative powers and financial relations.[225] The first reform of federalism included primarily: (1) ordering of the legislative competencies of the Federation and the *Länder*; (2) regulation of the Bundesrat's competence to approve federal and *Länder*'s legislation; (3) reduction of the "mixed financing," i.e. the overlapping financial powers of the Federation and the federated states; (4) adaptation of the Constitution to the deepening European integration.[226]

As a result of the shortcomings of the changes made and the disappointments resulting from them, the second reform of federalism was enacted in 2009 to complement the first.[227] Its main points were: (1) limiting selected regime changes from 2006; (2) reorganizing the financial relations between the Federation and the

---

realizing cooperation in the implementation of tasks legally designated as priorities (R. M. Bieniada, *Federalizm kooperatywny jako czynnik regionalizacji substruktur państwa. "Casus" Austrii, RFN i Szwajcarii* (Warszawa: Oficyna Wydawnicza ASPRA-JR, 2013), 35). Studies also draw attention to the analogous "model of intrastate federalism," based on the principle of cooperation (see, e.g., M. Olewińska, *Federalizm w Unii Europejskiej i w Niemczech. Modele i powiązania* (Kraków: Konrad Adenauer Stiftung, TN Societas Vistulana, 2007), 27). There is a distinct area of research in German studies on the economic aspects of federalism. This includes, among others, the perspective of political economy, new institutional economics or constitutional economics. See, e.g., K. Schmidt, ed., *Beiträge zu ökonomischen Problemen des Föderalismus* (Berlin: Duncker & Humblot, 1987); D. Sauerland, *Föderalismus zwischen Freiheit und Effizienz. Der Beitrag der ökonomischen Theorie zur Gestaltung dezentralisierter politischer Systeme* (Berlin: Duncker & Humblot, 1997); H. Pitlik, *Politische Ökonomie des Föderalismus. Föderative Kompetenzverteilung im Lichte der konstitutionellen Ökonomik* (Frankfurt am Main: Peter Lang, 1997).

224 Przybysz, "Pierwsza i druga 'reforma federalizmu'," 140–143.

225 *Gesetz zur Änderung des Grundgesetzes* (BGBl., Part I, 2006, No. 41, 2034–2038); *Gesetz zur Änderung des Grundgesetzes* (BGBl., Part I, 2009, No. 48, 2248–2250). The various amendment relating to socio-economic life, are referred to in various places in this study, especially in section 3.4.

226 Przybysz, "Pierwsza i druga 'reforma federalizmu'," 137–146.

227 There are opinions that the second reform of federalism limited or even negated the first reform (Przybysz, "Pierwsza i druga 'reforma federalizmu'," 152).

Länder. While the first reform of federalism focused primarily on systemic issues, the second reform oscillated mainly around financial issues. This is why the 2009 amendment is described as a reform of the "financial constitution," the financial system (*Reform der Finanzverfassung*).[228] In this context, it introduced, among other things: (1) new rules for the tax competence of the Federation and the federated states; (2) rules for avoiding and reducing debt; (3) obligation to protect public finances from the effects of economic downturns; (4) rules for the consolidation of existing debts; (5) system for recognizing budgetary emergencies and taking appropriate measures in this regard; (6) system of sanctions as a response to non-compliance with financial discipline; (7) establishment of a Stabilization Council; (8) regulation of financial assistance provided by the Federation to the *Länder* in disaster and emergency situations; (9) rules for borrowing by the federated states. From the point of view of the state as a whole, it is reasonable to conclude that the first reform of federalism attempted – which is assessed in different ways – to increase the autonomy of the *Länder*, while the second reform was carried out in a spirit of centralization.[229] It is also worth noting that the 2009 reform coincided with government measures against the effects of the 2008 financial crisis.[230]

From an economic point of view, the implementation of the West German institutional framework (established in particular in the Basic Law of the FRG) primarily involved the extension of the social market economy model as a West German established economic order to the new federated states. In this case, the models were drawn from ordoliberal thought and the experience of West Germany after World War II. Moszyński analyzed the transfer of Walter Eucken's theoretical (constitutive) principles of the established economic order into the practice of selected directions of the FRG authorities' economic policy after reunification, aimed at the transition of the new federated states. Details are presented in Table 4.

---

228 See W. Greite, "Finanzverfassung der Bundesrepublik Deutschland," in *Elemente der Sozialen Marktwirtschaft. Wirtschaftliche und rechtliche Rahmenbedingungen – Transformationsmöglichkeiten*, eds. K. Fasbender, M. Holthus, E. Thiel (Hamburg: Verlag Weltarchiv GmbH, 1991), 77–101. It should be emphasized, however, that both reforms of federalism reorganized the German financial system. More on this topic: C. Fuest, M. Thöne, "Der Finanzföderalismus in Deutschland und seine Reform," in Härtel, *Handbuch Föderalismus*, 265–321.

229 Przybysz, "Pierwsza i druga 'reforma federalizmu'," 146–153.

230 See more E. Cziomer, "Od światowego kryzysu finansowego do kryzysu strefy euro: implikacje wewnątrzpolityczne dla Niemiec w latach 2008–2011," *Rocznik Integracji Europejskiej* No. 5 (2011): 33–50. Cf. references of some aspects of the second reform of federalism to the state fiscal policy: section 4.8. in this study.

Table 4: *Walter Eucken's principles of established economic order and selected directions of the Eastern Länder's transition after German reunification in 1990*

Walter Eucken's principle of established economic order	Selected directions of the Eastern *Länder*'s transition
Creating a functional pricing system based on free competition	Release most prices and stop subsidizing most necessities
The primacy of stabilizing the value of money	The Bundesbank's restrictive policy and its high degree of independence
Open markets	Exposure of East German industry to open competition from the West, freedom of movement, and doing business
Private property of the means of production	Privatization and re-privatization of state assets, allowing private property of land
Freedom of contract. Accountability for management performance	Introduction of West German laws that guaranteed freedom of contract, choice of profession and place of work, and regulated responsibility for management performance (reference to Art. 14, Par. 2 GG and the statement that "property entails obligations")
Economic policy constancy	Credibility in monetary policy, stabilizing expectations of market participants. Consistency in the process of transition of the economy. A focus on order formation rather than interference in the economic process's course

Source: Moszyński, "Transformacja systemowa wschodnich Niemiec," 231, table 4.

Table 4 shows that an important place in the creation of the new economic policy of the FRG government after reunification was occupied by the Basic Law as the source of the institutional framework for the entire economic system and property rights as the basis for a free market economy based on respect for private property. The constancy of the state's economic policy, which consists of shaping and strengthening the established economic order rather than the economic process, confirms the existence of links between ordoliberal theory and institutional economics.[231]

The evolution of West Germany's socio-economic system since the 1960s towards a welfare state model has widened the gap between *de jure* and *de facto* institutions. Some authors find the source of Germany's later relatively poor macroeconomic performance in this process. It seems reasonable to conclude that the

231 Cf. section 4.1. in this work.

implementation of West German formal institutions – in line with the principles of ordoliberalism – shaped the economic order in the new federated states based on the model of a social market economy or at least outlined the general principles of this order, without assuming greater state interference in the economic process. In other words, the direction of change was set, allowing for some flexibility of action.[232] The Basic Law played a key role in this regard. However, government activity in the economic process in Eastern Germany was considerable, if only from the point of view of financial transfers.

It is difficult to establish a definite date for the end of the process of West German formal institutions' implementation in the new federated states.[233] It would be necessary to take into account the individual types of formal rules and separate chronologies of their implementation. While such a date can be proposed for constitutional rules (e.g. October 3, 1990), a similar caesura for property rights would be more debatable. However, it is doubtful whether looking for such dates for the discussed institutions is justified, as any proposals would have rather symbolic value. The formal implementation of constitutional and property rules was initiated in the period of shaping the institutional framework of German reunification (1990), while the realization of this process, which involved the adoption of specific West German institutions by the Eastern *Länder* and their modification to take account of current circumstances, was spread over subsequent years, especially the first half of the 1990s.[234]

---

232 Cf. Moszyński, "Idee ładu gospodarczego," 352–353.

233 A similar treatment of informal institutions would be even more difficult, if possible at all.

234 There are more or less successful attempts in the literature to set such a chronological framework. For example, Claus Schnabel points out that from an economic point of view, the entry into force of the monetary, economic, and social union on July 1, 1990, was more important than the formal (political) German reunification on October 3. The *Unification Treaty* of August 31 marked the beginning of the transition from a socialist economy to a social market economy (C. Schnabel, "Structural Adjustment and Privatization of the East German Economy," in Welfens, *Economic Aspects of German Unification*, 231. Cf. H. Klodt, "Government Support for Restructuring the East German Economy," in Welfens, *Economic Aspects of German Unification*, 262). Heather M. Stack distinguishes two dimensions of unification. Political unification (the transfer of West German laws to the GDR) began on June 21, 1990 (the enactment of the *Law on the Enactment of Legislation of the Federal Republic of Germany in the German Democratic Republic*). It ended formally when the GDR joined the FRG on October 3. Economic unification, on the other hand, was initiated on May 18, 1990 (*Treaty Establishing a Monetary, Economic and Social Union*). This process was complex and drawn out over time, although it culminated in privatization in the Eastern *Länder*. Due to the year of the article publication (1997), for Stack, this was not a closed sequence of events (Stack, "The 'Colonization' of East Germany?," 1215–1217).

CHAPTER 4 Relationship of the FRG Constitution to the German economy

4.1. Economic order and economic process

It is important to note the most critical aspects of the parallels between the category of institutions (especially the Basic Law) and the central concepts of ordoliberalism, i.e. economic order and economic process. This acquires particular importance in the context of the German economic system in 1990–2015.

The socio-economic ordoliberal doctrine emerged in the early 1930s. The authors of this concept were, above all, Alexander Rüstow, Walter Eucken, Franz Böhm and Wilhelm Röpke. An important role in its crystallization and in integrating the research community was played by the journal "ORDO. Jahrbuch für die Ordnung von Wirtschaft und Gesellschaft", in which the above-mentioned authors, among others, published their papers.[1] This doctrine is characterized by an integral analysis of the state, economy, and society on the basis of an economic and legal perspective. Ordoliberalism (*Ordoliberalismus*), the German version of liberalism, distinguishes between the economic process (*Wirtschaftsprozess*) and the legal and institutional framework, i.e. economic order (Latin *ordo*, German *Ordnung*) or socio-economic order (*Wirtschaftsordnung*). The economic process within this economic order is not subject to state interference. The state can only intervene in the economic order by creating or changing laws and institutions. However, the foundations of the order are individual freedom, private property, free competition, freedom of contract, and stable money. This creates the framework within which the economy functions.[2] It can be seen here as a certain reference to the

1 See *ORDO. Jahrbuch für die Ordnung von Wirtschaft und Gesellschaft* 1 (1948) and subsequent issues.

2 See key works by ordoliberalism theorists: A. Rüstow, *Das Versagen des Wirtschaftsliberalismus als religionsgeschichtliches Problem* (Heidelberg: Verlag Helmut Küpper, 1950); A. Rüstow, *Die Kehrseite des Wirtschaftswunders* (Hamburg: Hamburg Furche Verlag, 1961); W. Eucken, *Nationalökonomie – Wozu?* (Bad Godesberg: Verlag Helmut Küpper, 1947); W. Eucken, *Unser Zeitalter der Mißerfolge. Fünf Vorträge zur Wirtschaftspolitik* (Tübingen: Mohr, 1951); W. Eucken, *Kapitaltheoretische Untersuchungen* (Tübingen: Mohr, 1954); W. Eucken, *Grundsätze der Wirtschaftspolitik* (Tübingen: Mohr, 1955) (Polish translation: W. Eucken, *Podstawy polityki gospodarczej* (Poznań: Wydawnictwo Poznańskie, 2005)); W. Eucken, *Die Grundlagen der Nationalökonomie* (Berlin: Springer, 2011); F. Böhm, *Wettbewerb und Monopolkampf. Eine Untersuchung zur Frage des wirtschaftlichen Kampfrechts und zur Frage der rechtlichen Struktur der geltenden Wirtschaftsordnung* (Berlin: Carl Heymanns Verlag, 1933); F. Böhm, *Kartelle und Koalitionsfreiheit* (Berlin: Carl

division, occurring on the grounds of macroeconomics, into the regulatory and real spheres in the economy.

In ordoliberal doctrine, the state plays a special role in constituting economic order. This approach was represented in particular by Eucken (established order). A different view was held by Friedrich August von Hayek, who emphasized the spontaneous nature of order created by subsequent generations as a result of market discoveries (spontaneous order).[3] However, this does not mean that there is no feedback between these orders.[4]

At the end of the 1940s, the concept of the social market economy (*Soziale Marktwirtschaft*) grew out of ordoliberalism. The authors were Alfred Müller-Armack and Ludwig Erhard. The mutual dependence of these doctrines is so strong that it is difficult to separate them clearly. The same is true of their theorists, who often influenced both concepts. The economic system that is the social market economy is a mixed one. In essence, it combines potentially

---

Heymanns Verlag, 1933); F. Böhm, *Wirtschaftsordnung und Staatsverfassung* (Tübingen: Mohr, 1950); W. Röpke, *Die Gesellschaftskrisis der Gegenwart* (Erlenbach ZH: Rentsch, 1942); W. Röpke, *Civitas Humana. Grundfragen der Gesellschafts- und Wirtschaftsreform* (Erlenbach ZH: Rentsch, 1944); W. Röpke, *Internationale Ordnung* (Erlenbach ZH: Rentsch, 1945); W. Röpke, *Die Lehre von der Wirtschaft* (Erlenbach ZH: Rentsch, 1946); W. Röpke, *Maß und Mitte* (Erlenbach ZH: Rentsch, 1950); W. Röpke, *Jenseits von Angebot und Nachfrage* (Erlenbach ZH: Rentsch, 1958).

3 M. Moszyński, "Idee ładu gospodarczego w procesie transformacji systemowej byłej NRD – oczekiwania a rzeczywistość," *Prace Naukowe Uniwersytetu Ekonomicznego we Wrocławiu. Ekonomia* No. 245 (2012): 348–349.

4 Among the rich Polish literature on Eucken's and Hayek's concepts of economic order, especially in the context of their complementarity, see exemplary monographs: P. Pysz, A. Grabska, M. Moszyński, eds., *Ład gospodarczy a współczesna ekonomia* (Warszawa: WN PWN, 2014); P. Pysz, A. Grabska, M. Moszyński, eds., *Stanowione i spontaniczne elementów ładu gospodarczego w procesie transformacji – dryf ładu czy jego doskonalenie?* (Warszawa: PTE, 2014); A. Grabska, M. Moszyński, P. Pysz, *Stanowiony i spontaniczny ład gospodarczy w procesie transformacji systemowej Polski i byłej NRD* (Toruń: Instytut Badań Gospodarczych, PTE, 2014). Cf. also numerous papers by these authors on the issue in question. In this respect, a parallel can be drawn between "private order" (*ład zaprowadzany prywatnie*) and "public order" (*ład zaprowadzany publicznie*), as distinguished by Jerzy Wilkin. The latter remains the domain of public choice theory (J. Wilkin, "Pogoń za rentą przy pomocy mechanizmów politycznych," in *Teoria wyboru publicznego. Wstęp do ekonomicznej analizy polityki i funkcjonowania sfery publicznej*, ed. J. Wilkin (Warszawa: WN SCHOLAR, 2005), 218). The importance of both types of economic order in the process of systemic transition of post-communist countries is pointed out by Helmut Leipold (H. Leipold, "Der Zusammenhang zwischen gewachsener und gesetzer Ordnung: Einige Lehrer aus den postsozialistischen Reformerfahrungen," in *Institutionelle Probleme der Systemtransformation*, ed. D. Cassel (Berlin: Duncker & Humblot, 1997), 43–68).

contradictory elements: on the one hand, the market (treated as fundamental), and on the other, the social and state (interventionist). The state should intervene to ensure social justice in justified cases. In a way, this framework is fulfilled by the systemic form defined as a social market economy[5]. This is done according to the motto of Karl Schiller, West German Minister of Economic Affairs (1966–1972) and Minister of Finance (1971–1972) for the Social Democratic Party of Germany (*Sozialdemokratische Partei Deutschlands*, SPD): "As much market as possible, as much state as necessary" (*So viel Markt wie möglich, so viel Staat wie nötig*).[6]

The result of the implementation of the social market economy model was the "economic miracle" (*Wirtschaftswunder*) in West Germany in the 1950s and 1960s.

---

5 See major publications by authors of the concept of social market economy: A. Müller-Armack, *Studien zur sozialen Marktwirtschaft* (Köln: Institut für Wirtschaftspolitik an der Universität Köln, 1960); A. Müller-Armack, *Wirtschaftsordnung und Wirtschaftspolitik. Studien und Konzepte zur sozialen Marktwirtschaft und zur europäischen Integration* (Freiburg: Verlag Rombach, 1966); A. Müller-Armack, *Wirtschafts- und Finanzpolitik im Zeichen der sozialen Marktwirtschaft. Festgabe für Franz Etzel* (Stuttgart: Seewald, 1967); A. Müller-Armack, *Genealogie der Sozialen Marktwirtschaft. Frühschriften und weiterführende Konzepte* (Bern–Stuttgart: Haupt, 1974); L. Erhard, *Deutschland Rückkehr zum Weltmarkt* (Düsseldorf: Econ-Verlag, 1953); L. Erhard, *Wohlstand für Alle* (Düsseldorf: Econ-Verlag, 1957) (Polish translation: L. Erhard, *Dobrobyt dla wszystkich* (Warszawa: PTE, 2012)); L. Erhard, *Deutsche Wirtschaftspolitik. Der Weg der Sozialen Marktwirtschaft* (Düsseldorf: Econ, Knapp, 1962). Note the anthologies of texts by classics of ordoliberalism and social market economy: W. Stützel et al., eds., *Grundtexte zur Sozialen Martkwirtschaft. Zeugnisse aus zweihundert Jahren ordnungspolitischer Diskussion* (Stuttgart–New York: Ludwig-Erhard-Stiftung e. V. Bonn, Gustav Fischer Verlag, 1981); K. Hohmann et al., eds., *Grundtexte zur Sozialen Martkwirtschaft*, Vol. 2: *Das Soziale in der Sozialen Marktwirtschaft* (Stuttgart–New York: Ludwig-Erhard-Stiftung e. V. Bonn, Gustav Fischer Verlag, 1988).

6 Quoted in E. Egner, *Studien über Haushalt und Verbrauch*, Vol. 1: *Beiträge zur Ökonomie von Haushalt und Verbrauch* (Berlin: Duncker & Humblot, 1963), 267. A paraphrase of Karl Schiller's sentence was included in the SPD's programme, the aftermath of the party convention held on November 13–15, 1959, in Bad Godesberg: "Competition as far as possible – planning as far as necessary!" (*Wettbewerb soweit wie möglich – Planung soweit wie nötig!*) (*Grundsatzprogramm der Sozialdemokratischen Partei Deutschlands. Beschlossen vom Außerordentlichen Parteitag der Sozialdemokratischen Partei Deutschlands in Bad Godesberg vom 13. bis 15. November 1959* (facsimile, München: Archiv des Instituts für Zeitgeschichte München, 2006), 14). The literature on ordoliberalism and social market economy is extensive. Among exclusively Polish synthetic studies, it is worth mentioning: T. G. Pszczółkowski, *Ordoliberalizm. Społeczno-polityczna i gospodarcza doktryna neoliberalizmu w RFN* (Warszawa–Kraków: PWN, 1990); P. Pysz, *Społeczna gospodarka rynkowa. Ordoliberalna koncepcja polityki gospodarczej* (Warszawa: WN PWN, 2008); T. Włudyka, *Ordoliberalizm i społeczna gospodarka rynkowa w Niemczech* (Warszawa: Lex a Wolters Kluwer business, 2013).

It was a consequence of the policy of Erhard, Minister of Economic Affairs (1949–1963) and Chancellor of the FRG (1963–1966). In order to rescue the economy, which was overwhelmed by post-war destruction and crisis, as early as 1948, the authorities of the allied occupation zones introduced a program encompassing: the reform of money, price liberalization, and reform of the tax system. As a result, industrial production and foreign trade turnover increased significantly. Unemployment decreased, and the sign of the times was the growing prosperity of citizens.[7] The European Recovery Program (Marshall Plan), implemented by the USA between 1948 and 1952, also had a measurable influence on the revival of the country's economic situation. The FRG was one of the largest beneficiaries of the program (after Great Britain, France, and Italy), receiving a total of $1,389 million in aid.[8]

Eucken formulated a catalog of principles constituting the desired economic order. These are: (1) a functional price system based on free competition; (2) currency stability; (3) open markets; (4) private property of the means of production; (5) freedom of contract; (6) responsibility for economic performance; (7) constancy of economic policy. These principles should be implemented in a consistent manner, taking into account the current historical situation ("historical moment"). The ways of implementing the principles should be determined based on the context and a holistic view of the economy. The above set is complemented by four regulating principles that define the legitimacy of state interventionism in a situation of threat to the economic order. This concerns the occurrence of the

---

7 E. Cziomer, *Historia Niemiec współczesnych 1945–2005* (Warszawa: Wydawnictwo Neriton, 2006), 164–172; J. Krasuski, *Historia Niemiec* (Wrocław: Ossolineum, 2008), 524–532; A. Galos, "Najnowsza historia Niemiec od 1945 roku," in W. Czapliński, A. Galos, W. Korta, *Historia Niemiec* (Wrocław: Ossolineum, 2010), 739–742. More recent studies of *Wirtschaftswunder* are dominated by the perspective of selected economic sectors. See, e.g.: R. G. Stokes, "Technology and the West German 'Wirtschaftswunder'," *Technology and Culture* 32, No. 1 (1991): 1–22; S. Tolliday, "Enterprise and State in the West German Wirtschaftswunder: Volkswagen and the Automobile Industry, 1939–1962," *The Business History Review* 69, No. 3 (1995): 273–350.

8 K. Kowalski, *Plan Marshalla. Uwarunkowania i skutki gospodarczo-polityczne* (Łódź: Wydawnictwo UŁ, 2014): 206, table 4.8. However, there is no shortage of critical opinions about the significance of the Marshall Plan for the FRG economy. For example, Michał Moszyński cites the observations of German researchers, who indicate that this aid amounted to approximately $10 *per capita,* while in Austria, it was around $130 and in France $71. Transfers under the Plan amounted to less than 5 % of Germany's gross national product (GNP), a very large difference from the 11–15 % of GNP accounted for by the costs of the Allied occupation and reparations. In addition, around 1955, the FRG had already repaid a large part of the funds allocated under the Marshall Plan (M. Moszyński, "Transformacja systemowa wschodnich Niemiec w perspektywie "cudu gospodarczego" Ludwiga Erharda," in *Ordoliberalizm i społeczna gospodarka narodowa wobec wyzwań współczesności*, eds. P. Pysz, E. Mączyńska (Warszawa: PTE, 2013), 225–226).

following phenomena: (1) monopolies; (2) severe income inequality; (3) externalities; (4) abnormal supply.[9]

According to Michał Moszyński, "[t]he principles formulated by Eucken constitute an idealized institutional framework for free competition."[10] They are created by the state within the "policy of economic order" (*Ordnungspolitik*). Moreover, institutions in the ordoliberal view perform a control function against possible private monopolies, guaranteeing the protection of competition. Hence, one speaks of the economic order in terms of competitive order in the discussed approach to economics.[11] The literature emphasizes that the main elements of the theory and policy of shaping the economic order come down to the comprehensiveness and coherence of this policy and its orientation towards the long term.[12] This corresponds with the demands for far-sighted, strategic and effective formation of formal rules raised by institutional economics.[13] On the other hand, in ordoliberalism, it is pointed out that the effect of the implementation of Eucken's principles constituting an economic order is the functioning of a liberal market economy. The coexistence of the relevant components of established and spontaneous order, in turn, creates an institutional equilibrium.[14] Consequently, economic order policy is sometimes referred to as institutional policy.[15]

It is worth noting that Böhm and Eucken wrote about the "rules of the game" (*Spielregeln*) already in 1948, in the first issue of the cited journal "ORDO." They understood them as a "form of market" (*Marktform*) maintained by the state through the creation of specific "legal frameworks" (*Rechtsrahmen*) in order

---

9 Eucken, *Podstawy polityki gospodarczej*, 295–343. Admittedly, other representatives of ordoliberalism – Röpke and Müller-Armack – allowed deeper state interventionism than Eucken. However, all three stressed that it must be based on the logic and mechanisms of the market (A. Jurczuk, M. Moszyński, P. Pysz, "The Austrian School of Economics and Ordoliberalism – Socio-Economic Order," *Studies in Logic, Grammar and Rhetoric* No. 57 (70) (2019): 116).

10 Pol. *Zasady sformułowane przez Euckena stanowią wyidealizowane ramy instytucjonalne dla wolnej konkurencji* (M. Moszyński, "Koncepcje ładu stanowionego Waltera Euckena i ładu spontanicznego Friedricha Augusta von Hayeka – próba analizy porównawczej," *Acta Universitatis Nicolai Copernici. Ekonomia* 43, No. 2 (2012): 126).

11 Moszyński, "Koncepcje ładu," 128, 130; M. Moszyński, "Problemy teorii i polityki konkurencji w myśli ordoliberalnej," *Ekonomia i Prawo* 12, No. 2 (2013): 221–226.

12 M. Moszyński, P. Pysz, "Koncepcje polityki kształtowania ładu gospodarczego a reguły fiskalne w Republice Federalnej Niemiec," *Optimum. Studia Ekonomiczne* No. 4 (76) (2015): 74.

13 Cf. section 1.2.2. in this work.

14 P. Pysz, A. Jurczuk, M. Moszyński, "Ordoliberalizm a dynamika społeczno-gospodarcza," *Optimum. Economic Studies* No. 2 (96) (2019): 13.

15 Jurczuk, Moszyński, Pysz, "The Austrian School of Economics and Ordoliberalism," 115.

to realize the system, which is an "economy of full competition" (*vollständigen Wettbewerbs Wirtschaftsordnung*).[16]

Douglass C. North makes a distinction between formal and informal institutions, stressing the importance of the ways in which they are implemented. The former include constitutions.[17] Thus, he assumes that basic laws set the framework for the functioning of economies. This corresponds with the ordoliberal theory, leading to the conclusion that by enacting the Basic Law in 1949, the German legislator set the legal and institutional framework for the FRG's economic system (order), which consequently took the form of a social market economy. Moreover, according to the classification adopted by North, the German Constitution is an exemplification of the formal institution, which may serve as an object of economic and economic history research into the relations between this supreme legal act in the state and economic transformations.

It is important to remember the issue of the neutrality of the FRG Constitution with regard to economic policy, which was signaled earlier. It did not set a specific economic order. It could be created by the government, provided that constitutional rights and civil liberties were enforced.[18] This does not change the fact that the Basic Law constituted the foundation of the economic order, which in the literature on ordoliberal economics is identified with the concept of the economic system (the target (ideal) system of functioning of the economy in the normative sense) and the model of the social market economy.[19] Böhm and Eucken use the concept of an "economic constitution, an economic system" (*Wirtschaftsverfassung*) in this context.[20] It consists of the formal rules of the game (institutions) that determine the economic order. For Eucken, the coherence of the "economic constitution" depends on its top-down creation. It can therefore be referred to as the established economic order.[21] In other words, the Basic Law of the FRG, as a formal rule and the highest legal act in the state, set the framework not only for the political system but also for the socio-economic system.[22]

---

16 Cf. F. Böhm, W. Eucken, "Vorwort. Die Aufgabe des Jahrbuchs," *ORDO. Jahrbuch für die Ordnung von Wirtschaft und Gesellschaft* 1 (1948): VII–XI.

17 D. C. North, *Institutions, Institutional Change and Economic Performance* (Cambridge–New York: Cambridge University Press, 2009), 46–47.

18 See section 3.4. in this work.

19 See, e.g.: Moszyński, "Idee ładu gospodarczego," 350; Moszyński, "Koncepcje ładu," 123; Moszyński, "Transformacja systemowa wschodnich Niemiec," 230–231.

20 Moszyński, "Koncepcje ładu," 123; Moszyński, "Problemy teorii i polityki konkurencji," 224.

21 Jurczuk, Moszyński, Pysz, "The Austrian School of Economics and Ordoliberalism," 112, 115.

22 In another context, Böhm argues that it is the duty of the state to watch over the economic order, just as it is the duty of the constitution that determines the political order (cf. Moszyński, "Problemy teorii i polityki konkurencji," 224).

There are positions in ordoliberal economics that this approach, especially with respect to the theory of economic order, provides a possible platform for the integration (synthesis) of history and (theory) of economics[23] in order to formulate more effective economic policy assumptions and their implementation. This is a more desirable approach than the assumptions of neoclassical economics. The latter abstracts from retrospective references and relies more on static and abstract models that can be applied to any space-time continuum. Meanwhile, the study of the economy should take a holistic, multifaceted, and multifactorial perspective and take into account the historical context. Integration understood in such a way may be static (model and constitutive principles of economic order referring to different space-time continuums) or dynamic (permanent change of two complementary types of order – established and spontaneous – in different space-time continuums).[24] As noted by Piotr Pysz, Anna Jurczuk, and Moszyński, "[b]y underscoring the importance of institutions and history, the approach currently represented by Douglas C. North aligns with Eucken's intention to overcome the antinomy between economics and history. The Nobel Prize winner's achievements combine elements of neoclassical economic theory, theory of institutional change (as part of new institutional economics), and economic history."[25]

The above observations are all the more important since this work is an economic history study with theoretical references to institutional economics. Indeed, the study of the significance of selected formal institutions, i.e. constitutional and property rules, for the German economy in 1990–2015 can be considered in two dimensions. The first one – the level of economic order – would refer to the identification and characterization of the above formal rules. The second dimension – the level of the economic process – would concern the economic effects of these institutions.[26]

---

23 There is not enough space here to give a satisfactory account of the extensive discussion on this topic that has taken place in various streams of historical (humanistic) and economic (social) studies. Ordoliberalism is no exception in this regard. The problem of relations between history and economics in the field of economic history is discussed in section 1.3. in this work.

24 P. Pysz, A. Jurczuk, M. Moszyński, "Economics and History: Synthesis, Disintegration and Reintegration," *OIKONOMOS: Journal of Social Market Economy* No. 2 (8) (2017): 6–17; Pysz, Jurczuk, Moszyński, "Ordoliberalizm a dynamika społeczno-gospodarcza," 3–17.

25 Pysz, Jurczuk, Moszyński, "Economics and History," 10–11.

26 See the empirical study adopting the above analytical model: M. Moszyński, *Niemiecki model Społecznej Gospodarki Rynkowej – perspektywa rynku pracy* (Toruń: WN UMK, 2016), especially valuable Chap. 2, treating the theoretical and methodological links between ordoliberal and institutional theory: Moszyński, *Niemiecki model Społecznej Gospodarki Rynkowej*, 80–112.

4.2. Elementary civil rights and freedoms (the basic rights) in the FRG

The economic literature emphasizes the importance of civil rights and freedoms (more broadly: the democratic system) for economic growth. The catalog of these rights is variously defined, although property rights occupy an important place in it.[27]

---

27 See, e.g.: R. C. Kormendi, P. G. Meguire, "Macroeconomic Determinants of Growth: Cross-Country Evidence," *Journal of Monetary Economics* 16, No. 2 (1985): 141–163; G. W. Scully, "The Institutional Framework and Economic Development," *Journal of Political Economy* 96, No. 3 (1988): 652–662; K. B. Grier, G. Tullock, "An Empirical Analysis of Cross-National Economic Growth, 1951–1980," *Journal of Monetary Economics* 24, No. 2 (1989): 259–276; J. F. Helliwell, "Empirical Linkages Between Democracy and Economic Growth," *British Journal of Political Science* 24, No. 2 (1994): 225–248; X. de Vanssay, Z. A. Spindler, "Freedom and Growth: Do Constitutions Matter?," *Public Choice* 78, No. 3–4 (1994): 359–372; A. A. Goldsmith, "Democracy, Property Rights and Economic Growth," *The Journal of Development Studies* 32, No. 2 (1995): 157–174; D. A. Leblang, "Property Rights, Democracy and Economic Growth," *Political Research Quarterly* 49, No. 1 (1996): 5–26; J. de Haan, C. L. J. Siermann, "New Evidence on the Relationship Between Democracy and Economic Growth," *Public Choice* 86, No. 1–2 (1996): 175–198; J. de Haan, C. L. J. Siermann, "Further Evidence on the Relationship Between Economic Freedom and Economic Growth," *Public Choice* 95, No. 3–4 (1998): 363–380; W. Wu, O. A. Davis, "The Two Freedoms, Economic Growth and Development: An Empirical Study," *Public Choice* 100, No. 1–2 (1999): 39–64; J. de Haan, J.-E. Sturm, "On the Relationship Between Economic Freedom and Economic Growth," *European Journal of Political Economy* 16, No. 2 (2000): 215–241; J. C. Heckelman, "Economic Freedom and Economic Growth: A Short-Run Causal Investigation," *Journal of Applied Economics* 3, No. 1 (2000): 71–91; A. M. Ali, W. M. Crain, "Institutional Distortions, Economic Freedom, and Growth," *Cato Journal* 21, No. 3 (2002): 415–426; J. Gwartney, R. Lawson, "The Concept and Measurement of Economic Freedom," *European Journal of Political Economy* 19, No. 3 (2003): 405–430; J. W. Dawson, "Causality in the Freedom-Growth Relationship," *European Journal of Political Economy* 19, No. 3 (2003): 479–495; J. Fidrmuc, "Economic Reform, Democracy and Growth During Post-Communist Transition," *European Journal of Political Economy* 19, No. 3 (2003): 583–604; Ch. Doucouliagos, M. A. Ulubasoglu, "Economic Freedom and Economic Growth: Does Specification Make a Difference?," *European Journal of Political Economy* 22, No. 1 (2006): 60–81; W. N. W. Azman-Saini, A. Z. Baharumshah, S. H. Law, "Foreign Direct Investment, Economic Freedom and Economic Growth: International Evidence," *Economic Modelling* 27, No. 5 (2010): 1079–1089; W. Kasper, M. E. Streit, P. J. Boettke, *Institutional Economics. Property, Competition, Policies* (Cheltenham–Northampton: Edward Elgar, 2012), 483–524; D. Piątek, K. Szarzec, M. Pilc, "Economic Freedom, Democracy and Economic Growth: A Causal Investigation in Transition Countries," *Post-Communist Economies* 25, No. 3 (2013): 267–288. Cf. a critical review of the literature on this topic: S. Voigt, "Positive Constitutional Economics: A Survey," in *Constitutional Political Economy in a Public*

In the case of the Basic Law of the FRG, its content and form played a key role. For it appears that the arrangement of the chapters of the Constitution, i.e. its general systematics, had an impact on the interpretation of the individual provisions. According to the doctrine of German constitutionalism and the case law of the Federal Constitutional Court, these systematics indicated the meaning of the terms used and the relationship between the provisions.[28] In this context, it should be noted that the elementary rights and freedoms of citizens, the basic rights (*Grundrechte*), were the subject of Chap. I GG, while the state finances were not until Chap. X GG.[29] A number of other economic provisions were found in other chapters.[30]

It should be emphasized that among nineteen articles dealing with basic rights, four refer directly to socio-economic issues. These provisions concern: freedom of association and prohibition of actions against labor struggles (Art. 9 GG), freedom of choice of profession and prohibition of forced labor (Art. 12 GG), right to property and inheritance (Art. 14 GG), and nationalization (Art. 15 GG).[31]

Despite the predominance of political freedoms in the catalog of basic rights, the inclusion of even a few socio-economic provisions took on particular significance in the context of the principle of direct application of the Constitution. It consisted of certain provisions of the Basic Law being directly applicable, without the need to refer to lower-order acts. This could be enforced through judicial procedures, including a constitutional complaint. The principle of direct applicability applied both to the basic rights contained in Chap. I GG, as well as provisions contained in other chapters, but concerning the same matter.[32] The source of this principle was Art. 1 Par. 3 GG, which stated that basic rights were binding on the legislature, the executive, and the judiciary as "directly applicable law" (*unmittelbargeltendes Recht*).[33] Significantly, on the basis of Art. 142 GG, the provisions of the constitutions of the individual federated states that guaranteed basic rights were binding, despite the primacy of federal law over *Länder*'s law set out in Art. 31 GG.[34] It is also worth noting that under the Constitution, Germany

---

Choice Perspective, ed. Ch. K. Rowley (Drodrecht: Springer, 1997), 45–46. See economic history case study: A. Pieczewski, *Samodzierżawie a rozwój gospodarczy Królestwa Polskiego w ujęciu Jana Gottlieba Blocha* (Łódź: Wydawnictwo UŁ, 2019).

28 B. Banaszak, *System konstytucyjny Niemiec* (Warszawa: Wydawnictwo Sejmowe, 2005), 24.

29 Chaps. I, X GG.

30 Cf. section 3.4. in this study.

31 See section 3.4. in this book.

32 Banaszak, *System konstytucyjny Niemiec*, 24; B. Banaszak, *Wstęp*, in *Konstytucja Niemiec*, ed. B. Banaszak, A. Malicka (Warszawa: Wydawnictwo Sejmowe, 2008), 19.

33 Art. 1, Par. 3 GG.

34 Arts. 31, 142 GG.

made its participation in the EU conditional on its guaranteeing similar protection of basic rights.[35]

4.3. Role of Germany's systemic principles

It is difficult to question the bilateral links between the legal-political sphere and the economy.[36] In Germany, between 1990 and 2015, the FRG Constitution and the resulting law played a fundamental role in setting the framework for the functioning of the economic system.[37] Indeed, it should be emphasized that the economic consequences of the functioning of a given constitution are the result not only of its economic provisions but also of its political.[38]

When analyzing the systemic foundations of Germany, several elementary constitutional principles stand out. These are: the principle of national sovereignty, the principle of democracy, the principle of the rule of law, the principle of the social state, and the principle of the federal state.[39]

---

35 Art. 23, Par. 1 GG. For a more extensive discussion of the basic rights guaranteed by the German Constitution, see, e.g.: N. Luhmann, *Grundrechte als Institution. Ein Beitrag zur politischen Soziologie* (Berlin: Duncker & Humblot, 1965); M. Borowski, *Grundrechte als Prinzipien* (Baden-Baden: Nomos, 2007); R. Grawert, "Ustawa Zasadnicza w świetle ujętych w niej praw zasadniczych," *Przegląd Sejmowy* No. 6 (95) (2009): 33–44; B. Banaszak, Ł. Żukowski, "System środków ochrony praw podstawowych w RFN," *Przegląd Sejmowy* No. 6 (95) (2009): 45–64; J. W. Tkaczyński, *Prawo ustrojowe Niemiec* (Kraków: Wydawnictwo UJ, 2015), 85–144.

36 It is impossible to do even a cursory review of the literature on this vast issue. One of the numerous scholars who recalls the above relationship is Warren J. Samuels, who states: "The economic character of the politico-legal process must be conjoined with the political character of the economic process" (W. J. Samuels, "Interrelations between Legal and Economic Processes," in *Law and Economics: An Institutional Perspective*, eds. W. J. Samuels, A. A. Schmid (Boston: Martinus Nijhoff Publishing, 1981), 110).

37 W. Steffani, "Zum Selbstverständnis der Bundesrepublik Deutschland – Verfassungs – und verwaltungsrechtliche Grundlagen," in *Elemente der Sozialen Marktwirtschaft. Wirtschaftliche und rechtliche Rahmenbedingungen – Transformationsmöglichkeiten*, eds. K. Fasbender, M. Holthus, E. Thiel (Hamburg: Verlag Weltarchiv GmbH, 1991), 37–59; M. Weilepp, "Das System der rechtlichen Regelungen der Wirtschafts- und Sozialpolitik," in Fasbender, Holthus, Thiel, *Elemente der Sozialen Marktwirtschaft*, 61–76; F. Münzel, "Die Rolle des Rechtes in der Deutschen Marktwirtschaft," in Fasbender, Holthus, Thiel, *Elemente der Sozialen Marktwirtschaft*, 103–136.

38 Cf. J. Elster, "The Impact of Constitutions on Economic Performance," *The World Bank Economic Review* 1 (1994): 209–210.

39 Banaszak, *System konstytucyjny Niemiec*, 28–35; Banaszak, *Wstęp*, 20–23. In the former publication Bogusław Banaszak points to the principle of a democratic legal state, while in the latter he breaks it down into separate principles of democracy and the legal state.

Jan Wiktor Tkaczyński makes a distinction between the principles of the state system (*Staatsgrundlagen*) and the objectives of the state (*Staatsziele*), also called systemic objectives. By the former, he means permanent constitutional regulations that define the state system, giving it specificity and uniqueness. The author also refers to these principles as "systemic principles" (Pol. *zasady ustrojowe*) or "basic systemic solutions" (Pol. *podstawowe rozstrzygnięcia ustrojowe*), and includes among them: the principle of a democratic state, the principle of a parliamentary republic, the principle of the rule of law and the principle of a federal state.[40] On the other hand, Tkaczyński understands systemic objectives as political orders, temporary tasks or programs to be implemented in a specific time perspective within the constitutional order. They have a variable character. Among the objectives of the state, Tkaczyński points in particular to the social state, the fiscal state, and the ecological state.[41] At the same time, he is aware that it is difficult to unambiguously separate the systemic principles from the objectives of the state. This is the case, e.g., with the social state principle. Art. 79, Par. 3 GG defined the category of the social state as a principle. On the other hand, it was not explicitly laid out in the Basic Law but was intended to be implemented by the legislature, which makes it possible to view it as an objective. Tkaczyński concludes: "This, in turn, means that the systemic principle in question becomes at the same time the objective of the state, and gives grounds to state that the terminological distinction between the systemic principles of the state and its objectives cannot always be derived from the text of the German constitution."[42]

Nonetheless, one can venture to say that the principles of the system are connected with the positive dimension of the state, showing it as it is. The objectives, on the other hand, concern the normative dimension and give directions to the state, defining what it should be like.[43]

---

40 Tkaczyński, *Prawo ustrojowe Niemiec*, 150–188.

41 Tkaczyński, *Prawo ustrojowe Niemiec*, 151, 154, 188–221. Among other, more detailed systemic objectives, Tkaczyński lists: equal rights for women and men, ensuring equal conditions of development for children outside marriage, protecting animals and the environment (this objective is related to the concept of the FRG as an ecological state), maintaining international peace, maintaining the public railroad infrastructure, ensuring postal and telecommunication services, meeting the requirements of overall economic equilibrium, and supporting the idea of an open state as part of European integration (Tkaczyński, *Prawo ustrojowe Niemiec*, 154, 215–221). Some of these will be discussed in more detail later in work (see section 4.4. in this book).

42 Pol. *To zaś powoduje, że przedmiotowa zasada ustrojowa staje się równocześnie celem państwa i uprawnia do stwierdzenia, iż terminologiczne rozróżnienie pomiędzy zasadami ustrojowymi państwa a jego celami nie zawsze da się wyprowadzić z tekstu niemieckiej konstytucji* (Tkaczyński, *Prawo ustrojowe Niemiec*, 155).

43 There are approaches that identify systemic principles with the state objectives. See, e.g., Sz. Pawłowski, "Solidaryzm w Konstytucji Niemiec," in *Idea solidaryzmu*

It would seem that the social and fiscal dimensions of the state should be directly related to economic issues, regardless of which of the above classifications – referring only to systemic principles or both principles and objectives – is accepted as valid.[44] It turns out, however, that from the point of view of institutional economics, any political framework (institutions) can have an impact on the economy.[45] This was also the case in the FRG. Therefore, it is reasonable to outline the potential relationship of all German systemic principles with the economy (*de jure* institution). They presented Germany as a democratic, social, federal, republican state and a state under the rule of law.[46] According to Szymon Pawłowski, these principles stemmed directly from Art. 20 GG.[47]

The Basic Law defined Germany as a democratic state (*demokratischer Staat*).[48] The nation (sovereign) was recognized as the source of power.[49] This was a clear reference to the modern concept of popular sovereignty.[50] Interestingly, the definition of the nation embedded in the German constitutional law included a clear economic component. As Tkaczyński notes, this concept "is understood as a community of people aware of their group affiliation, also in the historical dimension, who are united by commonly shared basic values in the political, economic and cultural aspect, and who express the will to adopt and respect a uniform law, and therefore consider the establishment of common organs of state authority for that purpose as legitimate."[51] It should be noted that the nation thus understood, having the power of the sovereign, created – on the basis of the Constitution – the

---

we współczesnym prawie konstytucyjnym. Doświadczenia polskie i międzynarodowe, ed. A. Łabno (Warszawa: Wydawnictwo Sejmowe, 2015), 295.

44 Banaszak writes about the relative character of the systemic principles catalogs of any state, which are created by researchers (Banaszak, *System konstytucyjny Niemiec*, 28).

45 See, e.g., D. Acemoglu, J. A. Robinson, *Dlaczego narody przegrywają. Źródła władzy, pomyślności i ubóstwa* (Poznań: Zysk i S-ka Wydawnictwo, 2014), 56–57.

46 In this case, the findings of Tkaczyński, who enumerated the above five systemic principles of the German state, are taken as a basis (Tkaczyński, *Prawo ustrojowe Niemiec*, 152). However, in the further part of his work, he characterizes only four of them, while the category of the social state is presented not as a principle but as a systemic objective (Tkaczyński, *Prawo ustrojowe Niemiec*, 155–195).

47 Pawłowski, "Solidaryzm w Konstytucji Niemiec," 295–296; Art. 20 GG.

48 Art. 20, Par. 1 GG.

49 Art. 20, Par. 2 GG.

50 Cf., e.g., "Suwerenność," in K. Dziubka, B. Szlachta, L. M. Nijakowski, *Idee i ideologie we współczesnym świecie* (Warszawa: WN PWN, 2008), 270–275.

51 Pol. [Pod tym pojęciem] *rozumie się wspólnotę osób świadomych swojej grupowej przynależności, także – rzecz jasna – w wymiarze historycznym, które łączą wspólnie podzielane wartości podstawowe w aspekcie politycznym, gospodarczym i kulturowym oraz które wyrażają wolę przyjęcia oraz respektowania jednolitego prawa i w związku z tym uznają powołanie w tym celu wspólnych organów władzy państwowej za zasadne* (Tkaczyński, *Prawo ustrojowe Niemiec*, 156).

political and systemic framework (institutions), which co-shaped the economic and social system.

The people exercised power through elections, voting, and such bodies as the federal and *Länder*'s parliaments, representative bodies in the municipalities (*Gemeinderäte*) and districts (*Landräte*), and the chief municipal officials (*Bürgermeister, Landräte*). The *sine qua non of* a democratic system was decision-making by a majority vote. The Constitution referred this to both the Bundestag and the Federal Council.[52] Majority rule, however, respected the rights of minorities. The role of political parties should also be considered a characteristic feature of German democracy. The Basic Law guaranteed their freedom of establishment and equality.[53] Their importance was reflected in the designation of the FRG as the "party state" (*Parteienstaat*).[54] The democratization of political and social life was complemented by the basic rights guaranteed by the Constitution with regard to freedom of opinion, assembly, and association.[55]

Art. 20, Par. 2 GG explicitly invokes the Monteskian principle of the tripartite division of power.[56] The detailed powers of the three types of power are discussed in the individual passages of the Basic Law. According to the Constitution, the legislative branch consists of the federal parliament and the *Länder*'s parliaments.[57] The powers of the executive were vested in the federal government, headed by the Chancellor, and the federal president.[58] The judiciary, in turn, referred to the courts: Federal Constitutional Court, federal courts, and *Länder*'s courts.[59] Importantly, the framework for the legislature was set by the "constitutional order" (*verfassungsmäßige Ordnung*), while for the executive and judiciary – by acts and law.[60]

In Art. 20, Par. 1, the Basic Law of the FRG clearly indicated – apart from the democratic dimension – another important component of the system: social (*sozialer Staat*).[61] This position of the legislator allows the conclusion that the principle of the social state is one of the main pillars of the German political system. This principle was directly connected with the German model of the social market economy.

52 Art. 42, Par. 2; Art. 52, Par. 3 GG.
53 Art. 21, Par. 1 GG.
54 This term does not have its source in the German Basic Law but in the case law of the Federal Constitutional Court (Tkaczyński, *Prawo ustrojowe Niemiec*, 159).
55 Art. 5, Par. 1; Arts. 8–9 GG.
56 Art. 20, Par. 2 GG.
57 Arts. 38–48, 70–82 GG.
58 Arts. 54–69, 83–91 GG.
59 Arts. 92–104 GG.
60 Art. 20, Par. 3 GG. More on Germany as a democratic state: Banaszak, *System konstytucyjny Niemiec*, 28–31 (there also separate consideration of the principle of popular sovereignty); Tkaczyński, *Prawo ustrojowe Niemiec*, 155–159.
61 Art. 20, Par. 1 GG.

The social dimension of the state is indicated in Art. 20, Par. 1 GG, and additionally in Art. 79, Par. 3 GG as an unchangeable systemic principle. On the other hand, this principle was not articulated directly in the text of the Constitution. It thus became an object of implementation by the legislature. This, in turn, made it a systemic objective.[62]

The concept of the social state (welfare state) is variously defined. For example, Franz-Xaver Kaufmann distinguished three main approaches to this category. Firstly, the welfare state is interpreted as the expansion of services for the poorest segments of the population. Helping those who cannot help themselves is a moral obligation of the state. The second understanding presents the welfare state in the context of the "social question" (*Arbeiterfrage*). Here the guarantee of labor law and the expansion of social security play a key role. Finally, the third view emphasizes the social competence of the state for all citizens. The authorities should ensure the development of social rights.[63] Although the tradition of the welfare state dates back to the 19th century, it was not until after World War II that it especially developed in the economically prosperous countries of the capitalist West.[64]

The Constitution of the FRG has referred to this systemic principle on several occasions. In addition to the "social federal state"[65], it thus refers to "social principles" (*soziale Grundsätze*)[66] and the "social state governed by the rule of law" (*sozialer Rechtsstaat*).[67]

This principle remained a practical attempt to overcome the discrepancy between the categories of freedom and equality through the intervention of the state, which further ensured unity and solidarity in society. Sociality was concerned, among other things, with reducing social inequalities in access to power by supporting the weak and restricting the strong. Moreover, this principle meant being guided in political activity by the desire for an even increase in the welfare of the entire society, as well as a uniform distribution of public burdens. The goal of the state should be to remove all social extremes by providing real support and care for specific individuals or social groups. The government realized this obligation

---

62 Tkaczyński, *Prawo ustrojowe Niemiec*, 155, 188.

63 F.-X. Kaufmann, *Sozialpolitik und Sozialstaat: Soziologische Analysen* (Wiesbaden: VS Verlag für Sozialwissenschaften, 2009), 230.

64 Cf., e.g., J. Skodlarski, *Historia gospodarcza* (Warszawa: WN PWN, 2014), 331–334, 360–368, 388–408. Hugh Heclo presents an interesting concept of "stages of the welfare state." He distinguishes the following four stages of this idea's development: (1) experimentation (1870s–1920s); (2) consolidation (1930s–40s); (3) expansion (1950s–60s); (4) "re-formulation" (1970s and beyond) (H. Heclo, "Toward a New Welfare State?," [in:] *The Development of Welfare States in Europe and America*, eds. P. Flora, A. J. Heidenheimer (New Brunswick–London: Transaction Publishers, 2009), 386–387, table 11.1).

65 Art. 20, Par. 1 GG.

66 Art. 23, Par. 1 GG.

67 Art. 28, Par. 1 GG.

by securing the social minimum, social equalization, guaranteeing social security, and securing living conditions. However, state support was only necessary when the citizen needed it and was unable to help himself. On the other hand, the government was obliged to ensure the subsistence minimum for every citizen.[68]

The duties of the state in the implementation of this systemic principle boiled down, among other things, to the fact that all state bodies took specific legal, political, economic, or cultural measures to realize the social rights of citizens. Moreover, according to the jurisprudence of the Federal Constitutional Court, such basic rights as freedom of the arts and research, the right to life, education, marriage, personal inviolability, and the property right fulfilled the social function for the individual.[69]

A separate issue is the potential confrontation of the social state principle with other fundamental premises of the Basic Law. For example, there might be a contradiction between this principle and the constitutional requirement to maintain an overall economic equilibrium[70] or to protect basic rights (e.g., in the area of affluence). In that case, the state intervention had to meet the condition of proportionality, respect for the principle of the rule of law, and fair use of social assistance by contemporaries out of concern for future generations of citizens.[71]

The principle of the social state corresponded with other provisions of the German Constitution. These concerned: the prohibition of discrimination against persons with disabilities,[72] the state's obligation to provide protection and care for mothers,[73] the property right which should serve the community,[74] and the Federation's legislation on social law.[75] It is significant that practically the entire field of social law rested with the Federation rather than the *Länder*.[76]

The codification of social law also demonstrated the fundamental importance of the social state for the German system from 1969 to the present day, which resulted in the published *Social Law Code* (*Sozialgesetzbuch*).[77] This was supplemented by numerous rulings of the Federal Constitutional Court on social issues that were issued after 1949.[78]

---

68 Tkaczyński, *Prawo ustrojowe Niemiec*, 188–195.
69 Banaszak, *System konstytucyjny Niemiec*, 31–32.
70 Cf. Art. 104b, Par. 1, Pt. 1; Art. 109, Par. 2; Art. 115, Par. 1 GG.
71 Tkaczyński, *Prawo ustrojowe Niemiec*, 192.
72 Art. 3, Par. 3 GG.
73 Art. 6, Par. 4 GG.
74 Art. 14, Par. 2 GG.
75 Art. 73, Par. 1, Pt. 13; Art. 74, Par. 1, Pts. 6–7, 9–10, 12–16, 19–20, 26 GG.
76 Tkaczyński, *Prawo ustrojowe Niemiec*, 193–195.
77 Tkaczyński, *Prawo ustrojowe Niemiec*, 194.
78 More on the rulings of the Federal Constitutional Court on social issues: Tkaczyński, *Prawo ustrojowe Niemiec*, 190–193; Pawłowski, "Solidaryzm w Konstytucji Niemiec," 294–324.

The enforcement of the principle of the social state by the FRG authorities is illustrated by statistical data. In 1991, social spending was about 26 % of the German GDP, while in 2014, it was about 29 %. In 2009, during the financial crisis, this outlay exceeded 30 % of GDP.[79] Against this background, Germany stood out from other European countries.[80]

Art. 20, Par. 1 GG remained the foundation of the German federal system. It defines the FRG as a "democratic and social federal state" (*demokratischer und sozialer Bundesstaat*).[81] This federal dimension of the state was also the subject of other provisions of the Basic Law.[82]

A characteristic feature of the German federal state (*Bundesstaat*) is its decentralization, characterized by the supremacy of the central authority, i.e. the Federation (*Bund*) over the federated states (*Bundesländer*), which, however, enjoy autonomy in many areas. Moreover, the Federation as a whole and the individual *Länder* maintained their statehood and sovereignty. In order to avoid potential legal conflicts between the Federation and the federated states, however, a number of arrangements were put in place. These included the constitutional separation of powers between the central government and the *Länder*, including the previously discussed distinction between exclusive Federation legislation, competing legislation, and framework legislation (existing 1949–2006).[83] At the same time, this did not exclude the possibility of cross competences and their complementarity.[84]

Although both the Federation and the *Länder* were independent in their budgetary management, they had to respect the requirements of overall economic equilibrium. After all, the essential goal was to cover the demand for goods and services that were necessary to fulfill public tasks at the federal or *Länder* level.[85]

Over the decades, the trend of expanding the autonomy of the federated states has changed. Successive amendments to the Basic Law strengthened the powers

79 *Statistisches Jahrbuch. Deutschland und Internationales* (hereinafter: SJ DI), Vol. 2012 (Wiesbaden: Statistisches Bundesamt, 2012), 225; SJ DI, Vol. 2016 (Wiesbaden: Statistisches Bundesamt, 2016), 227.

80 Cf., e.g., V. Ziegelmayer, "Państwo socjalne w Niemczech: zmiana systemu?," in *Państwo socjalne w Europie. Historia – rozwój – perspektywy*, eds. K. Kraus, T. Geisen, K. Piątek (Toruń: WN UMK, 2008), 93–130. More extensively on Germany as a social state: Banaszak, *System konstytucyjny Niemiec*, 31–32; J. Czech-Rogosz, "Państwo socjalne – doświadczenia RFN," *Studia Ekonomiczne* No. 38 (2006): 97–114; Tkaczyński, *Prawo ustrojowe Niemiec*, 188–195.

81 Art. 20, Par. 1 GG.

82 Cf., e.g., Arts. 20–37, 50–53a, 70–87, 91a–91d, 92–99, 104a–109a, 115a–115l GG. Some of these articles are indirectly connected with the federal dimension of the German state.

83 Cf. section 3.4. in this work.

84 More extensively on Germany as a federal state: Banaszak, *System konstytucyjny Niemiec*, 32–35; Tkaczyński, *Prawo ustrojowe Niemiec*, 173–188.

85 Banaszak, *System konstytucyjny Niemiec*, 34.

of the Federation. As a result, by the beginning of the 21st century, the division of powers between the central government and the *Länder* had become complicated and unclear. This disturbed the functioning of the state and was a source of disputes. According to Bogusław Banaszak, this process weakened Germany's political and economic position in the world and had a negative impact on political decision-making in the EU.[86]

Leaving aside the discussion concerning the efficiency of the functioning of German federalism, one should notice the institutional component included in this feature of the FRG system defined by the Constitution. In this context, Tkaczyński is right when he argues: "The efficiency of the state is not impaired by the multiplicity of decision-making centers [i.e. the Federation and the federated states], but by the transparency of the rules of mutual conduct established in the federal state. It will therefore not be revealing to say that the place where this is established is naturally the constitution."[87] Thus, the Basic Law, analyzed as an institution, determined, among other things, the rules of federalism that influenced the political stability of the German state.[88]

Another systemic principle of Germany derived from Art. 20, Par. 1 GG was the republican state. Like the principle of the federal state, it was included directly in the name of the state.[89] Tkaczyński points out that the adjective "republican" (*republikanisch*)[90] means in German as much as: "people's government" (*volksstaatlich*) or "freedom" (*freiheitlich*). Moreover, a republic is a form of government that "embodies the idea of a democratic state."[91] Thus, the components of a republic coincide with the characteristics of a democratic state described earlier.

The sovereign people were recognized as the source of republican power. It could exercise it through elections, votes, and representative bodies. The role of the tripartite division of power was also important.[92] Majority rule took place while respecting the rights of minorities.[93] The key function in the state was performed by political parties.[94] Representative parliamentary democracy was identified as the foundation of the FRG political system. The great importance of the Bundestag

---

86 Banaszak, *System konstytucyjny Niemiec*, 34–35.

87 Pol. *Uszczerbku dla sprawności państwa nie należy bowiem szukać w wielości ośrodków decyzyjnych [tj. Federacji i landów], ale w przejrzystości ustanowionych w państwie federalnym reguł wzajemnego postępowania ustrojowego. Nie będzie wobec tego tutaj niczym odkrywczym, jeśli napiszemy, że miejscem, w którym takie ustanowienie następuje, jest naturalnie konstytucja* (Tkaczyński, *Prawo ustrojowe Niemiec*, 178).

88 See section 4.6. in this study.

89 Art. 20, Par. 1 GG.

90 Cf. Art. 28, Par. 1 GG.

91 Pol. *ucieleśnienie wyobrażenia demokratycznego państwa* (Tkaczyński, *Prawo ustrojowe Niemiec*, 160).

92 Art. 20, Par. 2 GG.

93 Art. 42, Par. 2; Art. 52, Par. 3 GG.

94 Art. 21, Par. 1 GG.

was connected with the dominant role of the federal government headed by the Chancellor. The system can thus be described as chancellor-parliamentary.[95]

From the Constitution came the fact of conceiving FRG in terms of the rule of law (*Rechtsstaat*).[96] Within this idea, two dimensions were distinguished. The first one concerned the rule of law in the formal sense and dependence on law (*Gesetzesstaat*). The second dimension, in turn, was connected to the binding of the state's power by law, the rule of law in the substantive sense (*Gerechtigkeitsstaat*).[97] The principle of the rule of law is clearly linked to the principle of a democratic state and – indirectly – a republican state.[98] Hence the frequently encountered in the literature concept of the institution of a democratic state under the rule of law.[99]

Particular elements of the idea of the rule of law can be found in certain provisions of the Basic Law. Tkaczyński indicates these. This was reflected in Art. 20, Par. 2 GG, which referred to the principle of the tripartite division of power.[100] Art. 20, Par. 3 GG treated the legislature as being bound by the constitutional order, while the executive and judiciary were bound by act and law.[101] Art. 28, Par. 1 GG stated that "[t]he constitutional order in the *Länder* must conform to the principles of a republican, democratic and social state governed by the rule of law within the meaning of this Basic Law."[102]

95 More on Germany as a republican state: Tkaczyński, *Prawo ustrojowe Niemiec*, 160–165.

96 Cf. Art. 28, Par. 1 GG.

97 Tkaczyński, *Prawo ustrojowe Niemiec*, 165. Cf. Banaszak, *System konstytucyjny Niemiec*, 29–30.

98 The indirect connection of the idea of a republican state with the rule of law and the democratic state results from the fact that the republic as a form of government is a reflection of the democratic system. Another realization of democracy, however, can be a monarchy, as e.g. in the following European countries: Andorra, Belgium, Denmark, Liechtenstein, Luxembourg, Monaco, the Netherlands, Norway, Spain, Sweden, and United Kingdom (cf. A. Ławniczak, *Monarchiczne i republikańskie głowy państwa w Europie* (Wrocław: Kolonia Limited, 2011)).

99 See, e.g.: J. Kowalski, *Państwo prawa. Demokratyczne państwo prawne. Antologia* (Warszawa: Oficyna Wydawnicza WSHiP im. R. Łazarskiego, 2008); M. Andruszkiewicz, A. Breczko, S. Oliwniak, eds., *Filozoficzne i teoretyczne zagadnienia demokratycznego państwa prawa* (Białystok: Wydawnictwo Temida 2, 2015). On the correlation between the rule of law and democracy in the perspective of institutional economics: J. Godłów-Legiędź, "Zasada rządów prawa i przemiany ustrojowe w Polsce," *Gospodarka Narodowa* No. 3 (2017): 5–13.

100 Art. 20, Par. 2 GG.

101 Art. 20, Par. 3 GG.

102 *Die verfassungsmäßige Ordnung in den Ländern muß den Grundsätzen des republikanischen, demokratischen und sozialen Rechtsstaates im Sinne dieses Grundgesetzes entsprechen* (Art. 28, Par. 1 GG).

Moreover, Tkaczyński points out that the state governed by the rule of law consists of the idea of a tripartite division of power combined with the rule of law.[103] He also states that the legal binding of the state authority in its actions resulting from Art. 20, Par. 3 GG testified to the systemic symbiosis of democracy and the rule of law.[104]

4.4. The FRG's systemic objectives related to the economy

As already mentioned, the literature on the subject points to the various systemic objectives of the German state contained in the Basic Law, regardless of whether they are identified with or separated from the systemic principles. They are directly or indirectly connected with the economy, thus justifying the thesis that the systemic framework determined by the Constitution has an impact on the entire German economic system. Tkaczyński identifies the systemic objectives: (1) the fiscal state; (2) the ecological state (including animal and environmental protection); (3) the promotion of an open state within the framework of European integration and international law; (4) the preservation of international peace; (5) the fulfillment of the requirements of overall economic equilibrium; (6) the maintenance of a public railroad infrastructure; (7) the provision of postal and telecommunication services; (8) equality between men and women; (9) the provision of equal conditions for the development of children outside marriage.[105]

The obvious nature of the objectives related to railroad infrastructure and postal and telecommunication services means that they do not require a detailed presentation. They result from a literal reading of the constitutional regulations pertaining to them.[106] Besides, the relevant provisions concerning this matter were discussed earlier.[107] The last two of these objectives, due to the least direct impact on the economy, will also not be discussed.

The constitutional source of the fiscal state as a systemic objective of Germany was Arts. 104a–115, collected in Chap. X GG. They have already been the subject of detailed characterization.[108] Interestingly, it turns out that Germany is one of the few countries in the world that has devoted a separate place to finance in its constitution.[109]

---

103 Tkaczyński, *Prawo ustrojowe Niemiec*, 153.

104 Tkaczyński, *Prawo ustrojowe Niemiec*, 158; Art. 20, Par. 3 GG. More on Germany as a state under the rule of law: Banaszak, *System konstytucyjny Niemiec*, 29–31, consideration of the principle of a democratic state under the rule of law; Tkaczyński, *Prawo ustrojowe Niemiec*, 165–173.

105 Tkaczyński, *Prawo ustrojowe Niemiec*, 154, 215–221. For the author, the systemic objective is also the social state (cf. section 4.3. in this work).

106 Tkaczyński, *Prawo ustrojowe Niemiec*, 220.

107 Cf. section 3.4. in this study.

108 Cf. section 3.4. in this book.

109 Tkaczyński, *Prawo ustrojowe Niemiec*, 195.

The realization of the objective of a fiscal state referred especially to issues related to public tributes (especially taxes), the separation of fiscal powers between the central government and the *Länder*, financial equalization between the Federation and the federated states, and fiscal management. According to Tkaczyński, the main goal of Chap. X GG was the equitable distribution of income and expenditures between the Federation and the *Länder*. It coincided with the distribution of their political and legal powers. Moreover, the separation of fiscal powers between the central and *Länder*'s authorities corresponded with the idea of an efficient federal state. It involved four types of the Federation's fiscal authority: legislative, executive (administrative), judicial, and that relating to the distribution of state revenues.[110]

An example of the impact of the above systemic objective on the economy is that state spending ranged from 42.8 % to 54.7 % of GDP between 1990 and 2015.[111] This is a characteristic of highly developed countries. In Germany, this information illustrates two things: the model of the social market economy with its social component and the strength of the state's influence on internal (especially socio-economic) transformations.[112]

The recognition of Germany as an ecological state in the context of its systemic objective resulted from Art. 20a GG, added to the Constitution in 1994.[113] This provision obliged the state to protect the "natural foundations of life" (*natürlichen Lebensgrundlagen*), i.e. the environment and – on the basis of the 2002 amendment[114] – animals. This was to be done in "responsibility towards future generations."[115]

As Tkaczyński notes, this article required the state not only to take certain actions but also to take into account the requirements and promote the protection of the environment. However, this provision should be juxtaposed with other constitutional principles or legal goods of the same rank. It turns out that the right to a clean environment was also related to the interpretation of Art. 2, Par. 1 GG or Art. 2, Par. 2, Sentence 1 GG.[116]

---

110 More on the fiscal state in the context of Germany's systemic objective: Tkaczyński, *Prawo ustrojowe Niemiec*, 195–209; D. Bębnowski, "Niemcy jako państwo fiskalne w perspektywie instytucjonalnej i historyczno-gospodarczej (1990–2015)," *Przegląd Zachodni* No. 1 (370) (2019): 41–58.

111 Cf. section 6.2.8. in this study.

112 Tkaczyński, *Prawo ustrojowe Niemiec*, 195.

113 *Gesetz zur Änderung des Grundgesetzes (Artikel 3, 20a, 28, 29, 72, 74, 75, 76, 77, 80, 87, 93, 118a und 125a) Vom 27. Oktober 1994*, Art. 1, Par. 2 (BGBl., Part I, 1994, No. 75, 3146).

114 *Gesetz zur Änderung des Grundgesetzes (Staatsziel Tierschutz) Vom 26. Juli 2002* (BGBl., Part I, 2002, No. 53, 2862).

115 [*I*]*n Verantwortung für die künftigen Generationen* (Art. 20a GG).

116 The first provision guarantees the individual's right to an unhindered development of personality, limited only by the rights of others, the constitutional order and the

On the other hand, the legislative practice of Germany shows that the laws on nature protection lacked a uniform and clearly defined aim of this protection. Therefore, Tkaczyński derives the goals of environmental protection from the assumptions of the 1971 federal government program concerning this matter. Thus, the said goals were political in nature. They were as follows: (1) to provide the individual with such an environment that guarantees a healthy life and a dignified existence; (2) to protect the goods of the environment, plants and animals from harmful human activity; (3) to remove damage or negative changes in the environment that are a consequence of human activity.

A separate issue remained the principles of environmental law, which included such rules as: (1) sustainable development and protection of the existing state (resources) of the environment; (2) treating economic development as permanent and long-term planning and use of environmental resources. Tkaczyński points out that it is possible to link the previously quoted constitutional provision on "responsibility towards future generations"[117] with the order of sustainable and balanced development. He concludes: "There is no doubt that the constitutional "responsibility" of the state indicated by the legislator must mean such a management of natural resources that will secure them for the future"[118].

Tkaczyński emphasizes that in Germany, the understanding of balanced and sustainable development is narrow. He adds that the noble recommendations of Art. 20a GG are difficult to implement in political practice unless far-reaching goals are conceptualized.[119]

The study of Henryk Runowski can be an exemplification of the channels of the relationship of the presented constitutional systemic objective with the economy. He compares the economic performance of organic and conventional farms in Germany in 2005–2006. Despite lower crop and milk yields and higher product prices, organic farms had higher incomes. This was due to the fact that organic farms received 39 % more subsidies than conventional farms. However, these subsidies were necessary because of the lower demand for organic products due to higher prices. In the analyzed period, subsidies accounted for 29.8 % of the income of the German organic farms compared to 23.6 % for the second group.[120]

---

dictates of morality (Art. 2, Par. 1 GG). The second confirms the universal right to life and physical integrity (Art. 2, Par. 2, Sentence 1 GG).

117 Art. 20a GG.

118 Pol. *Nie ulega bowiem wątpliwości, że wskazana przez ustawodawcę konstytucyjna "odpowiedzialność" państwa musi oznaczać takie gospodarowanie zasobami naturalnymi, jakie zabezpieczy je na przyszłość* (Tkaczyński, *Prawo ustrojowe Niemiec*, 214).

119 More on Germany as an ecological state (including the protection of animals and the environment) in the context of the systemic objective: Tkaczyński, *Prawo ustrojowe Niemiec*, 209–214, 216.

120 H. Runowski, "Rolnictwo ekologiczne – rozwój czy regres?," *Roczniki Nauk Rolniczych. Seria G* 96, No. 4 (2009): 189–190.

The objective of an open state (*offene Staatlichkeit*) complemented the principle of a democratic state under the rule of law. It did not imply its transparency but its openness to European integration and international law, as implied in the Preamble, Art. 1, Par. 2, and Arts. 23–26 GG.

The first sentence of the Preamble of the German Constitution refers, among other things, to the idea of European integration. The German nation defined itself as "an equal partner in a united Europe" (*gleichberechtigtes Glied in einem vereinten Europa*).[121]

Under Art. 1, Par. 2 GG, the German people affirmed: "inviolable and inalienable human rights as the basis of every community, of peace and of justice in the world."[122] This was a clear declaration of the FRG's openness to international law.

Originally, Art. 23 GG concerned the validity of the Basic Law in the FRG, providing for its extension after the incorporation of the Eastern *Länder*, brought together under the GDR.[123] On the basis of the *Unification Treaty* of 1990, this provision of the Constitution was abolished.[124] A new Art. 23 GG was added in 1992[125] and subsequently amended in 2006 and 2008.[126] It provided for the FRG's contribution to the development of the EU in order to "establishing a united Europe."[127] At the same time, the Federation required the EU to be based on democratic, the rule of law, social, federal, and subsidiarity principles, and similar protection of basic rights. The article provided for the possibility of transferring supreme rights to the Union by law with the consent of the Bundesrat. Its subsequent paragraphs regulated the competences of the respective state bodies (Bundestag, Bundesrat, and government) in the EU's affairs.[128]

The possibility of transferring sovereign rights not only to the EU but also to other international institutions was provided for in Art. 24 GG, amended in 1992.[129]

---

121 Preamble, Sentence 1 GG.

122 [*U*]*nverletzlichen und unveräußerlichen Menschenrechten als Grundlage jeder menschlichen Gemeinschaft, des Friedens und der Gerechtigkeit in der Welt* (Art. 1, Par. 2 GG).

123 Cf. *Grundgesetz für die Bundesrepublik Deutschland vom 23. Mai 1949.*, Art. 23 (BGBl., Part I, 1949, No. 1, 3–4).

124 Unification Treaty, Chap. 2, Art. 4, Par. 2 (BGBl., Part II, 1990, No. 35, 890).

125 *Gesetz zur Änderung des Grundgesetzes Vom 21. Dezember 1992*, Art. 1, Par. 1 (BGBl., Part I, 1992, No. 58, 2086).

126 *Gesetz zur Änderung des Grundgesetzes (Artikel 22, 23, 33, 52, 72, 73, 74, 74a, 75, 84, 85, 87c, 91a, 91b, 93, 98, 104a, 104b, 105, 107, 109, 125a, 125b, 125c, 143c) Vom 28. August 2006*, Art. 1, Par. 2 (BGBl., Part I, 2006, No. 41, 2034); *Gesetz zur Änderung des Grundgesetzes (Artikel 23, 45 und 93) Vom 8. Oktober 2008*, Art. 1, Par. 1 (BGBl., Part I, 2008, No. 45, 1926).

127 *Verwirklichung eines vereinten Europas* (Art. 23, Par. 1 GG).

128 Art. 23 GG.

129 *Gesetz zur Änderung des Grundgesetzes*, Art. 1, Par. 2 (BGBl., Part I, 1992, No. 58, 2086).

This applied both to the Federation and – under certain conditions – to the *Länder* and was done by law. The article also provided for the FRG's involvement in the system of international security and, for the purpose of conflict resolution, an international arbitration (*internationale Schiedsgerichtsbarkeit*).[130]

Art. 25 GG recognized international law as a component part of federal law. In addition, the provision indicated the superiority of the former over state rules. Citizens were obliged to observe the rights and obligations under international law.[131]

Also connected with the idea of an open state was Art. 26 GG confirming the unconstitutionality of any action that violated "the peaceful relations between nations" (*friedliche Zusammenleben der Völker*), especially "to prepare for a war of aggression" (*Führung lines Angriffskrieges vorzubereiten*).[132] The record suggested the imposition of punishment in this regard. Furthermore, the article noted that only with government approval could weapons of war be manufactured, transported, and traded.[133]

The FRG's subjective participation in the process of European integration after World War II and then in 1990–2015 testified to the realization of the discussed systemic objective resulting from the idea of an open state.[134] The same applies to global integration in its political, economic, and socio-cultural dimensions. Between 1990 and 2015, the German economy remained a European and even global leader in this process.

The FRG's systemic objective of maintaining international peace, which was formulated separately in the literature, had much in common with the previously discussed idea of an open state in the context of European integration and international law. It resulted, among other things, from the aforementioned Art. 26 GG, which condemns actions that breach the peace between the nations of the world and regulates the production and trade in weapons of war.[135] However, this objective was also rooted in the Preamble, in which the German people expressed their will "to promote world peace" (*Frieden der Welt zu dienen*).[136] Furthermore, the previously mentioned Art. 9 GG, which is part of the provisions guaranteeing the

---

130 Art. 24 GG.

131 Art. 25 GG.

132 Art. 26, Par. 1 GG.

133 Art. 26 GG. More on the support of the idea of an open state within the framework of European integration and international law in the context of Germany's systemic objective: K. Wójtowicz, "Otwarcie systemu konstytucyjnego Niemiec na sprawy jedności Europy," *Przegląd Sejmowy* No. 6 (95) (2009): 125–136; Tkaczyński, *Prawo ustrojowe Niemiec*, 216–220.

134 The literature on European integration is very rich. It captures the role of the FRG in this process. See the synthetic work: Z. Wysokińska, J. Witkowska, *Integracja europejska. Rozwój rynków* (Warszawa: WN PWN, 2002).

135 Art. 26 GG.

136 Preamble, Sentence 1 GG.

basic rights, prohibits associations whose aims or activities contradict the "concept of international understanding" (*Gedanke der Völkerverständigung*).[137] In the literature, these regulations are sometimes interpreted as an order for Germany to pursue an active policy aimed at maintaining world peace.[138]

The state's striving influenced the functioning of the German economic system to meet the requirements of overall economic equilibrium (*gesamtwirtschaftliches Gleichgewicht*). The following provisions of the Constitution addressed it: Art. 104b, Par. 1, Pt. 1, Art. 109, Par. 2, and Art. 115, Par. 1.[139]

As Tkaczyński notes, the above objective was to be achieved by fulfilling the four conditions of the "magic quadrilateral" (*magisches Viereck*). They were laid down in the *Act on the Postulates of Stability and Growth of the Economy* on June 8, 1967. Firstly, the price level should be stable, and the inflation rate should amount to around 2–4 %. Secondly, the act required full employment, that is, a situation in which there is only frictional unemployment of about 2–3 %.[140] Thirdly, the desired phenomenon was an external balance understood as the balance of Germany's trade with foreign countries, which should be reflected in a sustainable balance of payments. Fourthly, a condition of constant and adequate economic growth measured by the GDP growth rate was necessary.[141] It should be emphasized that between 1967 and 2015, the above goal was not achieved in the form of the aforementioned law.[142]

4.5. Selected indicators of German formal institutions' quality

There are databases that attempt to assess the quality of selected German formal institutions during the period under analysis by assigning specific measures to them.[143] The details of the formal rules related to the subject of this paper are summarized in Table 5.

---

137 Art. 9, Par. 2 GG.

138 More on the preservation of international peace in the context of Germany's systemic objective: Tkaczyński, *Prawo ustrojowe Niemiec*, 220.

139 Art. 104b, Par. 1, Pt. 1; Art. 109, Par. 2; Art. 115, Par. 1 GG. Cf. section 3.4. in this study.

140 Frictional unemployment should be understood as a type of lack of employment that refers to people who are unable to take up work due to various disabilities or to individuals who change jobs and, as a result, are temporarily unemployed. In economic theory, however, it is noted that this is a natural phenomenon in a dynamic economy, which remains the minimum amount of unemployment impossible to limit (D. Begg, G. Vernasca, S. Fischer, R. Dornbusch, *Makroekonomia* (Warszawa: PWE, 2014), 310).

141 *Gesetz zur Förderung der Stabilität und des Wachstums der Wirtschafts Vom 8. Juni 1967*, Par. 1 (BGBl., Part I, 1967, No. 32, 582).

142 Tkaczyński, *Prawo ustrojowe Niemiec*, 220–221.

143 Cf. methodological notes: *Introduction*, section *Research methods* in this book.

Table 5: *Examples of indicators of specific formal institutions' quality in Germany for selected years 1990–2015*

Database	Selected indicators, formal institutions considered	Scale, interpretation	Values for Germany in years:					
			1990	1995	2000	2005	2010	2015
World Governance Indicators (WGI), World Bank	(1) Political stability and absence of violence/terrorism (2) Government effectiveness (3) Regulatory quality (4) Rule of law	Quality of government from −2.5 to 2.5 (the higher the index, the higher the quality of the institution)	-	1996: (1) 1.29 (2) 1.72 (3) 1.48 (4) 1.61	(1) 1.41 (2) 1.89 (3) 1.51 (4) 1.64	(1) 0.89 (2) 1.51 (3) 1.52 (4) 1.66	(1) 0.80 (2) 1.57 (3) 1.57 (4) 1.63	(1) 0.70 (2) 1.74 (3) 1.72 (4) 1.79
Index of Economic Freedom (IEF), Heritage Foundation, "Wall Street Journal"	(1) Property rights (2) Government integrity (3) Government spending (4) Business freedom (5) Investment freedom	Indicators from 0 to 100 (the higher the indicator, the higher the level of economic freedom)	-	(1) 90.0 (2) 90.0 (3) 30.6 (4) 85.0 (5) 70.0	(1) 90.0 (2) 79.0 (3) 28.0 (4) 70.0 (5) 70.0	(1) 90.0 (2) 77.0 (3) 28.6 (4) 70.0 (5) 90.0	(1) 90.0 (2) 79.0 (3) 41.4 (4) 89.6 (5) 85.0	(1) 90.0 (2) 78.0 (3) 40.1 (4) 88.2 (5) 90.0
Economic Freedom of the World (EFW), Fraser Institute, Cato Institute	(1) Size of government (2) Legal systems and property rights (3) Regulation	Indicators from 0 to 10 (the higher the indicator, the higher the level of economic freedom)	(1) 5.73 (2) 8.35 (3) 5.56	(1) 5.34 (2) 9.13 (3) 5.70	(1) 5.97 (2) 8.58 (3) 6.50	(1) 6.59 (2) 8.80 (3) 6.45	(1) 6.19 (2) 7.97 (3) 7.02	(1) 6.41 (2) 7.45 (3) 7.85

Own compilation based on: "World Governance Indicators," https://info.worldbank.org/governance/wgi/ (accessed April 7, 2020); "2020 Index of Economic Freedom," https://www.heritage.org/index/ (accessed April 7, 2020); "Economic Freedom," https://www.fraserinstitute.org/economic-freedom/dataset/ (accessed April 7, 2020). Sources and methods of indicators' preparing are discussed in the individual databases.

The general conclusion from analyzing these indicators for the German economy after reunification is that the quality of the specified formal institutions was high during the period in question. Leaving aside detailed variations, it must also be mentioned that in international rankings comparing the countries of Europe and the world in these years from the point of view of these measures, Germany was highly placed.

The WGI indicators rate the quality of government in Germany highly. The values of regulatory quality increased between 1990 and 2015 (the similar EFW (3) measure showed a slight decline between 2000 and 2005) and the rule of law (with a slight decline between 2005 and 2010). Despite a clear improvement in the second half of the 1990s, government effectiveness declined in subsequent years, finally taking a level in 2015 close to the adequate one in 1995. Between 1995 and 2015, the index for political stability and the absence of violence or terrorism declined markedly.

The interpretation of measures of economic freedom, broadly defined, provides positive conclusions. Government spending (IEF (3)) at a relatively high level from 30.6 in 1995 to 40.1 in 2015 illustrates the social (welfare) dimension of the German market economy. This is confirmed by the increasing share of government spending in GDP (EFW (1)).

The very high score of 90.0 (IEF (1)) for property rights over the entire analyzed period attests to their effective enforcement and protection. On the other hand, the index of the EFW (2), which takes into account, among other things, the protection of property rights, the enforcement of contracts, and the regulatory costs of real estate sales (transferability), is slightly less optimistic (decrease from 8.35 in 1990 to 7.97 in 2015). However, this is coupled with the quality of the legal system, which – taking into account at least the decline in the WGI (1) or partly the IEF (2) in this regard – may have negatively affected the final assessment of property rights. Nevertheless, the quality of these rights' protection in Germany between 1990 and 2015 is rated high. The aftermath may have been the increasing measures of business freedom and investment freedom (IEF (4) and (5)). Sustainable and well-functioning property rights strengthened the sense of certainty for potential entrepreneurs and investors, allowing them to make long-term decisions. Development of entrepreneurship and investment progress, in turn, fostered economic growth.

4.6. Stability of the political system

Constitutional law emphasizes that the basic law should be stable as the basis of the state system and the created law. Then it remains a guarantor of social peace and protects the political, economic, and social relations system. An important asset of the constitution should be its concreteness, adequate detail, and unambiguity. Consequently, it may determine the character of the created system for a longer period, favoring long-term actions. This is conducive to building public confidence in the basic law. The permanence of constitutional rules has an integrating function in the state. It does not follow, however, that the constitution is immutable. It should be adapted to circumstances or social needs. Most often, however, basic laws implicitly assume the longest possible duration. Banaszak, from the position of legal comparative studies, formulates six interesting theses on the regularities related to the changes of the constitution: (1) the frequency of amendments to this act depends on the scope of its regulation, i.e., the fewer areas are regulated by the constitution, the rarer are its changes; (2) the frequency of changes of the basic law depends on the degree of generality of its provisions, i.e., the more general the provisions of the constitution, the rarer are its changes; (3) the frequency of amendments to the highest legal act in the state depends on the role of the Supreme Court or Constitutional Court in its adaptation to specific needs of social development, i.e. the more active one of these bodies is in formulating an interpretation regarding the basic law, the less frequently it is amended; (4) the frequency of changes of the constitution depends on the difficulty of amending it in relation to passing a new law; (5) the frequency of amendments to the basic law depends on the stability of the balance of political forces; (6) a constitution that is out of step with reality (which is typical of authoritarian and totalitarian states) is not often amended.[144]

The constitution determines the conditions for political decision-making. Constitutional amendments, therefore, determine changes in these conditions. Although the adaptation of the political sphere to changing framework conditions is considered a positive feature, this does not apply to constitutional rules. Their legitimacy depends on stability and reliability. In other words, sudden and frequent constitutional changes can have a destabilizing effect on the functioning of the state and society.[145] For example, there is a risk of diminishing returns on investment and the generation of additional transaction costs (resulting, among other things, from the time needed for individuals to become familiar with new regulations). Therefore, as Voigt points out, it is important to compare these costs with the potential benefits resulting from the introduced changes.[146]

Constitutional rules bind successive governments over the medium and long term.[147] This is done independently of short-term political constellations, limited

---

144 B. Banaszak, *Porównawcze prawo konstytucyjne współczesnych państw demokratycznych* (Warszawa: Wolters Kluwer Polska, 2007), 86–92.

145 A. Busch, "Verfassungspolitik: Stabilität und permanentes Austarieren," in *Regieren in der Bundesrepublik Deutschland. Innen- und Außenpolitik seit 1949*, eds. M. G. Schmidt, R. Zohlnhöfer (Wiesbaden: VS Verlag für Sozialwissenschaften, 2006), 33–56. Cf. R. G. Holcombe, *The Economic Foundations of Government* (London: Macmillan, 1994), 213–214.

146 Voigt, "Positive Constitutional Economics," 24.

147 Cf. M. Przybysz, "Pierwsza i druga 'reforma federalizmu' w Republice Federalnej Niemiec – zmiany Ustawy Zasadniczej z 2006 i 2009 r. w odniesieniu do kompetencji prawodawczych i stosunków finansowych Związku i krajów," *Przegląd Prawa Konstytucyjnego* No. 1 (35) (2017): 150.

to single terms of the legislature and the executive. This is why the stability of the political system is so important for the functioning of the economy.[148] It has its source and legitimacy in the basic law. This stability is strengthened by such systemic components (resulting from the constitution) as: division of power, bicameral parliament, executive veto,[149] tenure,[150] and property rights.[151] Jon Elster argues that constitutions influence economic development in terms of promoting certain values oscillating around stability, accountability and credibility. He concludes: "In more metaphorical language constitutions serve partly as flywheel, partly as feedback mechanism, and partly as precommitment device."[152]

From the point of view of the internal morality of law, attention is drawn to the essence of the certainty of the legal system and its relative (but not absolute) immutability over time. The legislator is obliged to ensure legal security by maintaining the permanence of the law over time. In this context, the German legal literature writes about the "guarantee of continuation" (*Kontinuitätsgewähr*) as a consequence of the rule of law. The changes undertaken to the system should have the character of continuity of the legal tradition and not a break with it. It is also important that they refer to the historical experience of the political community and its current problems.[153]

---

148 Cf. J. Hryniewicz, B. Jałowiecki, *System polityczny a rozwój gospodarczy* (Warszawa: Wydawnictwa EIRRiL, 1997), 96–97.

149 This is the right to veto laws vested in the executive power. In Polish law, in this context, one speaks of a legislative veto. In this work, however, the notion of executive veto is used due to its wide use in the literature (especially economic literature).

150 Cf. studies on the system of the United States: P. C. Ordeshook, "Constitutional Stability," *Constitutional Political Economy* 3, No. 2 (1992): 137–175.

151 Karol Dobrzeniecki and Marcin Romanowski write: "The property right, in addition to fulfilling a fundamental guarantee function for the subjectivity of natural persons, is a fair and inexpensive form of ensuring order and compliance with the law" (Pol. *Prawo własności, oprócz pełnienia fundamentalnej funkcji gwarancyjnej dla podmiotowości osób fizycznych, jest uczciwą i niekosztowną formą zapewnienia porządku i przestrzegania prawa*) (K. Dobrzeniecki, M. Romanowski, *Reprywatyzacja. Problemy tworzenia i stosowania prawa* (Warszawa: Wydawnictwo UKSW, 2015), 10–11).

152 Elster, "The Impact of Constitutions," 210.

153 Dobrzeniecki, Romanowski, *Reprywatyzacja*, 26–27, fn. 19; 36, 40 (relevant literature there). The authors rightly point out that the guarantee of continuation at the time of systemic transition only applies when the legislator refers to the legal tradition broken by the totalitarian regime, or to countries with a similar legal culture. The essence of transition is change (Dobrzeniecki, Romanowski, *Reprywatyzacja*, 26–27). This is why German legal science emphasizes the role of transitional regulations, which should facilitate a relatively smooth transition – as part of the whole systemic transition process – from the old to the new legal system. This is to protect this continuation from being interrupted (Dobrzeniecki, Romanowski, *Reprywatyzacja*, 36).

One of the economic functions of institutions is to reduce uncertainty.[154] However, it turns out that when relating this to the stability of the political system, it is difficult to unequivocally assess its importance for the economy due to its unmeasurable nature. Similar attempts usually concern a specific group of countries at a given time or have the character of subjective opinions of entities operating in a specific country.[155] Nevertheless, there are attempts to make estimations in this respect in economics.

Institutional economics recognizes the importance of political stability for the economy of a country, e.g. in terms of its investment attractiveness. This stability is related to such factors as the risk of political upheaval or the frequency of changes in legal norms, which in turn are reflected in the level of relative prices, the profitability of investments or the amount of transaction costs.[156] The impact of political stability on the level of inflation, or fiscal policy is discussed.[157] Moreover, there are studies justifying the importance of stability of the political system for economic growth.[158]

The positive approach of constitutional economics indicates that certain components of the political system can translate into the economic growth of a country. These are, e.g.: the political regime,[159] the rule of law,[160] forms of direct and indirect democracy (referenda), the rights of individuals, and the separation of powers.[161] In the last case, it can be talked about two dimensions of

154 H. Dietl, *Institutionen und Zeit* (Tübingen: J. C. B. Mohr (Paul Siebeck), 1993), 85–86.

155 Cf. Magdalena Owczarczuk's remarks on this topic in the context of stability and transparency of the legal system: M. Owczarczuk, "Atrakcyjność inwestycyjna Polski z perspektywy instytucjonalnej," *Studia Ekonomiczne* 184 (2014): 175.

156 Owczarczuk, "Atrakcyjność inwestycyjna Polski," 173–174. Cf. J. Svensson, "Investment, Property Rights and Political Instability: Theory and Evidence," *European Economic Review* 42, No. 7 (1998): 1317–1341; K. Baek, X, Quian, "An Analysis on Political Risks and the Flow of Foreign Direct Investment in Developing and Industrialized Economies," *Economics, Management, and Financial Markets* 6, No. 4 (2011): 60–91.

157 C. L. J. Siermann, *Politics, Institutions and the Economic Performance of Nations* (Cheltenham–Northampton: Edward Elgar, 1998).

158 See, e.g.: R. J. Barro, "Economic Growth in a Cross Section of Countries," *The Quarterly Journal of Economics* 106, No. 2 (1991): 407–443; A. Alesina, S. Özler, N. Roubini, P. Swagel, "Political Instability and Economic Growth," *Journal of Economic Growth* 1, No. 2 (1996): 189–211; V. Bergström, ed., *Government and Growth* (Oxford: Clarendon Press, 1997).

159 A. Przeworski, F. Limongi, "Political Regimes and Economic Growth," *Journal of Economic Perspectives* 7, No. 3 (1993): 51–69.

160 R. J. Barro, "Democracy and Growth," *Journal of Economic Growth* 1, No. 1 (1996): 1–27.

161 See review of relevant literature: Voigt, "Positive Constitutional Economics," 41–46. More on the importance of individual rights (defined as the basic rights in the FRG Constitution) for the German economy in 1990–2015: section 4.2. in this work. See other sample studies: D. C. North, B. R. Weingast, "Constitutions and

division: horizontal (a tripartite division of power) and vertical (e.g. federalism).[162] Analyses also take into account the size of the state and government (i.e. a share of state spending in GDP).[163] Some authors argue that political stability is strengthened, among other things, by the functioning of a bicameral parliament and an executive veto. These elements, in turn, stem from the constitution.[164] Other studies point to links between election results and economic growth.[165] There are also a number of studies showing the opposite relationship, i.e. the impact of economic growth on the quality of institutions.[166] For example, Matthes Buhbe argues that a democratic system and a free market economy are most conducive to the effective functioning of a property rights system.[167]

Analysis of the regulations concerning certain aspects of the political, systemic and social sphere, as well as of the amendments to the economic provisions of the FRG Constitution[168] allows the conclusion that there were no sudden (unexpected) or breakthrough (revolutionary) changes in the German constitutional system, and consequently in the political, systemic, economic or social sphere in 1990–2015. As Banaszak notes, despite such a key event in Germany's contemporary history as reunification, the stability of the Basic Law was guaranteed by the stability of the balance of political power.[169] The last thing was manifested, among others, by the long-standing strong political position of the CDU.

Commitment: The Evolution of Institutions Governing Public Choice in Seventeenth-Century England," *The Journal of Economic History* 49, No. 4 (1989): 803–832; B. R. Weingast, "The Economic Role of Political Institutions: Market-Preserving Federalism and Economic Development," *Journal of Law, Economics, & Organization* 11, No. 1 (1995): 1–31.

162 Voigt, "Positive Constitutional Economics," 41. Cf. studies on the importance of pro-market federalism for economic development: Weingast, "The Economic Role of Political Institutions."

163 G. W. Scully, *Constitutional Environments and Economic Growth* (Princeton: Princeton University Press, 1992), 200–211.

164 G. J. Miller, T. H. Hammond, "Stability and Efficiency in a Separation-of-Powers Constitutional System," in *The Federalist Papers and the New Institutionalism*, eds. B. Grofman, D. Wittman (New York: Agathon Press, 1989), 85–99.

165 A. Alesina, "Elections and the Economy: the Case of the United States, with Some Lessons for Europe," in *Economic and Political Institutions in Economic Policy*, ed. V. A. Muscatelli (Manchester–New York: Manchester University Press, 1996), 35–50.

166 A. Kacprzyk, *Instytucjonalne determinanty wzrostu gospodarczego* (Łódź: Wydawnictwo UŁ, 2014), *passim* (valuable review of research on this topic there).

167 M. Buhbe, *Ökonomische Analyse von Eigentumsrechten. Der Beitrag der Economics of Property Rights zur Theorie der Institutionen* (Frankfurt am Main: Peter D. Lang, 1980), 51–54.

168 Cf. sections 3.3.–3.4., 4.2.–4.4. in this book.

169 Banaszak, *Porównawcze prawo konstytucyjne*, 91.

On the other hand, it should be stressed that some of the provisions were exceptionally detailed. This was the case, e.g., with the structural changes in the state railroads (Art. 143a GG) or the German Federal Post Office (Art. 143b GG) in the 1990s. This is particularly evident in the context of provisions that were completely new or amended already in the 21st century, which reflected the current changes in socio-economic reality. This refers to solutions introduced during the financial crisis of 2008 (e.g. Art. 15, Par. 2; Art. 143c–143d GG) or the provisions responding to the challenges of modernization of the economy (e.g. Art. 91c GG). In the context of one of Banaszak's theses, according to which the generality of constitutional provisions is conducive to the durability of the basic law, a question arises as to whether the amendments to the FRG Constitution passed in the final years of the analyzed period were not too detailed, thus creating the possibility of more frequent changes to the Basic Law in the near future, and consequently weakening its durability, and thus that of the entire political, legal and socio-economic system.

In general, the amendments to the Basic Law passed during the period under review, which directly affect the economic system, can be divided into two groups. The first one includes the amendments from the years: 1990, 1992–1995, 1997, 2001, and 2014. They were ad hoc in nature, while their purpose was to clarify or correct specific provisions or to add completely new ones to reflect the current needs of socio-economic life. Consequently, these amendments served to improve the efficiency of governance and the functioning of the state and the economy. Thus, these amendments were – to use Jan Galster's term – adaptive and technical-organizational rather than structural in nature.[170]

The second group of constitutional modifications concerns the two great reforms of federalism of 2006 and 2009. Their importance is evaluated differently in the literature, especially in legal ones.[171] From an economic point of view, by 2015 it can be seen some effects of introduced amendments,[172] e.g., decreasing budget deficit and public debt. Admittedly, between 2006 and 2009, the FRG's deficit increased from −1.7 % to −3.7 % of GDP, but this was more a consequence of the financial crisis than of the ineffectiveness of the first reform of federalism, which mainly covered systemic issues. However, between 2009 and 2015, i.e. after the implementation of the second reform, the deficit decreased markedly, resulting

---

170 J. Galster, "Reforma konstytucyjna w zjednoczonych Niemczech," *Przegląd Sejmowy* 4, No. 3 (15) (1996): 57. The author's expressions – although referring to the constitutional changes in Germany from the first half of the 1990s. – can be applied to the first group of modifications discussed above.

171 See section 3.5. in this study.

172 It should be aware of the legitimacy of studying the economic effects of the first and second reforms of federalism after 2015, especially since the reference point for the work on the second reform was 2019 (Przybysz, "Pierwsza i druga 'reforma federalizmu'," 149, 153). However, this analysis goes beyond the chronological framework of this work.

in a small surplus of 0.9 % of GDP in 2015. A similar trend was observed in public debt. Between 2006 and 2009, debt increased from 64.5 % to 68.9 % of GDP. After the record year of 2010 (81.0 % of GDP), the debt level decreased to 71.2 % of GDP in 2015.[173] Naturally, the discussed trends were a consequence of the anti-crisis policy implemented primarily in 2008–2009. However, it cannot be excluded the positive impact of two reforms of federalism in this regard, especially the one of 2009, which significantly affected the state's financial system. The law amending the FRG Constitution of July 29, 2009, limited, among other things, the borrowing possibilities of the federated states.[174] It was both one of the government's anti-crisis measures[175] and a sanctioning of the second reform of federalism.

Despite the above classification, the conclusion should be drawn that the FRG's constitutional system in 1990–2015 was characterized by a high degree of stability and permanence. Both the individual amendments from the first group and the two major ones of 2006 and 2009 did not change the foundations of the state or economic system. Rather, they aimed at a more effective definition of intra-state relations under specific circumstances. First, it was a matter of regulating the political and systemic relations between the old and new federated states after reunification. This phase occurred more or less at the beginning of the enactment of the first group of amendments, especially in the first half of the 1990s. Then the circumstance of the alignment of relations between the Federation and the *Länder* came, which consisted of the reforms of 2006 and 2009. All these changes were to affect the economic performance of the entire German state.[176] The main components of the political and legal system of the state, i.e. the systemic principles and objectives, played an additional positive role in the economy.[177]

In view of the above, the FRG Constitution in 1990–2015 should be regarded as an example of a stable formal institution. This, in turn, influenced the stability of the political and economic system, the transformations of which were due not so much to endogenous factors (changes in the Basic Law), but to exogenous factors (the economic situation in the country, including the government's economic

---

173 More on the budget deficit and public debt in Germany between 1991 and 2015: section 4.8. in this book.

174 *Gesetz zur Änderung des Grundgesetzes (Artikel 91c, 91d, 104b, 109, 109a, 115, 143d) Vom 29. Juli 2009*, Art. 1, Par. 4, Pt. b; Par. 6, Pt. b (BGBl., Part I, 2009, No. 48, 2249).

175 This act is mentioned by Erhard Cziomer in this context, although he incorrectly dates it to May 29, 2009. (E. Cziomer, "Od światowego kryzysu finansowego do kryzysu strefy euro: implikacje wewnątrzpolityczne dla Niemiec w latach 2008–2011," *Rocznik Integracji Europejskiej* No. 5 (2011): 38).

176 The issue of the socio-economic effectiveness of German federalism in the context of constitutional and systemic changes is highlighted, e.g., by Marcin Przybysz (Przybysz, "Pierwsza i druga 'reforma federalizmu'," 140).

177 See sections 4.3.–4.4. in this book.

policy, and processes taking place in the global economy).[178] This can be applied to the "stability and growth policy" (*Stabilitäts- und Wachstumspolitik*) in the FRG described by Manfred Weilepp. Its foundations were laid down by law in 1967.[179]

The stability of the political system is co-shaped by legal stability, which in turn is made up of, among other things, the number of legal acts (laws and regulations) passed annually. The data for Germany is positive. According to Grant Thornton's calculations, the legal volatility index in Germany was 2.3 between 2012 and 2014 (taking into account both the number of laws passed and their average volume), one of the lowest in the EU. A better result was recorded only in Austria (2.1), Belgium (1.3), and Sweden (1.0). The highest levels of legal instability in the EU, understood in this way at the time, were recorded in Poland (55.6), Italy (53.0), Greece (46.2), Spain (44.8), France (42.9), and the United Kingdom (36.1).[180] The above result for Germany had improved compared to the 1990s, when under conditions of unification and integration of the two parts of the country, the ratio of the number of legal acts was higher.

Empirical studies confirm the high level of stability of the German political system. For example, Witold J. Henisz determined the degree of political hazard for Germany in 1980–1992 (taking into account especially the enforcement of the principle of the tripartite division of power) at 0.17, where 0 expresses no hazard and 1 – very high hazard. This very low index, which positively assesses the political stability of Germany, allowed the author to estimate the probability of international corporations investing in the FRG (and countries with similar results) at an average level of 84.8 % to 85.2 %.[181] Note that these calculations refer to the period before reunification and the first years of the 1990s when West German property rights were implemented in the Eastern federated states.

Political stability was also important for investors later on. According to some studies, in 2011, compared to 2005 (and thus after the financial crisis), the importance of economic and political stability in given EU countries for investors' decisions on investing there increased significantly. This was significant for

178 These conclusions are an expansion of the incomplete conclusions of the author's paper (Bębnowski, "Niemcy jako państwo fiskalne," 57). Cf. the analysis of indicators of formal institutions' quality in Germany between 1990 and 2015: section 4.5. in this study.

179 Weilepp, "Das System der rechtlichen Regelungen," 66–71. See *Gesetz zur Förderung der Stabilität und des Wachstums der Wirtschafts*, Par. 1 (BGBl., Part I, 1967, No. 32, 582).

180 *Polska liderem produkcji prawa w Unii Europejskiej. Barometr stabilności otoczenia prawnego w polskiej gospodarce. Edycja 2016* (Poznań: Grant Thornton, 2016), 9. Cf. data correction: "Wskaźnik zmienności prawa w UE," http://barometrprawa.pl/#wykresy (accessed April 18, 2019).

181 W. J. Henisz, "The Institutional Environment for Multinational Investment," *Journal of Law, Economics and Organization* 16 (2000): 334–364, especially 346, 349, table 1; 357, table 5.

Germany, as it was then ranked 4th in the EU in terms of the amount of foreign direct investments attracted.[182]

4.7. Economic growth[183]

The theory of constitutional economics suggests that the rules of the basic law may determine economic growth. This is because constitutionally imposed restrictions on government representatives increase the level of certainty among citizens about the fulfillment of promises made by politicians. The actions of those in power thus become more predictable. Then, the decisions of individuals can cover a longer time perspective. In the case of investment decisions, a strong sense of confidence in the stability and predictability of political power can generate investment growth, which in turn promotes economic growth.[184] There are studies that attempt to substantiate similar claims.[185]

The state can create such institutions that protect the functioning of the market and competition and define the relationship between economic actors. Efficient rules guarantee basic civil liberties and property rights, increase access to market information (reducing the cost of acquiring it), limit corruption, and strengthen the sense of confidence among individuals. Constitutions play a vital role in this regard, bringing together – through compromise – the interests of different social groups. Laszlo Bruszt refers to this type of system as "heterarchy." However, the

182 In 2005, only the United Kingdom, France and the Netherlands attracted more foreign direct investments, while in 2011 – Belgium, the United Kingdom and France (M. K. Stawicka, "Czynniki warunkujące wybór miejsca lokowania bezpośrednich inwestycji zagranicznych w Unii Europejskiej – studium komparatystyczne lat 2005 i 2011," *Zarządzanie i Finanse* 1, No. 2 (2013): 320, figure 1; 322, figure 2; 324, table 2; 326, table 4).

183 This section should be seen as complementary to the considerations made in this work on the relationship between property rights and economic growth in Germany between 1990 and 2015 (see section 6.2.9. in this study (detailed measures of economic growth there)).

184 Cf. J. Fałkowski, K. Metelska-Szaniawska, "Przyczyny ustanawiania i stabilność konstytucji państwa – perspektywa ekonomiczna," *Gospodarka Narodowa* 85/26, No. 3 (277) (2015): 94.

185 See, e.g.: Scully, *Constitutional Environments and Economic Growth*; A. Chhibber, "Institutions, Policies, and Development Outcomes," in *Evaluation & Development. The Institutional Dimension*, eds. R. Picciotto, E. Wiesner (New Brunswick–London: Transaction Publishers, 1998), pp. 34–46; S. Voigt, H.-J. Wagener, eds., *Constitutions, Markets and Law. Recent Experiences in Transition Economies* (Cheltenham–Northampton: Edward Elgar, 2002); T. Persson, G. Tabellini, *The Economic Effects of Constitutions* (Cambridge: The MIT Press, 2005); L. Blume, J. Müller, S. Voigt, C. Wolf, "The Economic Effects of Constitutions: Replicating – and Extending – Persson and Tabellini," *Public Choice* 139 (2009): 197–225.

poor quality of constitutions may contribute to the opposite of these effects. He divides basic laws into two groups. The first group concerns those acts that were created as a result of compromise debates that attempted to combine political and economic aspects. The second group includes those constitutions which place too much emphasis on political, systemic, or national issues, marginalizing economic rules or defining them too concisely, which in consequence encourages the emergence of interest groups, political rent-seeking,[186] corruption, low protection of citizens' economic rights and poor regulation of economic relations between individuals. Bruszt includes the constitutions of the USA and Germany in the first group, while the basic laws of the post-Soviet states and South-Eastern Europe in the second one.[187]

The economic growth that Germany experienced between 1990 and 2015 could have been conditioned, or at least supported, by rules derived from the Basic Law of the FRG *ceteris paribus*. As for empirical quantitative studies that would justify this view, it should be noted that most of them cover specific groups of countries. There is no clear-cut analysis of Germany alone in the period in question. Some attempts to draw conclusions about this country can be made only on the basis of aggregate economic analyses.

For example, there are studies showing that Anglo-Saxon countries belonging to the common law system were characterized by a faster economic growth than countries such as Germany, creating a system of continental law (civil law, public law, statutory law), referred to as private law. This was facilitated, among others, by greater protection of property and better developed financial markets in the first group of countries.[188] However, some studies show that in the 1990s, the German

186 On the phenomenon of rent-seeking, see Wilkin, "Pogoń za rentą," 204–219.

187 Cf. L. Bruszt, "Market-making as State-making. Constitutions and Economic Development in Postcommunist Eastern Europe," in Voigt, Wagener, *Constitutions, Markets and Law*, 129–157. He discusses in detail the process of institution building in post-communist countries. Bruszt's analysis should not be applied to the former GDR, as the new federated states adopted West German constitutional rules.

188 See, e.g., studies: Scully, *Constitutional Environments and Economic Growth*, 166–183; R. La Porta, F. Lopez-de-Silanes, A. Shleifer, R. W. Vishny, "Law and Finance," *Journal of Political Economy* 106 (1998): 1113–1155; R. La Porta, F. Lopez-de-Silanes, A. Shleifer, R. Vishny, "The Quality of Government," *Journal of Law, Economics, and Organization* 15, No. 1 (1999): 222–279; D. C. North, W. Summerhill, B. R. Weingast, "Order, Disorder, and Economic Change: Latin America versus North America," in *Governing for Prosperity*, eds. B. Dueno de Mequita, H. L. Root (New Haven–London: Yale University Press, 2000), 17–58; P. G. Mahoney, "The Common Law and Economic Growth: Hayek Might Be Right," *The Journal of Legal Studies* 30, No. 2 (2001): 503–525; D. S. Landes, *Bogactwo i nędza narodów. Dlaczego jedni się tak bogaci, a inni tak ubodzy* (Warszawa: Wydawnictwo Muza, 2000), especially Chaps. 19–20. Moreover, Gerald W. Scully argues that the common law system is more influential in expanding civil liberties (Scully, *Constitutional Environments and Economic Growth*, 148–165). Cf. research by Marie Möller who found that

legal system experienced economic growth results similar to those of the common law countries.[189] Moreover, it appears that in practical terms (e.g. in terms of doing business) the differences between the German system and the common law were actually imperceptible for individual entrepreneurs.[190]

Therefore, it is difficult to exclude the positive significance of the constitutional rules for German economic growth in 1990–2015. The stability of the political system was influenced by the durability of these rules.[191] The extension of the Basic Law to the annexed former GDR initiated the transition of the new federated states from plan to market. The West German constitutional rules outlined the original framework and directions for the process of unification, integration, and convergence of the two parts of the unified state. The eastern *Länder* were directly included in an efficient social market economy model. This was the fundamental difference in the development trajectory of the former GDR compared to the other economies of the former Eastern Bloc, which had to develop transition programs independently and from scratch. In this respect, the effects of the new federated states' transition should be assessed positively despite the high social costs.

The above conclusions are in line with part of the constitutional economics research, which shows that during the transition period, a basic law should primarily strengthen the state to implement appropriate economic policy coordinating the transition from plan to market by implementing correct economic reforms. In Germany, this was already evident in 1990 and thereafter. This required a strong concentration of power emanating from the Federation.[192]

4.8. Fiscal policy

A fundamental role in fiscal policy is played by its rules, also referred to as fiscal policy institutions (principles) or fiscal institutions (rules, principles). In a narrower sense, the term refers to permanent constraints on fiscal policy, while in a broader sense – to the type of budgetary institutions, which are the set of all rules under which the state budget is prepared, adopted, and implemented. Fiscal institutions

---

the quality of political institutions in 1996–2010 was not affected by the fact that a given country had a British colonial status in the past. Thus, countries liberated from Albion's domination did not have to implement British institutional solutions, including the common law system (M. Möller, "An Empirical Study of the Limits and Perspectives of Institutional Transfers" (working paper), Centrum für Interdisziplinäre Wirtschaftsforschung, No. 2 (2012), 1–26).

189 La Porta, Lopez-de-Silanes, Shleifer, Vishny, "The Quality of Government," 262.

190 C. Chance, "Legal Framework," in *Doing Business with Germany*, eds. R. Millar, J. Reuvid (London: Kogan Page, 1997), 311–312.

191 Cf. the analysis of indicators of formal institutions' quality in Germany between 1990 and 2015: section 4.5. in this work.

192 Cf. K. Metelska-Szaniawska, *Konstytucyjne czynniki reform gospodarczych w krajach postsocjalistycznych. Studium empiryczne* (Warszawa: Wydawnictwa UW, 2008), 168.

are most often related to stabilization policy (i.e., increasing budget expenditures in times of crisis and decreasing them in conditions of prosperity) and are characterized by greater complexity than monetary policy or exchange rate rules. These rules are most often exemplified by indicators reflecting the functioning of public finances.[193] The most common fiscal institutions understood in this way are summarized in Table 6.

Table 6: *Selected fiscal policy rules*

Scope of the rule	**Example constructions**
Budget balance	Balance between revenue and expenditures
Budget deficit	Acceptable level of the budget deficit (e.g., as a % of GDP or in total numbers)
Public debt	Acceptable level of the public finance sector's debt (as % of GDP)
Public debt brake	Balanced budget revenue and expenditures over the long term after accounting for business cycle fluctuations. Creating a compensating account to offset the negative impact of the economic downturn on the budget balance
Debt service expenses	Prohibition on exceeding a given income level by debt service expenditures
Borrowing by the government	Prohibit borrowing from domestic sources. Prohibition of financing of the budget deficit by the central bank or definition of an acceptable level in this regard. Loans taken out by the government for investment only

Source: Moszyński, "Wybrane reguły fiskalne," 115, table 1.

The rules listed above are among the most common ones. However, their construction, assumed variables, legal and institutional foundations, and implementation practice are different in individual countries. In the EU, as a result of the introduction of the Maastricht criteria of 1992, there has been an increase in the importance of the rules concerning the budget deficit and public debt in terms of their permissible level in relation to GDP (3 % and 60 % respectively).[194] The sources

193 M. Moszyński, "Wybrane reguły fiskalne w Szwajcarii i Republice Federalnej Niemiec – droga ku zrównoważonym finansom publicznym?," *Acta Universitatis Nicolai Copernici. Nauki Humanistyczno-Społeczne. Ekonomia* 40, No. 391 (2009): 114–115; Moszyński, Pysz, "Koncepcje polityki kształtowania ładu gospodarczego," 80.

194 The sustainability of public finances is one of the four convergence criteria of February 7, 1992, alongside price, exchange rate, and interest rate stability (Cf. "Consolidated Version of the Treaty on the Functioning of the European Union, Art. 126 (former Art. 104 of the Treaty establishing the European Community),"

of fiscal institutions can be threefold: (1) formal, finding its legal basis in the constitution or law; (2) informal, functioning on the basis of custom, declaration or decision of the government (e.g. the fiscal anchor); (3) international as a result of integration or agreements between individual countries (e.g. the mentioned convergence criteria, conditions for assistance formulated by the International Monetary Fund). The formal fiscal rules enshrined in the Constitution are considered the most durable from the point of view of their long-term validity. They are the most difficult to change. On the one hand, political teams interested in potentially changing these institutions would incur high costs. On the other hand, the government may justify its policy by the constitutionality of the rules. Embedding fiscal rules in the basic law strengthen their effectiveness, transparency, and credibility.[195]

Germany's fiscal policy institutions between 1990 and 2015 were defined in three complementary ways. These were: (1) the EU's rules (especially the convergence criteria); (2) constitutional rules; (3) other rules that responded to current challenges to public finances.[196]

The EU's rules are judged to be ineffective. In 1990–2015, Germany was among the EU countries that did not meet the Maastricht criteria several times. However, they

---

in *Consolidated Versions of the Treaty on European Union and the Treaty on the Functioning of the European Union* (Official Journal of the European Union, 26.10.2012, C 326, 99–102).; "Protocol (No 12) on the Excessive Deficit Procedure," in *Consolidated Versions* (Official Journal of the European Union, 26.10.2012, C 326, 279–280); "Protocol (No 13) on the Convergence Criteria," in *Consolidated Versions* (Official Journal of the European Union, 26.10.2012, C 326, 281–282)). These criteria were reiterated in the *Stability and Growth Pact* of June 17, 1997, and the *Treaty on Stability, Coordination and Governance in the Economic and Monetary Union* (the *Fiscal Compact*) of March 2, 2012.

195 Moszyński, "Wybrane reguły fiskalne," 115–116, 127; Moszyński, Pysz, "Koncepcje polityki kształtowania ładu gospodarczego," 80. On the importance of constitutional strictures on the fiscal system, see also Scully, *Constitutional Environments and Economic Growth*, 74–79.

196 No legal institutions directly addressed liability for violations of public finance discipline in Germany between 1990 and 2015. Rather, the legislation focused on the control and financial supervision of specific public entities. The Federal Court of Audit had only audit powers without being able to draw legal consequences resulting from abuses. The same was true of the courts of audit operating at the level of individual *Länder*. As a result, from the legal point of view, in the case of the FRG, one should not speak about the discipline of public finance or responsibility for its violation but about certain alternative solutions undertaken in order to spend public funds in an economical, effective and efficient way, to increase the quality of services provided by the public sector, and to promote reliability and diligence in managing public money (W. Bożek, "Odpowiedzialność za naruszenie dyscypliny finansów publicznych w Polsce na tle rozwiązań przyjętych we Francji, w Niemczech i Wielkiej Brytanii," in *Unia Europejska wobec wyzwań przyszłości. Aspekty prawne, finansowe i handlowe*, eds. E. Małuszyńska, G. Mazur, P. Idczak (Poznań: Wydawnictwo UE w Poznaniu, 2015), 146, 151–153). Germany also did not bear a similar responsibility for violating the Maastricht criteria in the

have not suffered any serious consequences for this, despite the fact that the EU law provides for the "excessive deficit procedure," which aims to influence the fiscal discipline of a country or even to punish it financially. Submission of Germany to this procedure in 2002–2007 and 2009–2012 was not, however, of major importance.[197]

The strongest and most solid anchoring of fiscal rules is found in the FRG Constitution. Germany was one of the few countries to dedicate a separate chapter of its Basic Law to finance (Chap. X GG). This has served the implementation of an important systemic objective – the fiscal state.[198] Some authors even indicate that the purpose of constitutional economics is to study the relevance of constitutional constraints on the fiscal, monetary and regulatory powers of the government.[199] This is not obvious, however, since, as Elster notes, constitutions of the late 20th century were unlikely to regulate issues such as the tax system or monetary institutions.[200] As can be seen, the problem of the object of study may come down to an understanding of the category of the constitution.

At the moment of reunification in 1990, the institutional order of public finance, binding so far only in West Germany, was extended to the new federated states. It had its source in the FRG Constitution and was subject to legal and system evolution, which was reflected in amendments to certain provisions of Chap. X GG, carried out in 1949–1990 and after reunification.[201] It should be stressed, however, that these changes did not constitute a turning point in the functioning of the system of public finance. They were aimed at better clarification of the existing rules and improvement of their efficiency and, consequently, of the whole sector. Therefore, it can be considered coherent. It has co-shaped a stable political system, which encouraged economic growth.[202] However, these considerations should be placed in the perspective of the dichotomy consisting of the distinction between *de jure* and *de facto* institutions. Indeed, it is legitimate to separate the constitutional framework of Germany's financial system from the country's economic reality between 1990 and 2015.[203]

The situation of Germany's public finances after reunification was dominated by the transition process of former East Germany and its integration with the Western *Länder*. A detailed summary of the budget deficit and public debt from 1991 to 2015 is presented in Table 7.

---

analyzed period (Moszyński, "Wybrane reguły fiskalne," 117–120; Moszyński, Pysz, "Koncepcje polityki kształtowania ładu gospodarczego," 80–82).

197 See more: Moszyński, "Wybrane reguły fiskalne," 117–120; M. Moszyński, "Ordoliberalism and the Macroeconomic Policy in the Face of the Euro Crisis," *Equilibrium. Quarterly Journal of Economics and Economic Policy* 10, No. 4 (2015): 52.

198 Tkaczyński, *Prawo ustrojowe Niemiec*, 195. See more section 4.4. in this study.

199 R. McKenzie, "Introduction," in *Constitutional Economics – Containing the Economic Powers of Government*, ed. R. McKenzie, (Lexington: Lexington Books, 1984), 1. Cited: Voigt, "Positive Constitutional Economics," 17.

200 Elster, "The Impact of Constitutions," 209.

201 See section 3.4. in this book.

202 See in more detail sections 4.6.–4.7. in this study.

203 Bębnowski, "Niemcy jako państwo fiskalne," 50–51.

Table 7: *Budget deficit and public debt in Germany in 1991–2015 (as % of GDP)*

Year	Budget deficit	Public debt
1991[a]	−4.0	39.1[b]
1992	−3.5	41.6
1993	−4.0	45.2
1994	−3.2	47.5
1995	−2.9	54.8
1996	−3.2	57.6
1997	−2.4	58.7
1998	−1.4	59.4
1999	−1.3	60.0
2000	−1.6	58.9
2001	−2.1	57.7
2002	−2.6	58.5
2003	−3.1	61.3
2004	−2.9	63.1
2005	−2.3	64.5
2006	−1.7	64.5
2007	0.0	62.1
2008	−0.4	61.6
2009	−3.7	68.9
2010	−3.1	81.0[c]
2011	−1.0	78.7
2012	−1.0	79.9
2013	−0.5	77.5
2014	0.1	74.9
2015	0.9	71.2

a Statistical sources cite data for reunified Germany starting in 1991.
b The amount of public debt for 1991–2001 is based on: *Verschuldung von Deutschland gemäß Maastricht-Vertrag in Prozent des BIP von 1991 bis 2016*, https://de.statista.com/statistik/daten/studie/154800/umfrage/deutsche-schuldenquote-seit-2003/ (accessed October 31, 2017).
c The Federal Ministry of Finance reported data for 2010 and thereafter according to a new system. A distinction was made between the share of total public debt in GDP (*Schulden der öffentlichen Haushalte, Öffentlicher Gesamthaushalt in Relation zum BIP in %*) from the Maastricht Treaty criteria (*Maastricht-Schuldenstand*). They differ due to the use of different methods (*Monatbericht des BMF. Dezember 2016*, (Berlin: Bundesministerium der Finanzen, 2016 (hereinafter: MB BMF)), 90, table 13b). For the years 2010–2015, the second group of data is cited.
Own compilation based on: *Monatbericht des BMF. Januar 2016* (Berlin: Bundesministerium der Finanzen, 2016), 93, table 13a; MB BMF, 90–91, tables 13b–14.

Table 7 clearly shows that the costs of German reunification from the point of view of public finances were very high. In the period in question, the FRG exceeded the Maastricht criterion for the size of the budget deficit as many as eight times (in 1991–1994, 1996, 2003 and 2009–2010), with 2009 being the worst year in this respect (−3.7 % of GDP, during the financial crisis). Recent years have brought an improvement in the situation.

The high public debt was a phenomenon parallel to the above. For 13 years (2003–2015), it exceeded the acceptable level of the convergence criterion (in 1999, the debt level remained at the limit of 60 % of GDP). After the debt peak in 2010 (81.0 % of GDP), coinciding with the financial crisis, the process of slow sanitation of public finances began. It is worth noting that against the background of the EU, Germany was not an exception in terms of non-compliance with the Maastricht criteria.[204]

The third level of fiscal policy institutions was complementary. The implementation of additional fiscal rules resulted from the need to reform the existing system on an ad hoc basis (although it was assumed to be long-term). A representative example is the second reform of federalism of 2009.[205] It proclaimed, among other things, the public debt brake rule (*Schuldenbremse*), modeled on the Swiss solutions and added to the Basic Law. The supplementary institution thus took on the character of a constitutional rule. It took effect in the 2011 fiscal year.[206] The basic principles of the new fiscal institution are presented in Table 8.

---

204 Bębnowski, "Niemcy jako państwo fiskalne," 52 (especially the literature in fn. 80). Cf. also: P. Kirchhof, "Staatsverschuldung im föderalen System der Bundesrepublik Deutschland," in *Handbuch Föderalismus – Föderalismus als demokratische Rechtsordnung und Rechtskultur in Deutschland, Europa und der Welt*, Vol. II: *Probleme, Reformen, Perspektiven des deutschen Föderalismus*, ed. I. Härtel (Berlin–Heidelberg: Springer-Verlag, 2012), 323–338; K. Marchewka-Bartkowiak, M. Wiśniewski, "Rola salda pierwotnego w stabilizowaniu długu publicznego w krajach członkowskich strefy euro w latach 1999–2013," in *Unia Europejska wobec wyzwań przyszłości*, 159–170.

205 More on the second reform of federalism section 3.5. in this work.

206 Moszyński, "Wybrane reguły fiskalne," 123–127; Moszyński, Pysz, "Koncepcje polityki kształtowania ładu gospodarczego," 80–82.

Table 8: *Main principles of the public debt brake in Germany effective since 2011*[a]

Subject of the principle	Description of the principle
Federal budget	Since 2016, under normal economic conditions, federal budget spending covered by new borrowing may not exceed 0.35 % of GDP
Länder's budgets	Since 2020, the *Länder* may not run a structural deficit. For the years 2011–2019, 800 million euros per year have been earmarked for consolidation aid for the *Länder* with the most difficult budgetary situation (Berlin, Bremen, Saarland, Saxony-Anhalt, Schleswig-Holstein)
Cyclical component	In weak economic conditions, the cyclical component may include budget deficits. However, in good times, budget surpluses are expected to occur in order to bring the business cycle into balance
Special control account	The special control (equalization) account is a corrective mechanism. Its size is 1.5 % of GDP. It accounts for deviations of actual expenditures from planned ones. These should be compensated by expenditures developments in subsequent years in order to consolidate the budget
Exceptional situations	In exceptional circumstances (e.g. natural disasters), special regulations require the consent of the Bundestag by a simple majority
Stabilization Council	A special body composed of the ministers of finance (federal and *Länder*'s) and the federal minister for economic affairs. The Council oversees the state of public finances

a The institution of a public debt brake in Germany was introduced as part of the second reform of federalism in 2009. It took effect from 2011.
Own compilation based on: Moszyński, "Wybrane reguły fiskalne," 124–125; Moszyński, Pysz, "Koncepcje polityki kształtowania ładu gospodarczego," 81.

These principles were introduced during the financial crisis, which speaks well for the German federal authorities trying to stabilize public finances. The constitutional legitimacy of the rules deserves additional emphasis. Under Germany's influence, the provisions of the 2012 *Fiscal Compact* for all EU member states were negotiated in a similar direction. The public debt brake in Germany is regarded as an attempt to find a middle mechanism between fiscal discipline and fiscal policy flexibility. Some researchers also see the following references to the ordoliberal concept of the economic order in this field: (1) self-restraint of the state, which creates rules and enforces them; (2) an attempt to balance public finances; (3) constancy of rules and economic policy to ensure stabilization of market actors' expectations; (4) strengthening of the ethical and moral dimension of the economy (universality of rules for both the state and citizens); (5) striving for a balance between the public and private sectors; (6) limiting the influence of lobbies advocating an increase in certain groups of expenditures.[207]

The positive effects of the public debt brake were evident in the first years of the new rule. Table 7 shows that between 2011 and 2015, the budget deficit decreased from −1.0 % to 0.9 % of GDP. A slight budget surplus was even generated in 2014 and 2015 (0.1 % and 0.9 % of GDP, respectively). Public debt was also steadily reduced: from 78.7 % of GDP in 2011 (an exceptional increase to 79.9 % of GDP in 2012) to 71.2 % of GDP in 2015. However, the ratio was still above the norm, representing one of the Maastricht criteria.

4.9. Summary of Chapters 3 and 4

The FRG Constitution's role in the integration of two different economic systems after German reunification was fundamental. The constitutional rules were primary in relation to the processes of transition of the Eastern *Länder* and the unification, integration, and convergence of the two parts of the state.

The Basic Law of the FRG rebuilt the political and legal system in Eastern Germany, which had been developing under the conditions of the communist regime, whose legitimacy had been rooted in the GDR Constitutions. Since 1990, regulations specifying the functioning of particular aspects of socio-economic life began to lay the foundations of a new economic system. Although it was a model of a social market economy, it should be stressed that the Basic Law was neutral towards the final economic order, guaranteeing only a catalog of basic rules defining it. Thus, the FRG Constitution outlined the framework for a new economic order in the Eastern *Länder*, identical to the West German order. This order defined the legal and institutional framework for the economic process.

In the dimension of *de jure* institutions, additional potential channels of linkage arose from the basic rights, systemic principles of the state, and systemic objectives of an economic nature. These factors reinforced the stability of the German political system during the period in question. The Basic Law was also characterized by durability, which was strengthened by its detailed nature (sometimes going too far) and relative concreteness and unambiguity in 1990–2015. The amendments to the Constitution, especially the first and second reforms of federalism, were intended to increase the system's effectiveness. Economic growth and the extension of the Basic Law's provisions to fiscal policy exemplified the functioning of *de facto* institutions. In order to maintain budgetary discipline, which had been undermined by the widening budget deficit and public debt in the 1990s as a result of the Eastern *Länder*'s transition, the second reform of federalism was adopted in 2009 (at the time of the financial crisis) and was of crucial importance. Its positive effects were already visible in subsequent years.

207 Moszyński, "Wybrane reguły fiskalne," 127; Moszyński, Pysz, "Koncepcje polityki kształtowania ładu gospodarczego," 81–83.

CHAPTER 5 The institution of property rights: Property regulations in the GDR and implementation of West German solutions

5.1. Property rights as a formal institution

In Douglass C. North's classification, property rights are indicated as an example of a formal institution.[1] The "institution of property"[2] or the "institution of private property" (*Institution des Privateigentums*)[3] are less frequently mentioned in the literature. The category of property sometimes occupies a central place in the consideration of socio-economic processes.[4] North admits that he once took property

---

1 See, e.g. D. C. North, "Institutions," *Journal of Economic Perspectives* 5, No. 1 (1991): 97.

2 M. Gottlieb, *A Theory of Economic Systems* (Orlando: Academic Press, Inc., 1984), 340–376. The author treats this institution as one of the factors that characterize economic systems.

3 H. Leipold, "Eigentum und wirtschaftliches Handeln in beiden deutschen Staaten," in *Materialien zum Bericht zur Lage der Nation im geteilten Deutschland 1987* (Bonn: Bundesministerium für innerdeutsche Beziehungen, 1987), 40; J. Schumann, "Wirtschaftliche Anreizwirkungen der Eigentumsordnung," in *Die Bedeutung der Eigentumsordnung für das Funktionieren einer Volkswirtschaft*, ed. J. Schumann (Bad Honnef: Bock und Herchen Verlag, 1991), 17.

4 From the more important synthetic works on the category of property in socio-economic and political-legal thought see: R. Schlatter, *Private Property. The History of an Idea* (New Brunswick–New Jersey: Rytgers University Press, 1951); D. Th. Heckel, ed., *Eigentum und Eigentumsverteilung als theologisches, rechtsphilosophisches und ökonomisches Problem. Vorträge gehalten auf der Tagung evangelischer Juristen 1961* (München: Evangelischer Presseverband für Bayern, 1962); F. Klüber, *Eigentumstheorie und Eigentumspolitik. Begründung und Gestaltung des Privateigentums nach katholisher Gesellschaftslehre* (Osnabrück: Verlag A. Fromm, 1963); F. Negro, *Das Eigentum. Geschichte und Zukunft. Versuch eines Überblicks* (München–Berlin: C. H. Beck, 1963); S. Kozyr-Kowalski, ed., *Własność: gospodarka a prawo. Studia o marksistowskiej teorii własności* (Warszawa: PWN, 1977); Cz. Strzeszewski, *Własność: zagadnienie społeczno-moralne* (Warszawa: Ośrodek Dokumentacji i Studiów Społecznych, 1981); A. Ryan, *Property* (Milton Keynes: Open University Press, 1987); J. F. Baur, ed., *Das Eigentum. Vorträge gehalten auf der Tagung der Joachim Jungius-Gesellschaft der Wissenschaften. Hamburg am 10., 11. und 12. Dezember 1987* (Göttingen: Vandenhoeck & Ruprecht, 1989); Schumann, "Wirtschaftliche Anreizwirkungen der Eigentumsordnung," 1–20; D. P. Ellerman,

rights and their evolution as the starting point of his institutional analysis of economic processes as if they were the explanation of everything. However, this is not the case, so the importance of other elements must be taken into account.[5]

Property and Contract in Economics. The Case for Economic Democracy (Oxford–Cambridge: Blackwell, 1992); J. M. Buchanan, *Property as a Guarantor of Liberty* (Cambridge: Edward Elgar, 1993); S. Kozyr-Kowalski, A. Przestalski, J. Tittenbrun, *Ownership and Society* (Poznań: Wydawnictwo Nakom, 1993); W. Kwaśnicki, *Historia myśli liberalnej. Wolność. Własność. Odpowiedzialność* (Warszawa: PWE, 2000), 244–286; R. Pipes, *Własność a wolność* (Warszawa: Warszawskie Wydawnictwo Literackie Muza S.A., 2000); H. Höfer, "Eigentum," in *Lexikon Soziale Marktwirtschaft. Wirtschaftspolitik von A bis Z*, eds. R. H. Hasse, H. Schneider, K. Weigelt (Paderborn: Ferdinand Schöningh, 2002), 156–159; M. Kuniński, "Własność i wolność," in *Kapitalizm po polsku. Państwo – prawo – gospodarka*, ed. M. Szułdrzyński (Kraków: Ośrodek Myśli Politycznej, 2003), 15–33; B. Szlachta, "O problemie wolności (dwie uwagi prawnika badającego historię myśli politycznej)," in Szułdrzyński, *Kapitalizm po polsku*, 35–46; G. D. Libecap, "Property Rights," in *The Oxford Encyclopedia of Economic History*, ed. J. Mokyr, Vol. 4: *Monte di Pietà – Spain* (Oxford: Oxford University Press, 2003), 268–274; L. Brace, *The Politics of Property. Labour, Freedom and Belonging* (New York–Basingstoke: Palgrave Macmillan, 2004); U. Zagóra-Jonszta, "Własność w ujęciu wybranych kierunków myśli ekonomicznej," *Ekonomia i Prawo* 3, No. 1 (2007): 39–59; U. Zagóra-Jonszta, "Ekonomia klasyczna wobec kategorii własności," *Studia Ekonomiczne* No. 54 (2008): 23–38; M. Lisak, "Pojęcie własności w ujęciu chrześcijaństwa i innych religii," in *Własność to odpowiedzialność – wiedza, praktyka, doświadczenie*, ed. B. Rogatko (Warszawa–Kraków: Europejski Instytut Nieruchomości, 2009), 17–30; A. Workowski, "Etyczne i moralne aspekty posiadania – w oparciu o różne tradycje filozoficzne," in Rogatko, *Własność to odpowiedzialność*, 31–47; J. Kolibski, "Własność jako podstawa efektywności gospodarczej i stosunków społecznych," in Rogatko, *Własność to odpowiedzialność*, 83–101; *Wrocławskie Studia Erazmiańskie/ Studia Erasmiana Wratislaviensia* 3 (2009): *Własność – idea, instytucje, ochrona*, eds. M. Sadowski, P. Szymaniec; D. Juruś, "Wstęp," in *Dzieje własności prywatnej. Od starożytności do współczesności*, ed. D. Juruś (Warszawa: Fijorr Publishing, 2014), 7–23; A. Suwalski, *Własność i jej przekształcenie* (Konin: PWSZ, 2014), 123–164; U. Zagóra-Jonszta, ed., *Kategoria własności w ujęciu wybranych kierunków myśli ekonomicznej* (Warszawa: Wydawnictwo WNT, 2015); W. Piątkowski, "Problem formy własności środków produkcji w ekonomii klasycznej i w myśli Karola Marksa," in W. Piątkowski, *Wokół idei ekonomicznych* (Łódź: author's own publishing, 2017), 7–20. A synthetic review of the more important German-language works on the category of property is made by Karol Dobrzeniecki and Marcin Romanowski (K. Dobrzeniecki, M. Romanowski, *Reprywatyzacja. Problemy tworzenia i stosowania prawa* (Warszawa: Wydawnictwo UKSW, 2015), 42, fn. 1).

5 Cf. D. C. North, "Pojmowanie zmian ekonomicznych i wzrostu gospodarczego," in *Globalizacja, marginalizacja, rozwój*, ed. G. Kołodko (Warszawa: Wydawnictwo WSPiZ im. Leona Koźmińskiego, 2003), 140.

The key role of property and its legal regulations in socio-economic transformations underpinned the emergence of a separate property rights theory (property rights economics) in the new institutional economics. Its conceptualization took place mainly in the 1960s. Academic literature on property rights theory is very rich. It includes both theoretical and methodological, as well as empirical studies. The main representatives of this approach – considered as late as in the 1980s and 1990s as a "new property rights approach"[6] – include: Howard Scott Gordon, Ronald H. Coase, Armen Alchian, Harold Demsetz, Steven Cheung, Louis de Alessi, Svetozar (Steve) Pejovich or Eirik G. Furubotn.[7]

In the discussed theory, the property is understood as a bundle of rights (*Rechtsbündel*) of the owner concerning a particular material or non-material good. It is not a sum, set, or aggregate of factors but just a bundle of relations differing in features and consequences and a specified whole, the essential element of which is the principle of exclusivity. Property presented in this way is a system of exclusions from access to material and non-material resources. Moreover, it is sanctioned by legal or social norms. Property rights understood in this way, however, do not refer to the relationship of the individual to things but to the relationship between individuals. They are therefore determined in relation to other people. Therefore,

---

6 F. L. Pryor, *A Guidebook to the Comparative Study of Economic Systems* (Englewood Cliffs: Prentice-Hall, Inc., 1985), 297, pt. A.2.; T. Eggertsson, *Economic Behavior and Institutions* (Cambridge: Cambridge University Press, 1995), 34, fn. 2.

7 As examples of the works of the mentioned representatives of the theory of property rights it is necessary to indicate: H. S. Gordon, "The Economics of Common Property Rights: The Fishery," *Journal of Political Economy* 62, No. 2 (1954): 124–142; R. Coase, "The Problem of Social Costs," *The Journal of Law and Economics* 3 (1960): 1–44; A. Alchian, *Some Economics of Property* (Santa Monica: Rand Corporation, 1961); H. Demsetz, "The Exchange and Enforcement of Property Rights," *The Journal of Law and Economics* 7 (1964): 11–26; S. N. S. Cheung, "Private Property Rights and Sharecropping," *Journal of Political Economy* 76, No. 6 (1968): 1107–1122; L. de Alessi, "Implications of Property Rights for Government Investment Choices," *American Economic Review* 59, No. 1 (1969): 13–24; L. de Alessi, "The Economics of Property Rights: A Review of Evidence," *Research in Law and Economics* 2 (1980): 1–47; L. de Alessi, "Development of the Property Right Approach," *Journal of Institutional and Theoretical Economics* 146 (1990): 6–11; S. Pejovich, "Toward a General Theory of Property Rights," *Zeitschrift für Nationalökonomie* 31, No. 1–2 (1971): 141–155; S. Pejovich, *The Economics of Property Rights: Towards a Theory of Comparative Systems* (Dordrecht: Kluwer Academic Publishers, 1990); E.G. Furubotn, S. Pejovich, "Property Rights and Economic Theory: A Survey of Recent Literature," *Journal of Economic Literature* 10, No. 4 (1972): 1137–1162; *The Economics of Property Rights*, eds. E.G. Furubotn, S. Pejovich (Cambridge: Ballinger Publishing Company, 1974). See also: Schumann, *Die Bedeutung der Eigentumsordnung*. According to Pejovich, the first researcher who presented a coherent theory of property rights was Karl Marx (S. Pejovich, "Karl Marx, Property Rigths School and the Process of Social Change," *Kyklos* 35, No. 3 (1982): 383–397).

according to the property rights theory, what is exchanged are bundles of property rights (or their components) to given goods and not the goods themselves. In this context, then, one speaks of the supply of such rights and the demand for them.[8]

Wacław Stankiewicz points out that the legal perspective dominates over the economic one in the property rights theory, which is evident in the definition of property, property rights, and its types. Moreover, the understanding of the category in question results from the Anglo-Saxon legal tradition.[9] The interest in property rights theory in German research has grown through American literature since the late 1970s and early 1980s. The concept gradually displaced concepts such as *Eigentumsrechte*, *Verfügungsrechte*, or *Handlungsrechte*.[10] In response, some West German scholars separated the understanding of property found in German law (especially in the Constitution of the FRG and the *Civil Code*) from the broader economic view proposed by the property rights theory.[11]

Jerzy Wilkin distinguishes between "property laws" (Pol. *prawa własności*) and "property rights" (Pol. *uprawnienia własnościowe*). While the former denote legal norms of property, the latter are connected with the right to use the object of property, which is regulated both by law and social norms. However, in the literature (e.g. in Poland), these terms are sometimes treated as synonyms.[12] Katarzyna Metelska-Szaniawska and Jarosław Bełdowski, on the other hand, point out that, e.g., Polish law is closer to the term "property right," which has its source in the uniform concept of property right. From an economic point of view, it is more accurate to talk about "property rights." These are the rights that make up the

---

8 See, e.g.: H.-B. Schäfer, C. Ott, *Lehrbuch der ökonomischen Analyse des Zivilrechts* (Berlin–Heidelberg: Springer, 2005), 97–99; W. Kasper, M. E. Streit, P. J. Boettke, *Institutional Economics. Property, Competition, Policies* (Cheltenham–Northampton: Edward Elgar, 2012), 187–190; W. Stankiewicz, *Ekonomika instytucjonalna. Zarys wykładu* (Warszawa: Wydawnictwo AON, 2014), 73–74, 77; J. Wilkin, *Instytucjonalne i kulturowe podstawy gospodarowania. Humanistyczna perspektywa ekonomii* (Warszawa: WN Scholar, 2016), 163–164, 167, 171; M. L. Stearns, T. J. Zywicki, T. J. Miceli, *Law and Economics: Private and Public* (St. Paul: West Academic Publishing, 2018), 222–225.

9 Stankiewicz, *Ekonomika instytucjonalna. Zarys wykładu*, 69, 73.

10 See, e.g.: A. Schüller, ed., *Property Rights und ökonomische Theorie* (München: Verlag Franz Vahlen, 1983); M. Neumann, ed., *Ansprüche, Eigentums- und Verfügungsrechte* (Berlin: Duncker & Humblot, 1984); K. Heuchert, "Das Eigentum in der Theorie der Property Rights," in Baur, *Das Eigentum*, 132; H. Dietl, *Institutionen und Zeit* (Tübingen: J. C. B. Mohr (Paul Siebeck), 1993), 57. The works cited are based on an impressive literature.

11 See, e.g.: Heuchert, "Das Eigentum," 125–141; Schumann, "Wirtschaftliche Anreizwirkungen der Eigentumsordnung," 2. See German handbook on the economic analysis of civil law with significant references to property rights in Germany: Schäfer, Ott, *Lehrbuch der ökonomischen Analyse des Zivilrechts, passim.* The authors equate the categories of property rights and *Handlungsrechte.*

12 Wilkin, *Instytucjonalne i kulturowe podstawy gospodarowania*, 145–146, fn. 6; 164.

property. The term "property law" refers to a separate field of law.[13] In this book, when writing about the property rights theory, one relies on the term "property rights." Extending the perspective to institutional economics, the terms "property rights institution" and "property rules" are used synonymously.

Property rights are applied to both material and non-material objects. The material dimension of property rights is the most elementary. In the latter case, one speaks of intellectual property rights, human rights, social relations, and norms, or human and social capital. There are also extreme positions according to which all rights can be property rights.[14]

Property rights form a certain whole, structure, most often referred to as the property rights system. Ernesto Screpanti writes about the "property rights regime," by which he means a system of normative, transactional, and behavioral institutions regulating wealth distribution and additional value. This regime determines who among the social actors is entitled to acquire property rights and who regulates their transfer. The norms in this regime indicate how to distribute residual gains and individual wealth. These norms derive from both law and informal institutions.[15]

The literature identifies various features of a desirable, effective property rights system, which relates to their analysis dimensions. The starting point for legal and economic perspectives are three basic aspects of property: (1) the right to use resources (Latin *usus*); (2) the right to returns on assets (Latin *usus fructus*); (3) the right to change the form, substance, or location of resources (Latin *abusus*).[16]

Some economists distinguish: (1) excludability, (2) divisibility, and (3) transferability.[17] Thráinn Eggertsson lists three categories of property rights that can be related to the mentioned dimensions. User rights concerning the use of property are related to exclusivity. The right to transfer rights to property (e.g., for sale) connects to the transferability dimension. Eggertsson indicates the right to derive income from property as a separate category (dimension) of property rights.[18] Along with exclusivity and transferability, Pejovich writes about a third dimension of the degree of completeness of property rights, which is the "constitutional guarantee of ownership." However, he does not limit it to the basic law but understands it broadly as the influence of political power on property.[19] Richard A. Posner, also

---

13 K. Metelska-Szaniawska, J. Bełdowski, "Nota redaktorska," in R. Cooter, T. Ulen, *Ekonomiczna analiza prawa* (Warszawa: Wydawnictwo C. H. Beck, 2011), XIV.

14 Cf. E. G. Furubotn, R. Richter, *Institutions and Economic Theory. The Contribution of the New Institutional Economics* (Ann Arbor: The University of Michigan Press, 2008), 86–96.

15 E. Screpanti, *The Fundamental Institutions of Capitalism* (London–New York: Routledge, 2001), 260.

16 Libecap, "Property Rights," 269.

17 Kasper, Streit, Boettke, *Institutional Economics*, 192–195, 205–207.

18 Eggertsson, *Economic Behavior and Institutions*, 34–35.

19 Cf. Pejovich, *The Economics of Property Rights*, 29. Institutional economics also distinguishes the "constitutional order" of organizational management as an

distinguishing exclusiveness and transferability of property rights, pays attention to their universality. He refers to the abstract situation of commonness of property and its individual use in such a way that each consumes his property freely, but without restricting the consumption of the other.[20] The degree of completeness of property rights and their enforcement and protection coincides with the main problems of property law. Robert Cooter and Thomas Ulen highlight the following aspects: (1) the manner in which property rights are established; (2) the subject matter of private property; (3) the ways in which owners dispose of their property; (4) the remedies when property rights are violated.[21] The economic analysis of German civil law mentions exclusivity and dilution (*Exklusivität und Verdünnung*), transferability (*Transferfähigkeit*) and protection (*Schutz*) of property rights.[22] Zbigniew Staniek refers to transferability mainly to the process of privatization, i.e. transfer of property rights between the state and companies, although he also emphasizes the importance of transfers between companies. The author identifies the protection of property rights with exclusiveness, writing that the latter *means exclusion of other entities from using the object of property.*[23]

Some authors propose more elaborate classifications. For example, Matthes Buhbe lists: (1) assignability, completeness (*Zuordnungsfähigkeit, Vollständigkeit*); (2) specificity, inclusiveness, integration (*Spezifizierbarkeit, Inklusivität*); (3) separability, exclusiveness (*Separierbarkeit, Exklusivität*); (4) controllability, monitoring, supervision (*Kontrollierbarkeit, Überwachung*); (5) sanctionability, enforcement (*Sanktionierbarkeit, Durchsetzung*); (6) disposability in terms of change of form and location (*Disponierbarkeit, Form- und Ortswechsel*); (7) transferability in terms of exchange between individuals (*Transferierbarkeit, personeller Wechsel*).[24]

---

alternative to hierarchical (vertical) and market (horizontal, democratic, dispersed) order. This, however, does not refer to the constitution understood as a basic law but to the rules determining the framework of the organization's functioning. See more: Ch. F. Sabel, "Constitutional Orders: Trust Building and Response to Change," in *Contemporary Capitalism. The Embeddedness of Institutions*, eds. J. R. Hollingsworth, R. Boyer (Cambridge: Cambridge University Press, 1998), 154–188.

20 Cf. R. A. Posner, *The Economic Analysis of Law* (Boston–Toronto: Little, Brown, 1972), 29; Furubotn, Richter, *Institutions and Economic Theory*, 84.

21 Cooter, Ulen, *Ekonomiczna analiza prawa*, 90.

22 Schäfer, Ott, *Lehrbuch der ökonomischen Analyse des Zivilrechts*, 99, 551–552.

23 Pol. [*O*]*znacza wyłączenie innych podmiotów z wykorzystywania przedmiotu własności* (Z. Staniek, *Ekonomia instytucjonalna. Dlaczego instytucje są ważne* (Warszawa: Wydawnictwo Difin, 2017), 117, 142).

24 M. Buhbe, *Ökonomische Analyse von Eigentumsrechten. Der Beitrag der Economics of Property Rights zur Theorie der Institutionen* (Frankfurt am Main: Peter D. Lang, 1980), 72–73. Elsewhere, in relation to private property, Buhbe writes about its three dimensions: universality (*Universalität*), accessibility (*Disponibilität*), and the aforementioned exclusivity (Buhbe, *Ökonomische Analyse von Eigentumsrechten*, 20).

Systematizing the above issues, it should be said that both the category of property and property rights belong to the central concepts in economics, especially the new institutional economics. The formalization of property rights is an example of the institutionalization of property relations. In discussed theory, these rights refer to the rights of concrete individuals who take actions concerning property regardless of their formal titles. They are guided by the aim of maximizing utility, which results from the fact that this theory is based on methodological individualism. The efficiency of the use of a given resource is determined by the individual's motivation, which depends on the degree of completeness of property rights. It constitutes the first dimension of the analysis of property rights and is defined in two fundamental aspects: exclusivity (*Exklusivität*) and transferability (*Transferfähigkeit*). Exclusivity is connected with the owner's sovereignty in the disposal of property rights in relation to the rights of others. Transferability, on the other hand, refers to the owner's freedom to transfer rights (in whole or in part) to other entities. Property rights must be simultaneously enforced and protected, which makes up the second dimension of their analysis. This is done through: (1) the state involvement based on law and coercive apparatus; (2) actions of owners themselves; (3) social norms. The degree of completeness of property rights and their enforcement and protection is reflected in socio-economic development. The more complete, better defined (i.e., assigned to specific individuals), enforced, and protected property rights are, the more efficient resource management is.[25] The two dimensions listed above provide a theoretical construct for the empirical analysis in the later parts of this book.[26] It is a fairly universal model.

At the same time, it should be noted that from the perspective of property rights theory, the sovereignty of the owner cannot be unlimited. In this context, one talks about natural limitations of property rights resulting from legal regulations or – following Oliver Hart and John Moore – "residual control rights over assets," which have not been reserved by contract.[27] One can also identify such restrictions that undermine the completeness of property rights by poor definition, insufficient enforcement, insufficient protection, or negative state influence.[28] Thus, as Wilkin notes, property rights are more effectively enforced and protected, the greater the

25 Wilkin, *Instytucjonalne i kulturowe podstawy gospodarowania*, 163–170, fn. 11. Cf. Schäfer, Ott, *Lehrbuch der ökonomischen Analyse des Zivilrechts*, 99, 552.

26 Karsten Heuchert writes about the validity of such an approach (K. Heuchert, "Das Eigentum in der Theorie der Property Rights," in Baur, *Das Eigentum*, 125–141).

27 Cf. O. Hart, J. Moore, "Property Rights and the Nature of the Firm," *Journal of Political Economy* 98, No. 6 (1990): 1120–1121, fn. 3. Researchers have taken this category from the work of Sanford J. Grossman and Oliver Hart (S. J. Grossman, O. D. Hart, "The Costs and Benefits of Ownership: A Theory of Vertical and Lateral Integration," *Journal of Political Economy* 94 (1986): 691–719).

28 Wilkin, *Instytucjonalne i kulturowe podstawy gospodarowania*, 168, 170.

congruence between the above factors: the law, the actions of citizens, and social norms.[29]

The property rights theory distinguishes three basic property systems: private, common, and state (public) property. The first of them is seen as wholly defined and complete rights, both in the dimension of exclusivity and transferability. In the light of the presented theory, it is the best property system because it motivates the individual to the greatest extent to act effectively. From this point of view, any state interference is detrimental to economic development. However, private property is a means and not an end in itself.[30] The latter system, common property, is undefined, non-exclusive and non-transferable, and therefore unorganized. This makes common property, to which every member of a group has access, but without assured exclusivity and transferability, ultimately inefficient.[31] Finally, the third system, the state (public) property, falls between private and common property. It is characterized by a relative organization (depending on the degree of exclusivity) and lack of transferability. Although the actual manager of public property is the government, which generates problems such as lobbying, corruption, and bureaucracy, from the perspective of property rights theory, its ultimate owner is the citizens (voters). However, their powers are limited. Because of this, the property rights theory assumes that state property is inefficient. As an example, the advantage of private enterprises over state-owned enterprises is often pointed out.[32] On

29 Wilkin, *Instytucjonalne i kulturowe podstawy gospodarowania*, 170, fn. 11.

30 Ch. Vogell, "Privateigentum, Manager und Property Rights," in Schumann, *Die Bedeutung der Eigentumsordnung*, 44.

31 The tragedy of the commons, coined in 1968 by Garret Hardin, an American ecologist, corresponds with the ineffectiveness of common property. It assumes the lack of responsibility for the damage done to the community (G. Hardin, "The Tragedy of the Commons," *Science* 162, No. 3859 (1968): 1243–1248). A little earlier, in 1965, Mancur Olson argued that members of a large group do not act to benefit the group without personal motivation (M. Olson, *The Logic of Collective Action. Public Goods and the Theory of Groups* (Cambridge: Harvard University Press, 1965)). These approaches are questioned by Elinor Ostrom in her research on the effective management of common goods (E. Ostrom, *Governing the Commons. The Evolution of Institutions for Collective Action* (Cambridge: Cambridge University Press, 1990)).

32 On the subject of inefficient management of public enterprises write, e.g., Saul Estrin and Virginie Pérotin (S. Estrin, V. Pérotin, "Does Ownership Always Matter?," *International Journal of Industrial Organization* 9, No. 1 (1991): 55–72). There are also studies devoted to the effective management of the state property. See, e.g.: D. W. Caves, L. R. Christiansen, "The Relative Efficiency of Public and Private Firms in a Competitive Environment: The Case of Canadian Railroads," *Journal of Political Economy* 88, No. 5 (1980): 958–976; M. Iwanek, *Analiza instytucji własności przedsiębiorstw. Przyczynek do problematyki efektywności i usprawnienia przedsiębiorstw publicznych* (Warszawa: WN PWN, 1996). Feliks Gross discusses two examples of socialized economy efficiency. Firstly, he characterizes the American project of the "Tennessee Valley Authority" (TVA) of the 1930s, a federal government

the one hand, the legitimacy of privatization processes is raised,[33] on the other hand – the implementation of effective management of both public and common property is postulated.[34]

The literature provides alternative classifications (systems, regimes) of property. As an example, open access, which means no right to exclude anyone from using a given resource, is sometimes distinguished as a separate sphere, as opposed to common property, which includes a defined group. The group can exclude anyone outside the group from using the resource.[35] However, there are those who treat open access as a type of common property ("open-access common pool resources"), e.g. access to water bodies, the atmosphere, space. It occurs next to the proper common property ("closed-access common pool resources"), related to a particular group.[36] Eggertsson lists four basic types of property: "private ownership," "state ownership," "communal ownership," and "common ownership." He identifies the last one with open access. Eggertsson emphasizes that the coexistence of various types of ownership is a characteristic feature of economies.[37] Screpanti writes

---

agency working with regional institutions and residents to coordinate the electrification of the Tennessee River Valley, promote the development of local agriculture and industry, combat mass unemployment, and initiate private and local government projects. Secondly, Gross positively evaluates the policy of the Labour Party government in Great Britain in 1945–1951, which nationalized key industries and carried out a number of social reforms (F. Gross, *Druga rewolucja przemysłowa. Zagadnienia współczesnego socjalizmu* (Paryż: Wydawnictwo Światło, 1958), 135–136, 138–141). However, it turns out that Gross's second example is not fully objective. He did not present a detailed balance sheet of the Labour governments, which collapsed as a result of, among others, economic problems. Moreover, Gross wrote his work from the position of humanistic socialism (social democratic thought). See more: F. Gross, *Socjalizm humanistyczny* (New York: Związek Socjalistów Polskich w Stanach Zjednoczonych, 1946); H. Sherman, *Radical Political Economy. Capitalism and Socialism from a Marxist-Humanist Perspective* (New York–London: Basic Books, Inc., Publishers, 1972).

33 More on the role of privatization processes in the light of the property rights theory: Staniek, *Ekonomia instytucjonalna*, 117–142.

34 Wilkin, *Instytucjonalne i kulturowe podstawy gospodarowania*, 171–174; Stankiewicz, *Ekonomika instytucjonalna. Zarys wykładu*, 79–80. These issues are partly within the scope of managerial economics. More on the three property systems (common, private, and public) in the context of the property rights theory: Stankiewicz, *Ekonomika instytucjonalna. Zarys wykładu*, 69–81. The author also discusses the issues of free access to resources, as well as group (communal) and intellectual property.

35 Stankiewicz, *Ekonomika instytucjonalna. Zarys wykładu*, 73; K. Bentkowska, *Ekonomia instytucjonalna. Zarys teorii i jej wymiar praktyczny* (Warszawa: Oficyna Wydawnicza SGH, 2020), 141.

36 Cf. E. G. Furubotn, R. Richter, *Institutions and Economic Theory*, 110.

37 Eggertsson, *Economic Behavior and Institutions*, 36–37.

about: "concentrated private property," "diffused private property," and "state property." In the case of the first one, wealth is concentrated in the hands of a privileged social group. Diffused private property refers to contemporary developed capitalist economies and is characterized by greater or lesser social diversification in access to resources. The state property, on the other hand, is formally owned by all citizens of a country and managed by the government.[38]

It is impossible to ignore the relationship of the property rights theory to other theories on the ground of the new institutional economics: agency, contract, and especially transaction costs.[39] The last category primarily includes the costs of defining, enforcing, and protecting property rights and their transfer. They affect the nature of these rights. Generally, the higher the transaction costs, the lower the degree of completeness of property rights. An increase in these costs also reduces the likelihood that property rights will be acquired by those who will use them efficiently. In addition, this theory assumes that the low value of a resource relative to its transaction costs affects the limitation of property rights.[40] However, as Wilkin notes, a given structure of property rights can be efficient despite high transaction costs. The condition is alternative structures that generate even higher transaction costs. Citing Louis de Alessi, he also emphasizes that the shape of certain property rights, in addition to efficiency, is also influenced by social preferences and political conditions.[41] From the point of view of the theoretical framework of this economic history study, it would be appropriate to superimpose on top of the above-mentioned factors broader categories such as formal and informal institutions.[42]

Property rights can be considered from the perspective of paradigms other than the new institutional economics. For example, Maciej Bałtowski and Maciej Miszewski relate this category to the economic systems theory, which they use to analyze economic transition. The analysis of a single economic system takes into account two spheres (characteristics or conditioning elements): property and regulation (mechanism of regulation and coordination of the economy concerning economic decision-making).

Property characteristics consist of the property structure and property rights. While the first category refers to the quantitative shares of given forms of property

38 Screpanti, *The Fundamental Institutions of Capitalism*, 260–261.

39 See, e.g., a review of agency and transaction cost theories embedded in the perspective of the new institutional economics: K. Sobiech-Grabka, J. Wallusch, B. Woźniak-Jęchorek, "Ekonomia instytucjonalna," in *Współczesne teorie ekonomiczne*, ed. M. Ratajczak (Poznań: Wydawnictwo UE w Poznaniu, 2012), 149–152.

40 Wilkin, *Instytucjonalne i kulturowe podstawy gospodarowania*, 163, 171, 174–177.

41 Wilkin, *Instytucjonalne i kulturowe podstawy gospodarowania*, 176; cf. L. de Alessi, "The Economics of Property Rights."

42 Cf. I. Böbel, *Eigentum, Eigentumsrechte und institutioneller Wandel* (Berlin: Springer-Verlag, 1988).

in the total economic property of a particular system, the latter refers to the sanctioned and customarily respected relations between resources and their owners. In this case, attention is paid to the owner's ability to choose efficient ways of using the resources and the rules that accompany this. Moreover, property rights are embedded in the context of social relations through the fact that they remain formal and informal rules of conduct for the economic property. Although, as the authors caution, property structure and property rights are distinct categories, they remain commensurate with each other: changes in property rights lead to transformations in property structure and *vice versa*.

Within the economic system's regulation mechanism, one can speak of coordinating principles and coordinating institutions (institutions of the regulatory sphere). The first component is based on codified and applied ways of determining, e.g., prices, demand, supply, exchange rates, or investments. In model terms, on one side, the regulator will be the market, and on the other, the state. In reality, each economic system is characterized by the coexistence of both regulators, while the dominance of one of them proves its specificity. The second element of the regulation mechanism consists of institutions responsible for establishing regulatory procedures, translating the principles of coordination into economic practice, and reducing uncertainty and indeterminacy of economic turnover. From the point of view of economic transition, the research on the transformation of formal institutions and organizations plays an important role.[43]

5.2. Characteristics of property rules in East Germany: Empowerment of property rights in the GDR Constitutions

Legal regulation of property is important in shaping a country's economic system. They influence a number of branches of law in a country.[44] The property order is a constitutive element of the entire economic order along with the issue of planning in the economy.[45] It follows that the degree of completeness, as well as the enforcement and protection of property rights in the GDR, were closely related to the model of a centrally planned economy and co-shaped it. After the establishment of the GDR in October 1949, some solutions were introduced in the country

43 M. Bałtowski, M. Miszewski, *Transformacja gospodarcza w Polsce* (Warszawa: WN PWN, 2006), 15–16, 52–56.

44 Cf. E. Gniewek, *Prawo rzeczowe* (Warszawa: Wydawnictwo C. H. Beck, 2016), 5.

45 H. Leipold, "Gesellschaftstheoretische Fundierung der Wirtschaftssysteme," in *Bundesrepublik Deutschland – DDR: Die Wirtschaftssysteme. Soziale Marktwirtschaft und Sozialistische Planwirtschaft im Systemvergleich*, ed. H. Hamel (München: Verlag C. H. Beck, 1983), 17–22.

to subordinate social and economic life to the political power of the communists.[46] These measures also included property.[47]

The basic role for the regulation of property rights in East Germany was played by provisions in the Constitutions passed during the GDR's existence: in 1949, 1968, and 1974.[48] All three guaranteed property but did so in a specific way, which resulted from Marxist legal and economic doctrine. In the 1949 document, the property was set in a social context. Property rights and their limitations were derived from the obligations of individuals to society. The state, guaranteeing inheritance rights, reserved a share of inherited property. Intellectual property was also constitutionally protected (Art. 22). Expropriation with compensation was to benefit the general public (Art. 23). The use of property that was obligated should have served the common good. Failure to comply with this principle justified expropriation without compensation. Enterprises of war criminals, Nazis, and entities implementing war policies were subject to nationalization. Private

---

46 Marxist philosophy in the GDR was subject to a process of evolution. See for a synthetic study of the problem: G. Raulet, *Filozofia niemiecka po 1945* (Warszawa: Oficyna Naukowa, 2013), 311–342.

47 See the transformation of the property system in the Soviet occupation zone and the GDR in the respective historical periods: J. Grünewald, *Das Eigentum und das Eigentumsrecht in der sowjetischen Besatzungszone Deutschlands* (Bonn: Ludwig Röhrscheid Verlag, 1961); H. E. Haase, *Das Wirtschaftssystem der DDR. Eine Einführung* (Berlin: Berlin Verlag, 1983), 41–44 (period 1945–1972); H. Hamel, "Ordnungspolitische Gestaltung der Wirtschaftssysteme," in Hamel, *Bundesrepublik Deutschland – DDR*, 77–80 (changes in property and business organization in the 1950s and 1960s); C. Schnabel, "Structural Adjustment and Privatization of the East German Economy," in *Economic Aspects of German Unification. National and International Perspectives*, ed. P. J. J. Welfens (Berlin–Heidelberg: Springer-Verlag, 1992), 242 (general overview); H.-W. Sinn, "Macroeconomic Aspects of German Unification," in Welfens, *Economic Aspects of German Unification*, 101–102 (general overview); V. Kreissig, R. Lungwitz, "Privatisation in East Germany and the Chance of Workers' Participation: A Problems Approach," in *International Privatisation. Strategies and Practices*, ed. T. Clarke, (Berlin–New York: Walter de Gruyter, 1994), 234–237 (period 1945–1972); S. Spangenberg, *The Institutionalised Transformation of the East German Economy* (Heidelberg–New York: Physica-Verlag. A Springer-Verlag Company, 1998), 117–120 (general overview); W. Waldner, "Private Property and the Transformation Process," in *East Germany's Economic Development since Unification. Domestic and Global Aspects*, eds. J. Hölscher, A. Hochberg (Basingstoke–London: Macmillan Press, 1998), 95–100 (period 1945–1976).

48 H. Leipold, "Eigentum und wirtschaftliches Handeln," 41–44; H. Hamel, "Die DDR-Wirtschaft auf dem Weg zum 'entwickelten Sozialismus'," in *Wirtschaftsreformen im Ostblock in den 80er Jahren. Länderstudien: Sowjetunion, DDR, Polen, Rumänien, Tschechoslowakei, Bulgarien, Ungarn*, ed. R. Schlüter (Paderborn: Ferdinand Schöningh, 1988), 59; Spangenberg, *The Institutionalised Transformation*, 119–120. See an overview of the GDR Constitutions: section 3.2. in this work.

monopolies were abolished. Land estates over 100 hectares were subject to expropriation without compensation and subsequent parcelization. The constitutional guarantee of private property of land granted to peasants as a result of land reform was also important (Art. 24).[49] Natural wealth and various heavy industries were nationalized (Art. 25). Cooperatives were also subordinated to the state (Art. 27). With regard to the transfer of public property rights, it has been stipulated that trade in real estate, factories or shares requires the consent of the respective representative bodies responsible for the legal personality of the object of the exchange (Art. 28). Property and income must be taxed in a progressive manner taking into account the current social context (Art. 29).[50]

The GDR's Constitution of 1968 placed property rights even more firmly in Marxist doctrine. It concludes that the socialist property of the means of production is an efficient model. It made it possible to combat the politics of war and exploitation through the abolition of monopolies, the expropriation of landowners, and the abandonment of capitalist economics (Art. 2, Par. 2; Art. 9, Par. 1). The document legalized the tripartition of socialist (social) property into (1) public (state) property, (2) cooperative property, and (3) social property of citizens' organizations. The latter was charged with the duty to protect and increase socialist property (Art. 10). The Constitution guaranteed inheritance rights and the right of citizens to personal property that satisfied their material and cultural needs. The state protected copyrights. However, any use of property could not conflict with the interests of the general public (Art. 11). The scope of social property included minerals and a number of branches of the economy (mines, power plants, reservoirs and dams, factories, banks, insurance institutions, public goods, roads, railroads, transport, postal services, communications). It could be managed only by state enterprises and institutions or – with the consent of the authorities – by cooperatives, social organizations, or associations, provided that this served social interests (Art. 12).[51] Cooperatives owned movable and immovable property, including inventories (Art. 13). The functioning of private enterprises was to serve social goals. The state was to promote cooperation between the socialist and private sectors, making it possible (if necessary) to transform the latter into social property. Expansive associations of private property were prohibited (Art. 14).[52]

49 It is worth noting that Art. 24 of the GDR Constitution of 1949 provided a legal basis for conveniently justifying the implemented policy of collectivization of agriculture and nationalization of the industry then.

50 "Gesetz über die Verfassung der Deutschen Demokratischen Republik vom 7. Oktober 1949.," in *Gesetz über die Konstituierung der Provisorischen Volkskammer der Deutschen Demokratischen Republik vom 7. Oktober 1949.* (GBl.-DDR, Part I, 1949, No. 1, 4–16).

51 Such broad social property meant nationalization in practice.

52 This type of provision facilitated the eradication of private property in the GDR.

The state extended special protection to land (Art. 15). Expropriation for the social good was permitted with compensation (Art. 16).[53]

In the new version of the GDR Constitution of 1974, the property regulations were retained in their previous form. The amended wording of some provisions (Art. 9, Par. 1; Art. 14) did not generate a different shaping of property relations. Art. 14, which dealt with the same issues as before, additionally mentioned small handicraft production.[54]

Additional regulation of property issues in the GDR remained the subject of a specific law. Civil law and criminal law were important in this regard.[55]

The way property rights were enshrined in the GDR Constitutions partly drew on the tradition of German constitutionalism from the period of the Weimar Republic. It resembled parallel regulations of the FRG in some places. However, this was limited only to the declarative sphere (*de jure* institution).[56] In reality, the state remained the depositary of property rights, limiting the influence of citizens in this respect (*de facto* institution).[57]

Socialist economics in the GDR, based on Marxist doctrine,[58] defined property as "a historically shaped form of appropriation of material

---

53 *Verfassung der Deutschen Demokratischen Republik vom 6. April 1968* (GBl.-DDR, Part I, 1968, No. 8, 199–222).

54 *Verfassung der Deutschen Demokratischen Republik vom 6. April 1968 in der Fassung des Gesetz zur Ergänzung und Änderung der Verfassung der Deutschen Demokratischen Republik vom 7. Oktober 1974* (GBl.-DDR, Part I, 1974, No. 47, 432–456).

55 H. Pohl, "Öffentliche und private Wirtschaft," in *Deutsche Wiedervereinigung. Die Rechtseinheit. Arbeitskreis Staats- und Verfassungsrecht*, Vol. II: *Zur Wiederherstellung der inneren Einheit*, Part 2: *Rundfunkrecht – Stasi-Akten – Wiedergutmachung – Öffentliche und Private Wirtschaft*, ed. K. Stern (Köln: Carl Heymanns Verlag KG, 1992), 136–139; F. Baur, J. F. Baur, R. Stürner, *Sachenrecht* (München: Verlag C. H. Beck, 2009), 887–891.

56 Cf. a broader discussion of the entrenchment of property rights in the FRG Constitution: section 6.1.1.1. in this study.

57 Spangenberg, *The Institutionalised Transformation*, 119–120; H. Höfer, "Eigentum," 157–158.

58 Although there are many synthetic studies on Marxian (Marxist) economics, especially in the history of economic thought, the following factual and organized works, which are in the nature of introductions to Marxist theory and consider economic issues, are worth noting: E. Mandel, *Marxistische Wirtschaftstheorie* (Frankfurt am Main: Suhrkamp Verlag, 1968); J. Schleifstein, *Einführung in das Studium von Marx, Engels und Lenin* (München: Verlag C. H. Beck, 1972), especially 63–123; J. F. Becker, *Marxian Political Economy. An Outline* (Cambridge: Cambridge University Press, 1977); H.-R. Peters, *Politische Ökonomie des Marxismus. Anspruch und Wirklichkeit* (Göttingen: Vandenhoeck & Ruprecht, 1980), especially 56–174; J. E. Roemer, *Free to Lose. An Introduction to Marxist Economic Philosophy* (Cambridge: Harvard University Press, 1988); D. M. Brennan et al., eds., *Routledge Handbook of Marxian Economics* (London–New York: Routledge, 2017). See also synthetic studies of the economics of socialism: B. Horvat, *The Political Economy of Socialism. A Marxist*

goods,"[59] characterizing the relationship between people in the process of production of these goods. Thus, it spoke of the property of the means of production (*Eigentum an den Produktionsmitteln*), which was seen as a fundamental type of property relations, developing according to the productive forces and the social division of labor. Property relations *sui generis* were, in turn, presented as the conclusive element of the production relations of a given socio-economic formation,[60] since they were supposed to express under which actual conditions of production individuals, social groups, classes, or entire societies found themselves. Thus, according to Marxists, property relations made it possible to distinguish particular epochs (or the aforementioned socio-economic formations) in the history of humanity. Their transformations were thus linked to such key issues as class and

---

Social Theory (Oxford: Martin Robertson, 1982); J. Wilczynski, *The Economics of Socialism. Principles Governing the Operation of the Centrally Planned Economies under the New System* (London: George Allen and Unwin, 1982); D. Lösch, *Sozialistische Wirtschaftswissenschaft. Die Wirtschaftstheorie im Sozialismus und ihre Bedeutung für die Wirtschaftspolitik* (Hamburg: Verlag Weltarchiv GmbH, 1987).

59 *[H]istorisch entstandene Form der Aneignung der materiellen Güter* ("Eigentum," in *Wörterbuch der Ökonomie Sozialismus*, eds. W. Ehlert et al. (Berlin: Dietz Verlag, 1969), 209–210).

60 In the *Manifesto of the Communist Party* (1848) Karl Marx and Frederick Engels stated: "All property relations in the past have continually been subject to historical change consequent upon the change in historical conditions. ... In all these movements [revolutionary movements], they [i.e. communists] bring to the front, as the leading question in each, the property question, no matter what its degree of development at the time." (Pol. *Wszystkie stosunki własności podlegały ciągłym zmianom historycznym, ciągłym przeobrażeniom historycznym. ... We wszystkich tych ruchach* [rewolucyjnych] *wysuwają oni* [tj. komuniści] *jako podstawowe zagadnienie ruchu zagadnienie własności, bez względu na to, czy przybrało ono bardziej czy mniej dojrzałą postać* (K. Marks, F. Engels, "Manifest partii komunistycznej," in K. Marks, F. Engels, *Manifest partii komunistycznej. Zasady komunizmu* (Warszawa: Książka i Wiedza, 1979), 53, 80)). The theory of socio-economic formations is not coherent and unified on the ground of classical Marxism. An excellent analysis of the evolution of historical materialism in the works of Marx and Engels, including the concept of socio-economic formations, was made by Andrzej Feliks Grabski (A. F. Grabski, *Dzieje historiografii* (Poznań: Wydawnictwo Poznańskie, 2006), 601–611). Generally, however, in the literature the following formations included in the works of the founders of Marxism are distinguished: primitive, Asiatic, ancient (slave), feudal, bourgeois (capitalist) and communist (D. Bębnowski, "The Social Change in the Marxism's Interpretation of History," in *Vade Nobiscum. Materiały Studenckiego Koła Naukowego Historyków Uniwersytetu Łódzkiego*, Vol. XIII: *Bunt, rebelia, rewolucja, strajk. Opór społeczeństwa wobec władzy na przestrzeni dziejów. Skąd przybyliśmy, dokąd zmierzamy? Źródła tożsamości. Gospodarka głupcze!*, eds. K. Banaś, R. Stasiak (Łódź: Piktor, 2014), 24).

power.[61] Property also remained decisive, though not the only, element of the base, which referred to the Marxist conception of the structure of society.[62]

Similarly, in the law of the GDR, based on the philosophical paradigm of Marxism,[63] property was understood as a type of social relations in which relationships are established between individuals in the process of production of goods and through appropriation for individual and productive consumption. However, with reference to Karl Marx's thought, property was not viewed autonomously as an individual's relationship to a thing or the fact of its ownership. It was seen in a social dimension, in which a designated authority determined the use of the means of production and its results. Thus defined property of the means of production was a fundamental type of social relations, defining society as such.[64]

In the GDR economics and law, there were two main types of property of the means of production: private (*Privat-Eigentum*) and social (*gesellschaftliches Eigentum*), sometimes referred to as socialist (*sozialistisches Eigentum*) or – depending on the translation – national, popular, public, state (*Volkseigentum*).[65]

---

61 "Eigentum," in Ehlert et al., *Wörterbuch*, 210.

62 Leipold, "Gesellschaftstheoretische Fundierung," 47. See the above observations on the importance of property relations in relation to Marxist economic historiography in the GDR: T. Kuczynski, *Politische Ökonomie*, [in:] *Handbuch Wirtschaftsgeschichte*, Vol. 1, eds. H. Radandt et al. (Berlin: Institut für Wirtschaftsgeschichte der Akademie der Wissenschaften der DDR, VEB Deutscher Verlag der Wissenschaften, 1981), 70–72. In Marxist theory, society is shown in a structural and storied way. A distinction is made between the base (relations of production, mode of production, relations between people in the labor process), which shapes the superstructure (non-economic, abstract elements of reality, e.g., the state, institutions, religion, social roles, social consciousness). Regardless of the base, the means of production (productive forces, tools, technology, people) function in conflict with it. The historical process results from dialectical relations between base and superstructure (D. Bębnowski, "Socjologiczny komponent historii gospodarczej. Résumé głównych paradygmatów w XX i XXI w." (unpublished manuscript), 8).

63 More on Marxist philosophy of law: M. Zirk-Sadowski, *Wprowadzenie do filozofii prawa* (Warszawa: Wolters Kluwer Polska, 2011), 63–66.

64 "Eigentum," in *Rechtslexikon*, eds. R. Brachmann et al. (Berlin: Staatsverlag der Deutschen Demokratischen Republik, 1988), 84. See also representative works written from a Marxist position: H. Luft, *Eigentum und Demokratie in ökonomischen System des Sozialismus* (Berlin: Institut für Gesellschaftswissenschaften beim Zentralkomitee der SED, 1970); M. Brie, *Wer ist Eigentümer im Sozialismus? Philosophische überlegungen* (Berlin: Dietz Verlag, 1990).

65 "Eigentum," in Ehlert et al., *Wörterbuch*, 210; "Eigentum," in Brachmann et al., *Rechtslexikon*, 84; "Sozialistisches Eigentum," in Brachmann et al., *Rechtslexikon*, 331; W. Behr, *Bundesrepublik Deutschland – Deutsche Demokratische Republik. Systemvergleich Politik – Wirtschaft – Gesellschaft* (Stuttgart: Verlag W. Kohlhammer, 1979), 109–110; Leipold, "Gesellschaftstheoretische Fundierung," 47–48. Other classifications can be found in the literature. For example, Rainer Waterkamp, in addition to the aforementioned property of means of production, distinguishes

Social property was linked to the state apparatus.[66] Helmut Leipold points in this context to the progressive centralization of social property in the GDR, consisting *de facto* of its gradual transformation into the state property.[67] Heidrun Pohl, in turn, writes about the "identification of the state property and socialism" (*Identifizierung von Staatseigentum und Sozialismus*) and the "monopolization of the function of the owner to the state" (*Monopolisierung der Eigentümerfunktion auf den Staat*), which demotivated producers and bureaucratized economic processes.[68] Indeed, the state property was seen in the Eastern Bloc as the best form of socialist property.[69] Leipold concludes that social property was the main reason for the GDR's weaker economic development in relation to the FRG.[70]

Private property was marginalized at the doctrinal level. Its economic and legal status was undermined, and its significance depreciated. Its inherently

---

Eigentum an Konsumgütern, i.e., property of consumer goods (R. Waterkamp, *Herrschaftssysteme und Industriegesselschaft: BRD und DDR* (Stuttgart: Verlag W. Kohlhammer, 1972), 42). Heidrun Pohl lists socialist property, personal property of citizens, and *Privateigentum von Handwerkern und Gewerbetreibenden*, i.e. private property of craftsmen and merchants (Pohl, "Öffentliche und private Wirtschaft," 135–136). In turn, Wolfram Waldner separates "socialist ownership of the means of production" from "private property of the citizens." It is worth noting the English distinction between the terms "ownership" and "property" (Waldner, "Private Property and the Transformation Process," 95). However, these are seemingly different classifications. The cited examples, in fact, refer to social and private property, with the latter being reduced *de facto* to personal property, which will be discussed later.

66 Hamel, "Die DDR-Wirtschaft," 59.

67 Leipold, "Gesellschaftstheoretische Fundierung," 56, 60. It should be noted at this point that the close relationship between the social, public, and state dimensions of property in the GDR reflects problems in translating the concepts discussed and classifying the different types of property.

68 H. Pohl, "Öffentliche und private Wirtschaft," 137.

69 However, this does not alter the fact that in Marxist thought the state property is only an intermediate stage on the road to communism. The state remains the expression of the interests of the people. Only social property ensures the status of workers as owners of the means of production. This was the direction followed by the reforms of the communist authorities in Yugoslavia, which developed workers' self-government in a special way (U. Baβeler, J. Heinrich, *Wirtschaftssysteme. Kapitalistische Marktwirtschaft und sozialistische Zentralplanwirtschaft* (Würzburg–Wien: Physica-Verlag, 1984), 57–58). The above understanding and classification of property resulted from the normative aspect of Marxist theory, showing how property relations should look like in the target communist formation (R. Baumeister, *Die Konzeption der Zukunftsgesellschaft bei Karl Marx, Friedrich Engels und bei neueren westeuropäischen Marxisten – eine ordnungspolitische Analyse* (Köln: Institut für Wirtschaftspolitik an der Universität zu Köln, 1976), 86–97; Baβeler, Heinrich, *Wirtschaftssysteme*, 57–58).

70 Leipold, "Eigentum und wirtschaftliches Handeln," 43.

individualistic character was placed in a collective context. It was emphasized that private property was the cause of the class division of society and the exploitation and oppression of the non-owning classes by the owners of the means of production. It was argued that the contradiction between the social character of production and private property (identified with the capitalism criticized by Marxists) was irreconcilable because it caused a violation of the "free socialist social order" (*freie sozialistische Gesellschaftsordnung*). It was stipulated that the use of the private property for profit-making purposes should serve social needs. A distinction was also made between the private capitalist property (*privatkapitalistisches Eigentum*), which was roundly criticized, and the "property of simple producers of raw materials" (*Eigentum einfacher Warenproduzenten*). The latter category was associated with the "personal property of citizens" (*persönliches Eigentum der Bürger*), guaranteed by the state, i.e., those results of work that satisfied the individual's needs. These included, e.g.: salaries, social benefits, savings, personal and everyday objects, household equipment, private residential and commercial buildings, summer cottages, gardens, garages, income from handicraft production, products from the homestead plots of peasants belonging to agricultural cooperatives, copyrights, acquired rights to a given property, insurance claims.[71]

---

71 "Eigentum," in Ehlert et al., *Wörterbuch*, 210–211; "Eigentumsform," in Ehlert et al., *Wörterbuch*, 211. Cf. K. Bolz, H. Clement, D. Lösch, *Wirtschaftssysteme. Marktwirtschaft – Kapitalismus. Planwirtschaft – Sozialismus* (München: Ehrenwirth Verlag, 1978), 96–97; Leipold, "Gesellschaftstheoretische Fundierung," 48; Waldner, "Private Property and the Transformation Process," 98. Waterkamp writes about the property of consumer goods (*Eigentum an Konsumgütern*), Pohl writes about the personal property of citizens and private property of craftsmen and merchants (*Privateigentum von Handwerkern und Gewerbetreibenden*), Waldner, in turn, writes about the "private property of the citizens." However, these categories are identical to personal property (Cf. Waterkamp, *Herrschaftssysteme und Industriegesselschaft*, 42; H. Pohl, "Öffentliche und private Wirtschaft," 135–136; Waldner, "Private Property and the Transformation Process," 95). More extensively on personal property: "Persönliches Eigentum," in Brachmann et al., *Rechtslexikon*, 267–268. Cf. a characteristic East German study that explains the legitimacy of social property in the GDR in an ideological manner, depreciating the importance of private property in the FRG: H. Meiβner, ed., *Bürgerliche Ökonomie im modernen Kapitalismus. Ideologische und praktische Bedeutung der westdeutschen Wirtschaftstheorie* (Berlin: Deutsche Akademie der Wissenschaften zu Berlin, Institut für Wirtschaftswissenschaften, Dietz Verlag, 1967), *passim*. The authors of the 746-page work write critically about, among other things, the "apologia of property" (*Eigentumsapologetik*) or the "demagogy of property" (*Eigentumsdemagogie*), often referring to Catholic social teaching, from which West German ordoliberal thought drew. According to them, private property is a manifestation of oppressive power and advantage over the weak (Meiβner, *Bürgerliche Ökonomie im modernen Kapitalismus*, 241–270, 535–537).

As shown above, personal property was permitted under the GDR Constitutions of 1968 and 1974.

Personal property (accepted by socialist doctrine) was contrasted with *de facto* contested private property. It should be noted that this was an example of the socialist nomenklatura replacing the universal concept of private property, reduced to elementary goods, with the term personal property. An excessive increase in ownership could be perceived as an unfavorable development of the much-fought private property. This, in turn, justified the policy of nationalization and collectivization. However, the complete elimination of private property was impossible. Hence, the basic goods owned by the individual citizen were defined as personal property. Thus, in socialist optics, this category should be considered semantically narrower than the concept of private property.

Leipold cites yet another classification of private property from the standpoint of the socialist theory of society. He relates it to those socio-economic formations that precede the formation of socialism and communism. Thus, he writes about slave ownership, as well as feudal and capitalist ownership.[72]

It was different with the social property. Marxist economic and legal theory defended its rationality and efficiency, which were supposed to stem from its collective character. It was pointed out that it removes exploitation, unites individuals in common work for the social interest, creates cooperation and mutual assistance in the production process, promotes democratic planning, management, and organization of the process of social reproduction and other areas of social life,[73] and finally serves the fair distribution of goods or exchange of products for goods.[74] The state and citizens had a special duty to protect and expand the socialist property.[75]

In the GDR, three forms of social property were distinguished. Firstly, there was general public property (*gesamtgesellschaftliches Volkseigentum*), also called state property (*staatliches Eigentum*) or social property (*gesellschaftliches Eigentum*). It was exemplified by state-owned enterprises. Secondly, there was the cooperative common property of working collectives (*genossenschaftliche Gemeineigentum werktätiger Kollektive*) or cooperative property (*genossenschaftliche Eigentum*), e.g. agricultural and crafts cooperatives. Thirdly, the property of social organizations of citizens (*Eigentum der gesellschaftlichen Organisationen der Bürger*) was singled

72 Leipold, "Gesellschaftstheoretische Fundierung," 48.

73 *Das Wesen des sozialistischen E.* [Eigentum] *im Sozialismus wird charakterisiert … durch die demokratische Planung, Leitung und Organisation des gesellschaftlichen Reproduktionsprozesses sowie aller übrigen Bereiche des gesellschaftlichen Lebens* ("Eigentum," in Ehlert et al., *Wörterbuch*, 210).

74 "Eigentum," in Ehlert et al., *Wörterbuch*, 210.

75 "Sozialistisches Eigentum," in Brachmann et al., *Rechtslexikon*, 331. See also: "Eigentumsschutz," in Brachmann et al., *Rechtslexikon*, 86–87. Cf. Leipold, "Gesellschaftstheoretische Fundierung," 48.

out.[76] These were, e.g., party facilities, publishing houses, or the headquarters of newspaper titles.[77] As already mentioned, the state retained an important share within a social property, regardless of its form.[78] The typology of property in the GDR in model terms is shown in Diagram 2.

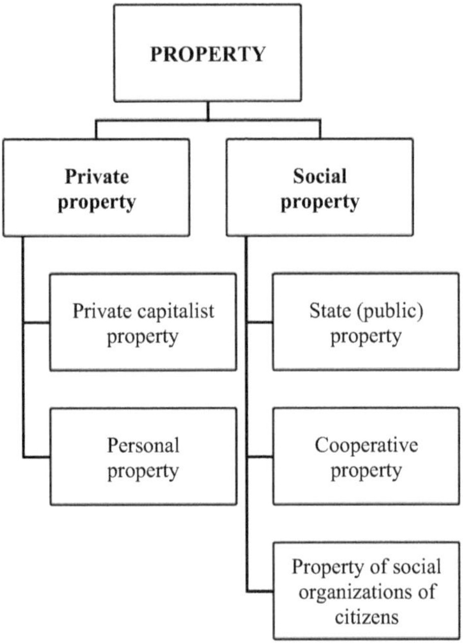

Diagram 2: *Property classification in the GDR*
Own compilation based on the cited literature.

76 "Eigentum," in Ehlert et al., *Wörterbuch*, 210; "Eigentumsform," in Ehlert et al., *Wörterbuch*, 211; "Eigentum," in Brachmann et al., *Rechtslexikon*, 84; "Sozialistisches Eigentum," [in:] Brachmann et al., *Rechtslexikon*, 331.
77 Haase, *Das Wirtschaftssystem der DDR*, 42.
78 Waldner cites a slightly different classification of social property that is inconsistent. He distinguishes between the "national property of the state," "co-operative property of the agricultural co-operatives," and the "property of the trades and crafts." As synonyms of the last two types the author indicates – discussed, by the way, elsewhere in this study – agricultural production cooperatives and craft production cooperatives (Waldner, "Private Property and the Transformation Process," 95). As the subsequent considerations will show, the last two types of cooperatives should be classified as belonging to the same form of social property, i.e. cooperative property. The general division of property into state, cooperative (together forming social property) and private property was characteristic of all Eastern Bloc countries (Bolz, Clement, Lösch, *Wirtschaftssysteme*, 94–97; W. Gumpel, *Die sozialistischen Staaten*, Vol. 1: *Sozialistische Wirtschaftssysteme* (München: Günter Olzog Verlag, 1983), 24–28).

As already presented, the above-mentioned classification of social property found its legitimacy in the GDR Constitution of 1968. It was confirmed in the Constitution of 1974.

The community of property (*Eigentumsgemeinschaft*) should also be placed on the ground of social property. They were referred to as the property of spouses, the community of inheritance, the community of citizens, the house community, and common property (*Eigentum der Ehegatten, Erbengemeinschaft, Gemeinschaften von Bürgern, Hausgemeinschaft, gemeinschafliches Eigentum*).[79]

An intermediate type between state and private property was enterprises with state participation (*Betriebe mit staatlicher Beteiligung*), which were called semi-state enterprises (*halbstaatliche Betriebe*). This group also included private trading plants linked with the state or cooperative enterprises by a commission agreement (*Betriebe mit Kommissionsvertrag*).[80]

The position of private property in the property structure was weakening during the GDR period. For example, in 1950, it accounted for 38.2 % of the total social product (*gesellschaftliches Gesamtprodukt*), while in 1967, it was only 6 %. At that time, the remaining part (94 %) of the total social product was produced by social property, of which 72.5 % was accounted for by state-owned enterprises, 14.3 % by cooperatives, and 7.2 % by plants with state participation or operating under a commission agreement.[81]

State (public) property of the means of production (*Volkseigentum an den Produktionsmitteln*) occupied a special place in the social and economic system of the GDR. It was seen as an inviolable achievement of the proletariat's revolution and the highest form of socialist property, as well as the basis for the aforementioned personal property of the citizen.[82] The East German system, guaranteed the state's disposal of all public facilities, as well as the creation and enforcement of appropriate legal norms in this regard. Importantly, the law stipulated that the state apparatus could manage the public property through cooperatives and social organizations, as well as interfere with the other two forms of socialist property in certain cases.[83]

From the point of view of the GDR law, property regulations remained the subject of property law (*Eigentumsrecht*). This consisted of the rights of individuals or groups to the means and fruits of production and the possession, use, and disposition of things in accordance with the dominant class interests within the given social order. Due to the special position of the state property in the East German

79 "Eigentumsgemeinschaft," in Brachmann et al., *Rechtslexikon*, 86.
80 "Eigentumsform," in Ehlert et al., *Wörterbuch*, 211; H. E. Haase, *Das Wirtschaftssystem der DDR*, 42.
81 "Eigentum," in Ehlert et al., *Wörterbuch*, 210.
82 "Eigentum," in Brachmann et al., *Rechtslexikon*, 84.
83 "Volkseigentum," in Brachmann et al., *Rechtslexikon*, 396.

property structure, a separate and important branch of property law was the state property law (*Volkseigentumsrecht*).[84]

Property law regulated, among other things, how the property could be disposed of. The "right of use" (*Nutzungsrecht*) was granted to the state bodies, e.g., the government, planning commissions, and economic ministries. On the other hand, the "right of disposal" (*Verfügungsrecht*) applied to economic entities, e.g. enterprises and management bodies.[85]

In GDR doctrine, there was also the category of property rights (*Eigentümerbefugnisse*), understood in a specific way. These were related to personal property, guaranteeing citizens the freedom to deal with the object of their property. These rights also included the protection of such property (*Eigentumsschutz*).[86] Property rights, property protection, and resulting obligations of citizens created the "legal status of the holder of personal property of a given thing" (*rechtliche Stellung des persönlichen Eigentümers von Sachen*). These rights were simultaneously connected with a guarantee of the individual's access to the property (e.g. money, savings). They were also placed in the context of transactions. It was even claimed that they result from contractual relations (*Vertragsbeziehungen*). Property rights were considered in a double way. On the one hand, the individual property right had a specific function in the enforcement of personal property. On the other hand, their close internal connection was emphasized. This resulted in a certain perception of the use of the personal property: the use of personal property on someone's own responsibility was pointed out as a manifestation of natural life processes.[87]

Property rights regulations directly affected how the GDR's most important economic sectors (i.e., industry, agriculture, trade, and finance) were organized. This was particularly true of their property structure.

The East German industry consisted of state, semi-state, cooperative, and private plants. State enterprises (*Volkseigener Betrieb*, VEB) played the most important

84 "Eigentumsrecht," in Ehlert et al., *Wörterbuch*, 211.

85 Spangenberg, *The Institutionalised Transformation*, 120.

86 See "Eigentumsschutz," in Brachmann et al., *Rechtslexikon*, 86–87.

87 "Eigentümerbefugnisse," in Brachmann et al., *Rechtslexikon*, 86. Although the last statement at first glance corresponds to the capitalist understanding of private property, it should be remembered that in the GDR economics and law, this view was limited exclusively to personal property, i.e., those goods that were the result of an individual's work and met individual needs. The legitimacy of private property as such was questioned in socialist doctrine. As argued earlier, the category of personal property was meaningfully narrower than the concept of private property. This is well illustrated by the example of a peasant belonging to a socialist agricultural cooperative. The goods he produced were given to the cooperative's board. The peasant himself could only freely dispose of the goods produced on his small homestead plot. See the later discussion in this section on the structure of agricultural property in the GDR. Cf. Waldner, "Private Property and the Transformation Process," 98.

role, both in terms of employment and production. They were concentrated within special management bodies: the unions of state enterprises (*Vereinigung Volkseigener Betriebe*, VVB) and combines (*Kombinat*).[88]

In semi-state enterprises, the state's shareholding was a majority, allowing it to set the production direction of a given plant. The GDR authorities, starting in 1956, applied various forms of pressure (especially in terms of taxes and employment limits) to make private firms allow government shares. For example, in the late 1960s, semi-state plants played an important role in the light, textile, and food industries. In terms of employment size, they were mostly small (up to 50 employees) or medium-sized (500 to 1,000 employees).[89]

Industrial cooperative production concerned especially craftsmen. They were also forced to join the production cooperatives of the craft in 1958 (*Produktionsgenossenschaft des Handwerks*, PGH).[90] However, the authorities did not succeed in fully eliminating private initiative in this area.[91]

The activity of private enterprises was accepted due to citizens' demand for certain goods and services; however, the size of this sector was systematically limited. As in the case of craft enterprises, this was done primarily on the basis of restrictive tax policies or employment limits. For example, by the end of the 1960s, private capital was especially present in the light and food industries and also played an important role in the production e.g., of luxury goods, work and business clothes, underwear, paper, and cardboard articles, clothing, sewing articles, fur and leather products. This sector consisted mainly of small plants.[92]

As Martin Schnitzer aptly observed: "The organization of industry [in the GDR] has to be considered as a basic part of the economic and political organization of the state. The state-owned enterprises form an integral part of the state economic organization and are indeed the foundation upon which this is built."[93] This was due to the policy of forcible industrialization, even at the expense of other sectors of the economy (especially agriculture), which was a characteristic of the socio-economic system of the entire Eastern Bloc in the post-war period.[94] Schnitzer adds that even semi-state and private enterprises co-created this system through

88 M. Schnitzer, *East and West Germany: A Comparative Economic Analysis* (New York: Praeger Publishers, 1972), 226, 230–238, chart 9.2.

89 Schnitzer, *East and West Germany*, 226–227, 233.

90 Martin Schnitzer cites the misnomer *Produktionsgenossenschaft des Handels* (Schnitzer, *East and West Germany*, 234).

91 Schnitzer, *East and West Germany*, 234, 239–240. Cf. Waterkamp, *Herrschaftssysteme und Industriegesselschaft*, 43.

92 Schnitzer, *East and West Germany*, 226–227, 233, 238–240.

93 Schnitzer, *East and West Germany*, 227.

94 More on the economic policy of Russia and the Soviet Union in 1917–1991 and the countries of Central and Eastern Europe in 1945–1991: J. Skodlarski, *Historia gospodarcza* (Warszawa: WN PWN, 2014), 317–330, 334–339, 368–371, 393–397, 403–404, 407–408, 451–454, 459, 464–466.

the strictly defined arrangement of purchase and supply contracts to which they were subject. Political authorities concentrated in the SED party leadership made all production decisions.[95] The transformation of the property structure in the East German industry in selected years 1955–1970 is shown in Table 9.

Table 9: *Property structure of the GDR industry in selected years 1955–1970 (excluding construction industry[a], in total numbers)*

Year	State enterprises (VEB)	Cooperative enterprises	Semi-state enterprises	Private enterprises	Total
1955	5,716	339	–	13,782	19,837
1960	4,589	518	4,455	6,476	16,038
1965	3,713	279	5,458	4,265	13,715
1970	2,437	311	5,632	3,184	11,564

a In German statistical material, the construction industry was often separated from the industrial sector.
Own calculations and compilation based on: *Statistisches Jahrbuch der Deutschen Demokratischen Republik* (hereinafter: SJ DDR), Vol. 1955 (Berlin: Staatlichen Zentralverwaltung für Statistik, VEB Deutscher Zentralverlag, 1956), 121, table 1; SJ DDR, Vol. 1960/1961 (Berlin: Staatlichen Zentralverwaltung für Statistik, VEB Deutscher Zentralverlag, 1962), 262, table 2; SJ DDR, Vol. 1966 (Berlin: Staatlichen Zentralverwaltung für Statistik, VEB Deutscher Zentralverlag, 1967), 114, table. 2; SJ DDR, Vol. 1971 (Berlin: Staatlichen Zentralverwaltung für Statistik, VEB Deutscher Zentralverlag, 1972), 103, table 7.

The decline in the total number of industrial enterprises between 1955 and 1970 (from 19,837 to 11,564) is noteworthy. However, this did not mean a decrease in the dynamics of industrialization. Its progress manifested itself, e.g., in the progressing concentration of production. This should also explain the only apparent weakening of social (state and cooperative) property in the industry. Although the number of enterprises was decreasing, the scope of their production – as part of unions of state enterprises or combines – was increasing. The 1960s were also beneficial for developing semi-state enterprises (there was an increase in their number by 26.4 %), which constituted the core of industrial production in the GDR and state plants. In turn, the private sector clearly declined. During the 15 years in question alone, more than 10,500 enterprises were liquidated.[96]

95 Schnitzer, *East and West Germany*, 227–229, chart 9.1. Cf. par. 3.2., Diagram 1 in this paper.

96 Waterkamp provides interesting information on the transformation of the property structure of the industry in the GDR. He used the share of individual sectors in East German gross industrial production as an indicator. His data complement the above statements. In 1948, the share of state plants in production was about

The proportions in the property structure of East German agriculture were somewhat different. As a result of the implemented collectivization policy, the most important role was played by cooperative farms, also referred to as collective farms, cooperative enterprises (*Genossenschaftliche Betriebe*),[97] or agricultural production cooperatives (*Landwirtschaftliche Produktionsgenossenschaft*, LPG).[98] They dominated both in terms of quantity and total area of cultivated land. The peasants grouped in them, after contributing their land and livestock (often as a result of external pressure), worked together on the land transferred to the cooperatives in perpetual use.[99] There were three types of socialization of agricultural production. The first type meant the exclusively common property of land. The second type included draught animals and equipment while maintaining private property of the remaining animals and meadows. The third type, on the other hand, involved the complete socialization of all the means of production with retaining the cooperative members' right to homestead plots (approximately 0.5 hectares per family), also called individual farms of cooperative members (*Individuelle Wirtschaften der Mitglieder*),[100] personal households of agricultural production cooperatives' members (*persönliche Hauswirtschaften der Mitglieder landwirtschaftlicher Produktionsgenossenschaften*)[101] or personally used areas (*persönlich genutzte*

39 %, while in 1955, it was 87.3 %. Waterkamp also notes an increase in the number of semi-state enterprises. While in 1956 there were only 144, in 1962 there were already 5,277 factories, while in 1967–5,562 plants. Their share in gross production increased from 3 % in 1956 to over 75 % in 1962 and about 85 % in 1967 (Waterkamp, *Herrschaftssysteme und Industriegesselschaft*, 42).

97 See, e.g., SJ DDR, Vol. 1955, 196, table 3.

98 The communist ideology emphasized the importance of collective production, seeing its sources, among others, in the alleged natural drive of peasants to form production communities. As early as 1949, this view was refuted by Władysław Wielhorski, a Polish sovietologist and economic historian living in exile in Great Britain after World War II. Analyzing the agrarian system of Russia and the Soviet Union, he proved that the natural aspiration of the peasants was individual management of the private property. This should explain their later resistance to the imposed policy of agriculture's collectivization (W. Wielhorski, *Ustrój agrarny Z.S.S.R.* (Londyn: Instytut Bliskiego i Środkowego Wschodu "Reduta," 1949), 1–20).

99 Cf. understanding of land property (*Grund-Eigentum*) in the GDR economics and law: "Eigentum," in Ehlert et al., *Wörterbuch*, 210–211. At the risk of a certain simplification, it is worth noting that the restriction of peasants' private property in the GDR and their use of land within agricultural production cooperatives resembled the feudal dependencies so strongly condemned by Marxist doctrine. The same was true of the state farms, which will be discussed later. In feudalism, there existed a double property of land: superior (full, lordly) and usable (incomplete, peasant). Cf. J. Szpak, *Historia gospodarcza powszechna* (Warszawa: PWE, 2007), 82.

100 See, e.g., SJ DDR, Vol. 1955, p. 196, table 3.

101 See, e.g., SJ DDR, Vol. 1960/1961, p. 419, table 1, fn. 2.

102 See, e.g., SJ DDR, Vol. 1976 (Berlin: Staatlichen Zentralverwaltung für Statistik, VEB Deutscher Zentralverlag, 1977), 176–177, table 5, fn. 1.

Fläche)[102] with personal livestock and equipment. It should be clearly emphasized that homestead plots were personal property. Although it was a type of private property, it functioned within the framework of cooperative farms, classified as social property.[103] The capital of a given collective farm was divided into fixed and circulating. While the former referred to buildings, their equipment, machinery, vehicles, animals, land, and orchards, the latter concerned the production process, stocks, and products for sale.[104]

There were also state agricultural enterprises. These were also called state or national farms (*Volkseigenes Gut*, VEG). They were larger than the collective farms in terms of area. They also employed more workers, focused on extensive cultivation, and implemented modern agricultural technology.[105] Regardless, they were less important in the production structure than cooperatives.[106] However, as in the case of the latter, state farms allocated homestead plots for employees.[107]

There were also private farms.[108] However, their role was systematically reduced.

---

103 Cf. earlier discussion of personal property in this section.

104 Schnitzer, *East and West Germany*, 242, 246–249, chart 9.5; 254.

105 Schnitzer, *East and West Germany*, 242, 244–246, 253–254.

106 The development of the cooperative sector and its domination over the state sector in the GDR's agriculture was a result of the situation prevailing in the Eastern Bloc after World War II. Cf. e.g. the analysis of this process in 1944–1968: J. Tomaszewski, *Europa Środkowo-Wschodnia 1944–1968. Powstanie, ewolucja i kryzys realnego socjalizmu* (Warszawa: Wydawnictwa UW, 1992), 73–79, 203–206, 271–279. The situation in Poland was different. In agriculture, the state sector prevailed over the cooperative sector. In addition, both sectors were giving way to the private sector, which was still in existence (see J. Skodlarski, *Zarys historii gospodarczej Polski* (Warszawa: WN PWN, 2005), 371–375, 400–404, 441–447, 469, 473–474, 477–480, 505–506, 511–513). See comparative studies of the problem: L. Kalinová, Z. Klusáková, "Przemiany społeczno-gospodarcze w krajach demokracji ludowej po roku 1948. Struktura klasowa i społeczna ludności krajów socjalistycznych," in *Rozwój gospodarczy europejskich krajów socjalistycznych*, ed. V. Průcha (Warszawa: Książka i Wiedza, 1981), 275–295; Z. Klusáková, "Rolnictwo," in Průcha, *Rozwój gospodarczy europejskich krajów socjalistycznych*, 549–555.

107 Kalinová, Klusáková, "Przemiany społeczno-gospodarcze," 290.

108 Schnitzer, *East and West Germany*, 242. The author claims that cooperative members were allowed to cultivate private plots of land. This statement sounds twofold. On the one hand, the impression is given that it refers to a situation where a private farmer was also a member of a cooperative. However, this would be unlikely. On the other hand, it can be assumed that Schnitzer has homestead plots in mind. If so, this view is imprecise. Indeed, it follows from the conception of property in GDR economics and law discussed in this section that homestead plots were an example of personal property. Although the latter was indicated as a type of private property, it was a semantically narrower category than private property *sensu stricto*. Moreover, it should be noted that homestead plots functioned within the framework of collective and state farms, i.e. social, not private, property. Thus, their legal and

The state enterprises of collection and purchase (*Volkseigener Erfassungs und Aufkaufbetrieb*, VEAB) dealt with the purchase and distribution of agricultural products. They were associated within the union of state enterprises of collection and purchase (*Vereinigung Volkseigener Erfassungs und Aufkaufbetriebe*, VVEAB). From an administrative point of view, industrial enterprises (state, semi-state, private ones, and cooperatives), farms (cooperative, state, private), and production cooperatives of the craft were governed by regional (district) economic councils (*Bezirkswirtschaftsrat*). Some plants, especially public utilities, were, in turn, governed by county economic councils.[109] The changes in the property structure in the GDR agriculture in selected years 1950–1989, based on the number of rural and forestry enterprises, are presented in Table 10.

economic status was limited by the social property framework. Allowing members of cooperatives to run individual farms and treating them as private property would be an internal contradiction of the GDR's property system, which, despite its inefficiency (as part of the centrally planned economy model), nevertheless had – at least in the theoretical level – its logic and coherence. The above statements are confirmed by statistical sources, which compile information on this type of farm together with data on production cooperatives, clearly distinguishing them from private agricultural enterprises (see, e.g., SJ DDR, Vol. 1955, 196, table 3).

109 Schnitzer, *East and West Germany*, 228–229, chart 9.1; 240–242, chart 9.3.

Table 10: *Property structure of the GDR agriculture in selected years 1950–1989 (rural and forestry enterprises, in total numbers)*

Year	State farms (VEG)	Other state or public farms[a]	Agricultural production cooperatives (LPG)		Private farms
			Cooperative enterprises	Homestead plots	
1950[b]	559	32,062	–	–	855,624
1955[c]	540	15,798	5,879	86,708	780,990
1960	669	9,449	19,276 (19,313)[d]	–	30,202[e]
1965[f]	660 (572)[g]	–	15,342 (15,139)[h]	–	13,839
1970	511	–	9,009	–	–
1975	463	–	4,621	–	–
1980	469	–	3,946	–	–
1985	465	–	3,905	–	–
1989	464	–	3,844	–	–

a *Sonstige volkseigene und öffentliche Betriebe.*
b For 1950–1958, rural and forestry enterprises above 0.5 hectares of economic area (*Wirtschaftsfläche*). Since 1959, enterprises above 1 hectare of utilized agricultural area (*Landwirtschaftliche Nutzfläche*), excluding households of agricultural production cooperatives' members.
c For 1955–1959, the number of agricultural production cooperatives is given together with horticultural production cooperatives (*Gärtnerische Produktionsgenossenschaften*) and fishermen's production cooperatives (*Produktionsgenossenschaften werktätiger Fischer*, PwF).
d Divergence of data (cf. e.g.: SJ DDR, Vol. 1960/1961, 419, table 1; SJ DDR, Vol. 1971, 182–183, table 5).
e For 1960–1965, private enterprises defined as "other" (*Übrige Betriebe*).
f Enterprises without other state or public agricultural enterprises and without other cooperative farms under the management of county councils.
g Divergence of data (cf. e.g.: SJ DDR, Vol. 1966, 259, table 1; SJ DDR, Vol. 1971, 182–183, table 5).
h Divergence of data (cf. e.g.: SJ DDR, Vol. 1966, 259, table 1; SJ DDR, Vol. 1971, 182–183, table 5).

The total number of enterprises is not given in the table, which results from methodological differences found in statistical materials. Since 1960 horticultural production cooperatives and fishermen's production cooperatives were distinguished (which had previously been included under agricultural production cooperatives). Later on, other types of cooperatives were distinguished in the data. They were not included in the above table. This would have disturbed the desired picture of property structure in the GDR agriculture.

Own calculations and compilation based on: SJ DDR, Vol. 1955, 196, table 3; SJ DDR, Vol. 1960/1961, 419, table 1; SJ DDR, Vol. 1966, 259, table 1; SJ DDR, Vol. 1971, 182–183, table 5; SJ DDR, Vol. 1976, 176–177, table 5; SJ DDR, Vol. 1981 (Berlin: Staatlichen Zentralverwaltung für Statistik, VEB Deutscher Zentralverlag, 1982), 162, table 3; SJ DDR, Vol. 1986 (Berlin: Staatlichen Zentralverwaltung für Statistik, VEB Deutscher Zentralverlag, 1987), 181, table 3; SJ DDR, Vol. 1990 (Berlin: Staatlichen Zentralverwaltung für Statistik, VEB Deutscher Zentralverlag, 1991), 212, table *Volkseigene und genossenschaftliche Landwirtschaftsbetriebe.*

The cited data lead to the conclusion that the transformations in the structure of agricultural property in the GDR took place in several complementary dimensions. Between 1950 and 1965, the private sector clearly weakened relative to the state and cooperative sectors, with a clear predominance of the latter. In just 15 years, the number of private agricultural enterprises fell dramatically by more than 840,000. However, even the nationalized or socialized agricultural sector did not prove too strong against the industry. Progressive industrialization did not favor the quantitative development of agricultural enterprises. The peak period for the growth in the number of state and cooperative farms was the turn of the 1950s and 1960s.[110] After that, a systematic fall took place in this respect. However, it should be emphasized that agricultural production was intensified by its concentration. First of all, it manifested itself in the increase of the crop area by state and cooperative enterprises. Besides the displacement of private property and the centralization of production, this was the second aspect of collectivization in the GDR. This is illustrated in Table 11.

110 The highest number of state farms (700) was recorded in 1958, while agricultural production cooperatives (19,276 or 19,313) were recorded in 1960 (SJ DDR, Vol. 1966, 259, table 1; SJ DDR, Vol. 1971, 182–183, table 5. Cf. earlier comment on table 10, fn. d in this section).

Table 11: *Property structure of GDR agriculture in selected years 1950–1989 (utilized agricultural area[a], in hectares)*

Year	State farms (VEG)	Agricultural production cooperatives (LPG)	Private farms[b]
1950[c]	177,410	–	6,157,034
1955	283,473	1,204,056	4,711,355
1960[d]	403,173 (395,663)	5,421,570 (5,408,064)	486,474
1965[e]	426,644	5,465,674	389,972
1970	442,638	5,392,416	–
1975	473,829 (105,938)[f]	769,314	–
1980	396,188 (407,845)[g]	5,033,215	–
1985	439,552	5,347,712	–
1989	446,397	5,346,203	–

a The East German statistical material distinguished between the category of economic area (*Wirtschaftsfläche*), encompassing the entire farm including the land, and the utilized agricultural area (*landwirtschaftliche Nutzfläche*), identified only with the crop area. The above summary is based on the second category.
b Private enterprises defined as "other" (*Übrige Betriebe*).
c For 1950–1965, including enterprises up to 1 hectare of the utilized agricultural area.
d For 1960–1975, the utilized agricultural area of production cooperatives includes the area of both cooperative enterprises and homestead plots. Divergence of data (cf. e.g.: SJ DDR, Vol. 1966, 259, table 1; SJ DDR, Vol. 1971, 182–183, table 5).
e Divergence of data (cf. e.g.: SJ DDR, Vol. 1966, 259, table 1; SJ DDR, Vol. 1971, 182–183, table 5).
f Divergence of data (cf. e.g.: SJ DDR, Vol. 1976, 176–177, table 5; SJ DDR, Vol. 1981, 163, table 4).
g Divergence of data (cf. e.g.: SJ DDR, Vol. 1981, 163, table 4; SJ DDR, Vol. 1986, 181, table 4).
Own calculations and compilation based on: SJ DDR, Vol. 1960/1961, 419, table 1; SJ DDR, Vol. 1966, 259, table 1; SJ DDR, Vol. 1971, 182–183, table 5; SJ DDR, Vol. 1976, 176–177, table 5; SJ DDR, Vol. 1981, 163, table 4; SJ DDR, Vol. 1986, 181, table 4; SJ DDR, Vol. 1990, 212, table *Landwirtschaftliche Nutzfläche in Bewirtschaftung volkseigener und genossenschaftlicher Landwirtschaftsbetriebe*.

Between 1950 and 1965, the private crop area radically decreased from over 6 million hectares to less than 400,000 hectares. The largest amount of land was concentrated by agricultural production cooperatives. Their utilized agricultural area stabilized at the level of well over 5 million hectares in 1960.[111] The size of the agricultural area belonging to state farms was also relatively constant from 1960–1961 (over 400,000 hectares).[112] The moment of collapse was the first half of the 1970s. The crop area cultivated by state farms and agricultural production cooperatives declined sharply. The sources of this phenomenon can be found in the first world energy crisis of 1973–1976. The recession was preceded by a global crop failure in 1972. The lack of fertilizers and increased production costs (especially for sowing and transport), resulting from increased oil and metal prices, limited the growth of agricultural production. Increasing world market purchases of grain by communist countries further upset the balance between food production and consumption. As a result, prices of agricultural commodities increased significantly. The energy crisis affected the highly developed capitalist countries the most, but its effects – although with some delay – were also felt in the Eastern Bloc countries, including the GDR.[113] There was a revival in the process of concentration of agricultural production and a return to the original trend in the second half of the 1970s.

Also, in the field of domestic trade (retail and wholesale), state and cooperative enterprises played a central role.[114] The entities of retail exchange were: state retail stores (*Verkaufsstellen des Volkseigenen Einzelhandels*), consumer cooperative retail stores (*Verkaufsstellen des Konsumgenossenschaftlichen Einzelhandels*), and enterprises with state partnership (semi-state). Parallel to these was the group of private retail stores (*private Einzelhändler*), which also included food and specialty stores (*privates Nahrungs und Genussmittelhandwerk*). The retail trade usually consisted of small and medium-sized stores with about 4–5 employees. They were affiliated with various state trade associations or trusts of regional or national scope.[115]

---

111 Between 1959 and 1960, the utilized agricultural area of production cooperatives increased from 2,586,140 hectares to 5,408,064 hectares (5,421,570 hectares), an increase of 109.1 % (109.6 %) (SJ DDR, Vol. 1966, 259, table 1; SJ DDR, Vol. 1971, 182–183, table 5).

112 Between 1959 and 1960, the utilized agricultural area of state farms increased from 388,753 hectares to 403,173 hectares (SJ DDR, Vol. 1966, 259, table 1). According to other data, the area was 395,663 hectares in 1960, rising to 400,429 hectares in 1961 (SJ DDR, Vol. 1971, 182–183, table 5. Cf. earlier comment on Table 11, fn. d in this section).

113 Cf. D. Wojnarski, *Powszechna historia gospodarcza* (Warszawa: Wydawnictwo Poltext, 2004), 371–375, 395–401.

114 Schnitzer, *East and West Germany*, 251, chart 9.6.; Waterkamp, *Herrschaftssysteme und Industriegesselschaft*, 43.

115 Schnitzer, *East and West Germany*, 248, 250.

As far as wholesale trade is concerned, it was handled by the Central Purchasing Bureaus (*Zentrale Einkäufe Büros*), which were state distribution bodies. The private commission brokers (*Kommissionshändler*), operating especially in the textile sector, were also part of this system. They organized the sale of products at a predetermined price, ensuring themselves an appropriate commission. The 1960s also saw the development of economic federations or production-distribution groups, which combined production with retail and wholesale trade. One such federation was, e.g., the clothing federation for the region of Leipzig and Karl-Marx-Stadt,[116] which integrated together the Karl-Marx-Stadt consumer cooperative enterprise, the Leipzig Centre, the Textile Wholesale Trade Directorate, and eight associations of textile state enterprises.[117]

The above undertakings were a manifestation of the vertical integration of individual sectors of the economy, i.e. industry, agriculture, and trade. This phenomenon appeared in the 1960s. Its effect was the creation of combines, called the cooperative unions in the GDR.[118]

Foreign trade enterprises (*Aussenhandelsbetrieb*, AHB) held a special place in the GDR's exchanges with other countries. These were subordinated to the Ministry of Foreign Trade. There were also more independent foreign trade enterprises supervised by industrial ministries or trusts.[119]

Significant state participation was also evident in the GDR's financial system, especially in the banking sector. The leading roles in it were played by: the GDR State Bank, the Industrial and Commercial Bank, the Agricultural Bank, the Foreign Trade Bank, Cooperative Bank for Handicrafts and Industry. A network of savings banks managed the majority of individual citizen deposits (60 %). The Ministry of Finance, the State Planning Commission, and the State Bank were responsible for coordinating the East German banking system. The banks' activities were correlated with the needs of industry, agriculture, and trade, especially in the execution of cyclical state economic plans. This was manifested, e.g., in the granting of short- and long-term loans to individual sectors of the economy or in the supervision of transactions of enterprises (primarily state and cooperative enterprises).[120]

---

116 It was the name of the city of Chemnitz in Saxony from 1953 to 1990 ("Chemnitz," in *Nowa Encyklopedia Powszechna PWN*, Vol. 1: *A-C*, ed. B. Petrozolin-Skowrońska (Warszawa: WN PWN, 1997), 694).

117 Schnitzer, *East and West Germany*, 250, 252.

118 Kalinová, Klusáková, "Przemiany społeczno-gospodarcze," 294, fn. 19.

119 Schnitzer, *East and West Germany*, 252.

120 Schnitzer, *East and West Germany*, 307–323, 328–329.

5.3. Implementation of West German property rules in the Eastern *Länder*

As early as 1953, Ludwig Erhard stated that the economic unification of the two German states would be based on two main factors: the middle class and enterprises. The latter, based on private property, he saw as the source of the power to initiate development. According to Erhard, competition would not weaken East German enterprises but would increase their productivity.[121]

From an economic point of view, one of the important issues on the threshold of German reunification was the need to regulate property rights in the new federated states.[122] The state played a vital role in this regard.[123] This was particularly important for entrepreneurs, potential investors and the rightful owners of property that had been expropriated during the Third Reich or after World War II.

The actions marking the beginning of the process of systemic transition in the GDR towards the free market took place in the 1980s, although they initially oscillated around maintaining and reforming the socialist system. On the one hand, it was a response to the deepening crisis of the centrally planned economy. On the other hand, it was a manifestation of the East German authorities' resistance to Mikhail Gorbachev's reforms (Rus. *perestroika*, *glasnost*, and *uskoreniye*) of 1985–1991, which were too bold in their view.[124]

German reunification, which was *de facto* the incorporation of the GDR into the FRG, meant, among other things, the implementation of West German regulations on property rights in the Eastern *Länder*. The framework for this process had already been set out in documents preceding the official reunification in October 1990.

---

121 Cf. M. Moszyński, "Idee ładu gospodarczego w procesie transformacji systemowej byłej NRD – oczekiwania a rzeczywistość," *Prace Naukowe Uniwersytetu Ekonomicznego we Wrocławiu. Ekonomia* No. 245 (2012): 351.

122 L. Hoffmann, "Integrating the East German States into the German Economy: Opportunities, Burdens and Options," in Welfens, *Economic Aspects of German Unification*, 63, 66, 70. See the impressive theoretical study devoted to the institutional analysis of the former GDR's transition in the first half of the 1990s with a special focus on property rights: Spangenberg, *The Institutionalised Transformation.*

123 G. Lehmbruch, "Zwischen Institutionentransfer und Eigendynamik: Sektorale Transformationspfade und ihre Bestimmungsgründe," in *Transformationspfade in Ostdeutschland*, eds. R. Czada, G. Lehmbruch (Frankfurt–New York: Campus Verlag, 1998), 34–40.

124 More on this issue, see: Hamel, "Die DDR-Wirtschaft," 53–77, especially 68–77; H. Betz, "Recent Changes in the System of Management in the German Democratic Republic," in *Economic Reforms in the Soviet Union and Eastern Europe since the 1960s*, ed. J. Adam (New York: St. Martin's Press, 1989), 208–224; P. J. Bryson, "East German Traditional Centralism: An Alternative Route to Economic Reconstruction," *The Annals of The American Academy of Political and Social Science* 507 (1990): 133–141.

Comparing the economic transformation in West Germany after World War II and the former GDR's transition, attention must be paid to the problem of property rights, especially private property rights. Despite the totalitarian regime and far-reaching state interventionism, private property was maintained in the Third Reich.[125] Therefore, the establishment of the social market economy model was easier in West Germany after 1945 than in East Germany after 1990. The centrally planned economy in the GDR undermined any meaning of private property both in terms of doctrine and economic policy. Consequently, the implementation of West German property rules in the new federated states after reunification was not a *de facto* reconstruction. It was rather a creation of the property rights system and the whole institutional system (economic order) from scratch.[126] Hence, it can be concluded that despite the implementation of West German constitutional regulations in the Eastern *Länder*, the entire economic order in the FRG was modified as a result of German reunification. The FRG's economic system started to operate under changed circumstances, which posed many challenges related to the transition, unification, integration, and convergence of the two parts of the state. In other words, it is reasonable to speak of two different systems of the social market economy. They are conventionally separated by the caesura of 1990.[127]

The assumption of property rights so far in force only in West Germany was a key aspect of the transition of the East German legal and economic system, which involved the rapid implementation of the West German order.[128] Otherwise, the costs of defining, specifying and then enforcing completely new property rules would have been much higher. Meanwhile, the takeover of the FRG's institutions was reflected, among other things, in lower transaction costs for investments or setting up businesses, which was particularly beneficial for investors from the old federated states. In addition, the costs of transferring West German property rights to the Eastern *Länder* were made cheaper because they were administered by a central government agency, the Trust Office. Its extensive powers and vast financial resources strengthened its autonomy and helped increase the pace and scope of the privatization process. The establishment of such a body made it possible to avoid the problem of diluted political responsibility for the negative effects of

125 The economic system of the Third Reich was dualistic in nature. On the one hand, certain elements of the free market economy were maintained, particularly private property. On the other hand, all social and economic life was subordinated to the interests of the state. This was done through centralism, administrative control, and planning (Wojnarski, *Powszechna historia gospodarcza*, 221).

126 Moszyński, "Idee ładu gospodarczego," 352–353.

127 In German literature, before and after reunification, there has been extensive discussion about the state and potential transformations of the economic order and the model of the social market economy.

128 Transition economics, which includes numerous comparative studies of this process in Central and Eastern Europe, emphasizes the importance of property rights.

property transformations, although, on the other hand, the Office's excessively strong position generated a number of abuses.[129]

The importance of consistent property rights for the economy of the future unified state is demonstrated by the fact that these issues were addressed in the *Treaty Establishing a Monetary, Economic and Social Union* of May 18, 1990, between the FRG and the GDR. The introductory provisions mentioned the adoption by the parties to the agreement of a social market economy model as the basis for economic union (*Grundlage der Wirtschaftsunion*) and a common economic order (*gemeinsame Wirtschaftsordnung*). As emphasized, this model was based on respect, especially for private property, competition, free price formation, and the free movement of labor, capital, goods, and services. Although the public property was allowed, it was stipulated that private entities could not be "discriminated against."[130] Several types of freedoms were guaranteed (contracts, business, settlement and occupation, choice of occupation, and choice of residence). Workers' and business associations were maintained, declaring support for them. The property of private entities investing in land and means of production was also recognized.[131]

The latter issue was dealt with in a separate Annex No. 9 attached to the treaty. Allowing private investors to acquire real estate was intended to create new jobs. The East German side was obliged to respect their property, including the land and means of production they acquired. It was concluded that the inability to acquire property in the GDR was a major obstacle to investment, as enterprises needed free access to land. Therefore, East Germany was obliged to solve this problem in order to attract investment from the FRG and other countries. This required a change in the East German legal system, including ensuring the right to acquire land as property. First of all, sufficiently numerous and large plots of land had to be made available for commercial or job-creating investments. This did not exclude urban locations (trade and services), which were to contribute to urban development. Land of state enterprises transformed into capital companies should become the property of these companies. The rationale was that this would make it easier to obtain loans and private investors and protect employees from dismissal. It was

---

129 Cf. H. Brücker, *Privatization in Eastern Germany: A Neo-Institutional Analysis* (London: Frank Cass, German Development Institute, 2005), 124–125, 128–129. See also section 6.2.1. in this book.

130 ... *soweit private Rechtsträger dadurch nicht diskriminiert werden* (Treaty Establishing a Monetary, Economic and Social Union, Art. 1, Par. 3 (BGBl., Part II, 1990, No. 20, 537)). Cf. Treaty Establishing a Monetary, Economic and Social Union, Art. 11, Par. 1 (BGBl., Part II, 1990, No. 20, 539).

131 Treaty Establishing a Monetary, Economic and Social Union, Art. 2, Par. 1 (BGBl., Part II, 1990, No. 20, 537). Cf. "Gemeinsames Protokoll über Leitsätze," Part A, Chap. II, Pts. 1–7; Chap. III, Pts. 1–4; Part B, Chap. III, in Treaty Establishing a Monetary, Economic and Social Union (BGBl., Part II, 1990, No. 20, 545–546).

also stipulated that during the transition period, the price of land was to be verified (taking into account market prices) and possibly changed.[132]

Additional arrangements concerning enterprises were included in other parts of the main document. The East German side declaring the transition to a social market economy model, undertook to support the development of "private initiative" (*Privatinitiative*), small and medium-sized enterprises, and to respect the free decisions of companies regarding production, investment, employment, prices, and profit distribution.[133] The GDR was also to conform to the economic policy goals of the European Communities,[134] liberalize foreign trade (especially on the basis of GATT regulations[135]) and continue its integration into the world economy with the support of the FRG[136] (while at the same time operating within the Comecon[137]). Implicit in this must have been, among other things, respect for private property and support for privatization processes. In a separate article, elaborating on the earlier issues, the East German government was obligated – within the budgetary possibilities – to undertake transitional measures (defined by the parties to the agreement) in terms of adjusting the structure of enterprises to the conditions of a market economy. This involved increasing their productivity, supporting private initiatives by creating diverse and modern economic structures, enabling small and medium-sized companies to operate, and creating additional and promising jobs.[138]

It was agreed that offenses relating to socialist property committed after the treaty's entry into force would not be settled under the criminal provisions of the GDR. They were to be subject to the provisions relating to other types of

132 "Anlage IX. Möglichkeiten des Eigentumserwerbs privater Investoren an Grund und Boden sowie an Produktionsmitteln zur Förderung gewerblicher arbeitsplatzschaffender Investitionen," in Treaty Establishing a Monetary, Economic and Social Union (BGBl., Part II, 1990, No. 20, 566).

133 Treaty Establishing a Monetary, Economic and Social Union, Art. 1, Par. 3; Art. 11, Pars. 1–2 (BGBl., Part II, 1990, No. 20, 537, 539).

134 Treaty Establishing a Monetary, Economic and Social Union, Art. 11, Par. 3; Art. 13, Par. 3 (BGBl., Part II, 1990, No. 20, 539).

135 It is the *General Agreement on Tariffs and Trade* (GATT) signed on October 30, 1947, in Geneva. It was in force until December 31, 1994. Since January 1, 1995, it has been replaced by the World Trade Organization (WTO) in Geneva. The primary goal of these initiatives was to liberalize international trade. More information see, e.g., M. Proczek, "Od Układu Ogólnego w Sprawie Taryf Celnych i Handlu do Światowej Organizacji Handlu," in E. Latoszek, M. Proczek, *Organizacje międzynarodowe. Założenia, cele, działalność* (Warszawa: WSHiFM, Dom Wydawniczy Elipsa, 2001), 131–151.

136 Cf. Treaty Establishing a Monetary, Economic and Social Union, Art. 13, Pars. 1, 3 (BGBl., Part II, 1990, No. 20, 539).

137 Cf. Treaty Establishing a Monetary, Economic and Social Union, Art. 13, Par. 2 (BGBl., Part II, 1990, No. 20, 539).

138 Treaty Establishing a Monetary, Economic and Social Union, Art. 14 (BGBl., Part II, 1990, No. 20, 539–540).

property.[139] From the point of view of agriculture, it was important to draw attention to the need to improve the competitiveness of agricultural enterprises, to develop their production in terms of quality and environment[140] and to avoid overproduction.[141] The monopoly of the East German state in the conduct of domestic and foreign trade,[142] as well as in the formation of the insurance[143] and financial system,[144] was abolished. It was announced that private banks could be established in the GDR, competing with state and cooperative banks.[145] The parties also settled issues related to such taxes as property, inheritance, and gift taxes.[146]

The document announced the compilation of an inventory of state assets (*volkseigene Vermögen*) in East Germany. This was to serve the "structural adjustment of the economy" (*Strukturanpassung der Wirtschaft*), i.e., its restructuring and the "restoration of the state budget" (*Sanierung des Staatshaushalts*) of the GDR.[147]

With regard to East German debts, it was agreed that the FRG would take them over. The debts from the GDR's loans taken out in 1990 were to be partly converted into trust assets (*Treuhandvermögen*) and partly covered by the federal government

139 "Gemeinsames Protokoll über Leitsätze," Part B, Chap. I, Pt. 5, in Treaty Establishing a Monetary, Economic and Social Union (BGBl., Part II, 1990, No. 20, 546).

140 It is worth noting that a separate and elaborate article of the analyzed document dealt with environmental protection (Treaty Establishing a Monetary, Economic and Social Union, Art. 16 (BGBl., Part II, 1990, No. 20, 540)).

141 Treaty Establishing a Monetary, Economic and Social Union, Art. 15, Pars. 2–4 (BGBl., Part II, 1990, No. 20, 540).

142 Cf. Treaty Establishing a Monetary, Economic and Social Union, Arts. 12–13 (BGBl., Part II, 1990, No. 20, 539); "Gemeinsames Protokoll über Leitsätze," Part B, Chap. II, Pt. 6, in Treaty Establishing a Monetary, Economic and Social Union (BGBl., Part II, 1990, No. 20, 546).

143 Cf. Treaty Establishing a Monetary, Economic and Social Union, Arts. 17–25 (BGBl., Part II, 1990, No. 20, 540–542); "Gemeinsames Protokoll über Leitsätze," Part B, Chap. II, Pt. 4, in Treaty Establishing a Monetary, Economic and Social Union (BGBl., Part II, 1990, No. 20, 546).

144 Cf. Treaty Establishing a Monetary, Economic and Social Union, Arts. 26–34 (BGBl., Part II, 1990, No. 20, 542–544); "Gemeinsames Protokoll über Leitsätze," Part B, Chap. II, Pts. 1–3, 5, in Treaty Establishing a Monetary, Economic and Social Union (BGBl., Part II, 1990, No. 20, 546).

145 Treaty Establishing a Monetary, Economic and Social Union, Art. 10, Par. 4 (BGBl., Part II, 1990, No. 20, 538).

146 Treaty Establishing a Monetary, Economic and Social Union, Arts. 31, 33–34 (BGBl., Part II, 1990, No. 20, 543–544). Cf. "Anlage IV. Von der Deutschen Demokratischen Republik neu zu erlassende Rechtsvorschriften," Art. III, Pars. 4–5, in Treaty Establishing a Monetary, Economic and Social Union (BGBl., Part II, 1990, No. 20, 559).

147 Treaty Establishing a Monetary, Economic and Social Union, Art. 26, Par. 4 (BGBl., Part II, 1990, No. 20, 542).

and the East German *Länder*.[148] It was mentioned that debts, rents, and leases would be converted into DM, which have been the common currency of the FRG and the GDR since July 1.[149]

The announcements of corresponding changes in the legislation of the FRG and the GDR, resulting from the conclusion of the *Treaty Establishing a Monetary, Economic and Social Union* between the two countries, included the eight remaining annexes to the agreement.[150] The parliaments of the German states ratified the treaty in June. The People's Chamber passed the relevant law on June 21.[151] On the same day, the East German parliament also passed the *Law on the Enactment of Legislation of the Federal Republic of Germany in the German Democratic Republic.* These concerned, among other things, the judiciary, administrative offenses, the credit system, banks (including the German Federal Bank), housing cooperatives, companies, deposits, the insurance system, competition protection, monopolies, atomic energy, trade, the Civil Code, economic cooperatives, the rights of employees in corporate management, collective bargaining agreements and employment protection. Some regulations were accompanied by exceptions, which resulted from the specificity of the East German system.[152]

Par. 22 of this law was relevant to property rights in the GDR. It implemented the *Act on the Conversion of Legal Entities* (*Transformation Act*) in East Germany, which was passed in West Germany on November 6, 1969.[153] The document of

148 Treaty Establishing a Monetary, Economic and Social Union, Art. 27, Par. 3 (BGBl., Part II, 1990, No. 20, 542).

149 Rents and leases were to be converted at a ratio of 1:1, while debts were to be converted at a ratio of 2:1 (Treaty Establishing a Monetary, Economic and Social Union, Art. 10, Par. 5, Pts. 2–3 (BGBl., Part II, 1990, No. 20, 538–539)).

150 Cf. "Anlage I–VIII," in Treaty Establishing a Monetary, Economic and Social Union (BGBl., Part II, 1990, No. 20, 547–565).

151 *Gesetz zum Vertrag über die Schaffung einer Währungs-, Wirtschafts- und Sozialunion zwischen der Deutschen Demokratischen Republik und der Bundesrepublik Deutschland vom 18. Mai 1990 (Verfassungsgesetz) vom 21. Juni 1990* (GBl.-DDR, Part I, 1990, No. 34, 331–357).

152 *Gesetz über die Inkraftsetzung von Rechtsvorschriften der Bundesrepublik Deutschland in der Deutschen Demokratischen Republik vom 21. Juni 1990* (GBl.-DDR, Part I, 1990, No. 34, 357–363).

153 *Bekanntmachung der Neufassung des Umwandlungsgesetzes Vom 6. November 1969* (BGBl., Part I, 1969, No. 119, 2081–2092). See amendments up 2015: December 19, 1985; October, 28, 1994; April, 19, 2007; July, 11, 2011 (*Gesetz zur Durchführung der Vierten, Siebenten und Achten Richtlinie des Rates der Europäischen Gemeinschaften zur Koordinierung des Gesellschaftsrechts (Bilanzrichtlinien-Gesetz – BiRiLiG) Vom 19. Dezember 1985* (BGBl, Part I, 1985, No. 62, 2355–2433); *Gesetz zur Bereinigung des Umwandlungsrechts (UmwBerG) Vom 28. Oktober 1994* (BGBl., Part I, 1994, No. 77, 3210–3266). Cf. the correction of this amendment of March 22, 1995: *Berichtigung des Gesetzes zur Bereinigung des Umwandlungsrechts Vom 22. März 1995* (BGBl., Part I, 1995, No. 16, 428). Subsequent amendments: *Zweites Gesetz zur Änderung des Umwandlungsgesetzes Vom 19. April 2007* (BGBl., Part I, 2007, No. 15, 542–548);

June 21, 1990, therefore, made it possible to change the legal structure of East German companies, enterprises, trade unions, and their assets.[154] The law in question entered into force on July 1.[155] It was already amended on July 6.[156]

The Bundestag, in ratifying the *Treaty Establishing a Monetary, Economic and Social Union* on June 25, additionally specified concrete amendments to the existing provisions resulting from its conclusion. The specific amendments concerned, among other things, property issues, which were the subject of the treaty.[157]

Two complementary issues should be noted at this point. Firstly, any modifications in East German legislation were temporary. At the moment of German reunification, the GDR became subject to the Basic Law of the FRG and the West German legal system. Secondly, as a result of the analyzed treaty, East German social (socialist) property lost its privileged legal status over private property. The latter form of property was to dispose of special legal protection. Moreover, the joint agreement between the FRG and the GDR opened up the possibility of privatization in East Germany in the future.

Property rights issues were also resolved in such a key document for German reunification as the *Unification Treaty* of August 31. It was agreed that East German state assets (*Verwaltungsvermögen*) would become the property of the FRG. Certain exceptions were made for assets serving administrative purposes of the *Länder*, municipalities (associations of municipalities), or other entities after October 1, 1989. The same applied to the assets of the Stasi,[158] unless they were used for other

---

Drittes Gesetz zur Änderung des Umwandlungsgesetzes Vom 11. Juli 2011 (BGBl., Part I, 2011, No. 35, 1338–1340)).

154 *Gesetz über die Inkraftsetzung von Rechtsvorschriften der Bundesrepublik Deutschland in der Deutschen Demokratischen Republik*, Par. 22 (GBl.-DDR, Part I, 1990, No. 34, 357–363).

155 *Gesetz über die Inkraftsetzung von Rechtsvorschriften der Bundesrepublik Deutschland in der Deutschen Demokratischen Republik*, Par. 34 (GBl.-DDR, Part I, 1990, No. 34, 357–363).

156 *Gesetz über die Änderung des Gesetzes vom 21. Juni 1990 über die Inkraftsetzung von Rechtsvorschriften der Bundesrepublik Deutschland in der Deutschen Demokratischen Republik vom 6. Juli 1990* (GBl.-DDR, Part I, 1990, No. 44, 713).

157 Cf. Treaty Establishing a Monetary, Economic and Social Union (BGBl., Part II, 1990, No. 20, 518–536).

158 It was the main security organ of the GDR, established in 1950. It was responsible for internal security, intelligence, and counterintelligence. The Stasi carried out agent activity, conducting numerous repressions and crimes against East German citizens. The structure of the Stasi was reorganized several times during the GDR's existence. In 1950–1953, it functioned as the Ministry for State Security (*Ministerium für Staatssicherheit*, MfS). Between 1953 and 1955, the work of the East German secret service was supervised by the Office of the State Secretary of State Security in the Ministry of the Interior (*Staatssekretariat für Staatssicherheit* (SfS) *des Ministerium des Inneren* (MdI)). From 1955 to 1989, the original name (MfS) was in use, while from 1989 to 1990, the Office for National Security (*Amt für Nationale Sicherheit*, AfNS)

purposes after that date. If these assets had not become federal, they were to be assigned to the competent administrative authority. If the assets were transferred to the authority free of charge by a third party, they were to be returned. The former assets of the Third Reich that remained in the GDR became the property of the FRG.[159]

The same was true of other public assets (*öffentliches Vermögen*), including state land assets, assets in agriculture and forestry, and GDR's financial assets (*Finanzvermögen*). The latter group was to be distributed half between the Federation and the *Länder*. The only exceptions were funds earmarked for social insurance (*Sozialversicherung*) and those at the disposal of the Trust Office, which coordinated the privatization process in the Eastern federated states,[160] or municipalities, cities, or *Länder*. The financial assets of the Stasi were to be managed by the Trust Office unless they were earmarked for other purposes since October 1, 1989. The agreement stipulated that until the legal settlement of the issues in question, the existing authorities managed the financial assets unless the FRG Minister of Finance decided otherwise. At the same time, the free flow of information and documents between the various public authorities was ensured. It was also agreed that separate rules would apply to the state housing capital. It was to pass (including debts) into the possession of the municipalities (*Kommune*), which were obliged to manage it according to the housing market conditions. Moreover, privatization processes in this sector were to be supported.[161] Social legislation also had to be adapted to West German and European requirements.[162]

A separate place was devoted to the issue of the GDR's debts. In principle, all debts (*Schulden*) were assumed by the FRG. Since reunification, East German debts (as of October 3, 1990) were to be serviced by a temporary special (purpose, trust) federal fund (*Sondervermögen*), supervised by the Federal Minister of Finance. It could borrow money to pay debt, interest, loan costs, or to purchase debt securities. Between October 3, 1990, and December 31, 1993, the federal government, together with the Trust Office, was to reimburse the special fund for half of the interest paid on the debt. In turn, on January 1, 1994 – with reference to the *Treaty Establishing a Monetary, Economic and Social Union* – the government, the *Länder*, and the Trust Office were obliged to take over the debt from the special fund finally.[163] The repayment was to be distributed proportionally to the individual federated

---

functioned. See, e.g., J. Gieseke, *Stasi. Historia 1945–1990* (Kraków: Wydawnictwo UJ, 2010).

159 Unification Treaty, Art. 21 (BGBl., Part II, 1990, No. 35, 895). With regard to the acquisition of the assets of the former Third Reich by the FRG, cf. Art. 134 GG.

160 The details of the Trust Office were regulated by Art. 25 of the *Unification Treaty* (Unification Treaty, Art. 25 (BGBl., Part II, 1990, No. 35, 897)). More on the activities of this body: section 6.2.1. in the present book.

161 Unification Treaty, Art. 22 (BGBl., Part II, 1990, No. 35, 895–896).

162 Cf. Unification Treaty, Arts. 30–33 (BGBl., part II, 1990, No. 35, 899–900).

163 Cf. Treaty Establishing a Monetary, Economic and Social Union, Art. 27, Par. 3 (BGBl., Part II, 1990, No. 20, 542).

states according to population, not including the population of West Berlin. In this way, the special fund was to be liquidated. The shares of the East German central bank (*Staatsbank Berlin*) were distributed among the *Länder*.[164] A separate article dealt with the details of the settlement of the GDR's debts to the FRG and to third countries (especially those that were part of the Comecon).[165] Elsewhere, issues related to the FRG's takeover of the East German railroads and post office were discussed.[166]

From the point of view of the convergence policy of the Eastern and Western *Länder*, the *Unification Treaty* pointed out, among other things, the importance of privatization. In this context, it spoke of "measures to strengthen the modernization and structural reorganization of the economy on the basis of restructuring concepts drawn up under the responsibility of the industry."[167] The possibility of writing off the debts of some enterprises was also indicated.[168]

The text of the *Joint Declaration of the Governments of the Federal Republic of Germany and the German Democratic Republic on the Settlement of Open Property Issues*, which was signed on June 15, 1990, was added as separate Annex No. 3 to the *Unification Treaty*. It was about maintaining the interferences with property undertaken in the Eastern *Länder* during the GDR period. This was justified by certain cases of the need to carry out key investments after reunification, especially in constructing enterprises and safeguarding existing jobs or creating new ones. Compensation was provided for the original owners.[169] A relevant provision in this regard, based on Art. 4, Par. 5 of the *Unification Treaty*, was even included in the FRG Constitution (Art. 143 GG).[170]

These issues were expanded in the aforementioned Annex No. 3. It was established that the authorities of the Soviet Union and the GDR lost the ability to carry out expropriations on the basis of internal law or occupation law from 1945–1949.[171] The future German parliament (after reunification) was to make the final decisions on possible compensations (Pt. 1).

---

164 Unification Treaty, Art. 23 (BGBl., Part II, 1990, No. 35, 896–897).

165 Unification Treaty, Art. 24 (BGBl., Part II, 1990, No. 35, 897). Cf. Unification Treaty, Art. 29 (BGBl., Part II, 1990, No. 35, 899).

166 Unification Treaty, Arts. 26–27 (BGBl., Part II, 1990, No. 35, 898).

167 *Maßnahmen zur verstärken Modernisierung und strukturellen Neuordnung der Wirtschaft auf der Grundlage von in Eigenverantwortung der Industrie erstellten Restrukturierungskonzepten* (Unification Treaty, Art. 28, Par. 2, Pt. 4 (BGBl., Part II, 1990, No. 35, 899)).

168 Unification Treaty, Art. 28, Par. 2, Par. 5 (BGBl., Part II, 1990, No. 35, 899).

169 Unification Treaty, Art. 41 (BGBl., Part II, 1990, No. 35, 903–904).

170 Unification Treaty, Art. 4, Par. 5 (BGBl., Part II, 1990, No. 35, 891); Art. 143 GG.

171 It is worth recalling that on October 1, 1990, at a session of the UN General Assembly in New York, France, the United Kingdom, the United States, and the Soviet Union renounced their rights and responsibilities with respect to Germany as of October 3, 1990 (see more fully section 2.2. in this paper).

Trusts and other restrictions on the property of land, production enterprises (crafts), and other property were abolished. Those citizens who had lost their property for various reasons (e.g., fleeing the GDR for the FRG) were declared to have it returned (Pt. 2).

The declaration provided for the return of expropriated property to the owners or their heirs. However, two caveats were made. Firstly, citizens were to receive compensation (if the GDR authorities had not already done so) if the seized property had changed its nature at the time this document was issued (e.g., it was assigned to public use, used for housing, commercial purposes, or incorporated into another economic entity). Secondly, in case the property was sold to a third party, the original owner was to receive another property of similar value or compensation. Separate regulations were to cover the determination of compensation, taking into account changes in the property's real value (Pt. 3). These regulations were to be applied to both private and state property (Pt. 4).

All tenant protection rights that had previously existed in East Germany were confirmed. This included the right to use real estate and buildings (Pt. 5).

The original owners were to recover the enterprises taken over by the GDR authorities. Enterprises nationalized in the GDR in 1972 were covered by the *Act on the Establishment and Operation of Private Enterprises and on Participation in Enterprises* of March 7, 1990, enacted there.[172] With reference to this act, state-owned shares in enterprises were to be sold to private entities. The decision to privatize was to be made on an internal proposal and not on the basis of guidelines from an external body (Pt. 6). Enterprises and shares nationalized between 1949 and 1972 were to be returned to their original owners (in full, in the form of shares or stocks) unless they demanded compensation (Pt. 7).

The declaration excluded the return of assets seized illegally. For example, it listed abuse of power, corruption, coercion, and fraud (Pt. 8). The document also addressed the unlawful recovery of property. The GDR committed to judicial consideration of such issues (Pt. 9).

It was decided to sell the shares in repayment of the loan from the FRG, taking into account the adoption of a common currency (Pt. 10). With the beginning of monetary, economic, and social union (July 1, 1990), all restrictions on payment transactions were to cease to apply (Pt. 11). All property under GDR state administration was to be returned to the original owners or their heirs (Pt. 12).

Furthermore, the GDR authorities were obliged to create essential legal procedures related to the document matter. Interested citizens were to be informed of the place and deadline (no longer than six months) for submitting the relevant applications. Compensation was to be paid from a separate fund, unconnected to the GDR budget. Refunds and compensation should be withheld until the deadline

172 Cf. *Gesetz über die Gründung und Tätigkeit privater Unternehmen und über Unternehmensbeteiligungen vom 7. März 1990* (GBl.-DDR, Part I, 1990, No. 17, 141–144).

for submitting the above applications by citizens. The GDR authorities also had to review unclear matters related to past restitutions (Pt. 13). Any remaining details were to be worked out by a joint group of experts appointed by both governments (Pt. 14).[173]

The People's Chamber ratified the *Unification Treaty* on September 20.[174] The West German ratification law of September 23 identified specific changes to the laws that resulted from the treaty between the two German states. These included property issues.[175]

With the formal reunification of Germany on October 3, the power of the FRG Constitution, in which property rights had a fundamental basis, was extended to the new federated states. In this context, Sabine Spangenberg writes about the "establishment of unambiguous property rights," referring to the constitutional guarantee of property rights, privatization, and re-privatization.[176]

---

173 "Anlage III. Gemeinsame Erklärung der Regierungen der Bundesrepublik Deutschland und der Deutschen Demokratischen Republik zur Regelung offener Vermögensfragen Vom 15. Juni 1990," in Unification Treaty (BGBl., Part II, 1990, No. 35, 1237–1238). In the literature, one can find a view that the *Unification Treaty* did not, however, specify a clear understanding of property. See, e.g., Waldner, "Private Property and the Transformation Process," 92. He adds that the category of the property was better defined (i.e. more precise) in the legislation of the GDR than that of the FRG.

174 *Gesetz zum Vertrag zwischen der Deutschen Demokratischen Republik und der Bundesrepublik Deutschland über die Herstellung der Einheit Deutschlands – Einigungsvertrag – vom 31. August 1990 (Verfassungsgesetz) vom 20. September* 1990 (GBl.-DDR, Part I, 1990, No. 64, 1627–1986). Cf. *Bekanntmachung über das Inkrafttreten des Vertrages zwischen der Deutschen Demokratischen Republik und der Bundesrepublik Deutschland über die Herstellung der Einheit Deutschlands – Einigungsvertrag – vom 29. September 1990* (GBl.-DDR, Part I, 1990, No. 65, 1988–1989).

175 Cf. Unification Treaty (BGBl., Part II, 1990, No. 35, 885–888).

176 Spangenberg, *The Institutionalised Transformation*, 132–159.

CHAPTER 6 Regulations of property rights in Germany after reunification and their relationship to the economy

6.1. Property rights in reunified Germany

Taking the risk of a certain simplification, the analysis of property rules in Germany after reunification will take into account two dimensions: (1) the degree of completeness of property rights from the point of view of their exclusivity and transferability; (2) the enforcement and protection of these rights, taking into account the role of the state, the actions of the owners and social norms. Although further considerations will show the interpenetration of these levels from the point of view of the studied sources' content, their separation is logical and has an ordering character.[1] The research of these dimensions was based primarily on German normative acts in force in Germany in 1990–2015, considered in the universally binding hierarchical order, starting with the FRG Constitution, and ending with specific laws. It turns out that a number of regulations had their source in the legal system of post-war West Germany. However, some solutions had a richer tradition.

6.1.1. Degree of completeness of property rights

6.1.1.1. Exclusivity: Empowerment of property rights in the FRG Constitution

The dimension of the degree of completeness of property rights in Germany after reunification stems from the way in which they are defined. This is reflected in the legal regulations of the time, starting with the Basic Law. The first level of analysis of the degree of completeness of property rights is exclusivity, which means the owner's exclusive rights to property. The owner possesses sovereignty within the framework of disposing of them in relation to other individuals. Between 1990 and 2015, there were a number of regulations in Germany guaranteeing owners the exclusivity of their rights. They concerned various aspects.

It should be mentioned that in German law, the concept of "property" (*Eigentum*) is distinguished from "possession" and "assets" (*Besitz*). The nouns *Eigentum* and *Eigentümer* ("owner") refer to property rights that the owner has. They have a non-material and abstract dimension. This corresponds to the view of property rights theory. *Besitz* and *Besitzer*, on the other hand, refer to the actual disposition over a given thing, the material and concrete use of the object of property by both the

---

1 See para. 5.1. in this book.

owner and the person authorized by him.[2] Thus, the last noun can be translated as "possessor," "user."[3]

Germany's property rights (*Eigentumsrechte*) have their basic foundation in the Basic Law. The importance of property regulations is demonstrated by the fact that in German literature, they are sometimes referred to as the "property constitution" or "property system" (*Eigentumsverfassung*).[4] In the German jurisprudence, it is stated that property is included in the framework of public law in this case (*Rahmen des öffentlichen Rechts*).[5]

The importance of property rights for the German social and economic system is confirmed by regulations included in Chap. I GG, dedicated to the basic rights. It is also important to note that a significant part of constitutional provisions concerning property referred to the Weimar Constitution (actually: the Constitution of the German Reich, or the Weimar Republic) from August 11, 1919. Thus, the authors of the Basic Law of 1949 referred to the republican and democratic traditions of the state that had grown on the ruins of the Second Reich.[6] A comparison of the relevant sections of both constitutions is presented in Table 12.

---

2 W. Theil, "Eigentum und Verpflichtung. Einige juristische Aspekte," in *Verpflichtungsökonomik. Eigentum, Freiheit und Haftung in der Geldwirtschaft*, ed. H.-J. Stadermann (Marburg: Metropolis Verlag, 2001), 181, table 2.

3 More on the category of *Besitz* in German law and how it differs from *Eigentum*: F. Baur, J. F. Baur, R. Stürner, *Sachenrecht* (München: Verlag C. H. Beck, 2009), 64–103; J. Wilhelm, *Sachenrecht* (Berlin–New York: De Gruyter, 2010), 58–80, 209–243; T. Zerres, *Bürgerliches Recht. Eine Einführung in das Zivilrecht und die Grundzüge des Zivilprozessrecht* (Heidelberg: Springer, 2010), 353–360; E. Klunzinger, *Einführung in das Bürgerliche Recht. Grundkurs für Studierende der Rechts- und Wirtschaftswissenschaften* (München: Verlag Franz Vahlen, 2011), 529–536.

4 P. Häberle, "Vielfalt der Property Rights und der verfassungsrechtliche Eigentumsbegriff," in *Ansprüche, Eigentums- und Verfügungsrechte*, ed. M. Neumann (Berlin: Duncker & Humblot, 1984), 63–102; H. Leipold, "Eigentum und wirtschaftliches Handeln in beiden deutschen Staaten," in *Materialien zum Bericht zur Lage der Nation im geteilten Deutschland 1987* (Bonn: Bundesministerium für innerdeutsche Beziehungen, 1987), 38–41; G. Brunner, "Verfassungsrechtliche Rahmenbedingungen der wirtschaftlichen Transformation," in *Transformationsprozesse in sozialistischen Wirtschaftssystemen. Ursachen, Konzepte, Instrumente*, eds. K.-H. Hartwig, H. J. Thieme (Berlin: Springer-Verlag, 1991), 206. Cf. S. Spangenberg, *The Institutionalised Transformation of the East German Economy* (Heidelberg–New York: Physica-Verlag. A Springer-Verlag Company, 1998), 132–134; H. Höfer, "Eigentum," in *Lexikon Soziale Marktwirtschaft. Wirtschaftspolitik von A bis Z*, eds. R. H. Hasse, H. Schneider, K. Weigelt (Paderborn: Ferdinand Schöningh, 2002), 158.

5 Wilhelm, *Sachenrecht*, 312, table 15.

6 More on the similarities between the German constitutions of 1919 and 1949, see, e.g.: E. M. Hucko, ed., *The Democratic Tradition: Four German Constitutions* (Leamington: Berg Publishers, 1987), *passim*. The constitutions of the GDR also bear some similarities in this regard. Due to the totalitarian nature of the communist regime, however, the regulations there were of a declarative nature (cf. section 3.2. in this work).

Table 12: *Comparison of the provisions of the Weimar Constitution and the FRG Constitution regarding property*[a]

Language version	**Weimar Constitution of August 11, 1919**	**The FRG Constitution of May 23, 1949**
Translation in English	*Article 153* [Paragraph 1] *Property shall be guaranteed by the constitution. Its nature and limits shall be prescribed by law.*	*Article 14* *(1) Property and the right of inheritance shall be guaranteed. Their content and limits shall be defined by the laws.*
	[Paragraph 2] *Expropriation shall take place only for the general good and only on the basis of law. It shall be accompanied by payment of just compensation unless otherwise provided by national law. In case of dispute over the amount of compensation recourse to the ordinary courts shall be permitted, unless otherwise provided by national law. Expropriation by the Reich over against the states, municipalities, and associations serving the public welfare may take place only upon the payment of compensation.*	*(2) Property entails obligations. Its use shall also serve the public good.*
	[Paragraph 3] *Property imposes obligations. Its use by its owner shall at the same time serve the public good.* *Article 154* [Paragraph 1] *The right of inheritance shall be guaranteed according to the provisions of the civil code.* [Paragraph 2] *The share of the state in estates shall be determined by law.*	*(3) Expropriation shall only be permissible for the public good. It may only be ordered by or pursuant to a law that determines the nature and extent of compensation. Such compensation shall be determined by establishing an equitable balance between the public interest and the interests of those affected. In case of dispute concerning the amount of compensation, recourse may be had to the ordinary courts.*
Original in German	*Artikel 153* [Paragraph 1] *Das Eigentum wird von der Verfassung gewährleistet. Sein Inhalt und seine Schranken ergeben sich aus den Gesetzen.*	*Artikel 14* *(1) Das Eigentum und das Erbrecht werden gewährleistet. Inhalt und Schranken werden durch die Gesetze bestimmt.*

(*Continued*)

Table 12: (*Continued*)

Language version	Weimar Constitution of August 11, 1919	The FRG Constitution of May 23, 1949
	[Paragraph 2] *Eine Enteignung kann nur zum Wohle der Allgemeinheit und auf gesetzlicher Grundlage vorgenommen werden. Sie erfolgt gegen angemessene Entschädigung, soweit nicht ein Reichsgesetz etwas anderes bestimmt. Wegen der Höhe der Entschädigung ist im Streitfalle der Rechtsweg bei den ordentlichen Gerichten offen zu halten, soweit Reichsgesetze nichts anderes bestimmen. Enteignung durch das Reich gegenüber Ländern, Gemeinden und gemeinnützigen Verbänden kann nur gegen Entschädigung erfolgen.*	*(2) Eigentum verpflichtet. Sein Gebrauch soll zugleich dem Wohle der Allgemeinheit dienen.*
	[Paragraph 3] *Eigentum verpflichtet. Sein Gebrauch soll zugleich Dienst sein für das Gemeine Beste.* *Artikel 154* [Paragraph 1] *Das Erbrecht wird nach Maßgabe des bürgerlichen Rechtes gewährleistet.* [Paragraph 2] *Der Anteil des Staates am Erbgut bestimmt sich nach den Gesetzen.*	*(3) Eine Enteignung ist nur zum Wohle der Allgemeinheit zulässig. Sie darf nur durch Gesetz oder auf Grund eines Gesetzes erfolgen, das Art und Ausmaß der Entschädigung regelt. Die Entschädigung ist unter gerechter Abwägung der Interessen der Allgemeinheit und der Beteiligten zu bestimmen. Wegen der Höhe der Entschädigung steht im Streitfalle der Rechtsweg vor den ordentlichen Gerichten offen.*

a Translations of the provisions of the Weimar Constitution: "Germany," in *The New Constitutions of Europe*, eds. H. L. McBain, L. Rogers (New York: Doubleday, Page & Company, 1922), 167–212. Translations of the provisions of the FRG Constitution: *Basic Law for the Federal Republic of Germany*, Federal Ministry of Justice, Federal Office of Justice, https://www.gesetze-im-internet.de/englisch_gg/ (accessed May 18, 2022). Cf. L. Janicki, ed., *Ustawa Zasadnicza (Konstytucja) Republiki Federalnej Niemiec z 23 maja 1949 r./Grundgesetz für die Bundesrepublik Deutschland vom 23. Mai 1949* (Poznań: Instytut Zachodni, 2007), 87; "Grundgesetz für die Bundesrepublik Deutschland vom 23. Mai 1949/Ustawa Zasadnicza Republiki Federalnej Niemiec z 23 maja 1949," in J. W. Tkaczyński, *Prawo ustrojowe Niemiec* (Kraków: Wydawnictwo UJ, 2015), 463–464.

Own compilation based on: *Die Verfassung des Deutschen Reichs. Vom 11. August 1919.*, Arts. 153–154 (*ReichsGesetzblatt* (hereinafter: RGBl.), 1919, No. 152/6982, 1412–1413); *Grundgesetz für die Bundesrepublik Deutschland vom 23. Mai 1949.*, Art. 14 (BGBl., Part I, 1949, No. 1, 3).

The similarities between the German constitutions of 1919 and 1949 with regard to property concern both the matter and the manner in which it is defined. Some formulations sound almost identical. In both acts, the existence of property and the right of inheritance is ensured, with the details of this being included in the laws. There is also an important statement about the social obligation arising from the disposition of property. However, while the Weimar Constitution stipulated that the use of property should serve the "public good," or rather "common good" (*Gemeine Beste*), 30 years later, the legislature specified the "public good" (*Wohl der Allgemeinheit*) in Art. 14 GG.[7] The latter category was the common point of reference for the expropriation regulated in both analyzed constitutions. It should be the subject of the respective laws. The act of 1919 provided for legal solutions concerning "just compensation" (*angemessene Entschädigung*), while the FRG Constitution was more precise and mentioned statutory solutions concerning the "nature and extent of compensation" (*Art und Ausmaß der Entschädigung*). Moreover, the document of 1949 expressed the expectation that compensation would be determined on the "equitable balance between the public interest and the interests of those affected" (*unter gerechter Abwägung der Interessen der Allgemeinheit und der Beteiligten*),[8] reinforcing the social component of the economic system in postwar West Germany. Both basic laws provided for the possibility of appealing the cases in question to ordinary courts.[9]

The constitutional regulations of 1919 should be placed in the social and legal context of Europe at the time. After World War I, as a result of the development of the workers' movement and the social teachings of the Roman Catholic Church,[10]

---

7 Interestingly, there is another English translation of the phrase *Wohl der Allgemeinheit*, contained in Art. 14, Par. 2 GG: "general good" (see Table 12 in this study). The same problems are in other languages, e.g. in Polish. Jan Wiktor Tkaczyński translates this phrase as "public benefit" (Pol. *pożytek publiczny*), while the same one present in the next paragraph as the "public good" (Pol. *dobro ogółu*) ("Grundgesetz für die Bundesrepublik Deutschland," Art. 14, Pars. 2–3, in Tkaczyński, *Prawo ustrojowe Niemiec*, 464).

8 Tkaczyński proposes a translation: "on the basis of a fair balancing of the interests of the public and those concerned" (Pol. *na podstawie sprawiedliwego wyważenia interesów ogółu i osób zainteresowanych*) ("Grundgesetz für die Bundesrepublik Deutschland,", Art. 14, Par. 3, in Tkaczyński, *Prawo ustrojowe Niemiec*, 464).

9 On the empowerment of property in the Weimar Constitution see: W. Böhmer, "Eigentum aus verfassungsrechtlicher Sicht. Grundfragen der verfassungsrechtlichen Gewährleistung des Eigentums in der Rechtsprechung des Bundesverfassungsgerichts," in *Das Eigentum. Vorträge gehalten auf der Tagung der Joachim Jungius-Gesellschaft der Wissenschaften. Hamburg am 10., 11. und 12. Dezember 1987*, ed. J. F. Baur (Göttingen: Vandenhoeck & Ruprecht, 1989), 44–45, 71–74. See comments on Art. 14 GG: H. Dreier, ed., *Grundgesetz. Kommentar*, Vol. I: *Präambel, Artikel 1–19* (Tübingen: Mohr Siebeck, 2004), 1228–1329; M. Sachs, ed., *Grundgesetz. Kommentar* (München: C. H. Beck, 2018), 603–669.

10 It refers to the Roman Catholic Church's teaching on social issues. The publication of Pope Leo XIII's encyclical *Rerum novarum* in 1891 is the beginnings of its

the role of "social rights" increased. Their enforcement was associated with positive state interference, which was an important difference from civil liberties. On the basis of specific principles, the authorities could restrict, e.g., the inviolability of private property. Examples of basic laws passed in this spirit were the Weimar Constitution and the Polish March Constitution of 1921.[11] The regulations of 1949, through their links to the Weimar Constitution, indirectly referred to this context.

The above provisions correspond to Art. 15 GG, which provides for the legal possibility of nationalization of ground, land, natural resources, and means of production. Based on the law, they could be transformed into a common property or any form of common management with compensation.[12] However, as Lech Janicki noted, this provision remained a dead letter.[13]

On the other hand, Art. 143 GG, attached on the basis of the *Unification Treaty* of August 31, 1990, in certain cases maintained previous interferences with the property that had taken place in the former GDR. This was justified by the need for key investments. Specific provisions regulated compensation to the original owner.[14]

The legal and economic interpretation of the constitutional provisions on property in West Germany has received many studies, especially in the German study. Several important points should be noted. The property guarantee in the FRG Constitution was universal and inclusive. In principle, everyone had the right to acquire and dispose of property, in contrast to the extractive constitutional regulations in the GDR, where certain objects of property were assigned to separate groups of owners, excluding others. In West Germany, no differentiation was made between productive and utilitarian objects. Art. 14 GG defined and protected the right to acquire and dispose of any type of property (material, non-material, insurance rights, commercial rights, etc.) in both private and public dimensions.

---

conceptualization (Leon XIII, *Encyklika papieża Leona XIII wszystkim czcigodnym Braciom Patriarchom, Prymasom, Arcybiskupom świata katolickiego, łaskę i społeczność ze Stolicą Apostolską mającym Rerum Novarum o kwestii socjalnej. 15 V 1891 r.* (Warszawa: Wydawnictwo Te Deum, 2001)). The Leo XIII's successors developed this teaching (cf. *Kompendium nauki społecznej Kościoła* (Kielce: Papieska Rada Iustitia et Pax, Wydawnictwo Jedność, 2005)). On the current reading of the encyclical of the "pope of the workers" in the context of Catholic entrepreneurship, see, e.g., D. Bębnowski, "Wokół przedsiębiorczości katolickiej. Reminiscencje z odczytania 'Rerum Novarum' Leona XIII na nowo," *Łódzkie Studia Teologiczne* 27, No. 3 (2018): 197–210.

11 S. Krukowski, "Konstytucja Rzeczypospolitej Polskiej z 1921 r.," in *Konstytucje Polski. Szkice monograficzne z dziejów polskiego konstytucjonalizmu*, ed. M. Kallas (Warszawa: PWN, 1990), 114–115.

12 Art. 15 GG.

13 L. Janicki, "Wprowadzenie," in Janicki, *Ustawa Zasadnicza*, 19.

14 Art. 143 GG. Cf. Unification Treaty, Art. 4, Par. 5; Art. 41 (BGBl., Part II, 1990, No. 35, 891, 903–904). More on this issue, see: section 5.3. in this work.

This included the right to private business. Among the most important economic effects of such a definition of property, Helmut Leipold includes e.g.: enabling households to manage their property in various ways, increasing investment, higher levels of prosperity, developing the enterprise sector and entrepreneurship as such, stimulating competition.[15]

Heinrich Höfer writes about several basic functions of property, especially with regard to private property. These concerned: (1) individual and family development (*Entfaltungs- und Familienfunktion*); (2) decentralization to foster optimal and innovative solutions to problems in a spirit of competition (*Dezentralisierungsfunktion*); (3) motivation of individuals (*Motivationsfunktion*); (4) civil liberties (*Freiheitsfunktion*); (5) sustainability in the context of the social obligation of owners (*Nachhaltigkeitsfunktion*).[16]

The literature sometimes presents two perspectives of presenting the category of property contained in the German Constitution. The first one, human (*menschliche*), refers to the personal right (*persönliches Recht*) of an individual to an object of property. The material perspective (*sachliche*), on the other hand, concerned the fact that property as a specific thing constituted a concrete "embodied asset" (*verkörperter Vermögenswert*).[17] This coincided with the demonstration of the dual function of the constitutional guarantee of property: the right to establish and operate a business based on the principles of profitability, risk and profit maximization, and the right to private property of the means of production.[18]

Three additional dimensions can be discerned in the constitutional guarantee of property in West Germany. Firstly, it resulted in the guarantee of the *status quo* (*Bestandsgarantie*), referring to the protection of property in a concrete form belonging to a specific owner. This, in turn, entailed the right of the individual to formulate a claim against the authorities with respect to the object of property. Secondly, the consequence of Art. 14 GG was the guarantee of the property as a legal institution (*Institutsgarantie*). The Basic Law imposed the requirement that property is properly constituted. It was the task of the government to create an institutional infrastructure that would ensure the sovereignty of individuals with regard to the exclusiveness (exclusivity) and transfer (transferability) of property rights. The state also had a constitutional obligation to enforce and protect the institutional infrastructure it had created. However, the property rights of

15 Leipold, "Eigentum und wirtschaftliches Handeln," 39–41. In the context of the mentioned economic effects, the author writes about the institution of private property (Leipold, "Eigentum und wirtschaftliches Handeln," 40).

16 Höfer, "Eigentum," 157–159.

17 Böhmer, "Eigentum aus verfassungsrechtlicher Sicht," 42–43.

18 R. Scholz, E. Lieser-Triebnigg, "Grundgesetz und Wirtschaftsordnung in der Bundesrepublik Deutschland," in *Materialien zum Bericht zur Lage der Nation im geteilten Deutschland 1987* (Bonn: Bundesministerium für innerdeutsche Beziehungen, 1987), 29.

individual citizens were "socially bound." Thirdly, the constitutional guarantee of property was embedded in the context of a specific economic policy, which was based on the model of a social market economy in the FRG. Thus, Art. 14 GG co-shaped the German economic system (*Wirtschaftsverfassung*).[19]

There were two prerequisites for the legal entrenchment of property in the FRG. Firstly, there were the rights to dispose of property (*Verfügungsrechte*), which included the purchase or sale of all kinds of goods and services. Secondly, German regulations conditioned rights of appropriation (*Aneignungsrechte*), which concerned the proceeds from the enforcement of the rights of property's disposal and the liability associated with its use.[20]

In constitutional economics, it is pointed out that the guarantee of property rights is the basic circumstance of enacting a basic law in a country. These considerations are therefore grounded in property rights theory. The analysis of the German Basic Law shows that it guaranteed property rights as a public good. The FRG Constitution was an example of a social contract that regulated the behavior and obligations of the parties to certain interactions. The "state–citizen" ("government–society") relationship played a primary role there. In this case, the Basic Law limited potential losses resulting from poorly defined property rights or their complete lack. It should be added that the FRG Constitution clarified the competencies of state bodies and set out the principles of enforcing and protecting property rights, thus reducing the risk of the emergence of the phenomenon of political (negative) rent-seeking or abuse of power in seizing property. Thus, the Basic Law increased the position of citizens *vis-à-vis* the government in potential confrontation. This situation was further strengthened by the tri-partite division of power, appropriate mechanisms for controlling political elites and holding them accountable, and German federalism. The distribution of power in society was thus balanced, which some authors even interpret as a concession by the elite to the citizens.[21]

---

19 Cf. K. Dobrzeniecki, M. Romanowski, *Reprywatyzacja. Problemy tworzenia i stosowania prawa* (Warszawa: Wydawnictwo UKSW, 2015), 44–45.

20 B. Tietz, *Optionen für Deutschland. Szenariem und Handlungsalternativen für Wirtschaft und Gesellschaft. Ein Handbuch für Entscheidungsträger* (Landsberg/Lech: Verlag Moderne Industrie, 1990), 94.

21 The above interpretation is a part of one of the three perspectives of research on the constitutional guarantee of property rights realized from the position of constitutional economics. Jan Fałkowski and Katarzyna Metelska-Szaniawska also describe the other two perspectives. Firstly, the constitutional guarantee of property rights as a private good, which results from the privileged position of interest groups and concerns in some African, Asian, and post-communist countries. Secondly, they distinguish an intermediate model, i.e. the constitutional guarantee of property rights as a public good, which represents a consensus between the ruling elites and the general public with the simultaneous high position of pressure groups, as a result of which the constitution guarantees property rights as a private good. This refers to the situation in some South American countries

The enshrinement of property rights in the Basic Law limited state interference with these rights. Although property guarantees applied to all types of property, the most important role was played by the constitutional protection of private property – as Zbigniew Staniek puts it – "from the rule of the "majority" and the ruling political elites. This principle makes it possible to separate economic wealth from political power. Wealth is not directly dependent on the place occupied in the system of political power."[22] In the context of the entrenchment of property rights in the FRG Constitution, their political dimension from their economic one can be distinguished.[23]

Another interesting category contained in the analyzed provisions of the FRG Constitution and already mentioned is the "public good."[24] It can also be found in Art. 87e, Par. 4 GG, which deals with rail transport.[25] It can also be found indirectly in Art. 72, Par. 2 GG, which deals with competition law, and in Art. 91a, Par. 1 GG, which regulated the issues related to federal participation in the execution of tasks of the *Länder*. The first one referred to the "national interest" (*gesamtstaatliche Interesse*).[26] Between 1949 and 1994, this provision mentioned the "interests of the

---

(J. Fałkowski, K. Metelska-Szaniawska, "Przyczyny ustanawiania i stabilność konstytucji państwa – perspektywa ekonomiczna," *Gospodarka Narodowa* 85/26, No. 3 (277) (2015): 88–91).

22 Pol. *przed rządami "większości" i rządzących elit politycznych. Zasada ta pozwala oddzielić bogactwo ekonomiczne od siły politycznej. Bogactwo nie jest bezpośrednio zależne od miejsca zajmowanego w systemie władzy politycznej* (cf. Z. Staniek, *Ekonomia instytucjonalna. Dlaczego instytucje są ważne* (Warszawa: Wydawnictwo Difin, 2017), 142).

23 Cf. W. A. Niskanen, "Conditions Affecting the Survivial of Constitutional Rules," *Constitutional Political Economy* 1, No. 2 (1990): 54.

24 This issue was presented by the author in the paper "Kategoria dobra ogółu w ekonomicznych zapisach Konstytucji RFN" ["The Category of the Public Good in the Economic Provisions of the FRG Constitution"], delivered at the XXI International Scientific Conference *Ethics in Economic Life*, organized on May 11–12, 2017, at the University of Lodz by the Department of Statistical Methods, Department of Econometrics and Department of History of Economic Thought and Economic History (Faculty of Economics and Sociology, University of Lodz, Poland). I especially thank Prof. Grzegorz Szulczewski of the Warsaw School of Economics for his constructive comments on my paper.

25 However, the official English translation does not include this term: "The Federation shall ensure that, in developing and maintaining the federal railway system, as well as in offering services over this system, other than local passenger services, due account is taken of the interests and especially the transportation needs of the public" (*Der Bund gewährleistet, daß dem Wohl der Allgemeinheit, insbesondere den Verkehrsbedürfnissen, beim Ausbau und Erhalt des Schienennetzes der Eisenbahnen des Bundes sowie bei deren Verkehrsangeboten auf diesem Schienennetz, soweit diese nicht den Schienenpersonennahverkehr betreffen, Rechnung getragen wird* (Art. 87e, Par. 4 GG)).

26 Art. 72, Par. 2 GG.

whole" (*Interessen der Gesamtheit*).[27] The second article spoke of "important responsibilities to society as a whole" (*bedeutsame Aufgaben für die Gesamtheit*).[28] Art. 14, Par. 3 GG, cited earlier, contains a similar category of "public interest" (*Interessen der Allgemeinheit*).[29] However, it may be concluded that the content of the specified terms overlapped in meaning with the concept of the "public good." Moreover, the mention of the above-mentioned articles, in which this category appeared directly, does not exclude the possibility that it was included indirectly in other constitutional provisions, e.g. in terms of the interpretative context.

The presented "public good" indicated social responsibility and obligation. The concept enshrined in the Basic Law also determined the directions of socio-economic measures taken by the state and individuals, which can be associated with the ordoliberal doctrine.[30] In the context of the reflections made here, which present property in the perspective of the "public good," three types of social responsibility should be distinguished. They refer to the state, citizens, and property itself. Their fundamental source is Catholic social teaching.

One of the elements of the social market economy system is the idea of social responsibility of the state, which for the benefit of the citizens, sets the legal and institutional framework for the economic process, in the proper course of which – at least in theory – it does not interfere. Referring to the German Constitution, one can point to this obligation of the state to social responsibility on the example of the aforementioned articles, in which the Federation, as an embodiment of the state, was obliged – in the specific circumstances indicated therein – to act for the "public good" and "national interest."[31]

Szymon Pawłowski identifies the constitutional approach to private property with the concept of solidarism. Based on the analysis of the jurisprudence of the Federal Constitutional Court, he argues that the content and limits of the property right determined by the legislator should take into account the social aspect. The stronger the relationship between the object of property and its social function is, the greater the possibility for the state to restrict property for the "public good." In other words, the state interference could be greater, the weaker the relationship between use and the provision of the constitutional right to freedom and self-realization. At the same time, the Basic Law implied differentiation of property protection, which consisted in the fact that the property of socially "weaker" individuals was better protected than the property of, e.g., large capital companies. Although Pawłowski states that the German constitution did not express the idea of solidarism *expressis verbis*, its normative expression was an order to use

---

27 *Grundgesetz für die Bundesrepublik Deutschland vom 23. Mai 1949.*, Art. 72, Par. 2 (BGBl., Part I, 1949, No. 1, 9).
28 Art. 91a, Par. 1 GG.
29 Art. 14, Par. 3 GG.
30 See section 4.1. in this book.
31 Cf. Art. 14, Pars. 2–3; Art. 72, Par. 2; Art. 87e, Par. 4 GG.

property rights for the "public good," next to the principle of the social state and the system of compensatory payments.[32]

The Basic Law also stipulated that citizens should have a sense of community responsibility, the object of which was the "public good." Private property, which was a social "obligation" for these citizens, should "serve" this purpose.[33]

The category of the "public good" corresponds to the concept of the "common good" characterized as a collective value that is achieved by communities through: (1) developing the natural capacities of individuals, (2) realizing individualized interests, or (3) respecting the rights of individuals combined with bringing the community closer to certain goals.[34] It should be noted that the "public good" as laid out in the German Basic Law was qualitatively related to the last element of the definition of the "common good." This can be seen again in the provision on private property. The constitutionally guaranteed right to property (Art. 14, Par. 1 GG) was a safeguard of one of the elementary rights of individuals (the basic rights). At the same time, it was supposed to entail socially "obligations," serving the "public good" (Art. 14, Par. 2 GG), thus directing the community of individuals toward collective responsibility.[35] Moreover, as emphasized earlier, a comparison of the provisions of the Weimar Constitution and the FRG Constitution shows that the category of the "common good" from the 1919 document was replaced by the concept of the "public good" in the Basic Law of 1949.[36]

German social and legal philosophy also distinguishes the principle of social responsibility of property (*Sozialpflichtigkeit des Eigentums*, *Sozialbindung des Eigentums*). It is connected with the mentioned Art. 14, Par. 2 GG.[37] The obligation

---

32 Sz. Pawłowski, "Solidaryzm w Konstytucji Niemiec," in *Idea solidaryzmu we współczesnym prawie konstytucyjnym. Doświadczenia polskie i międzynarodowe*, ed. A. Łabno (Warszawa: Wydawnictwo Sejmowe, 2015), 306–323. Cf. the research of Barry R. Weingast, who analyzes the discrepancies between the legal protection of property rights and the state's powers to confiscate property. In his opinion, economic development is served by "market-preserving federalism," which is confirmed by the examples of Great Britain in the 17th–18th centuries, the United States in the period from the late 18th century to the 1930s, and China in the 1980s. (B. R. Weingast, "The Economic Role of Political Institutions: Market-Preserving Federalism and Economic Development," *Journal of Law, Economics, & Organization* 11, No. 1 (1995): 1–31). See also Émile Durkheim's concept of organic solidarity (understood as a social bond), which can be applied to constitutional law: J. Szacki, *Historia myśli socjologicznej* (Warszawa: WN PWN, 2002), 382–386.

33 Art. 14, Par. 2 GG.

34 "Dobro wspólne," in K. Dziubka, B. Szlachta, L. M. Nijakowski, *Idee i ideologie we współczesnym świecie* (Warszawa: WN PWN, 2008), 48. More on this topic: W. Arndt, F. Longchamps de Bérier, K. Szczucki, *Dobro wspólne. Teoria i praktyka* (Warszawa: Wydawnictwo Sejmowe, Fundacja "Utriusque Iuris", 2013).

35 Cf. Art. 14, Pars. 1–2 GG.

36 Cf. Table 12.

37 Art. 14, Par. 2 GG.

arising from the disposition of property is not limited to an individual perspective. It is much broader. Property is considered in community terms, which means that other members of society should be its beneficiaries in a certain way. This is the basis of the above-mentioned notions of "serve," "public good," and "social responsibility" considered in the context of property.[38] Within the social responsibility of property, corporate social responsibility (CSR) is sometimes distinguished, which remains a separate subject of study in the literature.[39] Suffice it to say that in this context, property in the form of an enterprise is obliged to socially responsible practices.

To exemplify the realization of the social responsibility of property, which should serve the "public good," it can be pointed to the case of a landowner who has the right to erect real estate. However, he had to comply with the construction law (*Baurecht*). It took into account, among others, the issues related to spatial development, protection of landscape, environment, and monuments, or safety of inhabitants.[40] The above discussion confirms the key significance of the "public good" for the German socio-economic system, contained in specific economic provisions of the FRG Constitution.[41]

---

38 The concept of social responsibility of property was popular in the FRG even before reunification, as evidenced by works published at the time. See, among others: K. Rudolph, *Die Bindungen des Eigentums. Eine rechtsvergleichende Studie* (Tübingen: Mohr Siebeck, 1960); W. Leisner, *Sozialbindung des Eigentums* (Berlin: Duncker & Humblot, 1972). See also examples of studies published after 1990: J. Rozek, *Die Unterscheidung von Eigentumsbindung und Enteignung. Eine Bestandsaufnahme zur dogmatischen Struktur des Art. 14 GG nach 15 Jahren "Naßauskiesung"* (Tübingen: Mohr Siebeck, 1998), 64–71; Theil, "Eigentum und Verpflichtung," 175–200.

39 From general studies see, e.g.,: A. Crane et al., eds., *The Oxford Handbook of Corporate Social Responsibility*, (New York: Oxford University Press, 2009); J. Witkowska, "Społeczna odpowiedzialność biznesu," in Z. Wysokińska, J. Witkowska, *Zrównoważony rozwój. Wybrane aspekty makro- i mikroekonomiczne* (Łódź: Wydawnictwo UŁ, 2016), 95–166.

40 Construction law in the FRG was codified on June 23, 1960, in the form of the Building Code (*Baugesetzbuch*, BauGB) and came into force on October 30 (*Bundesbaugesetz Vom 23. Juni 1960* (BGBl., Part I, 1960, No. 30, 341–388 as amended)).

41 Among the rich German legal literature treating the empowerment of property in the FRG Constitution, see, e.g.: Häberle, "Vielfalt der Property Rights," 63–102; Böhmer, "Eigentum aus verfassungsrechtlicher Sicht," 39–82; P. Badura, "Der Verfassungsauftrag der Eigentumsgarantie im wiedervereinigten Deutschland," *Deutsches Verwaltungsblatt* No. 105 (1990): 1256–1263; P. Badura, "Eigentum," in *Handbuch des Verfassungsrechts der Bundesrepublik Deutschland*, eds. E. Benda, W. Maihofer, H.-J. Vogel (Berlin–New York: Walter de Gruyter, 1994), 327–390; H.-J. Papier, "Grundgesetz und Wirtschaftsordnung," in Benda, Maihofer, Vogel, *Handbuch des Verfassungsrechts*, 805–808; Baur, Baur, Stürner, *Sachenrecht*, 308–311; Wilhelm, *Sachenrecht*, 128–163. There is further extensive literature in these studies.

Other regulations on property rights were complementary to the Basic Law.[42] Among the most important is the civil law (*Bürgerliches Recht*).[43] The *Civil Code* (*Bürgerliches Gesetzbuch*, BGB) was enacted in the German Empire on August 18, 1896, and came into force on January 1, 1900.[44] It has been amended many times. The biggest one was made in 2002.[45] The empowerment of property in the *Civil Code* placed it within the framework of private law (*Rahmen des Privatrechts*).[46] The branch of civil law that regulates property is property law. In principle, it includes norms determining absolute subjective rights (effective for all) that relate to things.[47] In Germany, a separate third book of the *Civil Code* (§§ 854–1296 BGB) is devoted to it: *Property Law* (*Sachenrecht*).[48] Nevertheless, individual provisions concerning property remained the subject (at least in part) also of books two (*Law of Obligations, Recht der Schuldverhältnisse*, §§ 241–853 BGB)[49] and five (*Law of Succession, Erbrecht*, §§ 1922–2385 BGB).[50]

As part of the research on the institution of property rights in Germany in 1990–2015, it is necessary to look at the most important provisions of the *Civil Code* treating the subject matter. German civil law in § 872 BGB defined the owner (*Eigenbezitzer*) as the one "who possesses a thing as belonging to him" (*Wer eine Sache als ihm gehörend besitzt*),[51] with the juridical understanding of a thing

42 More on the legal property (rights) regulations in the FRG: Rudolph, *Die Bindungen des Eigentums*, comparative analysis of German, British and American rules; H. Eichler, *Die Rechtsidee des Eigentums. Eine rechtsdogmatische und rechtspolitische Betrachtung* (Berlin: Duncker & Humblot, 1994), comparative analysis of Austrian, German and Swiss rules.

43 See professional introductions: Zerres, *Bürgerliches Recht*; Klunzinger, *Einführung in das Bürgerliche Recht.*

44 *Bürgerliches Gesetzbuch. Vom 18. August 1896.* (RGBl., 1896, No. 21/2322, 195–603 as amended).

45 *Bekanntmachung der Neufassung des Bürgerlichen Gesetzbuchs Vom 2. Januar 2002* (BGBl., Part I, 2002, No. 2, 42–341).

46 Baur, Baur, Stürner, *Sachenrecht*, 312, table 15.

47 Z. Radwański, A. Olejniczak, *Prawo cywilne – część ogólna* (Warszawa: Wydawnictwo C. H. Beck, 2017), 14.

48 §§ 854–1296 (*Bürgerliches Gesetzbuch*, Bundesministerium der Justiz und für Verbraucherschutz, Berlin 2017, as of July 20, 2017 (hereinafter: BGB)). The use of the 2017 edition of the *Civil Code* is justified insofar as the provisions in question for the years 1990–2015 have not changed in their essential meaning so much as to distort the picture presented. See professional introductions: H. J. Wieling, *Sachenrecht* (Berlin–Heidelberg: Springer, 2007); Baur, Baur, Stürner, *Sachenrecht*; Wilhelm, *Sachenrecht.*

49 §§ 241–853 BGB.

50 §§ 1922–2385 BGB.

51 § 872 BGB. See commentary H. Prütting, G. Wegen, G. Weinreich, *Bürgerliches Gesetzbuch. Kommentar* (Köln: Luchterhand Verlag, Wolters Kluwer Deutschland, 2018), 1885–1886. English translation: *German Civil Code BGB*, Federal Ministry of

referring to material, physical objects (§ 90 BGB).[52] General provisions concerning land property were regulated in §§ 873–902 BGB.[53] In § 903 BGB the rights of the owner were defined. He could deal with his property as he saw fit, excluding others, unless the law or the rights of third parties provided otherwise. Another restriction was that the owner of the animal was obliged to follow the relevant rules in this regard. From the point of view of the theory of property rights, it is important to note that this provision referred to property "rights" (*Befugnisse*).[54] The literature points out that § 903 BGB confirmed the unlimited right of an individual to a thing. It is at the same time compared with Art. 14 GG.[55] The problem of social costs (using Ronald H. Coase's term[56]), resulting from the use of property, was resolved in § 906 BGB.[57] Other major issues related to the property remained the subject of §§ 903–924 BGB.[58]

The above analysis of the most important provisions of the *Civil Code* shows that under certain conditions, German law allowed third parties to interfere in a given resource (even if it was someone's property) or limited the powers of its owner. On the grounds of economic analysis of law, it is pointed out that this way of defining property rights promotes efficient use of resources. According to Coase's theorem, this only applies when the transaction costs of a potential voluntary agreement between actors are too high.[59]

The various issues comprising the matter of property rights in Germany between 1990 and 2015 remained the subject of specific legislation. It suffices to limit analysis to a few exemplifications. The *Act on the Ownership of Apartments and the Permanent Residential Right* (*Wohnungseigentumsgesetz*, WEG) of March 15, 1951, regulated property of real estate. Its last amendment during the period in question

---

Justice, Federal Office of Justice, https://www.gesetze-im-internet.de/englisch_bgb/ (accessed July 1, 2022).

52 § 90 BGB.

53 §§ 873–902 BGB. See more Wieling, *Sachenrecht*, 341–377.

54 § 903 BGB. See commentary Prütting, Wegen, Weinreich, *Bürgerliches Gesetzbuch*, 1921–1925.

55 W. Waldner, "Private Property and the Transformation Process," in *East Germany's Economic Development since Unification. Domestic and Global Aspects*, eds. J. Hölscher, A. Hochberg (Basingstoke–London: Macmillan Press, 1998), 94. See also D. Olzen, "Aktuelle zivilrechtliche Probleme des Eigentums," in Baur, *Das Eigentum*, 103–124.

56 R. H. Coase, *Firma, rynek i prawo* (Warszawa: Oficyna a Wolters Kluwer Business, 2013), 10–15.

57 § 906 BGB. See commentary Prütting, Wegen, Weinreich, *Bürgerliches Gesetzbuch*, 1928–1935.

58 §§ 903–924 BGB.

59 H.-B. Schäfer, C. Ott, *Lehrbuch der ökonomischen Analyse des Zivilrechts* (Berlin–Heidelberg: Springer, 2005), 550–551. Cf. Coase, *Firma, rynek i prawo*, 10–15.

took place in 2014.[60] This act consisted of four parts. The first one, entitled *Apartment Ownership* (*Wohnungseigentum*, §§ 1–30), was composed of four chapters: *Creation of Title in Respect of Apartments* (*Begründung des Wohnungseigentums*, §§ 2–9), *Community of Apartment Owners* (*Gemeinschaft der Wohnungseigentümer*, §§ 10–19), *Administration* (*Verwaltung*, §§ 20–29) and *Heritable Building Right in Respect of an Apartment* (*Wohnungserbbaurecht*, § 30). The subject matter of Part II, titled *Permanent Residential Right* (*Dauerwohnrecht*, §§ 31–42) were: the requirements for registration (*Voraussetzungen der Eintragung*), contents of the permanent residential right (*Inhalt des Dauerwohnrechts*), rights of the owner and of the persons entitled to the permanent residential right (*Ansprüche des Eigentümers und der Dauerwohnberechtigten*), restrictions on disposal (*Veräußerungsbeschränkung*), reversionary claim (*Heimfallanspruch*), leases (*Vermietung*), legal succession (*Eintritt in das Rechtsverhältnis*), enforced auction (*Zwangsversteigerung*), payments as subject to a charge (*Haftung des Entgelts*), special provisions applying to long-term permanent residential rights (*Besondere Vorschriften für langfristige Dauerwohnrechte*), encumbrance of heritable building right (*Belastung eines Erbbaurechts*). Section III, entitled *Procedural Rules* (*Verfahrensvorschriften*, §§ 43–58) formed three chapters: *Procedures for Voluntary Jurisdiction in Apartment Ownership Cases* (*Verfahren der freiwilligen Gerichtsbarkeit in Wohnungseigentumssachen*, §§ 43–50), *Competence in Legal Disputes* (*Zuständigkeit für Rechtsstreitigkeiten*, §§ 51–52) and *Procedures for Auction of Apartment Ownership* (*Verfahren bei der Versteigerung des Wohnungseigentums*, §§ 53–58). Section IV, *Supplementary Provisions* (*Ergänzende Bestimmungen*, §§ 59–63), discusses implementing regulations for building authorities, issues related to spousal housing, the assessment of the tax value of housing, the status of single-family homes, and the transition of existing legal relationships.[61]

Precise regulations also covered particular aspects of socio-economic life. With regard to real estate law, the following should be mentioned in

---

60 *Gesetz zur Erleichterung der Umsetzung der Grundbuchamtsreform in Baden-Württemberg sowie zur Änderung des Gesetzes betreffend die Einführung der Zivilprozessordnung und des Wohnungseigentumsgesetzes Vom 5. Dezember 2014* (BGBl., Part I, 2014, No. 57, 1962–1963).

61 *Gesetz über das Wohnungseigentum und das Dauerwohnrecht (Wohnungseigentumsgesetz). Vom 15. März 1951* (BGBl., Part I, 1951, No. 13, 175–185 as amended). English translation: *Act on the Ownership of Apartments and the Permanent Residential Right (Wohnungseigentumsgesetz, WEG)*, Federal Ministry of Justice, Federal Office of Justice, http://www.gesetze-im-internet.de/englisch_woeigg/ (accessed July 1, 2022). Some translations are from the author. More on a residential property in the light of property law: Baur, Baur, Stürner, *Sachenrecht*, 374–403. Claus Schnabel draws attention to the issue of expanding private property of housing in the Eastern *Länder* just after reunification (C. Schnabel, "Structural Adjustment and Privatization of the East German Economy," in *Economic Aspects of German Unification. National and International Perspectives*, ed. P. J. J. Welfens (Berlin–Heidelberg: Springer-Verlag, 1992), 245–247).

particular: joint property (*Gesamthandeigentum*), house right (*Hausrecht*), fractional property (*Bruchteilseigentum*), special property (*Sondereigentum*), special right of use (*Sondernutzungsrecht*), residential plot (*Anliegerflurstück*), fishing law (*Fischereirecht*), limited personal easement (*beschränkte persönliche Dienstbarkeit*), permanent residential right (*Dauerwohnrecht*), heritable building right (*Erbbaurecht*), mining property (*Bergwerkseigentum*), and commercial law (*Gewerberecht*). These sections and categories of property defined in detail the property relations, the relationship between owner and user, the issues of transferability and indicated the appropriate legal sanctions for their violation.[62] In addition, property law regulated issues related to the agricultural land property (*landwirtschaftliche Grundeigentum*), including land lease (*einschließlich Landpacht*), water law (*Wasserrecht*), forest law (*Forstrecht*), hunting and fishing law (*Jagd- und Fishereirecht*).[63] Separate provisions applied to the property of enterprises (*Unternehmenseigentum*) and movable property (*Eigentum an Mobilien*).[64]

The public register, which determined the legal status of a given property, was the land register (*Grundbuch*). It registered the subject of property, rights to it, and existing encumbrances. The rules governing the operation of land registers were laid down in the *Land Register Act* (*Grundbuchordnung*, GBO) of March 24, 1897.[65] A major revision was carried out in 1994.[66] This is supplemented by the *Ordinance on the Implementation of the Land Register Act* (*Verordnung zur Durchführung der Grundbuchordnung*), or the *Land Register Order* (*Grundbuchverfügung*, GBV) of August 8, 1935.[67] It was amended, among others, in 1995.[68]

The regulations for doing business were contained in the *Commercial Code* (*Handelgesetzbuch*, HGB), enacted on May 10, 1897, and amended several times later.[69] The document discusses rules primarily concerning: the commercial status of a company (*Handelsstand*, §§ 1-104a), commercial companies and silent companies

---

62 J. M. Paasch, *Classification of Real Property Rights – A Comparative Study of Real Property Rights in Germany, Ireland, the Netherlands and Sweden* (Stockholm: KTH Royal Institute of Technology, 2011), *passim*.

63 Wieling, *Sachenrecht*, 343–401; Baur, Baur, Stürner, *Sachenrecht*, 348–367.

64 Baur, Baur, Stürner, *Sachenrecht*, 367–374, 630–635.

65 *Grundbuchordnung. Vom 24. März 1897.* (RGBl., 1897, No. 15/2374, 139–157 as amended).

66 *Bekanntmachung der Neufassung der Grundbuchordnung Vom 26. Mai 1994* (BGBl., Part I, 1994, No. 32, 1114–1132).

67 *Allgemeine Verfügung über die Einrichtung und Führung des Grundbuchs* (Reichsministerialblatt der inneren Verwaltung, 1935, 637 as amended).

68 *Bekanntmachung der Neufassung der Grundbuchverfügung Vom 24. Januar 1995* (BGBl., Part I, 1995, No. 6, 114–133). See in more detail: Baur, Baur, Stürner, *Sachenrecht*, 167–234; Wilhelm, *Sachenrecht*, 243–313.

69 *Handelsgesetzbuch. Vom 10. Mai 1897.* (RGBl., 1897, No. 23/2388, 219–436 as amended).

(*Handelsgesellschaften*, §§ 105–237), commercial transactions (*Handelsgeschäfte*, §§ 343-475h), and maritime trade (*Seehandel*, §§ 476–619)[70].

Some quantitative studies recognize the impact of government performance on political, economic, and cultural institutions and consequently on economic development. This is an indicator that includes the level of government interference in the private sector (e.g., the enforcement of private property rights), the efficiency of the public sector, the productivity of public goods, the size of the public sector, and the extent of political freedom. It is shown, e.g., that there was a positive relationship between the legal system (which includes a company or commercial law) and the property rights index (which measures the degree of enforcement and protection of private property) in Germany (and in other countries taking their cues from the German legal system) in the 1990s.[71] This confirms the thesis of the legal (constitutional and systemic) embeddedness of property rights and the positive influence of the legal system on the quality of property rights institutions in Germany between 1990 and 2015, as the analyzed property rights regulations did not change much in the first two decades of the 21st century.

6.1.1.2. Transferability

The second of the indicated dimensions of the degree of completeness of property rights, which is transferability, concerns their portability. The owner is free to transfer property rights to another entity. It can be transferred in whole or in part. Various forms (ways) of transferability were permitted in Germany between 1990 and 2015. Civil law distinguished between acquire (*Erwerb*) and loss (*Verlust*) of property.

There were many ways of acquiring property to different extents (full, partial, under certain conditions, or similar to the *Besitz* category[72]). Each of them was subject to detailed regulations, especially the *Civil Code*. It should be noted that German civil law regulated ways of acquiring and losing "property," not "property rights." Therefore, adopting a broader – economic – perspective, the most important ways of acquiring certain property rights, along with references to the basic sources of law, are presented in Table 13.

---

70 *Handelsgesetzbuch*, Bundesministerium der Justiz und für Verbraucherschutz, Berlin 2019, legal as of December 12, 2019. The use of the 2019 edition of the *Commercial Code* is justified insofar as the provisions in question for the years 1990–2015 have not changed in their essential meaning so much as to distort the picture presented.

71 R. La Porta, F. Lopez-de-Silanes, A. Shleifer, R. W. Vishny, "The Quality of Government," *Journal of Law, Economics and Organization* 15, No. 1 (1999): 222–279, especially 234–238, table 1; 246, table 4; 261–262. It is worth mentioning that the authors proved the negative impact of the socialist and French law systems on the quality of property rights institutions.

72 See section 6.1.1.1. in this study.

Table 13: *The most important ways of acquiring certain property rights in Germany and their main legal regulations in 1990–2015*[a]

Way of acquiring property rights	Main regulations
Obligations (*Schulden*), including: (1) purchase (*Kauf*) (2) exchange (*Tausch*) (3) loan contract, financing assistance and contracts for delivery by instalments between an entrepreneur and a consumer (*Darlehensvertrag, Finanzierungshilfen und Ratenlieferungsverträge zwischen einem Unternehmer und einem Verbraucher*) (4) donation (*Schenkung*) (5) lease (*Miete*) (6) usufructuary lease (*Pacht*) (7) gratuitous loan (*Leihe*) (8) loan of a thing (*Sachdarlehen*)	§§ 241–853, 952 BGB, including: (1) §§ 433–479 BGB (2) §§ 480 BGB (3) §§ 488–515 BGB (4) §§ 516–534 BGB (5) §§ 535–580a BGB (6) §§ 581–597 BGB (7) §§ 598–606 BGB (8) §§ 607–610 BGB
Surrogation (*Surrogation*)	§§ 281, 285, 718, 966, 975, 979, 1046, 1075, 1127, 1219, 1247, 1287, 1370, 2019, 2041 BGB
Agreement (*Einigung*)	§§ 873, 925 BGB
Transfer (*Übertragung*)	§§ 929–936 BGB
Good faith acquisition (*Gutgläubiger Erwerb*)	§§ 932–936 BGB
Acquisition by prescription (*Ersitzung*)	§§ 937–945 BGB
Combination (*Verbindung*)	§§ 946–947, 949, 951 BGB
Intermixture (*Vermischung*)	§§ 948–949, 951 BGB
Processing (*Verarbeitung*)	§§ 950–951 BGB
Acquisition of products and other components of a thing (*Erwerb von Erzeugnissen und sonstigen Bestandteilen einer Sache*), acquisition of fruits, harvests, crops (*Fruchterwerb*)	§§ 953–957 BGB
Appropriation (*Aneignung*)	§§ 928, 958–964 BGB
Finding (*Fund*)	§§ 965–984 BGB
Co-ownership (*Miteigentum*)	§§ 1008–1011 BGB
Easement (*Grunddienstbarkeit*)	§§ 1018–1029 BGB
Usufruct (*Nießbrauch*)	§§ 1030–1089 BGB
Restricted personal easement (*Beschränkte persönliche Dienstbarkeit*)	§§ 1090–1093 BGB
Right of preemption (*Vorkaufsrecht*)	§§ 1094–1104 BGB

Table 13: (*Continued*)

Way of acquiring property rights	Main regulations
Succession (*Erbe*)	§§ 1922–2385 BGB
Heritable building right (*Erbbaurecht*)	ErbbauVO (since 2007 ErbbauRG)[b]

a Translation of German terms by author or based on: *German Civil Code BGB*, https://www.gesetze-im-internet.de/englisch_bgb/ (accessed July 1, 2022).
b *Verordnung über das Erbbaurecht. Vom 15. Januar 1919.* (RGBl., 1919, No. 14/6654, 72–82 as amended. (Heritable Building Right Ordinance, *Erbbaurechtsverordnung*, ErbbauVO)) [The ordinance of January 15, 1919, was raised to the status of law on November 23, 2007 (*Zweites Gesetz über die Bereinigung von Bundesrecht im Zuständigkeitsbereich des Bundesministeriums der Justiz Vom 23. November 2007*, Art. 25 (BGBl, Part I, 2007, No. 59, 2617))]; *Gesetz über das Erbaurecht (Erbbaurechtsgesetz – ErbbauRG)* (Berlin: Bundesministerium der Justiz und für Verbraucherschutz, 2013), as of October 1, 2013 (ErbbauRG).
Own compilation based on: BGB, *passim*, and documents from fn. b.

Transferability of property rights is characterized by feedback, i.e., it involves two parties to the transaction. Acquiring property rights in one of the above-mentioned ways was most often associated with the loss of those rights by the original owner. In the German *Civil Code*, acquire and loss of property are referred to separately to real estate (*Erwerb und Verlust des Eigentums an Grundstücken*) and movables (*Erwerb und Verlust des Eigentums an beweglichen Sachen*). These regulations included, respectively: §§ 925–928 and §§ 929–984 BGB. Within the last group, the following were specified: transfer, acquisition by prescription, combination, intermixture, processing, acquisition of products and other components of a thing, appropriation, and finding.[73] The specialized literature makes an additional distinction between acquiring of property from a person entitled (*Erwerb vom Berechtigten*) and acquire of such property from a person not entitled (*Erwerb vom Nichtberechtigten*).[74] Adopting the theory of property rights allows, however, to distinguish other ways of acquiring property rights listed in the table, classified in civil law e.g. as obligations.[75] This is due to the signalized broader economic perspective of the theory of property rights in comparison to the approach to the category of property in German law.

It is important to note a separate group of the most important ways of losing property rights to various extents, which – with the exception of those presented above – were regulated primarily in civil law. They also had bilateral character. The

73 §§ 925–984 BGB.
74 Wieling, *Sachenrecht*, 95–162; Baur, Baur, Stürner, *Sachenrecht*, 635–743; Wilhelm, *Sachenrecht*, 343–487; Zerres, *Bürgerliches Recht*, 375–396; Klunzinger, *Einführung in das Bürgerliche Recht*, 546–562.
75 §§ 241–853, 952 BGB.

loss of property rights could take place in favor of another subject who acquired them. Although German civil law spoke of the category of *Verlust* in this context, it should be noted that some of the discussed ways concerned only the limitation of the relevant property rights. Details are shown in Table 14. Some of the manners remained subject to other laws, especially criminal law, which places them within the scope of the enforcement and protection of property rights in Germany discussed later. This concerned, e.g., the loss of property rights due to the destruction of property.[76]

Table 14: *Other most important ways of losing or limiting certain property rights in Germany and their main legal regulations in 1990–2015*[a]

Way of losing or limiting property rights	Main regulations
Transfer of property for security (*Übereignung zur Sicherung*)	§§ 158, 929–931 BGB
Waiver (*Verzicht*)	§§ 397, 875, 928, 959, 1064, 1165, 1168–1169, 1175, 1178, 1942–1966, 2180 BGB
Abandonment, neglect, dereliction of property (*Eigentumsaufgabe, Dereliktion*)	§§ 928, 959 BGB
Charges on land (*Realllasten*)	§§ 1105–1112 BGB
Mortgage (*Hypothek*)	§§ 1113–1190 BGB
Land charge (*Grundschuld*)	§§ 1191–1198 BGB
Annuity land charge (*Rentenschuld*)	§§ 1199–1203 BGB
Pledge (*Pfand*)	§§ 1204–1296 BGB
Expropriation (*Enteignung*)	Art. 14, Par. 3 GG; §§ 85–122 BauGB[b]
Compulsory enforcement (*Zwangsvollstreckung*)	§§ 704–959 ZPO[c]
Enforced auction (*Zwangsversteigerung*)	ZVG[d]

a Translation of German terms by author or based on: *German Civil Code BGB*, https://www.gesetze-im-internet.de/englisch_bgb/ (accessed July 1, 2022).
b *Bundesbaugesetz* (BGBl., Part I, 1960, No. 30, 341–388). See the more important amendments: *Gesetz über städtebauliche Sanierungs- und Entwicklungsmaßnahmen in den Gemeinden (Städtebauförderungsgesetz) Vom 27. Juli 1971* (BGBl., Part I, 1971, No. 72, 1125–1156); *Gesetz über das Baugesetzbuch Vom 8. Dezember 1986* (BGBl, Part I, 1986, No. 63, 2191–2236); *Gesetz zur Anpassung des Baugesetzbuchs an EU-Richtlinien*

76 More on the enforcement and protection of property rights: section 6.1.2. in this work.

Table 14: (*Continued*)

(Europarechtsanpassungsgesetz Bau – EAG Bau) Vom 24. Juni 2004 (BGBl, Part I, 2004, No. 31, 1359–1382); *Gesetz zur Erleichterung von Planungsvorhaben für die Innenentwicklung der Städte Vom 21. Dezember 2006* (BGBl., Part I, 2006, No. 64, 3316–3321).
c *Zivilprozessordnung* (Berlin: Bundesministerium der Justiz und für Verbraucherschutz, 2019), legal as of February 20, 2019. The use of the 2019 edition of the *Code of Civil Procedure* is justified insofar as the provisions in question for the years 1990–2015 have not changed in their essential meaning so much as to distort the picture presented. Translation of German term: *Code of Civil Procedure*, Federal Ministry of Justice, Federal Office of Justice, https://www.gesetze-im-internet.de/englisch_zpo/ (accessed July 12, 2022).
d *Gesetz über die Zwangsversteigerung und die Zwangsverwaltung. Vom 24. März 1897.* (RGBl., 1897, No. 14/2372, 97–134 as amended). Translation of German term: *Act on Enforced Auction and Receivership (Gesetz über die Zwangsversteigerung und die Zwangsverwaltung)*, Federal Ministry of Justice, Federal Office of Justice, https://www.gesetze-im-internet.de/englisch_zvg/ (accessed July 12, 2022).
Own compilation based on: BGB, *passim*, and documents from fns. b–d.

It should be added that Eugen Klunzinger defines the loss of property rights through expropriation or enforced auction as the acquisition of property by a sovereign act (*Hoheitsakt*). So he looks at this issue from the point of view of the state as the acquiring entity.[77]

Transferability restrictions arose from its particular ways of acquiring and losing property rights and from the general provisions of civil law. This is well illustrated in particular by § 134 BGB, according to which any transaction contrary to the law was void.[78] In contrast, § 138 BGB nullified transactions that were immoral, usurious, or that took advantage of the other party's lack of experience, judgment, or other weakness.[79]

Specific legislation further clarified the rules for the transfer of property rights. For example, the acquisition of real estate was regulated by the provisions on land registers.[80]

On the basis of the discussion so far, it should be noted that German law in 1990–2015 provided for a wide range of ways of acquiring and losing property rights. From an economic perspective, this was conducive to increasing the efficiency of resource allocation and realizing adaptive efficiency. Resources could be transferred to entities and domains that operated most efficiently in a given

---

77 Klunzinger, *Einführung in das Bürgerliche Recht*, 560. More on the expropriation from the point of view of the economic analysis of civil law: Schäfer, Ott, *Lehrbuch der ökonomischen Analyse des Zivilrechts*, 575–587.

78 § 134 BGB.

79 § 138 BGB. See in more detail on this topic: Schäfer, Ott, *Lehrbuch der ökonomischen Analyse des Zivilrechts*, 552, 563–564.

80 See: GBO, GBV.

market. In other words, the regulations in question facilitated the transfer of property rights to better uses. Importantly, the resulting restrictions on transferability were not severe. Thus, they did not undermine the efficiency of the entire system of property rights and did not limit the economic (positive) rent-seeking. Instead, they safeguarded the interests of the individual parties to the contract by reducing transaction costs.[81]

6.1.2. Enforcement and protection of property rights

It was pointed out earlier that the theory of property rights mentions three factors enforcing and protecting property rights: the state on the basis of law and coercive apparatus, individuals who are the holders of these rights, and social norms.[82] Naturally, the system of state legal protection plays the greatest role in this respect.[83] It is worth noting that the sphere of enforcement and protection of property rights refers to the issue of implementation of formal and informal institutions, i.e. their enforcement and the system of sanctions, which North points out.[84] The economic analysis of property rights sometimes points to two additional aspects of protection of property rights: legal protection claims, the "property rules" (*Sachenrechtliche Abwehransprüche*) and compensation claims, the "liability rules" (*Haftungsrechtliche Ansprüche*). Both were present in German law in 1990–2015.[85]

6.1.2.1. Law

As a starting point, it should be stated that the enforcement and protection of property rights in Germany in 1990–2015 were closely related to their definition within the degree of completeness. In other words, the legal regulation of the exclusivity and transferability of property rights showed a strong connection with the enforcement and protection of these rights. Thus, there was feedback between these two dimensions. Nevertheless, taking into account the risk of considerable simplification of the examined matter, it seems logical to separate these two levels in order to organize the analyzed problem.

In addition to the previously discussed sources of German law (especially the FRG Constitution and civil law),[86] it is also possible to identify other major

81 Cf. Schäfer, Ott, *Lehrbuch der ökonomischen Analyse des Zivilrechts*, 563–565; Staniek, *Ekonomia instytucjonalna*, 117.
82 See section 5.1. in this book.
83 R. Richter, *Institutionen ökonomisch analysiert. Zur jüngeren Entwicklung auf einem Gebiet der Wirtschaftstheorie* (Tübingen: J. C. B. Mohr (Paul Siebeck), 1994), 53–55.
84 See section 1.2.2. in this study.
85 Schäfer, Ott, *Lehrbuch der ökonomischen Analyse des Zivilrechts*, 551.
86 Cf. section 6.1.1. in this work.

regulations securing property that were in force in Germany in 1990–2015. Thus, they should be regarded as complementary to the previously presented regulations.

Property in the German system was protected, among other things, under European law to which Germany was subject. The guarantee of private property became the subject of Art. 1 of the *Protocol* of March 20, 1952, to the *Convention for the Protection of Human Rights and Fundamental Freedoms* (*European Convention on Human Rights*) of November 4, 1950.[87] An additional safeguard of private property at the EU level was Art. 17, Par. 1 of the *Charter of Fundamental Rights of the European Union* of December 7, 2000.[88]

The constitutional guarantee of property, expressed in Art. 14 GG, was linked to Art. 13 GG, which concerned one of the basic rights: the inviolability of the home (Par. 1). Searches, acoustical surveillance or inspections of the home could only take place with the consent of the court or, in case of danger of urgency, the relevant authorities (Pars. 2–5). Any interference with or restriction of this right was intended to prevent danger to the public or individual citizens (Par. 7).[89]

Protection of the property has been ensured through key provisions of the *Civil Code.* The most relevant of these, which are further highlighted in the literature, should be pointed out. § 823 BGB ensured the right to compensation for damage caused to someone's property.[90] Under § 985 BGB, the owner was entitled

87 "Every natural or legal person is entitled to the peaceful enjoyment of his possessions. No one shall be deprived of his possessions except in the public interest and subject to the conditions provided for by law and by the general principles of international law. The preceding provisions shall not, however, in any way impair the right of a State to enforce such laws as it deems necessary to control the use of property in accordance with the general interest or to secure the payment of taxes or other contributions or penalties" ("Protocol to the Convention for the Protection of Human Rights and Fundamental Freedoms. Paris, 20.III.1952," Art. 1, in *European Convention on Human Rights as Amended by Protocols Nos. 11, 14 and 15 Supplemented by Protocols Nos. 1, 4, 6, 7, 12, 13 and 16* (Strasbourg: European Court of Human Rights, 2021), 33).

88 "Everyone has the right to own, use, dispose of and bequeath his or her lawfully acquired possessions. No one may be deprived of his or her possessions, except in the public interest an in the cases and under the conditions provided for by law, subject to fair compensation being paid in good time for their loss. The use of property may be regulated by law in so far as is necessary for the general interest" (*Charter of Fundamental Rights of the European Union*, Art. 17, Par. 1 (Official Journal of the European Union, 26.10.2012, C 326, 399)). More on the EU property guarantee in relation to the FRG: Wilhelm, *Sachenrecht*, 163–167. It is worth mentioning that in the quoted EU documents – by placing the protection of private property in the social context ("public (general) interest") or by making expropriation conditional on adequate compensation – reference is made to the German guarantee of property in Art. 14 GG.

89 Art. 13 GG.

90 § 823 BGB. See commentary Prütting, Wegen, Weinreich, *Bürgerliches Gesetzbuch*, 1747–1798.

to demand the return of the property by its user.[91] § 1004 BGB provided the owner's right to require the perpetrator to remove the damage done to the property.[92]

Among other civil law regulations, it is worth noting, e.g., § 94 BGB, according to which real estate consisted of both buildings, land, and all elements connected with them.[93] Similarly, § 905 BGB extended the right of the real estate owner to the space both above and below the surface.[94] According to § 906 BGB, a citizen could not prohibit the owner of another estate from generating social costs at an acceptable level in the form of gases, steam, smells, smoke, soot, warmth, noise, vibration, etc.[95] §§ 226–231 BGB indicate the situations permitting trespass on someone's property: causing harm to another based on one's own rights and damaging someone's property under conditions of necessary defense (*Notwehr*) or self-help (*Selbsthilfe*).[96] Companies (*Gesellchaften*) and communities (*Gemeinschaften*) dealt with respectively: §§ 705–740 and §§ 741–758 BGB. They resolved, among other things, issues related to the management of disposed property.[97] The provisions governing claims arising from property (*Ansprüche aus dem Eigentum*) remained the subject of §§ 985–1007 BGB. These primarily covered the relationship of owner and possessor (*Eigentümer-Besitzer-Verhältnis*, EBV, §§ 987–1003 BGB).[98] Rules concerning the administration of marital property within the framework of a community of property (*Gütergemeinschaft*) or separation of property (*Gütertrennung*) were the subject of §§ 1363–1563 BGB.[99]

---

91 "The owner may require the possessor to return the thing" (*Der Eigentümer kann von dem Besitzer die Herausgabe der Sache verlangen* (§ 985 BGB)). See commentary Prütting, Wegen, Weinreich, *Bürgerliches Gesetzbuch*, 2000–2004. On the difference between the nouns *Eigentümer* and *Besitzer*, which results from the distinction in German law between the terms *Eigentum* and *Besitz* see section 6.1.1.1. in this work. The possessor who is at the same time the owner of an object is referred to as *Eigenbesitzer* in civil law, which can be translated as: "proprietary possessor" (§ 872 BGB). The *Civil Code* also distinguished between a "possessor" (*Besitzer*, § 854 BGB) and an "agent in possession" (*Besitzdiener*, § 855 BGB). English translations: *German Civil Code BGB*, https://www.gesetze-im-internet.de/englisch_bgb/ (accessed July 1, 2022).

92 § 1004 BGB. See commentary Prütting, Wegen, Weinreich, *Bürgerliches Gesetzbuch*, 2019–2021.

93 § 94 BGB.

94 § 905 BGB.

95 § 906 BGB.

96 §§ 226–231 BGB.

97 §§ 705–758 BGB.

98 §§ 985–1007 BGB.

99 §§ 1363–1563 BGB. More on the protection of property in German civil law: Wieling, *Sachenrecht*, 163–201; Wilhelm, *Sachenrecht*, 487–581; Zerres, *Bürgerliches Recht*, 363–366; Klunzinger, *Einführung in das Bürgerliche Recht*, 537–546.

The *Code of Civil Procedure* (*Zivilprozessordnung*, ZPO) became the source of separate rules for civil enforcement proceedings. It was enacted on January 30, 1877.[100] It has subsequently been subject to numerous amendments. Between 1990 and 2015, Book 8 ZPO (§§ 704–959) regulated the various types of compulsory enforcement (*Zwangsvollstreckung*) relating to: monetary claims (*Geldforderungen*), movable property (*bewegliche Vermögen*), physical objects (*körperliche Sachen*), claims and other property rights (*Forderungen und andere Vermögensrechte*), immovable property (*unbewegliche Vermögen*), legal persons under public law (*juristische Personen des öffentlichen Rechts*), obtaining the surrender of objects or ensuring that actions are taken or refrained from (*Erwirkung der Herausgabe von Sachen und zur Erwirkung von Handlungen oder Unterlassungen*). Furthermore, the *Code of Civil Procedure* addressed issues such as the list of debtors (*Schuldnerverzeichnis*), seizure and injunction (*Arrest und einstweilige Verfügung*), or cross-border attachment of bank accounts (*Grenzüberschreitende vorläufige Kontenpfändung*).[101] Additional issues concerning the enforcement of court decisions on execution auctions are found in the *Act on Enforced Auction and Receivership* of March 24, 1897, later amended several times.[102]

Criminal law is one of the branches of law that defines the acts that are considered crimes, the penalties and measures that can be taken for committing them, and the rules of criminal responsibility.[103] The German *Criminal Code* (*Strafgesetzbuch*, StGB) was passed in the Second Reich on May 15, 1871. It entered into force on January 1, 1872. Over the following decades, it has undergone many revisions.[104] Parts 19 to 22 (§§ 242–266b StGB) contained the most provisions concerning penalties for violation of property rights: *Theft and misappropriation* (*Diebstahl und Unterschlagung*), *Robbery and extortion* (*Raub und Erpressung*), *Aiding after the fact and handling stolen goods* (*Begünstigung und Hehlerei*), *Fraud and embezzlement* (*Betrug und Untreue*).[105] Part 27 (§§ 303–305a StGB) also addressed these issues: *Criminal damage* (*Sachbeschädigung*).[106] As with the *Civil Code*, it is important

100 *Civilprozeßordnung. Vom 30. Januar 1877.* (RGBl., 1877, No. 6/1166, 83–243 as amended).

101 §§ 704–959 ZPO. English translation: *Code of Civil Procedure*, https://www.gesetze-im-internet.de/englisch_zpo/ (accessed July 12, 2022). Some translations are from the author.

102 *Gesetz über die Zwangsversteigerung und die Zwangsverwaltung* (RGBl., 1897, No. 14/2372, 97–134 as amended).

103 L. Gardocki, *Prawo karne* (Warszawa: Wydawnictwo C. H. Beck, 2017), 1.

104 *Gesetz, betreffend die Redaktion des Strafgesetzbuchs für den Norddeutschen Bund als Strafgesetzbuch für das Deutsche Reich. Vom 15. Mai 1871.* (RGBl., 1871, No. 24/651, 127–205 as amended).

105 §§ 242–266b (*Strafgesetzbuch* (Berlin: Bundesministerium der Justiz und für Verbraucherschutz, 2017), legal as of November 1, 2017. The use of the 2017 edition of the *Criminal Code* is justified insofar as the provisions in question for the years 1990–2015 have not changed in their essential meaning so much as to distort the picture presented).

106 §§ 303–305a StGB.

to highlight only some of the most relevant provisions in the *Criminal Code* that addressed the enforcement and protection of property rights in Germany in 1990–2015.

Theft or attempted theft of movable property was punishable by a fine or imprisonment of up to five years.[107] "[E]specially serious cases of theft" (*besonders schwerer Fall des Diebstahls*) were punishable by imprisonment from three months to ten years,[108] while theft with a weapon, committed by a gang or burglary was punishable by six months to ten years.[109] The more serious crimes of theft committed by gangs (*schwerer Bandendiebstahl*) were punishable by imprisonment from one to ten years.[110] Attempting or committing misappropriation was punished with a fine or imprisonment of up to three years, and ordering someone to do it was punished with a fine or imprisonment of up to five years.[111] Separate regulations governed the theft of vehicles and electricity.[112] Assault and robbery with the intent to steal was punishable by at least one year in prison, in milder cases by six months to five years, in more severe cases by a minimum of three years, and in the case of the victim's death by ten years to life imprisonment.[113] The crime of handling stolen goods was punishable by a fine or imprisonment for up to five years, while handling stolen goods for profit or as part of a gang was punishable by six months to ten years. A gang member involved in handling stolen goods for profit was punishable by imprisonment from one to ten years (in milder cases – from six months to five years).[114] Specific provisions provided penalties for fraud, including computer fraud, relating to subsidy, capital investments, insurance, fee, credit or sports betting.[115]

A separate section of the *Criminal Code* provisions covered damage to property. In the case of private property, the penalty was a fine or imprisonment of up to two years.[116] Damage to public property was punishable by a fine or imprisonment of up to three years,[117] and to the foreign property by a fine or imprisonment of up to five years.[118] Appropriate penalties were also applied to the destruction of certain types of work equipment.[119]

---

107 § 242 StGB.
108 The cited provision lists seven different situations of this type (§ 243 StGB).
109 § 243 StGB.
110 § 244a StGB.
111 § 246 StGB.
112 §§ 248b–248c StGB.
113 §§ 249–251 StGB.
114 §§ 259–260a StGB.
115 §§ 263–265e StGB.
116 § 303 StGB.
117 § 304 StGB.
118 § 305 StGB.
119 § 305a StGB. English translation: *German Criminal Code (Strafgesetzbuch – StGB)*, Federal Ministry of Justice, Federal Office of Justice, https://www.gesetze-im-internet.de/englisch_stgb/ (accessed July 13, 2022).

Frank Münzel illustrates the degree of enforcement within the legal and economic order by, among other things, data on the number of courts. The degree of subjective diversification of judicial bodies is important in his interpretation. Additionally, according to the author's findings, just before reunification, the higher legal culture of West Germany was illustrated by the fact that in 1989 there were 17,627 judges and 37,000 lawyers in the FRG, while in the GDR, there were 1,500 judges and 600 lawyers.[120]

A decreasing number of thefts can be observed between 2002 and 2014. In 2002, there were 2,983,269 reported thefts and 59,414 robberies, predatory extortion, and predatory attacks on drivers.[121] In 2014, there were 2,440,060 reported thefts and 45,475 robberies, predatory extortion, and predatory attacks on drivers.[122] However, it turns out that Germany's theft rate per 100,000 population (1,701) was one of the highest in Europe in 2014.[123]

The discussion so far allows a positive assessment of the system of regulations enforcing and protecting property rights in Germany after reunification. Effective protection of property could have encouraged investments, capital formation, setting long-term economic goals, and contracting while reducing transaction costs. The system was also not overregulated and thus too costly. The costs of enforcing and protecting property rights, adequately reduced by the state apparatus, should ensure that owners in the formal legal sense are owners in the economic sense. In other words, individuals should be able to derive economic benefits from the fact of having legal title to an object of property.[124]

It is worth noting that the FRG law *sensu largo* was perceived as effective in social perception. Twenty-five years after reunification, Germans were generally positive about the functioning of the law. According to "Roland Rechtsreport," 74 % of the inhabitants of former West Germany expressed high or fairly high confidence in the FRG law in 2014. However, the same opinion was represented by only 55 % of those surveyed in the Eastern *Länder*.[125] This significant discrepancy

120 F. Münzel, "Die Rolle des Rechts in der Deutschen Marktwirtschaft," in *Elemente der Sozialen Marktwirtschaft. Wirtschaftliche und rechtliche Rahmenbedingungen – Transformationsmöglichkeiten*, eds. K. Fasbender, M. Holthus, E. Thiel, (Hamburg: Verlag Weltarchiv GmbH, 1991), 132–133.

121 SJ BRD, Vol. 2002 (Wiesbaden: Statistisches Bundesamt, 2002), 348, table 15.6.

122 SJ DI, Vol. 2016, 311, table 11.2.1.

123 SJ DI, Vol. 2016, 655, table A.11.

124 Cf. Staniek, *Ekonomia instytucjonalna*, 142–143.

125 Similar differences, although much smaller, pertained to trust in other institutions: small and medium-sized enterprises (respectively: Western *Länder* – 85 %, Eastern *Länder* – 79 %), the police (76 % and 63 %), courts (65 % and 57 %), the federal government (50 % and 48 %), administration (49 % and 36 %), the press (47 % and 38 %), trade unions (41 % and 37 %), the Church (37 % and 25 %). Interestingly, the opposite distribution of opinions was true of large economic enterprises, which 40 % of the Eastern *Länder*'s inhabitants trusted to a great extent or quite a lot,

may have been caused, above all, by the high social costs of the systemic transition in the former GDR. The report also shows that over the course of a quarter of a century, the East Germans' trust in the law has declined somewhat. In 1991, 59 % of respondents declared great or quite great trust in this institution, while in 2014–55 %.[126]

6.1.2.2. *Owners*

The costs of enforcing and protecting property rights are also borne by the individuals with the greatest interest in doing so, namely the owners.[127] The following can be cited as their actions: purchasing property insurance, owning weapons and using alarm systems, among others. Examining these examples captures the potential involvement of German citizens in the protection of private property in 1990–2015.

Considering property insurance (analyzed on the example of the damage insurance sector (*Schadenversicherung*), which includes property damage and accident insurance (*Unfallversicherung*), hereinafter: SUV), it is important to note the increase in its importance in German society between 1990 and 2015. Data from the German Insurance Association (*Gesamtverband der Deutschen Versicherungswirtschaft*) show that the insurance sector grew during this period. Although there was a decrease in the number of insurance companies at the time (from 729 in 1990 to 539 in 2015), including SUV companies (from 322 to 205), the total value of SUV contributions increased by 95.6 % (from 32,939 million to 64,422 million euros). In general, this trend covered both the Western and Eastern parts of the country.[128] During the same period, total SUV real estate insurance contributions increased from 8,351 million to 18,006 million euros, including private real estate insurance contributions that rose from 3,697 million to

---

compared to 33 % of respondents in Western Germany. This was due to historical reasons, when the communist authorities in the GDR invested mainly in large industry, and a large part of the population found employment there. The role of propaganda was not insignificant, which presented such a model of social and economic development exclusively in a positive light (*Roland Rechtsreport 2015* (Köln: Institut für Demoskopie Allensbach, Roland Rechtsschutz-Versicherungs-AG, 2015), 16, figure 5).

126 The level of trust in institutions such as large economic enterprises (from 45 % in 1991 to 40 % in 2014), trade unions (from 46 % to 37 %) and the Church (from 35 % to 25 %) also recorded a decline. Twenty-five years after reunification, East Germans trusted more: the police (increase in trust level from 35 % in 1991 to 63 % in 2014), the press (from 14 % to 38 %), and the administration (from 22 % to 36 %) (*Roland Rechtsreport 2015*, 17, figure 6). This was a result of the liberation of these institutions from the communist regime.

127 Staniek, *Ekonomia instytucjonalna*, 143.

128 Own calculations based on: *Statistisches Taschenbuch der Versicherungswirtschaft*, Vol. 2016, (Berlin: Gesamtverband der Deutschen Versicherungswirtschaft e. V., 2016), tables 1, 4.

9,762 million euros.[129] While in 1990 there were 200,320 thousand contracts in the SUV sector in Germany, in 2015 there were 304,290 thousand contracts. Between 1995 and 2015, the number of private real estate insurance contracts increased from 52.1 million to 54.8 million.[130] The system can be considered stable since the number of claims found in the SUV sector as a whole has remained relatively constant over the period analyzed (22,965 thousand in 1990 and 23,492 thousand in 2015).[131]

The SUV industrial, commercial, and agricultural insurance sector developed in parallel. In 1990, contributions to it amounted to 3,649 million euros, and in 2015–6,244 million euros. In the field of transport and aviation, progress was no longer as dynamic: 1,214 million euros in 1990 and 1,849 million euros in 2015. However, the same cannot be said for credit, surety and employee loyalty insurance. The contributions of this SUV division increased from 629 million to 1,646 million euros.[132]

Access to weapons in Germany was regulated by law. In terms of legislation during the period in question, it was the subject in particular of the *Weapons Law* (*Waffengesetz*, WaffG) of March 8, 1976.[133] It was substantially amended on 11 October 2002, creating a *de facto* new, more restrictive, law.[134] This trend continued as the law was tightened again on July 17, 2009.[135] On the other hand, the process of decentralization in the area of issuing gun permits progressed over the

---

129 *Statistisches Taschenbuch*, tables 66–67.

130 *Statistisches Taschenbuch*, tables 63–64.

131 *Statistisches Taschenbuch*, table 63.

132 *Statistisches Taschenbuch*, tables 71, 73, 75.

133 *Bekanntmachung der Neufassung des Waffengesetzes (WaffG) Vom 8. März 1976* (BGBl., Part I, 1976, No. 23, 432–455). This act was a new version of the briefly applicable law of September 19, 1972 (*Waffengesetz (WaffG) Vom 19. September 1972* (BGBl., Part I, 1972, No. 105, 1797–1817)).

134 *Gesetz zur Neuregelung des Waffenrechts (WassRNeuRegG) Vom 11. Oktober 2002* (BGBl., Part I, 2002, No. 73, 3970–4014). Cf. corrigenda to the law: *Berichtigung des Gesetzes zur Neuregelung des Waffenrechts Vom 19. Dezember 2002* (BGBl., Part I, 2002, No. 86, 4592); *Berichtigung des Gesetzes zur Neuregelung des Waffenrechts Vom 19. September 2003* (BGBl., Part I, 2003, No. 49, 1957). Cf. the amendment to the law reorganizing the previous provisions: *Gesetz zur Änderung des Waffengesetzes und weiterer Vorschriften Vom 26. März 2008* (BGBl., Part I, 2008, No. 11, 426–440). A significant influence on the shape of the new law of October 11, 2002, limiting access to weapons, was the Erfurt school massacre of April 26, 2002 (K. W., A. P., "Zginęło 17 osób. Masakra w gimnazjum," *Rzeczpospolita* April 27–28, 2002, No. 99 (6176), A1; K. W., AP, Reuters, DPA, "Strzelanina w Erfurcie. 18 osób nie żyje. Prawdopodobnie zemsta ucznia. Masakra w gimnazjum," *Rzeczpospolita*, April 27–28, 2002, No. 99 (6176), A4).

135 *Viertes Gesetz zur Änderung des Spregstoffgesetzes Vom 17. Juli 2009*, Art. 3, Par. 5 (BGBl., Part I, 2009, No. 44, 2088–2090). The reason for the new tightening of regulations concerning access to weapons was the school shooting in Winnenden on March 11, 2009 (P. Gillert, P. Jednroszczyk, mszy, "Masakry w Niemczech i USA," *Rzeczpospolita*, March 12, 2009, No. 60 (8265), A1; P. Jendroszczyk, "Masakra w niemieckiej szkole," *Rzeczpospolita*, March 12, 2009, No. 60 (8265), A10; H. Merkens,

following years. The *Länder* were responsible for this and their certain regional offices.[136] On the basis of estimations, it can be assumed that out of 82 million inhabitants of Germany, approximately 3 million people had a gun permit in 2006. At the same time, it is assumed that there is an arsenal of about 10 million weapons in the FRG then.[137]

These numbers decreased in 2015. Available data shows that with relatively the same population, 970,401 people had gun permits. The number of weapons registered was 5,096,227 at that time. Interestingly, in terms of the number of permits and the size of the arsenal, the Western *Länder* such as Bavaria, North Rhine-Westphalia, Lower Saxony, and Baden-Württemberg dominated.[138] Leaving aside the distribution of the above numbers by categories of gun owners and the fact that these were mainly permits for sportsmen and hunters in the period in question,[139] it can be assumed that one of the key reasons for the decline in both the number of gun permits and the number of guns were the amendments to the *Waffengesetz* in 2002–2009, which were characterized by progressive legal strictness.

New technologies are conducive to lowering the cost of protecting property rights.[140] A fairly popular form in this regard, especially in relation to real estate, is alarm systems. Data from the Swedish company Berg Insight shows that there is a correlation between GDP *per capita* and demand for alarm services. In particular, economic development, the standard of living, new housing construction, and the quality of services provided by professionals in this field are cited as factors for the increase in demand for such systems in the residential sector. In 2016, the highest penetration rate of monitored alarm systems was recorded in Norway (17 %), Ireland (12 %), and Sweden (11 %). However, in Germany, it was relatively low at only 2 %.[141]

It has been pointed out that the reason for this is the memory of repression and surveillance during the Third Reich and the GDR.[142] In addition, the FRG

P. Jendroszczyk, "Trudno temu zapobiec," *Rzeczpospolita*, March 12, 2009, No. 60 (8265), A10).

136 M. Mróz, *Prawo do broni w Polsce i Europie. Posiadanie broni strzeleckiej przez osoby fizyczne w ustawodawstwie wybranych państw Unii Europejskiej* (Warszawa: Wydawnictwo Sejmowe, 2011), 113.

137 Mróz, *Prawo do broni w Polsce i Europie*, 113.

138 Own calculations based on: F. Boeselager, "Deutschland, deine Waffen," http://www.deutschlandfunkkultur.de/statistik-deutschland-deine-waffen.976.de.html?dram:article_id=346481 (accessed January 11, 2018). Data for Brandenburg are not included in the article.

139 Mróz, *Prawo do broni w Polsce i Europie*, 113–114.

140 Staniek, *Ekonomia instytucjonalna*, 143.

141 "Active Monitored Alarm Systems in Europe and North America Reached 41 Million at the End of 2016," https://www.iot-now.com/2017/04/19/60882-active-monitored-alarm-systems-europe-north-america-reached-41-million-end-2016/ (accessed January 12, 2018).

142 "It's Different in Germany," http://www.professionalsecurity.co.uk/reviews/its-different-in-germany/ (accessed January 12, 2018).

Constitution set out freedoms that protected citizens from a too powerful state,[143] while the *Federal Data Protection Act* (*Bundesdatenschutzgesetz*, BDSG) of January 27, 1977, contained strict regulations in this regard.[144] These acts were supplemented by the internal laws of the individual *Länder*. In 1999, the number of closed-circuit television (CCTV) systems in Germany was estimated at 30,000. CCTV was one of the fastest-growing sectors of electronic security systems in the FRG in the second half of the 1990s. For example, in 1998 it grew by 18 %, and two years later – by 8 %. The burglar alarm sector was much less dynamic. Between 1996 and 2000, the entire electronic security systems market in Germany grew by 221 %.[145]

Analyses of the phenomenon of rent-seeking, made from the position of public choice theory, point to the social costs of theft. It turns out that theft is not just a transfer of wealth between one person (victim) and another (thief). The potential costs and benefits can be considered from the perspective of both the thief and the victim. Institutional arrangements that adequately regulate the costs of theft and prevention activities play an important role. A high level of such protection discourages potential thieves from activity, securing the property of individuals.[146] It follows that by far the greater role in securing property is played by the state through the creation and enforcement of appropriate formal institutions, while the actions of citizens in this area play a complementary role. This is confirmed in the case of Germany in 1990–2015.

6.1.2.3. Social norms

Institutional economics emphasizes the influence of informal institutions on socio-economic change.[147] It also highlights the importance of ideologies, as well as social

---

143 Cf. Arts. 1–19 GG (the basic rights).

144 *Gesetz zum Schutz vor Mißbrauch personenbezogener Daten bei der Datenverarbeitung (Bundesdatenschutzgesetz – BDSG) Vom 27. Januar 1977* (BGBl., Part I, 1977, No. 7, 201–214). See the new version of the law of January 14, 2003: *Bekanntmachung der Neufassung des Bundesdatenschutzgesetzes Vom 14. Januar 2003* (BGBl., Part I, 2003, No. 3, 66–88). See the amendments: *Gesetz zur Änderung des Bundesdatenschutzgesetzes Vom 29. Juli 2009* (BGBl., Part I, 2009, No. 48, 2254–2257); *Gesetz zur Umsetzung der Verbraucherkreditrichtlinie, des zivilrechtlichen Teils der Zahlungsdiensterrichtlinie sowie zur Neuordnung der Vorschriften über das Widerrufs- und Rückgaberecht Vom 29. Juli 2009*, Art. 5 (BGBl, Part I, 2009, No. 49, 2384); *Gesetz zur Änderung datenschutzrechtlicher Vorschriften Vom 14. August 2009*, Art. 1 (BGBl., Part I, 2009, No. 54, 2814–2819).

145 "It's Different in Germany," http://www.professionalsecurity.co.uk/reviews/its-different-in-germany/ (accessed January 12, 2018). This article is based on 2001 data compiled by the agency MSI Market Research for Industry in Great Britain.

146 G. Tullock, "The Welfare Costs of Tariffs, Monopolies, and Theft," *Economic Inquiry* 5, No. 3 (1967): 224–232; Wilkin, *Instytucjonalne i kulturowe podstawy gospodarowania*, 206–210, 212.

147 These issues were presented by the author in a paper "Normy społeczne jako sposób egzekwowania i ochrony praw własności. Przykład Niemiec w latach 1990–2015"

norms and values.[148] However, empirical demonstration of these relationships is difficult because these categories are unmeasurable in nature.[149]

Social norms are understood as specific rules of behavior that demonstrate and embody the values of a particular culture. Norms promote, sanction, or negate a given behavior. Values, on the other hand, are abstract ideas professed by both individuals and social groups. They indicate what is good, right, and necessary and what is not. They provide a sense of meaning, acting as a guidepost for social interaction. They decide on cultural differences while embedding the individual in a cultural context. Anthony Giddens states that values and norms together create for members of culture ways to behave in their particular environment. Values and cultural norms evolve under the influence of time.[150] Piotr Sztompka, also writing about values and cultural norms, identifies the former with goals, while the latter with the means to achieve them. For example, the diligent study will remain the norm if one's value is thorough education. Sometimes, however, as Sztompka notes, "values are understood as ... superior, fundamental rules, concerning matters of the highest importance, whose concrete implications are the norms regulating more mundane matters."[151]

It is worth trying to capture such social norms (values) that were conducive to the enforcement and protection of property rights by German citizens in 1990–2015. According to the understanding provided by institutional economics, social norms are an example of informal rules that interact with formal institutions, in this case, property rights. In doing so, one should not forget the feedback loop. Formal institutions influence informal rules, although the latter are characterized by greater permanence.[152]

At the same time, social norms are a component of a broader phenomenon, namely social capital. Social capital is sometimes distinguished from human capital or cultural capital.[153]

["Social Norms as a Way to Enforce and Protect Property Rights. The Example of Germany in 1990–2015"], delivered at the XXII International Scientific Conference *Ethics in Economic Life*, organized on May 23–24, 2019, at the University of Lodz, Poland, by the Department of History of Economic Thought and Economic History (Faculty of Economics and Sociology, University of Lodz).

148 Cf. T. Eggertsson, *Economic Behavior and Institutions* (Cambridge: Cambridge University Press, 1995), 73–75.

149 See for an exemplary attempt to econometrically demonstrate the relationship between social values and norms and economic development: S. Voigt, S.-M. Park, "Die Bedeutung von Werten und Normen für langfristige wirtschaftliche Entwicklung," in *Vom Sozialismus zur Marktwirtschaft. Wandlungsprozesse, Ergebnisse und Perspektiven*, eds. K. von Delhaes, W. Quaisser, K. Ziemer (München: Olzog, 2009), 183–218.

150 A. Giddens, *Socjologia* (Warszawa: WN PWN, 2006), 45–47, 727, 737.

151 P. Sztompka, *Socjologia. Analiza społeczeństwa* (Kraków: Wydawnictwo Znak, 2010), 258–259.

152 Cf. section 1.2.2. in this study.

153 See a cross-sectional study on this topic: P. Sztompka, *Kapitał społeczny. Teoria przestrzeni międzyludzkiej* (Kraków: Wydawnictwo Znak, 2016).

Characterizing the economic culture of contemporary Germany, the literature draws attention to the importance of key national characteristics. The following are mentioned above all: uniformity, respect for social norms, high level of organization, dutifulness, diligence, regularity and effectiveness of work, accuracy, perfection, unambiguity, predictability, concreteness, faithfulness to priorities, punctuality, efficiency, commitment, reliability, stability, ambition, methodicalness, scrupulosity, individualism, thrift, the rationality of thinking, respect for authorities and power, politeness, good manners, attaching importance to competence and professionalism, and hierarchy. In research, the Germans stressed the importance of diligence (instilled in children from an early age), thoroughness (important in the educational process, socio-economic activity, and contributing to the acceptance of predetermined rules of conduct), and conformity (defined as the ability to adapt to specific norms of conduct). Protestant and bourgeois ethics played an important role in this ethos.[154]

A general characteristic of the contemporary economic culture in Germany (sometimes referred to as business culture) emphasizes, among other things, the technical approach of German entrepreneurs to their activities and their focus on the high quality of manufactured goods. This has even given rise to some controversy, as some have accused Germans of overemphasizing these aspects at the expense of effective marketing and sales. More recent research shows that entrepreneurs pursued a strategic, long-term policy, while implementing new solutions was usually faster, making it possible to correct possible mistakes. Accuracy in the execution of specific tasks was, therefore, dominant over speed. The high quality of goods and services offered by German companies was complemented by strict health and safety regulations and environmental protection regulations.[155]

Business culture in the FRG is often depicted as formalized. The importance of economic and social solidarity is emphasized, which manifests itself in such areas as: cooperation between businesses and banks, implementation of common goals by individual sectors, and hidden protectionism, making it difficult for foreign entities

---

154 I. Ścibiorska-Kowalczyk, "Kultura ekonomiczna w Niemczech na przykładzie Euroregionu Nysa," *Pogranicze. Polish Borderlands Studies* 5, No. 2 (2017): 136–138. Cf. e.g.: A. Müller-Armack, *Religion und Wirtschaft. Geistesgeschichtliche Hintergründe unserer europäischen Lebensform* (Stuttgart: W. Kohlhammer Verlag, 1959); M. Weber, *The Protestant Ethic and the Spirit of Capitalism* (New York: Charles Scribner's Sons, 1958); J. Skodlarski, "Stosunek judaizmu, chrześcijaństwa i islamu do działalności gospodarczej," in *Rola Kościołów w życiu gospodarczym ziem polskich*, eds. K. Kowalski, R. Matera, A. Pieczewski (Łódź: Wydawnictwo UŁ, 2017), 23–24; J. Skodlarski, *Religia a gospodarka. Judaizm – chrześcijaństwo – islam* (Łódź: Wydawnictwo UŁ, 2020), 53–69. See also the polemical voice with Weber's thesis: Bębnowski, "Wokół przedsiębiorczości katolickiej," 197–210.

155 Environmental regulations were even included in the FRG Constitution. These issues were also drawn attention to in the documents regulating German reunification. See sections 3.4.–3.5., 5.3. in this study.

to penetrate the market. In some surveys, Germans indicated the following business goals as the most important: social responsibility, responsibility towards employees, innovation, creativity, profits in a time horizon of 10 years, and enforcement of ethical standards. On the other hand, power, patriotism, national pride, personal wealth, enterprise growth, and profits in a given year were less important for them.[156]

However, the above description is only a model. It does not fully reflect the social, cultural, and mental transformations that took place in Germany after reunification.[157] The literature still lacks a comprehensive picture of this process. Various works highlight its individual aspects.[158]

Sabine Spangenberg points out that the change in the economic, legal and political system in the new federated states coincided with the transformation of the social system. This, in turn, resulted from the implementation in Eastern Germany of the West German ordoliberal concept of economic policy. The change in social norms had already begun in the early 1990s. The turning point in this regard was to be the first national election on December 2, 1990, which showed the approval of Eastern German society for reunification.[159] The change in norms from then was aimed at strengthening personal freedom and individual freedom of action. Individuals and private enterprises became the main actors in consumption and production. The importance of individual interests, utility (satisfaction), rationality, personal motivation, and behavioral function (showing money as a determinant of individual behavior) increased. Periodic economic plans were replaced by individual planning of economic agents. This went hand in hand with the decentralization and marketization of decision-making, the rise of private property, and the democratization and pluralization of public life. In other words, social life, forming a superstructure in the Marxist system, which was only a consequence of the base, i.e., the economic system, evolved in a democratic and capitalist direction. As a result, the economic system became part of a much broader and internally differentiated social system. According to Spangenberg, the occurrence of the discussed change in social norms in the Eastern *Länder* in a relatively short period (first half of the 1990s) testified to the proper adjustment of the systemic, structural, and institutional framework.[160]

---

156 Ścibiorska-Kowalczyk, "Kultura ekonomiczna w Niemczech," 137–139.

157 This applies, among others, to different entrepreneurial cultures (*Unternehmenskultur*) represented by the FRG and the GDR companies (G. Aβmann, K. Backhaus, J. Hilker, eds., *Deutsh-deutsche Unternehmen. Ein unternehmenskulturelles Anpassungsproblem* (Stuttgart: C. E. Poeschel Verlag, 1991)).

158 This gap is partially filled by the following books: B. Nuss, *Das Faust Syndrom. Ein Versuch über die Mentalität der Deutschen* (Bonn–Berlin: Bouvier, 1993); N. Elias, *Studies on the Germans. Power Struggles and the Development of Habitus in the Nineteenth and Twentieth Centuries* (Dublin: University College Dublin Press, 2013); K. Gazdar, *Germany's Balanced Development. The Real Wealth of a Nation* (Westport–London: Quorum Books, 1998).

159 The author incorrectly dates the first all-German parliamentary elections to 1991 (Spangenberg, *The Institutionalised Transformation*, 242).

160 Cf. Spangenberg, *The Institutionalised Transformation*, 240–247.

Robert Rohrschneider, in his valuable research, points out that the dichotomous division of the set of economic values in Western Germany and the new *Länder* was largely based on two separate economic systems created after World War II. While the FRG's development was based on a social market economy and respect for private property, the GDR was dominated by a centrally planned economy that saw private property as the source of inequality and poverty in capitalist countries.[161]

On this basis, Rohrschneider distinguished two ideal types of economies (economic cultures) that were present in the German social consciousness after reunification. The first type, the "ideal-typical free market culture," was characterized by such economic values (beliefs) as: the right to private property, the right to maximize profits, distribution of income based on the criterion of achievement, perfect market efficiency, income inequality initiating economic activity, minimal involvement of the state in the economy, limited role of trade unions as political actors. As Rohrschneider stresses, this model was accepted by the majority of German society after 1990. The second model, the ideal-typical socialist culture,[162] was in opposition to the above-mentioned economic values (beliefs). Their adherents, e.g.: questioned the importance of private property and income inequality as factors initiating economic processes, emphasized the role of the state, which with the support of trade unions, regulated the economy, limited inequalities, and showed profit as an inappropriate motive for economic activity. Naturally, Rohrschneider's models are only ideal types, so, according to Max Weber's understanding, they are abstract theoretical constructs created for the purpose of analysis. Thus, they do not exist in reality in their pure form.[163] Furthermore, the West German model of a social market economy, which was implemented in the new *Länder* after reunification, was, as Rohrschneider points out, a combination of a free market and socialist (social) order.[164]

German society's social norms related to the economy were significantly shaped in the first half of the 1990s. Although the directions of their transformation generally followed the West (old *Länder*) – East (new *Länder*) axis, they did not always follow the dichotomy outlined above, resulting from different economic models in the FRG and the GDR in the period preceding reunification. However,

---

161 R. Rohrschneider, *Learning Democracy. Democratic and Economic Values in Unified Germany* (Oxford: Oxford University Press, 1999), 160. Other authors, such as Adam Przeworski, also point in this context to the fundamental importance of the two different economic systems in the FRG and the GDR (A. Przeworski, *Democracy and the Market. Political and Economic Reforms in Eastern Europe and Latin America* (Cambridge: Cambridge University Press, 1991), 121).

162 Rohrschneider does not use this name. With reference to the first model, he inconsistently writes about the "set of ideal-typical socialist economic values," "socialist value system," or "ideal-typical socialist economy." Cf. Rohrschneider, *Learning Democracy*, 163. In other places, Rohrschneider writes simply about "market/socialistic values." See Rohrschneider, *Learning Democracy, passim.*

163 M. Weber, "'Obiektywność' poznania w naukach społecznych," in *Problemy socjologii wiedzy*, eds. A. Chmielecki et al. (Warszawa: PWN, 1985), 45–100.

164 Rohrschneider, *Learning Democracy*, 163–164.

as Rohrschneider states, in the early 1990s, the inhabitants of the new federated states were more able to support the values characteristic of socialist culture, i.e. those that referred to "economic protection" of the state. This occurred under systemic transition conditions perceived as a fundamental change of the previous economic order. Consequently, Eastern German society was more supportive of interventionist measures to rebuild the economy in the former GDR.[165]

Rohrschneider analyzed in this context the evolution of attitudes of German parliamentarians in 1992–1995 as those who represented their electorate in the Bundestag and thus – at least indirectly – expressed the values adhered to by voters. He divided them into two groups according to the *Länder* of origin: old or new federated states. Although egalitarian values were much more characteristic of Eastern German parliamentarians, it can be seen a fundamental change in their views on economic issues in the above years.[166] Details are presented in Table 15.

Table 15: *Summary of economic values declared by German parliamentarians in 1992 and 1995 (distribution of parliamentarians by group of Western and Eastern Länder, in %)*

Economic value	**Western *Länder***	**Eastern *Länder***	
	1992	**1992**	**1995**
(A) Social market economies generally lead to acceptable differences in income distribution	67.4	49.4	56.9
(B) The profit motive often brings out the worst in human nature	51.7	73.4	66.2
(C) Democracy is only possible if individuals not only participate in general elections, but can also participate in important management decisions at their workplace	68.5	81.0	73.9
(D) The poor are poor because they often do not make use of available opportunities which the economic system provides	16.9	8.9	21.5
(E) The national government should play a greater role in the management of the economy	27.0	40.5	53.9
(F) Unions should have more power in German society	23.6	48.1	38.5
(G) When private industry is allowed to make as much money as it can, everyone profits in the long run	31.5	13.9	13.9

Source: Rohrschneider, *Learning Democracy*, 169, table 8.1.

165 Rohrschneider, *Learning Democracy*, 167.

166 Rohrschneider, *Learning Democracy*, p. 169. See also R. Rohrschneider, "Cultural Transmission Versus Perceptions of the Economy: The Sources of Political Elites' Economic Values in the United Germany," *Comparative Political Studies* 29, No. 1 (1996): 78–104.

A definite turn in 1992–1995 of Eastern German political elites towards values typical of free market culture is presented by item (D), while (B) reflects a relative weakening of socialist culture. Some items also show a strengthening of values that should be associated with the social market economy model: (A), (C),[167] and partly (E)[168]. Although it is based on the free market, the state plays an important coordinating role in it.[169] The change in attitudes among parliamentarians from the Eastern *Länder*, noticed by Rohrschneider, is all the more significant because it took place within just three years and coincided with the years of intensive systemic transition, generating high social costs, especially the high unemployment. As he notes, optimism about the future played an important role in this case. Citizens who believed in economic development after 1990 were generally more likely to adhere to pro-market values.[170] However, despite the mentioned direction in the new federated states, these values were still not as popular as among Western German parliamentarians. On the other hand, items (D), (F), and (G) show that Eastern German elites did not always identify with a socialist culture, while Western German elites did not always identify with a free-market culture.[171] This confirms the earlier statement about these cultures as ideal types that do not necessarily coincide with the West-East axis.

Although Rohrschneider writes about economic values in Germany after reunification, in his otherwise interesting research, it is often difficult to separate the economic values declared by German political elites from their opinions on the economic changes in the FRG after 1990, which would reflect social moods rather than values, let alone norms. Among the accounts of Eastern German politicians analyzed by Rohrschneider, a rather populist statement by a representative of the post-communist Party of Democratic Socialism (*Partei des Demokratischen Sozialismus*, PDS) is telling. He stated, among other things, that in the new socio-economic reality, the new property relations are the worst, where citizens lose their

---

167 This position should be linked to the model of the social market economy due to the extensive system of employee participation in Germany. More on this topic, see section 6.2.5. in this study.

168 The strong support for state interventionism among Eastern German elites may also stem from a socialist culture. This is how Rohrschneider interprets it (Rohrschneider, *Learning Democracy*, 169).

169 Hence, in the theory of varieties of capitalism, developing since the 1990s and characterizing different models (cultures) of capitalism, the German system is sometimes referred to as a "coordinated market economy." See, e.g.: P. A. Hall, D. Soskice, "An Introduction to Varieties of Capitalism," in *Varieties of Capitalism. The Institutional Foundations of Comparative Advantage*, eds. P. A. Hall, D. Soskice (New York: Oxford University Press, 2001), 19; P. A. Hall, D. W. Gingerich, "Varieties of Capitalism and Institutional Complementarities in the Political Economy: An Empirical Analysis," *British Journal of Political Science* 39, No. 3 (2009): 452–453.

170 Rohrschneider, *Learning Democracy*, 167.

171 Cf. Rohrschneider, *Learning Democracy*, 170.

property every day.[172] Such assessments, however, were rare. As Rohrschneider found, in the mid-1990s, most parliamentarians from the Western *Länder* and a small proportion of politicians from the Eastern *Länder* stressed the higher efficiency of the market economy, the importance of personal freedom, individual self-reliance, and responsibility.[173]

Summing up Rohrschneider;s findings, and at the risk of considerable simplification, it should be stated that the discussed evolution of economic values declared by parliamentarians from the new federated states between 1992 and 1995 may have revealed (at least indirectly) values characteristic of their constituents.[174] Thus, his results have to be considered valuable from the point of view of the values adhered to by the whole or at least a representative part of the Eastern German society.

The growing importance of values that fit into the free market culture model in Eastern Germany in the first half of the 1990s must therefore be pointed to as a factor supporting property rights in the former GDR. As Rohrschneider argues, private property was a key component of this ideal type. In the years that followed, pro-market values were generally expanded and strengthened, especially in Eastern German society. They evolved into the social market economy model already proven in the postwar FRG.

However, this process was slow and complicated. In the literature of the 1990s, which provided an ongoing commentary on the social and economic transformations in the Eastern *Länder*, it was pointed out that a significant part of the population there was disillusioned with the transition and consequently distrusted the federal government. This was largely due to uncertainty about individual property, the privatization of state enterprises, and high unemployment. This situation created a reluctance to get involved in economic affairs and deepened antagonism between citizens from both parts of Germany. For this reason, some people at the time viewed reunification and transition of the former GDR as "colonization" or "occupation." The new federated states were to become an "economic colony of West German capital." Comparisons were also made to a "political colony," as cadres from Western Germany were recruited to high political positions in the Eastern *Länder*. Restitution of property to its rightful owners was to be a form of compensation for the transformation of the property. However, the formula for re-privatization was complex and controversial.[175] The conviction that Eastern

---

172 Rohrschneider, *Learning Democracy*, 174.

173 Rohrschneider, *Learning Democracy*, 172.

174 See the book – which is actually an appeal or even a manifesto of the author – on the importance of elites for systemic transition and economic development: H. H. Karg, *Nationalökonomie und Elitenbildung. Eine grundlegende Wirtschaftstheorie an die Adresse der nachkommunistischen Menschheit* (Hamburg: Verlag Dr. Kovač, 1996). The author states, among other things, that the mentality of elites constitutes a social value (Karg, *Nationalökonomie und Elitenbildung*, 64–66).

175 More on re-privatization in Germany after reunification: section 6.2.1. in this work.

German citizens had been deprived of their property ("lack of ownership") deepened. The new owners of the privatized or re-privatized property were usually Germans from the Western part of the country (the original owners of nationalized property largely originated from there) or foreign investors. The residents of the new federated states, who had been stuck in a centrally planned economy for years, were disoriented because they did not understand the free market rules. This was a form of their specific exclusion from the process of social and economic development within the democratic and capitalist system.[176]

Nevertheless, the authors emphasized the importance of privatization for the systemic transition of the former GDR. They also stressed the need to popularize property transformations in Eastern German society. For example, Gerd H. Wächter wrote at the time about the need to develop a kind of "privatization philosophy."[177]

---

176 H. M. Stack, "The 'Colonization' of East Germany?: A Comparative Analysis of German Privatization," *Duke Law Journal* 46 (1997): 1212–1213, 1221, 1228–1230, 1236–1239. Cf. P. Christ, R. Neubauer, *Kolonie im eigenen Land. Die Treuhand, Bonn und die Wirtschaftskatastrophe der fünf neuen Länder* (Berlin: Rowohlt, 1991); Schnabel, "Structural Adjustment and Privatization," 240; D. M. W. N. Hitchens, K. Wagner, J. E. Birnie, *East German Productivity and the Transition to the Market Economy. Comparisons with West Germany and Northern Ireland* (Aldershot–Brookfield: Avebury, 1993), 99–100; D. Landua, "The Social Aspects of German Reunification," in *The Economics of German Unification*, eds. A. G. Ghanssy, W. Schäfer (London–New York: Routledge, 1993), 92–109; H. J. Maaz, "Transformationsprobleme aus psychosozialer Sicht," in *Transformationsprozesse in Deutschland*, ed. H. Sahner (Opladen: Leske + Budrich, 1995), 105–115; G. Trommsdorff, "Identitätsprozesse in kulturellen Kontext und im sozialen Wandel," in Sahner, *Transformationsprozesse in Deutschland*, 116–148; P. Wiles, "Capitalist Triumphalism in the Eastern European Transition," in *The Transformation of the Communist Economies. Against the Mainstream*, eds. H.-J. Chang, P. Nolan (New York: St. Martin's Press, 1995), 61–65. Over time, therefore, the enthusiastic view of some researchers, such as Heinz-Dieter Haustein, who stated in 1991 that the advantage of the citizens of the former GDR was the social memory of a market economy with a long historical tradition, was not confirmed (H.-D. Haustein, "Experiences and Prospects: The Case of the GDR," in *Towards a Market Economy in Central and Eastern Europe*, ed. H.-D. Haustein (Berlin–Heidelberg: Springer-Verlag, 1991), 151). It is worth mentioning that he came from East Germany (Haustein, "Experiences and Prospects," 169). The importance of the historical experience of Eastern German society regarding the private property was also pointed out by Volkmar Kreissig and Ralph Lungwitz in 1994 (V. Kreissig, R. Lungwitz, "Privatisation in East Germany and the Chance of Workers' Participation: A Problems Approach," in *International Privatisation. Strategies and Practices*, ed. T. Clarke (Berlin–New York: Walter de Gruyter, 1994), 234–237). As it later turned out, this was also too optimistic.

177 G. H. Wächter, "Privatization in East Germany: Success or Failure? Questions from a Transactional Perspective," in *Democracy, Market Economy, and the Law. Legal,*

It should therefore be concluded that the Eastern German elites more quickly perceived the positive aspects of Germany's economic unification than the general public in the Eastern *Länder*. In the latter case, the implemented West German formal rules (constitutional and property rules) functioned (at least partly) as political and economic extractive institutions.

At the turn of the 20th and 21st centuries, a discussion arose in Germany about the legitimacy of maintaining a social market economy model. Its critics raised the following problems: the decline of private initiative, lack of courage, abandonment of savings, and limited sense of responsibility in the collective dimension. In addition, some of them pointed out that the *de facto* welfare state model in the FRG undermines the free market and creates a dangerous dependence of the individual citizen on the state.[178] However, such voices were not dominant and did not force a fundamental reformulation of the functioning model of economic development before 2015.[179]

Nevertheless, in the literature from the first years of the 21st century summarising the progress of social and economic unification in Germany, attention is drawn, among other things, to the problem of the "subsidy mentality" of the inhabitants of the Eastern *Länder*. Although the state's role in the integration and transition of the former GDR was crucial, some authors point out that the interventionism of financial transfers in the 1990s was too high. Consequently, Eastern German society did not break out of its communist mentality. It had exaggerated expectations of the state, which was seen as the only entity that could solve all problems. Social attention was focused primarily on government support programs rather than on individual responsibility. The inhabitants of the new federated states were characterized by relative apathy and reluctance to become active. Welfare played a key role in this case. The model of a social market economy established from above became, in popular perception, an equivalent of the once imposed model of a centrally planned economy. Naturally, there is no equal sign between the two. At the time of reunification (thanks to the state sphere), East Germans received the most important (formal) institutions within the social market economy. However, these same people, seen as an entrepreneurial group, were not empowered through social – and thus their own – initiative. Consequently, development was not stimulated from below, and the state was seen as the author of any change to the existing order. This had negative social consequences (psychological, emotional, cultural) in both parts of the formally unified state. In the opinion of the inhabitants of the Eastern *Länder* (contemptuously called *Ossi* in Western Germany), the federal government did not do everything to even out the differences in development. On the

---

Economic, and Political Problems of Transition to Democracy, eds. W. F. Ebke, D. F. Vagts (Heidelberg: Verlag Recht und Wirtschaft GmbH, 1995), 258.

178 Ścibiorska-Kowalczyk, "Kultura ekonomiczna w Niemczech," 141.

179 In the German literature, discussions about the condition of the social market economy system were actually ongoing both in the 1980s, which preceded the chronological framework of this paper, and in the 1990–2015 period.

other hand, the *Wessi* from the Western *Länder* felt overburdened with the financial costs of aid transfers and accused their fellow countrymen of being too passive and mismanaged.[180]

The Eastern Germans were also disillusioned by the ostentatious violation of their previous mental system. Researchers highlight the problem of questioning the existing values so far, identity, and the compulsion to adapt to new rules of the game, both formal and informal. One of the main disappointments of this kind was the sharp rise in unemployment in the new federated states in the 1990s.[181]

---

180 Cf. J. Czech-Rogosz, "Gospodarka wschodnich Niemiec w 12 lat po zjednoczeniu – niedokończony proces unifikacji gospodarczej. Wybrane problemy," in *Unifikacja gospodarek europejskich. Szanse i zagrożenia*, eds. A. Manikowski, A. Psyk (Warszawa: WN WZ UW, 2004), 102; M. Moszyński, "Zjednoczenie Niemiec – dwie dekady konwergencji," *Ekonomia i Prawo* 7 (2011): 265; M. Moszyński, "Idee ładu gospodarczego w procesie transformacji systemowej byłej NRD – oczekiwania a rzeczywistość," *Prace Naukowe Uniwersytetu Ekonomicznego we Wrocławiu. Economia* No. 245 (2012): 354; M. Zawilska-Florczuk, A. Ciechanowicz, *Jeden kraj, dwa społeczeństwa? Niemcy 20 lat po zjednoczeniu* (Warszawa: OSW, 2011), 15–38. One can see here a certain parallel to the *Homo sovieticus* model, a category coined in the 1980s by Alexander Zinoviev and Mikhail Heller. In Poland, this concept was reinterpreted and popularized by Józef Tischner. In general, the "Soviet man" is characterized primarily by: enslavement, clientelism, lack of initiative, inability to think critically, entitlement attitude towards the state and others, dependence on authority (social organization, group), falling into complexes, megalomania, conformism, lack of respect for common property. See, e.g.: J. Tischner, *Nieszczęsny dar wolności* (Kraków: Wydawnictwo Znak, 2015); J. Tischner, *Etyka solidarności oraz Homo sovieticus* (Kraków: Wydawnictwo Znak, 2018). Przemysław Dakowicz uses the concept of aphasia when referring to Polish society experienced by two 20th-century totalitarianisms (P. Dakowicz, *Afazja polska* (Warszawa: Wydawnictwo Sic!, 2015); P. Dakowicz, *Afazja polska 2* (Warszawa: Wydawnictwo Sic!, 2016)). With some obvious differences, they can be applied to society from the former GDR. Heather M. Stack writes about the colonial mentality of Eastern German society (Stack, "The 'Colonization' of East Germany?," 1240, 1247–1248, 1252). He also cites in this context such terms as the "emotional divide between east and west" and the "spiritual and mental version of the Berlin Wall" (Stack, "The 'Colonization' of East Germany?," 1212, fn. 9).

181 Cf. M. Moszyński, "Transformacja systemowa wschodnich Niemiec w perspektywie "cudu gospodarczego" Ludwiga Erharda," in *Ordoliberalizm i społeczna gospodarka rynkowa wobec wyzwań współczesności*, eds. P. Pysz, E. Mączyńska (Warszawa: PTE, 2013), 233. Cf. theoretical considerations on mental models from the perspective of new institutional economics: K. Fijałkowski, "Instytucjonalna teoria zmiany społeczno-ekonomicznej w historii gospodarczej Douglassa C. Northa," in *Społeczeństwo i gospodarka w badaniach historycznych – dokonania i perspektywy. W 60-lecie polskich badań statystycznych i gospodarczych na Dolnym Śląsku*, eds. E. Kościk, T. Głowiński (Wrocław: Wydawnictwo GAJT, 2006), 63–71; A. T. Denzau, D. C. North, "Shared Mental Models: Ideologies and Institutions," *Kyklos* No. 47 (1994): 3–31.

6.2. Relationship of property rights to the German economy

In the literature, there are positions that the West German model of privatization, resulting from the system of property rights previously operating in the FRG, paradoxically contributed to weakening the economic potential of the Eastern *Länder* and hindered the process of convergence.[182] Property rights were imposed on the new federated states. This resulted in ready-made and preconceived (through political decisions) outline of the privatization process and certain models of management.[183]

Such views, however, do not dominate the literature. From the point of view of the formal institutions analyzed in this study, it is reasonable to conclude that the West German constitutional and property rules set an institutional framework for the economy of the former GDR that produced generally favorable economic effects. Rather, the weakening of economic growth in the individual years of the period in question or the convergence process was due to other factors widely discussed in the literature (e.g., inefficient transfers to the Eastern *Länder*, missed infrastructure investments, reunification costs, exogenous factors), as well as those cited in various places in this work.

On the basis of the theory of property rights, the relationship between the institution of property rules and economic change is sought, taking as a criterion, in particular, changes in economic growth or economic development rates. Quantitative studies even propose the use of specific indicators to assess the quality of this institution and then its impact on the economy. However, it turns out that there is a lack of uniform measures of property rights institutions (especially in the dimension of their enforcement and protection, taking into account, e.g., the degree of enforceability of contracts or the risk of expropriation), so researchers usually rely

182 The literature on the convergence of the Eastern and Western *Länder* after German reunification is very rich. Empirical analyses focus on the common conclusion that this process has not been completed in the first decades of the 21st century, its pace has clearly slowed down, and the developmental differences (measured by various indicators) between the old and new federated states are significant (to the detriment of the latter). See examples of synthetic reviews of this literature: M. Berlemann, M. Thum, "Mittelfristige Perspektiven der Ost-West-Konvergenz," *ifo Dresden berichtet* 13, No. 1 (2006): 34–39; M. Götz, "Przyczyny słabszego wzrostu gospodarczego wschodnich krajów RFN w ocenie literatury naukowej," *Przegląd Zachodni* No. 2 (2010): 203–213.

183 Götz, "Przyczyny słabszego wzrostu gospodarczego wschodnich krajów RFN," 204. Cf., e.g., D. J. Snower, Ch. Merkl, "The Caring Hand that Cripples: The East German Labor Market after Reunification," *American Economic Review* 96, No. 2 (2006): 375–382 (the authors present the negative consequences of the unification model imposed by the FRG on the labor market).

on "broader" indicators measuring the quality of political institutions *sensu largo*, such as political stability, political freedom or civil liberties. They include, among others, property rights.[184]

6.2.1. Property transformations: Legal and institutional framework

With reference to the theory of economic systems, the concept of property transformations can be identified with the transformations of the property structure, i.e. changes in the quantitative shares of given forms of property in the total economic property of a particular system. Property structure is complementary to property rights. It remains the result of transformations of these rights and vice versa: property regulations are the consequence of changes in the structure of property in a given economic system.[185]

Strengthening property rights, especially through the institutionalization of private property, is one of the most important aspects of the transition process.

184 This is pointed out, among others, by Stephen Knack and Philip Keefer, citing representative studies (S. Knack, P. Keefer, "Institutions and Economic Performance: Cross-Country Tests Using Alternative Institutional Measures," *Economics and Politics* 7, No. 3 (1995): 207–208). See also: J. Gwartney, R. Lawson, "The Concept and Measurement of Economic Freedom," *European Journal of Political Economy* 19, No. 3 (2003): 405–430. Cf. section 4.5. in this book.

185 Cf. M. Bałtowski, M. Miszewski, *Transformacja gospodarcza w Polsce* (Warszawa: WN PWN, 2006), 53–54. Admittedly, referring to the authors' deliberations and their distinction of the property characteristics of the economic system (see more: section 5.1. in this work), the notion of property transformations can also include transformations of property rights. However, only the property structure has been consciously singled out here and synonymously linked to the category of property transformations, as the changes in property rights in Germany are dealt with elsewhere (see section 6.1. in this study). Such a perspective is often found in economic history studies, in which property transformations in transition economies, such as Poland after 1989, are identified with changes in the property structure based on privatization (see, e.g.: M. Kozaczka, *Gospodarka Polski w latach 1989–2009* (Lublin: Norbertinum, 2012), *passim*; J. Kaliński, "Przekształcenia własnościowe," in *Problemy gospodarcze Trzeciej Rzeczypospolitej*, ed. A. Jarosz-Nojszewska (Warszawa: Oficyna Wydawnicza SGH, 2017), 91–104). Besides, Maciej Bałtowski and Maciej Miszewski also do so. Although they show "property changes during the transition period" (Pol. *zmiany własnościowe w okresie transformacji*) in both of the above dimensions (Bałtowski, Miszewski, *Transformacja gospodarcza w Polsce*, 221), they characterize the transformation of the property structure in Poland after 1989 precisely as "property changes in the economy" (Pol. *zmiany własnościowe gospodarki*) in their analysis (Bałtowski, Miszewski, *Transformacja gospodarcza w Polsce*, 221–254).

Privatization and re-privatization play an important role in this regard.[186] Janusz Skodlarski, writing about the systemic transition in Poland in the late 1980s and early 1990s, analyzes its three dimensions: (1) the construction of a new legal and institutional system; (2) property transformations (with privatization at the forefront); (3) the restructuring of the national economy. The last dimension refers basically to the increase in the share of services in the generation of GDP against the decline in the share of industry and agriculture.[187] Following the path outlined above, in this section, it will be important to look at the legal and institutional framework of property transformation in Germany at the dawn of reunification, and then at selected effects of privatization processes, in order to trace some aspects of economic restructuring in the next section.

Property transformation (change of property structure) in Germany after reunification had two main dimensions: re-privatization and privatization. This process primarily involved the new federated states.[188]

Re-privatization should be understood as a process aimed at returning property to the original owners or their legal successors or granting and paying appropriate compensation. As a rule, this is done on the basis of a law reversing or compensating for the consequences of the nationalization and collectivization carried out in the past.[189]

The literature emphasizes that the successful and relatively quick resolution of the re-privatization problem in the former GDR was a consequence of the West German legal order in particular (first and foremost of the Basic Law provisions on the property), extended to the Eastern *Länder*.[190] On the other hand, there is a view that the basis for property claims was not Art. 14 GG, but the axiology underlying the legal guarantee of property in the said article. This axiology, in turn, gave

---

186 J. Tucker-Mohl, *Property Rights and Transitional Justice: Restitution in Hungary and East Germany* (Cambridge: MIT Open Course Ware, 2005), 2.

187 Cf. J. Skodlarski, *Historia gospodarcza* (Warszawa: WN PWN, 2014), 544–548.

188 Heather M. Stack distinguishes two types of privatization in Germany after reunification: "sale of formerly state-owned property," understood as proper privatization coordinated by the Trust Office, and restitution, i.e. re-privatization (Stack, "The 'Colonization' of East Germany?," 1218–1227). See a detailed legal analysis of privatization and re-privatization in the former GDR: A. M. Welker, "Privatisierung und Restitution. Zivilrechtliche Probleme bei der Rückübereignung in den neuen Bundesländern" (PhD diss., Frankfurt am Main: Fakultät der Rechtswissenschaft der Johann Wolfgang Goethe-Universität, 1999).

189 Dobrzeniecki, Romanowski, *Reprywatyzacja*, 10. Gerhard Opitz compiles the most important legal acts under which expropriations were carried out in the Third Reich, the Soviet occupation zone, and the GDR (G. Opitz, "Enteignung und Restitution (Begründung, Durchführung, Auswirkungen)," in *Ökonomische Erfolge und Mißerfolge der deutsche Vereinigung – Eine Zwischenbilanz*, eds. G. Gutmann, U. Wagner (Stuttgart: Gustav Fischer Verlag, 1994), 73–74).

190 Stack, "The 'Colonization' of East Germany?," 1222.

rise to the normative content of an objective nature, which was the basis for the claims and the relevant regulations. According to Karol Dobrzeniecki and Marcin Romanowski, "the content of the Constitution determined that the settlement law was to be more than simply resolving collisions between two legal systems [of the GDR and the FRG]. Its essence, based on the axiological foundations of property guarantees, was to revise communist lawlessness by bringing property relations into line with Western standards."[191]

Re-privatization legislation in reunified Germany regulated the return of property to former East German citizens who had formulated property claims against the communist regime. This group of regulations primarily includes: *Ordinance on the Filling of Property Claims* of July 11, 1990 (amended on August 21), issued by the GDR authorities;[192] certain provisions of the *Unification Treaty* (e.g., Art. 41, concerning the primacy of key investments over claims and the question of compensation for the original owners in this regard,[193] or the Annex No. 3 to the *Unification Treaty*[194]); *Law on Special Investments in the German Democratic Republic*;[195] *Law*

191 Pol. *Treść Konstytucji przesądziła, że prawo rozliczeniowe miało być czymś więcej niż tylko rozwiązywaniem kolizji między dwoma systemami prawnymi. Jego istotą, opartą na aksjologicznych podstawach gwarancji własności, była rewizja komunistycznego bezprawia poprzez dopasowanie stosunków własnościowych do zachodnich standardów* (Dobrzeniecki, Romanowski, *Reprywatyzacja*, 42). It should be noted that in the literature, one can find positions questioning the legitimacy of restitution. For example, Jon Elster argues that restitution was compensation only for one group of the communist regime's victims (the original owners), while the whole society suffered. Therefore, one should compensate everyone or no one. The same reasoning is applied by Elster to punishing people connected with the repressive apparatus (J. Elster, "On Doing What One Can: An Argument Against Restitution and Retribution as a Means of Overcoming the Communist Legacy," *East European Constitutional Review* 1, No. 2 (1992): 15–17). Such views, however, are isolated.

192 *Verordnung über die Anmeldung vermögensrechtlicher Ansprüche vom 11. Juli 1990* (GBl.-DDR, Part I, 1990, No. 44, 718–719); *Zweite Verordnung über die Anmeldung vermögensrechtlicher Ansprüche vom 21. August 1990* (GBl.-DDR, Part I, 1990, No. 56, 1260).

193 Unification Treaty, Art. 41 (BGBl., Part II, 1990, No. 35, 891, 903–904). Cf. Art. 143 GG.

194 "Anlage III. Gemeinsame Erklärung der Regierungen der Bundesrepublik Deutschland und der Deutschen Demokratischen Republik zur Regelung offener Vermögensfragen Vom 15. Juni 1990," in Unification Treaty (BGBl., Part II, 1990, No. 35, 1237–1238). See for a detailed discussion of the contents of Annex No. 3 to the *Unification Treaty*: section 5.3. in this work.

195 "Gesetz über besondere Investitionen in der Deutschen Demokratischen Republik," in Unification Treaty, Anlage II, Chap. III, Field B, Section I, Pt. 4 (BGBl., Part II, 1990, No. 35, 1157–1158). See the amendment: *Gesetz zur Beseitigung*

on the Regulation of Open Property Issues, or the *Property Law* (*Vermögensgesetz*, VermG)[196] (both passed by the GDR parliament on September 23 and subsequently incorporated into the *Unification Treaty*); *Law on Priority for Investments in the Case of Claims for Reassignment under the Property Law* of July 14, 1992;[197] *Law on Compensation under the Law on the Regulation of Open Property Issues and on State Compensation for Expropriation under Occupation Law or Occupation Sovereignty Law* (*Compensation and Equalization Law*) of September 27, 1994;[198] specific

---

von Hemmnissen bei der Privatisierung von Unternehmen und zur Förderung von Investitionen Vom 22. März 1991, Art. 2 (BGBl., Part I, 1991, No. 20, 774–777).

196 "Gesetz zur Regelung offener Vermögensfragen," in Unification Treaty, Anlage II, Chap. III, Field B, Section I, Pt. 5 (BGBl., Part II, 1990, No. 35, 1159–1167). See the more important amendments: *Gesetz zur Beseitigung von Hemmnissen bei der Privatisierung von Unternehmen und zur Förderung von Investitionen*, Art. 1 (BGBl., part I, 1991, No. 20, 766–774); *Bekanntmachung der Neufassung des Vermögensgesetzes Vom 18. April 1991* (BGBl, part I, 1991, No. 26, 957–970); *Gesetz zur Änderung des Vermögensgesetzes und anderer Vorschriften (Zweites Vermögensrechtsänderungsgesetz – 2.VermRÄndG) Vom 14. Juli 1992*, Art. 1 (BGBl, Part I, 1992, No. 33, 1257–1265); *Bekanntmachung der Neufassung des Vermögensgesetzes Vom 4. August 1997* (BGBl, part I, 1997, No. 56, 1974–1995); *Gesetz zur Bereinigung vermögensrechtlicher und anderer Vorschriften (Vermöge nsrechtsbereinigungsgesetz – VermBerG) Vom 20. Oktober 1998*, Arts. 1, 7 (BGBl, Part I, 1998, No 71, 3180–3184, 3187); *Bekanntmachung der Neufassung des Vermögensgesetzes Vom 9. Februar 2005* (BGBl., Part I, 2005, No 9, 205–228).

197 "Gesetz über den Vorrang für Investitionen bei Rückübertragungsansprüchen nach dem Vermögensgesetz (Investitionsvorranggesetz – InVorG)," in *Gesetz zur Änderung des Vermögensgesetzes und anderer Vorschriften*, Art. 6 (BGBl., Part I, 1992, No. 33, 1268–1275). See the amendments: *Bekanntmachung der Neufassung des Investitionsvorranggesetzes Vom 4. August 1997* (BGBl., Part I, 1997, No. 56, 1996–2005); *Zehnte Zuständigkeitsanpassungsverordnung Vom 31. August 2015*, Art. 588 (BGBl., Part I, 2015, No. 35, 1559).

198 *Gesetz über die Entschädigung nach dem Gesetz zur Regelung offener Vermögensfragen und über staatliche Ausgleichsleistungen für Enteignungen auf besatzungsrechtlicher oder besatzungshoheitlicher Grundlage (Entschädigungs- und Ausgleichsleistungsgesetz – EALG) Vom 27. September 1994* (BGBl., Part I, 1994, No. 65, 2624–2639). See the more important amendments: *Gesetz zur Bereinigung vermögensrechtlicher und anderer Vorschriften*, Art. 3 (BGBl., part I, 1998, No. 71, 3185); *Bekanntmachung der Neufassung des Ausgleichsleistungsgesetzes Vom 13. Juli 2004* (BGBl, part I, 2004, No. 37, 1665–1670); *Gesetz zur Neuorganisation der Bundesfinanzverwaltung und zur Schaffung eines Reffinanzierungsregisters Vom 22. September 2005*, Art. 4, Par. 38 (BGBl, Part I, 2005, No. 60, 2813); *Zweites Gesetz zur Änderung der Vorschriften zum begünstigten Flächenerwerb nach § 3 des Ausgleichsleistungsgesetzes und der Flächenerwerbsverordnung (Zweites Flächenerwerbsänderungsgesetz – 2. FlErwÄndG) Vom 21. März 2011* (BGBl, Part I, 2011, No. 12, 450–451).

regulations for persecuted persons and political prisoners in the GDR.[199] The main legal and institutional framework for the re-privatization process was set by the *Property Law*.

By the end of August 1990, an estimated 1,565 small enterprises had been returned to their rightful owners.[200] By the end of August 1992, of the 16,712 enterprises claimed by the original owners, 6,338 plants had been privatized.[201] By June 1994, a total of 10,158 enterprise claims had been processed. Of these 1,585 plants supervised by the Trust Office (which coordinated the privatization and re-privatization process in 1990–1994),[202] 2,714 parts of enterprises and 2,064 company assets were re-privatized. By the end of its existence (December 31, 1994), the Office managed 11,937 enterprises, while 1,588 (13.3 %) of them were re-privatized.[203]

By the end of 1992, the relevant offices had processed a total of about 1.2 million applications for property restitution in the Eastern *Länder*. They concerned more than 2 million real estates, covering more than 50 % of the former GDR's territory.[204] In September 1995, there were already approximately 2.7 million applications, of which about 33 % were processed.[205] By 2003, decisions had been issued on 96 % of the restitution applications of individuals (excluding enterprises). Among this part, in 18 % of cases, restitution was admitted, in 42 % of cases, the applications were rejected, in 13 % of cases, the applicants themselves gave up their efforts for restitution, while in 27 % of cases, compensation was paid.[206] By the end of 2007, decisions were made to return 419,820 land plots. No decision was issued for 21,979 cases.[207]

---

199 Dobrzeniecki, Romanowski, *Reprywatyzacja*, 59. See, e.g.: "Gesetz über die Rehabilitierung und Entschädigung von Opfern rechtsstaatswidriger Strafverfolgungsmaβnahmen im Beitrittsgebiet (Strafrechtliches Rehabilitierungsgesetz – StrRehaG)," in *Erstes Gesetz zur Bereinigung von SED-Unrecht (Erstes SED-Unrechtsbereinigungsgesetz – 1. SED-UnBerG) Vom 29. Oktober 1992*, Art. 1 (BGBl, Part I, 1992, No. 50, 1814–1819). See the amendments: *Bekanntmachung der Neufassung des Strafrechtlichen Rehabilitierungsgesetzes Vom 17. Dezember 1999* (BGBl, Part I, 1999, No. 60, 2664–2670); *Fünftes Gesetz zur Verbesserung rehabilitierungsrechtlicher Vorschriften für Opfer der politischen Verfolgung in der ehemaligen DDR Vom 22. Dezember 2014*, Art. 1 (BGBl., Part I, 2014, No. 63, 2408).

200 Schnabel, "Structural Adjustment and Privatization," 249.

201 W. Gruhler, *Unternehmens bezogene Umstrukturierung in den neuen Bundesländern – Zwischenbilanz* (Köln: Deutscher Instituts-Verlag, 1992), 13, table 2.

202 For a more extensive discussion of the operations of the Trust Office, see the remainder of this section.

203 Spangenberg, *The Institutionalised Transformation*, 140, table 3.5.; 175, table 4.1.

204 A. Falkowska, "Restytucja, odszkodowanie czy inwestycje? – reprywatyzacja majątku Niemieckiej Republiki Demokratycznej," *Ekonomia i Prawo* 7 (2011): 279.

205 Stack, "The 'Colonization' of East Germany?," 1236.

206 Tucker-Mohl, *Property Rights and Transitional Justice*, 18–19, fn. 56.

207 Baur, Baur, Stürner, *Sachenrecht*, 900.

It should be noted that re-privatization did not include land expropriations from 1945–1949. It was decided to accept the effects of, among other things, the land reform carried out in East Germany in 1945.[208] Initially, there were also no plans to pay any compensation in this regard. This was only changed by the aforementioned *Compensation and Equalization Law* of 1994. Such instrumental treatment of the law and claims (especially of large landowners) caused a great deal of controversy in the FRG after 1990.[209]

German re-privatization legislation was one of the first in Central and Eastern Europe undergoing systemic transition. The original re-privatization formula was

---

208 On the basis of a proclamation issued on September 8, 1945, the East German communists divided up large land ownership. About 7,000 owners were expropriated without compensation. Consequently, about 2.5 million hectares of land were taken over. In addition, about 600,000 hectares of Nazi land and state farms were parceled out. In total, this represented approximately 35 % of the country's agricultural area. The land was distributed mainly among agricultural workers, displaced persons, refugees, and smallholders. Approximately 33 % of the acquired land was transferred to municipalities, districts, and *Länder* (E. Cziomer, *Zarys historii Niemiec powojennych 1945–1995* (Warszawa–Kraków: WN PWN, 1997), 39).

209 There is no consensus in the literature on the reasons for this. It is sometimes argued that maintaining the effects of the expropriations of 1945–1949 was one of the Soviet Union's conditions for agreeing to German reunification. Other scholars claim that it was the result of earlier pressure from the FRG government on the GDR, which did not want to deal with land restitution or compensation in the future (Stack, "The 'Colonization' of East Germany?," 1222–1223; Dobrzeniecki, Romanowski, *Reprywatyzacja*, 20–21). There is also a view that it was the GDR government that protested against the re-privatization of property nationalized by the Soviet occupation authorities in 1945–1949, for which it did not want to bear responsibility. However, as Erhard Cziomer notes, the initiative concerning, e.g., the land reform of 1945 came from the East German communists, which was accepted by the authorities of the Soviet occupation zone (Cziomer, *Zarys historii Niemiec powojennych*, 39). Moreover, the sum of this group of claims was estimated at around 8 billion DM, which exceeded the budgetary possibilities of the GDR and the FRG. Also important was the fact that the bulk of the expropriated property was agricultural land, concentrated within the social agricultural sector. East German citizens later acquired the remaining plots of land and invested considerable funds in them. Regarding the mentioned ultimatum from the Soviet Union, some authors stress that Gorbachev denied this version of events in 1994 (Stack, "The 'Colonization' of East Germany?," 1222–1223; Falkowska, "Restytucja, odszkodowanie czy inwestycje?," 270, fn. 5; 271; A. Moszyńska, M. Moszyński, "Reprywatyzacja a konflikt interesów ekonomicznych jednostek i państwa – Polska na tle pozostałych krajów transformacji," *Ekonomia i Prawo* 8, No. 1 (2012): 128, fn. 28). More on the restitution of landed estates in Germany after reunification: D. B. Southern, "Restitution or Compensation: The Land Question in East Germany," *International & Comparative Law Quarterly* 42, No. 3 (1993): 690–697; Tucker-Mohl, *Property Rights and Transitional Justice*, 14–19.

broad. It covered real estate taken over by the state during the Third Reich (1933–1939) and the GDR (1949–1990), although the fundamental point of reference for the regulation was 1949, i.e. the establishment of the GDR.[210] The first legal acts of July–August 1990 guaranteed the primacy of restitution over compensation (with some exceptions).[211] However, in subsequent regulations issued since September 1990 (the *Property Law* and its amendments, the law on special investments of 1990, and the law on priority for investments of 1992), the position of persons seeking restitution of property was gradually weakened. Restitution was limited by additional restrictions, which were followed by appropriate decision-making practice. This was justified by the need to modernize the new federated states, especially in terms of stimulating private investment. This, in turn, required precisely defined property rights.[212] It is worth emphasizing that the disputed issues of re-privatization were resolved efficiently, although not without mistakes and controversies. The most important legal acts were passed as early as 1990–1992, later amended as needed. The last significant re-privatization settlement took place in 1994 (compensation for expropriations between 1945 and 1949). Similar regulations were introduced at different speeds in other post-communist countries. Only Poland has not yet enacted a re-privatization law.[213]

---

210 This is sometimes referred to as "the 49 Rule" in the literature. The communist state decisions in question, which were deemed illegal, had to be reversed if possible. Hans-Werner Sinn claims: "Everything expropriated before 1949 is treated as a result of history and does not qualify for compensation other than that already given to those who lost their properties in the East ... The wheel of history is turned back to 1949" (H.-W. Sinn, "Macroeconomic Aspects of German Unification," in Welfens, *Economic Aspects of German Unification*, 102–103). The author refers to the equalization of war burdens (*Lastenausgleich*). On the basis of the law of August 14, 1952, the FRG government paid compensation to the "expellees" (*Vertriebene*), i.e. German citizens who had lost their property as a result of the change in the borders of the German state after World War II (*Gesetz über den Lastenausgleich (Lastenausgleichsgesetz – LAG). Vom 14. August 1952.* (BGBl., Part I, 1952, No. 34, 446–533). See the amendments: *Bekanntmachung der Neufassung des Lastenausgleichsgesetzes Vom 2. Juni 1993* (BGBl., Part I, 1993, No. 28, 845–897); *Berichtigung der Neufassung des Lastenausgleichsgesetzes Vom 14. Februar 1995* (BGBl., Part I, 1995, No. 10, 248)). Sinn, however, omits the question of the re-privatization of assets acquired by the state during the Third Reich.

211 Shortly after reunification, some scholars raised this as an obstacle in strengthening the certainty of future investors about property rights in the Eastern *Länder*. See, e.g., L. Hoffmann, "Integrating the East German States into the German Economy: Opportunities, Burdens and Options," in Welfens, *Economic Aspects of German Unification*, 63.

212 See also section 6.2.6. in this study.

213 More on the model of re-privatization in Germany after reunification: A. B. Shingleton, V. Ahrens, P. Ries, "Property Rights in Eastern Germany: An Overview of the Amended Property Law," *Georgia Journal of International and Comparative*

However, the privatization of state property, primarily industrial plants, played the most important role in the property transformation in the Eastern *Länder*. It was a fundamental structural mechanism aimed at unifying Eastern and Western Germany within a single social and economic system based on the implementation of the social market economy model in the former GDR.[214]

Even while the reunification formula was still being crystallized and the West German formal institutions were being gradually implemented,[215] the GDR authorities took steps to prepare the ground for future privatization processes. It should be emphasized, however, that the regime's initial intention was to maintain power and reform (not liquidate) the centrally planned economy system, taking into account the relative marketization and democratization of social and economic life. Legal regulations were of fundamental importance. Among the numerous normative acts reforming the state and cooperative property sectors, the most relevant should be indicated.[216] The GDR government's ordinance of January 25, 1990, suspended the privatization of state enterprises while introducing regulations

Law 21 (1991): 345–357; G. Sinn, H.-W. Sinn, *Jumpstart: The Economic Unification of Germany* (Cambridge: MIT Press, 1992), 87–96; D. Southern, "Restitution or Compensation: the Open Property Question," *German Politics* 2, No. 3 (1993): 436–449; H. Willgerodt, "Wiedereinsetzung der Alteigentümer (Reprivatisierung)," in *Treuhandanstalt. Das Unmögliche wagen*, eds. W. Fischer, H. Hax, H. K. Schneider (Berlin: Akademie Verlag, 1993), 241–262; R. Frank, "Privatization in Eastern Germany: A Comprehensive Study," *Vanderbilt Journal of Transnational Law* 27, No. 4 (1994): 809–868; Opitz, "Enteignung und Restitution," 59–75; P. E. Quint, *The Imperfect Union. Constitutional Structures of German Unification* (Princeton: Princeton University Press, 1997), 124–153; Stack, "The 'Colonization' of East Germany?," 1221–1227, 1236–1239; Spangenberg, *The Institutionalised Transformation*, 134–143; C. Offe, *Drogi transformacji. Doświadczenia wschodnioeuropejskie i wschodnioniemieckie* (Warszawa–Kraków: WN PWN, 1999), 146–181; Baur, Baur, Stürner, *Sachenrecht*, 896–901; J. Busche, "Die Privatisierung der volkseigenen Unternehmen der ehemaligen DDR. Der rechtliche und wirtschaftliche Umbruch im Zuge der Wiedervereinigung," in *Staat und Recht in Teilung und Einheit*, eds. J. Krüper, H. Sauer (Tübingen: Mohr Siebeck, 2011), 137; Falkowska, "Restytucja, odszkodowanie czy inwestycje?," 269–284; Moszyńska, Moszyński, "Reprywatyzacja a konflikt interesów ekonomicznych jednostek i państwa," 127–129; Dobrzeniecki, Romanowski, *Reprywatyzacja*, 17–66.

214 Sinn, "Macroeconomic Aspects of German Unification," 101; Z. Klimiuk, "Trendy rozwojowe w gospodarce niemieckiej po 1990 r.," *Roczniki Ekonomii i Zarządzania* 5 (41) (2013): 68.

215 More on the implementation of constitutional and property rules in the Eastern *Länder* at the turn of the 1980s and 1990s: sections 3.5., 5.3. in this work.

216 Heidrun Pohl compiled the most important legal acts initiating the processes in question in the GDR between December 1, 1989, and June 22, 1990 (H. Pohl, "Öffentliche und private Wirtschaft," in *Deutsche Wiedervereinigung. Die Rechtseinheit. Arbeitskreis Staats- und Verfassungsrecht*, Vol. II: *Zur Wiederherstellung der inneren Einheit*, Part 2: *Rundfunkrecht – Stasi-Akten – Wiedergutmachung – Öffentliche und Private Wirtschaft*, ed. K. Stern (Köln: Carl Heymanns Verlag KG, 1992), 144–148).

intended to encourage the inflow of foreign investment into East Germany.[217] The conditions for the establishment of private enterprises were specified in the *Law on the Establishment and Operation of Private Enterprises and on Participation in Enterprises* of March 7.[218] In turn, the amendment to the GDR Constitution of June 17 introduced a relative guarantee of private property of means of production.[219]

The GDR government's decision of March 1 to establish the Office for Trust Administration of Public Property, the Trust Office (*Anstalt zur treuhänderischen Verwaltung des Volkseigentums, Treuhandanstalt*, THA, or *Treuhand*, less commonly referred to as: *Ur-Treuhandanstalt*, UrTHA, i.e., "great-Trust Office," "great-THA;" Eng. *First Trusteeship Law*[220]) was of key importance. It was responsible for the supervision (trusteeship) of all public property with the exception of the assets of cities, municipalities, and areas where state enterprises were to be established, as well as those assets that were used by agricultural production cooperatives. The Office had no managerial or decision-making powers. Its task was to protect, defend, and preserve (*Wahrung*) the public property entrusted to it. The UrTHA was subordinate to the government and was to function until the adoption of a new constitution.[221] An additional ordinance of the same date allowed the transformation ("conversion," *Umwandlung*) of combines and most state-owned enterprises into capital companies ("corporations," *Kapitalgesellschaften*) under the UrTHA's control. These could have been limited liability companies (*Gesellschaften mit beschränkten Haftung*, GmbH) or joint stock companies (*Aktiengesellschaften*, AG). Other forms of conversions were decided by the Office.[222] A separate statute of March 15 defined the organizational structure of the UrTHA, which consisted of the Directorate (*Direktorium*) and the Administrative Council (*Verwaltungsrat*).

---

217 *Verordnung über die Gründung und Tätigkeit von Unternehmen mit ausländischer Beteiligung in der DDR vom 25. Januar 1990* (GBl.-DDR, Part I, 1990, No. 4, 16–19).

218 *Gesetz über die Gründung und Tätigkeit privater Unternehmen und über Unternehmensbeteiligungen vom 7. März 1990* (GBl.-DDR, Part I, 1990, No. 17, 141–144).

219 *Gesetz zur Änderung und Ergänzung der Verfassung der Deutschen Demokratischen Republik (Verfassungsgrundsätze) vom 17. Juni 1990* (GBl.-DDR, Part I, 1990, No. 33, 299–300). More extensively on this thread: Pohl, "Öffentliche und private Wirtschaft," 144–148; Busche, "Die Privatisierung," 127–132.

220 The UrTHA terms cited from: Sinn, Sinn, *Jumpstart*, 96; W. Fischer, H. Schröter, "Die Entstehung der Treuhandanstalt," in Fischer, Hax, Schneider, *Treuhandanstalt*, 26.

221 *Beschluss zur Gründung der Anstalt zur treuhänderischen Verwaltung des Volkseigentums (Treuhandanstalt) vom 1. März 1990* (GBl.-DDR, Part I, 1990, No. 14, 107). In terms of the establishment of the UrTHA, it followed the example of Hungary, where the Property Agency (Hung.: *Allami Vagyonügy-nökség*) was established in parallel. See Brunner, "Verfassungsrechtliche Rahmenbedingungen," 212–213.

222 *Verordnung zur Umwandlung von volkseigenen Kombinaten, Betrieben und Einrichtungen in Kapitalgesellschaften vom 1. März 1990* (GBl.-DDR, Part I, 1990, No. 14, 107–108).

It was finally decided that control over the UrTHA would, however, be exercised by the People's Chamber. It also stated that the Office is to supervise state assets "in the public interest" (*im Interesse der Allgemeinheit*).[223] The official goal of the UrTHA's creation by the GDR authorities was the denationalization of the economy, the transformation of enterprise structures and the protection of social property.[224]

The UrTHA took over the control of 8,000 state enterprises consisting of 45,000 plants.[225] The Office took care of their "conversion," i.e. transformation into capital companies ("corporations") in order to make them marketable. However, the state still remained the owner of the reorganized enterprises. Although their privatization was formally possible, the consent of the People's Chamber was necessary.[226] The effects of the Office's work (among other things, due to disputes between economic ministries) were not spectacular. By April 30, the UrTHA had converted only 75 entities into capital companies. It is also telling that on May 23, the Office published a report on its assessment of the competitiveness of 2,200 selected enterprises in the GDR. The document showed that 597 (27.1 %) enterprises were at risk of bankruptcy. Only 683 (31 %) enterprises could be profitable after entry into the monetary union (no subsidies were planned for them), while 920 (41.8 %) were expected to make losses.[227] Privatization was limited to some small enterprises, forcibly sold to the state in 1972.[228]

Sabine Spangenberg refers to this period as the "corporatisation of nationally-owned enterprises."[229] According to Sinn, the establishment of UrTHA by the

---

223 *Statut der Anstalt zur treuhänderischen Verwaltung des Volkseigentums (Treuhandanstalt) – Beschluss des Ministerrates – vom 15. März 1990* (GBl.-DDR, Part I, 1990, No. 18, 167–169).

224 Spangenberg, *The Institutionalised Transformation*, 123.

225 Spangenberg, *The Institutionalised Transformation*, 123. The German legal system distinguished between enterprises (*Unternehmen*) and plants (*Betriebe*). This classification is also present in the analyzed statistical materials. An enterprise was the smallest legal unit to which individual plants, which were local branches of the enterprise, were assigned. Thus, a single enterprise could consist of a certain number of plants. In other words, one company could have a given number of factories in different locations in the country (SJ BRD, Vol. 1990, 173). Therefore, the number of plants was higher than the number of enterprises, as opposed to the number of people employed. Enterprises generally employed more workers than individual plants combined. This is because the additional personnel worked for the company as a whole rather than individual plants.

226 Spangenberg, *The Institutionalised Transformation*, 123–124.

227 "Treuhandgesetz und Treuhandanstalt," https://deutsche-einheit-1990.de/ministerien/ministerium-fuer-wirtschaft/treuhandgesetz-und-treuhandanstalt/ (accessed August 5, 2019).

228 Sinn, Sinn, *Jumpstart*, 96; Busche, "Die Privatisierung," 129–130.

229 Spangenberg, *The Institutionalised Transformation*, 123–124.

GDR authorities was "a desperate attempt to prevent the privatization of state owned property."[230] The state property was to operate under partially free market conditions. It was a kind of "third way" for the transforming GDR economy.[231]

As a result of the conclusion of the *Treaty Establishing a Monetary, Economic and Social Union* between the FRG and the GDR, which addressed, among other things, property issues,[232] a reorganization of the UrTHA began.[233] New tasks had to be set for it and its competence had to be expanded.[234]

Based on the *Law on the Privatization and Reorganization of Nationally Owned Assets* of June 17 (which came into force on July 1, as did the *Treaty Establishing a Monetary, Economic and Social Union*), the People's Chamber established a new Trust Office based in Berlin (*Second Trusteeship Law*[235]). The revised regulations gave the THA greater powers than before to manage the nation's assets. The introduction to the document stated that the purpose of the enacted regulations was to "restore the state's economic activity as quickly and as broadly as possible through privatization"[236], as well as to guarantee the competitiveness of enterprises, protect existing jobs and create new ones, and secure land for economic activity. The Office was to function on behalf of the government, which was accountable to the People's Chamber in this regard (Par. 1, Pts. 2–3). It was up to the head of government to supervise the activities of the THA (Par. 2, Pt.2).[237] In principle, national assets were to be privatized; however, the possibility of transferring (under separate

---

230 Sinn, "Macroeconomic Aspects of German Unification," 104.

231 Sinn, Sinn, *Jumpstart*, 96. The concept of the "third way" developed in Marxist economics of the Eastern Bloc countries in the 1970s and 1980s. It was a proposal to reform centrally planned economies by partially implementing market solutions. A considerable literature emerged at the time, the most extensive study of which was done by Ota Šik (O. Šik, *Der Dritte Weg. Die marxistisch-leninistische Theorie und die modern Industriegesellschaft* (Hamburg: Hoffmann und Campe, 1972)).

232 See in more detail: section 5.3. in this study.

233 "Treuhandgesetz und Treuhandanstalt," https://deutsche-einheit-1990.de/ministerien/ministerium-fuer-wirtschaft/treuhandgesetz-und-treuhandanstalt/ (accessed August 5, 2019).

234 Cziomer, *Zarys historii Niemiec powojennych*, 293. More on the origins and activities of the UrTHA see: Fischer, Schröter, "Die Entstehung der Treuhandanstalt," 17–40, valuable discussion of the political discussion surrounding the UrTHA; Busche, "Die Privatisierung," 127–134.

235 Definition of the THA establishment law from: Sinn, Sinn, *Jumpstart*, 96.

236 *[D]ie unternehmerische Tätigkeit des Staates durch Privatisierung so rasch und so weit wie möglich zurückzuführen* (*Gesetz zur Privatisierung und Reorganisation des volkseigenen Vermögens (Treuhandgesetz) vom 17. Juni 1990* (GBl.-DDR, Part I, 1990, No. 33, 300)).

237 After reunification, the Federal Ministry of Finance, in cooperation with the Federal Ministry of Economic Affairs and Energy and, on an ad hoc basis, the relevant ministry, provided technical and legal oversight of the THA's activities.

rules) certain assets to municipalities, cities, districts, or lands was allowed (Par. 1, Pt. 1). The Office was the owner of the shares of capital companies resulting from past or future transformations of social property, excluding in particular: the assets of the postal service, railroads, waterway and land way administration, and certain enterprises owned by the state, municipalities, cities, districts and federated states (Par. 1, Pts. 4–5).[238] In the case of the agricultural and forestry sector, appropriate trusteeship regulations had to be established, taking into account the economic, ecological and structural specificities of the area concerned (Par. 1, Pt. 6).[239] The Trust Office had the status of a public law institution (*Anstalt öffentlichen Rechts*). It was to supervise the privatization and reorganization of national assets process on the basis of the model of a social market economy (Par. 2, Pt. 1).[240] The Office should therefore support the restructuring of the economy according to market demand by privatizing state enterprises and promoting the competitiveness of companies. The "efficient economic structure" (*effiziente Wirtschaftsstruktur*) referred to in the law would be a consequence of these processes (Par. 2, Pt. 6). State enterprises that had not yet been converted into capital companies were to be included in this reorganization, excluding in particular: the postal service, railroads, waterway and land way administration, certain enterprises owned by municipalities, cities, districts, and *Länder*, foreign trade enterprises in liquidation, state land assets and state forestry enterprises (Par. 11, Pts. 1, 3). The law also regulated further details regarding the THA's management of assets of privatized and reorganized national assets.[241]

---

238 In German civil law a separate category of "trust property" or "fiduciary property" (*Treuhandeigentum, fiduziarisches Eigentum*) was distinguished, which can be referred to the competence of the THA (Zerres, *Bürgerliches Recht*, 362; Klunzinger, *Einführung in das Bürgerliche Recht*, 537–538).

239 More on the changes in Eastern German agriculture after reunification: section 6.2.3. in this book.

240 The THA was given the status of a federal public law institution with legal capacity (*rechtsfähige bundesunmittelbare Anstalt des öffentlichen Rechts*) after reunification. In addition, it was stated that the Office's shares were indirect assets of the Federation.

241 *Gesetz zur Privatisierung und Reorganisation des volkseigenen Vermögens* (GBl.-DDR, Part I, 1990, No. 33, 300–304). The law has been amended several times. After reunification, it was adapted to the FRG legal system, including, among others, to the administrative structure, drawing out the relevant relations of the THA to the federal ministries (cf., e.g., earlier footnotes). See for a detailed and critical legal analysis of the new role of the THA after the *Unification Treaty*: R. Bärwaldt, "Die Treuhandanstalt nach dem Inkrafttreten des Einigungsvertrages," *Deutsch-Deutsche Rechts-Zeitschrift* No. 9 (1990), 347–348. See the latest amendment during the period in question: *Zehnte Zuständigkeitsanpassungsverordn ung*, Art. 590 (BGBl., Part I, 2015, No. 35, 1559). See other legal acts defining the THA: R. Drewnicki et al., eds., *Dokumentation 1990–1994*, Vol. 1 (Berlin: Treuhandanstalt, 1994).

On July 16, the Trust Office took over the competencies of the former body, coordinating the process of privatization, re-privatization, and reorganization of state property in the GDR and, after reunification, in the Eastern *Länder*.[242] It functioned until December 31, 1994. As of January 1, 1995, the Federal Office for Special Unification Tasks (*Bundesanstalt für vereinigungsbedingte Sonderaufgaben*, BvS) was established in its place.[243] It was responsible, among other things, for completing the privatization process, including renegotiating the agreements concluded by the THA in this regard.[244]

Other types of property rights relating to East German national assets, which were excluded from the competence of the Trust Office, were assigned to separate bodies. Table 16 provides details.

242 Spangenberg wrongly states that private property rights in the former GDR were institutionalized through the creation of the THA. Moreover, she describes the THA as a "state institution," whereas – in the light of institutional theory and North's approach – it was an organization (Spangenberg, *The Institutionalised Transformation*, 176). Although the THA played a key role in the process of privatization of state property in the new federated states, it carried out political and economic practice within the institutional framework set by law, especially the FRG Constitution.

243 *Gesetz zur abschließenden Erfüllung der verbliebenen Aufgaben der Treuhandanstalt Vom 9. August 1994* (BGBl, Part I, 1994, No. 54, 2062–2065); *Verordnung zur Übertragung von liegenschaftsbezogenen Aufgaben und Liegenschaftsgesellschaften der Treuhandanstalt (Treuhandliegenschaftsübertragungsverordnung – TreuhLÜV) Vom 20. Dezember 1994* (BGBl, Part I, 1994, No. 92, 3908–3909); *Verordnung zur Übertragung von unternehmensbezogenen Aufgaben und Unternehmensbeteiligungen der Treuhandanstalt (Treuhandunternehmensübertragungsverordnung – TreuhUntÜV) Vom 20. Dezember 1994* (BGBl, Part I, 1994, No. 92, 3910–3912); *Verordnung über die Umbenennung und die Anpassung von Zuständigkeiten der Treuhandanstalt (Tre uhandanstaltumbenennungsverordnung – TreuhUmbenV) Vom 20. Dezember 1994* (BGBl., Part I, 1994, No. 92, 3913).

244 See in more detail: D. Bös, "Privatization in Eastern Germany: The Never-Ending Story of the Treuhand," in *Privatization at the End of the Century*, ed. by H. Giersch (Berlin: Egon-Sohmen-Foundation, Springer, 1997), 175–197. The author also identifies other government agencies and companies that took over the tasks of the THA (Bös, "Privatization in Eastern Germany," 175–176, table 1; 194–195).

Table 16: *Assignment of rights to the GDR's national property in 1990*

Type of property rights (national assets) of the GDR	Body (public institution)
State enterprises, combines, other economic entities listed in the register of state enterprises, administrative and financial assets of the *Stasi* and GDR army	Trust Office
Railroad infrastructure	German Reich Railways (*Deutsche Reichsbahn*)
Postal infrastructure	German Post (*Deutsche Post*)
Administrative and financial assets of local and regional authorities of the GDR	Federal government, Eastern *Länder* authorities, municipalities
Housing stock management corporations	Urban municipalities

Own elaboration based on: H. Brücker, *Privatization in Eastern Germany: A Neo-Institutional Analysis* (London: Frank Cass, German Development Institute, 2005), 125–126.

It can be seen from the above list that the assignment of particular rights to the GDR's national property reflected the system adopted in the FRG after World War II.[245] This was another dimension of the implementation of West German property rules in the new federal states.

The other most important normative acts that set the legal and institutional framework for the privatization process in Germany were as follows: *Law on the Property of Municipalities, Cities and Districts* (*Municipal Property Law*) of July 6, 1990 (passed by the People's Chamber);[246] the aforementioned *Law on Special Investments in the German Democratic Republic*[247] and *Property Law* of September

245 Brücker, *Privatization in Eastern Germany*, 126.

246 *Gesetz über das Vermögen der Gemeinden, Städte und Landkreise (Kommunalvermögensgesetz – KVG) vom 6. Juli 1990* (GBl.-DDR, Part I, 1990, No. 42, 660–662). See the amendments: *Gesetz zur Änderung und Ergänzung des Gesetzes über das Vermögen der Gemeinden, Städte und Landkreise vom 6. Juli 1990 (Kommunalvermögensgesetz – KVG) vom 13. September 1990* (GBl.-DDR, Part I, 1990, No. 61, 1537–1538); "Gesetz über die Feststellung der Zuordnung von ehemals volkseigenem Vermögen (Vermögenszurordnungsgesetz – VZOG)," in *Gesetz zur Beseitigung von Hemmnissen bei der Privatisierung von Unternehmen und zur Förderung von Investitionen*, Art. 7 (BGBl., Part I, 1991, No. 20, 784–786).

247 *Gesetz über besondere Investitionen in der Deutschen Demokratischen Republik* (BGBl., Part II, 1990, No. 35, 1157–1158). See the amendment: *Gesetz zur Beseitigung von Hemmnissen bei der Privatisierung von Unternehmen und zur Förderung von Investitionen*, Art. 2 (BGBl., Part I, 1991, No. 20, 774–777).

23. The last two laws were passed in West Germany. They supplemented the *Unification Treaty* (Annex No. 2). The *Law on the Removal of Barriers to the Privatization of Enterprises and the Promotion of Investment* of March 22, 1991,[248] had already been passed by the Bundestag after reunification.[249] The enactment of the last mentioned legal act closed the process of creating a comprehensive and compact legal system for regulating privatization.[250] Some privatization regulations (including later ones) also referred to issues related to property claims (re-privatization) and vice versa.[251]

The Trust Office played a key role in the property transformation in the Eastern *Länder*. Its activities were part of the broader *Aufbau Ost* project. Nevertheless, it has raised a number of controversies. The main accusations against the THA concern its mismanagement, implementation of a forced and unconditional privatization, liquidation of a large number of industrial plants combined with mass layoffs of workers, and corruption present in its structures.[252] This resulted in massive

248 *Gesetz zur Beseitigung von Hemmnissen bei der Privatisierung von Unternehmen und zur Förderung von Investitionen* (BGBl., Part I, 1991, No. 20, 766–789). See correction: *Berichtigung des Gesetzes zur Beseitigung von Hemmnissen bei der Privatisierung von Unternehmen und zur Förderung von Investitionen Vom 12. September 1991* (BGBl., Part I, 1991, No. 54, 1928). See the amendment: *Gesetz zur Änderung des Vermögensgesetzes und anderer Vorschriften*, Art. 7 (BGBl., part I, 1992, No. 33, 1275).

249 See also: J. Ditges, "Privatisierungsstrategien in den neuen Bundesländern," in Gutmann, Wagner, *Ökonomische Erfolge und Mißerfolge der deutsche Vereinigung*, 56–57.

250 B. Petz, "Przekształcenia własnościowe w krajach Europy Środkowej," *Informacja. Kancelaria Sejmu. Biuro Studiów i Ekspertyz. Wydział Analiz Ekonomicznych i Społecznych* No. 185 (1994): 4.

251 Cf. Opitz, "Enteignung und Restitution," 74–75.

252 Detailed documentation of the THA's activities is contained in the volumes: R. Drewnicki et al., eds., *Dokumentation*, Vols. 1–15. The literature on the THA is extensive. Most publications were written in the first half of the 1990s. They analyzed the course of privatization in the former GDR on an ongoing basis. Among newer studies see, e.g.: C. Goschler, *Studie zur Wahrnehmung und Bewertung der Arbeit der Treuhandanstalt im Auftrag des Bundesministeriums für Wirtschaft und Energie* (Bochum: Ruhr-Universität Bochum, 2017); J. E. Howard, *The Treuhandanstalt and Privatisation in the Former East Germany: Stakeholder Perspectives* (London: Routledge, 2018); "Die Treuhandanstalt im Spiegel der wissenschaftlichen Forschung," *Deutscher Bundestag, Wissenschaftliche Dienste, Ausarbeitung* No. WD 1-3000-010/19 (2019): 1–15; M. Böick, *Die Treuhand. Idee – Praxis – Erfahrung 1990–1994* (Göttingen: Wallstein Verlag, 2018); D. Hoffmann, ed., *Transformation einer Volkswirtschaft. Neue Forschungen zur Geschichte der Treuhandanstalt* (Berlin: Metropol Verlag, 2020); A. Malycha, *Vom Hoffnungsträger zum Prügelknaben. Die Treuandanstalt zwischen wirtschaftlichen Erwartungen und politischen Zwängen 1989–1994* (Berlin: C. H. Links Verlag, 2022); M. Trecker,

social protests. The case of the murder of Detlev Karsten Rohwedder, Chairman of the THA's Administrative Council, who was shot dead on April 1, 1991, by terrorists from the extreme left-wing Red Army Faction (*Rote Armee Fraktion*, RAF, also known as the Baader-Meinhof Group), was very loud.[253]

Three main methods (models, strategies) of privatization implemented by the Trust Office in 1990–1994 should be distinguished. They were as follows: (1) liquidation of inefficient companies; (2) support for companies whose future prognosis was positive; (3) sale of companies.[254]

In the beginning, the THA managed 8,500 enterprises consisting of 44,000 plants. At the time of liquidation, out of the 11,937 enterprises managed, the Office re-privatized 1,588 companies, returning them to their rightful owners, while 265 were transferred to local authorities for management. Full privatization (100 %) involved 6,321 enterprises, half privatization (50 %) involved 225 companies, and partial privatization involved 7,374 entities. 3,561 enterprises were liquidated. Organizations functioning after the Trust Office took over 475 enterprises. The process of selling state enterprises in the Eastern *Länder* was most intense between

---

Neue Unternehmer braucht das Land. Die Genese des ostdeustchen Mittelstands nach der Wiedervereinigung (Berlin: C. H. Links Verlag, 2022). Relevant literature there. Germany has also produced a number of documentaries on the THA activities.

253 "RAF zastrzelił szefa Urzędu Powierniczego w Niemczech. Antykapitalistyczny mord," *Gazeta Wyborcza*, April 3, 1991, No. 78 (547), 1; A. Kaniewski, "Niemcy. Łańcuch przemocy," *Gazeta Wyborcza*, April 3, 1991, No. 78 (547), 6.

254 Spangenberg, *The Institutionalised Transformation*, 144–145. Modifications of this tripartition can be found in the literature. For example, Claus Schnabel distinguishes: (1) free transfers as a tool for liquidating inefficient companies or as an incentive for managerial acquisitions between companies; (2) public sale of the privatized company shares; (3) direct sale of company shares to or a merger with foreign investors (Schnabel, "Structural Adjustment and Privatization," 251). Cf., e.g.: K.-D. Schmidt, U. Siegmund, "Strategien der Privatisierung," in Fischer, Hax, Schneider, *Treuhandanstalt*, 211–240; M. Myant, F. Fleischer, K. Hornschild, R. Vintrová, K. Zeman, Z. Souček, *Successful Transformations? The Creation of Market Economies in Eastern Germany and the Czech Republic* (Cheltenham–Brookfield: Edward Elgar, 1996), 56–62; Brücker, *Privatization in Eastern Germany*, *passim*. Georg Brunner, in a representative comparative study of privatization processes in the transition economies of Central and Eastern Europe, distinguishes three types of privatization. The first – spontaneous – involved the creation of new small and medium-sized enterprises. Small privatization involved small state enterprises, e.g., retail stores, restaurants, and some services. On the other hand, large privatization involved property transformations of large state enterprises, most often industrial ones (Brunner, "Verfassungsrechtliche Rahmenbedingungen," 207–215).

January 1991 and December 1992 (from 2,175 to 2,868 companies), with a peak in January–June 1992 (2,965 enterprises).[255] An internal report summarizing more than 4 years of the Office's work shows that on December 31, 1994, the THA's budget posted a not inconsiderable loss of DM 256 billion. Expenditures of DM 332 billion were matched by revenues of only DM 76 billion.[256]

6.2.2. Progress of privatization

In the 1990s, some state enterprises were privatized, and some federal companies were liquidated. However, official information from the federal government shows that the effects of this process were unsatisfactory, as the revenues obtained were not in line with those previously anticipated. Details are presented in Table 17.

---

255 Spangenberg, *The Institutionalised Transformation*, 140, table 3.5.; 156–157, tables 3.8.–3.9. The above categories of companies overlapped. Hence simply summing up all the numbers does not give a result of 11,937. For example, companies placed under local authorities' management may have been subsequently privatized. It should be emphasized that different data are indicated in various publications. Spangenberg relies on the official THA statistics, which should also be treated with a dose of caution.

256 Bös, "Privatization in Eastern Germany," 180, table 3. Other figures for the THA losses between 1990 and 1994 also appear in the literature. See, e.g.: K.-D. Schmidt, "Requirements for Successful Privatization – Lessons from the Treuhandanstalt's Approach," *Kiel Working Paper* No. 696 (1995): 11 (DM 270 billion); K. H. Domdey, "Privatisation in the New Bundesländer: A Critical Assessment of the Treuhand," in *The Political Economy of German Unification*, eds. T. Lange, J. R. Shackleton (Providence–Oxford: Berghahn Books, 1998), 52 (more than DM 300 billion); T. Lange, G. Pugh, "The Treuhand: A Positive Account," in Lange, J. R. Shackleton, *The Political Economy of German Unification*, 59, table 5.1 (DM 275 billion); Moszyński, "Zjednoczenie Niemiec," 255, fn. 4 (DM 205 billion, Moszyński also quotes Rohwedder's own estimate of the value of the GDR assets at the disposal of the Trust Office at DM 600 billion). The Bundestag established several committees of inquiry investigating in detail various aspects of the THA's controversial activities. See, e.g., the final report (running to 848 pages) from 1994: "Beschlußempfehlung und Bericht des 2. Untersuchungsausschusses 'Treuhandanstalt' nach Artikel 44 des Grundgesetzes," *Deutscher Bundestag. 12. Wahlperiode. Sachgebiet 1101. Drucksache* No. 12/8404 (1994): 1–848.

Table 17: *Projected and actual revenues from the full or partial privatization of state enterprises in Germany in 1990–1999 (as of 2000, DM million)*

Year	Number of fully or partially privatized state enterprises	Forecasted revenues	Actual revenues
1990	–	500.00	–
1991	2	556.00	555.70
1992	–	1,000.00	–
1993	5	840.00	122.50
1994	3	675.00	1,117.90
1995	4	1,500.00	285.10
1996	2	9,000.00	2,189.80
1997	6	5,370.00	5,392.40
1998	7	28,700.00	19,860.88
1999	3	12,000.00	5,055.44
Total	**32**	**60,141.00**	**34,579.72**

Own calculations and compilation based on: "Antwort der Bundesregierung auf die Große Anfrage der Abgeordneten Hans Jochen Henke, Susanne Jaffke, Dietrich Austermann, weiterer Abgeordneter und der Fraktion der CDU/CSU – Drucksache 14/3556 –," *Deutscher Bundestag. 14. Wahlperiode. Drucksache* No. 14/4696 (2000): 8.

The overview shows that the actual revenues from the full or partial privatization of state enterprises in 1990–1999 covered only 57.5 % of the projected amounts. Thus, in 2000 the federal budget was short of DM 25,561.28 million from privatization. Despite the explanations provided by the government, the scale of the above gap aroused controversy. In the second half of the 1990s, the government distributed the privatization revenues among the individual federated states. This amounted to a total of DM 27,679.9 million in 1995–1999.[257]

In subsequent decades, the process of privatization of state enterprises continued. Details in this regard – from the perspective of state shareholdings in enterprises – are presented in Table 18.

257 "Antwort der Bundesregierung," 9, 23.

Table 18: *State shareholdings in enterprises in Germany in selected years 2001–2015*

Year	Enterprises with direct state shareholdings[a]	Enterprises with indirect state shareholdings[b]	Dominant federal ministries as shareholders	
			by number of direct shareholdings	by the amount of the nominal share capital
2001	122	321[c]	Federal Ministry of Transport, Building and Housing (51)[d]	Federal Ministry of Finance (DM 19,445.9 million)[e]
2005	108	369[f]	Federal Ministry of Transport, Building and Housing (41)	Federal Ministry of Finance (14,548.7 million euros), Federal Ministry of Transport, Building and Housing (3,717.3 million euros)[g]
2010	107	363	Federal Ministry of Transport, Building and Urban Affairs (34)	Federal Ministry of Finance (15,014.6 million euros), Federal Ministry of Transport, Building and Urban Affairs (2,761.9 million euros)[h]
2015	108	508	Federal Ministry of Education and Research (12), Federal Ministry of Finance (11), Federal Ministry of Transport and Digital Infrastructure (9)	Federal Ministry of Finance (16,824.5 million euros), Federal Ministry of Transport and Digital Infrastructure (2,684.3 million euros)[i]

a *Unmittelbare Beteiligungen.*
b *Mittelbare Beteiligungen.*
c Only at least 25 % indirect state shareholdings in companies with a minimum nominal share capital of DM 100,000.
d For 2005 and 2010 regardless of the nominal share capital and the size of the shareholding.
e Status as of December 31, 2000, excluding the Federal Office of Posts and Telecommunications *Deutsche Bundespost* and the Federal Office for Special Unification Tasks.
f For 2005–2015, only at least 25 % indirect state shareholdings in companies with a minimum nominal share capital of 50,000 euros.
g Status as of December 31, 2004.
h Status as of December 31, 2009.
i Status as of December 2014.

Own calculations and compilation based on: *Beteiligungsbericht* (hereinafter: BB), Vol. 2001 (Bonn: Bundesministerium der Finanzen, 2001), 1–2; BB, Vol. 2005 (Berlin: Bundesministerium der Finanzen, 2005), 1–2; *Die Beteiligungen des Bundes. Beteiligungsbericht* (hereinafter: BB BB), Vol. 2010 (Berlin: Bundesministerium der Finanzen, 2011), 3–4; BB BB, Vol. 2015 (Berlin: Bundesministerium der Finanzen, 2016), 16, 179–180; BB BB, Vol. 2016 (Berlin: Bundesministerium der Finanzen, 2017), 11, 16.

The information in Table 18 indicates that the privatization of direct state shareholdings in enterprises progressed from 2001 to 2015. However, by simultaneously increasing indirect shareholdings by 58.3 %, the federal government continued to influence the operation of key entities. Moreover, the above overview shows an interesting shift towards an innovative economy between 2010 and 2015, for which federal economic policy was largely responsible. This was evident, among other things, in the increasing participation of the relevant ministries (i.e. those responsible for education and research and digital infrastructure) in the structure of direct state shareholdings both from the point of view of their number and nominal share capitals.

Taking a broad perspective, it should be stated that the privatization of state enterprises in Germany in 1991–2015 – as measured by the number of direct state shareholdings in companies – was carried out with varying intensity, although in a characteristic way. The details are shown in Figure 1.

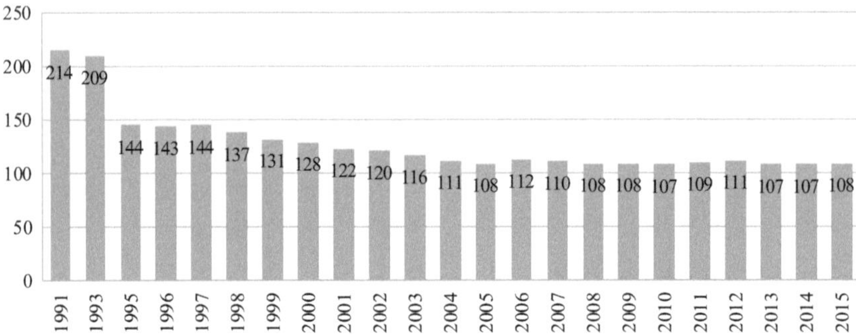

Figure 1: *Privatization of direct state shareholdings in enterprises in Germany in selected years 1991–2015 (in total numbers)*[a]

a The above figures refer to the number of enterprises (companies under public or private law) in which the Federation or special funds (*Sondervermögen*) have a direct shareholdings in a given year.

Own compilation based on: BB, Vol. 2002 (Bonn: Bundesministerium der Finanzen, 2002), insert between p. 2 and 3; BB, Vol. 2005, 3; BB BB, Vol. 2011 (Berlin: Bundesministerium der Finanzen, 2011), 2, 4; BB BB, Vol. 2013 (Berlin: Bundesministerium der Finanzen, 2014), 10; BB BB, Vol. 2014 (Berlin: Bundesministerium der Finanzen, 2015), 11; BB BB, Vol. 2015, 11; BB BB, Vol. 2016, 11.

There was an increase in direct state shareholdings in 1991 due to the incorporation of the new federated states into the FRG. However, a systematic process of their privatization began then. The significant decrease in the number of shareholdings (by 31.1 %) between 1993 and 1995 was mainly due to the transformation of direct shares of special funds (*Sondervermögen*) in the postal, telecommunications, and railroad sectors into indirect shareholdings of the Federation.[258]

258 BB BB, Vol. 2011, 4.

Privatization was put on hold in 2005, henceforth keeping the number of direct state shareholdings relatively constant until the end of the period in question. Interestingly, a slight increase in this regard was recorded in 2006 and in 2011–2012. The first case occurred during the first government of Chancellor Angela Merkel (2005–2009) and not – as it might seem – during the Social Democratic government led by Gerhard Schröder (1998–2002 and 2002–2005) when the privatization process was consistently continued. The second case of a slight increase in the state's share in the property structure of enterprises occurred after the financial crisis, which resulted from the government's anti-crisis policy.

Taking into account, in turn, only larger direct state shareholdings in enterprises (i.e., at least 25 % in companies with a minimum nominal share capital of 50,000 euros), it is worth noting a privatization trend for the years 1991–2011 that in some respects coincides with the one discussed above. The details are presented in Figure 2.

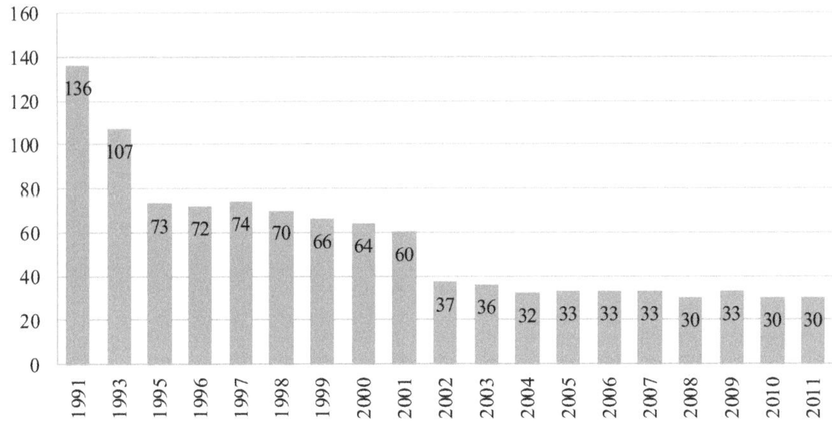

Figure 2: *Privatization of larger direct state shareholdings in enterprises in Germany in selected years 1991–2011 (in total numbers)*[a]

a The above figures refer to the number of enterprises (companies under public or private law) in which the Federation or special funds (*Sondervermögen*) had direct shareholdings in a given year. Only larger direct state shareholdings (i.e., at least 25 % in companies with a minimum nominal share capital of 50,000 euros) have been selected.

Own compilation based on: BB, Vol. 2002, insert between p. 2 and 3; BB, Vol. 2005, 3; BB BB, Vol. 2011, 2, 4.

As in the previous case, privatization of larger direct state shareholdings was intensively pursued in the first half of the 1990s. The reasons for this process were also similar. The significant decrease in shareholdings between 1993 and 1995 (by 31.8 %) was due to the above-mentioned shareholding transformations. However, the discussed process of property changes slowed down in 2002 and more markedly than the earlier one. The privatization of federal railroad assets was significant at that time.[259] From then on, the state held larger direct shareholdings in about 33 companies. The exception was during the financial crisis when these shareholdings declined slightly.

In March 2017, the Federal Ministry of Finance compiled a summary of privatization transactions in state enterprises in 1959–2016. These should be understood as all reorganizations of property structures of companies with direct federal shareholdings in a given year. They included both full and partial privatization of state enterprises or direct state shareholdings in companies, as well as mergers of certain companies.[260] The progress of this process is shown in Figure 3.

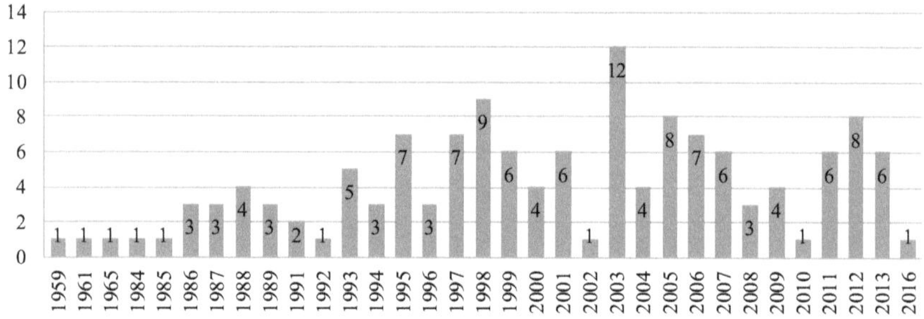

Figure 3: *Privatization transactions in state enterprises in Germany in 1959–2016 (in total numbers)*[a]

a Figures include all reorganizations of property structures of companies with direct federal shareholdings in a given year, i.e., full and partial privatization of state enterprises or direct state shareholdings in companies, as well as mergers of companies. Omitted years mean that privatization was not implemented in a given year. In some years the property (shareholding) structures of the same companies were reorganized.

Own calculations and compilation based on: *Veräußerung/Verwertung...*, https://www.bundesfinanzministerium.de/Content/DE/Standardartikel/Themen/Bundesvermoegen/Privatisierungs_und_Beteiligungspolitik/Privatisierungspolitik/privatisierungspolitik-anlage-2-uebersicht-privatisierungen-des-bundes.pdf?__blob=publicationFile&v=4 (accessed 13.09.2019).

Based on Figure 3, it can be concluded that the largest scale of privatization of federal enterprises occurred in the period after German reunification, i.e., after the takeover of post-GDR state property. This process covers the chronological framework of this work. It is possible to distinguish three key phases of privatization, coinciding with the specific economic policy of subsequent federal governments.

259 BB, Vol. 2005, 3.

260 "Veräußerung/Verwertung von Bundesunternehmen. Unmittelbare Beteiligungsunternehmen des Bundes," Bundesministerium der Finanzen, https://www.bundesfinanzministerium.de/Content/DE/Standardartikel/Themen/Bundesvermoegen/Privatisierungs_und_Beteiligungspolitik/Privatisierungspolitik/privatisierungspolitik-anlage-2-uebersicht-privatisierungen-des-bundes.pdf?__blob=publicationFile&v=4 (accessed September 13, 2019).

The first phase, which lasted from 1993 to 1998, coincided with the Christian democracy (CDU) government led by Kohl (1991–1994 and 1994–1998). The federal authorities then intensified the privatization process in the new Länder, with the exception of 1994 and 1996. It should be noted, however, that 1994 was still an election campaign, and Kohl's party was seeking the next term in office, which may have contributed to the government deliberately slowing down the pace of privatization, a source of social controversy, especially in view of rising unemployment in the Eastern *Länder*. However, the literature shows that the rapid and intensive privatization and restructuring processes saved the federal government from having to subsidize inefficient industries, which would have generated high costs.[261]

The second phase during the Schröder government (1998–2002 and 2002–2005), led by the social democrats (SPD), is interesting. After the new government took power, which in principle advocated greater participation of the state in the regulatory sphere of the economy, the privatization process declined, only to pick up again in 2000–2001. In the election year 2002, only one privatization transaction was recorded (according to the data processing methods shown in Figure 3). During Schröder's second government, privatization – as measured by the number of privatization transactions defined above – reached its peak. In 2003, as many as 12 reorganizations of property structures of companies with state shareholdings were completed. Therefore, the level three times lower in the following year could only be a kind of "scale effect." The increasing level of privatization transactions in 2004–2005 could have been one of the reasons for the collapse of the SPD government and the return of the CDU to power, this time with Merkel in the lead (2005–2009, 2009–2013, 2013–2018 and 2018–2021).

This marked the step to the third phase of privatization identified here. The process slowed down markedly during the first Christian democrats' government (2005–2009), although the number of property transformations increased slightly in 2009 when Merkel was running for re-election. This coincided with the global financial crisis and the need to seek additional funds for the federal budget. Only one transaction was completed in 2010, which can be explained by the increased state interventionism during the crisis. A clear revival of privatization processes took place in 2011–2013. The next property reorganization was realized only in 2016. The above cautious and non-exclusive interpretation of the results takes into account the political factor in the form of current party-government constellations, referring to the political theory of the business cycle.[262] It thus complements the seemingly contradictory picture emerging from the earlier analysis of the privatization progress of direct state shareholdings in enterprises between 1991 and 2015.

In 1989, only 5.3 % of the workforce in the GDR worked in private enterprises, while 2.1 % were self-employed.[263] Transformations in the structure of employment by property sector were one of the consequences of privatization in Germany in the 1990s. Changes for the state sector in this regard for 1991–1997 are presented in Table 19.

261 See, e.g., Moszyński, "Zjednoczenie Niemiec," 255.

262 See more P. Minford, D. Peel, "The Political Theory of the Business Cycle," *European Economic Review* 17, No. 2 (1982): 253–270.

263 Schnabel, "Structural Adjustment and Privatization," 232–233, table 1.

Table 19: *Employment in the state sector in Germany in 1991–1997 (annual average in thousands of people)*

Year	**Germany**			**Western *Länder***			**Eastern *Länder***		
	Workforce[a]	**Total employees**[b]	**State sector**	**Workforce**	**Total employees**	**State sector**	**Workforce**	**Total employees**	**State sector**
1991	**39,165**	36,510	*5,811*	**30,662**	29,189	*4,307*	**8,503**	7,321	*1,504*
1992	**38,838**	35,844	*5,755*	**30,943**	29,457	*4,329*	**7,895**	6,387	*1,426*
1993	**38,640**	35,221	*5,624*	**30,947**	29,002	*4,302*	**7,693**	6,219	*1,322*
1994	**38,670**	34,986	*5,524*	**30,872**	28,656	*4,275*	**7,798**	6,330	*1,249*
1995[c]	**38,429**	34,880	*5,409*	–	28,464	*4,210*	–	6,416	*1,199*
1996[c]	**38,329**	34,415	*5,320*	–	28,156	*4,164*	–	6,259	*1,156*
1997[c]	**38,261**	33,928	*5,218*	–	27,875	*4,116*	–	6,053	*1,102*

a *Erwerbspersonen.*
b *Erwerbstätige im Inland.*
c For 1995–1997, estimates from 1998.
Own calculations and compilation based on: SJ BRD, Vol. 1998 (Wiesbaden–Stuttgart: Statistisches Bundesamt, Metzler-Poeschel Verlag, 1998), 104–106, tables 6.4.1–6.4.2.

The summary shows that between 1991 and 1997, privatization resulted in a systematic decrease in the level of employment in the state sector in the whole country. In quantitative terms, however, this process was more dynamic in the new federated states. While in the Western *Länder*, 191,000 people lost their jobs in state enterprises in the analyzed period, in the former GDR, the number was as high as 402,000. This scale becomes even more significant if one takes into account the then existing workforce in both parts of Germany.

Between 1991 and 1997, there were characteristic transformations in the state sector's share in GDP creation. This was particularly evident in the Eastern part of the country. Precise data on this are provided in Table 20.

Table 20: *Share of the state sector in Germany's GDP in 1991–1997 (in billion DM)*[a]

Indicator	Year						
	1991	**1992**	**1993**	**1994**	**1995**[b]	**1996**[b]	**1997**[b]
at current prices							
GDP of Germany	2,853.60	3,078.60	3,163.70	3,328.20	3,459.60	3,541.50	3,641.80
- of which state share	*317.43*	*349.21*	*365.99*	*372.88*	*384.79*	*389.59*	*390.63*
GDP of Western *Länder*	2,647.60	2,813.00	2,840.50	2,962.10	3,062.20	3,128.30	3,219.70
- of which state share	*271.19*	*290.67*	*300.36*	*306.39*	*314.89*	*318.97*	*320.91*
GDP of Eastern *Länder*	206.00	265.60	323.20	366.10	397.40	413.20	422.10
- of which state share	*46.24*	*58.54*	*65.63*	*66.49*	*69.90*	*70.62*	*69.72*
at constant 1991 prices							
GDP of Germany	2,853.60	2,916.40	2,881.90	2,960.20	3,013.80	3,054.50	3,121.20
- of which state share	*317.43*	*320.79*	*320.71*	*322.69*	*321.75*	*321.89*	*319.37*
GDP of Western *Länder*	2,647.60	2,694.30	2,639.10	2,694.00	2,733.70	2,769.00	2,831.00
- of which state share	*271.19*	*277.15*	*278.74*	*282.20*	*281.77*	*282.41*	*280.59*
GDP of Eastern *Länder*	206.00	222.10	242.80	266.20	280.10	285.50	290.20
- of which state share	*46.24*	*43.64*	*41.97*	*40.49*	*39.98*	*39.48*	*38.78*

a Data only cover the years 1991–1997, because German statistical yearbooks changed the method of presenting the structure of GDP by property sectors and economy sectors (*Wirtschaftsbereichen*) in 1999. The share of the state sector in the GDP creation was not distinguished since then. See, e.g.: SJ BRD, Vol. 1999 (Wiesbaden–Stuttgart: Statistisches Bundesamt, Metzler-Poeschel Verlag, 1999), 667, table 24.2 (share of the government consumption expenditure (*Konsumausgaben des Staates*) in GDP); 670–671, table 24.4.
b For 1995–1997, estimates from 1998.
Own calculations and compilation based on: SJ BRD, Vol. 1998, 658, table 24.6.1; 660, 662, table 24.6.2.

The above table is one of the illustrations confirming the great developmental differences between the old and new federated states after German reunification. The GDP of the West *Länder* at constant 1991 prices was on average 11 times (9 times in current prices) the GDP of the former GDR in the analyzed period. Moreover, the share of only the state sector in real GDP creation (i.e. at constant 1991 prices) of the old federated states exceeded the level of real GDP of all Eastern *Länder* in 1991–1995 (in current prices, this advantage covered only the years 1991–1992). The process of the Eastern and Western *Länder*'s convergence was not completed by 2015, and significant developmental differences between the two parts of the country continued.[264]

It should be noted that the state sector's share in GDP creation increased along with its growth in 1991–1997. However, this phenomenon concerned the Western *Länder* and Germany as a whole. In the case of the new federated states, the share of the state was decreasing. This is confirmed by Figure 4, showing the percentage share of the state in the real GDP structure (at constant 1991 prices).

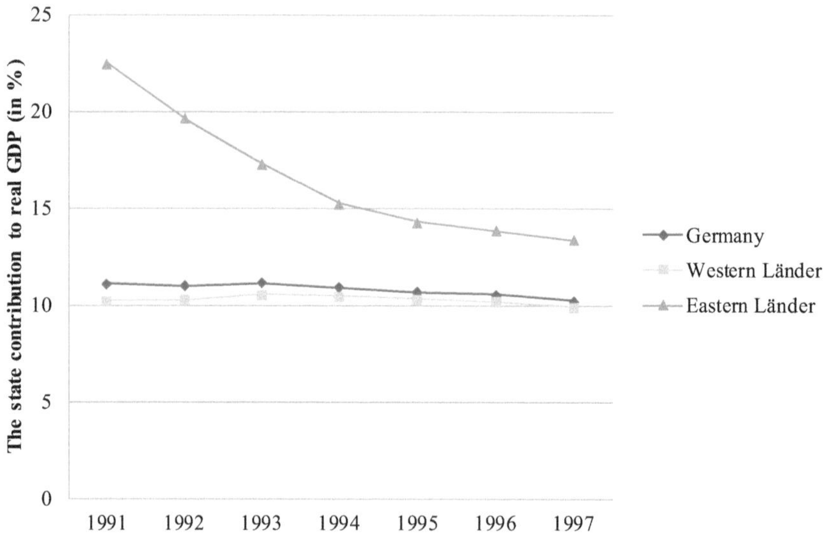

Figure 4: *Share of the state sector in Germany's real GDP in 1991–1997 (in %, at constant 1991 prices)*[a]

a For 1995–1997, estimates from 1998.

Own calculations and compilation based on: SJ BRD, Vol. 1998, 658, table 24.6.1; 662, table 24.6.2.

264 More on Germany's economic growth after reunification: section 6.2.9. in this work.

It turns out that the privatization of the 1990s clearly weakened the state's contribution to real GDP (at constant 1991 prices) only in the new federated states. While in 1991 the level was 22.4 % of GDP, in 1997, it was 13.4 %. However, this did not impinge on the property structure of GDP in the whole country. This was the result of the state sector's share in GDP remaining relatively constant in the economically stronger Western *Länder*, with a slight decline in this regard (10.2 % of GDP in 1991 and 9.9 % in 1997). Consequently, the state participated in real GDP creation at the level of 11.1 % in 1991 and 10.2 % in 1997.[265]

One effect of privatization in the 1990s was a transformation in the structure of German enterprises. As a result of property changes, the number of large production plants decreased significantly, especially in heavy industry. They were the largest employers in the region and determined its industrial fabric (e.g. the chemical industry in Saxony-Anhalt, shipbuilding in Mecklenburg-Vorpommern, engineering in Saxony-Anhalt, Saxony, and Brandenburg, and the metallurgical and railroad industries in Brandenburg). The number of small and medium-sized enterprises (up to 500 employees) has increased at the same time.[266]

6.2.3. Restructuring of the economy

Generally, the term "restructuring" means the reconstruction of a given structure in order to modernize it and increase its efficiency, rationality, effectiveness, and progress. Therefore, restructuring of the national economy should be understood as the process of intensifying the development of production of a group (groups) of products, industry (industries), or the entire sector (sectors) of the economy at the expense of others. This is done in order to improve the macroeconomic performance of a given economy, increase its competitiveness in the world and increase the quality of society's life. The state's activity plays a key role in this respect, e.g., through the reallocation of investment funds from traditional to innovative industries. Andrzej Karpiński calls this type of restructuring "macro-restructuring" (Pol. *makrorestrukturyzacja*) and distinguishes it from "micro-restructuring" (Pol. *mikrorestrukturyzacja*), limited to a single enterprise.[267] In economic history studies, the concept of restructuring often refers to long-term processes of the

---

265 SJ BRD, Vol. 1998, 658, table 24.6.1; 662, table 24.6.2.

266 Myant, Fleischer, Hornschild, Vintrová, Zeman, Souček, *Successful Transformations?*, 66–85.

267 Cf. A. Karpiński, *Restrukturyzacja gospodarki w Polsce i na świecie* (Warszawa: PWE, 1986), 19–23. It is important to mention that the concept of restructuring is primarily a key category in management science and refers to the reorganization of an enterprise. See, e.g., R. Borowiecki, ed., *Zarządzanie restrukturyzacją przedsiębiorstw i gospodarki. Uwarunkowania – procesy – efekty* (Kraków: Fundacja UE w Krakowie, 2014).

national income structure's transformations from the point of view of changes in the shares of the three main economic sectors (industry, agriculture, and services) in its creation.[268] In contemporary economic literature it is sometimes argued that the traditional three-sector division should be diversified, thus broadening the perspective for the analysis of the transformations of the individual economies' structures.[269]

The West German economy began to adopt a modern macrostructure[270] in the 1950s. This was a process typical of highly developed capitalist countries in Western

---

268 See, e.g.: R. Matera, J. Skodlarski, *Gospodarka światowa. Geneza i ewolucja do czasów pandemii* (Warszawa: WN PWN, 2021), *passim*; Skodlarski, *Historia gospodarcza*, *passim*. Cf. monographic study: E. Kwiatkowski, *Teoria trzech sektorów gospodarki. Prezentacja i próba oceny* (Warszawa: PWN, 1980). Andrzej Karpinski stresses, however, that it is a mistake to link restructuring only with changes in the branch-industry structure of the economy. All types of structures within a single economy as a system are combined with the structure of economic growth, including the structure of national income creation and distribution, the rate of investment, or social factors (Karpiński, *Restrukturyzacja gospodarki*, 17). However, he wrongly depreciates the spontaneity of the restructuring processes, stressing that the state remains their only *spiritus movens* (Karpiński, *Restrukturyzacja gospodarki*, 22–23, 25–28). This is a consequence of the fact that Karpiński's work was written from a Marxist position. Moreover, he reduces the category of restructuring to a certain doctrine of economic policy after World War II. Economic history, however, shows that a number of changes in this regard were a consequence of the natural developmental processes of the world economy, although a particular acceleration of macro-restructuring took place in capitalist countries in the second half of the 20th century. Although the economic policies of governments played a key role in this case, they were not exclusive.

269 See, e.g., Śliwa, Waląg, Tabor, "Ewolucja struktur produkcji i zatrudnienia w gospodarkach rynkowych. Wnioski dla Polski," *Prace Komisji Geografii Przemysłu Polskiego Towarzystwa Geograficznego* No. 30 (3) (2016): 49–50.

270 By macrostructure, Karpiński means "the relationship of the individual parts of the system in the most aggregate terms, that is, as a rule, on the scale of the entire national economy. Structural changes at this level consist of production, international exchange, and distribution transformations. In the production sphere, they concern the increase in the share of particular sectors or branches of the economy fulfilling separate functions at the expense of a decrease in the share of others" (Pol. *stosunek poszczególnych części układu w najbardziej zagregowanym ujęciu, czyli z reguły w skali całej gospodarki narodowej. Zmiany strukturalne na tym szczeblu polegają na przekształceniach sfery produkcji, wymiany międzynarodowej i podziału. W sferze produkcji dotyczą one zwiększania się udziału poszczególnych sektorów lub działów gospodarki spełniających odrębne funkcje kosztem zmniejszenia udziału innych*) (Karpiński, *Restrukturyzacja gospodarki*, 16). In this work, as a rule, three sectors are taken into account (i.e. industry, agriculture, and services), unless indicated otherwise. Karpiński adds: "In the sphere of distribution the elements of macrostructure include the structure of the basic elements of the national income

Europe and North America. Employment in services systematically increased at the expense of agriculture. The rapid growth of industrial production was dominated by the dynamic development of the service sector.[271] Nevertheless, industrial production – properly modernized – continued to play a key role in Germany's economic development both in the post-war period and after reunification.[272]

In the first half of the 1990s, the new federated states gradually made their macrostructure similar to Western *Länder* as a result of property transformations and integration with their economy under a unified economic system.[273] Details of this process from the perspective of the growth rate of gross value added in selected years 1992–2015 are presented in Table 21.

---

distribution across the economy, i.e. its parts allocated to exports, consumption or investment" (Pol. *W sferze podziału do elementów makrostruktury zalicza się strukturę podstawowych elementów podziału dochodu narodowego w skali całej gospodarki, a więc jego części przeznaczone na eksport, konsumpcję lub inwestycje*) (Karpiński, *Restrukturyzacja gospodarki*, 16–17).

271 H. Giersch, K.-H. Paqué, H. Schmieding, *The Fading Miracle. Four Decades of Market Economy in Germany* (Cambridge: Cambridge University Press, 1992), 7–9. See a detailed economic history study on this topic: W. Polster, K. Voy, "Die Entfaltung der Industriewirtschafts – Zum Strukturwandel von Wirtschaft und Erwerbsarbeit in der Industriegesellschaft," in *Marktwirtschafts und politische Regulierung. Beiträge zur Wirtschafts- und Gesellschaftsgeschichte der Bundesrepublik Deutschland (1949–1989)*, Vol. 1, eds. K. Voy, W. Polster, C. Thomasberger (Marburg: Metropolis-Verlag, 1991), 25–85. See the comparative perspective for capitalist states: Skodlarski, *Historia gospodarcza*, 388–393, 396–397.

272 W. Plumpe, *German Economic and Business History in the 19th and 20th Centuries* (London: Palgrave Macmillan, 2016), 239–280.

273 Hoffmann, "Integrating the East German States into the German Economy," 59–62; F.-W. Henning, *Das industrialisierte Deutschland 1914 bis 1992* (Paderborn: Ferdinand Schöningh, 1993), 318–323; M. Eli, C. Vögtle, "Dienstleistungen: Dynamisches Wachstum verspricht Zukunftschancen," in *Wiedervereinigung nach sechs Jahren: Erfolge, Defizite, Zukunftsperspektiven im Transformationsprozeß*, ed. by K. H. Oppenländer (Berlin–München: Duncker & Humblot, 1997), 469–479.

Table 21: *Year-on-year growth rate of gross value added in Germany in the main economic sectors in selected years 1992–2015 (in %, constant prices)*

Area	Economic sector	1992	1995	2000	2005	2010	2011	2012	2013	2014	2015
Berlin	Agriculture, forestry, fishing	−21.4	−8.3	−7.9	−14.5	−35.7	−26.4	34.1	−23.7	8.3	−2.6
	Processing industry	−7.9	−0.0[a]	3.0	1.5	6.3	9.2	−6.1	−5.4	1.4	0.7
	Construction	14.0	−0.2	−9.0	−7.6	11.3	5.7	−3.6	1.7	10.5	1.9
	Services	4.9	2.3	2.2	1.8	2.2	3.5	0.5	1.0	1.9	3.2
New federated states[b]	Agriculture, forestry, fishing	−5.5	9.1	−8.5	−36.5	−21.0	−10.1	14.0	2.4	9.0	−5.8
	Processing industry	−5.2	8.4	13.6	5.4	16.6	4.6	−2.4	3.0	4.0	1.1
	Construction	27.1	2.5	−10.8	−7.9	6.4	4.9	−1.0	−2.9	2.6	−0.9
	Services	12.8	8.4	1.7	0.2	0.6	2.1	0.4	0.3	0.3	1.6
Eastern Germany[c]	Agriculture, forestry, fishing	−5.7	9.0	−8.5	−36.5	−21.1	−10.2	14.1	2.4	9.0	−5.8
	Processing industry	−6.4	5.7	11.2	4.7	14.6	5.4	−3.1	1.5	3.6	1.0
	Construction	23.9	2.0	−10.5	−7.9	7.1	5.0	−1.4	−2.2	3.9	−0.4
	Services	9.4	6.3	1.9	0.7	1.1	2.5	0.4	0.5	0.8	2.1

Area	Economic sector	1992	1995	2000	2005	2010	2011	2012	2013	2014	2015
Western Germany[d]	**Agriculture, forestry, fishing**	−2.0	0.6	−2.9	−25.2	−25.3	−10.4	3.5	4.9	7.0	−0.6
	Processing industry	−2.5	−0.8	6.9	1.3	18.9	8.9	−1.4	0.8	2.2	1.8
	Construction	3.4	−5.3	0.8	−3.3	7.7	3.5	−1.1	−1.0	2.3	0.4
	Services	3.0	2.8	2.9	1.2	0.5	3.1	0.6	0.3	1.4	1.4
Germany	**Agriculture, forestry, fishing**	−2.7	2.4	−4.2	−27.9	−24.4	−10.3	5.9	4.3	7.5	−1.8
	Processing industry	−2.8	−0.3	7.3	1.6	18.4	8.5	−1.5	0.9	2.3	1.7
	Construction	7.1	−3.1	−2.1	−4.3	7.6	3.8	−1.2	−1.2	2.6	0.3
	Services	3.8	3.3	2.8	1.2	0.6	3.0	0.6	0.3	1.3	1.5

a A rounded negative value higher than −1.0.
b New federated states (*Neue Länder*) – the area of the former GDR (1949–1990) without Berlin, i.e.: Brandenburg, Mecklenburg-Vorpommern, Saxony, Saxony-Anhalt and Thuringia.
c Eastern Germany (*Ostdeutschland*) – new federated states with Berlin.
d Western Germany (*Westdeutschland*) – the area of the former FRG (1949–1990) without Berlin.
Source: *Wirtschaftsdaten neue Länder. August 2016* (Berlin: Bundesministerium für Wirtschaft und Energie, 2016), 4, table 1.2.

The above summary shows the continuation of the restructuring process of the Western German economy, which began in the 1950s. The highest dynamics of growth in gross value added covered services in 1992–2015, while the lowest dynamics covered agriculture. The negative values for the processing industry in the first half of the 1990s were due to the costs of German reunification. The collapse of industrial production in the former GDR affected the Western part of the country. Processing industry and construction were still important in the structure of the economy of the new federated states in 1992–2015, to a lesser extent, agriculture. Nevertheless, the growth rates of the service sector (in some years higher than in Western Germany) point to the process of the incorporated *Länder*'s inclusion into the Western German macrostructure, initiated in 1990. As a result, the structure of the economy of the whole country moved towards strengthening the position of services at the expense of the processing industry and construction, and to an even greater extent, agriculture, in 1992–2015. In turn, the dynamics of gross value added in Berlin show the metropolitan character of this state. In the same period, the services sector was of key importance for the capital city's economy, to a lesser extent processing industry and construction.

It is also interesting to note that since the early 1990s, there has been a progressive production (structural) specialization of individual *Länder*, presented in the literature as a sign of regionalization. Often it had its roots in the earlier decades.[274]

274 D. Dathe, "Der wirtschaftliche Strukturwandel in ausgewählten Stadtregionen der neuen Bundesländer in den Jahren 1989 bis 1993/94," in *Regionen im Vergleich. Gesellschaftlicher Wandel in Ostdeutschland am Beispiel ausgewählter Regionen*, ed. H. Bertram (Opdalen: Leske + Budrich, 1996), 41–66; R. Koll, "Der räumliche Strukturwandel in Ostdeutschland. Was ist neu in den neuen Bundesländern?," in Oppenländer, *Wiedervereinigung nach sechs Jahren*, 520, table 6; Spangenberg, *The Institutionalised Transformation*, 210–211, table 5.8.; U. Busch, W. Kühn, K. Steinitz, *Schrumpfung und Entwicklung in Ostdeutschland. Aktuelle Probleme im 20. Jahr der Einheit* (Hamburg: VSA-Verlag, 2009), 103–112, until ca. 2006; I. Mieck, *Kleine Wirtschaftsgeschichte der neuen Bundesländer* (Stuttgart: Franz Steiner Verlag, 2009), 227–318, until ca. 2007. A separate research challenge remains the fact that regional development diversification not only concerns the West-East axis. The developmental dividing line in Germany also runs along the North-South axis, especially taking into account the development of individual *Länder* and lower levels of the German administrative division. The literature on this subject is abundant. As representative studies it is worth pointing out, e.g. M. Götz, "Od Republiki Federalnej do 'Regierungsbezirke' – niemiecki krajobraz wiedzy na różnych poziomach analizy," *Studia Regionalne i Lokalne* No. 1 (35) (2009): 5–31. This approach refers to the trend of new geographical economics, which examines the economic polarization of a country by developmental inequalities of its regions (M. Götz, "Konwergencja dochodów w Niemczech w latach 1991–2007," *Ruch Prawniczy, Ekonomiczny i Socjologiczny* 72, No. 1 (2010): 113, fn. 32).

Some researchers relate this issue to the problem of sectoral institution transfer (*sektorales Institutionentransfer*) or reorganization of sectoral property rights (*Reorganisation der sektorspezifischen Eigentumsrechte*). As a result of state policy resulting from reunification documents, privatization did not extend to strategic sectors in reunified Germany. In other words, the state property in the Eastern *Länder* was maintained in those sectors that had also been nationalized in the FRG. This included three groups of sectors: (1) typically state-owned (e.g. telecommunications, research science system, health care system); (2) indirect, i.e. combining market and government involvement (e.g. agriculture, energy); (3) sectors over which the FRG directly assumed full supervision from the GDR and reorganized property rights based on the THA.[275]

The literature notes that immediately after reunification, as part of the transition crisis, the largest losses in the Eastern *Länder* were in the industrial sector. Some researchers point to the effects of the currency union. Eastern German plants were not able to compete with companies from Western Germany and abroad. Increased labor costs, unprofitability of production, and shifting demand for goods from Western Germany caused the collapse of many enterprises, which in turn increased unemployment. The last factor simultaneously contributed to a decline in the level of industrial production.[276]

The highest growth in Eastern Germany in the 1990s was in the automotive and metal industries, while the lowest was in the food and chemical industries.[277] Already at the beginning of reunification, the machinery industry was considered the most competitive branch.[278]

The processing industry was an important sector intensifying economic growth in the Eastern *Länder*. Between 1991 and 2002, the gross value added it produced increased from 13,612 thousand to 31,996 thousand euros, but the level of employment in this industry declined from 1,751 thousand to 879 thousand people. However, the gross value added per 1 employee increased by 368 %. The share of the processing industry in gross value added per 1 employee was subject to

275 G. Lehmbruch, "Zwischen Institutionentransfer und Eigendynamik: Sektorale Transformationspfade und ihre Bestimmungsgründe," in *Transformationspfade in Ostdeutschland*, eds. R. Czada, G. Lehmbruch (Frankfurt–New York: Campus Verlag, 1998), 36–40.

276 Hoffmann, "Integrating the East German States into the German Economy," 50–55; Sinn, "Macroeconomic Aspects of German Unification," 94; H. Klodt, "Government Support for Restructuring the East German Economy," in Welfens, *Economic Aspects of German Unification*, 262–264, 268–271, especially: 263, figure 1; 266, table 2; 268, figure 2; Hitchens, Wagner, Birnie, *East German Productivity and the Transition to the Market Economy*, 103–118; Moszyński, "Zjednoczenie Niemiec," 254; Klimiuk, "Trendy rozwojowe," 61.

277 Klimiuk, "Trendy rozwojowe," 70.

278 Hoffmann, "Integrating the East German States into the German Economy,", pp. 61–62.

periodical fluctuations. While in 1991, it accounted for 17.2 % in relation to the old federated states, and between 1991 and 1996, it amounted to 27.7 %, it decreased to 6.7 % in 1996–2001.[279]

The construction sector also played an important role in the development of Eastern Germany. As a result of numerous infrastructure investments in the first half of the 1990s, demand in the construction industry reached a high level. However, in the following years, the sector started to record losses due to overcapacity. Gross value added per 1 employee declined from an average level of 5.4 % in 1991–1996 to 1.5 % for the period 1996–2001. The effects were particularly felt in housing construction, projects carried out by *Länder* and municipalities, as well as in the transport industry and trade in construction materials. Between 1991 and 1996, the number of building permits issued increased from 5,484 to 186,155, while in 2002, it was only 42,075. A similar trend was observed in the rate of completed investments. In 1997 their number rose to 177,829 from 16,670 in 1991, while in 2002, there were already 49,013 completed projects. The crisis in the construction sector also resulted in an increase in unemployment. Only in 1999, about 40,000 people lost their jobs in the sector.[280]

As Michał Moszyński noted, the share of the entire industrial sector in the creation of gross value added in the Eastern *Länder* increased from 93 % in 1991 to 98 % in 2009 in relation to the old federated states. However, this was an apparent convergence. The construction industry was overdeveloped (226 % in 1991 and 145 % in 2009), while the collapse of processing and production industries in the early 1990s resulted in the underdevelopment of these sectors compared to the Western *Länder* (respectively: 49 % and 70 % in 1991 and 81 % and 89 % in 2009).[281]

It is noteworthy that the only Eastern German sector with higher productivity than in Western Germany was agriculture.[282] However, in the late 1980s and early 1990s, the agricultural sector in the GDR absorbed 10 % of the labor force, while it was 5 % in the FRG. The Eastern *Länder* were also characterized by higher inputs, over-employment, inefficient organization of the production process, outdated or defective means of production, and consequently higher production costs and prices of agricultural commodities.[283] It should be recalled that the property structure of agriculture in the GDR was dominated by the social sector, especially the cooperative one. This concerned both the number of farms and the crop area.[284]

---

279 Czech-Rogosz, "Gospodarka wschodnich Niemiec w 12 lat po zjednoczeniu," 96.

280 Czech-Rogosz, "Gospodarka wschodnich Niemiec w 12 lat po zjednoczeniu," 96–97; Klimiuk, "Trendy rozwojowe," 65.

281 Moszyński, "Zjednoczenie Niemiec," 263–264, table 4.

282 Cf. Busch, Kühn, Steinitz, *Schrumpfung und Entwicklung in Ostdeutschland*, 28–29; Klimiuk, "Trendy rozwojowe," 70.

283 Hoffmann, "Integrating the East German States into the German Economy," 59–60.

284 See in more detail: section 5.2. in this work.

The transformations in the structure of the FRG agriculture after World War II, in turn, remained consistent with the corresponding changes in other Western European countries. It consisted mainly of a gradual decrease in the total number of farms, especially small ones (or their share in the area structure of production units), and a progressive concentration of land in large farms, which increased in the number or their share in the area structure of farms. Since the 1960s, this process has been particularly intensified both from the point of view of the European Communities' agricultural policy and individual governments' actions. As a result of the systemic transition, different tendencies took place in Central and Eastern Europe in the 1990s and in the first years of the 21st century: a general decrease in the number of production units with a strong fragmentation and a high numerical and percentage share of small farms in the area structure.[285]

From a national perspective, it should be mentioned that the number of agricultural units in Germany decreased from 653.6 thousand to 370.5 thousand in the 1989/1990–2007 economic years. The dynamics of this process in individual periods were very high, although it was relatively weakened: 1985–1989/1990–88.3 %, 1989/1990–1995–86.7 %, 1995–2000–83.3 %, and 2000–2007–78.5 %. In turn, the average size of farms increased from 26.1 to 48.4 hectares. Between 1989/1990 and 2007, the share of small production units in the area structure of farms decreased from 33.4 % to 22.6 %, while large entities (50 hectares and more) increased from 8.6 % to 23.0 %. Medium area groups recorded a slight decrease in participation, maintaining their *de facto* status: from 34.5 % to 32.3 % (5–20 ha) and from 23.4 % to 22.1 % (20–50 hectares).[286]

Between 2004/2005 and 2012/2013, entities focused on crop and milk production (in the latter case, this was mainly the case in the Northern *Länder*) recorded the highest competitiveness (measured as the ratio of net income from the farm to the opportunity cost of own factors of production in the agricultural unit). An average level of competitiveness concerned pig and poultry producers, although among them, farmers from Northern Germany were more profitable. The lowest results were reported by cattle farms (especially those producing beef and located in the Southern federated states). Werner Kleinhanss' research also shows that in the same period, 40–50 % of German farms fully covered their opportunity costs, 40–50 % – only partially, and about 10 % were unable to do so due to negative net income.[287]

---

285 J. Babiak, "Zmiany w strukturze rolnictwa krajów Unii Europejskiej," *Rocznik Integracji Europejskiej* No. 4 (2010): 87–97.

286 Babiak, "Zmiany w strukturze rolnictwa," 88–89, table 2; 90, table 3; 91–93, table 4; 94, table 5.

287 W. Kleinhanss, "Konkurencyjność głównych typów gospodarstw rolniczych w Niemczech," *Zagadnienia Ekonomiki Rolnej* No. 1 (2015): 25–41.

Based on a law of the People's Chamber of June 29, 1990, East German agricultural production cooperatives were converted into new forms of cooperatives.[288] An amendment to the law adopted by the parliament of reunified Germany on July 3, 1991, introduced the additional possibility of converting the former LPGs into partnerships or capital companies.[289] Most members of the former cooperatives continued their cooperative production activities under the changed legal forms. Individual agricultural enterprises, on the other hand, were often larger than in the Western part of the country, able to carry out mass production to a greater extent. By August 1992, about 3,000 agricultural enterprises had been registered. Among them, cooperatives dominated with an average area of 1,136 hectares, and thus smaller on average than the former LPGs. Relatively quickly, agricultural cooperatives achieved higher production than cooperatives in the GDR due to their rationalization. This included, among other things: outsourcing of existing non-economic services (utilities) to external firms, structural and administrative restrictions, and staff reductions. For example, in 1993, agriculture in the Eastern *Länder* employed about 2.8 people per 1 hectare, while in the old federated states, it was about 5.5 people. At the beginning of the 21st century, the agriculture of the new *Länder* was competitive. It was dominated by large farms with high productivity. Their profitability was good, and production was usually environmentally friendly. Even the income situation of farmers from the East was relatively better than that of producers in Western Germany. The impressive agricultural development in the new *Länder*, however, reflected the weakness of their industrial potential. This was especially true in Mecklenburg-Vorpommern. After reunification, agricultural cooperatives loosened their ties with the region as a result of the abandonment of non-economic functions. They reduced their influence on the modernization of the local infrastructure. They also provided work for a relatively small number of people from the region.[290]

---

288 *Gesetz über die strukturelle Anpassung der Landwirtschaft an die soziale und ökologische Marktwirtschaft in der Deutschen Demokratischen Republik – Landwirtschaftsanpassungsgesetz – vom 29. Juni 1990* (GBl.-DDR, Part I, 1990, No. 42, 642–649).

289 *Bekanntmachung der Neufassung des Landwirtschaftsanpassungsgesetzes Vom 3. Juli 1991* (BGBl., Part I, 1991, No. 40, 1418–1429). See the most recent amendment: *Zweites Gesetz zur Modernisierung des Kostenrechts (2. Kostenrechtsmodern isierungsgesetz – 2. KostRMoG) Vom 23. Juli 2013*, Art. 40 (BGBl., Part I, 2013, No. 42, 2708). See Baur, Baur, Stürner, *Sachenrecht*, 894.

290 B. Martens, "Landwirtschaft in Ostdeutschland: der späte Erfolg der DDR," https://www.bpb.de/geschichte/deutsche-einheit/lange-wege-der-deutschen-einheit/47157/landwirtschaft?p=all (accessed March 9, 2020).

6.2.4. Enterprise sector

German reunification brought a breakthrough in the development of East German entrepreneurship. It was limited to the number of enterprises (*Unternehmen*) in this section.[291] However, it should be aware that there is an ongoing dispute in the economic literature about the validity of using this kind of indicator.[292]

The new favorable conditions for the establishment of private companies in the former GDR resulted primarily from: the transition from the plan to the market, guarantee of private property, privatization and re-privatization, and restructuring of the economy. However, the evaluation of this breakthrough is not unequivocal.

The changes resulting from the circumstances discussed above are illustrated by data on the number of private enterprise start-ups and liquidations in Germany between 1990 and 2015. Table 22 provides details in this regard.

291 More on the difference between enterprises (*Unternehmen*) and plants (*Betriebe*): section 6.2.1. in this work.

292 However, there is no place here to discuss the concept of entrepreneurship and its potential measures, although a broad (interdisciplinary) approach to this category should be supported (see a classic synthetic study: B. Glinka, S. Gudkova, *Przedsiębiorczość* (Warszawa: Wolters Kluwer Polska, 2011)), consciously reducing the analysis to the most relevant data from the point of view of these considerations. The aim is to show the significance of property rights for the development of the private enterprise sector in reunified Germany.

Table 22: *New and liquidated enterprises in Germany in 1991–2015 (in total numbers)*

Year	All sectors						Processing sector					
	New enetrprises[a]		Liquidated enterprises[a]		Balance per 100,000 inhabitants[a]		New enterprises[a]		Liquidated enterprises[a]		Balance per 100,000 inhabitants[a]	
	New *Länder*[b]	Western Germany[c]	New *Länder*[b]	Western Germany[c]	New *Länder*[b]	Western Germany[c]	New *Länder*[b]	Western Germany[c]	New *Länder*[b]	Western Germany[c]	New *Länder*[b]	Western Germany[c]
1991[d]	140,000	391,000	11,000	297,000	882	147	–	–	–	–	–	–
1992[d]	96,000	398,000	24,000	288,000	499	170	–	–	–	–	–	–
1993[d]	79,000	407,000	41,000	298,000	265	167	–	–	–	–	–	–
1994[d]	74,000	419,000	44,000	328,000	211	139	–	–	–	–	–	–
1995[d]	76,000	452,000	49,000	358,000	191	143	–	–	–	–	–	–
1996[d]	86,000	421,000	74,000	344,000	69	120	–	–	–	–	–	–
1997[e]	72,700	355,600	56,500	273,700	116	128	–	–	–	–	–	–
1998	76,600	358,100	60,100	277,900	118	125	–	–	–	–	–	–
1999	72,300	345,400	60,900	288,600	82	89	–	–	–	–	–	–
2000	66,100	335,400	60,700	266,000	39	108	–	–	–	–	–	–
2001	63,700	327,000	60,400	264,400	24	97	–	–	–	–	–	–
2002	60,300	328,700	57,300	270,800	22	89	–	–	–	–	–	–
2003[f]	76,200	346,700	60,300	309,700	118	57	–	–	–	–	–	–
2004	91,700	391,800	59,000	304,000	245	135	–	–	–	–	–	–
2005	70,800	345,200	61,900	317,200	67	43	2,500	12,700	2,400	13,500	1	–1
2006	62,900	331,100	58,000	312,600	37	29	2,500	11,800	2,200	12,600	2	–1

Table 22: *Continued*

2007	51,000	300,900	55,600	300,000	−35	1	2,100	10,700	2,200	11,800	−1	−2
2008[g]	48,300	282,800	55,500	300,300	−57	−27	2,100	9,600	2,100	10,700	–	−2
2009	46,900	297,200	49,300	288,700	−19	13	1,900	10,100	2,100	11,100	−2	−2
2010	45,400	304,900	46,500	285,800	−9	30	1,700	10,200	1,700	10,500	–	−0[h]
2011	41,400	293,600	45,000	286,700	−29	11	1,500	9,700	1,700	10,300	−2	−1
2012	33,100	250,200	42,800	276,900	−77	−41	1,200	7,800	1,600	10,400	−3	−4
2013	31,100	245,100	40,400	265,000	−74	−31	1,200	7,400	1,600	10,000	−3	−4
2014	29,300	220,900	38,700	260,900	−75	−62	1,000	6,900	1,600	9,400	−5	−4
2015	27,900	213,100	38,200	242,600	−82	−45	1,000	6,500	1,600	9,100	−5	−4

a Excluding free professions, agricultural, forestry and other non-commercial "self-employed activities" (*weitere nichtgewerbliche sog. sonstige selbstständige Tätigkeiten*).
b *Neue Länder* – the area of the former GDR (1949–1990) without Berlin; the new federated states: Brandenburg, Mecklenburg-Vorpommern, Saxony, Saxony-Anhalt and Thuringia. For 1996, including Berlin.
c *Westdeutschland* – the area of the former FRG (1949–1990) without Berlin. Until 1995 with West Berlin.
d Data based on commercial advertisements of selected federated states.
e Since 1997, calculations based on company registrations and deregistrations throughout the FRG by the Federal Statistical Office (*Statistischen Bundesamt*).
f The change in the calculation method in 2003 allows limited comparison of data from earlier years.
g The change in the business classification in 2008 allows limited comparison of data from earlier years. Possible rounding.
h A rounded negative value higher than −1.
Source: *Wirtschaftsdaten neue Länder*, 12, table 1.6.

This comparison for the entire analyzed period shows a clear disparity between the old and new federated states. Taking all sectors into account, until 1995, new enterprises were established much more intensively in the Eastern part of Germany. This was the result of the initiation of the systemic transition of the former GDR, involving the implementation of West German law (constitutional rules and property rights), the capitalist system, as well as progressive privatization and re-privatization processes.[293] However, the positive balance per 100,000 inhabitants were gradually decreasing in relation to the old *Länder*. In 1996, the proportions were reversed as a result of a kind of saturation, a stabilization of the trend, and the increasingly stronger economic predominance of Western Germany. It persisted (sometimes very significantly) until the end of the analyzed period, with the exception of 2003–2006. This was one of the reasons why the convergence process between the two parts of Germany was hindered. Importantly, the general crisis in terms of start-ups spread throughout Germany at the onset of the financial crisis. In 2007, however, the new federated states felt it much more strongly. Since then, the situation has not been reversed. Between 2007 and 2015, more enterprises were liquidated in the Eastern *Länder* than new ones were founded. However, the situation was similar in the West. The negative balance covered the years 2008 and 2012–2015. For the period 2005–2015, stagnation was observed in the processing sector from the point of view of new enterprises' development in both parts of Germany.

Most likely, the above statistics are highly inflated. The actual number of newly established firms, especially in the East in the 1990s, is not precisely known, and the differences in the data may even reach hundreds of thousands. Researchers point out that some potential entrepreneurs registered their businesses without starting them at all. Some were starting a business while working elsewhere. Still, others registered several enterprises at once, postponing the decision on running a particular business for the future. Less controversial is the data on the creation of new companies as a result of the division of large state plants and their privatization.[294]

The analysis is complemented by data on enterprise bankruptcies, understood as the declaration of insolvency by them. This is presented in Table 23 for the period 1991–2007.

293 Busch, Kühn, Steinitz, *Schrumpfung und Entwicklung in Ostdeutschland*, 75–76.

294 L. von Schuttenbach, R. Ganter, *Sektor małych i średnich przedsiębiorstw w Republice Federalnej Niemiec* (Warszawa: PAB-Font, 2000), 48–50.

Table 23: *Enterprise bankruptcies in Germany in 1991–2007 (in total numbers)*

Year	Eastern Germany[a]	Western Germany[b]
1991	392	8,445
1992	1,092	9,828
1993	2,327	12,821
1994	3,911	14,913
1995	5,874	16,470
1996	7,419	18,111
1997	8,126	19,348
1998	8,615	19,213
1999[c]	7,567	16,772
2000	8,047	18,062
2001	8,506	21,664
2002	8,847	26,638
2003	7,575	29,584
2004	7,296	30,015
2005	7,104	28,017
2006	5,736	23,240
2007	4,471	23,261

a Until 1998 with East Berlin, since 1999 without East Berlin.
b Until 1998 with West Berlin, since 1999 without West Berlin.
c Since 1999, including a small business.
Source: Busch, Kühn, Steinitz, *Schrumpfung und Entwicklung in Ostdeutschland*, 70, table 11.

The lower number of firm bankruptcies in the new federated states between 1991 and 2007 was due to the Western part of the country's entrepreneurial advantage. In the old federated states, the enterprise sector grew longer and more dynamically, which included both start-ups and bankruptcies. The vast majority of bankrupt entities in the East (sometimes about 90 %) were micro enterprises (less than ten employees). For some researchers, this was indicative of the conjunctural nature of Eastern German enterprises' development.[295] According to more recent data, 31,998 firms went bankrupt across Germany in 2010. In 2015, there were 23,123 companies, of which 4,008 were in the new *Länder* (including Berlin).[296] The trend has therefore not fluctuated much.

295 Busch, Kühn, Steinitz, *Schrumpfung und Entwicklung in Ostdeutschland*, 79.
296 Own calculations based on: SJ DI, Vol. 2016, 518, tables 20.4.1.–20.4.2.

The entry into force of the monetary union on July 1, 1990, favored the establishment of new enterprises in East Germany. This was encouraged by the favorable ratio of German currencies for citizens. Only between January and September 1990 197,286 new companies were established in the GDR, of which 96,804 (49.1 %) were between July and September. However, competitive challenges quickly emerged. A total of 12,328 entities failed between January and September 1990, with 8,872 firms (72.0 %) between July and September.[297]

There were also other problems. By selling more expensive and lower quality products, enterprises from the new federated states were not able to compete with the Western German companies' offers. Consumer demand from the Eastern *Länder* naturally shifted to the desired products from Western Germany or abroad. In addition, service companies had hitherto been dominated by industrial plants.[298]

From the enterprises' point of view, the West German property rights implemented in the new federated states were, in some respects, a *de jure* institution. In reality, there were informal dependencies of East German entrepreneurs on larger entities from the old *Länder* or abroad. These included participation in business ventures, the establishment of contracts, supply agreements, and financial relations.[299] This increased the transaction costs for new entrepreneurs from the East.

Additional problems resulted from the nature of the East German transition. Due to the strong rivalry with the FRG, private property in the GDR was particularly fought against. There was little knowledge of the free market in the East. The rapid and short-lived implementation of West German legal rules hindered initiative. This was due first to the recognition of West German competence, then to the growing antagonism between *Ossi* and *Wessi*. Moreover, the institutional system developing in the FRG evolved over the following decades, while its imposition on East Germany did not stimulate small, individual, grassroots initiatives in the first years of transition. Certain regulatory issues (obtaining selected concessions, high environmental or labor law standards) further complicated the situation of entrepreneurs in the East. As a result, the development of the small and medium-sized enterprises sector was slower there than, e.g., in Poland, the Czech Republic or Hungary.[300]

In the early 1990s, advances in property concentration were observed in privatized East German enterprises. This was especially true for large companies.[301]

The establishment of new firms is positively influenced, among other things, by the stability of legal norms resulting from the stability of the political system. This

297 Own calculations based on: Klodt, "Government Support," 270, table 3.

298 Klodt, "Government Support," 267–269.

299 Busch, Kühn, Steinitz, *Schrumpfung und Entwicklung in Ostdeutschland*, 77.

300 von Schuttenbach, Ganter, *Sektor małych i średnich przedsiębiorstw*, 53–54.

301 Spangenberg, *The Institutionalised Transformation*, 253–256; Busch, Kühn, Steinitz, *Schrumpfung und Entwicklung in Ostdeutschland*, 80–81. There is separate literature on this topic, which is not the subject of this discussion.

includes, among others, procedures related to the registration of new companies. Their transparency, vastness, and length influence the level of transaction costs, which in turn results in the investment attractiveness of a given country and the creation of new enterprises.[302] According to World Bank data (*Doing Business* project) available for the years 2004–2015, the time required to set up a company in Germany decreased from 45 days in 2004 to 14.5 days in 2015. This period was associated with the completion of a total of nine procedures (the same result for 2004 and 2015). In this respect, Germany's situation stood out positively among other European countries. Germany fared worse against the Old Continent in terms of property registration. In 2015, this process required 52 days and six procedures.[303]

Despite the fact that Eastern German companies developed quantitatively at the beginning of the 21st century,[304] they were still inferior to companies from Western Germany. This was especially true for the size of employment, the level of innovation, research and development expenditures,[305] generation of added value, level of exports, cost structure, or amount of profits.[306]

The size structure of Eastern German companies gradually resembled that of companies in the old federated states. A characteristic feature was the strong dominance of micro and small enterprises, possibly small and medium-sized enterprises. Large enterprises were the least numerous group. For example, in 2005, 3,475,094 plants (*Betriebe*) were registered throughout the country, including 3,121,753 micro plants (*Kleinstbetriebe*, less than 10 employees), 278,634 small plants (*Kleinbetriebe*, less than 50 employees), 63,627 medium-sized plants (*Mittelbetriebe*, less than 250 employees), and 11,080 large plants (*Großbetriebe*, 250 or more employees). Out of a total of 2,836,413 plants in Western Germany at that time, the following were accounted for: 2,552,257 micro, 223,976 small, 50,893 medium, and 9,287 large plants. In contrast, in 2005, there were 497,197 plants in Eastern Germany, including: 439,413 micro, 45,875 small, 10,605 medium, and 1,304 large. The situation was similar in the capital city of Berlin. In the same year, 141,484 plants were registered there, among them: 130,083 micro, 8,783 small, 2,129 medium, and 489 large. In 2005, micro plants in both parts of Germany thus represented respectively: 90.0 % (West) and 88.4 % (East) of the total number of plants (excluding Berlin).[307]

---

302 Cf. M. Owczarczuk, "Atrakcyjność inwestycyjna Polski z perspektywy instytucjonalnej," *Studia Ekonomiczne* 184 (2014): 174.

303 "Doing Business. Measuring Business Regulations," https://www.doingbusiness.org/en/custom-query# (accessed April 9, 2020).

304 For example, in 2006, there were 380 firms per 10,000 inhabitants in the East (excluding Berlin), while in 2013–404 (S. Pastuszka, "Polityka rozwoju Wschodnich Niemiec – cele, narzędzia, efekty," *Optimum. Studia Ekonomiczne* No. 6 (84) (2016): 67, table 5).

305 The issues of innovation and research and development expenditures are the subject of section 6.2.6. in this work.

306 Busch, Kühn, Steinitz, *Schrumpfung und Entwicklung in Ostdeutschland*, 78–79.

307 Own calculations based on: Busch, Kühn, Steinitz, *Schrumpfung und Entwicklung in Ostdeutschland*, 78, table 13.

6.2.5. Employee participation

In the case of enterprises, various forms of employee interest representation (*Arbeitnehmervertretung*) play an important role. The term is generally understood as a set of institutions, methods, and measures aimed at protecting, supporting, and developing the rights of employees. This is usually carried out by employees' organizations (e.g. trade unions) which influence the employers or their representatives through negotiations, agreements, or forceful confrontations (e.g. strikes).[308] The representation of employee interests includes, among other things, employee participation in management (employee participation), which refers to the participation of employees in complicity or co-determination of general or specific enterprise issues. It is indicated in different types in the literature, e.g.: capital, property, information, negotiation, decision-making, and consultation, where the last two are further divided into direct and representative participation.[309]

The process of spreading property by the capitalist countries' governments in the 20th century (especially after World War II) went hand in hand with the implementation of various participation programs, although their scale was not massive.[310] The German model of employee participation is called "co-determination" (*Mitbestimmung*). Its origins go back to the 1840s. After World War II, the most important (but not the only) regulations on employee participation were enacted in 1951–1952, 1972, 1976, and 2004.[311] These laws primarily provided for: (1) the appointment of supervisory boards in mining and metallurgical plants (over 1,000 people) including representatives of employees and investors (1951); (2) the normalization of the rules of co-determination in the enterprise, whereby the works council was to co-determine in social, personnel and economic matters (1952, a new form of the law – 1972); the extension of the provisions of the 1951 law to

---

308 See more: G. Goździewicz, ed., *Reprezentacja praw i interesów pracowniczych* (Toruń: TNOiK, Dom Organizatora, 2001).

309 See, e.g., A. Stabryła, *Podstawy zarządzania firmą. Modele, metody, praktyka* (Warszawa: WN PWN, 1995), 125, 127. Cf. the review of definitions of participation, employee participation and exemplary classifications: M. Kozłowski, *Pracownicza partycypacja finansowa. Geneza, uwarunkowania rozwoju, rezultaty* (Łódź: Wydawnictwo UŁ, 2013), 24–29.

310 Kozłowski, *Pracownicza partycypacja finansowa*, 23–24.

311 *Gesetz über die Mitbestimmung der Arbeitnehmer in den Aufsichtsräten und Vorständen der Unternehmen des Bergbaus und der Eisen und Stahl erzeugenden Industrie. Vom 21. Mai 1951* (BGBl., Part I, 1951, No. 24, 347–349 as amended); *Betriebsverfassungsgesetz. Vom 11. Oktober 1952.* (BGBl., Part I, 1952, No. 43, 681–694 as amended); *Betriebsverfassungsgesetz Vom 15. Januar 1972* (BGBl., Part I, 1972, No. 2, 13–43 as amended); *Gesetz über die Mitbestimmung der Arbeitnehmer (Mitbestimmungsgesetz – MitbestG) Vom 4. Mai 1976* (BGBl, Part I, 1976, No. 51, 1153–1165 as amended); *Zweites Gesetz zur Vereinfachung der Wahl der Arbeitnehmervertreter in den Aufsichtsrat Vom 18. Mai 2004* (BGBl., Part I, 2004, No. 25, 974–979 as amended).

such establishments with more than 2,000 persons as: joint stock companies, associations, limited joint-stock partnerships, limited liability companies (1976); providing employees with 1/3 of the supervisory board in capital companies with more than 500 persons (2004).[312]

The implementation of employee participation in Germany transformed the traditional structure of property of means of production in enterprises. In addition to the previous dichotomy, i.e., property by shareholders and managers, the third group of owners, the employees, emerged. The labor power they offered consisted partly of their private property and partly, in combination with the other workers, of their collective property. In addition, the workers were collective co-owner of the means of production (capital) in the plant. Andrzej Przestalski calls this kind of economic organization, resulting from the triple property structure of the enterprise, a participatory mode of production. Despite this, as he stresses, in the literature, the prevailing view is that employee participation is a non-property phenomenon.[313] Therefore, it should not be identified with common property analyzed from the property rights theory perspective[314] even though participation is related to this theoretical approach in three main aspects: (1) voting rights; (2) profit and residual rights; (3) net asset rights.[315] In other words, while employee participation may refer to specific participation of employees in the property management, it is not itself a separate form of property.[316]

In the GDR, employee participation was exemplified by employee self-government (*Arbeiterselbstverwaltung*) in state and cooperative enterprises. The

312 M. Koppernock, "Niemiecki model partycypacji. Pracownicy we współzarządzaniu i jako współwłaściciele," *Dialog. Pismo Dialogu Społecznego* No. 3 (26) (2010): 4–5.

313 A. Przestalski, "Własnościowe aspekty partycypacji pracowniczej," *Uniwersyteckie Czasopismo Socjologiczne* No. 8 (2013): 21–22, 24–26, 28, 30. Przestalski discusses, among others, selected theoretical concepts of employee participation and its types. He also argues for not equating with property (according to the economic understanding, consistent with, e.g., the property rights theory) employee participation in company profits or individual property of company shares. On the other hand, the collective property of company shares brings employees closer (although only to a certain extent) to the status of cooperatives (especially with a share exceeding 50 %), which, on the basis of the property rights theory, is an example of common property.

314 Cf. section 5.1. in this study.

315 Spangenberg, *The Institutionalised Transformation*, 91.

316 This problem is pointed out by Maciej Kozłowski, who, in outlining the origins of employee participation, points out that its sources should be sought in the ideas of social solidarity and Christian solidarity. While these approaches proposed a form of co-management, leftist currents (socialist, Marxist) postulated the introduction of a certain type of co-ownership (cf. Kozłowski, *Pracownicza partycypacja finansowa*, 21–23). Nevertheless, Kozłowski considers employee participation as a separate form of property (Kozłowski, *Pracownicza partycypacja finansowa*, *passim*).

director, who represented the company externally, was elected by the employees. This form of management stemmed from the Marxist concept of direct democracy, classless society, and the eventual collapse of a state institution.[317] However, it should be remembered that the participation of cadres in enterprise management was only formal (*de jure* institution). Real decisions were made outside of it and were made by the political authorities within a system of central planning (*de facto* institution).[318]

After World War II, the West German *Mitbestimmung* model oscillated around the idea of social partnership, only to move towards co-management after German reunification. While in the post-war FRG, the state focused on deepening democratization processes, after 1990, it stood guard over respect for competition. After 1945, management in that model aimed to raise the importance of labor, while in reunified Germany, it focused on the "shareholder-value paradigm." In the first period, trade unions played a key political role in the FRG, while after reunification – as part of deeper decentralization processes – they focused on enforcing framework agreements. For the post-war workers, the reconstruction of the country was a special experience, hence the high importance of quality of life, while after 1990, their expectations turned to the process of individualization.[319]

Employee participation was in accordance with the German Basic Law, including Art. 14 GG, which guarantees property rights. In this context, however, the protection of property was an element of respect for the personal freedom of individuals. This protection became weaker when the subject of property was set in the social dimension. This is because of the interests of others ("public good").[320] The beginnings of the *Mitbestimmung* model's spreading after reunification were difficult. In the early 1990s,

317 K. Bolz, H. Clement, D. Lösch, *Wirtschaftssysteme. Marktwirtschaft – Kapitalismus. Planwirtschaft – Sozialismus* (München: Ehrenwirth Verlag, 1978), 96.

318 Cf. section 3.2., Diagram 1 in this work.

319 G. Jackson, "Contested Boundaries: Ambiguity and Creativity in the Evolution of German Codetermination," in *Beyond Continuity. Institutional Change in Advanced Political Economies*, eds. W. Streeck, K. Thelen (New York: Oxford University Press, 2005), 237, table 9.1. More on these processes, see: Jackson, "Contested Boundaries," 236–249. Gregory Jackson's findings on the shareholder-value paradigm cover the period before the 2008 financial crisis. The methodology of management sciences recognizes the importance of the recession at that time for the transformation of the value management concept. See, e.g., A. Jaki, "Prowartościowy paradygmat i koncepcja zarządzania wartością – mechanizmy i obszary ewolucji," *Przegląd Organizacji* No. 1 (2016): 9–15.

320 Cf. the relevant case law of the Federal Constitutional Court on this issue: *Mitbestimmung – eine gute Sache. Alles über die Mitbestimmung und ihre rechtlichen Grundlagen* (Bonn: Bundesministerium für Arbeit und Soziales, 2018), 78. Cf. section 6.1.1.1. in this work.

workers in the new *Länder* showed less personal initiative in their workplaces than their counterparts in Western Germany.[321]

The literature sometimes highlights the negative economic consequences of certain legal regulations on employee participation in Germany. They concern, among others, the costs of its functioning in companies.[322] On the other hand, among the positive effects, the increased productivity of some companies, where the functioning of works councils was studied, is pointed out.[323] The *Mitbestimmung* model contributed to a more attractive wage and personnel policy of the management. It also increased the profitability of selected companies[324]. Works councils reduced labor force fluctuations in some places, influenced higher productivity of large plants, and did not inhibit the innovation activities of companies.[325] However, a significant number of researchers argue that there is still a lack of comprehensive research and resulting conclusive assessments of the economic effects of employee participation in Germany.[326]

6.2.6. Investment level

One of the factors determining the investments of economic entities is the sphere of expectations, which concerns their confidence in the economy. The greater the confidence of potential investors (domestic and foreign) in the institutional conditions of economic life, the higher the level of investment.[327] In turn, the feeling

321 M. Frese, W. Kring, A. Soose, J. Zempel, "Personalinitiative at Work: Differences between East and West Germany," *Academy of Management Journal* No. 39 (1996): 37–63.

322 See, e.g., W. Franz, "Die deutsche Mitbestimmung auf dem Prüfstand: Bilanz und Vorschläge für eine Neuausrichtung," *Zeitschrift für Arbeitsmarkt Forschung/ Journal for Labour Market Research* 38, No. 2/3 (2005): 268–283.

323 U. Jirjahn, "Ökonomische Wirkungen der Mitbestimmung in Deutschland. Überblick über den Stand der Forschung und Perspektiven für zukünftige Studien," *Sozialer Fortschritt* 55, No. 9 (2006): 215–226.

324 U. Jirjahn, "Ökonomische Wirkungen der Mitbestimmung in Deutschland. Ein Update" (working paper), No. 186 (Düsseldorf: Hans-Böckler-Stiftung, 2010).

325 J. T. Addison, C. Schnabel, J. Wagner, "Works Councils in Germany: Their Effects on Establishment Performance," *Oxford Economic Papers* 53, No. 4 (2001): 659–694.

326 The literature on German employee participation is extensive. It was recently collected by Tristan Graefen (T. Graefen, *Bibliographie zur Mitbestimmung. Stand: März 2018* (Düsseldorf: Hans-Böckler-Stiftung, 2018)). An important role in researching and promoting *Mitbestimmung* is played by the German Hans Böckler Foundation (*Hans-Böckler-Stiftung*), which was established in 1977 in Düsseldorf on the initiative of the German Trade Union Confederation (*Deutscher Gewerkschaftsbund*, DGB), the largest trade union federation in the FRG (https://www.boeckler.de (accessed March 18, 2019)).

327 Cf. B. Martinet, *Wywiad gospodarczy. Pozyskiwanie i ochrona informacji* (Warszawa: PWE, 1999), 105; M. Razjer, *Strategie dywersyfikacji przedsiębiorstw*

of such confidence is influenced by, among others, legal regulations on property. In other words, precisely defined property rights in terms of their completeness (both in terms of exclusivity and transferability), as well as enforcement and protection *ceteris paribus*, positively affect the level of investment (domestic and foreign), which in turn promotes economic growth. This is confirmed by numerous empirical studies (especially econometric studies) on specific countries and regions in different historical periods.[328]

(Warszawa: PWE, 2001), 209, 211; S. Fuller, *Knowledge Management Foundation* (Boston: Butterworth-Heinemann, 2002), 17; A. Michalak, *Finansowanie inwestycji w teorii i praktyce* (Warszawa: WN PWN, 2007), 41–43.

328 Some studies also emphasize the importance of other institutions (especially formal, as well as political and economic institutions, though to a lesser extent informal ones) for the level of investment in a particular space-time. See, e.g.: R. C. Kormendi, P. G. Meguire, "Macroeconomic Determinants of Growth: Cross-Country Evidence," *Journal of Monetary Economics* 16, No. 2 (1985): 141–163; K.-J. Kuss, *Rechtliche Rahmenbedingungen für Investitionen in Polen* (Baden-Baden: Nomos Verlagsgesellschaft, 1991); T. Besley, "Property Rights and Investment Incentives: Theory and Evidence from Ghana," *Journal of Political Economy* 103 (1995): 903–937; Knack, Keefer, "Institutions and Economic Performance," 207–227; J. Svensson, "Investment, Property Rights and Political Instability: Theory and Evidence," *European Economic Review* 42, No. 7 (1998): 1317–1341; La Porta, Lopez-de-Silanes, Shleifer, Vishny, "The Quality of Government," 222–279; W. J. Henisz, "The Institutional Environment for Multinational Investment," *Journal of Law, Economics and Organization* 16 (2000): 334–364; M. Olson, *Power and Prosperity: Outgrowing Communist and Capitalist Dictatorships* (New York: Basic Books, 2000); D. Acemoglu, S. Johnson, J. A. Robinson, "The Colonial Origins of Comparative Development: An Empirical Investigation," *American Economic Review* 91, No. 5 (2001): 1369–1401; D. Acemoglu, S. Johnson, J. A. Robinson, "Reversal of Fortune: Geography and Institutions in the Making of the Modern World Income Distribution," *The Quarterly Journal of Economics* 117, No. 4 (2002): 1231–1294; B. Marona, "Bariery realizacji inwestycji zależne od gminy a atrakcyjność inwestycyjna polskich miast," *Studia Ekonomiczne* 155 (2013): 241–251; Owczarczuk, "Atrakcyjność inwestycyjna Polski," 168–180; B. Buczkowski, A. Kuna-Marszałek, "Motywy polskich inwestycji bezpośrednich: przykład przedsiębiorstw z województwa łódzkiego," *Studia i Prace WNEiZ US* 41, No. 2 (2015): 121–133; M. Jaworek, M. Kuczmarska, W. Lizińska, "Kreowanie klimatu inwestycyjnego na rzecz przyciągania inwestorów zagranicznych przez jednostki samorządu terytorialnego w wybranych województwach Polski," *Acta Universitatis Nicolai Copernici. Ekonomia* 47, No. 1 (2016): 53–72. See also a synthetic review of major studies on the importance of institutions for the level of foreign investment: K. Stachowiak, *Instytucjonalne uwarunkowania bezpośrednich inwestycji zagranicznych w Polsce* (Poznań: Bogucki Wydawnictwo Naukowe, 2007), 43–48. Cf. Stachowiak's empirical research on the influence of the institutional environment on the level of direct foreign investment in the countries of Central and Eastern Europe during the transition period: Stachowiak, *Instytucjonalne uwarunkowania*, 49–92. The influence of well-defined and protected property rights on lowering transaction

It follows that in the case of Germany, rising investment rates in certain periods exemplify the increasing quality of property regulations as one of the determinants of investment in the country.[329] Detailed data on gross fixed capital formation in Germany between 1990 and 2015 are presented in Table 24.

Table 24: *Gross fixed capital formation in Germany in 1990–2015 (in billion euros and %)*

Year	Gross fixed capital formation[a]	
	in billion euros	in %, compared to previous year
1990	422.4	+8.0
1991	442.3	+4.7
1992	460.5	+4.1
1993	441.2	−4.2
1994	457.2	+3.6
1995	457.1	−0.0[b]
1996	454.8	−0.5
1997	458.4	+0.8
1998	476.2	+3.9
1999	498.3	+4.6
2000	510.0	+2.3
2001	497.1	−2.5
2002	468.4	−5.8
2003	462.2	−1.3

(*Continued*)

costs and increasing investment is also recognized by legal literature. See, e.g., Dobrzeniecki, Romanowski, *Reprywatyzacja*, 63.

329 Hans-Werner Sinn refers in this context to Ronald H. Coase's theory, which implies that the better the property rights are defined and the lower the transaction costs, the greater the efficiency of a given market (see Coase, *Firma, rynek i prawo*, 10–15). Sinn relates this to the level of investment in Eastern Germany, pointing out that uncertainty about property rights discouraged entities from investing capital in the new federated states (Sinn, "Macroeconomic Aspects of German Unification," 103). Cf. Schnabel, "Structural Adjustment and Privatization," 249–250. See also Spangenberg's polemic on positive transaction costs in the Eastern *Länder*. However, she focuses on the THA activities in the new federated states in the first half of the 1990s (Spangenberg, *The Institutionalised Transformation*, 180).

Table 24: *(Continued)*

Year	Gross fixed capital formation[a]	
	in billion euros	in %, compared to previous year
2004	462.4	+0.0[c]
2005	465.8	+0.7
2006	500.8	+7.5
2007	521.2	+4.1
2008	529.2	+1.5
2009	475.8	−10.1
2010	501.4	+5.4
2011	537.4	+7.2
2012	533.9	−0.7
2013	527.8	−1.1
2014	545.9	+3.4
2015	555.2	+1.7

a Based on adjusted purchase price (amortized cost).
b A rounded negative value higher than −1.0.
c A rounded positive value less than +1.0.
Source: MB BMF, 115, table 6.

The years 1990–1996 were characterized by a relatively constant level of nominal gross fixed capital formation. An average of 447.9 billion euros per year was allocated to investment in that period.[330] Only in comparison with 1989 (391.1 billion euros)[331] the investment growth rate increased in 1990 by as much as 8.0 %. The second half of the 1990s saw a steady increase in investment expenditures. Their level increased from 454.8 billion euros in 1996 to 510 billion euros in 2000. After a few years of decline (2000–2003), which coincided with the implementation of the tax reform of 2000,[332] investments again increased: from 462.2 billion euros in 2003 to 529.2 billion euros in 2008. The financial crisis interrupted this trend. As in other countries, it manifested itself, among other things, in reduced investment outlays. Only in 2008–2009, their value dropped by 10.1 %. The process of increasing the level of investments was resumed after the crisis and continued until the end of the analyzed period, with slight deviations in 2012–2013. In 2015,

330 Own calculations.
331 MB BMF, 115, table 6.
332 More on the 2000 tax reform: para. 6.2.7.1. in this study.

the total value of gross fixed capital formation reached a record level of 555.2 billion euros.

In discussed years, Germany played a key role in the global economy, being the leading supplier of foreign direct investment. The dynamics of their outflows from Germany to other countries were similar to that presented above. In the first half of the 1990s, the level was relatively stable and averaged $21,547.1 million.[333] A sharp increase in this respect took place in the years 1994–1999: from $18,859.4 million to $108,688.4 million (with a slight decline in 1996–1997). After the tax reform of 2000, the level of foreign direct investment outflows dropped significantly to $5,568.1 million in 2003. A renewed growth trend (with a record $169,319.9 million in 2007) was abruptly interrupted by the financial crisis: $71,506.7 million in 2008 and $68,541.0 million in 2009. After a short increase in German foreign direct investment ($125,450.8 million in 2010), it declined again to $42,270.6 million in 2013. The discussed question culminated in an increase of $108,177.3 million in 2015.[334] It should be noted that only between 2007 and 2012 Germany was among the ten countries that located the most foreign direct investment in the world.[335]

The level of investment expenditures *per capita* varied geographically. This was due to the different developmental trajectories of the Western and Eastern *Länder* after German reunification. This is illustrated in Table 25.

333 Own calculations for 1990–1994 based on: "FDI Outflows, by Region and Economy, 1990–2017," World Investment Report 2018, UNCTAD, https://worldinvestmentreport.unctad.org/annex-tables/ (accessed April 9, 2019).

334 "FDI Outflows," https://worldinvestmentreport.unctad.org/annex-tables/ (accessed April 9, 2019).

335 In addition to Germany these were: the United States, Japan, China, Hong Kong, United Kingdom, Canada, Russia, France and Sweden (G. Górniewicz, "Determinanty i konsekwencje bezpośrednich inwestycji zagranicznych," *Studia z Zakresu Prawa, Administracji i Zarządzania UKW* 4 (2013): 63, table 2). On the other hand, there are positions claiming that foreign direct investment flowing into Germany has not played a significant role in bridging the development gap between the Western and Eastern *Länder*. For example, only in 1998–2001, a total of DM 6.7 billion in foreign direct investment was realized in the FRG, which accounted for only 5 % of annual investment in the manufacturing sector. In addition, macroeconomic conditions for the inflow of foreign direct investment to Germany are considered unfavorable (B. Brocka-Palacz, "Zjednoczenie Niemiec – bilans po 25 latach," *Zeszyty Naukowe Uczelni Vistula* No. 48 (3) (2016): 32).

Table 25: *Investment expenditures per capita in Germany in 1991–2015 (in euros, current prices)*

Year	Investment in the economy *per capita*				Investment in the processing sector *per capita*			
	New equipment		New buildings		New equipment		New buildings	
	New *Länder*[a]	Western Germany[b]	New *Länder*	Western Germany	New *Länder*	Western Germany	New *Länder*	Western Germany
1991	1,466	2,883	1,834	2,543	–	–	–	–
1992	1,694	2,806	2,980	2,744	–	–	–	–
1993	1,840	2,445	3,931	2,711	–	–	–	–
1994	2,053	2,371	5,040	2,805	–	–	–	–
1995	2,140	2,384	5,185	2,794	534	899	174	63
1996	2,185	2,453	4,847	2,676	565	918	141	69
1997	2,127	2,571	4,637	2,624	562	953	110	61
1998	2,278	2,797	4,256	2,742	571	1,032	94	74
1999	2,395	3,013	3,975	2,840	582	1,102	74	78
2000	2,497	3,276	3,562	2,860	605	1,148	78	81
2001	2,172	3,336	2,983	2,823	708	1,200	91	81
2002	1,863	3,194	2,722	2,669	588	1,148	63	70
2003	1,798	3,140	2,711	2,607	569	1,146	46	61
2004	1,992	3,209	2,560	2,554	652	1,114	104	53
2005	2,013	3,338	2,432	2,476	646	1,091	71	54
2006	2,264	3,625	2,389	2,730	728	1,155	72	60

Year	**Investment in the economy *per capita***				**Investment in the processing sector *per capita***			
	New equipment		**New buildings**		**New equipment**		**New buildings**	
	New *Länder*[a]	**Western Germany[b]**	**New *Länder***	**Western Germany**	**New *Länder***	**Western Germany**	**New *Länder***	**Western Germany**
2007	2,474	3,906	2,522	2,866	792	1,277	92	80
2008	2,572	4,052	2,554	2,968	821	1,351	101	88
2009	2,127	3,461	2,552	2,901	689	1,182	67	67
2010	2,490	3,694	2,528	3,065	753	1,199	64	56
2011	2,636	3,964	2,664	3,482	873	1,332	94	67
2012	2,659	3,916	2,834	3,541	844	1,397	83	85
2013	2,577	3,889	2,709	3,623	790	1,383	71	90
2014	2,681	4,113	2,811	3,770	750	1,462	65	97
2015	2,702	4,336	2,735	3,747	784	1,517	72	96

a *Neue Länder* – the area of the former GDR (1949–1990) without Berlin; the new federated states: Brandenburg, Mecklenburg-Vorpommern, Saxony, Saxony-Anhalt and Thuringia.
b *Westdeutschland* – the area of the former FRG (1949–1990) without Berlin.
Source: *Jahresbericht der Bundesregierung zum Stand der Deutschen Einheit 2018* (Berlin: Der Beauftragte der Bundesregierung für die neuen Bundesländer, Bundesministerium für Wirtschaft und Energie, 2018) (hereinafter: JB BR SDE), 94, table 1.4.

Table 25 clearly shows the worse position of the Eastern *Länder* in terms of investment expenditures *per capita*, generally with the exception of new buildings in the manufacturing sector.[336] Also, between 1992 and 2004, *per capita* investment in new buildings in the overall economy was higher in Eastern Germany, reflecting the modernization of the economy there. Rising investment in the Eastern federated states in the 1990s was a consequence of the implementation of West German property rights and the convergence effect. Subsequent fluctuations in these amounts were largely in line with the dynamics of investment in the Western *Länder* and were due to other endogenous (e.g. government economic policy) or exogenous reasons (e.g. the economic advantage of the old federated states, economic fluctuations).[337] These transformations were similar to the trends in gross fixed capital formation and outflows of foreign direct investment from Germany in the period discussed above.

After reunification, the federal authorities were forced to pursue a pro-investment policy, especially in Eastern Germany. This included the promotion of both public and private investment.[338] In the latter case, (re-)privatization legislation played a fundamental role.[339] Investments were one of the key exceptions to the general broad re-privatization formula applied in German law and based on property restitution. The *Property Law*, passed on September 23, 1990, allowed claims to be disregarded when the purpose or use of the real estate had been substantially changed through appropriate financial expenditures, thus serving the general public, and when the real estate had been acquired by a public person or organization (e.g., a religious organization) in "an honest manner" (*in redlicher Weise).* Petitioners then got compensation.[340] The *Law on Special Investments in the German Democratic Republic* of September 23 provided for the payment of compensation, instead of direct restitution, to estates with special investment purposes

336 This situation may have resulted from the fact that the industry in the Eastern *Länder* was, as Bogumiła Brocka-Palacz puts it, "an extended production line of Western German factories" (Pol. *przedłużoną taśmą produkcyjną fabryk zachodnioniemieckich*) (B. Brocka-Palacz, *Wspieranie rozwoju gospodarki wschodniej części Niemiec – zamierzenia, instrumenty, efekty* (Warszawa: IGŚ SGH, 2008), 7). Moreover, according to Joanna Czech-Rogosz, manufacturing was the most dynamic sector in the Eastern federated states in 1990–2002 (Czech-Rogosz, "Gospodarka wschodnich Niemiec w 12 lat po zjednoczeniu," 94, 96–97, figure 2). Branches of Western German enterprises which were located in the Eastern *Länder* in the period in question belonged mainly to the processing sector (Zawilska-Florczuk, Ciechanowicz, *Jeden kraj, dwa społeczeństwa?*, 60).

337 Cf. JB BR SDE, 95.

338 Henning, *Das industrialisierte Deutschland*, 323–324.

339 More on privatization and re-privatization legislation, see: section 6.2.1. in this study.

340 *Gesetz zur Regelung offener Vermögensfragen* (BGBl., Part II, 1990, No. 35, 1159–1167).

(*Besondere Investitionszwecke*).[341] Disappointments with the functioning of these regulations (above all with regard to their restrictiveness, the complexity of the administrative procedures and a large number of claims) did not initiate increased investment and consequently triggered the need for new regulations. On March 22, 1991, the *Law on the Removal of Barriers to the Privatization of Enterprises and the Promotion of Investment* was passed. It provided investors with a significant advantage over those applying for restitution of property.[342] The new regulation contributed to an increase in the pace of privatization and investment. However, the effects were not satisfactory. The regulation was supplemented by the *Law on Priority for Investments in the Case of Claims for Reassignment under the Property Law* of July 14, 1992. It further strengthened the legal position of investors.[343] Noteworthy are the quick and effective responses of the federal authorities to resolve (re-)privatization issues, which were important for increasing certainty of property rights for future investors in the new federated states. Successive amendments or completely new regulations have gradually clarified the complexity of the matter. They also strengthened the interests of investors at the expense of former owners or their heirs.[344]

Another dimension of the federal government's pro-investment policy was the various programs to initiate investment and the establishment of new enterprises. The first group included programs to encourage the inflow of foreign capital (*ERP-Regionalförderprogramm, KfW-Unternehmerkredit, Bürgschaften und Rückbürgschaften des Bundes*), to support domestic capital (*ERP-Beteiligungsprogramm, Mezzanin-Dachfonds für Deutschland* (MDD), *Mikromezzaninfonds Deutschland, Rückgarantien des Bundes, High-Tech Gründerfonds, Coparion-Fonds*) and grants (*Bund-Länder-Gemeinschaftsaufgabe «Verbesserung der regionalen Wirtschaftsstruktur»* (GRW)).

The second group consisted of programs that facilitated the establishment of new enterprises. This consisted of three subgroups. Firstly, there were strategies that involved receiving direct funding. These were divided into those addressed to foreign capital (*ERP-Gründerkredit (StartGeld/Universell), ERP-Kapital für Gründungen, Mikrokreditfonds Deutschland*), German capital (most programs), including share capital, and innovation (*Coparion-Fonds, ERP/EIF-Dachfonds,*

341 *Gesetz über besondere Investitionen in der Deutschen Demokratischen Republik* (BGBl., Part II, 1990, No. 35, 1157–1158).

342 *Gesetz zur Beseitigung von Hemmnissen bei der Privatisierung von Unternehmen und zur Förderung* (BGBl., Part I, 1991, No. 20, 766–789).

343 *Gesetz über den Vorrang für Investitionen bei Rückübertragungsansprüchen nach dem Vermögensgesetz* (BGBl., Part I, 1992, No. 33, 1268–1275).

344 Falkowska, "Restytucja, odszkodowanie czy inwestycje?," 272–282; Moszyńska, Moszyński, "Reprywatyzacja a konflikt interesów ekonomicznych jednostek i państwa," 129. Cf. Southern, "Restitution or Compensation," 436–449; Frank, "Privatization in Eastern Germany," 809–868; Spangenberg, *The Institutionalised Transformation*, 143.

Mikromezzaninfonds, European Angels Fonds (EAF), *High-Tech Gründerfonds, INVEST – Zuschuss für Wagniskapital, ERP-Digitalisierungs- und Innovationskredit*) and others (*Bürgschaftsbanken, Gründungszuschuss nach dem SGB III*). Secondly, some of the programs were in the area of knowledge and practical assistance for new entrepreneurs (*EXIST, Förderung der Beratungen von Handwerksunternehmen durch Kammern und Fachverbände, Förderung unternehmerischen Know-hows, German Accelerator Program*). Thirdly, there were strategies including support in areas such as strengthening entrepreneurial attitudes (*Gründerwettbewerb – «Digitale Innovationen», Initiative «Unternehmergeist in Schulen», Gründerwoche Deutschland*), enterprise succession (*Nexxt-Initiative Unternehmensnachfolge mit Nachfolgebörse)* and others (*Programme zur Gründungsunterstützung der großen Forschungsorganisationen*).[345]

The sources of funding for the above programs were diversified: the federal budget, budgets of the Western *Länder*, the Trust Office, the "German Unity" Fund (*Fonds "Deutsche Einheit,"* operating in 1990–1994, with total transfers of 82.2 billion euros), solidarity packages (the first one in 1995–2004 with a value of approximately 105 billion euros and the second one in 2005–2019 with a value of 156.5 billion euros), the solidarity tax, the social security system, the budget of the Federal Employment Office, funds granted to the FRG as part of the Marshall Plan, and structural funds of the European Communities (the EU since 1993). Most of the transfers came from the federal budget, within which a fund for the "reconstruction of the East" (*Aufbau Ost*) was set aside. Its purpose was to reconstruct and develop the Eastern German economy and institutions.[346]

An additional manifestation of the restructuring of the Eastern German economy[347] was transformations in the sectoral distribution of investment expenditures. Details for 1991–2005 are presented in Table 26.

---

345 JB BR SDE, 20–23. Cf. also programs supporting innovation, research, internationalization of German entrepreneurship, economic clusters, and digital transition: JB BR SDE, pp. 23–31. For example, Brocka-Palacz points to a different classification of the most important support instruments in Germany as a whole, although this was particularly important for the convergence of the Eastern *Länder*. The criterion for division are the support areas: (1) productive investments; (2) infrastructure; (3) science and innovation, education, environmental protection and others. A separate type of support instruments are funds from the collection of a special tax, solidarity surcharge (Brocka-Palacz, *Wspieranie rozwoju gospodarki wschodniej części Niemiec*, 14–24). More on the solidarity tax, see section 6.2.7.1. in this work.

346 Brocka-Palacz, *Wspieranie rozwoju gospodarki wschodniej części Niemiec*, 15; Zawilska-Florczuk, Ciechanowicz, *Jeden kraj, dwa społeczeństwa?*, 54–56, figure 8; Moszyński, "Transformacja systemowa wschodnich Niemiec," 223, table 3; Pastuszka, "Polityka rozwoju Wschodnich Niemiec," 59–63.

347 More on the restructuring of the former GDR's economy, see section 6.2.3. in this work.

Table 26: *Investments in new plants in selected economic sectors in the FRG Eastern Länder in selected years 1991–2005 (in billion euros)*

Economic sector	Year								
	1991	**1993**	**1995**	**1997**	**1999**	**2001**	**2002**	**2003**	**2004**	**2005**
Total sectors	**50.9**	**85.2**	**105.5**	**96.2**	**88.4**	**76.1**	**68.7**	**66.9**	**67.2**	**65.3**
Manufacturing sector	14.4	21.7	21.2	16.9	15.5	14.3	12.4	11.5	12.4	11.6
Processing sector	9.5	12.4	10.9	9.7	9.5	10.3	8.9	8.6	9.6	8.9
Construction sector	2.4	3.2	2.2	1.5	1.3	1.0	0.8	0.7	0.6	0.6
Services	35.8	62.5	82.8	78.1	71.5	60.5	55.1	54.2	53.7	52.5

Source: Busch, Kühn, Steinitz, *Schrumpfung und Entwicklung in Ostdeutschland*, 68, table 9.

It should be noted that the largest part of investment expenditures in the Eastern *Länder* in 1991–2005 was occupied by services (from 70.3 % to 80.4 %). A particular development of services occurred in the first half of the 1990s, along with a nominal increase in investment outlays for individual sectors in Eastern Germany. After 1995, the amount of expenditures on services decreased along with the level of total investment expenditures, although the service sector still clearly dominated in the structure of investment funds. Other sectors, which were particularly crucial for the structure of the GDR economy, became increasingly less important as investment expenditures decreased. The share of the manufacturing sector in the structure of investments in 1991–2005 decreased from 28.3 % to 17.8 %. In the case of the processing sector, it decreased from 18.7 % to 13.6 %, and in the construction sector from 4.7 % to 0.9 %.[348] These changes may suggest a progressive modernization of the Eastern German economy.

Deepening the analysis, however, reveals significant gaps in the modernization process, which in turn slowed down the convergence of the two parts of Germany. This is evident from Table 27.

Table 27: *Investments in new plants in selected economic sectors in the FRG Eastern German Länder (with East Berlin) in selected years 1992–2005 (in %, compared to previous year)*

Economic sector	Year									
	1992	**1993**	**1995**	**1997**	**1999**	**2001**	**2002**	**2003**	**2004**	**2005**
Total sectors	**38.4**	**21.1**	**3.0**	**–4.5**	**–3.4**	**–9.2**	**–9.7**	**–2.7**	**0.5**	**–2.8**
Manufacturing sector	39.3	7.9	–2.6	–15.3	–3.1	–1.3	–13.8	–6.9	7.5	–6.2
Processing sector	15.9	12.5	–13.6	–7.3	1.7	6.3	–14.0	–2.8	11.3	–6.7
Construction sector	24.7	4.0	–32.0	–22.0	1.5	–20.8	–20.0	–12.6	–8.1	–5.0
Services	52.8	36.2	8.4	4.0	–6.2	–11.0	–9.0	–1.6	–0.9	–2.2

Source: Busch, Kühn, Steinitz, *Schrumpfung und Entwicklung in Ostdeutschland*, 69, table 10.

Although the modernization of the Eastern German economy may be evidenced by a systematic decline in the shares of the manufacturing, processing, and construction sectors in total investment expenditures, it turns out that the growth of the last one has gradually declined. This also applied to services. The percentage change in outlays for this sector compared to the previous year was lower and

348 Own calculations based on Table 26.

lower. To sum up, although the restructuring process set the right direction for the development of the Eastern *Länder*'s economy, the scope and intensity of these transformations were insufficient. Although indicators of investment *per capita* for selected groups of outlays look promising for the period in question, significant differences can still be seen in comparison with the old federated states. Details in this regard are shown in Table 28.

Table 28: *Ratios of some investment groups per capita in the FRG Eastern German Länder in selected years 1991–2005 (Western Länder = 100)*

Investment group	**Year**									
	1991	**1993**	**1995**	**1997**	**1999**	**2001**	**2002**	**2003**	**2004**	**2005**
New equipment	58.9	89.0	103.2	92.2	87.8	84.1	84.3	83.6	85.2	85.7
Construction	71.4	137.5	175.4	161.5	129.2	103.5	98.2	94.4	92.4	95.9
Capital resources	34.8	40.6	48.0	55.1	61.1	65.8	67.3	68.4	68.6	70.7

Source: Busch, Kühn, Steinitz, *Schrumpfung und Entwicklung in Ostdeutschland*, 70, table 11.

In the area of new equipment and construction, *per capita* investment in the new *Länder* exceeded the Western German level by several times. This was the result of the then culmination of financial transfers to the new federated states and the development of the construction sector, which was important for the local economy. Since the end of the 1990s, spending on new equipment has stabilized at approximately 85.1 % of the Western German level. Much more important for the modernization of the former GDR's economy, investments in capital resources have taken a relatively stable level of 67.0 % of such expenditures in the old federated states since the late 1990s.[349] According to more recent data, gross investment in production plants *per capita* in the Eastern *Länder* increased between 1991 and 2015 from 61.0 % to 71.0 % of the Western German level. In contrast, capital resources investment *per capita* increased from 45.0 % to 80.0 % of the old *Länder*'s level over the same period.[350] These statistics support the thesis that the convergence process between the two parts of Germany had not been completed by 2015 and was stagnating for a prolonged period.

One of the positive results of investments in the new *Länder* was the development of innovative branches of the economy there. This even fits into the broader development strategy of the Eastern federated states advocated by some

349 Own calculations.

350 *Wirtschaftsdaten neue Länder*, 26, table 4.3.

economists in the 1990s. The "high-wage, high-tech strategy" was dependent primarily on state transfers and, to a lesser extent, on associations and private enterprises. It relied on a rapid realignment of wages in the Eastern *Länder* relative to the Western federated states. Since this wage growth would exceed the productivity growth of Eastern German production, more public funds would be needed. These could be used for investments to intensify production in Eastern Germany and for the payment of social benefits there to even out wage differences or to help the unemployed. An important role was to be played here by investments in modern technologies (although not exclusively) to replace the often obsolete equipment of the Eastern German industry. It would also be important to increase the Horndal effect, i.e. the increase in employee productivity due to learning by doing. According to this strategy, the effect would be the production of high-quality goods. This would be combined with an increased income elasticity of demand. In parallel, private investment would be stimulated. The sequence of these factors would lead to favorable export performance and high economic growth. The opposite strategy – the "low-wage, low-tech strategy" – would produce low-quality goods and lower the income elasticity of demand. This would hinder economic growth and, consequently, the process of convergence of the Eastern and Western *Länder*.[351]

The importance of high technology in industry was already recognized in the GDR. It turns out that in 1991 the share of "high-tech and medium-tech" in the

351 T. Lange, G. Pugh, "Catching Up with the West: The Achievements and Limitations of Creative Destruction," in Hölscher, Hochberg *East Germany's Economic Development since Unification*, 141–160, especially 155, figure 9.1. The "high-wage, high-tech strategy" was described in 1992 by Gerlinde Sinn and Hans-Werner Sinn as an alternative for the development of the Eastern *Länder* after German reunification. They also pointed to the possibility of basing development on a "maintenance strategy" and an "organic system transformation" strategy. The first one would involve keeping wages low in order to maintain employment in Eastern Germany at the current level. Due to the deepening phenomenon of migration from the Eastern to Western *Länder* and the slowdown in economic growth and convergence, this strategy, according to Sinn and Sinn, could not be effective. The "organic system transformation," on the other hand, was to be a compromise and involve a gradual transformation of the price structure, which would follow the gradual transformation of the production model. Wages in this strategy would remain higher than in the "maintenance strategy," but lower than in the "high-wage, high-tech strategy." Sinn and Sinn favored the last model (cf. Sinn, Sinn, *Jumpstart*, 141–168). There are analyzes of income (wage) convergence in the Eastern and Western *Länder* in 1991–2015. The new federated states were then characterized by higher growth dynamics in this regard (M. Götz, "Konwergencja dochodów," 93–114; S. Pastuszka, "Zmiany w spójności gospodarczej i społecznej niemieckich landów w latach 2000–2015," *Studia Prawno-Ekonomiczne* 107 (2018): 348–350). This is typical of the catch-up effect.

industry of the Eastern *Länder* (57.9 %) did not differ from, and even exceeded a similar share in highly industrialized countries in 1990: West Germany (55 %), Japan (55 %), the United States (51 %), France (47 %), United Kingdom (44 %) and Italy (40 %).[352] In 1994, the share of high and medium technology in Eastern German industry was 65 %.[353] This resulted positively to exports there in the first years of the transition.[354]

Indeed, after reunification, one can notice the significant position of modern branches of the economy in the investment structure in the Eastern *Länder*. Just in 1991–1994, when the growth of investment in the enterprise sector was 93 %, the following industries were the most successful: housing (182 %), utilities (96 %), transport and communications (65 %), agriculture, forestry and fishing (58 %) and construction (53 %).[355]

However, the literature from the 1990s does not lack positions that research and development expenditures in Eastern Germany at that time were still significantly lower than in the old federated states. For example, in 1992, research and development expenditures in the Eastern German chemical industry amounted to 1.6 % of such funds for the whole of the FRG, in the engineering industry – 6.6 %, in the automotive industry – 0.3 %, in electrical engineering – 2.4 %, in precision mechanics and optics – 5.6 %. At that time, total research and development spending in the industrial sector in the Eastern *Länder* did not exceed 2.4 % of the funds for Germany as a whole.[356] According to some researchers, this was a sign of "structural weakness" in the new federated states. This was a consequence of, e.g., the closure or privatization of research centers at failing large industrial plants in Eastern Germany and the opening of only branches of Western German enterprises in the Eastern *Länder* with laboratories located in their parent centers.[357]

In later years, the importance of innovative branches for the Eastern German economy's development grew. Renewable energy sources (bioenergy, wind, solar,

---

352 Lange, Pugh, "Catching Up with the West," 148–149, tables 9.3–9.4. The distinction between high, medium, and low technology was taken from the OECD classification (Lange, Pugh, "Catching Up with the West," 146–147, table 9.1).

353 Lange, Pugh, "Catching Up with the West," 156–157, table 9.6.

354 See more: Lange, Pugh, "Catching Up with the West," 156–160, tables 9.7–9.8, figure 9.2. Cf. Hitchens, Wagner, Birnie, *East German Productivity and the Transition to the Market Economy*, 102. The GDR industry strengthened the potential of the East German economy, which distinguished the country from other countries of the former Eastern Bloc and facilitated the subsequent transition (Sinn, "Macroeconomic Aspects of German Unification," 83).

355 Lange, Pugh, "Catching Up with the West," 156, table 9.5. Cf. Pastuszka, "Polityka rozwoju Wschodnich Niemiec," 64.

356 Myant, Fleischer, Hornschild, Vintrová, Zeman, Souček, *Successful Transformations?*, 89, table 3.1.

357 Myant, Fleischer, Hornschild, Vintrová, Zeman, Souček, *Successful Transformations?*, 85–91.

geothermal, hydroelectric energy) occupied an important place. For example, in the first decade of the 21st century, the solar industry employed about 10,000 people in the new federated states, producing more than 75 % of the total solar modules in the whole of Germany. The main source of financing for these investments funded from the second solidarity package. In the period in question, investments (often co-financed by the federal budget or the Western *Länder*'s budgets) also covered the construction sector (especially in the first half of the 1990s), the banking sector, and, at the beginning of the 21st century, the industrial and service sectors. Thriving industrial centers have developed in the Southern group of the Eastern *Länder*: Thuringia, Saxony, and Saxony-Anhalt (similar to Western Germany). This coincided with the division of the country into a richer (industrial) South and a poorer (agricultural) North. However, the new *Länder* were dominated by branches of enterprises located in the old federated states. Outlays on research and development increased slightly and were still much lower than in Western Germany. This resulted negatively in the level of enterprises innovation in the East, hampering the economic growth of the region.[358] In addition, the clusters of Eastern German industrial enterprises in urban agglomerations, although growing in quantitative terms after 1990, were still characterized by a relatively low level of production quality compared to the Western *Länder*, especially in terms of innovation.[359]

358 Busch, Kühn, Steinitz, *Schrumpfung und Entwicklung in Ostdeutschland*, 61–66; Zawilska-Florczuk, Ciechanowicz, *Jeden kraj, dwa społeczeństwa?*, 7, 70–73. Some researchers see in increased investment in modern economic sectors a development opportunity for the Eastern *Länder* after 2015. This would support the continuation and deepening of the convergence process (see, e.g.: Brocka-Palacz, "Zjednoczenie Niemiec," 32, 36; Moszyński, "Zjednoczenie Niemiec," 265–266). Cf. T. Hellmann, M. Kullas, "Das ökonomische Innovationsregime der Bundesländer im föderalen Deutschland," in *Handbuch Föderalismus – Föderalismus als demokratische Rechtsordnung und Rechtskultur in Deutschland, Europa und der Welt*, Vol. II: *Probleme, Reformen, Perspektiven des deutschen Föderalismus*, ed. I. Härtel (Berlin–Heidelberg: Springer-Verlag, 2012, 137–163).

359 M. T. W. Rosenfeld, P. Franz, G. Heimpold, "Economic 'Clusters' in East Germany: Evidence on the Location and Characteristics of Spatially Concentrated Industries," *Post-Communist Economies* 19, No. 1 (2007): 73–93. Cf. R. Sternberg, T. Litzenberger, "Regional Clusters in Germany – Their Geography and Their Relevance for Entrepreneurial Activities," *European Planning Studies* 12, No. 6 (2004): 767–791; K.-H. Röhl, P. von Speicher, *Ostdeutschland 20 Jahre nach dem Mauerfall. Ist die Investitionsförderung Triebfeder von Industriewachstum und regionaler Entwicklung?* (Köln: Deutscher Instituts-Verlag, 2009), especially 11–12, figures 2–3; 13–18. On the other hand, there is a view in the literature that the convergence of the two German regions can be fostered by the agglomerations' development or, more broadly, urbanization processes and the promotion of settlement in urban centers (see, e.g., J. Ragnitz, "Angleichung der Lebensverhältnisse in Ostdeutschland: Eine regional differenzierte Analyse," *ifo Dresden berichtet* 16, No. 4 (2009): 28–38).

Investments in the new federated states accounted for a significant part of Western Germany's financial transfers, amounting to around 4 % of the old *Länder*'s GDP annually in the 1990s and the first years of the 21st century. However, the dominant share in the structure of this financial support's spending in 1991–1999 was recorded in social benefits (from 45.4 % to 54.0 %), while investments (funds for economic infrastructure and economic support) – from 14.7 % to 21.1 %. Some researchers indicate that this share may have reached a maximum of 25 % in the 1990s, which is assessed as insufficient in terms of accelerating convergence.[360]

360 Own calculations based on: Brocka-Palacz, *Wspieranie rozwoju gospodarki wschodniej części Niemiec*, 13–14, table 7. Brocka-Palacz also draws attention to the strong structural links between the economies of Western and Eastern Germany after reunification and the dependence of the new federated states on the economic situation in Western Germany (Brocka-Palacz, *Wspieranie rozwoju gospodarki wschodniej części Niemiec*, 5, 7, 13, 25–26). In the literature (regardless of the length of the period studied) there are extremely different estimates of the size of investment outlays. According to some data, between 1991 and 1998, public investments and investment grants accounted for 25.2 % of gross transfers for the Eastern *Länder* (Pastuszka, "Polityka rozwoju Wschodnich Niemiec," 60, table 2. Sławomir Pastuszka cites various German estimates of the transfers' amounts in specific years). Other calculations indicate that between 1990 and 2009, of the total sum of 1.3 trillion euros in transfers, only around 10 % was earmarked for investment (Zawilska-Florczuk, Ciechanowicz, *Jeden kraj, dwa społeczeństwa?*, 56). Similar controversies concern the amount of social funds. Pastuszka points out that problems with an unambiguous calculation of the transfers' size to the new federated states result from several reasons. Firstly, financial aid had different sources and forms. Secondly, there were as many as two currency reforms in the analyzed period: in 1990, the West German mark was introduced in the GDR, and in 2002 the euro replaced the DM. In turn, the ECU (European Currency Unit), the unit of account in the EU countries, was used until 1998 (more on German integration into the eurozone see, e.g., P. Albiński, M. Chrzanowski, "Dochodzenie do euro: studium przypadków gospodarki niemieckiej i austriackiej," *Bank i Kredyt* No. 8 (2008): 3–25). Thirdly, in 1999, the federal authorities stopped publishing official reports on the costs of convergence. This was justified, among other things, by the unjustifiability of summing up transfers' amounts due to the dynamics of relations between different types of personnel and material costs and inflation (Pastuszka, "Polityka rozwoju Wschodnich Niemiec," 59–60). Another important reason, which was the political-propaganda context, cannot be excluded. The federal authorities may have been unwilling to disclose the real size of transfers in the face of effects that did not meet initial expectations. Regardless of the size of the already high financial aid to the Eastern *Länder* in 1990–2015, it reached its peak in 1995. Total transfers were 1/3 of the former GDR's GDP then. After 1995, the flows gradually decreased (Pastuszka, "Polityka rozwoju Wschodnich Niemiec," 60). See also: U. Busch, *Am Tropf. Die ostdeutsche Transfergesellschaft* (Berlin: trafo verlag, 2002).

Ulrich Busch distinguished four levels of financial transfer flows. The first one included taxes and contributions paid by contributors in Western Germany. The second level referred to intermediary financing institutions. These were primarily: the Federation, special federal budgets, the Western *Länder* and municipalities, the EU, the Federal Employment Agency (*Bundesagentur für Arbeit*), and pension benefits (Western bodies). In the third level, he included intermediate recipient institutions, especially: local authorities in the *Länder*, unemployment insurance, and pension benefits (Eastern bodies). The fourth level consisted of the direct disbursement of funds in the East according to general and specific criteria. This included private households, enterprises, companies based in Western Germany or abroad, and recipients of transfers and tax credits.[361]

In the early 1990s, Western German transfers were financed mainly with loans, which had a negative effect on public finances. In the second half of the 1990s, as much as 2/3 of net transfers were spent on social expenses.[362] Furthermore, some of the new federated states misused the allocated funds, which gave rise to political controversies.[363]

The economic development of Eastern Germany was in the interest of the old federated states and the country as a whole. It stimulated prosperity in the West in a Keynesian sense. The intensification of development in the former GDR and the consequent stimulation of demand there encouraged investments in Western Germany, which in turn created new jobs, expanded services, and boosted consumption. The emigration from the Eastern part of Germany ensured an influx of skilled labor force in the West. New development strategies were implemented in the Eastern *Länder*, including modern manufacturing industries. During the

361 Busch, *Am Tropf*, 139–145, figures 3.1.-1.–3.1.-5.

362 Czech-Rogosz, "Gospodarka wschodnich Niemiec w 12 lat po zjednoczeniu," 99–100. Cf. Zawilska-Florczuk, Ciechanowicz, *Jeden kraj, dwa społeczeństwa?*, pp. 54, 56; Brocka-Palacz, "Zjednoczenie Niemiec," 31. This problem was compounded by the fact that the amount of financial assistance depended on the number of a given Eastern federated state's residents. In the 1990s, the Eastern *Länder* were constantly depopulated. This was a consequence of declining population growth and the residents' emigration (mainly the young and well-educated persons) to the Western *Länder* (Czech-Rogosz, "Gospodarka wschodnich Niemiec w 12 lat po zjednoczeniu," 98, 100). Another criterion for the allocation of aid was the level of economic development of a given federated state (Pastuszka, "Polityka rozwoju Wschodnich Niemiec," 60).

363 For example, in 2003, Thuringia spent 32.5 % of the funds not as planned, Brandenburg – 54.8 %, Saxony-Anhalt – 66.6 %, Mecklenburg-Vorpommern – 71.3 %, Berlin (as a federated state) – 100 % (Zawilska-Florczuk, Ciechanowicz, *Jeden kraj, dwa społeczeństwa?*, 55–56). Brocka-Palacz notes that around 2005, thanks to Western German transfers, the Eastern *Länder* produced only 16 % of GDP, excluding administration and social security (Brocka-Palacz, "Zjednoczenie Niemiec," 34. See also: Brocka-Palacz, "Zjednoczenie Niemiec," 37–38).

privatization period, the THA preferred Western German investors to foreign ones. The gradual increase in GDP *per capita* in the new federated states contributed to improvements in the FRG's public finances. Supporting the development of the former GDR strengthened Germany's position in the world economy, which had been relatively weakened by the costs of reunification. It was, therefore, necessary to take into account the developmental differences between concrete Eastern *Länder*, to use their potential, and to eliminate the problems of internal social unification. Social dissatisfaction could result, among other things, in the increased popularity of extreme political groups. Trade unions from Western Germany were very influential in the East. One of their goals was to strive for higher wages to curb emigration to the old *Länder*.[364]

There are econometric studies that confirm the high quality of institutions – especially formal (political) ones – in Germany after reunification and their influence on investment levels. Among these, the importance of property rights is highlighted. For example, some cross-sectional analyzes for the second half of the 20th century (up to 1989) see a positive impact of measures of property rights enforcement and protection on economic growth and investment level. Moreover, there is a positive relationship between the quality of property rules and the efficiency of investment expenditures.[365] This is important because the well-functioning property rules in the FRG were implemented in the former GDR after 1990. The increase in investment rates in Germany (especially Eastern Germany) immediately after reunification (in the first half of the 1990s) was due to the positive effects of the new *Länder*'s inclusion in the Western German property regime. The dynamics of investment in later years were rather a consequence of other circumstances (both internal and external).

In the years 1990–2015, there were no significant changes in the property rights regulation, with the exception of their implementation in the new *Länder* after reunification and privatization and re-privatization legislation. Therefore, it can be assumed that the above statements resulting from the quantitative analysis of the problem in question are also valid for the second half of the 1990s and the first two decades of the 21st century.

At the same time, one should notice regularity in the fact that investment expenditures in 1990–2015 were higher in the Western *Länder* than in the Eastern ones. This represented more developed private entrepreneurship in the old federated states. This, in turn, was due to informal institutions. Earlier property regulations and its structure in the FRG in 1949–1990 emphasized the importance

---

364 W. R. Smyser, *The Economy of United Germany. Colossus at the Crossroads* (New York: St. Martin's Press, 1992), 164–168; Busch, Kühn, Steinitz, *Schrumpfung und Entwicklung in Ostdeutschland*, 149–157.

365 Cf. cross-sectional studies for the second half of the 20th century (before German reunification): Knack, Keefer, "Institutions and Economic Performance," 207–227, especially 220–224, tables 5–6.

of private property, fostering the development of individualistic attitudes (related, e.g., to the risks arising from investments), while the legal and structural domination of social (state and cooperative) property in the GDR sanctioned and developed behaviors in the spirit of collectivism (communitarianism).[366] Consequently, the clear differences in the size of investment outlays in the Western and Eastern *Länder* in 1990–2015 were attempted to be bridged by the federal authorities on the basis of special programs to support investment and the creation of new enterprises. During the period in question, these measures – although partially effective – were not fully successful.

6.2.7. Taxes

6.2.7.1. Overview of main property taxes

At this point, it is worthwhile to make at least a cursory review of the most important taxes on property that were in force in Germany in 1990–2015. Some of the regulations based on which certain taxes were levied were enacted before the period under analysis. It should also be mentioned that property is understood here in a broad sense and includes everything that is at an individual's disposal (income, purchased goods and services, movable and immovable property). This corresponds to the property rights theory, which defines it as a bundle of the owner's rights to a specific material or non-material good.[367] This, in turn, is subject to taxation by the state.

Between 1990 and 2015, the German tax system distinguished three groups of levies based on the subject of taxation. These were: turnover taxes, consumption taxes, and property taxes.

The turnover taxes (*Verkehrsteuer*) belonging to the first group concerned the transfer of property of goods (e.g., through sale) or the performance of certain legal acts (e.g., the provision of services). The most important among them were: value added tax, land transfer tax, and insurance tax.

Value-added tax (VAT, *Umsatzsteuer*) was paid as a consequence of the purchase of goods and services. Its legal basis was the law of July 26, 1918,[368] amended in 1979 and 2005.[369]

Land transfer tax (*Grunderwerbsteuer*) was paid by those who purchased real estate. Its rate depended on the location of the acquired property. Details were

---

366 Cf. Moszyński, "Transformacja systemowa wschodnich Niemiec," 232–234.

367 See section 5.1. in this study.

368 *Umsatzsteuergesetz. Vom 26. Juli 1918.* (RGBl., 1918, No. 95/6399, 779–797).

369 *Gesetz zur Neufassung des Umsatzsteuergesetzes und zur Änderung anderer Gesetze Vom 26. November 1979* (BGBl., Part I, 1979, No. 69, 1953–1979); *Bekanntmachung der Neufassung des Umsatzsteuergesetzes Vom 21. Februar 2005* (BGBl., Part I, 2005, No. 13, 386–433).

regulated by the law of December 17, 1982.[370] The amendments were made in 1997.[371]

Premiums and contributions resulting from certain insurance contracts were subject to insurance tax (*Versicherungsteuer*). It was levied based on the law of April 8, 1922.[372] Its amendments were made in 1996 and 2015.[373]

The group of excise taxes (*Verbrauchsteuer*) included taxes on luxury goods (e.g., on tobacco, beer, spirits, coffee), but also on energy or electricity. Their collection was regulated in detail by separate laws.[374]

Wealth taxes (*Besitzsteuer*) were divided into two subgroups: income taxes (*Erstragsteuer*) and taxes related to fixed assets, the "property substance" (*Substanzsteuer*). The first one included taxes related to income obtained, e.g., as a result of work, sale of goods, or conducting specific activities. These included the following taxes: personal income tax, payroll tax, corporate income tax, tax on industrial and commercial activity, church tax, and solidarity surcharge.

The collection of personal income tax (PIT, *Einkommensteuer*) was regulated by the law of October 16, 1934.[375] It was amended in 2009.[376] The tax was levied on income earned by individuals from, e.g., work or rent.

The same laws regulated the collection of wage tax (*Lohnsteuer*). This covered income from the "dependent work" (*unselbständige Arbeit*). It involved work for an employer as opposed to self-employment (e.g., running a business). Its rate was determined by variables such as the tax class of the payer, marital status, and having children.

---

370 *Grunderwerbsteuergesetz (GrEStG 1983) Vom 17. Dezember 1982* (BGBl., Part I, 1982, No. 52, 1777–1789).

371 *Bekanntmachung der Neufassung des Grunderwerbsteuergesetzes Vom 26. Februar 1997* (BGBl., Part I, 1997, No. 14, 418–425). Cf. *Berichtigung der Bekanntmachung der Neufassung des Grunderwerbsteuergesetzes Vom 2. Juli 1997* (BGBl., Part I, 1997, No. 48, 1804).

372 *Versicherungssteuergesetz* (RGBl., Part I, 1922, No. 30, 400–405).

373 *Bekanntmachung der Neufassung des Versicherungsteuergesetzes Vom 10. Januar 1996* (BGBl., part I, 1996, No. 2, 22–27); *Bekanntmachung der Neufassung der Versicherungsteuer-Durchführungsverordnung Vom 10. Januar 1996* (BGBl, Part I, 1996, No. 2, 28–29); *Gesetz zur Umsetzung der Transparenzrichtlinie-Änderungsrichtlinie Vom 20. November 2015*, Art. 25 (BGBl., Part I, 2015, No. 46, 2051).

374 See, e.g., the fourth amendment of the excise tax law of July 15, 2009: *Viertes Gesetz zur Änderung von Verbrauchsteuergesetzen Vom 15. Juli 2009* (BGBl., Part I, 2009, No. 42, 1870–1938).

375 *Einkommensteuergesetz (EStG) Vom 16. Oktober 1934* (RGBl., Part I, 1934, No. 119, 1005–1030).

376 *Bekanntmachung der Neufassung des Einkommensteuergesetzes Vom 8. Oktober 2009* (BGBl., Part I, 2009, No. 68, 3366–3533); *Berichtigung der Bekanntmachung der Neufassung des Einkommensteuergesetzes Vom. 8 Dezember 2009* (BGBl., Part I, 2009, No. 78, 3862).

Corporate income tax (CIT, *Körperschaftsteuer*) remained the subject of a separate law of October 16, 1934.[377] It was amended in 1976 and 2002.[378] The levy covered certain income of legal persons.

The conduct of business in any form was subject to the tax on industrial and commercial activity (*Gewerbesteuer*). Details were regulated by the law of December 1, 1936,[379] amended in 2002.[380]

Laws on church tax (*Kirchensteuer*), passed at the level of individual *Länder*, regulated the issues related to the levy resulting from the fact of professing a particular religion. The tax was based on the income of individuals and legal persons. Employees' monthly salaries were reduced by a specific amount of tax. Entrepreneurs paid the tax together with corporate income tax.

After German reunification, the solidarity tax (*Solidaritätszuschlag*, or *Soli*), levied for the purpose of convergence of the Eastern and Western *Länder*, was promulgated by the law of June 24, 1991, and later amended several times.[381] Its subject remained the income of individuals and legal persons. The rules of its collection were similar to those of the church tax.

The second subgroup of property taxes – taxes related to fixed assets – concerned the possession or acquiring of the "property substance." They included, e.g., taxes on inheritance and donations, land tax, and tax on second home.

Based on the law of July 3, 1906,[382] amended in 1974 and 1997,[383] inheritance and donation tax (*Erbschaft- und Schenkungsteuer*) was enforced. Its amount depended on the tax group in which the recipient fell in relation to the donee.

---

377 *Körperschaftsteuergesetz (KStG) Vom 16. Oktober 1934* (RGBl., Part I, 1934, No. 119, 1031–1034).

378 *Körperschaftsteuerreformgesetz Vom 31. August 1976* (BGBl., Part I, 1976, No. 114, 2597–2628); *Bekanntmachung der Neufassung des Körperschaftsteuergesetzes Vom 15. Oktober 2002* (BGBl., Part I, 2002, No. 75, 4144–4166).

379 *Gewerbesteuergesetz (GewStG) Vom 1. Dezember 1936* (RGBl., Part I, 1936, No. 112, 979–985).

380 *Bekanntmachung der Neufassung des Gewerbesteuergesetzes Vom 15. Oktober 2002* (BGBl., Part I, 2002, No. 75, 4167–4179); *Bekanntmachung der Neufassung der Gewerbesteuer-Durchführungsverordnung Vom 15. Oktober 2002* (BGBl., Part I, 2002, No. 75, 4180–4183).

381 *Gesetz zur Einführung eines befristeten Solidaritätszuschlags und zur Änderung von Verbrauchsteuer- und anderen Gesetzen (Solidaritätsgesetz) Vom 24. Juni 1991* (BGBl., Part I, 1991, No. 38, 1318–1321 as amended).

382 "Anlage 4: Erbschaftssteuergesetz.," in *Gesetz, betreffend die Ordnung des Reichshaushalts und die Tilgung der Reichsschuld. Vom 3. Juni 1906.* (RGBl., 1906, No. 31, 654–674).

383 *Gesetz zur Reform des Erbschaftsteuer- und Schenkungsteuerrechts Vom 17. April 1974* (BGBl., Part I, 1974, No. 42, 933–947); *Bekanntmachung der Neufassung des Erbschaftsteuer- und Schenkungsteuergesetzes Vom 27. Februar 1997* (BGBl., Part I, 1997, No. 13, 378–392).

Land tax (*Grundsteuer*) was levied by law on August 7, 1973.[384] It was amended in 2008.[385] The tax was levied on immovable property, and its value determined the amount of the tax.

Legislation at the level of the individual federated states, on the other hand, regulated the rules for collecting tax on the second home (*Zweitwohnungsteuer*). The tax obligation arises in the situation of having a second address of residence.[386]

Changes in the top rates of selected property taxes discussed above that were in Germany between 1990 and 2015 are shown in Table 29. It also includes social security contributions.

Table 29: *Top rates of selected property taxes and social security contributions in Germany in 1990–2015 (as % of tax base)*

Year	**Taxes**			**Social security contributions**[a]
	VAT	**PIT**	**CIT**	
1990	–	–	–	35.6
1991	–	–	–	–
1992	–	–	–	–
1993	–	–	–	–
1994	–	–	–	–
1995	–	57.0	56.8	–
1996	–	57.0	56.7	–
1997	–	57.0	56.7	–
1998	–	55.9	56.0	–

(*Continued*)

384 *Gesetz zur Reform des Grundsteuerrechts Vom 7. August 1973* (BGBl., Part I, 1973, No. 66, 965–974).

385 *Jahressteuergesetz 2009 (JStG 2009) Vom 19. Dezember 2008*, Art. 38 (BGBl., Part I, 2008, No. 63, 2844).

386 "Niemcy – opodatkowanie w Niemczech," http://gia-polska.pl/praktyczne-wskazowki/niemcy-opodatkowanie-w-niemczech/ (accessed March 25, 2019). See other examples of taxes classifications in contemporary Germany: Tkaczyński, *Prawo ustrojowe Niemiec*, 196–201; K.-D. Drüen, *Allgemeines Steuerrecht* (Münster: Verlag Alpmann und Schmidt Juristische Lehrgänge, Technische Universität Kaiserslautern, 2017), 12; *Steuern von A bis Z* (Berlin: Bundesministerium der Finanzen, 2018), 26–27. More on the division of taxing powers between the Federation and the *Länder*, see: A. Leisner-Egensperger, "Gesetzgebungs- und Verwaltungskompetenzen von Bund und Ländern im Bereich der Steuern," in Härtel, *Handbuch Föderalismus*, 365–387.

Table 29: (*Continued*)

Year	Taxes			Social security contributions[a]
	VAT	PIT	CIT	
1999	–	55.9	51.6	–
2000	16.0	53.8	51.6	41.0
2001	16.0	51.2	38.3	40.95
2002	16.0	51.2	38.3	41.35
2003	16.0	51.2	39.6	42.0
2004	16.0	47.5	38.3	41.75
2005	16.0	44.3	38.7	42.53
2006	16.0	44.3	38.3	41.95
2007	19.0	47.5	38.4	40.6
2008	19.0	47.5	29.5	39.91
2009	19.0	47.5	29.4	39.98
2010	19.0	47.5	29.4	39.53
2011	19.0	47.5	29.4	40.33
2012	19.0	47.5	29.5	40.08
2013	19.0	47.5	29.6	39.46
2014	19.0	47.5	29.6	39.46
2015	19.0	47.5	29.65	39.56

a Total social security contributions incurred by both employers and employees.
Own compilation based on: "Trading Economics," https://pl.tradingeconomics.com/germany/ (accessed March 26, 2019).

Table 29 shows that it was typical to reduce the rates of direct taxes (*direkte Steuern*) PIT and CIT for the period in question in Germany. Between 1995 and 2015, the former was successively reduced from 57.0 % to 47.5 %. The trend for CIT was similar (falling from 56.8 % in 1995 to 29.65 % in 2015). However, the years 2002–2003, 2004–2005, 2006–2007, and 2011–2015 saw slight increases. The data indicate that the German authorities have pursued a fiscal policy rather in the direction of increasing budget revenues from indirect taxes (*indirekte Steuern*). This is reflected in the increase in the VAT rate in 2007 from 16.0 % to 19.0 %. This situation was maintained until the end of the analyzed period. In turn, the level of social security contributions remained relatively stable (average: 40.36 %).[387] The growing importance of indirect taxes in German fiscal policy between 1990 and 2015 is also illustrated in Table 30.

387 Own calculations.

Table 30: *Budget revenues from direct and indirect taxes in Germany in 1991–2015 (in billion euros and %)*

Year	Total tax revenues (billion euro)	Share of direct taxes (in %)	Share of indirect taxes (in %)
1991	338.4	55.9	44.1
1992	374.1	56.0	44.0
1993	383.0	54.2	45.8
1994	402.0	52.3	47.7
1995	416.3	53.8	46.2
1996	409.0	52.2	47.8
1997	407.6	51.4	48.6
1998	425.9	52.0	48.0
1999	453.1	51.9	48.1
2000	467.3	52.1	47.9
2001	446.2	49.0	51.0
2002	441.7	47.9	52.1
2003	442.2	47.5	52.5
2004	442.8	47.8	52.2
2005	452.1	48.4	51.6
2006	488.4	50.5	49.5
2007	538.2	50.6	49.4
2008	561.2	51.7	48.3
2009	524.0	48.4	51.6
2010	530.6	48.2	51.8
2011	573.4	49.3	50.7
2012	600.0	50.6	49.4
2013	619.7	51.7	48.3
2014	643.6	52.2	47.8
2015	673.3	52.6	47.4

Source: MB BMF, 84–85, table 10.

Based on Table 30, it can be found that between 1991 and 2015, there was an increase in the share of indirect taxes in total tax revenues (from 44.1 % in 1991 to 47.4 % in 2015). Between 2001 and 2005 (i.e. after the tax reform of 2000[388]) indirect levies even accounted for more than half of this group of budget revenues. A similar situation took place between 2009 and 2011. Firstly, this could be a consequence of the VAT rate increase. Secondly, increasing indirect taxes was less controversial during the financial crisis.

According to the above, it can be concluded that Germany was characterized by weakening fiscalism between 1990 and 2015. This included at least private property of citizens taking the form of income.

6.2.7.2. Property taxation and the economy

There can be found the view in economic history and sociology that state property, which is the legal reflection of national property (also referred to as common and social[389]), can exist in corporal or non-corporal forms. While the former refers to public economic and non-economic objects (e.g., resources, rivers, forests, roads, state plants), the latter involves public participation in material and non-material objects of private property. In modern times, this is usually done through taxation. Private property, as a result of taxation, takes the form of a monetary resource, which then becomes the object of state (public, national) property.[390] The latter

---

388 The main elements of the tax reform of 2000, carried out during the first government of Chancellor Gerhard Schröder (1998–2002), were as follows: (1) reduction of CIT rates; (2) reduction of depreciation allowances; (3) change in the method of PIT and CIT integration; (4) reduction of capital income tax rates; (5) replacement of the personal tax liability of owners of unincorporated firms with a special credit for the standardized amount of local tax on industrial and commercial activities; (6) abolition of CIT on capital gains on a parent company's shares in a subsidiary (P. B. Sørensen, "The German Business Tax Reform of 2000: A General Equilibrium Analysis," *German Economic Review* 3, No. 4 (2002): 359, table 3). The literature, especially polemical literature, on the tax reform of 2000 is abundant. Its main causes, assumptions and effects are discussed, among others, by: M. Keen, "The German Tax Reform of 2000," *International Tax and Public Finance* 9, No. 5 (2002): 603–621; A. Truger, W. Jacoby, "Tax Reforms and 'Modell Deutschland': Lessons from Four Years of Red-Green Tax Policy," in *Germany at Fifty-Five. Berlin ist nicht Bonn?*, ed. J. Sperling (Manchester–New York: Manchester University Press, 2004), 386–410.

389 However, these additional terms should be approached with caution because of their application on the grounds of property rights theory and Marxist theory, which are the focus of attention in the book. Common property and social property are understood in them in a specific way (see: sections 5.1.–5.2. in this study).

390 S. Kozyr-Kowalski, *Socjologia, społeczeństwo obywatelskie i państwo* (Poznań: WN UAM, 2004), 178–180; Przestalski, "Własnościowe aspekty

is expressed by taxes, defining it insofar as the given objects are taxed. The state, through taxes, collects revenues flowing from different types of property of individual members of society. Depending on the needs, these are transformed into other forms of property, especially as a result of budget expenditures (e.g. for state investments). Thus, e.g., a private owner of a taxable object is only a private owner in a formal and legal sense. In the economic and actual dimension, the state (national community) remains the co-owner of this good. The same is true of the contemporary taxpaying employee, who – in the light of the above understanding – is only formally (partially) the owner of the labor force he offers to the employer. This is a criterion that distinguishes him, e.g., from a worker in the 19th-century factory who was not burdened with taxes. Consequently, it can told about the "property character of taxes," the change of property relations resulting from the tax system,[391] or the influence of taxes on the organization of property in a given country.

Thus, a clear distinction can be seen here between (property) rights as *de jure* institution (legal, formal dimension) and *de facto* institution (economic, actual dimension). It is reasonable to try to grasp the relationship of property rights to the German economy in the analyzed period from the point of view of budget revenues from taxes. This is because they are paid by entities owning property and constitute the most important item in the structure of the state revenues. This, in turn, affects the state of public finances.[392] The transformation of German budget revenues from taxes and social contributions as a share of GDP between 1990 and 2015 is shown in Figure 5.

partycypacji pracowniczej," 28–29. In economic history, the issue of corporate and non-corporate property appears, e.g., in Jan Rutkowski's research on land property in the 17th century Brittany (J. Rutkowski, *Wieś europejska późnego feudalizmu (XVI–XVIII w.)*, ed. J. Topolski (Warszawa: PIW, 1986), 272–273).

391 Cf. Przestalski, "Własnościowe aspekty partycypacji pracowniczej," 28–30.

392 Cf. observations on one of Germany's systemic objectives of a fiscal state: section 4.4. in this study.

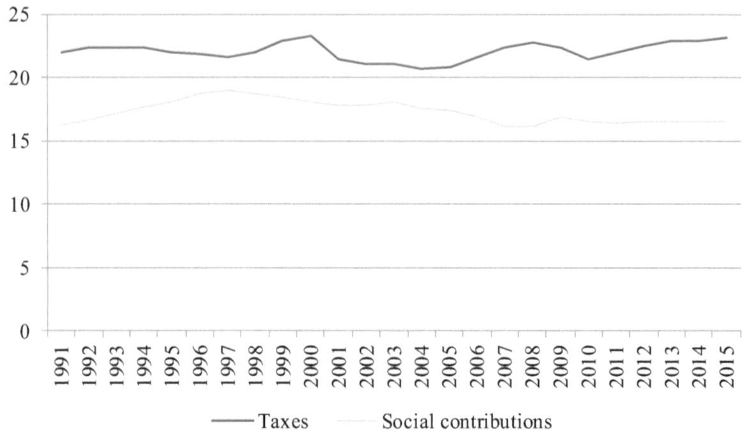

Figure 5: *Budget revenues from taxes and social contributions in Germany in 1991–2015 (as % of GDP)*[a]

a In statistical sources, data for reunified Germany appear since 1991. For 2013–2015, estimates are provided as of August 2016.

Own compilation based on: MB BMF, 86, table 11.

As shown in Figure 5, between 1991 and 2015, the share of taxes in the GDP structure oscillated between 22.0 % in 1991 and 23.1 % in 2015. They recorded the highest share of GDP in 2000 (23.2 %) and the lowest in 2004 (20.6 %). Periods of increasing fiscalism were short and included the following years: 1991–1992 (from 22.0 % to 22.4 % of GDP), 1993–1994 (from 22.3 % to 22.4 % of GDP), 1997–2000 (from 21.5 % to 23.2 % of GDP), 2002–2003 (from 21.0 % to 21.1 % of GDP), 2004–2008 (from 20.6 % to 22.7 % of GDP), and 2010–2015 (from 21.4 % to 23.1 % of GDP).

The dynamics of the share of social contributions in GDP were also not strong. During the analyzed period, the level ranged from 16.3 % in 1991 to 16.5 % of GDP in 2015, with the highest value in 1997 (19.0 % of GDP) and the lowest one in 2007–2008 (16.1 % of GDP). The following periods of increasing share of social contributions in the structure of German GDP can be distinguished: 1991–1997 (from 16.3 % to 19.0 %), 2002–2003 (from 17.8 % to 18.0 %), 2008–2009 (from 16.1 % to 16.9 %) and 2011–2012 (from 16.4 % to 16.5 %).

It is also interesting to trace the dynamics of the total participation of taxes and social contributions in Germany's GDP. It fluctuated from 38.3 % in 1991 to 39.6 % of GDP in 2015. The increase in the share of taxes and social contributions in GDP occurred in the years: 1991–1996 (from 38.3 % to 40.5 %), 1997–1999 (from 40.4 % to

41.4 %), 2002–2003 (from 38.8 % to 39.1 %), 2005–2009 (from 38.2 % to 39.3 %) and 2010–2015 (from 37.9 % to 39.6 %).[393]

Under the assumption that taxes burden property (especially private property), it can be concluded that the analyzed period in Germany was not a time of increasing fiscalism. Although periods of increasing tax share in GDP were dominant in the years under study, they were not significant. The level of participation of taxes in GDP was relatively constant.

The level of fiscalism in the FRG was among the lower in Europe in the same period. For example, in 1995, the share of taxes in Germany's GDP was 22.1 % (according to other data than previously). Lower levels were recorded only by: Czech Republic (20.4 %), Greece (18.8 %), Spain (20.0 %), Portugal (21.6 %), Slovenia (21.9 %) and Switzerland (18.6 %). The overall composition of this group of countries did not change much. In 2005, taxes accounted for 20.4 % of Germany's GDP, while a lower index applied to countries such as the Czech Republic (19.7 %), Estonia (19.8 %), Greece (20.2 %), Slovakia (18.9 %), and Switzerland (20.2 %). In 2015, Germany, whose taxes shaped GDP at 22.9 %, was characterized by greater fiscalism than: Czech Republic (19.0 %), Estonia (22.4 %), Spain (22.5 %), Ireland (19.7 %), Slovakia (18.5 %), Slovenia (22.1 %) and Switzerland (21.0 %).[394]

6.2.8. State expenditures

An indicator of the relationship between the market and the state in Germany in 1990–2015, as proposed by Stanisław Kozyr-Kowalski, can be the share of government expenditures in national income. These are the consumed monetary resources, which are the form of non-corporal state property derived from taxation of property (usually private property). As a result, the higher the participation

393 MB BMF, 86, table 11. See also D. Bębnowski, "Niemcy jako państwo fiskalne w perspektywie instytucjonalnej i historyczno-gospodarczej (1990–2015)," *Przegląd Zachodni* No. 1 (370) (2019): 54.

394 MB BMF, 94, table 17. Cf. critical studies: U. Wagschal, "Deutschlands Steuerstaat und die vier Welten der Besteuerung," in *Wohlfahrtsstaatliche Politik. Institutionen, politischer Prozess und Leistungsprofil*, ed. M. G. Schmidt (Opdalen: Leske + Budrich, 2001), 125–142; U. Wagschal, "Entwicklung, Determinanten und Vergleich der Staatsfinanzen," in *Regieren in der Bundesrepublik Deutschland. Innen- und Außenpolitik seit 1949*, eds. M. G. Schmidt, R. Zohlnhöfer (Wiesbaden: VS Verlag für Sozialwissenschaften, 2006), 57–85; B. Zbroińska, A. Gierałka, "Obciążenia podatkowe w Polsce i w Niemczech," *Ekonomika i Organizacja Przedsiębiorstwa* No. 1 (2007): 23–29; A. Peichl, T. Schaefer, "Wie progressiv ist Deutschland? Das Steuer- und Transfersystem im europäischen Vergleich," *SOEPpapers on Multidisciplinary Panel Data Research* No. 102 (2008): 1–28; Bębnowski, "Niemcy jako państwo fiskalne," 55.

of government spending (i.e. non-corporal state property) in the national income structure, the greater the participation of the state in the economy and society.[395]

In the analyzed statistical materials of the Federal Ministry of Finance for the period in question, e.g., both the overall "expenditures of the federal budget" (*Ausgaben des Bundeshaushalts*), presented in total numbers,[396] and the "government share in relation to GDP in percentages" (*Staatsquote in Relation zum BIP in Prozente*) were positioned. In order to grasp the relationship in question here, it is necessary to rely on the second category.[397] Data for the years 1991–2015 are presented in Figure 6.

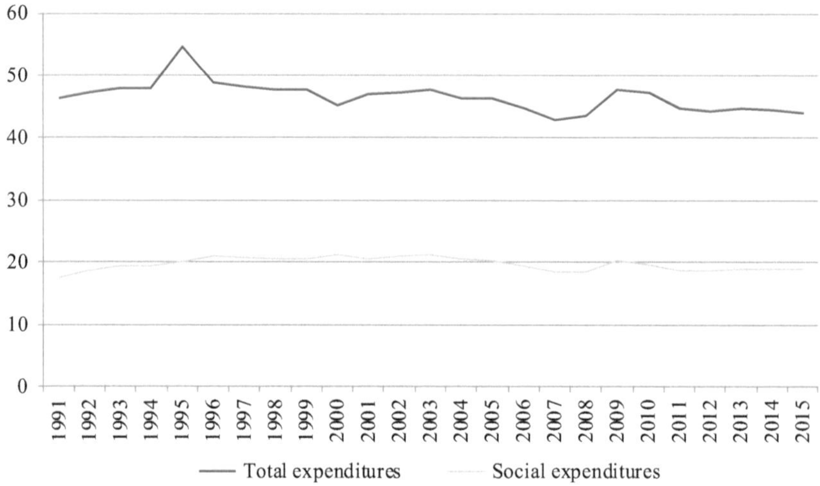

Figure 6: *State expenditures in Germany in 1991–2015 (as % of GDP)*[a]

a Data include direct expenditures only. For 1995, the assumption of debts of the Trust Office and the housing industry of the former GDR are not included. For 2013–2015, estimates are provided as of August 2016.

Own compilation based on: MB BMF, 87, table 12.

395 Cf. Kozyr-Kowalski, *Socjologia*, 180. See also section 6.2.7.2. in this study.

396 See, e.g., MB BMF, 41.

397 Interpretation discrepancies concerning the category of public expenditures or budget expenditures occur, e.g., in Polish law. See more on this topic: K. Nizioł, "Analiza pojęć 'wydatków publicznych,' 'wydatków budżetu państwa' oraz 'rozchodów publicznych' na gruncie ustawy o finansach publicznych," *Studia Lubuskie* 7 (2011): 325–339.

Figure 6 shows that in 1991 state spending totaled 46.4 % of GDP. In the first half of the 1990s, this ratio increased (a slight deviation in 1994–47.9 % of GDP). It reached its highest level in 1995 (54.7 % of GDP). In the second half of the decade, the expenditure share declined, returning almost to its initial value (47.7 % of GDP in 1999). After the introduction of the tax reform in 2000,[398] the share of state expenditures in GDP increased again (from 45.1 % in 2000 to 47.8 % in 2003). The following years saw a downward trend. In 2007, state spending oscillated at 42.8 % of GDP. This trend was interrupted by the financial crisis, during which the share of expenditures in GDP clearly increased from 43.6 % in 2008 to 47.6 % in 2009. In the last years of the period under review, there was a gradual decline in this regard: from 47.3 % in 2010 to 44.0 % in 2015, with a slight increase between 2012 and 2013 (from 44.3 % to 44.7 % of GDP).

A significant share in the structure of state spending was occupied by social insurance (*Sozialversicherung*), referred to here as social expenditures. Between 1990 and 2015, the trends in their size were similar to total expenditures, although they were characterized by much lower intensity. In 1991, the share of social expenditures in German GDP was the lowest (17.5 %), while in 2003, it was the highest (21.3 %).[399]

Compiling the above illustration with the proposed interpretive concept of Kozyr-Kowalski, it should be stated that from the point of view of the government spending participation in national income (expressed in GDP), the participation of the state in the economy and society increased in the following periods: 1991–1995, 2000–2003, 2007–2009 and 2012–2013. The social dimension of state interventionism[400] specifically reflects the share of social spending in the GDP structure. Growth trends were recorded in similar periods as the previous ones: 1991–1996 (from 17.5 % to 20.9 % of GDP), 1998–2000 (from 20.5 % to 21.2 % of GDP), 2001–2003 (from 20.6 % to 21.3 % of GDP), 2008–2009 (from 18.4 % to 20.3 % of GDP) and 2012–2015 (from 18.7 % to 19.0 % of GDP).[401]

The highest growth rates – both at the level of total and social expenditures – occurred in two key periods: in the first half of the 1990s and in 2007–2009. In the first one, the increase in state interventionism resulted from German reunification and the beginning of the convergence process between the Eastern and Western *Länder*. In the second period, it was caused by the financial crisis. However, there is an important difference between these phenomena. The convergence process in

398 More on the tax reform of 2000: section 6.2.7.1. in this study.
399 MB BMF, 87, table 12. See also: Bębnowski, "Niemcy jako państwo fiskalne," 53–54.
400 Abstracting from the rich literature, the concept of interventionism should be understood here broadly as the intervention of state authorities in the economy.
401 MB BMF, p. 87, table 12.

1991–2015 was permanent and ultimately not fully completed. In contrast, interventionism during the crisis was ad hoc and short.[402]

The increase in interventionism, manifested in the rise of state expenditures share in GDP, was accomplished through increased monetary resources in the form of non-corporal state property. This, in turn, came from the taxation of property (usually private property).

It follows from Kozyr-Kowalski's conception that state interference in the economy and society is a consequence of the growing government spending share in national income, while taxes are the source of that. Thus, the participation of taxes in the structure of GDP can be considered an independent (explanatory) variable, while the share of state expenditures in GDP – is a dependent (response) variable.[403] The relationship between them can be examined by calculating the Pearson correlation coefficient.

However, it is difficult to capture the causal relationship between the above variables. The Pearson correlation coefficient only measures the relationship between two variables, determining its strength and direction. The existence of a relationship between variables does not necessarily correspond to a deterministic relationship in reality.[404]

The calculations made show that the Pearson correlation coefficient for these variables (25 observations for 1991–2015) is −0.2991, while the critical value (with a two-sided 5 % critical area) is equal to 0.3961.[405] As the absolute value of the coefficient does not exceed the critical value, there are no grounds to reject the null hypothesis assuming that there is no relationship between the variables. In other

402 See, e.g., comparative studies by Stanisław Swadźba, who compared economic freedom indicators for 27 EU countries, the United States, and Japan in selected years 2007–2015, concluding that the increase in state interventionism in these countries was an ad hoc and temporary response of governments to the financial crisis of 2008. Thus, according to him, the crisis did not permanently affect the changes in the regulatory sphere of the analyzed economies (S. Swadźba, "Przyczyny i skutki kryzysu pierwszej dekady XXI wieku," in *Europa XX-XXI wieku. Społeczno-polityczne konsekwencje kryzysów*, eds. M. Gruszczyk, L. Krzyżanowski, M. Skrzypek (Katowice: Wydawnictwo UŚ, 2017), 303–308). It should be noted that this was in contrast to the great economic crisis of 1929–1933 (1935), which revolutionized economic theory (triumph of John Maynard Keynes' views) and the economic policies of the countries affected by the crisis (development of the state interventionism).

403 Cf. M. Sobczyk, *Statystyka* (Warszawa: WN PWN, 2007), 256.

404 Cf. J. Topolski, *Metodologia historii* (Warszawa: PWN, 1973), 462–465; G. Koop, *Wprowadzenie do ekonometrii* (Warszawa: Oficyna a Wolters Kluwer Business, 2014), 30–38, 44–49.

405 Own calculations made in Gretl on the basis of data: MB BMF, 86, table 11; 87, table 12. See in more detail: T. Kufel, *Ekonometria. Rozwiązywanie problemów z wykorzystaniem programu GRETL* (Warszawa: WN PWN, 2007).

words, there is no relationship between tax participation in German GDP and state expenditures shared in it between 1991 and 2015.

This is a reason to question Kozyr-Kowalski's thesis that the increase in interventionism was dictated by the rising state spending share (non-corporal state property), and this, in turn, by the increasing tax share in GDP. Moreover, there was no marked rise in fiscalism in the FRG in the analyzed period. This partly confirms the thesis formulated above.[406] The taxes share in Germany's GDP was relatively stable, as was state expenditures share in GDP (only in 1995 did it exceed 50 %). This was important if only from the point of view of the fact that there was no full convergence of the inhabitants' incomes in the Eastern and Western *Länder* in the analyzed years. In 1991, the level of income *per capita* in the new federated states (excluding Berlin) was 7,247.47 euros, while in Western Germany, it was 13,787.58 euros. In contrast, in 2014, the average inhabitant of the Eastern *Länder* had an income of 18,044.87 euros, while a citizen from the Western part of the state had 21,840.88 euros. The ratio of *per capita* income in the Eastern federated states to that in the Western *Länder* has thus increased from 53 % to 83 %.[407] However, this does not change the fact that even periodic deviations from the trends of relatively stable taxes and state expenditures shares in GDP have determined certain actions of the authorities.[408]

6.2.9. Economic growth[409]

The property rights theory recognizes the regularity that well-defined and protected property rights (referring especially to private property) *ceteris paribus* generate economic growth. Examples in this regard are provided by research in institutional economics and economic history.[410]

---

406 See: sections 6.2.7.1.–6.2.7.2. in this study.

407 *Wirtschaftsdaten neue Länder*, 22, table 3.1.

408 See, e.g.: J. Czech-Rogosz, "Reformy gospodarcze w Niemczech w ramach programu 'Agenda 2010'," *Studia Ekonomiczne. Zeszyty Naukowe Uniwersytetu Ekonomicznego w Katowicach* No. 34 (2005): 117–142; D. Bębnowski, "Niemcy jako państwo fiskalne," 49–57.

409 This section should be seen as complementary to the considerations made in this work on the relationship between constitutional rules and economic growth in Germany between 1990 and 2015 (see section 4.7. in this study).

410 See, e.g.: J. Röpke, "Handlungsrechte und wirtschaftliche Entwicklung," in *Property Rights und ökonomische Theorie*, ed. A. Schüller (München: Verlag Franz Vahlen, 1983), 111–144; G. W. Scully, "The Institutional Framework and Economic Development," *Journal of Political Economy* 96, No. 3 (1988): 652–662; J. Torstensson, "Property Rights and Economic Growth: An Empirical Study," *Kyklos* 47, No. 2 (1994): 231–247; A. A. Goldsmith, "Democracy, Property Rights and Economic Growth," *The Journal of Development Studies* 32, No. 2 (1995): 157–174; Knack, Keefer, "Institutions and Economic Performance," 207–227; D. A. Leblang, "Property

As property rights are primarily anchored in the Basic Law, also studies on (positive) constitutional economics recognize the correlation between civil rights and liberties (e.g. property rights) and economic growth. And in this case, retrospective studies are important.[411]

Reunified Germany between 1990 and 2015 was characterized by variable economic growth rates. A summary of selected classical measures in this regard for the period 1991–2000 is presented in Table 31.

Rights, Democracy and Economic Growth," *Political Research Quarterly* 49, No. 1 (1996): 5–26; E. Weede, "Eigentum und Freiheit als Determinanten der wirtschaftlichen Entwicklung," in *Neuer Institutionalismus. Zur soziologischen Erklärung von Organisation, Moral und Vertrauen*, eds. A. Maurer, M. Schmid (Frankfurt–New York: Campus Verlag, 2002), 87–106; G. D. Libecap, "Property Rights," in *The Oxford Encyclopedia of Economic History*, ed. J. Mokyr, Vol. 4: *Monte di Pietà – Spain* (Oxford: Oxford University Press, 2003), 269–270; M. Zalesko, "Prawa własności filarem rozwoju gospodarczego," *Ekonomia* No. 4 (25) (2013): 92–102; A. Kacprzyk, *Instytucjonalne determinanty wzrostu gospodarczego* (Łódź: Wydawnictwo UŁ, 2014), *passim*.

411 See sample literature at the beginning of section 4.7. in this work.

Table 31: *Main economic growth indicators for Germany in 1991–2000 (DM billion)*[a]

Indicator	**Year**									
	1991	**1992**	**1993**	**1994**	**1995**	**1996**	**1997**	**1998**	**1999**	**2000**
at current prices										
Gross value added[b]	2,639.74	2,848.54	2,918.06	3,063.16	3,193.10	3,273.80	3,367.66	–	–	–
Gross domestic product (GDP)[c] **– incl. Eastern *Länder* without Berlin/ with Berlin**	2,938.0 –/–	3,155.2 –/–	3,235.4 318.64/ 460.88	3,394.4 368.16/ 514.82	3,523.0 393.27/ 544.50	3,586.5 409.69/ 558.73	3,666.5 417.15/ 564.30	3,784.4 425.03/ 573.05	3,877.2 433.84/ 583.76	3,976.1 436.14/ 586.34
Net domestic product (NDP) at market prices[d]	2,492.45	2,684.76	2,743.09	2,892.76	3,007.89	3,079.93	3,169.26	–	–	–
NDP at factor costs (net value added)[e]	2,247.54	2,401.99	2,435.44	2,545.93	2,656.70	2,707.56	2,779.63	2,878.37	–	–
Gross national product (GNP)[f]	2,955.7	3,170.6	3,248.9	3,380.6	3,504.4	3,570.9	3,648.6	3,758.6	3,845.9	3,946.9
GNP *per capita* (DM)[g]	*37,000*	*39,300*	*40,000*	*41.500*	*42,900*	*43,600*	*44,500*	*45,800*	*46,900*	*48,100*
Net national product (NNP) at market prices[h]	2,520.95	2,703.76	2,748.19	2,884.76	2,990.99	3,053.73	3,139.66	–	–	–
NNP at factor costs (national income)[i]	2,282.8	2,430.3	2,456.2	2,547.9	2,657.3	2,702.5	2,753.1	2,832.4	2,871.2	2,945.6

(Continued)

Table 31: (*Continued*)

National income *per capita* (DM)[j]	*28,500*	*30,200*	*30,300*	*31,300*	*32,500*	*33,000*	*33,600*	*34,500*	*35,000*	*35,900*
at permanent prices[k]										
Gross value added[l]	2,639.74	2,695.51	2,663.71	2,730.63	2,785.65	2,826.72	2,889.80	–	–	–
GDP[m]	3,346.0	3,421.0	3,383.8	3,463.2	3,523.0	3,550.0	3,599.6	3,673.5	3,730.7	3,840.8
NDP at market prices[n]	2,492.45	2,535.81	2,484.68	2,551.87	2,594.79	2,626.28	2,684.35	–	–	–
GNP[o]	3,369.0	3,440.8	3,399.7	3,449.7	3,504.4	3,536.5	3,584.2	3,650.7	3,703.3	3,815.5
NNP at market prices[p]	2,520.95	2,553.81	2,489.38	2,544.77	2,579.89	2,603.48	2,658.95	–	–	–

a The data in the table are most complete for the years 1991–1997 (according to 1998 statistical information). In 1999, the German statistical yearbooks changed the method of presenting national accounts (*Volkswirtschaftliche Gesamtrechnungen*). Some measures were dropped at that time (cf. SJ BRD, Vol. 1999, 665–666, table 24.1; 667, table 24.2).
b *Bruttowertschöpfung*. Data from 1998. Estimates for 1995–1997.
c *Bruttoinlandsprodukt*, BIP. Data from 2001. Estimates for 1997–2000.
d *Nettoinlandsprodukt zu Marktpreisen*. Data from 1998. Estimates for 1995–1997.
e *Nettoinlandsprodukt zu Faktorkosten*. This measure is equated with net value added (*Nettowertschöpfung*). Data from 1999. Estimates for 1995–1998.
f *Bruttosozialprodukt*, BSP. Data from 2001. Estimates for 1997–2000.
g *Bruttosozialprodukt je Einwohner*. Data from 2001. Estimates for 1997–2000.
h *Nettosozialprodukt zu Marktpreisen*. Data from 1998. estimates for 1995–1997.
i *Nettosozialprodukt zu Faktorkosten*. This measure is equated with national income (*Volkseinkommen*). Data from 2001. Estimates for 1997–2000.

j *Nettosozialprodukt zu Faktorkosten (Volkseinkommen) je Einwohner.* Data from 2001. Estimates for 1997–2000.
k At constant 1991 or 1995 prices. cf. footnotes to specific indicators.
l At constant 1991 prices. Data from 1998. Estimates for 1995–1997.
m At constant 1995 prices. Data from 2001. Estimates for 1997–2000.
n At constant 1991 prices. Data from 1998. Estimates for 1995–1997.
o At constant 1995 prices. Data from 2001. Estimates for 1997–2000.
p At constant 1991 prices. Data from 1998. Estimates for 1995–1997.
Own compilation based on: SJ BRD, Vol. 1998, 656, table 24.4; SJ BRD, Vol. 1999, 667, table 24.2; SJ BRD, Vol. 2001 (Wiesbaden: Statistisches Bundesamt, 2001), 655, table 24.1; 673, table 24.17.

The summary shows that in the early 1990s, the costs of reunification resulted in weaker economic growth for Germany as a whole. Between 1992 and 1993, real GDP fell from DM 3,421.0 to DM 3,383.8 billion. In 1994, this trend was reversed. However, the vast majority of GDP was created by the more developed Western *Länder*. Between 1993 and 2000, the new federated states (excluding Berlin) generated between 9.8 % and 11.0 % of the nominal GDP of the entire country.

In 2002, German statistical yearbooks began to present the dynamics of economic growth in the euro due to the adoption of the new currency by Germany.[412] Sometimes values in US dollars were given.[413] The values for the previous period were standardized. Detailed data on the dynamics of Germany's GDP between 1991 and 2015 are presented in Table 32.

Table 32: *Changes in the size of Germany's GDP in 1991–2015 (in billion euros and %)*

Year	**Nominal GDP**			**Real GDP**[a]	
	in billion euro	**in %, compared to previous year**	**GDP *per capita* (euro)**	**in billion euro**	**in %, compared to previous year**
1991	1,579.8	+8.4	19,754	2,038.5	+5.2
1992	1,695.3	+7.3	21,060	2,077.7	+1.9
1993	1,748.6	+3.1	21,601	2,057.9	−1.0
1994	1,830.3	+4.7	22,555	2,108.4	+2.5
1995	1,898.9	+3.7	23,354	2,145.1	+1.7
1996	1,926.3	+1.4	23,646	2,162.6	+0.8
1997	1,967.1	+2.1	24,133	2,202.6	+1.8
1998	2,018.2	+2.6	24,780	2,246.2	+2.0
1999	2,064.9	+2.3	25,360	2,290.8	+2.0
2000	2,116.5	+2.5	25,983	2,358.7	+3.0
2001	2,179.9	+3.0	26,741	2,398.7	+1.7
2002	2,209.3	+1.4	27,082	2,398.7	+0.0
2003	2,220.1	+0.5	27,224	2,381.7	−0.7
2004	2,270.6	+2.3	27,875	2,409.5	+1.2
2005	2,300.9	+1.3	28,288	2,426.5	+0.7
2006	2,393.3	+4.0	29,483	2,516.3	+3.7

412 See SJ BRD, Vol. 2002, 632, table 24.2.

413 See, e.g., SJ BRD, Vol. 2010 (Wiesbaden: Statistisches Bundesamt, 2010), 724, table A.24.1.

Table 32: (*Continued*)

Year	Nominal GDP			Real GDP[a]	
	in billion euro	in %, compared to previous year	GDP *per capita* (euro)	in billion euro	in %, compared to previous year
2007	2,513.2	+5.0	31,031	2,598.4	+3.3
2008	2,561.7	+1.9	31,719	2,626.5	+1.1
2009	2,460.3	−4.0	30,569	2,478.9	−5.6
2010	2,580.1	+4.9	32,137	2,580.1	+4.1
2011	2,703.1	+4.8	33,673	2,674.5	+3.7
2012	2,758.3	+2.0	34,296	2,687.6	+0.5
2013	2,826.2	+2.5	35,045	2,700.8	+0.5
2014	2,923.9	+3.5	36,105	2,743.9	+1.6
2015	3,032.8	+3.7	37,127	2,791.1	+1.7

a At constant 2010 prices.
Source: MB BMF, 109–110, table 4; SJ BRD, Vol. 2017 (Wiesbaden: Statistisches Bundesamt, 2017), 327, table 12.1.

A look at the entire period analyzed in this study allows distinguishing several key phases of Germany's economic growth after 1990. The direct economic effect of reunification was a weakening economic growth dynamics due to the incorporation of the much less developed territory of the former GDR to the FRG. This resulted in a slowdown in GDP growth for the whole country. This was all the more important because, at the turn of the 1980s and 1990s, the West German economy recorded a clear increase in GDP.[414] Between 1992 and 1993, the level of real GDP decreased from 2,077.7 to 2,057.9 billion euros (negative economic growth of −1.0 %). From 1994 to 2000, the German economy generated growth averaging 2.0 %, reaching a maximum of 3.0 % in 2000.

Between 2000 and 2003, real GDP growth slowed down again. There was a phase of stagnation in 2002 and a recession of −0.7 % a year later (real GDP fell from 2,398.7 billion to 2,381.7 billion euros). The subsequent (i.e. for 2004–2007) strong recovery (except for 2005) peaked at 3.7 % in 2006 and 3.3 % in 2007. This prosperity was abruptly interrupted by the global financial crisis. The dynamics clearly weakened in 2008, while the bottom of the recession occurred in 2009 (−5,6 %). The implementation of anti-crisis solutions brought visible results. Already in 2010, GDP grew by 4.1 %, and it exceeded the pre-crisis level in 2011 (2,674.5 billion

414 Cf. section 2.1. in this work.

euros). In the final years of the analyzed period, the German economy entered a new phase of slower economic growth, which nevertheless remained at an average level of 1.1 %.

Between 1991 and 2015, nominal GDP *per capita* increased regularly. Only the bottom of the financial recession was an exception (falling from 31,719 in 2008 to 30,569 euros in 2009), but already the following year, GDP *per capita* reached a level higher than before the crisis. This trend was consistent for the Western and Eastern *Länder*, although the new federated states (excluding Berlin) in the analyzed years recorded significantly lower values of this indicator.[415]

According to different estimates, in 1991, the average GDP *per capita* in Germany was 19,186 euros. In the Western part of the country, it was registered 22,004 euros (i.e. 14.7 % more than the all-German average). The Eastern *Länder* (excluding Berlin) generated a value of 7,278 euros or 37.9 % of the all-German average and 33.1 % of the Western German level. In contrast, in 2013, the average value of the index for Germany as a whole was 33,355 euros. The old federated states recorded a smaller lead this time: 35,391 euros, i.e., 6.1 % more than the statewide average. The GDP *per capita* in the former GDR increased by 224 % (a value of 23,585 euros). This represented 70.7 % of the average for Germany as a whole and 66.6 % of the product of the Western *Länder*.[416] Although the convergence progress in terms of GDP *per capita* is evident in the analyzed period, the process was not completed by 2015.

Other data, published by the Federal Ministry of Economic Affairs and Energy, approximates the dynamics of economic growth in Germany, taking into account the division into old and new federated states. Detailed information in this regard for the period 1992–2015 is presented in Figure 7.

415 JB BR SDE, 89.
416 Pastuszka, "Polityka rozwoju Wschodnich Niemiec," 66, table 4.

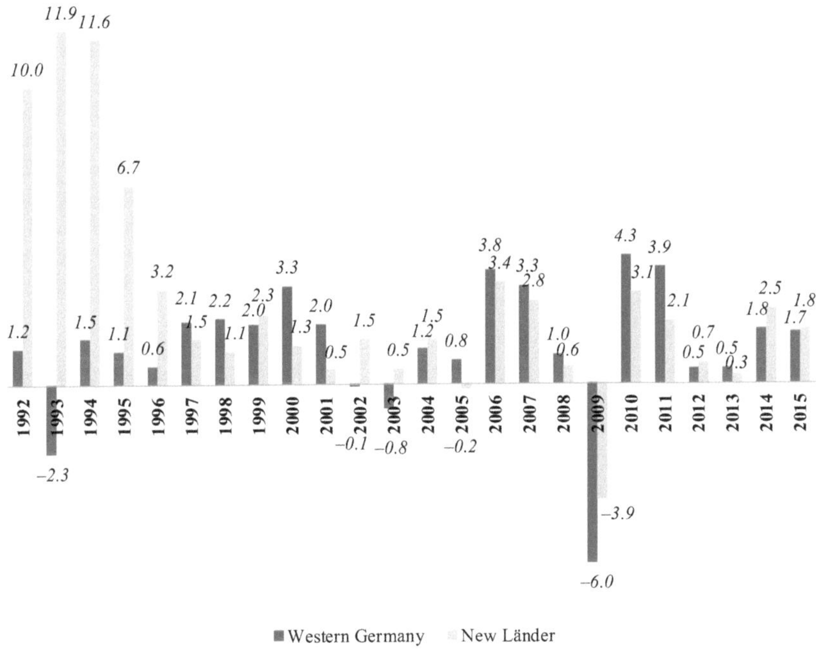

Figure 7: *Growth rates of real GDP compared to the previous year in the Western and Eastern Länder in Germany in 1992–2015 (in %)*

Western Germany (*Westdeutschland*) – the area of the former FRG (1949–1990) without Berlin.

New *Länder* (*Neue Länder*) – the area of the former GDR (1949–1990) without Berlin, i.e.: Brandenburg, Mecklenburg-Vorpommern, Saxony, Saxony-Anhalt and Thuringia.

Source: JB BR SDE, 89.

Figure 7 clearly shows that the rate of economic growth (measured by the rate of real GDP related to the previous year) in the former GDR was highest in the first half of the 1990s. From 1992 to 1996, the GDP rate in the Eastern *Länder* was several times higher than in the old federated states. The greatest disproportion occurred in 1993: GDP growth in Eastern Germany was as high as 11.9 % (the highest level in the entire analyzed period), while Western *Länder* even recorded negative growth of –2.3 %. This situation resulted from deep developmental differences between the two parts of Germany. Highly developed Western Germany was characterized by a slower but relatively stable GDP growth rate (even taking into account the problems arising from reunification and the temporary weakening of their potential), while less developed new federated states were intensively catching up.[417] The Western German financial transfers were an additional factor initiating economic growth in the Eastern *Länder*.[418]

However, already in 1995, the economic growth rate of the new federated states, and thus the convergence rate, weakened significantly (a decline of 4.9 percentage points). In 1997 the relationship was reversed, and the Western German economy has since generated more growth than the Eastern *Länder*. This advantage actually lasted until 2015. The higher GDP growth recorded in the new federated states in 1999, 2002–2004, 2009, 2012, and 2014–2015 belonged rather to exceptional situations, and the resulting differences were not as significant as at the beginning of the period in question.

In 1992–2015, several sub-periods of prosperity can be distinguished for both parts of the FRG. The previously mentioned weakening of German economic growth due to the incorporation of the less developed territory of the former GDR was particularly felt by the old federated states. In the late 1980s and early 1990s, West Germany experienced a significant increase in GDP.[419] The decline in this growth rate to 1.2 % in 1992 and even to −2.3 % in 1993 shows the scale of the burden of reunification borne by the Western German economy at that time. Although the years 1994–1996 brought an improvement, the disproportion was still significant. Only the period between 1997 and 2001 was favorable for the Western *Länder*, when the GDP growth rate exceeded the Eastern German level and reached values between 2.1 % and 2.0 %, with the best result in 2000 (3.3 %). A significant slowdown occurred between 2002 and 2005 (negative growth in 2002 and 2003). The rapid recovery of 2006 and 2007 (over 3 % growth rate) was interrupted by the financial crisis in 2008 and especially in 2009 (−6,0 %). A significant

417 This observation is an exemplification of the convergence theory, which, among other things, assumes that underdeveloped countries tend to record higher economic growth results than highly developed countries. In this context, it is told about the catching up effect. Cf., e.g., S. Kuznets, *Wzrost gospodarczy narodów. Produkt i struktura produkcji* (Warszawa: PWE, 1976), 13–58, especially tables with statistical data.

418 Klimiuk, "Trendy rozwojowe," 61–62.

419 See section 2.1. in this work. According to the data of the Federal Statistical Office from 2001, the real GDP of West Germany (at constant 1991 prices) in 1990–1991 increased by 5.0 %: from DM 2,520.4 billion to DM 2,647.6 billion. After reunification, due to the incorporation of the GDR into the FRG, the value of the index (at constant 1995 prices) increased and amounted to DM 3,346.0 billion in 1991 (for 1991, statistical sources quote data for both West Germany before reunification and the reunified FRG). Nevertheless, between 1992 and 1993, there was a decline in this figure: from DM 3,421.0 billion to DM 3,383.8 billion. The GDP growth rate was thus −1.1 %. Although these figures are not complementary to those presented in the discussed Figure 7, they illustrate the weakening of Western Germany's economic potential after reunification (SJ BRD, Vol. 2001, 655, table 24.1).

upturn followed the recession and covered the years 2010–2011 (the GDP growth rate of the Western *Länder* in 2010 reached the maximum level for the entire analyzed period, i.e. 4.3 %). After a slowdown in 2012 and 2013, the growth of the old federated states stabilized (1.8 % in 2014 and 1.7 % in 2015).

The dynamics of economic growth in the Eastern *Länder* in the first half of the 1990s developed in a different direction. Despite the initial collapse of production, resulting from the privatization of great manufacturing plants and deindustrialization of Eastern Germany due to the low competitiveness of enterprises there,[420] the years 1992–1996 saw a significant increase in GDP within the convergence process. However, from 1997 to 2015, the direction of the trend of the examined indicator was already essentially the same (with some exceptions) as in the case of the Western *Länder*, of course, taking into account all the differences between the growth rates in the old and new federated states. This was a consequence of Germany's progressive (though not completed) integration in creating a single economic system. It should also be noted that since 1995, the differences in real GDP growth rates in the two parts of the country gradually narrowed actually until 2015 (with few exceptions). It is worth mentioning that from the point of view of the indicator in question, Eastern Germany went through the bottom of the economic recession in 2009 somewhat more smoothly than the Western part of the country.

The literature draws attention to several specific issues concerning the trends of German economic growth in 1990–2015. Firstly, the process of convergence of the Eastern and Western *Länder* was dynamic. It was most intense in the first half of the 1990s. Some authors estimate that in 1992–1996 the total GDP growth of the former GDR amounted to 44.4 %, while the Western *Länder* reached a total of 1.8 %. This was a consequence of the property transformations, the growing importance of private capital, and transfers to Eastern Germany, which were highest in 1995. Investments mainly included road infrastructure and housing construction. Later, however, this trend was reversed. Between 1997 and 2014, the aggregate GDP growth of the new federated states was 19.5 %, while it was 24.7 % for Western Germany. Nevertheless, between 1991 and 2013, the GDP of the former GDR was to grow by a total of 181.8 %, while the old federated states generated GDP growth of 70.9 %. The Eastern *Länder* were the most successful in this respect: Thuringia (205.3 %), Brandenburg (203.1 %), Saxony (178.9 %), Saxony-Anhalt (162.2 %), and Mecklenburg-Vorpommern (160.3 %). Interestingly, Berlin – despite being the state capital – did not generate a relatively high level of GDP (cumulative growth of 60 %

420 According to Czech-Rogosz, the GDP level of the Eastern part of Germany fell by 12.5 % in 1990 (compared to the previous year) and by another 21.5 % in 1991 (Czech-Rogosz, "Gospodarka wschodnich Niemiec w 12 lat po zjednoczeniu," 94, fn. 5).

between 1991 and 2013), although it dominated among the all new federated states in single years.[421]

As far as the dynamics of GDP *per capita* are concerned, it is essential to note that between 1991 and 2013, the same Eastern *Länder* as mentioned above converged most closely to the all-German level: Thuringia (from 33.6 % to 69.5 %), Saxony (from 39.5 % to 72.6 %), Saxony-Anhalt (from 37.0 % to 69.5 %), Brandenburg (from 39.7 % to 71.2 %), and Mecklenburg-Vorpommern (from 38.9 % to 68.4 %). The highest level of GDP *per capita* was recorded in Berlin: 99.6 % of the statewide average in 1991 and 91.9 % in 2013. This was fundamentally influenced by the high economic position of the former West Berlin.[422] It should be mentioned that there are positions stating that the intensive growth of GDP *per capita* in the new federated states was the result of deferred domestic demand. The number of jobs in the construction and service sectors then increased.[423] Some researchers see the reason for the increase in GDP per *capita* in the Eastern *Länder* throughout the period in question in the massive emigration of young and educated residents to Western German centers.[424]

The revival of economic growth in the new federated states in the early 1990s resulted from increased labor productivity there. This resulted from the privatization and restructuring of Eastern German enterprises, increased investment, and reduction of over-employment. As a result, in 1992–2009 (with the exception of 1998 and 2007), the rate of real GDP per worker was higher than in the Western part of the country. Nevertheless, full convergence has not been achieved in this area either. For example, in the first decade of the 21st century, the Eastern German labor productivity per worker was about 79 % of the value of this indicator for the old federated states.[425]

Secondly, a number of reasons contributed to the significant decline in the initially high rate of GDP growth in the Eastern part of Germany that occurred around the mid-1990s (various data cited in studies), thus slowing down the convergence process. Among them, the literature most often mentions: (1) the reduction of the so far high transfers from the old federated states, especially after 1995; (2) the adoption of: (2.1.) an excessively high exchange rate between the GDR marks and the FRG marks (although the 1: 1 ratio was attractive to citizens due to increased real incomes, it hindered the development of enterprises, which

421 Cf. Pastuszka, "Polityka rozwoju Wschodnich Niemiec," 64, fn. 1; 65–66, table 4. There is a separate German literature on the economic role of Berlin.

422 Pastuszka, "Polityka rozwoju Wschodnich Niemiec," 66, table 4.

423 Czech-Rogosz, "Gospodarka wschodnich Niemiec w 12 lat po zjednoczeniu," 95.

424 See, e.g., Brocka-Palacz, *Wspieranie rozwoju gospodarki wschodniej części Niemiec*, 6. Cf. Pastuszka's polemics points to the greater significance of the growth rate than the population's outflow from the Eastern *Länder*: Pastuszka, "Polityka rozwoju Wschodnich Niemiec," 66, fn. 2.

425 Moszyński, "Zjednoczenie Niemiec," 259–260, table 3.

henceforth competed on prices in DM) and (2.2.) Western German wage policy (nominally identical wage rates, which in Eastern Germany were inadequate for the level of development, which in turn resulted in a "wage–productivity" gap, i.e. faster growth in wages than in productivity, as well as growing unemployment and economic stagnation); (3) weaker position of Eastern German workers in the labor market, resulting from the less developed education system in the GDR; (4) low efficiency of private enterprises in the Eastern *Länder* (determined by: old production assets, technological backwardness, low labor productivity, poor management); (5) external factors (transformations resulting from the world economy, globalization, European integration); (6) internal factors (decline in industrial production and low domestic demand resulting from low dynamics of consumption growth, reduced investment and unemployment).[426]

As an alternative to the above – one could say objective – interpretation, some researchers point to a more subjective factor, the "base effect." It is methodological in nature and consists in changing the starting point of the analysis, resulting in relatively smaller increments in subsequent periods of the study.[427]

From the point of view of the dynamics of GDP *per capita* in both parts of Germany, it is noted that the convergence involved only the growth rates of this indicator, not its absolute values. For example, in 2006, the overall German GDP *per capita* level (about 27.0 thousand euros) ranked the country 10th in the EU, while the value in the Western *Länder* was much higher (30.8 thousand euros, 3rd place in the EU), and in the new federated states much lower (19.8 thousand euros, 17th place in the EU). Taking into account the dynamics of GDP *per capita* in the Eastern *Länder* only, its value in 2007 was three times higher than in 1991, but in relation to the average for the old federated states (as a reference value), it turns out that the convergence process slowed down significantly in 1997. The difference in the value of this indicator between the two parts of Germany has remained relatively constant since then (about 10–11 thousand euros).[428]

Thirdly, the recovery period in GDP growth in 1994–2000 was not uniform. The slowdown in economic growth in 1994–1996 coincided with changes in the values of the indicators discussed earlier (e.g., investment, budget tax revenues, government expenditures). This resulted in a slowdown of the unification (convergence) process.[429] Moreover, due to the close ties between the two parts of Germany

---

426 See summaries of the mentioned reasons with exemplary literature references: Czech-Rogosz, "Gospodarka wschodnich Niemiec w 12 lat po zjednoczeniu," 94–95, 97; Götz, "Konwergencja dochodów," 94–95; Moszyński, "Zjednoczenie Niemiec," 254; Moszyński, "Idee ładu gospodarczego w procesie transformacji systemowej byłej NRD," 352–353; Klimiuk, "Trendy rozwojowe," 63–64.

427 This is done, e.g., by Marta Götz (Götz, "Konwergencja dochodów," 94).

428 Götz, "Konwergencja dochodów," 95, 97, 113.

429 Czech-Rogosz, "Gospodarka wschodnich Niemiec w 12 lat po zjednoczeniu," 94. Cf. 6.2.6., 6.2.7.2., 6.2.8. in this study.

in terms of industrial production (branches of Western German factories in the Eastern *Länder*), the slowdown in the economic growth of the old federated states after 1995 significantly weakened the economic potential of the Eastern *Länder*, and consequently of the whole country.[430] It can be assumed that this was the result of the convergence of the directions of real GDP growth dynamics, which was observed above since 1997.

Fourthly, the slowdown in growth in 2001–2002 was due to a decline in the level of production in the industrial, agricultural, and construction sectors. This situation was preceded by a global increase in oil prices, a weaker global economy, a decline in the FRG's exports, and chaos after the terrorist attacks in the United States on September 11, 2001. The situation was not much better after the introduction of the euro in Germany in 2002. At that time, the prices of consumer goods and services of first necessity increased by 4.8 %. A significant price increase also occurred between 2003 and 2005. The economic downturn of that time was the basis for the introduction of the economic reform package of the Schröder government in 2003, called *Agenda 2010*. These reforms were continued even after Merkel took power.[431]

Fifthly, the revival of economic growth in Eastern Germany in 2006–2007 was a consequence of the increased performance of industrial production and exports there, as well as the end of several years of crisis in the construction industry. The latter resulted from the systematic liquidation of the sector's overcapacity, the source of which was the subsidizing of the construction industry in the first half of the 1990s.[432] Reducing unemployment and increasing investment expenditures also had a positive impact on economic growth.[433]

---

430 Brocka-Palacz, *Wspieranie rozwoju gospodarki wschodniej części Niemiec*, 5, 7, 25–26.

431 Klimiuk, "Trendy rozwojowe," 64, 71–72. The literature on *Agenda 2010* is extensive. The main elements of the 2003 reform package were: (1) reduction of workers' privileges under the law protecting against unjustified termination; (2) reduction of the duration of unemployment benefits; (3) merger of unemployment assistance and social assistance into a single unemployment benefit; (4) transformation of the Federal Employment Office into the Federal Employment Agency; (5) change in the reimbursement system for certain medications; (6) increase in the number of paid medical services; (7) introduction of full payment of sickness benefits by insured persons; (8) one-time suspension of pension and disability benefit indexation (July 1, 2004); (9) charging pensions and disability benefits with a contribution for nursing insurance; (10) reducing early retirement privileges; (11) continuing the tax reform of 2000 with specific changes (Czech-Rogosz, "Reformy gospodarcze," 129–133).

432 Brocka-Palacz, *Wspieranie rozwoju gospodarki wschodniej części Niemiec*, 7.

433 Klimiuk, "Trendy rozwojowe," 73–74. See also a detailed analysis of the convergence of the Eastern and Western *Länder* until the financial crisis of 2008: M. Kullas, *Der Konvergenzprozess zwischen Ost- und Westdeutschland. Hemmnisse und politische Handlungsmöglichkeiten* (Hamburg: Verlag Dr. Kovač, 2011).

Sixthly, from a GDP perspective, the new federated states came through the financial crisis in 2009 relatively more smoothly than the Western part of Germany. This was due to the fact that Eastern-dominant small and medium-sized enterprises occupied a much weaker position in the structure of German exports than large Western German firms. The significant share of the agri-food sector in the production of the Eastern *Länder* was also important. This structure of the Eastern German economy was less exposed to the consequences of the world market recession. Its effects were felt primarily by concerns and the industrial sector concentrated in Western Germany. The development-promoting transfers implemented at that time within the Second Solidarity Pact for 2005–2019 played an additional protective role for the Eastern German economy.[434] The dependence of the FRG economy on exports meant that the recession on world markets had a strong impact on the situation in Germany. It is telling that until 2008, Germany had the largest share in global exports, after which it gave way to China.[435]

Seventhly, among the post-crisis pro-growth factors, the following are particularly mentioned: increased foreign trade, increased investment levels, and increased consumption. This is especially true for 2010 and 2011.[436] Moreover, there are studies showing that the Eastern *Länder* (excluding Berlin) grew faster than the Western part of Germany between 2000 and 2015. Suffice it to say that during this period, the difference in the size of real GDP *per capita* between the poorest federated state (Mecklenburg-Vorpommern) and the richest one (Hamburg) decreased by 17.2 percentage points. Compared to the all-German average, the gap narrowed by 3.8 percentage points. In 2000, Mecklenburg-Vorpommern generated 63.3 % of the statewide average level of real GDP *per capita*, while Hamburg generated 179.8 %. In 2015, these figures were respectively: 67.1 % and 166.4 %. The first decades of the 21st century were thus conducive to narrowing the disparity between the old and new federated states. This was not even disrupted by the financial crisis. However, the pace of this process was slow, so it had not been completed by 2015.[437]

It should be mentioned that there are various estimates in the literature about the time perspective of the completion of the convergence process of the Eastern and Western *Länder*, including from the perspective of GDP levels. Without reviewing such forecasts, it is worth noting some observations interesting from the point of view of this study.[438] In the light of the convergence theory, it is assumed,

434 Moszyński, "Zjednoczenie Niemiec," 259; Pastuszka, "Polityka rozwoju Wschodnich Niemiec," 64; Pastuszka, "Zmiany w spójności gospodarczej i społećznej," 347–348.

435 Klimiuk, "Trendy rozwojowe," 74–75, 77–82.

436 Klimiuk, "Trendy rozwojowe," 76–78.

437 Pastuszka, "Zmiany w spójności gospodarczej i społecznej," 346, table 2; 355–356.

438 The current forecast by Pastuszko and Jurand Skrzypek can be cited as representative. Taking the period 2000–2015 as a starting point and assuming unchanged political and economic conditions, they analyzed the rate of change of GDP *per capita* of the Eastern and Western *Länder* in the medium term and *sigma*

among other things, that the differences in economic growth rates in both parts of Germany will gradually decrease through lowering the Eastern German growth rate in relation to the Western German *Länder*. The main reason for this is catching up with the old federated states in the sphere of capital and labor. In order to continue the process of convergence, it is necessary to look for more permanent tools than – as Moszyński puts it – sources of growth of a one-off nature, i.e., property transformations, enterprise restructuring, or infrastructure investments. The next stage of generating growth should primarily be technology, as well as labor and capital.[439] It should be mentioned that these elements, which make up the economic process, should function within an effective economic order.

6.3. Summary of Chapters 5 and 6

The implementation of Western German property rights took place while the GDR was still in existence and during the formulation of the reunification concept in 1990. In an attempt to reform the political and economic system, the East German authorities, under the influence of the FRG, partially allowed the private sector into the economy. However, further elements of the West German model were gradually incorporated into the GDR. The extension of the Basic Law of the FRG to the GDR, i.e., the formal reunification of Germany, was of fundamental importance in this respect. The qualitative relationship between the institutions under study, i.e., constitutional and property rules, can be clearly seen here. Thus, the institution of West German property rights significantly contributed to economic transformations, first in the GDR (at the end of its existence) and then in the new federated states, which were an integral part of the reunified FRG.

The institution of property rights, previously functioning in West Germany (in some aspects with a much richer tradition), reformulated the previous system of property rules in the GDR. West German property rights were strongly anchored in the FRG Constitution, unlike the situation in East Germany, where the gap between civil liberties in the GDR Constitutions (*de jure* institution) and social reality (*de facto* institution) was large. Moreover, private property, which was the most efficient for the economy, was depreciated already on the doctrinal level and then limited or liquidated in the economic practice of East Germany.

West German property regulations played a key role in the transition of the Eastern *Länder* and in the unification, integration, and convergence of the two

---

convergence. Their calculations show that the developmental differences between the two parts of Germany will be eliminated around 2069–2081 (S. Pastuszka, J. Skrzypek, "Regionalne zróżnicowanie poziomu PKB w Niemczech," *Modern Management Review* 23, No. 25 (2018): 191–211). Events related to a coronavirus pandemic starting in 2020, Russian aggression against Ukraine, and the resulting economic crisis may slow the pace of this process, extending the time horizon for its completion.

439 Cf. Moszyński, "Zjednoczenie Niemiec," 265–266.

parts of Germany. Private property was precisely defined in law, from the Basic Law through civil law to specific legislation. Individual rights were embedded in a social context (the "public good"), a characteristic of the social market economy model. A wide range of ways of acquiring and losing property rights, regulated primarily by civil law, increased resource allocation efficiency, protecting the interests of parties exchanging these rights, and reducing transaction costs. In terms of enforcing and protecting property rights, the law with the state coercive apparatus played the most important role. This was particularly important in the context of Eastern German society's disillusionment with the increasing costs of transition and the slower evolution of informal institutions in the form of post-communist social norms.

After reunification, it was a priority to initiate privatization in the Eastern *Länder*. The adoption of specific legislation helped to intensify this process, already producing tangible results in the first half of the 1990s. A negative symbol of the haste in this regard and the accompanying chaos and sluggishness were the controversial aspects of the Trust Office. Re-privatization issues were settled fairly quickly in the former GDR. Between 1990 and 1994, further legislation was introduced in Germany that resolved questionable property situations, increasingly favoring potential investors in the Eastern *Länder*. Through decisive transformations of their property structure, the new federated states had already embarked on restructuring processes in the early 1990s. The private service sector played an increasingly important role there, displacing inefficient and ineffective heavy industry. The Eastern German agricultural sector remained in good economic condition. The German property tax system should also be viewed favorably. Studies on it and state interventionism from the point of view of budget expenditures showed that Germany was not an example of a fiscal state that burdened private property in the discussed period.

The period of transition of the Eastern *Länder* and their integration into the Western part of the country was not free of problems. In addition to the social costs widely discussed in the literature, attention should be paid to the disproportion in the development of the enterprise sector. Despite promising trends shortly after reunification, the economic predominance of Western German companies became increasingly apparent from the mid-1990s onwards. In the former GDR, it was more difficult to develop the model of employee participation, which had been functioning well in the West for decades. Regardless of increasing transfers to the Eastern *Länder*, the investment expenditures there were lower than in the West. Nevertheless, the new federated states concentrated investments in the high-tech sector. These difficulties resulted in a transformation in Germany's economic growth in 1990–2015. While up until the mid-1990s, the Eastern *Länder* grew significantly faster than the old federated states, due to the catch-up effect, in the second half of the 1990s, as a result of the growing disparity between the East and West of the country, the growth rate slowed significantly, often giving way to the results for the old *Länder*. These factors have contributed to the weakening of the convergence process and failure to complete it by 2015.

SUMMARY

The research conducted allows positive verification of the main research hypothesis of the dissertation. The analyzed formal institutions, i.e. the FRG Constitution and property rights, played a fundamental role in the economic transformations in Germany in 1990–2015. In doing so, they set the legal and institutional frameworks for the economic transition of the Eastern *Länder*, as well as the economic unification of the two parts of Germany. The answers to the four formulated specific research questions formed the content of the summaries of the relevant chapters of the study.

(1) In the social science literature, institutions are most often understood in two ways. One shows them as groups of people or organizations aimed at achieving a specific goal. Another view is the one that identifies institutions with norms or frameworks that provide boundaries for individuals to function. Management science and political science represent an understanding of institutions similar to the common perception, considering them as organizations.

An impressive theoretical body of work on the conceptualization of institutions was recorded by economics in the 19th to 21st centuries within the framework of separate currents, i.e. the old and new institutional economics. However, while in the first phase, the understanding of the category in question oscillated around a sociological and psychological point of view (as in Thorstein Veblen and Wesley C. Mitchell), the new institutional economics adopted more of an economic or socio-political perspective. Understood in this way, institutions regulate human relations, determine exchanges, define the terms of transactions, and stimulate development. The concept of Douglass C. North, which is the broadest, universalizes the spectrum of the impact of formal and informal rules on socio-economic reality.

In the case of history and economic history, the theoretical literature on institutions is much more modest. Nevertheless, rules of various kinds remain an important subject of historical and economic-historical research, even though their understanding is often not clearly defined and differs from that of institutional economics. For example, institutions and organizations are not infrequently juxtaposed synonymously in historical research. On the theoretical level, the perception of institutions in economic history is most often developed at the interface between history and the humanities on the one hand and economics and the social sciences on the other. This is due to the ontology of the discipline itself and its direct interdisciplinarity. Within the framework of indirect interdisciplinarity, economic history borrows concepts of institutions, most often from law and sociology. However, this is done most often in an ad hoc manner, at the level of research empirics, without theoretical and methodological deliberations. This should therefore be assessed as a gap to be filled.

However, positive examples can also be seen in this regard. Today, these are the results of the promising development of separate approaches to economic history research that emphasize the importance of rules, such as the new institutional economic history or the institutional approach in economic history research. A key role in this regard is played by historians inspired by the achievements of the new institutional economics. These currents have two additional advantages. Firstly, they emphasize the role of direct historical sources, although this is not obvious in institutional economic history studies conducted from economic positions. Secondly, empirical research is accompanied by important theoretical and methodological considerations. This is done in accordance with Werner Sombart's motto from 1929: "No theory – no history! Theory is the prerequisite to any scientific writing of history."[1] Ewa Domańska even calls for the creation of new theories based on the empirical material analyzed.[2] This acquires special significance when it is emphasized that economic history is a multiparadigmatic study.[3]

Significant and ongoing problems in institutional research in economics and economic history include: the lack of a general, consistent, unambiguous, and universally accepted definition of institutions; the difficulty of explaining causal relationships between rules and economic change; the reduction of research to a quantitative perspective and the related controversy with measuring institutions. The dominant role in the study of institutions in economics and economic history is played by formal rules as those that interact directly with socio-economic processes.

(2) Macroeconomic differences in terms of economic structures between the FRG and the GDR in the late 1980s and early 1990s were fundamental. West Germany maintained a clear advantage over the GDR's economic potential from the point of view of the most important segments of the economy, i.e. industry, agriculture, public finance, foreign trade, transport, and economic growth. West German society recorded a much higher standard of everyday life.

One of the consequences of West Germany's economic superiority was its political dominance. This allowed the FRG, with the backing of the superpowers, to achieve state reunification. Despite alternative East German projects aimed at maintaining separateness and subjectivity or reforming the political and economic system in a democratic and market-oriented direction, the West German vision of reunification was imposed on East Germany and implemented, eventually leading to the abolition of the GDR as a separate state and the incorporation of its territory within the borders of the FRG.

Among the most important factors responsible for the demonstrated differences in economic structures are the constitutional and property rules that set the basis for the different economic systems of the FRG and the GDR, i.e. the social market economy and the centrally planned economy. After reunification, they also

---

1 W. Sombart, "Economic Theory and Economic History," *The Economic History Review* 2, No. 1 (1929): 3.

2 Cf. D. Bębnowski, "The Attractiveness of the Project of Practical Methodology and Virtue Epistemology for Economic History Research," *Annales. Ethics in Economic Life* 20, No. 5 (2017): 107–125.

3 D. Bębnowski, "Socjologiczny komponent historii gospodarczej. Résumé głównych paradygmatów w XX i XXI w." (unpublished manuscript), 30.

determined the basic framework of Germany's development trajectory, especially that of the new federated states.

(3) Research has shown that the basis for the process of unification and integration of the two disparate economic systems after 1990 was the Basic Law of the FRG. The resulting constitutional rules outlined the framework for the culmination of the political reunification process itself. With the incorporation of the GDR into the FRG in October 1990, the force of this supreme legal act was extended to the territory of the Eastern *Länder*. Thus, the Constitution set the course for the further transition process of the new federated states, as well as the unification, integration, and convergence of the two parts of Germany. From this point of view, the particular significance of the Basic Law institution for the economy of the reunified state came in the late 1980s and early 1990s (still at the end of the GDR's existence) and the first half of the 1990s.

Although the FRG Constitution itself remained neutral on economic order, it set its most important premises. As a result, it can be considered the basic formal institution defining the framework of the social market economy system. Reunification was followed by a reformulation of Eastern Germany's political and legal system along the lines of the West German model. The Basic Law also implemented the main regulations of social and economic life there. On this basis, the Constitution incorporated the new *Länder* into the FRG's economic order, outlining the legal and institutional framework for the economic process. In other words, the Basic Law, while helping to shape the economic order, left space for the market to function. The beginning of the process of implementing the West German constitutional rules came at a time when the formula for the process of German reunification was being crystallized, and this process was underway. The basic steps in this regard were carried out as early as 1990.

The analysis proved the impact of the Basic Law institution on the German economy in 1990–2015. Institutional economics and positive constitutional economics provide theoretical references in this field. Although important results in this regard are provided by empirical econometric studies, they should be considered insufficient in qualitative-quantitative analysis. The methods of economic history, which allow to look at the object of study in a holistic, contextual, retrospective, interdisciplinary way, as well as integrating description with the analysis of statistical data, reveal important networks of relationships between the institution of the FRG Constitution and specific areas of the economy. Two dimensions of these can be distinguished: *de jure* and *de facto* institutions.

The first sphere included potential channels for the relationship between the political and systemic components of the Constitution and the German economy. These referred to the economic order, the catalog of the most important civil rights (the basic rights), systemic principles, and systemic objectives of an economic nature. Constitutional references to European integration, international law, and peace or environmental protection should be regarded as relevant to the economy. The provisions of the Basic Law can be considered durable, detailed (sometimes too much so), and relatively specific and unambiguous. This strengthened the stability of the country's political system after reunification. In the case of concreteness and unambiguity, contentious issues were resolved by the Federal Constitutional Court, whose line of jurisprudence on the subject has evolved. However, this was not the aim of this research. The amendments to the Basic Law, including the most important in the period under review, i.e. the first and second reforms of federalism of 2006 and 2009, contributed to increasing the effectiveness of constitutional rules. This status of them fostered long-term decision-making by economic entities, reducing their sense of uncertainty. This, in turn, determined the growth of investment and, consequently, economic growth. The latter, along with fiscal policy, counted among the second dimension of the Constitution's impact on the FRG economy during the period under review – *de facto* institutions. Despite the costs of reunification, including a growing budget deficit and public debt, as well as the weakening pace of convergence between the two parts of Germany, the country managed to maintain a high level of economic growth. From a fiscal policy perspective, the permanent embedding of Germany's fiscal rules in the Constitution promoted their effectiveness, transparency, and credibility. The second reform of federalism as a "remedy" to the financial crisis of 2008, introducing specific institutional arrangements to maintain fiscal discipline, had positive effects.

The above conclusions are in line with the high values of the formal institutional indicators for Germany in 1990–2015. They concern both categories related to constitutional rules and the institution of property rights. Germany stood out compared to other European countries in terms of political stability, government effectiveness, regulatory quality, the rule of law, property rights, government integrity, government spending, business and investment freedom, size of government, and legal system (considered together with property rights).

(4) West German property rules also played a key role in the economic transformation of the new federated states. Some solutions originated in the second half of the 19th century or the first half of the 20th century. The process of their implementation began in 1990 before the formal reunification of Germany. The property changes thus extended to the still-existing GDR.

East Germany's communist government, while attempting to reform its political and economic system, agreed under the FRG influence to some reforms in the free market spirit, partially allowing the private sector into the East German economy, especially in terms of creating new enterprises, attracting foreign investment, promoting competition and even initiating privatization and re-privatization. Further elements of the West German social market economy model were gradually adopted in the Eastern *Länder*. The extension of the force of the FRG Constitution to the GDR in October 1990 was of fundamental importance in this regard. This provides an additional argument justifying the qualitative link between constitutional rules and the institution of property rights.

The property rights theory sets the theoretical limits of the analysis of property rules in Germany. Private property as the most efficient for the economy was questioned even at the level of the Marxist doctrine of law and economics in the GDR. Successive East German Constitutions have extended more and more protection over social (state and cooperative) property. The libertarian provisions of the documents concerning civil rights (*de jure* institution) diverged from the reality of life under the communist regime (*de facto* institution). The private sector was consistently fought or at least restricted in all sectors of the economy by the GDR's economic policy.

Given the exclusivity within the degree of completeness of property rights, it should be said that in the Basic Law of the FRG, property rights found strong guarantees within the framework of the basic rights catalog that makes up Chap. I GG. Owners' rights were set in a broader social context, which was based on the ordoliberal doctrine and the social market economy model. Private property was intended to serve the "public good." Property rules were further defined in civil law and specific legislation. From the point of view of transferability, the wide range of ways of acquiring and losing property rights is noteworthy. It was specified especially by civil law. It increased resource allocation efficiency, protected both parties' interests in the contract, and reduced transaction costs. On the other hand, law played the most crucial role in Germany after reunification when it came to enforcing and protecting property rights. The tools for the state coercive apparatus were provided in this regard by European regulations, as well as civil and criminal law. This was particularly important in the prevailing realities. This is because the actions of the owners themselves played a complementary role, while post-communist social norms, characteristic of Eastern German society, evolved towards market-oriented values much more slowly, as is typical of informal institutions.

Consequently, the role of West German property regulations in the processes of transition of the new federated states, as well as unification, integration, and convergence of the two parts of the country, was crucial. The implemented rules remodeled the previous property order of Eastern Germany, which involved transitioning from the dominance of social property to strengthening the private sector's position in the property structure.

The introduction of regulations initiating property transformations in the new federated states was of primary importance. The first privatization decisions were made even at the end of the GDR during the formation of the reunification formula. Tangible results in this regard appeared in the first half of the 1990s. The role of coordinating this process was performed by the Trust Office, whose activities aroused much controversy. While the creation of a central body to manage state property and oversee property changes is appreciated, the effects of its activities have been criticized.

Noteworthy is the fact of the relatively rapid resolution of re-privatization cases in Germany. The relevant legislation in this regard was enacted in 1990–1994. They gradually strengthened potential investors, weakening the position of those persons formulating claims and seeking compensation. Although morally questionable from the point of view of the aggrieved, this type of mechanism fostered an increase in investment in the Eastern *Länder* and a process of convergence.

The progressive restructuring processes resulted from property transformations in the new *Länder*. Beginning in the 1990s, the importance of the state-heavy industry in the manufacturing sphere declined in favor of a growing private service sector. Significantly, the agricultural sector maintained a fairly strong potential, even recording higher productivity compared to Western Germany. In parallel, the process of regionalization of the Eastern *Länder*, i.e. their manufacturing specialization, deepened.

It is important to note that between 1990 and 2015, the FRG did not exhibit the characteristics of a fiscal state overburdening private property. This is confirmed by an analysis of the system of taxes covering property at the time, as well as budget expenditures related to the level of state interventionism.

The high social costs of the Eastern German transition, especially rapidly rising unemployment, were not the only negative consequence of German reunification. From the point of view of the formal institutions studied, the problem of uneven development of the enterprise sector should be noted. Thanks to property transformations, until the mid-1990s, there was a dynamic growth of new companies in the East due to the catch-up effect. However, the situation was later reversed. Firms in the new federated states were lagging behind the Western German companies in terms of the quality of goods produced, the size of employment, innovations, resources for research and development, value-added produced, exports, the size of costs and profits, or informal dependencies on partners from the old *Länder* or abroad. The result was a widening quantitative gap in this regard.

Despite the experience of the communist period in terms of particularly state-supported social activism and collectivism, the West German model of employee participation in the Eastern *Länder* encountered development difficulties. This may have been due to the earlier oppressiveness of the authorities, as well as the activities of the enterprises themselves implementing political guidelines in the production process, which was characteristic of the GDR. While abundant, the literature now provides divergent conclusions on the effectiveness of the *Mitbestimmung* model for the German economy.

The convergence of the 1990s also extended to the dynamics of capital expenditures. Although transfers from Western Germany were increasing, the development disparity between the two parts of the country also affected this area. The old federated states recorded higher nominal investment in subsequent years. The Eastern *Länder*, however, stood out with their thriving high-tech sector, especially the renewable energy industry.

It is important to note, considering economic growth, the characteristic catch-up effect of faster growth of the new federated states relative to the old *Länder*, falling in the first half of the 1990s. A slowdown in the convergence process and deepening development inequalities weakened this trend in the second half of the 1990s. Many times the economic growth rate of the Eastern *Länder* has since been lower than in the West. However, the weaker export potential of the former GDR's dominant small and medium-sized companies meant that the consequences of the economic crisis of 2008 were milder for this part of the country. Nevertheless, the year 2015, which closes the consideration, did not bring the end of the convergence process between Eastern and Western Germany, still maintaining clear development differences between the old and new federated states. Thus, despite the right directions, as well as the legal and institutional framework for the systemic transition of the Eastern *Länder*, it is difficult to consider that the process of their unification and integration has been completed.

An assessment of the formal institutions' effects on unified Germany's economy should be positive. They were appropriately selected components of economic order. They can be considered sufficiently general, certain and open.[4] It is also justified to speak of the permanence of German constitutional and property rules, understood as their constancy, continuity, and validity over a long period. They were entrenched in the Basic Law of the FRG and the most important areas of law, making them difficult to modify. These institutions were effective from the point of view of sanctions in situations of rule-breaking and functional, i.e. useful, which some authors refer to as the precision of the institutions' definition and their transparency and transparency.[5]

Constitutional rules and property rights laid the foundation for the FRG's socio-economic success in the post-war period. The problems with their implementation and effectiveness in the former GDR were not due to the quality of these rules but to factors exogenous to them. These, in turn, related to the not fully anticipated difficulties associated with the systemic transition of the new federated states, their unification and integration with the old *Länder*, and the initiation and promotion of convergence between the two parts of Germany. This complex and multidimensional process had not been completed by 2015.

Potential directions for further study can be identified based on the research conducted. An important research postulate would certainly be to set Germany's economic transformation under the influence of constitutional and property regulations in a broader comparative context. This involves capturing the similarities and differences between the post-reunification FRG and the other Eastern Bloc countries and considering the situation in other federal states or regions with strong integrationist tendencies.

From the point of view of the importance of the institutions under study for the German economy in a similar period, it would be interesting to conduct a broader analysis that would include the political discussion around the implementation of individual legal and institutional regulations, especially in the late 1980s and early

---

4 Cf. J. Groenewegen, A. Spithoven, A. van den Berg, *Institutional Economics. An Introduction* (New York: Palgrave Macmillan, 2010), 29.

5 Cf. M. Moszyński, "Wybrane reguły fiskalne w Szwajcarii i Republice Federalnej Niemiec – droga ku zrównoważonym finansom publicznym?," *Acta Universitatis Nicolai Copernici. Nauki Humanistyczno-Społeczne. Ekonomia* 40, No. 391 (2009): 116.

1990s. A little researched issue is the genesis and activities of the UrTHA in 1990. The directions of socio-economic transformations may also have been significantly influenced by the evolution of the Federal Constitutional Court's jurisprudence on constitutional and property rules, as well as the changes in informal institutions.

BIBLIOGRAPHY

SOURCES

Normative acts

THE SECOND REICH

Act on Enforced Auction and Receivership (Gesetz über die Zwangsversteigerung und die Zwangsverwaltung), Federal Ministry of Justice, Federal Office of Justice. https://www.gesetze-im-internet.de/englisch_zvg/.

Bürgerliches Gesetzbuch. Vom 18. August 1896. (RGBl., 1896, No. 21/2322, 195–603 as amended).

Civilprozeßordnung. Vom 30. Januar 1877. (RGBl., 1877, No. 6/1166, 83–243 as amended).

Gesetz über die Zwangsversteigerung und die Zwangsverwaltung. Vom 24. März 1897. (RGBl., 1897, No. 14/2372, 97–134 as amended).

Gesetz, betreffend die Ordnung des Reichshaushalts und die Tilgung der Reichsschuld. Vom 3. Juni 1906. (RGBl., 1906, No. 31/3248, 620–674).

Gesetz, betreffend die Redaktion des Strafgesetzbuchs für den Norddeutschen Bund als Strafgesetzbuch für das Deutsche Reich. Vom 15. Mai 1871. (RGBl., 1871, No. 24/651, 127–205 as amended).

Grundbuchordnung. Vom 24. März 1897. (RGBl., 1897, No. 15/2374, 139–157 as amended).

Handelsgesetzbuch. Vom 10. Mai 1897. (RGBl., 1897, No. 23/2388, 219–436 as amended).

Umsatzsteuergesetz. Vom 26. Juli 1918. (RGBl., 1918, No. 95/6399, 779–797).

WEIMAR REPUBLIC

Die Verfassung des Deutschen Reichs. Vom 11. August 1919. (RGBl., 1919, No. 152/6982, 1383–1418).

"Germany." In *The New Constitutions of Europe*, eds. H. L. McBain, L. Rogers, 167–212. New York: Doubleday, Page & Company, 1922.

Verordnung über das Erbbaurecht. Vom 15. Januar 1919. (RGBl., 1919, No. 14/6654, 72–82 as amended).

Versicherungssteuergesetz (RGBl., Part I, 1922, No. 30, 400–405).

THE THIRD REICH

Allgemeine Verfügung über die Einrichtung und Führung des Grundbuchs (Reichsministerialblatt der inneren Verwaltung, 1935, 637 as amended).

Einkommensteuergesetz (EStG) Vom 16. Oktober 1934 (RGBl., Part I, 1934, No. 119, 1005–1030).

Gewerbesteuergesetz (GewStG) Vom 1. Dezember 1936 (RGBl., Part I, 1936, No. 112, 979–985).

Körperschaftsteuergesetz (KStG) Vom 16. Oktober 1934 (RGBl., Part I, 1934, No. 119, 1031–1034).

GERMAN DEMOCRATIC REPUBLIC

Constitutions

"Gesetz über die Verfassung der Deutschen Demokratischen Republik vom 7. Oktober 1949." In *Gesetz über die Konstituierung der Provisorischen Volkskammer der Deutschen Demokratischen Republik vom 7. Oktober 1949.* (GBl.-DDR, Part I, 1949, No. 1, 4–16).

Verfassung der Deutschen Demokratischen Republik vom 6. April 1968 (GBl.-DDR, Part I, 1968, No. 8, 199–222).

Verfassung der Deutschen Demokratischen Republik vom 6. April 1968 in der Fassung des Gesetz zur Ergänzung und Änderung der Verfassung der Deutschen Demokratischen Republik vom 7. Oktober 1974 (GBl.-DDR, Part I, 1974, No. 47, 432–456).

Amendments to the Constitutions

Gesetz zur Änderung und Ergänzung der Verfassung der Deutschen Demokratischen Republik (Verfassungsgrundsätze) vom 17. Juni 1990 (GBl.-DDR, Part I, 1990, No. 33, 299–300).

Gesetz zur Ergänzung und Änderung der Verfassung der Deutschen Demokratischen Republik vom 7. Oktober 1974 (GBl.-DDR, Part I, 1974, No. 47, 425–432).

Verfassungsgesetz über Schulen in freier Trägerschaft vom 22. Juli 1990 (GBl.-DDR, Part I, 1990, No. 52, 1036–1038).

Other laws

Gesetz über das Vermögen der Gemeinden, Städte und Landkreise (Kommunalvermögensgesetz – KVG) vom 3. Juli 1990 (GBl.-DDR, Part I, 1990, No. 42, 660–662).

Gesetz über die Änderung des Gesetzes vom 21. Juni 1990 über die Inkraftsetzung von Rechtsvorschriften der Bundesrepublik Deutschland in der Deutschen Demokratischen Republik vom 6. Juli 1990 (GBl.-DDR, Part I, 1990, No. 44, 713).

Gesetz über die Gründung und Tätigkeit privater Unternehmen und über Unternehmensbeteiligungen vom 7. März 1990 (GBl.-DDR, Part I, 1990, No. 17, 141–144).

Gesetz über die Inkraftsetzung von Rechtsvorschriften der Bundesrepublik Deutschland in der Deutschen Demokratischen Republik vom 21. Juni 1990 (GBl.-DDR, Part I, 1990, No. 34, 357–363).

Gesetz über die strukturelle Anpassung der Landwirtschaft an die soziale und ökologische Marktwirtschaft in der Deutschen Demokratischen Republik – Landwirtschaftsanpassungsgesetz – vom 29. Juni 1990 (GBl.-DDR, Part I, 1990, No. 42, 642–649).

Gesetz zum Vertrag über die Schaffung einer Währungs-, Wirtschafts- und Sozialunion zwischen der Deutschen Demokratischen Republik und der Bundesrepublik Deutschland vom 18. Mai 1990 (Verfassungsgesetz) vom 21. Juni 1990 (GBl.-DDR, Part I, 1990, No. 34, 331–357).

Gesetz zum Vertrag zwischen der Deutschen Demokratischen Republik und der Bundesrepublik Deutschland über die Herstellung der Einheit Deutschlands – Einigungsvertrag – vom 31. August 1990 (Verfassungsgesetz) vom 20. September 1990 (GBl-DDR, Part I, 1990, No. 64, 1627–1986).

Gesetz zur Änderung und Ergänzung des Gesetzes über das Vermögen der Gemeinden, Städte und Landkreise vom 6. Juli 1990 (Kommunalvermögensgesetz – KVG) vom 13. September 1990 (GBl.-DDR, Part I, 1990, No. 61, 1537–1538).

Gesetz zur Durchführung eines Volksentscheides über die Verfassung der Deutschen Demokratischen Republik vom 28. März 1968 (GBl.-DDR, Part I, 1968, No. 7, 192–195).

Gesetz zur Privatisierung und Reorganisation des volkseigenen Vermögens (Treuhandgesetz) vom 17. Juni 1990 (GBl.-DDR, Part I, 1990, No. 33, 300–304).

Ordinances, resolutions, announcements

Bekanntmachung über das Inkrafttreten des Vertrages zwischen der Deutschen Demokratischen Republik und der Bundesrepublik Deutschland über die Herstellung der Einheit Deutschlands – Einigungsvertrag – vom 29. September 1990 (GBl.-DDR, Part I, 1990, No. 65, 1988–1989).

Beschluss zur Gründung der Anstalt zur treuhänderischen Verwaltung des Volkseigentums (Treuhandanstalt) vom 1. März 1990 (GBl.-DDR, Part I, 1990, No. 14, 107).

Statut der Anstalt zur treuhänderischen Verwaltung des Volkseigentums (Treuhandanstalt) – Beschluss des Ministerrates – vom 15. März 1990 (GBl.-DDR, Part I, 1990, No. 18, 167–169).

Verordnung über die Anmeldung vermögensrechtlicher Ansprüche vom 11. Juli 1990 (GBl.-DDR, Part I, 1990, No. 44, 718–719).

Verordnung über die Gründung und Tätigkeit von Unternehmen mit ausländischer Beteiligung in der DDR vom 25. Januar 1990 (GBl.-DDR, Part I, 1990, No. 4, 16–19).

Verordnung zur Umwandlung von volkseigenen Kombinaten, Betrieben und Einrichtungen in Kapitalgesellschaften vom 1. März 1990 (GBl.-DDR, Part I, 1990, No. 14, 107–108).

Zweite Verordnung über die Anmeldung vermögensrechtlicher Ansprüche vom 21. August 1990 (GBl.-DDR, Part I, 1990, No. 56, 1260).

FEDERAL REPUBLIC OF GERMANY

Constitution

Banaszak, B., Malicka, A., eds. *Konstytucja Niemiec.* Warszawa: Wydawnictwo Sejmowe, 2008.

Basic Law for the Federal Republic of Germany, Federal Ministry of Justice, Federal Office of Justice. https://www.gesetze-im-internet.de/englisch_gg/.

Grundgesetz für die Bundesrepublik Deutschland vom 23. Mai 1949. (BGBl., Part I, 1949, No 1, 1–20).

"Grundgesetz für die Bundesrepublik Deutschland vom 23. Mai 1949/Ustawa Zasadnicza Republiki Federalnej Niemiec z 23 maja 1949." In J. W. Tkaczyński, *Prawo ustrojowe Niemiec*, 453–562. Kraków: Wydawnictwo UJ, 2015.

Janicki, L., ed. *Ustawa Zasadnicza (Konstytucja) Republiki Federalnej Niemiec z 23 maja 1949 r./Grundgesetz für die Bundesrepublik Deutschland vom 23. Mai 1949.* Poznań: Instytut Zachodni, 2007.

Amendments to the Constitution

Achtundzwanzigstes Gesetz zur Änderung des Grundgesetzes (Artikel 74a GG) Vom 18. März 1971 (BGBl., Part I, 1971, No. 23, 206).

Dreißigstes Gesetz zur Änderung des Grundgesetzes (Artikel 74 GG – Umweltschutz) Vom 12. April 1972 (BGBl., Part I, 1972, No. 31, 593).

Dreizehntes Gesetz zur Änderung des Grundgesetzes Vom 16. Juni 1965 (BGBl., Part I, 1965, No. 26, 513).

Einunddreißigstes Gesetz zur Änderung des Grundgesetzes Vom 28. Juli 1972 (BGBl., Part I, 1972, No. 76, 1305).

Einundzwanzigstes Gesetz zur Änderung des Grundegesetzes (Finanzreformgesetz) Vom 12. Mai 1969 (BGBl., Part I, 1969, No. 37, 359–362).

Fünfzehntes Gesetz zur Änderung des Grundgesetzes Vom 8. Juni 1967 (BGBl., Part I, 1967, No. 32, 581).

Gesetz zur Änderung des Artikels 107 des Grundgesetzes. Vom 20. April 1953. (BGBl., Part I, 1953, No. 16, 130).

Gesetz zur Änderung des Grundgesetzes (Artikel 106, 106b, 107, 108) Vom 19 März 2009 (BGBl., Part I, 2009, No. 16, 606).

Gesetz zur Änderung des Grundgesetzes (Artikel 108) Vom 26. November 2001 (BGBl., Part I, 2001, No. 61, 3219).

Gesetz zur Änderung des Grundgesetzes (Artikel 22, 23, 33, 52, 72, 73, 74, 74a, 75, 84, 85, 87c, 91a, 91b, 93, 98, 104a, 104b, 105, 107, 109, 125a, 125b, 125c, 143c) Vom 28. August 2006 (BGBl., Part I, 2006, No. 41, 2034–2038).

Gesetz zur Änderung des Grundgesetzes (Artikel 23, 45 und 93) Vom 8. Oktober 2008 (BGBl., Part I, 2008, No. 45, 1926).

Gesetz zur Änderung des Grundgesetzes (Artikel 28 und 106) Vom 20. Oktober 1997 (BGBl., Part I, 1997, No. 69, 2470).

Gesetz zur Änderung des Grundgesetzes (Artikel 3, 20a, 28, 29, 72, 74, 75, 76, 77, 80, 87, 93, 118a und 125a) Vom 27. Oktober 1994 (BGBl., Part I, 1994, No. 75, 3146–3148).

Gesetz zur Änderung des Grundgesetzes (Artikel 87d) Vom 29. Juli 2009 (BGBl., Part I, 2009, No. 48, 2247).

Gesetz zur Änderung des Grundgesetzes (Artikel 91b) Vom 23. Dezember 2014 (BGBl., Part I, 2014, No. 64, 2438).

Gesetz zur Änderung des Grundgesetzes (Artikel 91c, 91d, 104b, 109, 109a, 115, 143d) Vom 29. Juli 2009 (BGBl., Part I, 2009, No. 48, 2248–2250).

Gesetz zur Änderung des Grundgesetzes (Artikel 91e) Vom 21. Juli 2010 (BGBl., Part I, 2010, No. 38, 944).

Gesetz zur Änderung des Grundgesetzes (Staatsziel Tierschutz) Vom 26. Juli 2002 (BGBl., Part I, 2002, No. 53, 2862).

Gesetz zur Änderung des Grundgesetzes Vom 14. Juli 1992 (BGBl., Part I, 1992, No. 33, 1254).

Gesetz zur Änderung des Grundgesetzes Vom 20. Dezember 1993 (BGBl., Part I, 1993, No. 68, 2089–2090).

Gesetz zur Änderung des Grundgesetzes Vom 21. Dezember 1992 (BGBl., Part I, 1992, No. 58, 2086–2087).

Gesetz zur Änderung des Grundgesetzes Vom 3. November 1995 (BGBl., Part I, 1995, No. 57, 1492).

Gesetz zur Änderung des Grundgesetzes Vom 30. August 1994 (BGBl., Part I, 1994, No. 58, 2245).

Gesetz zur Änderung und Ergänzung der Finanzverfassung (Finanzverfassungsgesetz). Vom 23. Dezember 1955. (BGBl., Part I, 1955, No. 47, 817–818).

Gesetz zur Änderung und Ergänzung des Artikels 106 des Grundgesetzes. Vom 24. Dezember 1956. (BGBl., Part I, 1956, No. 54, 1077).

Gesetz zur Einfügung eines Artikels 120a in das Grundgesetz. Vom 14. August 1952 (BGBl., Part I, 1952, No. 34, 445).

Gesetz zur Einfügung eines Artikels 135a in das Grundgesetz. Vom 22. Oktober 1957. (BGBl., Part I, 1957, No. 58, 1745).

Gesetz zur Einfügung eines Artikels über die Luftverkehrsverwaltung in das Grundgesetz (11. Änderung des Grundgesetzes) Vom 6. Februar 1961 (BGBl., Part I, 1961, No. 7, 65).

Gesetz zur Ergänzung des Grundgesetzes. Vom 23. Dezember 1959. (BGBl., Part I, 1959, No. 56, 813).

Gesetz zur Ergänzung des Grundgesetzes. Vom 26. März 1954. (BGBl., Part I, 1954, No. 6, 45).

Neunundzwanzigstes Gesetz zur Änderung des Grundgesetzes Vom 18. März 1971 (BGBl., Part I, 1971, No. 23, 207).

Siebenundzwanzigstes Gesetz zur Änderung des Grundgesetzes Vom 31. Juli 1970 (BGBl., Part I, 1970, No. 76, 1161).

Siebzehntes Gesetz zur Ergänzung des Grundgesetzes Vom 24. Juni 1968 (BGBl., Part I, 1968, No. 41, 709–713).

Vierunddreißigstes Gesetz zur Änderung des Grundgesetzes (Artikel 74 Nr. 4a) Vom 23. August 1976 (BGBl., Part I, 1976, No. 107, 2383).

Vierundzwanzigstes Gesetz zur Änderung des Grundgesetzes Vom 28. Juli 1969 (BGBl., Part I, 1969, No. 68, 985).

Vierzehntes Gesetz zur Änderung des Grundgesetzes Vom 30. Juli 1965 (BGBl., Part I, 1965, No. 34, 649).

Zwanzigstes Gesetz zur Änderung des Grundgesetzes Vom 12. Mai 1969 (BGBl, Part I, 1969, No. 37, 357–358).

Zweites Gesetz zur Änderung des Artikels 107 des Grundgesetzes. Vom 25. Dezember 1954. (BGBl., Part I, 1954, No. 45, 517).

Zweiundzwanzigstes Gesetz zur Änderung des Grundgesetzes Vom 12. Mai 1969 (BGBl., Part I, 1969, No. 37, 363).

Other laws

Act on the Ownership of Apartments and the Permanent Residential Right (Wohnungseigentumsgesetz, WEG), Federal Ministry of Justice, Federal Office of Justice. http://www.gesetze-im-internet.de/englisch_woeigg/.

Betriebsverfassungsgesetz Vom 15. Januar 1972 (BGBl., Part I, 1972, No. 2, 13–43 as amended).

Betriebsverfassungsgesetz. Vom 11. Oktober 1952. (BGBl., Part I, 1952, No. 43, 681–694 as amended).

Bundesbaugesetz Vom 23. Juni 1960 (BGBl., Part I, 1960, No. 30, 341–388 as amended).

Bürgerliches Gesetzbuch. Berlin: Bundesministerium der Justiz und für Verbraucherschutz, 2017, as of 20.07.2017.

Code of Civil Procedure, Federal Ministry of Justice, Federal Office of Justice. https://www.gesetze-im-internet.de/englisch_zpo/.

Drittes Gesetz zur Änderung des Umwandlungsgesetzes Vom 11. Juli 2011 (BGBl., Part I, 2011, No. 35, 1338–1340).

Erstes Gesetz zur Bereinigung von SED-Unrecht (Erstes SED-Unrechtsbereinigungsgesetz – 1. SED-UnBerG) Vom 29. Oktober 1992 (BGBl., Part I, 1992, No. 50, 1814–1821).

Fünftes Gesetz zur Verbesserung rehabilitierungsrechtlicher Vorschriften für Opfer der politischen Verfolgung in der ehemaligen DDR Vom 22. Dezember 2014 (BGBl., Part I, 2014, No. 63, 2408).

German Civil Code BGB, Federal Ministry of Justice, Federal Office of Justice. https://www.gesetze-im-internet.de/englisch_bgb/.

German Criminal Code (Strafgesetzbuch – StGB), Federal Ministry of Justice, Federal Office of Justice. https://www.gesetze-im-internet.de/englisch_stgb/.

Gesetz über das Baugesetzbuch Vom 8. Dezember 1986 (BGBl., Part I, 1986, No. 63, 2191–2236).

Gesetz über das Erbaurecht (Erbbaurechtsgesetz – ErbbauRG). Berlin: Bundesministerium der Justiz und für Verbraucherschutz, 2013, as of 01.10.2013.

Gesetz über das Wohnungseigentum und das Dauerwohnrecht (Wohnungseigentumsgesetz). Vom 15. März 1951. (BGBl., Part I, 1951, No. 13, 175–185 as amended).

Gesetz über den Lastenausgleich (Lastenausgleichsgesetz – LAG). Vom 14. August 1952. (BGBl., Part I, 1952, No. 34, 446–533).

Gesetz über die Entschädigung nach dem Gesetz zur Regelung offener Vermögensfragen und über staatliche Ausgleichsleistungen für Enteignungen auf besatzungsrechtlicher oder besatzungshoheitlicher Grundlage (Entschädigungs- und Ausgleichsleistungsgesetz – EALG) Vom 27. September 1994 (BGBl., Part I, 1994, No. 65, 2624–2639).

Gesetz über die Mitbestimmung der Arbeitnehmer (Mitbestimmungsgesetz – MitbestG) Vom 4. Mai 1976 (BGBl., Part I, 1976, No. 51, 1153–1165 as amended).

Gesetz über die Mitbestimmung der Arbeitnehmer in den Aufsichtsräten und Vorständen der Unternehmen des Bergbaus und der Eisen und Stahl erzeugenden Industrie. Vom 21. Mai 1951. (BGBl., Part I, 1951, No. 24, 347–349 as amended).

Gesetz über städtebauliche Sanierungs- und Entwicklungsmaßnahmen in den Gemeinden (Städtebauförderungsgesetz) Vom 27. Juli 1971 (BGBl., Part I, 1971, No. 72, 1125–1156).

Gesetz zu dem Vertrag vom 12. September 1990 über die abschließende Regelung in bezug auf Deutschland Vom 11. Oktober 1990 (BGBl., Part II, 1990, No. 38, 1317–1329).

Gesetz zu dem Vertrag vom 18. Mai 1990 über die Schaffung einer Währungs-, Wirtschafts- und Sozialunion zwischen der Bundesrepublik Deutschland und der Deutschen Demokratischen Republik Vom 25. Juni 1990 (BGBl., Part II, 1990, No. 20, 518–568).

Gesetz zu dem Vertrag vom 3. August 1990 zur Vorbereitung und Durchführung der ersten gesamtdeutschen Wahl des Deutschen Bundestages zwischen der Bundesrepublik Deutschland und der Deutschen Demokratischen Republik sowie dem Änderungsvertrag vom 20. August 1990 Vom 29. August 1990 (BGBl., Part II, 1990, No. 31, 813–832).

Gesetz zu dem Vertrag vom 31. August 1990 zwischen der Bundesrepublik Deutschland und der Deutschen Demokratischen Republik über die Herstellung der Einheit Deutschlands – Einigungsvertragsgesetz – und der Vereinbarung vom 18. September 1990 Vom 23. September 1990 (BGBl., Part II, 1990, No. 35, 885–1245).

Gesetz zum Schutz vor Mißbrauch personenbezogener Daten bei der Datenverarbeitung (Bundesdatenschutzgesetz – BDSG) Vom 27. Januar 1977 (BGBl., Part I, 1977, No. 7, 201–214).

Gesetz zur abschließenden Erfüllung der verbliebenen Aufgaben der Treuhandanstalt Vom 9. August 1994 (BGBl., Part I, 1994, No. 54, 2062–2065).

Gesetz zur Anpassung des Baugesetzbuchs an EU-Richtlinien (Europarechtsanpassungsgesetz Bau – EAG Bau) Vom 24. Juni 2004 (BGBl., Part I, 2004, No. 31, 1359–1382).

Gesetz zur Änderung datenschutzrechtlicher Vorschriften Vom 14. August 2009 (BGBl., Part I, 2009, No. 54, 2814–2820).

Gesetz zur Änderung des Bundesdatenschutzgesetzes Vom 29. Juli 2009 (BGBl., Part I, 2009, No. 48, 2254–2257).

Gesetz zur Änderung des Vermögensgesetzes und anderer Vorschriften (Zweites Vermögensrechtsänderungsgesetz – 2.VermRÄndG) Vom 14. Juli 1992 (BGBl., Part I, 1992, No. 33, 1257–1286).

Gesetz zur Änderung des Waffengesetzes und weiterer Vorschriften Vom 26. März 2008 (BGBl., Part I, 2008, No. 11, 426–440).

Gesetz zur Bereinigung des Umwandlungsrechts (UmwBerG) Vom 28. Oktober 1994 (BGBl., Part I, 1994, No. 77, 3210–3266).

Gesetz zur Bereinigung vermögensrechtlicher und anderer Vorschriften (Vermögensr echtsbereinigungsgesetz – VermBerG) Vom 20. Oktober 1998 (BGBl., Part I, 1998, No. 71, 3180–3187).

Gesetz zur Beseitigung von Hemmnissen bei der Privatisierung von Unternehmen und zur Förderung von Investitionen Vom 22. März 1991 (BGBl., Part I, 1991, No. 20, 766–789).

Gesetz zur Durchführung der Vierten, Siebenten und Achten Richtlinie des Rates der Europäischen Gemeinschaften zur Koordinierung des Gesellschaftsrechts (Bilanzrichtlinien-Gesetz – BiRiLiG) Vom 19. Dezember 1985 (BGBl., Part I, 1985, No. 62, 2355–2433).

Gesetz zur Einführung eines befristeten Solidaritätszuschlags und zur Änderung von Verbrauchsteuer- und anderen Gesetzen (Solidaritätsgesetz) Vom 24. Juni 1991 (BGBl., Part I, 1991, No. 38, 1318–1321 as amended).

Gesetz zur Erleichterung der Umsetzung der Grundbuchamtsreform in Baden-Württemberg sowie zur Änderung des Gesetzes betreffend die Einführung der Zivilprozessordnung und des Wohnungseigentumsgesetzes Vom 5. Dezember 2014 (BGBl., Part I, 2014, No. 57, 1962–1963).

Gesetz zur Erleichterung von Planungsvorhaben für die Innenentwicklung der Städte Vom 21. Dezember 2006 (BGBl., Part I, 2006, No. 64, 3316–3321).

Gesetz zur Förderung der Stabilität und des Wachstums der Wirtschafts Vom 8. Juni 1967 (BGBl., Part I, 1967, No. 32, 582–589).

Gesetz zur Neufassung des Umsatzsteuergesetzes und zur Änderung anderer Gesetze Vom 26. November 1979 (BGBl., Part I, 1979, No. 69, 1953–1979).

Gesetz zur Neuorganisation der Bundesfinanzverwaltung und zur Schaffung eines Reffinanzierungsregisters Vom 22. September 2005 (BGBl., Part I, 2005, No. 60, 2809–2819).

Gesetz zur Neuregelung des Waffenrechts (WassRNeuRegG) Vom 11. Oktober 2002 (BGBl., Part I, 2002, No. 73, 3970–4014).

Gesetz zur Reform des Erbschaftsteuer- und Schenkungsteuerrechts Vom 17. April 1974 (BGBl., Part I, 1974, No. 42, 933–947).

Gesetz zur Reform des Grundsteuerrechts Vom 7. August 1973 (BGBl., Part I, 1973, No. 66, 965–974).

Gesetz zur Umsetzung der Transparenzrichtlinie-Änderungsrichtlinie Vom 20. November 2015 (BGBl., Part I, 2015, No. 46, 2029–2052).

Gesetz zur Umsetzung der Verbraucherkreditrichtlinie, des zivilrechtlichen Teils der Zahlungsdiensterrichtlinie sowie zur Neuordnung der Vorschriften über das Widerrufs- und Rückgaberecht Vom 29. Juli 2009 (BGBl., Part I, 2009, No. 49, 2355–2408).

Grunderwerbsteuergesetz (GrEStG 1983) Vom 17. Dezember 1982 (BGBl., Part I, 1982, No. 52, 1777–1789).

Handelsgesetzbuch. Berlin: Bundesministerium der Justiz und für Verbraucherschutz, 2019, as of 12.12.2019.

Jahressteuergesetz 2009 (JStG 2009) Vom 19. Dezember 2008 (BGBl., Part I, 2008, No. 63, 2794–2845).

Körperschaftsteuerreformgesetz Vom 31. August 1976 (BGBl., Part I, 1976, No. 114, 2597–2628).

Strafgesetzbuch. Berlin: Bundesministerium der Justiz und für Verbraucherschutz, 2017, as of 01.11.2017.

Viertes Gesetz zur Änderung des Spregstoffgesetzes Vom 17. Juli 2009 (BGBl., Part I, 2009, No. 44, 2062–2090).

Viertes Gesetz zur Änderung von Verbrauchsteuergesetzen Vom 15. Juli 2009 (BGBl., Part I, 2009, No. 42, 1870–1938).

Waffengesetz (WaffG) Vom 19. September 1972 (BGBl., Part I, 1972, No. 105, 1797–1817).

Zehnte Zuständigkeitsanpassungsverordnung Vom 31. August 2015 (BGBl., Part I, 2015, No. 35, 1474–1564).

Zivilprozessordnung. Berlin: Bundesministerium der Justiz und für Verbraucherschutz, 2019, as of 20.02.2019.

Zweites Gesetz über die Bereinigung von Bundesrecht im Zuständigkeitsbereich des Bundesministeriums der Justiz Vom 23. November 2007 (BGBl., Part I, 2007, No. 59, 2614–2630).

Zweites Gesetz zur Änderung der Vorschriften zum begünstigten Flächenerwerb nach § 3 des Ausgleichsleistungsgesetzes und der Flächenerwerbsverordnung (Zweites Flächenerwerbsänderungsgesetz – 2. FlErwÄndG) Vom 21. März 2011 (BGBl., Part I, 2011, No. 12, 450–451).

Zweites Gesetz zur Änderung des Umwandlungsgesetzes Vom 19. April 2007 (BGBl., Part I, 2007, No. 15, 542–548).

Zweites Gesetz zur Modernisierung des Kostenrechts (2. Kostenrechtsmodernisierungs gesetz – 2. KostRMoG) Vom 23. Juli 2013 (BGBl., Part I, 2013, No. 42, 2586–2712).

Zweites Gesetz zur Vereinfachung der Wahl der Arbeitnehmervertreter in den Aufsichtsrat Vom 18. Mai 2004 (BGBl., Part I, 2004, No. 25, 974–979 as amended).

Ordinances, announcements, corrections

Bekanntmachung der Neufassung der Gewerbesteuer-Durchführungsverordnung Vom 15. Oktober 2002 (BGBl., Part I, 2002, No. 75, 4180–4183).

Bekanntmachung der Neufassung der Grundbuchordnung Vom 26. Mai 1994 (BGBl., Part I, 1994, No. 32, 1114–1132).

Bekanntmachung der Neufassung der Grundbuchverfügung Vom 24. Januar 1995 (BGBl., Part I, 1995, No. 6, 114–133).

Bekanntmachung der Neufassung der Versicherungsteuer-Durchführungsverordnung Vom 10. Januar 1996 (BGBl., Part I, 1996, No. 2, 28–29).

Bekanntmachung der Neufassung des Ausgleichsleistungsgesetzes Vom 13. Juli 2004 (BGBl., Part I, 2004, No. 37, 1665–1670).

Bekanntmachung der Neufassung des Bundesdatenschutzgesetzes Vom 14. Januar 2003 (BGBl., Part I, 2003, No. 3, 66–88).

Bekanntmachung der Neufassung des Bürgerlichen Gesetzbuchs Vom 2. Januar 2002 (BGBl., Part I, 2002, No. 2, 42–341).

Bekanntmachung der Neufassung des Einkommensteuergesetzes Vom 8. Oktober 2009 (BGBl., Part I, 2009, No. 68, 3366–3533).

Bekanntmachung der Neufassung des Erbschaftsteuer- und Schenkungsteuergesetzes Vom 27. Februar 1997 (BGBl., Part I, 1997, No. 13, 378–392).

Bekanntmachung der Neufassung des Gewerbesteuergesetzes Vom 15. Oktober 2002 (BGBl., Part I, 2002, No. 75, 4167–4179).

Bekanntmachung der Neufassung des Grunderwerbsteuergesetzes Vom 26. Februar 1997 (BGBl., Part I, 1997, No. 14, 418–425).

Bekanntmachung der Neufassung des Investitionsvorranggesetzes Vom 4. August 1997 (BGBl., Part I, 1997, No. 56, 1996–2005).

Bekanntmachung der Neufassung des Körperschaftsteuergesetzes Vom 15. Oktober 2002 (BGBl., Part I, 2002, No. 75, 4144–4166).

Bekanntmachung der Neufassung des Landwirtschaftsanpassungsgesetzes Vom 3. Juli 1991 (BGBl., Part I, 1991, No. 40, 1418–1429).

Bekanntmachung der Neufassung des Lastenausgleichsgesetzes Vom 2. Juni 1993 (BGBl., Part I, 1993, No. 28, 845–897).

Bekanntmachung der Neufassung des Strafrechtlichen Rehabilitierungsgesetzes Vom 17. Dezember 1999 (BGBl., Part I, 1999, No. 60, 2664–2670).

Bekanntmachung der Neufassung des Umsatzsteuergesetzes Vom 21. Februar 2005 (BGBl., Part I, 2005, No. 13, 386–433).

Bekanntmachung der Neufassung des Umwandlungsgesetzes Vom 6. November 1969, (BGBl., Part I, 1969, No. 119, 2081–2092).

Bekanntmachung der Neufassung des Vermögensgesetzes Vom 18. April 1991 (BGBl., Part I, 1991, No. 26, 957–970).

Bekanntmachung der Neufassung des Vermögensgesetzes Vom 4. August 1997 (BGBl., Part I, 1997, No. 56, 1974–1995).

Bekanntmachung der Neufassung des Vermögensgesetzes Vom 9. Februar 2005 (BGBl., Part I, 2005, No. 9, 205–228).

Bekanntmachung der Neufassung des Versicherungsteuergesetzes Vom 10. Januar 1996 (BGBl., Part I, 1996, No. 2, 22–27).

Bekanntmachung der Neufassung des Waffengesetzes (WaffG) Vom 8. März 1976 (BGBl., Part I, 1976, No. 23, 432–455).

Bekanntmachung des Schreibens der Präsidentin der Volkskammer der Deutschen Demokratischen Republik vom 25. August 1990 und des Beschlusses der Volkskammer vom 23. August 1990 über den Beitritt der Deutschen Demokratischen Republik zum Geltungsbereich des Grundgesetzes der Bundesrepublik Deutschland Vom 19. September 1990 (BGBl., Part I, 1990, No. 49, 2057–2058).

Bekanntmachung einer Erklärung der Außenminister Frankreichs, der Sowjetunion, des Vereinigten Königreichs und der Vereinigten Staaten im Zusammenhang mit dem in Moskau am 12. September 1990 unterzeichneten Vertrag über die abschließende Regelung in bezug auf Deutschland Vom 2. Oktober 1990 (BGBl., Part II, 1990, No. 38, 1331–1332).

Berichtigung der Bekanntmachung der Neufassung des Einkommensteuergesetzes Vom. 8 Dezember 2009 (BGBl., Part I, 2009, No. 78, 3862).

Berichtigung der Bekanntmachung der Neufassung des Grunderwerbsteuergesetzes Vom 2. Juli 1997 (BGBl., Part I, 1997, No. 48, 1804).

Berichtigung der Neufassung des Lastenausgleichsgesetzes Vom 14. Februar 1995 (BGBl., Part I, 1995, No. 10, 248).

Berichtigung des Gesetzes zur Bereinigung des Umwandlungsrechts Vom 22. März 1995 (BGBl., Part I, 1995, No. 16, 428).

Berichtigung des Gesetzes zur Beseitigung von Hemmnissen bei der Privatisierung von Unternehmen und zur Förderung von Investitionen Vom 12. September 1991 (BGBl., Part I, 1991, No. 54, 1928).

Berichtigung des Gesetzes zur Neuregelung des Waffenrechts Vom 19. Dezember 2002 (BGBl., Part I, 2002, No. 86, 4592).

Berichtigung des Gesetzes zur Neuregelung des Waffenrechts Vom 19. September 2003 (BGBl., Part I, 2003, No. 49, 1957).

Verordnung über die Umbenennung und die Anpassung von Zuständigkeiten der Treuhandanstalt (Treuhandanstaltumbenennungsverordnung – TreuhUmbenV) Vom 20. Dezember 1994 (BGBl., Part I, 1994, No. 92, 3913).

Verordnung zur Übertragung von liegenschaftsbezogenen Aufgaben und Liegenschaftsgesellschaften der Treuhandanstalt (Treuhandliegenschaftsübertrag ungsverordnung – TreuhLÜV) Vom 20. Dezember 1994 (BGBl., Part I, 1994, No. 92, 3908–3909).

Verordnung zur Übertragung von unternehmensbezogenen Aufgaben und Unternehmensbeteiligungen der Treuhandanstalt (Treuhandunternehmensübertr agungsverordnung – TreuhUntÜV) Vom 20. Dezember 1994 (BGBl., Part I, 1994, No. 92, 3910–3912).

European Union normative acts

Charter of Fundamental Rights of the European Union (Official Journal of the European Union, 26.10.2012, C 326, 391–407).

"Consolidated Version of the Treaty on the Functioning of the European Union." In *Consolidated Versions of the Treaty on European Union and the Treaty on the Functioning of the European Union* (Official Journal of the European Union, 26.10.2012, C 326, 47–199).

European Convention on Human Rights as Amended by Protocols Nos. 11, 14 and 15 Supplemented by Protocols Nos. 1, 4, 6, 7, 12, 13 and 16. Strasbourg: European Court of Human Rights, 2021.

"Protocol (No 12) on the Excessive Deficit Procedure." In *Consolidated Versions of the Treaty on European Union and the Treaty on the Functioning of the European Union* (Official Journal of the European Union, 26.10.2012, C 326, 279–280).

"Protocol (No 13) on the Convergence Criteria." In *Consolidated Versions of the Treaty on European Union and the Treaty on the Functioning of the European Union* (Official Journal of the European Union, 26.10.2012, C 326, 281–282).

Statistical materials

"2020 Index of Economic Freedom." https://www.heritage.org/index/.

"Active Monitored Alarm Systems in Europe and North America Reached 41 Million at the End of 2016." https://www.iot-now.com/2017/04/19/60882-active-monitored-alarm-systems-europe-north-america-reached-41-million-end-2016/.

Beteiligungsbericht, Vol. 2001. Bonn: Bundesministerium der Finanzen, 2001.

Beteiligungsbericht, Vol. 2002. Bonn: Bundesministerium der Finanzen, 2002.

Beteiligungsbericht, Vol. 2005. Berlin: Bundesministerium der Finanzen, 2005.

Boeselager, F. "Deutschland, deine Waffen." http://www.deutschlandfunkkultur.de/statistik-deutschland-deine-waffen.976.de.html?dram:article_id=346481.

Die Beteiligungen des Bundes. Beteiligungsbericht, Vol. 2010. Berlin: Bundesministerium der Finanzen, 2011.

Die Beteiligungen des Bundes. Beteiligungsbericht, Vol. 2011. Berlin: Bundesministerium der Finanzen, 2011.

Die Beteiligungen des Bundes. Beteiligungsbericht, Vol. 2013. Berlin: Bundesministerium der Finanzen, 2014.

Die Beteiligungen des Bundes. Beteiligungsbericht, Vol. 2014. Berlin: Bundesministerium der Finanzen, 2015.

Die Beteiligungen des Bundes. Beteiligungsbericht, Vol. 2015. Berlin: Bundesministerium der Finanzen, 2016.

Die Beteiligungen des Bundes. Beteiligungsbericht, Vol. 2016. Berlin: Bundesministerium der Finanzen, 2017.

"Doing Business. Measuring Business Regulations." https://www.doingbusiness.org/en/custom-query#.

"Economic Freedom." https://www.fraserinstitute.org/economic-freedom/dataset/.

Ergebnisse früherer Bundestagswahlen. Stand: 18. August 2017. Informationen des Bundeswahlleiters. Wiesbaden: Der Bundeswahlleiter, 2017.

Europäisches System Volkswirtschaftlicher Gesamtrechnungen – ESVG 2010. Luxemburg: Eurostat, Europäische Kommission, Amt für Veröffentlichungen der Europäischen Union, 2014.

"FDI Outflows, by Region and Economy, 1990–2017." World Investment Report 2018, UNCTAD. https://worldinvestmentreport.unctad.org/annex-tables/.

"It's Different in Germany." http://www.professionalsecurity.co.uk/reviews/its-different-in-germany/.

Jahresbericht der Bundesregierung zum Stand der Deutschen Einheit 2018. Berlin: Der Beauftragte der Bundesregierung für die neuen Bundesländer, Bundesministerium für Wirtschaft und Energie, 2018.

Maddison, A. *The World Economy*, Vol. 1: *A Millennial Perspective*. Paris: OECD, 2006.

Materialien zum Bericht zur Lage der Nation im geteilten Deutschland 1987. Bonn: Bundesministerium für innerdeutsche Beziehungen, 1987.

Mitchell, B. R. *International Historical Statistics. Europe 1750–1988*. New York: M Stockton Press, 1993.

Monatbericht des BMF. Dezember 2016. Berlin: Bundesministerium der Finanzen, 2016.

Monatbericht des BMF. Januar 2016. Berlin: Bundesministerium der Finanzen, 2016.

Polska liderem produkcji prawa w Unii Europejskiej. Barometr stabilności otoczenia prawnego w polskiej gospodarce. Edycja 2016. Poznań: Grant Thornton, 2016.

Roland Rechtsreport 2015. Köln: Institut für Demoskopie Allensbach, Roland Rechtsschutz-Versicherungs-AG, 2015.

Smith-Morris, M., ed. *Welt Wirtschaft in Zahlen*. Düsseldorf: Wirtschaftswoche, The Economist Books, 1991.

Statistisches Jahrbuch der Deutschen Demokratischen Republik, Vol. 1955. Berlin: Staatlichen Zentralverwaltung für Statistik, VEB Deutscher Zentralverlag, 1956.

Statistisches Jahrbuch der Deutschen Demokratischen Republik, Vol. 1960/1961. Berlin: Staatlichen Zentralverwaltung für Statistik, VEB Deutscher Zentralverlag, 1962.

Statistisches Jahrbuch der Deutschen Demokratischen Republik, Vol. 1966. Berlin: Staatlichen Zentralverwaltung für Statistik, VEB Deutscher Zentralverlag, 1967.

Statistisches Jahrbuch der Deutschen Demokratischen Republik, Vol. 1971. Berlin: Staatlichen Zentralverwaltung für Statistik, VEB Deutscher Zentralverlag, 1972.

Statistisches Jahrbuch der Deutschen Demokratischen Republik, Vol. 1976. Berlin: Staatlichen Zentralverwaltung für Statistik, VEB Deutscher Zentralverlag, 1977.

Statistisches Jahrbuch der Deutschen Demokratischen Republik, Vol. 1981. Berlin: Staatlichen Zentralverwaltung für Statistik, VEB Deutscher Zentralverlag, 1982.

Statistisches Jahrbuch der Deutschen Demokratischen Republik, Vol. 1986. Berlin: Staatlichen Zentralverwaltung für Statistik, VEB Deutscher Zentralverlag, 1987.

Statistisches Jahrbuch der Deutschen Demokratischen Republik, Vol. 1990. Berlin: Staatlichen Zentralverwaltung für Statistik, VEB Deutscher Zentralverlag, 1991.

Statistisches Jahrbuch für die Bundesrepublik Deutschland, Vol. 1990. Wiesbaden–Stuttgart: Statistisches Bundesamt, Metzler-Poeschel Verlag, 1990.

Statistisches Jahrbuch für die Bundesrepublik Deutschland, Vol. 1998. Wiesbaden–Stuttgart: Statistisches Bundesamt, Metzler-Poeschel Verlag, 1998.

Statistisches Jahrbuch für die Bundesrepublik Deutschland, Vol. 1999. Wiesbaden–Stuttgart: Statistisches Bundesamt, Metzler-Poeschel Verlag, 1999.

Statistisches Jahrbuch für die Bundesrepublik Deutschland, Vol. 2001. Wiesbaden: Statistisches Bundesamt, 2001.

Statistisches Jahrbuch für die Bundesrepublik Deutschland, Vol. 2002. Wiesbaden: Statistisches Bundesamt, 2002.

Statistisches Jahrbuch für die Bundesrepublik Deutschland, Vol. 2010. Wiesbaden: Statistisches Bundesamt, 2010.

Statistisches Jahrbuch für die Bundesrepublik Deutschland, Vol. 2017. Wiesbaden: Statistisches Bundesamt, 2017.

Statistisches Jahrbuch. Deutschland und Internationales, Vol. 2012. Wiesbaden: Statistisches Bundesamt, 2012.

Statistisches Jahrbuch. Deutschland und Internationales, Vol. 2016. Wiesbaden: Statistisches Bundesamt, 2016.

Statistisches Taschenbuch der Versicherungswirtschaft, Vol. 2016. Berlin: Gesamtverband der Deutschen Versicherungswirtschaft e. V., 2016.

"Trading Economics." https://pl.tradingeconomics.com/germany/.

Veräußerung/Verwertung von Bundesunternehmen. Unmittelbare Beteiligungsunternehmen des Bundes, Bundesministerium der Finanzen. https://www.bundesfinanzministerium.de/Content/DE/Standardartikel/Themen/Bundesvermoegen/Privatisierungs_und_Beteiligungspolitik/Privatisierungspolitik/privatisierungspolitik-anlage-2-uebersicht-privatisierungen-des-bundes.pdf?__blob=publicationFile&v=4.

"Verschuldung von Deutschland gemäß Maastricht-Vertrag in Prozent des BIP von 1991 bis 2016." https://de.statista.com/statistik/daten/studie/154800/umfrage/deutsche-schuldenquote-seit-2003/.

Wirtschaftsdaten neue Länder. August 2016. Berlin: Bundesministerium für Wirtschaft und Energie, 2016.

"World Governance Indicators." https://info.worldbank.org/governance/wgi/.

"Wskaźnik zmienności prawa w UE." http://barometrprawa.pl/#wykresy.

Press

Gazeta Wyborcza, 1989–1991.

Rzeczpospolita, 2002, 2009.

Others

177. Sitzung. Bonn, Dienstag, den 28. November 1989 (Deutscher Bundestag. Stenografischer Bericht, Plenarprotokoll 11/177, 13510–13514).

"Antwort der Bundesregierung auf die Große Anfrage der Abgeordneten Hans Jochen Henke, Susanne Jaffke, Dietrich Austermann, weiterer Abgeordneter und der Fraktion der CDU/CSU – Drucksache 14/3556 –." *Deutscher Bundestag. 14. Wahlperiode. Drucksache* No. 14/4696 (2000): 1–24.

"Beschlußempfehlung und Bericht des 2. Untersuchungsausschusses "Treuhandanstalt" nach Artikel 44 des Grundgesetzes." *Deutscher Bundestag. 12. Wahlperiode. Sachgebiet 1101. Drucksache* No. 12/8404 (1994): 1–848.

Deutscher Gewerkschaftsbund, DGB. https://www.boeckler.de.

Drewnicki, R. et al., eds. *Dokumentation 1990–1994*, Vol. 1–15. Berlin: Treuhandanstalt, 1994.

Grundsatzprogramm der Sozialdemokratischen Partei Deutschlands. Beschlossen vom Außerordentlichen Parteitag der Sozialdemokratischen Partei Deutschlands in Bad Godesberg vom 13. bis 15. November 1959. Facsimile. München: Archiv des Instituts für Zeitgeschichte München, 2006.

Kompendium nauki społecznej Kościoła. Kielce: Papieska Rada Iustitia et Pax, Wydawnictwo Jedność, 2005.

Leon XIII. *Encyklika papieża Leona XIII wszystkim czcigodnym Braciom Patriarchom, Prymasom, Arcybiskupom świata katolickiego, łaskę i społeczność ze Stolicą Apostolską mającym Rerum Novarum o kwestii socjalnej. 15 V 1891 r.* Warszawa: Wydawnictwo Te Deum, 2001.

Marks, K., Engels, F. *Manifest partii komunistycznej. Zasady komunizmu.* Warszawa: Książka i Wiedza, 1979.

ENCYCLOPEDIAS, LEXICONS, DICTIONARIES

Bator, A., ed. *Wprowadzenie do nauk prawnych. Leksykon tematyczny.* Warszawa: Lexis Nexis Polska, 2012.

Brachmann, R. et al., eds. *Rechtslexikon.* Berlin: Staatsverlag der Deutschen Demokratischen Republik, 1988.

Dziubka, K., Szlachta, B., Nijakowski, L. M. *Idee i ideologie we współczesnym świecie.* Warszawa: WN PWN, 2008.

Ehlert, W. et al., eds. *Wörterbuch der Ökonomie Sozialismus.* Berlin: Dietz Verlag, 1969.

Hasse, R. H., Schneider, H., Weigelt, K. *Lexikon Soziale Marktwirtschaft. Wirtschaftspolitik von A bis Z.* Paderborn: Ferdinand Schöningh, 2002.

Kopaliński W. *Słownik wyrazów obcych i zwrotów obcojęzycznych.* Warszawa: Wiedza Powszechna, 1990.

Mokyr, J., ed. *The Oxford Encyclopedia of Economic History*, Vol. 4: *Monte di Pietà – Spain.* Oxford: Oxford University Press, 2003.

Opara, S. et al., eds. *Mały słownik politologii.* Toruń: Wydawnictwo Adam Marszałek, 2007.

Petrozolin-Skowrońska, B. *Nowa Encyklopedia Powszechna PWN*, Vol. 1: *A–C.* Warszawa: WN PWN, 1997.

LITERATURE

Acemoglu, D., Johnson, S., Robinson, J. A. "The Colonial Origins of Comparative Development: An Empirical Investigation." *American Economic Review* 91, No. 5 (2001): 1369–1401.

Acemoglu, D., Johnson, S., Robinson, J. A. "Reversal of Fortune: Geography and Institutions in the Making of the Modern World Income Distribution." *The Quarterly Journal of Economics* 117, No. 4 (2002): 1231–1294.

Acemoglu, D., Robinson, J. A. *Dlaczego narody przegrywają? Źródła władzy, pomyślności i ubóstwa.* Poznań: Zysk i S-ka Wydawnictwo, 2014.

Acemoglu, D. "Świat, jaki odziedziczą nasze wnuki." In *Gospodarka za 100 lat. Najważniejsi ekonomiści przewidują przyszłość*, ed. I. Palacios-Huerta, 23–70. Warszawa: Kurhaus, 2014.

Addison, J. T., Schnabel, C., Wagner, J. "Works Councils in Germany: Their Effects on Establishment Performance." *Oxford Economic Papers* 53, No. 4 (2001): 659–694.

Albiński, P., Chrzanowski, M. "Dochodzenie do euro: studium przypadków gospodarki niemieckiej i austriackiej." *Bank i Kredyt* No. 8 (2008): 3–25.

Alchian, A. A., Demsetz, H. "Production, Information Costs, and Economic Organization." *American Economic Review* 62, No. 5 (1972): 777–795.

Alchian, A. *Some Economics of Property*. Santa Monica: Rand Corporation, 1961.

Alesina, A. "Elections and the Economy: the Case of the United States, with Some Lessons for Europe." In *Economic and Political Institutions in Economic Policy*, ed. V. A. Muscatelli, 35–50. Manchester–New York: Manchester University Press, 1996.

Alesina, A., Özler, S., Roubini, N., Swagel, P. "Political Instability and Economic Growth." *Journal of Economic Growth* 1, No. 2 (1996): 189–211.

Alessi, L. de. "Development of the Property Right Approach." *Journal of Institutional and Theoretical Economics* 146 (1990): 6–11.

Alessi, L. de. "Implications of Property Rights for Government Investment Choices." *American Economic Review* 59, No. 1 (1969): 13–24.

Alessi, L. de. "The Economics of Property Rights: A Review of Evidence." *Research in Law and Economics* 2 (1980): 1–47.

Alewell, K., Bohnet, A., eds. *Leistungswille und Leistungsanreize im Systemvergleich. Wirtschaftswissenschaftliches Symposium anläβlich des 10-jährigen Bestehens der Partnerschaft zwischen den Universitäten Gieβen und Łódź. Schloβ Rauischholzhausen bei Gieβen 12.–17. Juni 1988. Tagungsband.* Gieβen: Justus-Liebig-Universität, 1988.

Ali, A. M., Crain, W. M. "Institutional Distortions, Economic Freedom, and Growth." *Cato Journal* 21, No. 3 (2002): 415–426.

"All Prizes in Economic Sciences." http://www.nobelprize.org/nobel_prizes/economic-sciences/laureates/.

Andruszkiewicz, M., Breczko, A., Oliwniak, S., eds. *Filozoficzne i teoretyczne zagadnienia demokratycznego państwa prawa*. Białystok: Wydawnictwo Temida 2, 2015.

Arndt, W., Longchamps de Bérier, F., Szczucki, K., eds. *Dobro wspólne. Teoria i praktyka*. Warszawa: Wydawnictwo Sejmowe, Fundacja "Utriusque Iuris," 2013.

Aβmann, G., Backhaus, K., Hilker, J., eds. *Deutsh-deutsche Unternehmen. Ein unternehmenskulturelles Anpassungsproblem.* Stuttgart: C. E. Poeschel Verlag, 1991.

Azman-Saini, W. N. W., Baharumshah, A. Z., Law, S. H. "Foreign Direct Investment, Economic Freedom and Economic Growth: International Evidence." *Economic Modelling* 27, No. 5 (2010): 1079–1089.

Babiak, J. "Zmiany w strukturze rolnictwa krajów Unii Europejskiej." *Rocznik Integracji Europejskiej* No. 4 (2010): 87–97.

Badura, P. "Der Verfassungsauftrag der Eigentumsgarantie im wiedervereinigten Deutschland." *Deutsches Verwaltungsblatt* No. 105 (1990): 1256–1263.

Badura, P. "Eigentum." In *Handbuch des Verfassungsrechts der Bundesrepublik Deutschland*, eds. E. Benda, W. Maihofer, H.-J. Vogel, 327–390. Berlin–New York: Walter de Gruyter, 1994.

Baek, K., Quian, X. "An Analysis on Political Risks and the Flow of Foreign Direct Investment in Developing and Industrialized Economies," *Economics, Management, and Financial Markets* 6, No. 4 (2011): 60–91.

Bałtowski, M., Miszewski, M. *Transformacja gospodarcza w Polsce*. Warszawa: WN PWN, 2006.

Banaszak, B. *System konstytucyjny Niemiec*. Warszawa: Wydawnictwo Sejmowe, 2005.

Banaszak, B. *Porównawcze prawo konstytucyjne współczesnych państw demokratycznych*. Warszawa: Wolters Kluwer Polska, 2007.

Banaszak, B., Żukowski, Ł. "System środków ochrony praw podstawowych w RFN." *Przegląd Sejmowy* No. 6 (95) (2009): 45–64.

Barro, R. J. "Democracy and Growth." *Journal of Economic Growth* 1, No. 1 (1996): 1–27.

Barro, R. J. "Economic Growth in a Cross Section of Countries." *The Quarterly Journal of Economics* 106, No. 2 (1991): 407–443.

Baβeler, U., Heinrich, J. *Wirtschaftssysteme. Kapitalistische Marktwirtschaft und sozialistische Zentralplanwirtschaft*. Würzburg–Wien: Physica-Verlag, 1984.

Bärwaldt, R. "Die Treuhandanstalt nach dem Inkrafttreten des Einigungsvertrages." *Deutsch-Deutsche Rechts-Zeitschrift* No. 9 (1990): 347–348.

Baumeister, R. *Die Konzeption der Zukunftsgesellschaft bei Karl Marx, Friedrich Engels und bei neueren westeuropäischen Marxisten – eine ordnungspolitische Analyse*. Köln: Institut für Wirtschaftspolitik an der Universität zu Köln, 1976.

Baur, F., Baur, J. F., Stürner, R. *Sachenrecht*. München: Verlag C. H. Beck, 2009.

Baur, J. F., ed. *Das Eigentum. Vorträge gehalten auf der Tagung der Joachim Jungius-Gesellschaft der Wissenschaften. Hamburg am 10., 11. und 12. Dezember 1987*. Göttingen: Vandenhoeck & Ruprecht, 1989.

Becker, J. F. *Marxian Political Economy. An Outline*. Cambridge: Cambridge University Press, 1977.

Begg, D., Vernasca, G., Fischer, S., Dornbusch, R. *Makroekonomia*. Warszawa: PWE, 2014.

Behr, W. *Bundesrepublik Deutschland – Deutsche Demokratische Republik. Systemvergleich Politik – Wirtschaft – Gesellschaft.* Stuttgart: Verlag W. Kohlhammer, 1979.

Below, G. von. *Probleme der Wirtschaftsgeschichte. Eine Einführung in das Studium der Wirtschaftsgeschichte.* Tübingen: Verlag von J. C. B. Mohr (Paul Siebeck), 1926.

Benda, E. "Grundgesetz und Wirtschaftsordnung." In *Handbuch Marktwirtschaft*, eds. R. Vaubel, H. D. Barbier, 144–149. Weinsberg: Neske, 1986.

Bentkowska, K. *Ekonomia instytucjonalna. Zarys teorii i jej wymiar praktyczny.* Warszawa: Oficyna Wydawnicza SGH, 2020.

Berg, H. von. *Die Anti-Ökonomie des Sozialismus. Zur Reformfähigkeit parteimonopolistischer Staatswirtschaften.* Würzburg: Creator, 1989.

Berghoff, H., Vogel, J., eds. *Wirtschaftsgeschichte als Kulturgeschichte. Dimensionen eines Perspektivenwechseln.* Frankfurt–New York: Campus Verlag, 2004.

Bergström, V., ed. *Government and Growth.* Oxford: Clarendon Press, 1997.

Berlemann, M., Thum, M. "Mittelfristige Perspektiven der Ost-West-Konvergenz." *ifo Dresden berichtet* 13, No. 1 (2006): 34–39.

Besley, T. "Property Rights and Investment Incentives: Theory and Evidence from Ghana." *Journal of Political Economy* 103 (1995): 903–937.

Betz, H. "Recent Changes in the System of Management in the German Democratic Republic." In *Economic Reforms in the Soviet Union and Eastern Europe since the 1960s*, ed. J. Adam, 208–224. New York: St. Martin's Press, 1989.

Beutin, L. *Einführung in die Wirtschaftsgeschichte.* Köln–Graz: Böhlau Verlag, 1958.

Beutin, L., Kellenbenz, H. *Grundlagen des Studiums der Wirtschaftsgeschichte.* Köln–Wien: Böhlau Verlag, 1973.

Bębnowski, D. "Czy historia jest nauką tylko o przeszłości?" *Transformacje. Pismo Interdyscyplinarne* No. 1–2 (88–89) (2016): 30–44.

Bębnowski, D. "Czy istnieje przyjaźń między naukami? Polskie spojrzenie na historię gospodarczą, czyli o związkach historii i ekonomii raz jeszcze." Unpublished manuscript.

Bębnowski, D., Matera, R. "Przegląd regulacji praw własności w Polsce w pierwszych miesiącach niepodległości (listopad 1918 – luty 1919)." In *Społeczny bilans otwarcia polskiej niepodległości w 1918 roku*, eds. T. Głowiński, M. Zawadka, 117–136. Wrocław: Wydawnictwo GAJT, 2018.

Bębnowski, D. "Niemcy jako państwo fiskalne w perspektywie instytucjonalnej i historyczno-gospodarczej (1990–2015)." *Przegląd Zachodni* No. 1 (370) (2019): 41–58.

Bębnowski, D. "Socjologiczny komponent historii gospodarczej. Résumé głównych paradygmatów w XX i XXI w." Unpublished manuscript.

Bębnowski, D. "The Attractiveness of the Project of Practical Methodology and Virtue Epistemology for Economic History Research." *Annales. Ethics in Economic Life* 20, No. 5 (2017): 107–125.

Bębnowski, D. "The Social Change in the Marxism's Interpretation of History." In *Vade Nobiscum. Materiały Studenckiego Koła Naukowego Historyków Uniwersytetu Łódzkiego*, Vol. XIII: *Bunt, rebelia, rewolucja, strajk. Opór społeczeństwa wobec władzy na przestrzeni dziejów. Skąd przybyliśmy, dokąd zmierzamy? Źródła tożsamości. Gospodarka głupcze!*, eds. K. Banaś, R. Stasiak, 23–27. Łódź: Piktor, 2014.

Bębnowski, D. "Wokół przedsiębiorczości katolickiej. Reminiscencje z odczytania Rerum Novarum Leona XIII na nowo." *Łódzkie Studia Teologiczne* 27, No. 3 (2018): 197–210.

Biedenkopf, K. H. *Offene Grenze Offener Markt. Voraussetzungen für die Erneuerung der DDR-Volkswirtschaft.* Wiesbaden: Gabler, Bertelsmann, 1990.

Bieniada, R. M. *Federalizm kooperatywny jako czynnik regionalizacji substruktur państwa.* Casus *Austrii, RFN i Szwajcarii.* Warszawa: Oficyna Wydawnicza ASPRA-JR, 2013.

Bischoff, J., Menard, M. *Marktwirtschaft und Sozialismus. Der Dritte Weg.* Hamburg: VSA-Verlag, 1990.

Bjørnskov, Ch., Voigt, S., Khesali, M. "Unconstitutional States of Emergency." Working paper, Institute of Law and Economics (ILE) Working Paper Series, No. 51 (2021), 1–34.

Blanchard, O., Dornbusch, R., Krugman, P., Layard, R., Summers, L. *Reform in Eastern Europe.* Cambridge–London: The MIT Press, 1991.

Blaug. M. *Teoria ekonomii. Ujęcie retrospektywne.* Warszawa: WN PWN, 2000.

Blume, L., Müller, J., Voigt, S., Wolf, C. "The Economic Effects of Constitutions: Replicating – and Extending – Persson and Tabellini." *Public Choice* 139 (2009): 197–225.

Bolz, K., Clement, H., Lösch, D. *Wirtschaftssysteme. Marktwirtschaft – Kapitalismus. Planwirtschaft – Sozialismus.* München: Ehrenwirth Verlag, 1978.

Bolz, K., ed. *Die Wirtschaft der osteuropäischen Ländern an der Wende zu den 90er Jahren.* Hamburg: Verlag Weltarchiv GmbH, 1990.

Borkowska, B., Klimczak, M., Klimczak, B. *Ekonomia instytucjonalna.* Wrocław: Wydawnictwo UE we Wrocławiu, 2019.

Borowiecki, R., ed. *Zarządzanie restrukturyzacją przedsiębiorstw i gospodarki. Uwarunkowania – procesy – efekty.* Kraków: Fundacja UE w Krakowie, 2014.

Borowski, M. *Grundrechte als Prinzipien.* Baden-Baden: Nomos, 2007.

Bożek, W. "Odpowiedzialność za naruszenie dyscypliny finansów publicznych w Polsce na tle rozwiązań przyjętych we Francji, w Niemczech i Wielkiej Brytanii." In *Unia Europejska wobec wyzwań przyszłości. Aspekty prawne, finansowe i handlowe*, eds. E. Małuszyńska, G. Mazur, P. Idczak, 146–158. Poznań: Wydawnictwo UE w Poznaniu, 2015.

Böbel, I. *Eigentum, Eigentumsrechte und institutioneller Wandel.* Berlin: Springer-Verlag, 1988.

Böhm, F., Eucken, W. "Vorwort. Die Aufgabe des Jahrbuchs." *ORDO. Jahrbuch für die Ordnung von Wirtschaft und Gesellschaft* 1 (1948): VII–XI.

Böhm, F. *Kartelle und Koalitionsfreiheit.* Berlin: Carl Heymanns Verlag, 1933.

Böhm, F. *Wettbewerb und Monopolkampf. Eine Untersuchung zur Frage des wirtschaftlichen Kampfrechts und zur Frage der rechtlichen Struktur der geltenden Wirtschaftsordnung.* Berlin: Carl Heymanns Verlag, 1933.

Böhm, F. *Wirtschaftsordnung und Staatsverfassung.* Tübingen: Mohr, 1950.

Böhmer, W. "Eigentum aus verfassungsrechtlicher Sicht. Grundfragen der verfassungsrechtlichen Gewährleistung des Eigentums in der Rechtsprechung des Bundesverfassungsgerichts." In *Das Eigentum. Vorträge gehalten auf der Tagung der Joachim Jungius-Gesellschaft der Wissenschaften. Hamburg am 10., 11. und 12. Dezember 1987*, ed. J. F. Baur, 39–82. Göttingen: Vandenhoeck & Ruprecht, 1989.

Böick, M. *Die Treuhand. Idee – Praxis – Erfahrung 1990–1994.* Göttingen: Wallstein Verlag, 2018.

Bös, D. "Privatization in Eastern Germany: The Never-Ending Story of the Treuhand." In *Privatization at the End of the Century*, ed. H. Giersch, 175–197. Berlin: Egon-Sohmen-Foundation, Springer, 1997.

Brace, L. *The Politics of Property. Labour, Freedom and Belonging.* New York–Basingstoke: Palgrave Macmillan, 2004.

Braudel, F. *Gramatyka cywilizacji.* Warszawa: Oficyna Naukowa, 2006.

Bräuer, K. *Kritische Studien zur Literatur und Quellenkunde der Wirtschaftsgeschichte.* Leipzig: Verlag von Veit & Comp., 1912.

Brennan, D. M. et al., eds. *Routledge Handbook of Marxian Economics.* London–New York: Routledge, 2017.

Brie, M. *Wer ist Eigentümer im Sozialismus? Philosophische überlegungen.* Berlin: Dietz Verlag, 1990.

Brocka-Palacz, B. *Wspieranie rozwoju gospodarki wschodniej części Niemiec – zamierzenia, instrumenty, efekty.* Warszawa: IGŚ SGH, 2008.

Brocka-Palacz, B. "Zjednoczenie Niemiec – bilans po 25 latach," *Zeszyty Naukowe Uczelni Vistula* No. 48 (3) (2016): 25–41.

Brocka-Palacz, B., ed. *Dokąd zmierzają Niemcy. Reformy polityczne, gospodarcze i społeczne.* Warszawa: SGH, 2008.

Brunner, G. "Verfassungsrechtliche Rahmenbedingungen der wirtschaftlichen Transformation." In *Transformationsprozesse in sozialistischen*

Wirtschaftssystemen. Ursachen, Konzepte, Instrumente, eds. K.-H. Hartwig, H. J. Thieme, 201–225. Berlin: Springer-Verlag, 1991.

Brus, W., Łaski, K. *Von Marx zum Markt. Die sozialistischen Länder auf der Suche nach einem neuen Wirtschaftssystem.* Marburg: Metropolis-Verlag, 1990.

Bruszt, L. "Market-making as State-making. Constitutions and Economic Development in Postcommunist Eastern Europe." In *Constitutions, Markets and Law. Recent Experiences in Transition Economies*, eds. S. Voigt, H.-J. Wagener, 129–157. Cheltenham–Northampton: Edward Elgar, 2002.

Brücker, H. *Privatization in Eastern Germany: A Neo-Institutional Analysis.* London: Frank Cass, German Development Institute, 2005.

Bryson, P. J. "East German Traditional Centralism: An Alternative Route to Economic Reconstruction." *The Annals of The American Academy of Political and Social Science* 507 (1990): 133–141.

Buchanan, J. M. *Property as a Guarantor of Liberty.* Cambridge: Edward Elgar, 1993.

Buchanan, J. M. *The Limits of Liberty. Between Anarchy and Leviathan.* Indianapolis: Liberty Fund, 2000.

Buchanan, J. M., Tullock, G. *The Calculus of Consent. Logical Foundations of Constitutional Democracy.* Indianapolis: Liberty Fund, 1999.

Buczkowski, B., Kuna-Marszałek, A. "Motywy polskich inwestycji bezpośrednich: przykład przedsiębiorstw z województwa łódzkiego." *Studia i Prace WNEiZ US* 41, No. 2 (2015): 121–133.

Buhbe, M. *Ökonomische Analyse von Eigentumsrechten. Der Beitrag der Economics of Property Rights zur Theorie der Institutionen.* Frankfurt am Main: Peter D. Lang, 1980.

Bujak, F. *Wybór pism*, Vol. I. Warszawa: PWN, 1976.

Bukowski, A. "Przegląd publikacji z historii gospodarczej na łamach 'Explorations in Economic History' w latach 2001–2010." In *Przegląd badań nad historią gospodarczą w XXI wieku*, eds. R. Matera, A. Pieczewski, 225–234. Łódź: Wydawnictwo UŁ, 2011.

Burakowski, A., Gubrynowicz, A., Ukielski, P. *1989 – Jesień Narodów.* Warszawa: Collegium Civitas, ISP PAN, Wydawnictwo Trio, 2009.

Burchard-Dziubińska, M. "Rola instytucji w kształtowaniu ładu ekonomicznego." In *W poszukiwaniu nowego ładu ekonomicznego*, ed. S. Owsiak, A. Pollok, 17–29. Warszawa: PTE, 2013.

Burkhardt, G. et al., eds. *Rat für gegensetige Wirtschaftshilfe. Strukturen und Probleme.* Bonn: Ostkolleg der Bundeszentrale für politische Bildung, 1987.

Busch, A. "Verfassungspolitik: Stabilität und permanentes Austarieren." In *Regieren in der Bundesrepublik Deutschland. Innen- und Außenpolitik seit 1949*, eds. M. G. Schmidt, R. Zohlnhöfer, 33–56. Wiesbaden: VS Verlag für Sozialwissenschaften, 2006.

Busch, U. *Am Tropf. Die ostdeutsche Transfergesellschaft.* Berlin: trafo verlag, 2002.

Busch, U., Kühn, W., Steinitz, K. *Schrumpfung und Entwicklung in Ostdeutschland. Aktuelle Probleme im 20. Jahr der Einheit.* Hamburg: VSA-Verlag, 2009.

Busche, J. "Die Privatisierung der volkseigenen Unternehmen der ehemaligen DDR. Der rechtliche und wirtschaftliche Umbruch im Zuge der Wiedervereinigung." In *Staat und Recht in Teilung und Einheit,* eds. J. Krüper, H. Sauer, 127–141. Tübingen: Mohr Siebeck, 2011.

Cameron, R., Neal, L. *Historia gospodarcza świata. Od paleolitu do czasów najnowszych.* Warszawa: Książka i Wiedza, 2004.

Campbell, J. L. "Institutional Analysis and the Role of Ideas in Political Economy." In *The Rise of Neoliberalism and Institutional Analysis,* eds. J. L. Campbell, O. K. Pedersen, 159–189. Princeton–Oxford: Princeton University Press, 2001.

Cassel, D. et al., eds. *Inflation und Schattenwirtschaft im Sozialismus. Bestandaufnahme, Erklärungsansätze und Reformvorschläge für die Volksrepublik Polen.* Hamburg: Steuer- und Wirtschaftsverlag, 1989.

Caves, D. W., Christiansen, L. R. "The Relative Efficiency of Public and Private Firms in a Competitive Environment: The Case of Canadian Railroads." *Journal of Political Economy* 88, No. 5 (1980): 958–976.

Chance, C. "Legal Framework." In *Doing Business with Germany,* eds. R. Millar, J. Reuvid, 311–315. London: Kogan Page, 1997.

Cheung, S. N. S. "Private Property Rights and Sharecropping." *Journal of Political Economy* 76, No. 6 (1968): 1107–1122.

Chhibber, A. "Institutions, Policies, and Development Outcomes." In *Evaluation & Development. The Institutional Dimension,* eds. R. Picciotto, E. Wiesner, 34–46. New Brunswick–London: Transaction Publishers, 1998.

Christ, P., Neubauer, R. *Kolonie im eigenen Land. Die Treuhand, Bonn und die Wirtschaftskatastrophe der fünf neuen Länder.* Berlin: Rowohlt, 1991.

Christoph, K.-H. "Das Vereinigungsgesetz der DDR." *Deutsch-Deutsche Rechts-Zeitschrift* No. 8 (1990): 257–261.

Chumiński, J., Popiński, K. "Dominanty i zaniechania w badaniach PRL – historia gospodarcza po 1989 r." In *Z Jeleniej Góry do Wrocławia i z powrotem. Wokół historii społecznej i gospodarczej. Tom studiów dedykowany Profesor Elżbiecie Kościk,* ed. T. Głowiński, 195–216. Wrocław: Wydawnictwo TUM, 2018.

Chumiński, J., Popiński, K. "Gospodarka PRL w historiografii polskiej 1989–2010." In *Przegląd badań nad historią gospodarczą w XXI wieku,* eds. R. Matera, A. Pieczewski, 45–57. Łódź: Wydawnictwo UŁ, 2011.

Cichy, E. U. *Wirtschaftsreform und Ausweichwirtschaft im Sozialismus. Zur Rolle der Ausweichwirtschaft im Reformprozeß sozialistischer Planwirtschaften dargestellt am Beispiel der DDR, Polens und Ungarns.* Hamburg: Verlag Weltarchiv GmbH, 1990.

Clapham, J. H. "Economic History as a Discipline." In *The Varieties of History. From Voltaire to the Present*, ed. F. Stern, 308–313. New York: Meridian Books, 1956.

Coase, R. H. *Firma, rynek i prawo*. Warszawa: Oficyna a Wolters Kluwer Business, 2013.

Coase, R. H. "The Problem of Social Costs." *The Journal of Law and Economics* 3 (1960): 1–44.

Commons, J. R. *Institutional Economics. Its Place in Political Economy*. New York: The Macmillan Company, 1934.

Cooter, R., Ulen, T. *Ekonomiczna analiza prawa*. Warszawa: Wydawnictwo C. H. Beck, 2011.

Crane, A. et al., eds. *The Oxford Handbook of Corporate Social Responsibility*. New York: Oxford University Press, 2009.

Currie, D. P. *The Constitution of the Federal Republic of Germany*. Chicago–London: The University of Chicago Press, 1994.

Czaja, S., *Blaski i cienie Nagrody Nobla*. Wrocław: Wydawnictwo I-BiS, 2002.

Czapliński, W., Galos, A., Korta, W., *Historia Niemiec*. Wrocław: Ossolineum, 2010.

Czech, A., Czech, S. "Nowe trendy w ekonomii w perspektywie instytucjonalizmu." In *Instytucje w teorii i praktyce. Przeszłość – teraźniejszość – przyszłość*, eds. H. Pondel, S. Kuźmar, 38–47. Poznań: Wydawnictwo UE w Poznaniu, 2020.

Czech-Rogosz, J. "Gospodarka wschodnich Niemiec w 12 lat po zjednoczeniu – niedokończony proces unifikacji gospodarczej. Wybrane problemy." In *Unifikacja gospodarek europejskich. Szanse i zagrożenia*, eds. A. Manikowski, A. Psyk, 93–102. Warszawa: WN WZ UW, 2004.

Czech-Rogosz, J. "Państwo socjalne – doświadczenia RFN." *Studia Ekonomiczne* No. 38 (2006): 97–114.

Czech-Rogosz, J. "Reformy gospodarcze w Niemczech w ramach programu 'Agenda 2010'." *Studia Ekonomiczne. Zeszyty Naukowe Uniwersytetu Ekonomicznego w Katowicach* No. 34 (2005): 117–142.

Cziomer, E. *Historia Niemiec współczesnych 1945–2005*. Warszawa: Wydawnictwo Neriton, 2006.

Cziomer, E. "Od światowego kryzysu finansowego do kryzysu strefy euro: implikacje wewnątrzpolityczne dla Niemiec w latach 2008–2011." *Rocznik Integracji Europejskiej* No. 5 (2011): 33–50.

Cziomer, E. *Polityka zagraniczna Niemiec. Kontynuacja i zmiana po zjednoczeniu ze szczególnym uwzględnieniem polityki europejskiej i transatlantyckiej*. Warszawa: Dom Wydawniczy Elipsa, 2005.

Cziomer, E. *Zarys historii Niemiec powojennych 1945–1995*. Warszawa–Kraków: WN PWN, 1997.

Dahl, M. "Europejski kryzys imigracyjny i jego konsekwencje dla Republiki Federalnej Niemiec – aspekty polityczne, społeczne i gospodarcze." *Studia Polityczne* No. 4 (44) (2016): 241–262.

Dahl, M. "Wpływ europejskiego kryzysu imigracyjnego na procesy dezintegracyjne w Unii Europejskiej." *Roczniki Nauk Społecznych* 10 (46), No. 3 (2018): 33–44.

Dakowicz, P. *Afazja polska.* Warszawa: Wydawnictwo Sic!, 2015.

Dakowicz, P. *Afazja polska 2.* Warszawa: Wydawnictwo Sic!, 2016.

Dathe, D. "Der wirtschaftliche Strukturwandel in ausgewählten Stadtregionen der neuen Bundesländer in den Jahren 1989 bis 1993/94." In *Regionen im Vergleich. Gesellschaftlicher Wandel in Ostdeutschland am Beispiel ausgewählter Regionen,* ed. H. Bertram, 41–66. Opdalen: Leske + Budrich, 1996.

Dawson, J. W. "Causality in the Freedom-Growth Relationship." *European Journal of Political Economy* 19, No. 3 (2003): 479–495.

Demsetz, H. "The Exchange and Enforcement of Property Rights." *The Journal of Law and Economics* 7 (1964): 11–26.

Denzau, A. T., North, D. C. "Shared Mental Models: Ideologies and Institutions." *Kyklos* No. 47 (1994): 3–31.

"Die Treuhandanstalt im Spiegel der wissenschaftlichen Forschung." *Deutscher Bundestag, Wissenschaftliche Dienste, Ausarbeitung* No. WD 1-3000-010/19 (2019): 1–15.

Diebolt, C., Haupert, M., eds. *Handbook of Cliometrics.* Berlin–Heidelberg: Springer Reference, 2016.

Dietl, H. *Institutionen und Zeit.* Tübingen: J. C. B. Mohr (Paul Siebeck), 1993.

Ditges, J. "Privatisierungsstrategien in den neuen Bundesländern." In *Ökonomische Erfolge und Mißerfolge der deutsche Vereinigung – Eine Zwischenbilanz,* eds. G. Gutmann, U. Wagner, 37–58. Stuttgart: Gustav Fischer Verlag, 1994.

Dobrzeniecki, K., Romanowski, M. *Reprywatyzacja. Problemy tworzenia i stosowania prawa.* Warszawa: Wydawnictwo UKSW, 2015.

Domagała, M. *Pozycja konstytucyjnoprawna kraju w systemie federalnym RFN na przykładzie Hesji.* Łódź: Wydawnictwo UŁ, 1990.

Domdey, K. H. "Privatisation in the New Bundesländer: A Critical Assessment of the Treuhand." In *The Political Economy of German Unification,* eds. T. Lange, J. R. Shackleton, 44–55. Providence–Oxford: Berghahn Books, 1998.

Doucouliagos, Ch., Ulubasoglu, M. A. "Economic Freedom and Economic Growth: Does Specification Make a Difference?" *European Journal of Political Economy* 22, No. 1 (2006): 60–81.

Dreier, H., ed. *Grundgesetz. Kommentar,* Vol. I: *Präambel, Artikel 1–19.* Tübingen: Mohr Siebeck, 2004.

Drüen, K.-D. *Allgemeines Steuerrecht.* Münster: Verlag Alpmann und Schmidt Juristische Lehrgänge, Technische Universität Kaiserslautern, 2017.

Dudek, A. *Historia polityczna Polski 1989–2012.* Kraków: Wydawnictwo Znak, 2013.

Dzionek-Kozłowska, J. "Koncepcja path dependence w historii gospodarczej: przegląd najnowszych publikacji." In *Przegląd badań nad historią gospodarczą w XXI wieku*, eds. R. Matera, A. Pieczewski, 265–280. Łódź: Wydawnictwo UŁ, 2011.

Edeling, T. "Organisationen als Institutionen." In *Neuer Institutionalismus. Zur soziologischen Erklärung von Organisation, Moral und Vertrauen*, eds. A. Maurer, M. Schmid, 219–235. Frankfurt–New York: Campus Verlag, 2002.

Eggertsson, T. *Economic Behavior and Institutions.* Cambridge: Cambridge University Press, 1995.

Egner, E. *Studien über Haushalt und Verbrauch*, Vol. 1: *Beiträge zur Ökonomie von Haushalt und Verbrauch.* Berlin: Duncker & Humblot, 1963.

Eichler, H. *Die Rechtsidee des Eigentums. Eine rechtsdogmatische und rechtspolitische Betrachtung.* Berlin: Duncker & Humblot, 1994.

Eli, M., Vögtle, C. "Dienstleistungen: Dynamisches Wachstum verspricht Zukunftschancen." In *Wiedervereinigung nach sechs Jahren: Erfolge, Defizite, Zukunftsperspektiven im Transformationsprozeß*, ed. K. H. Oppenländer, 469–479. Berlin–München: Duncker & Humblot, 1997.

Elias, N. *Studies on the Germans. Power Struggles and the Development of Habitus in the Nineteenth and Twentieth Centuries.* Dublin: University College Dublin Press, 2013.

Ellerman, D. P. *Property and Contract in Economics. The Case for Economic Democracy.* Oxford–Cambridge: Blackwell, 1992.

Elster, J. "On Doing What One Can: An Argument Against Restitution and Retribution as a Means of Overcoming the Communist Legacy." *East European Constitutional Review* 1, No. 2 (1992): 15–17.

Elster, J. "The Impact of Constitutions on Economic Performance." *The World Bank Economic Review* 1 (1994): 209–226.

Erhard, L. *Deutsche Wirtschaftspolitik. Der Weg der Sozialen Marktwirtschaft.* Düsseldorf: Econ, Knapp, 1962.

Erhard, L. *Deutschland Rückkehr zum Weltmarkt.* Düsseldorf: Econ-Verlag, 1953.

Erhard, L. *Dobrobyt dla wszystkich.* Warszawa: PTE, 2012.

Erhard, L. *Wohlstand für Alle.* Düsseldorf: Econ-Verlag, 1957.

Estrin, S., Pérotin, V. "Does Ownership Always Matter?" *International Journal of Industrial Organization* 9, No. 1 (1991): 55–72.

Eucken, W. *Die Grundlagen der Nationalökonomie.* Berlin: Springer, 2011.

Eucken, W. *Grundsätze der Wirtschaftspolitik.* Tübingen: Mohr, 1955.

Eucken, W. *Kapitaltheoretische Untersuchungen.* Tübingen: Mohr, 1954.

Eucken, W. *Nationalökonomie – Wozu?* Bad Godesberg: Verlag Helmut Küpper, 1947.

Eucken, W. *Podstawy polityki gospodarczej.* Poznań: Wydawnictwo Poznańskie, 2005.

Eucken, W. *Unser Zeitalter der Mißerfolge. Fünf Vorträge zur Wirtschaftspolitik.* Tübingen: Mohr, 1951.

Fair-Schulz, A., Kessler, M., eds. *East German Historians Since Reunification. A Discipline Transformed.* New York: SUNY Press, 2017.

Falkowska, A. "Restytucja, odszkodowanie czy inwestycje? – reprywatyzacja majątku Niemieckiej Republiki Demokratycznej." *Ekonomia i Prawo* 7 (2011): 269–284.

Fałkowski, J., Metelska-Szaniawska, K. "Przyczyny ustanawiania i stabilność konstytucji – spojrzenie z perspektywy ekonomicznej." *Gospodarka Narodowa* No. 3 (2015): 79–105.

Fidrmuc, J. "Economic Reform, Democracy and Growth During Post-Communist Transition." *European Journal of Political Economy* 19, No. 3 (2003): 583–604.

Fiedor, B. "Instytucje formalne i nieformalne w kształtowaniu trwałego rozwoju," *Zeszyty Naukowe Uniwersytetu Szczecińskiego. Studia i Prace Wydziału Nauk Ekonomicznych i Zarządzania* No. 40 (2015), Vol. 2: *Problemy współczesnej ekonomii*: 83–107.

Fijałkowski, K. "Instytucjonalna teoria zmiany społeczno-ekonomicznej w historii gospodarczej Douglassa C. Northa." In *Społeczeństwo i gospodarka w badaniach historycznych – dokonania i perspektywy. W 60-lecie polskich badań statystycznych i gospodarczych na Dolnym Śląsku*, eds. E. Kościk, T. Głowiński, 58–71. Wrocław: Wydawnictwo GAJT, 2006.

Fischer, W., Schröter, H. "Die Entstehung der Treuhandanstalt." In *Treuhandanstalt. Das Unmögliche wagen*, eds. W. Fischer, H. Hax, H. K. Schneider, 17–40. Berlin: Akademie Verlag, 1993.

Florczak, A. "Organizacja Bezpieczeństwa i Współpracy w Europie." In *Organizacje w stosunkach międzynarodowych. Istota – mechanizmy działania – zasięg*, ed. T. Łoś-Nowak, 138–164. Wrocław: Wydawnictwo UWr, 2004.

Foster, N. "The German 'Grundgesetz' After the 1990 Unification Treaty of the Two Germanies." *Netherlands International Law Review* 38, No. 3 (1991): 360–372.

Frambach, H. *Die neoklassische »Geschichte« der Ökonomie. Bemerkungen zur Standortbestimmung von Douglass C. North's Theorie vom Wandel der Institutionen.* Wuppertal: Bergische Universität Gesamthochschule Wuppertal, 2001.

Frank, R. "Privatization in Eastern Germany: A Comprehensive Study." *Vanderbilt Journal of Transnational Law* 27, No. 4 (1994): 809–868.

Franz, W. "Die deutsche Mitbestimmung auf dem Prüfstand: Bilanz und Vorschläge für eine Neuausrichtung." *Zeitschrift für Arbeitsmarkt Forschung/Journal for Labour Market Research* 38, No. 2/3 (2005): 268–283.

Frese, M., Kring, W., Soose, A., Zempel, J. "Personalinitiative at Work: Differences between East and West Germany." *Academy of Management Journal* No. 39 (1996): 37–63.

Fuest, C., Thöne, M. "Der Finanzföderalismus in Deutschland und seine Reform." In *Handbuch Föderalismus – Föderalismus als demokratische Rechtsordnung und Rechtskultur in Deutschland, Europa und der Welt*, Vol. II: *Probleme, Reformen, Perspektiven des deutschen Föderalismus*, ed. I. Härtel, 265–321. Berlin–Heidelberg: Springer-Verlag, 2012.

Fuller, S. *Knowledge Management Foundations.* Boston: Butterworth-Heinemann, 2002.

Furubotn, E. G., Pejovich, S. "Property Rights and Economic Theory: A Survey of Recent Literature." *Journal of Economic Literature* 10, No. 4 (1972): 1137–1162.

Furubotn, E. G., Pejovich, S., eds. *The Economics of Property Rights.* Cambridge: Ballinger Publishing Company, 1974.

Furubotn, E. G., Richter, R. *Institutions and Economic Theory. The Contribution of the New Institutional Economics.* Ann Arbor; The Univeristy of Michigan Press, 2008.

Gabrielczak, P. "Główne nurty w rosyjskiej historii gospodarczej w nowym millennium." In *Przegląd badań nad historią gospodarczą w XXI wieku*, eds. R. Matera, A. Pieczewski, 149–159. Łódź: Wydawnictwo UŁ, 2011.

Galster, J. "Reforma konstytucyjna w zjednoczonych Niemczech." *Przegląd Sejmowy* 4, No. 3 (15) (1996): 57–68.

Gardocki, L. *Prawo karne.* Warszawa: Wydawnictwo C. H. Beck, 2017.

Garner, R., Ferdinand, P., Lawson, S. *Introduction to Politics.* Oxford: Oxford University Press, 2020.

Gaweł, T., Klimczak, M. "Pojęcie instytucji w prawie i ekonomii." In *Ład instytucjonalny w gospodarce*, Vol. I, eds. B. Polszakiewicz, J. Boehlke, 73–86. Toruń: Wydawnictwo UMK, 2005.

Gazda, Z. *Historia gospodarcza*, Vol. 1. Kielce: Wydział Zarządzania i Administracji Wyższej Szkoły Pedagogicznej, 1998.

Gazdar, K. *Germany's Balanced Development. The Real Wealth of a Nation.* Westport–London: Quorum Books, 1998.

Giddens, A. *Socjologia.* Warszawa: WN PWN, 2006.

Giersch, H., Paqué, K.-H., Schmieding, H. *The Fading Miracle. Four Decades of Market Economy in Germany.* Cambridge: Cambridge University Press, 1992.

Giersch, H. "Some General Lessons from West Germany's Postwar Experiences." In *Towards a Market Economy in Central and Eastern Europe*, ed. H. Giersch, 1–21. Berlin–Heidelberg: Springer-Verlag, 1991.

Gieseke, J. *Stasi. Historia 1945–1990.* Kraków: Wydawnictwo UJ, 2010.

Ginsburg, T., Elkins, Z., Blount, J. "Does the Process of Constitution-Making Matter?" *Annual Review of Law and Social Science* 5 (2009): 201–223.

Giza, W. "Niemiecki 'cud gospodarczy' jako efekt realizacji ordoliberalnej polityki gospodarczej – analiza krytyczna." *Optimum. Studia Ekonomiczne* No. 4 (52) (2011): 107–118.

Glinka, B., Gudkova, S. *Przedsiębiorczość*. Warszawa: Wolters Kluwer Polska, 2011.

Gniewek, E. *Prawo rzeczowe*. Warszawa: Wydawnictwo C. H. Beck, 2016.

Godlewska, M. "Wpływ instytucji formalnych i nieformalnych na działalność innowacyjną polskich przedsiębiorstw sektora MSP." *Nierówności Społeczne a Wzrost Gospodarczy* No. 54 (2018): 289–300.

Godłów-Legiędź, J. "Aneks do wydania polskiego" In H. Landreth, D. C. Colander, *Historia myśli ekonomicznej*, 547–575. Warszawa: WN PWN, 2005.

Godłów-Legiędź, J. "Instytucje i koszty transakcji jako podstawowe pojęcia nowej ekonomii instytucjonalnej." In *Instytucje i transformacja*, ed. J. Godłów-Legiędź, 11–32. Toruń: Wydawnictwo Adam Marszałek, 2009.

Godłów-Legiędź, J., Legiędź, T. "Interaction between Formal and Informal Institutions in the Process of Transformation from a Planned to a Market Economy." *Comparative Economic Research. Central and Eastern Europe* 11, No. 1–2 (2008): 105–124.

Godłów-Legiędź, J. *Współczesna ekonomia. Ku nowemu paradygmatowi?* Warszawa: Wydawnictwo C. H. Beck, 2010.

Godłów-Legiędź, J. "Wstęp." In *Instytucje i transformacja*, ed. J. Godłów-Legiędź, 4–10. Toruń: Wydawnictwo Adam Marszałek, 2009.

Godłów-Legiędź, J. "Zasada rządów prawa i przemiany ustrojowe w Polsce." *Gospodarka Narodowa* No. 3 (2017): 5–27.

Goetz, K. H., Cullen, P. J., eds. *Constitutional Policy in Unified Germany*. London: Frank Cass, 1995.

Goldsmith, A. A. "Democracy, Property Rights and Economic Growth." *The Journal of Development Studies* 32, No. 2 (1995): 157–174.

Goodman, N. *Wstęp do socjologii*. Poznań: Zysk i S-ka, 2001.

Gordon, H. S. "The Economics of Common Property Rights: The Fishery." *Journal of Political Economy* 62, No. 2 (1954): 124–142.

Górniewicz, G. "Determinanty i konsekwencje bezpośrednich inwestycji zagranicznych." *Studia z Zakresu Prawa, Administracji i Zarządzania UKW* 4 (2013): 61–78.

Goschler, C. *Studie zur Wahrnehmung und Bewertung der Arbeit der Treuhandanstalt im Auftrag des Bundesministeriums für Wirtschaft und Energie*. Bochum: Ruhr-Universität Bochum, 2017.

Gottlieb, M. *A Theory of Economic Systems*. Orlando: Academic Press, Inc., 1984.

Goździewicz, G., ed. *Reprezentacja praw i interesów pracowniczych*. Toruń: TNOiK, Dom Organizatora, 2001.

Götz, M. "Konwergencja dochodów w Niemczech w latach 1991–2007." *Ruch Prawniczy, Ekonomiczny i Socjologiczny* 72, No. 1 (2010): 93–114.

Götz, M. "Od Republiki Federalnej do 'Regierungsbezirke' – niemiecki krajobraz wiedzy na różnych poziomach analizy." *Studia Regionalne i Lokalne* No. 1 (35) (2009): 5–31.

Götz, M. "Przyczyny słabszego wzrostu gospodarczego wschodnich krajów RFN w ocenie literatury naukowej." *Przegląd Zachodni* No. 2 (2010): 203–213.

Grabska, A., Moszyński, M., Pysz, P. *Stanowiony i spontaniczny ład gospodarczy w procesie transformacji systemowej Polski i byłej NRD*. Toruń: Instytut Badań Gospodarczych, PTE, 2014.

Grabski, A. F. *Dzieje historiografii*. Poznań: Wydawnictwo Poznańskie, 2006.

Grabski, A. F. *Zarys historii historiografii polskiej*. Poznań: Wydawnictwo Poznańskie, 2006.

Graefen, T. *Bibliographie zur Mitbestimmung. Stand: März 2018*. Düsseldorf: Hans-Böckler-Stiftung, 2018.

Grala, D. "Badania nad dziejami reform gospodarczych w Polsce po roku 1989. Cele, obiekty i metody." In *Przegląd badań nad historią gospodarczą w XXI wieku*, eds. R. Matera, A. Pieczewski, 59–73. Łódź: Wydawnictwo UŁ, 2011.

Grawert, R. "Ustawa Zasadnicza w świetle ujętych w niej praw zasadniczych." *Przegląd Sejmowy* No. 6 (95) (2009): 33–44.

Greite, W. "Finanzverfassung der Bundesrepublik Deutschland." In *Elemente der Sozialen Marktwirtschaft. Wirtschaftliche und rechtliche Rahmenbedingungen – Transformationsmöglichkeiten*, eds. K. Fasbender, M. Holthus, E. Thiel, 77–101. Hamburg: Verlag Weltarchiv GmbH, 1991.

Grier, K. B., Tullock, G. "An Empirical Analysis of Cross-National Economic Growth, 1951–1980." *Journal of Monetary Economics* 24, No. 2 (1989): 259–276.

Griffin, R. W. *Podstawy zarządzania organizacjami*. Warszawa: WN PWN, 2004.

Grimm, K. *Socjalna gospodarka rynkowa w RFN. Koncepcja – rozwój – problematyka*. Warszawa: Fundacja im. Friedricha Eberta, 1992.

Grodek, A. "Czego historią jest historia gospodarcza." In *Pamiętnik trzydziestolecia Szkoły Głównej Handlowej w Warszawie 1906–1936*, 46–62. Warszawa: SGH, 1938.

Groenewegen, J., Spithoven, A., Berg, A. van den. *Institutional Economics. An Introduction*. New York: Palgrave Macmillan, 2010.

Gröpl, Ch. *Staatsrecht I. Staatsgrundlagen, Staatsorganisation, Verfassungsprozess mit Einführung in das juristische Lernen*. München: C. H. Beck, 2018.

Gross, F. *Druga rewolucja przemysłowa. Zagadnienia współczesnego socjalizmu*. Paryż: Wydawnictwo Światło, 1958.

Gross, F. *Socjalizm humanistyczny*. New York: Związek Socjalistów Polskich w Stanach Zjednoczonych, 1946.

Grossman, S. J., Hart, O. D. "The Costs and Benefits of Ownership: A Theory of Vertical and Lateral Integration." *Journal of Political Economy* 94 (1986): 691–719.

Gruhler, W. *Unternehmens bezogene Umstrukturierung in den neuen Bundesländern – Zwischenbilanz*. Köln: Deutscher Instituts-Verlag, 1992.

Grünewald, J. *Das Eigentum und das Eigentumsrecht in der sowjetischen Besatzungszone Deutschlands*. Bonn: Ludwig Röhrscheid Verlag, 1961.

Gruszewska, E. "Transformacja instytucji nieformalnych w Polsce." *Gospodarka Narodowa* 80 (11), No. 3 (247) (2012): 61–83.

Gruszewska, E. "Wpływ interakcji instytucji formalnych i nieformalnych na przedsiębiorczość w Polsce." In *Zrozumieć kapitalizm. Podejście ewolucyjno-instytucjonalne*, eds. A. Ząbkowicz, M. Miszewski, P. Chmielnicki, S. Czech, 197–215. Sosnowiec–Kraków: Forum Myśli Instytucjonalnej, Oficyna Wydawnicza "Humanitas," 2018.

Gumpel, W. *Die sozialistischen Staaten*, Vol. 1: *Sozialistische Wirtschaftssysteme*. München: Günter Olzog Verlag, 1983.

Gutmann, J., Metelska-Szaniawska, K., Voigt, S. "The Comparative Constitutional Compliance Database." Working paper, Institute of Law and Economics (ILE) Working Paper Series, No. 57 (2022), 1–44.

Gutmann, J., Voigt, S. "Militant Constitutionalism: A Promising Concept to Make Constitutional Backsliding less likely?" *Public Choice* (2021). https://link.springer.com/content/pdf/10.1007/s11127-021-00874-1.pdf.

Gutmann, J., Voigt, S. "Quantitative Analysis of Constitutions." Working paper, Institute of Law and Economics (ILE) Working Paper Series, No. 56 (2022), 1–32.

Gwartney, J., Lawson, R. "The Concept and Measurement of Economic Freedom." *European Journal of Political Economy* 19, No. 3 (2003): 405–430.

Haan, J. de, Siermann, C. L. J. "Further Evidence on the Relationship Between Economic Freedom and Economic Growth." *Public Choice* 95, No. 3–4 (1998): 363–380.

Haan, J. de, Siermann, C. L. J. "New Evidence on the Relationship Between Democracy and Economic Growth." *Public Choice* 86, No. 1–2 (1996): 175–198.

Haan, J. de, Sturm, J.-E. "On the Relationship Between Economic Freedom and Economic Growth." *European Journal of Political Economy* 16, No. 2 (2000): 215–241.

Haase, H. E. *Das Wirtschaftssystem der DDR. Eine Einführung*. Berlin: Berlin Verlag, 1983.

Haase, H. E. *Entwicklungstendenzen der DDR-Wirtschaft für die 80er Jahre – Eine Prognose der Probleme*. Berlin: Osteuropa-Instituts an der Freien Universität Berlin, 1980.

Häberle, P. "Vielfalt der Property Rights und der verfassungsrechtliche Eigentumsbegriff." In *Ansprüche, Eigentums- und Verfügungsrechte*, ed. M. Neumann, 63–102. Berlin: Duncker & Humblot, 1984.

Haendcke-Hoppe, M., ed. *Außenwirtschaftssysteme und Außenwirtschaftsreformen sozialistischer Länder. Ein intrasystemarer Vergleich.* Berlin: Duncker & Humblot, 1988.

Hall, P. A., Gingerich, D. W. "Varieties of Capitalism and Institutional Complementarities in the Political Economy: An Empirical Analysis." *British Journal of Political Science* 39, No. 3 (2009): 449–482.

Hall, P. A., Soskice, D. "An Introduction to Varieties of Capitalism." In *Varieties of Capitalism. The Institutional Foundations of Comparative Advantage*, eds. P. A. Hall, D. Soskice, 1–68. New York: Oxford University Press, 2001.

Hamel, H. "Die DDR-Wirtschaft auf dem Weg zum 'entwickelten Sozialismus'." In *Wirtschaftsreformen im Ostblock in den 80er Jahren. Länderstudien: Sowjetunion, DDR, Polen, Rumänien, Tschechoslowakei, Bulgarien, Ungarn*, ed. R. Schlüter, 53–77. Paderborn: Ferdinand Schöningh, 1988.

Hamel, H. "Ordnungspolitische Gestaltung der Wirtschaftssysteme." In *Bundesrepublik Deutschland – DDR: Die Wirtschaftssysteme. Soziale Marktwirtschaft und Sozialistische Planwirtschaft im Systemvergleich*, ed. H. Hamel, 61–115. München: Verlag C. H. Beck, 1983.

Hardin, G. "The Tragedy of the Commons." *Science* 162, No. 3859 (1968): 1243–1248.

Hart, O., Moore, J. "Property Rights and the Nature of the Firm." *Journal of Political Economy* 98, No. 6 (1990): 1119–1158.

Haustein, H.-D. "Experiences and Prospects: The Case of the GDR." In *Towards a Market Economy in Central and Eastern Europe*, ed. H.-D. Haustein, 143–154. Berlin–Heidelberg: Springer-Verlag, 1991.

Hayek, F. A. von *The Law, Legislation and Liberty. A New Statement of the Liberal Principles of Justice and Political Economy.* London–New York: Routledge, 2013.

Heckel, D. Th., ed. *Eigentum und Eigentumsverteilung als theologisches, rechtsphilosophisches und ökonomisches Problem. Vorträge gehalten auf der Tagung evangelischer Juristen 1961.* München: Evangelischer Presseverband für Bayern, 1962.

Heckelman, J. C. "Economic Freedom and Economic Growth: A Short-Run Causal Investigation." *Journal of Applied Economics* 3, No. 1 (2000): 71–91.

Heclo, H. "Toward a New Welfare State?" In *The Development of Welfare States in Europe and America*, eds. P. Flora, A. J. Heidenheimer, 383–406. New Brunswick–London: Transaction Publishers, 2009.

Helliwell, J. F. "Empirical Linkages Between Democracy and Economic Growth." *British Journal of Political Science* 24, No. 2 (1994): 225–248.

Hellmann, T., Kullas, M. "Das ökonomische Innovationsregime der Bundesländer im föderalen Deutschland." In *Handbuch Föderalismus – Föderalismus als demokratische Rechtsordnung und Rechtskultur in Deutschland, Europa und der Welt*, Vol. II: *Probleme, Reformen, Perspektiven des deutschen Föderalismus*, ed. I. Härtel, 137–163. Berlin–Heidelberg: Springer-Verlag, 2012.

Henisz, W. J. "The Institutional Environment for Multinational Investment." *Journal of Law, Economics and Organization* 16 (2000): 334–364.

Henning, F.-W. *Das industrialisierte Deutschland 1914 bis 1992.* Paderborn: Ferdinand Schöningh, 1993.

Heslop, J., Roberto, J. "Property Rights in the Unified Germany: A Constitutional, Comparative, and International Legal Analysis." *Boston University International Law Journal* 11, No. 2 (1993): 243–298.

Hettling, M. et al., eds. *Was ist Gesellschaftsgeschichte? Positionen, Themen, Analysen.* München: Verlag C. H. Beck, 1991.

Heuchert, K. "Das Eigentum in der Theorie der Property Rights." In *Das Eigentum. Vorträge gehalten auf der Tagung der Joachim Jungius-Gesellschaft der Wissenschaften. Hamburg am 10., 11. und 12. Dezember 1987*, ed. J. F. Baur, 125–141. Göttingen: Vandenhoeck & Ruprecht, 1989.

Heuer, U.-J., Riege, G., eds. *Neues Deutschland. Neue Verfassung?!* Bonn: Pahl-Rugenstein, 1992.

Hitchens, D. M. W. N., Wagner, K., Birnie, J. E. *East German Productivity and the Transition to the Market Economy. Comparisons with West Germany and Northern Ireland.* Aldershot–Brookfield: Avebury, 1993.

Hodgson, G. M. *The Evolution of Institutional Economics. Agency, Structure and Darwinism in American Institutionalism.* London–New York: Routledge, 2004.

Hoffmann, D., ed. *Transformation einer Volkswirtschaft. Neue Forschungen zur Geschichte der Treuhandanstalt.* Berlin: Metropol Verlag, 2020.

Hoffmann, L. "Integrating the East German States into the German Economy: Opportunities, Burdens and Options." In *Economic Aspects of German Unification. National and International Perspectives*, ed. P. J. J. Welfens, 49–71. Berlin–Heidelberg: Springer-Verlag, 1992.

Hohmann, K. et al., eds. *Grundtexte zur Sozialen Martkwirtschaft*, Vol. 2: *Das Soziale in der Sozialen Marktwirtschaft.* Stuttgart–New York: Ludwig-Erhard-Stiftung e. V. Bonn, Gustav Fischer Verlag, 1988.

Holcombe, R. G. *The Economic Foundations of Government.* London: Macmillan, 1994.

Holmes Jr, R. M., Miller, T., Hitt, M. A., Salmador, M. P. "The Interrelationships Among Informal Institutions, Formal Institutions, and Inward Foreign Direct Investment." *Journal of Management* 39, No. 2 (2013): 531–566.

Holona, M., ed. M. Weber, *Racjonalność, władza, odczarowanie.* Poznań: Wydawnictwo Poznańskie, 2004.

Holzer, J. *Europa zimnej wojny*. Kraków: Wydawnictwo Znak, ISP PAN, 2012.

Horvat, B. *The Political Economy of Socialism. A Marxist Social Theory*. Oxford: Martin Robertson, 1982.

Howard, J. E. *The Treuhandanstalt and Privatisation in the Former East Germany: Stakeholder Perspectives*. London: Routledge, 2018.

Hryniewicz, J., Jałowiecki, B. *System polityczny a rozwój gospodarczy*. Warszawa: Wydawnictwa EIRRiL, 1997.

Hucko, E. M., ed. *The Democratic Tradition: Four German Constitutions*. Leamington: Berg Publishers, 1987.

Iggers, G. G. *Historiografia XX wieku. Przegląd kierunków badawczych*. Warszawa: WN PWN, 2010.

Iwanek, M. *Analiza instytucji własności przedsiębiorstw. Przyczynek do problematyki efektywności i usprawnienia przedsiębiorstw publicznych*. Warszawa: WN PWN, 1996.

Jabłkowska, J., Żyliński, L., eds. *O kondycji Niemiec. Tożsamość niemiecka w debatach intelektualistów po 1945 roku*. Poznań: Wydawnictwo Poznańskie, 2008.

Jackson, G. "Contested Boundaries: Ambiguity and Creativity in the Evolution of German Codetermination." In *Beyond Continuity. Institutional Change in Advanced Political Economies*, eds. W. Streeck, K. Thelen, 236–249. New York: Oxford University Press, 2005.

Jaki, A. "Prowartościowy paradygmat i koncepcja zarządzania wartością – mechanizmy i obszary ewolucji." *Przegląd Organizacji* No. 1 (2016): 9–15.

Janicka, D. *Ustawa Zasadnicza w praktyce Republiki Federalnej Niemiec (1949–1989)*. Toruń: WN UMK, 2009.

Jasiński, L. J. *Nobel z ekonomii. Poglądy laureatów w zarysie*. Warszawa: Wydawnictwo Key Text, 2008.

Jaskułowski, T. *Ostatnie miesiące NRD*. Wrocław: CSNiE UWr, Oficyna Wydawnicza Atut, 2010.

Jaskułowski, T. *Pokojowa rewolucja w Niemieckiej Republice Demokratycznej w latach 1989–1990. Geneza – przebieg – efekty*. Wrocław: CSNiE UWr, Oficyna Wydawnicza Atut, 2007.

Jaworek, M., Kuczmarska, M., Lizińska, W. "Kreowanie klimatu inwestycyjnego na rzecz przyciągania inwestorów zagranicznych przez jednostki samorządu terytorialnego w wybranych województwach Polski." *Acta Universitatis Nicolai Copernici. Ekonomia* 47, No. 1 (2016): 53–72.

Jirjahn, U. "Ökonomische Wirkungen der Mitbestimmung in Deutschland. Überblick über den Stand der Forschung und Perspektiven für zukünftige Studien." *Sozialer Fortschritt* 55, No. 9 (2006): 215–226.

Jirjahn, U. "Ökonomische Wirkungen der Mitbestimmung in Deutschland. Ein Update." Working paper, No. 186. Düsseldorf: Hans-Böckler-Stiftung, 2010.

Jung, H., ed. *Der staatsmonopolistische Kapitalismus. Einführungen in marxistische Analysen aus der DDR, Frankreich und der Sowjetunion*. Frankfurt/Main: Verlag Marxistische Blätter, 1973.

Jurczuk, A., Moszyński, M., Pysz, P. "The Austrian School of Economics and Ordoliberalism – Socio-Economic Order." *Studies in Logic, Grammar and Rhetoric* No. 57 (70) (2019): 105–121.

Juruś, D. "Wstęp." In *Dzieje własności prywatnej. Od starożytności do współczesności*, ed. D. Juruś, 7–23. Warszawa: Fijorr Publishing, 2014.

Kacprzyk, A. *Instytucjonalne determinanty wzrostu gospodarczego*. Łódź: Wydawnictwo UŁ, 2014.

Kalinová, L., Klusáková, Z. "Przemiany społeczno-gospodarcze w krajach demokracji ludowej po roku 1948. Struktura klasowa i społeczna ludności krajów socjalistycznych." In *Rozwój gospodarczy europejskich krajów socjalistycznych*, ed. V. Průcha, 275–295. Warszawa: Książka i Wiedza, 1981.

Kaliński, J. "Przekształcenia własnościowe." In *Problemy gospodarcze Trzeciej Rzeczypospolitej*, ed. A. Jarosz-Nojszewska, 91–104. Warszawa: Oficyna Wydawnicza SGH, 2017.

Kałużny, R. "Układ Warszawski 1955–1991." *Zeszyty Naukowe Wyższej Szkoły Oficerskiej Wojsk Lądowych* No. 1 (147) (2008): 190–198.

Karg, H. H. *Nationalökonomie und Elitenbildung. Eine grundlegende Wirtschaftstheorie an die Adresse der nachkommunistischen Menschheit*. Hamburg: Verlag Dr. Kovač, 1996.

Karpiński, A. *Restrukturyzacja gospodarki w Polsce i na świecie*. Warszawa: PWE, 1986.

Kasper, W., Streit, M. E., Boettke, P. J. *Institutional Economics. Property, Competition, Policies*. Cheltenham–Northampton: Edward Elgar, 2012.

Kaufmann, F.-X. *Sozialpolitik und Sozialstaat: Soziologische Analysen*. Wiesbaden: VS Verlag für Sozialwissenschaften, 2009.

Keen, M. "The German Tax Reform of 2000." *International Tax and Public Finance* 9, No. 5 (2002): 603–621.

Kelley, D. R. *Granice historii. Badanie przeszłości w XX wieku*. Warszawa: WN PWN, 2009.

Kelley, D. R. *Losy historii. Badanie przeszłości od Herdera do Huizingi*. Warszawa: WN PWN, 2010.

Kelley, D. R. *Oblicza historii. Badanie przeszłości od Herodota do Herdera*. Warszawa: WN PWN, 2010.

Kirchhof, P. "Staatsverschuldung im föderalen System der Bundesrepublik Deutschland." In *Handbuch Föderalismus – Föderalismus als demokratische*

Rechtsordnung und Rechtskultur in Deutschland, Europa und der Welt, Vol. II: *Probleme, Reformen, Perspektiven des deutschen Föderalismus*, ed. I. Härtel, 323–338. Berlin–Heidelberg: Springer-Verlag, 2012.

Kiwerska, J., Koszel, B., Tomczak, M., Żerko, S. *Polityka zagraniczna zjednoczonych Niemiec*. Poznań: Instytut Zachodni, 2011.

Kleinhanss, W. "Konkurencyjność głównych typów gospodarstw rolniczych w Niemczech." *Zagadnienia Ekonomiki Rolnej* No. 1 (2015): 25–41.

Klimczak, B. *Wybrane problemy i zastosowania ekonomii instytucjonalnej*. Wrocław: Wydawnictwo AE we Wrocławiu, 2006.

Klimiuk, Z. "Trendy rozwojowe w gospodarce niemieckiej po 1990 r." *Roczniki Ekonomii i Zarządzania* 5 (41) (2013): 57–87.

Klodt, H. "Government Support for Restructuring the East German Economy." In *Economic Aspects of German Unification. National and International Perspectives*, ed. P. J. J. Welfens, 261–285. Berlin–Heidelberg: Springer-Verlag, 1992.

Kloepfer, M. *Verfassungsrecht I. Grundlagen, Staatsorganisationsrecht, Bezüge zum Völker- und Europarecht*. München: C. H. Beck, 2011.

Klüber, F. *Eigentumstheorie und Eigentumspolitik. Begründung und Gestaltung des Privateigentums nach katholisher Gesellschaftslehre*. Osnabrück: Verlag A. Fromm, 1963.

Klunzinger, E. *Einführung in das Bürgerliche Recht. Grundkurs für Studierende der Rechts- und Wirtschaftswissenschaften*. München: Verlag Franz Vahlen, 2011.

Klusáková, Z. "Rolnictwo." In *Rozwój gospodarczy europejskich krajów socjalistycznych*, ed. V. Průcha, 549–555. Warszawa: Książka i Wiedza, 1981.

Knack, S., Keefer, P. "Institutions and Economic Performance: Cross-Country Tests Using Alternative Institutional Measures." *Economics & Politics* 7, No. 3 (1995): 207–227.

Kocka, J. *Sozialgeschichte. Begriff – Entwicklung – Probleme*. Göttingen: Vandenhoeck & Ruprecht, 1986.

Kocka, J., ed. *Sozialgeschichte im internationalen Überblick. Ergebnisse und Tendenzen der Forschung*. Darmstadt: Wissenschaftliche Buchgesellschaft, 1989.

Kolibski, J. "Własność jako podstawa efektywności gospodarczej i stosunków społecznych." In *Własność to odpowiedzialność – wiedza, praktyka, doświadczenie*, ed. B. Rogatko, 83–101. Warszawa–Kraków: Europejski Instytut Nieruchomości, 2009.

Koll, R. "Der räumliche Strukturwandel in Ostdeutschland. Was ist neu in den neuen Bundesländern?" In *Wiedervereinigung nach sechs Jahren: Erfolge, Defizite, Zukunftsperspektiven im Transformationsprozeß*, ed. K. H. Oppenländer, 505–525. Berlin–München: Duncker & Humblot, 1997.

Koop, G. *Wprowadzenie do ekonometrii*. Warszawa: Oficyna a Wolters Kluwer Business, 2014.

Koppernock, M. "Niemiecki model partycypacji. Pracownicy we współzarządzaniu i jako współwłaściciele." *Dialog. Pismo Dialogu Społecznego* No. 3 (26) (2010): 3–12.

Kormendi, R. C., Meguire, P. G. "Macroeconomic Determinants of Growth: Cross-Country Evidence." *Journal of Monetary Economics* 16, No. 2 (1985): 141–163.

Korybski, A., Leszczyński, L., Pieniążek, A. *Wstęp do prawoznawstwa.* Lublin: Wydawnictwo UMCS, 2007.

Kościk, E. " 'Wrocławskie Spotkania z Historią Gospodarczą' próbą ożywienia badań historycznych nad gospodarką i społeczeństwem." In *Przegląd badań nad historią gospodarczą w XXI wieku,* eds. R. Matera, A. Pieczewski, 39–44. Łódź: Wydawnictwo UŁ, 2011.

Kościk, E., Głowiński, T., eds. *Społeczeństwo i gospodarka w badaniach historycznych – dokonania i perspektywy. W 60-lecie polskich badań statystycznych i gospodarczych na Dolnym Śląsku.* Wrocław: Wydawnictwo GAJT, 2006.

Koselleck, R. *Dzieje pojęć. Studia z semantyki i pragmatyki języka społeczno-politycznego.* Warszawa: Oficyna Naukowa, 2009.

Koselleck, R. *Semantyka historyczna.* Poznań: Wydawnictwo Poznańskie, 2001.

Kosman, M. M. *Zjednoczone Niemcy w procesie integracji europejskiej (1990–2002).* Toruń: Wydawnictwo Adam Marszałek, 2005.

Kostro, K. "Nieformalne instytucje w życiu gospodarczym." *Studia Ekonomiczne* No. 1–2 (2004): 71–94.

Kowalski, J. *Państwo prawa. Demokratyczne państwo prawne. Antologia.* Warszawa: Oficyna Wydawnicza WSHiP im. R. Łazarskiego, 2008.

Kowalski, K. "Nowe trendy w historii gospodarczej. 'The Economic History Review' w latach 2001–2009." In *Przegląd badań nad historią gospodarczą w XXI wieku,* eds. R. Matera, A. Pieczewski, 193–211. Łódź: Wydawnictwo UŁ, 2011.

Kowalski, K. *Plan Marshalla. Uwarunkowania i skutki gospodarczo-polityczne.* Łódź: Wydawnictwo UŁ, 2014.

Kozaczka, M. *Gospodarka Polski w latach 1989–2009.* Lublin: Norbertinum, 2012.

Kozłowski, M. *Pracownicza partycypacja finansowa. Geneza, uwarunkowania rozwoju, rezultaty.* Łódź: Wydawnictwo UŁ, 2013.

Kozyr-Kowalski, S. *Socjologia, społeczeństwo obywatelskie i państwo.* Poznań: WN UAM, 2004.

Kozyr-Kowalski, S., ed. *Własność: gospodarka a prawo. Studia o marksistowskiej teorii własności.* Warszawa: PWN, 1977.

Kozyr-Kowalski, S., Przestalski, A., Tittenbrun, J. *Ownership and Society.* Poznań: Wydawnictwo Nakom, 1993.

Krastev, I., Peeva, R. "Invisible Context, Invisible Constraints. The Limits of the Normative Explanation of Constitutional Change." In *Constitutions, Markets and*

Law. Recent Experiences in Transition Economies, eds. S. Voigt, H.-J. Wagener, 113–128. Cheltenham–Northampton: Edward Elgar, 2002.

Krasuski, J. *Historia Niemiec*. Wrocław: Ossolineum, 2008.

Kreissig, V., Lungwitz, R. "Privatisation in East Germany and the Chance of Workers' Participation: A Problems Approach." In *International Privatisation. Strategies and Practices*, ed. T. Clarke, 234–244. Berlin–New York: Walter de Gruyter, 1994.

Krukowski, S. "Konstytucja Rzeczypospolitej Polskiej z 1921 r." In *Konstytucje Polski. Szkice monograficzne z dziejów polskiego konstytucjonalizmu*, ed. M. Kallas, 19–140. Warszawa: PWN, 1990.

Kuciński, J. "Miejsce historii gospodarczej w systemie nauk ekonomicznych." *Acta Universitatis Lodziensis. Zeszyty Naukowe Uniwersytetu Łódzkiego. Nauki Ekonomiczne i Socjologiczne* No. 17 (1977): 3–22.

Kuczynski, J. *Studien zur Geschichte der Weltwirtschaft*. Berlin: Dietz Verlag, 1952.

Kuczynski, T. "Politische Ökonomie." In *Handbuch Wirtschaftsgeschichte*, Vol. 1, eds. H. Radandt et al., 64–79. Berlin: Institut für Wirtschaftsgeschichte der Akademie der Wissenschaften der DDR, VEB Deutscher Verlag der Wissenschaften, 1981.

Kuczynski, T., ed. *Wirtschaftsgeschichte und Mathematik. Beiträge zur Anwendung mathematischer insbesondere statistischer Methoden in der wirtschafts- und sozialhistorischen Forschung*. Berlin: Akademie-Verlag, 1985.

Kuder, D. "Pojęcie instytucji w teorii ekonomii." *Nierówności Społeczne a Wzrost Gospodarczy* No. 19 (2011): 84–93.

Kufel, T. *Ekonometria. Rozwiązywanie problemów z wykorzystaniem programu GRETL*. Warszawa: WN PWN, 2007.

Kuhn, T. S. *Struktura rewolucji naukowych*. Warszawa: Fundacja Aletheia, 2001.

Kühne, K. *Geschichtskonzept und Profitrate im Marxismus*. Neuwied: Luchterhand, 1976.

Kukułka, J. *Historia współczesna stosunków międzynarodowych 1945–2000*. Warszawa: WN Scholar, 2003.

Kula, W. *Problemy i metody historii gospodarczej*. Warszawa: PWN, 1983.

Kullas, M. *Der Konvergenzprozess zwischen Ost- und Westdeutschland. Hemmnisse und politische Handlungsmöglichkeiten*. Hamburg: Verlag Dr. Kovač, 2011.

Kuniński, M. "Własność i wolność." In *Kapitalizm po polsku. Państwo – prawo – gospodarka*, ed. M. Szułdrzyński, 15–33. Kraków: Ośrodek Myśli Politycznej, 2003.

Kuss, K.-J. *Rechtliche Rahmenbedingungen für Investitionen in Polen*. Baden-Baden: Nomos Verlagsgesellschaft, 1991.

Kuznets, S. *Wzrost gospodarczy narodów. Produkt i struktura produkcji*. Warszawa: PWE, 1976.

Kwaśnicki, W. *Historia myśli liberalnej. Wolność. Własność. Odpowiedzialność*. Warszawa: PWE, 2000.

Kwiatkowski, E. *Teoria trzech sektorów gospodarki. Prezentacja i próba oceny.* Warszawa: PWN, 1980.

La Porta, R., Lopez-de-Silanes, F., Shleifer, A., Vishny, R. W. "Law and Finance." *Journal of Political Economy* 106 (1998): 1113–1155.

La Porta, R., Lopez-de-Silanes, F., Shleifer, A., Vishny, R., "The Quality of Government." *Journal of Law, Economics, and Organization* 15, No. 1 (1999): 222–279.

Landes, D. S. *Bogactwo i nędza narodów. Dlaczego jedni się tak bogaci, a inni tak ubodzy.* Warszawa: Wydawnictwo Muza, 2000.

Landreth, H., Colander, D. C. *Historia myśli ekonomicznej.* Warszawa: WN PWN, 2005.

Landua, D. "The Social Aspects of German Reunification." In *The Economics of German Unification*, eds. A. G. Ghanssy, W. Schäfer, 92–109. London–New York: Routledge, 1993.

Lange, O. *Ekonomia polityczna*, Vol. I: *Zagadnienia ogólne.* Warszawa: PWN, 1959.

Lange, T., Pugh, G. "Catching Up with the West: The Achievements and Limitations of Creative Destruction." In *East Germany's Economic Development since Unification. Domestic and Global Aspects*, eds. J. Hölscher, A. Hochberg, 141–165. Basingstoke–London: Macmillan Press, 1998.

Lange, T., Pugh, G. "The Treuhand: A Positive Account." In *The Political Economy of German Unification*, eds. T. Lange, J. R. Shackleton, 56–71. Providence–Oxford: Berghahn Books, 1998.

Latoszek, E., Proczek, M. *Organizacje międzynarodowe. Założenia, cele, działalność.* Warszawa: WSHiFM, Dom Wydawniczy Elipsa, 2001.

Ławniczak, A. *Monarchiczne i republikańskie głowy państwa w Europie.* Wrocław: Kolonia Limited, 2011.

Leblang, D. A. "Property Rights, Democracy and Economic Growth." *Political Research Quarterly* 49, No. 1 (1996): 5–26.

Legiędź, T. "Instytucjonalna teoria przemian gospodarczych – rozwój gospodarczy z perspektywy nowej ekonomii instytucjonalnej." *Ekonomia* No. 4 (21) (2012): 30–45.

Lehmbruch, G. "Zwischen Institutionentransfer und Eigendynamik: Sektorale Transformationspfade und ihre Bestimmungsgründe." In *Transformationspfade in Ostdeutschland*, eds. R. Czada, G. Lehmbruch, 17–57. Frankfurt–New York: Campus Verlag, 1998.

Leipold, H. "Der Zusammenhang zwischen gewachsener und gesetzer Ordnung: Einige Lehrer aus den postsozialistischen Reformerfahrungen." In *Institutionelle Probleme der Systemtransformation*, ed. D. Cassel, 43–68. Berlin: Duncker & Humblot, 1997.

Leipold, H. "Eigentum und wirtschaftliches Handeln in beiden deutschen Staaten." In *Materialien zum Bericht zur Lage der Nation im geteilten Deutschland 1987*, 38–44. Bonn: Bundesministerium für innerdeutsche Beziehungen, 1987.

Leipold, H. "Gesellschaftstheoretische Fundierung der Wirtschaftssysteme." In *Bundesrepublik Deutschland – DDR: Die Wirtschaftssysteme. Soziale Marktwirtschaft und Sozialistische Planwirtschaft im Systemvergleich*, ed. H. Hamel, 17–60. München: Verlag C. H. Beck, 1983.

Leisner, W. *Sozialbindung des Eigentums*. Berlin: Duncker & Humblot, 1972.

Leisner-Egensperger, A. "Gesetzgebungs- und Verwaltungskompetenzen von Bund und Ländern im Bereich der Steuern." In *Handbuch Föderalismus – Föderalismus als demokratische Rechtsordnung und Rechtskultur in Deutschland, Europa und der Welt*, Vol. II: *Probleme, Reformen, Perspektiven des deutschen Föderalismus*, ed. I. Härtel, 365–387. Berlin–Heidelberg: Springer-Verlag, 2012.

Lewkowicz, J., Metelska-Szaniawska, K. "De jure and de facto Institutions – Disentangling the Interrelationships." *The Latin American and Iberian Journal of Law and Economics* 2, No. 2 (2016): 1–26.

Libecap, G. D. "Property Rights in Economic History: Implications for Research." *Explorations in Economic History* 23 (1986): 227–252.

Lippe, P. von der "The Political Role of Official Statistics in the Former GDR (East Germany)." *Historical Social Research* 24, No. 4 (1999): 3–28.

Lisak, M. "Pojęcie własności w ujęciu chrześcijaństwa i innych religii." In *Własność to odpowiedzialność – wiedza, praktyka, doświadczenie*, ed. B. Rogatko, 17–30. Warszawa–Kraków: Europejski Instytut Nieruchomości, 2009.

Llewellyn, K. N. "The Constitution as an Institution." *Columbia Law Review* 34, No. 1 (1934): 1–40.

Lösch, D. *Sozialistische Wirtschaftswissenschaft. Die Wirtschaftstheorie im Sozialismus und ihre Bedeutung für die Wirtschaftspolitik*. Hamburg: Verlag Weltarchiv GmbH, 1987.

Ludwikowski, R. R. *Prawo konstytucyjne porównawcze*. Toruń: TNOiK "Dom Organizatora," 2000.

Luft, H. *Eigentum und Demokratie in ökonomischen System des Sozialismus*. Berlin: Institut für Gesellschaftswissenschaften beim Zentralkomitee der SED, 1970.

Luhmann, N. *Grundrechte als Institution. Ein Beitrag zur politischen Soziologie*. Berlin: Duncker & Humblot, 1965.

Łepkowski, T. *Przeszłość miniona i teraźniejsza*. Warszawa: PIW, 1980.

Maaz, H. J. "Transformationsprobleme aus psychosozialer Sicht." In *Transformationsprozesse in Deutschland*, ed. H. Sahner, 105–115. Opladen: Leske + Budrich, 1995.

Mahoney, P. G. "The Common Law and Economic Growth: Hayek Might Be Right." *The Journal of Legal Studies* 30, No. 2 (2001): 503–525.

Malycha, A. *Vom Hoffnungsträger zum Prügelknaben. Die Treuandanstalt zwischen wirtschaftlichen Erwartungen und politischen Zwängen 1989–1994*. Berlin: C. H. Links Verlag, 2022.

Małysz, J. "Instytucje a koszty transakcyjne w świetle neoinstytucjonalnej ekonomii." *Ekonomista* No. 3 (2003): 315–339.

Mampel, S. "Die verfassungsrechtlichen und die politischen Grundlagen der DDR-Wirtschaft." In *Materialien zum Bericht zur Lage der Nation im geteilten Deutschland 1987*, 33–38. Bonn: Bundesministerium für innerdeutsche Beziehungen, 1987.

Mandel, E. *Marxistische Wirtschaftstheorie*. Frankfurt am Main: Suhrkamp Verlag, 1968.

Marchewka-Bartkowiak, K., Wiśniewski, M. "Rola salda pierwotnego w stabilizowaniu długu publicznego w krajach członkowskich strefy euro w latach 1999–2013." In *Unia Europejska wobec wyzwań przyszłości. Aspekty prawne, finansowe i handlowe*, eds. E. Małuszyńska, G. Mazur, P. Idczak, 159–170. Poznań: Wydawnictwo UE w Poznaniu, 2015.

Marks, B., Skodlarski, J. "Uwagi dotyczące nauczania historii gospodarczej na kierunkach ekonomicznych." *Studia Prawno-Ekonomiczne* 52 (1995): 225–228.

Marona, B. "Bariery realizacji inwestycji zależne od gminy a atrakcyjność inwestycycjna polskich miast." *Studia Ekonomiczne* 155 (2013): 241–251.

Martens, B. "Landwirtschaft in Ostdeutschland: der späte Erfolg der DDR." https://www.bpb.de/geschichte/deutsche-einheit/lange-wege-der-deutschen-einheit/47157/landwirtschaft?p=all.

Martinet, B. *Wywiad gospodarczy. Pozyskiwanie i ochrona informacji*. Warszawa: PWE, 1999.

Matera, P., Matera, R. "Problem światowego bogactwa i ubóstwa jako element badań historii gospodarczej – studia z przełomu mileniów." In *Przegląd badań nad historią gospodarczą w XXI wieku*, eds. R. Matera, A. Pieczewski, 247–263. Łódź: Wydawnictwo UŁ, 2011.

Matera, R. "Czy odwrót historii? Rozważania na temat miejsca historii w nauce." In *Z historii myśli ekonomicznej i historii gospodarczej. Księga jubileuszowa prof. dr. hab. Wiesława Piątkowskiego*, ed. J. Skodlarski, 93–105. Łódź: Wydawnictwo UŁ, 2006.

Matera, R. *G8 jako instytucja gospodarki światowej*. Łódź: Wydawnictwo UŁ, 2009.

Matera, R. "Gospodarka światowa w anglosaskiej historii gospodarczej w pierwszej dekadzie trzeciego millennium." In *Przegląd badań nad historią gospodarczą w XXI wieku*, eds. R. Matera, A. Pieczewski, 177–191. Łódź: Wydawnictwo UŁ, 2011.

Matera, R. "Interdyscyplinarny charakter historii gospodarczej. Perspektywy rozwoju dyscypliny w XXI wieku." In *Rzeczywistość społeczna w badaniach młodych naukowców*, eds. Z. Dziemanko, W. Stach, 287–306. Poznań: Wydawnictwo Maiuscula, 2012.

Matera, R. "Jak pisać historię gospodarczą – inspiracje z lektury 'Fałszywej ekonomii' Alana Beattiego." In *Przegląd badań nad historią gospodarczą w XXI wieku*, eds. R. Matera, A. Pieczewski, 281–297. Łódź: Wydawnictwo UŁ, 2011.

Matera, R. "Łączenie ekonomii i polityki w badaniach interdyscyplinarnych. Wyzwania dla ekonomisty, politologa i historyka." In *Polityczna kreacja ładu ekonomicznego. Teoria i praktyka*, eds. M. Kalinowski, A. Pieczewski, 17–34. Łódź: Wydawnictwo UŁ, 2013.

Matera, R., Skodlarski, J. *Gospodarka światowa. Geneza i ewolucja do czasów pandemii.* Warszawa: WN PWN, 2021.

Matera, R. "Studia nad bogactwem i ubóstwem narodów na przełomie mileniów – wkład Darona Acemoglu i Jamaesa A. Robinsona." *Ruch Prawniczy, Ekonomiczny i Socjologiczny* 76, No. 1 (2014): 269–282.

Mazur, Z. *Droga Niemiec do zjednoczenia wewnętrznego.* Poznań: Instytut Zachodni, 2015.

Mazur, Z., Orłowski, H., Wagińska-Marzec M. *Kultura zjednoczonych Niemiec. Wybrane problemy.* Poznań: Instytut Zachodni, 2013.

Meiβner, H., ed. *Bürgerliche Ökonomie im modernen Kapitalismus. Ideologische und praktische Bedeutung der westdeutschen Wirtschaftstheorie.* Berlin: Deutsche Akademie der Wissenschaften zu Berlin, Institut für Wirtschaftswissenschaften, Dietz Verlag, 1967.

Mejía, J. "The Evolution of Economic History since 1950: From Cliometrics to Cliodynamics." *Tiempo & Economía* 2, No. 2 (2015): 79–103.

Metelska-Szaniawska, K. "Constitutions and Economic Reforms in Transition: An Empirical Study." *Constitutional Political Economy* 1 (2009): 1–41.

Metelska-Szaniawska, K. *Economic Effects of Post-Socialist Constitutions 25 Years from the Outset of Transition. The Constitutional Political Economy Approach.* Frankfurt am Main: Peter Lang International Academic Publishers, 2016.

Metelska-Szaniawska, K. "Ekonomia konstytucyjna – ekonomia polityczna ładu gospodarczego." In *Teoria wyboru publicznego. Główne nurty i zastosowania*, ed. J. Wilkin, 109–136. Warszawa: WN Scholar, 2012.

Metelska-Szaniawska, K. "Ekonomia konstytucyjna – ekonomia polityczna ładu gospodarczego." In *Teoria wyboru publicznego. Wstęp do ekonomicznej analizy polityki i funkcjonowania sfery publicznej*, ed. J. Wilkin, 87–110. Warszawa: WN Scholar, 2005.

Metelska-Szaniawska, K. "Konstytucja w świetle nauk ekonomicznych." *Przegląd Sejmowy* No. 1 (2010): 49–62.

Metelska-Szaniawska, K. *Konstytucyjne czynniki reform gospodarczych w krajach postsocjalistycznych. Studium empiryczne.* Warszawa: Wydawnictwa UW, 2008.

Metelska-Szaniawska, K. "Post-Socialist Constitutions: The de jure–de facto Gap, Its Effects and Determinants." *Economics of Transition and Institutional Change* 29 (2021): 175–196.

Metelska-Szaniawska, K., Bełdowski, J. "Nota redaktorska." In R. Cooter, T. Ulen, *Ekonomiczna analiza prawa*, XIII–XV. Warszawa: Wydawnictwo C. H. Beck, 2011.

Metelska-Szaniawska, K., Lewczuk, A. "Constitutional Overperformance: An Empirical Study of de facto Protection of Rights with No de jure Equivalents." *European Journal of Law and Economics* 53 (2022): 289–317.

Metelska-Szaniawska, K., Lewkowicz, J. "Post-socialist 'illiberal democracies:' Do 'de jure' Constitutional Rights Matter?" *Constitutional Political Economy* 32 (2021): 233–265.

Michalak, A. *Finansowanie inwestycji w teorii i praktyce.* Warszawa: WN PWN, 2007.

Mickiewicz, T. *Economics of Institutional Change. Central and Eastern Europe Revisited.* New York: Palgrave Macmillan, 2010.

Mieck, I. *Kleine Wirtschaftsgeschichte der neuen Bundesländer.* Stuttgart: Franz Steiner Verlag, 2009.

Mierzwa, E. A. *Historia historiografii*, Vol. 1: *Starożytność-Średniowiecze.* Toruń: Wydawnictwo Adam Marszałek, 2002.

Mierzwa, E. A. *Historia historiografii*, Vol. 2: *Renesans-Oświecenie.* Warszawa: Wydawnictwo Neriton, 2007.

Mierzwa, E. A. *Historia historiografii. Wiek XIX*, Vol. 3: *Historiografia niemieckojęzyczna.* Piotrków Trybunalski: Naukowe Wydawnictwo Piotrkowskie przy Filii UJK w Kielcach, 2015.

Miller, G. J., Hammond, T. H. "Stability and Efficiency in a Separation-of-Powers Constitutional System." In *The Federalist Papers and the New Institutionalism*, eds. B. Grofman, D. Wittman, 85–99. New York: Agathon Press, 1989.

Miller, T., ed. *Prager Frühling und Reformpolitik heute. Hintergründe, Entwicklungen und Vergleiche der Reformen in Osteuropa.* München: Olzog Verlag, 1989.

Minford, P., Peel, D. "The Political Theory of the Business Cycle." *European Economic Review* 17, No. 2 (1982): 253–270.

Mitbestimmung – eine gute Sache. Alles über die Mitbestimmung und ihre rechtlichen Grundlagen. Bonn: Bundesministerium für Arbeit und Soziales, 2018.

Mitchell, W. C. "The Rationality of Economic Activity. I." *Journal of Political Economy* 18, No. 2 (1910): 97–113.

Mitchell, W. C. "The Rationality of Economic Activity. II." *Journal of Political Economy* 18, No. 3 (1910): 197–216.

Morawski, W. "Czego historią jest historia gospodarcza?" In *Przegląd badań nad historią gospodarczą w XXI wieku*, eds. R. Matera, A. Pieczewski, 15–25. Łódź: Wydawnictwo UŁ, 2011.

Morawski, W. *Dzieje gospodarcze Polski*. Warszawa: Wydawnictwo Difin, 2010.

Morawski, W., ed. *Tradycje szkolnictwa ekonomicznego w Polsce po 1945 roku*. Warszawa: Oficyna Wydawnicza SGH, 2007.

Morf, O. *Geschichte und Dialektik in der politischen Ökonomie. Zum Verhältnis von Wirtschaftstheorie und Wirtschaftsgeschichte bei Karl Marx*. Frankfurt–Wien: Europäische Verlagsanstalt, Europa Verlag, 1970.

Moszczeńska, W. *Metodologii historii zarys krytyczny*. Warszawa: PWN, 1968.

Moszyńska, A., Moszyński, M. "Reprywatyzacja a konflikt interesów ekonomicznych jednostek i państwa – Polska na tle pozostałych krajów transformacji." *Ekonomia i Prawo* 8, No. 1 (2012): 119–136.

Moszyński, M. "Idee ładu gospodarczego w procesie transformacji systemowej byłej NRD – oczekiwania a rzeczywistość." *Prace Naukowe Uniwersytetu Ekonomicznego we Wrocławiu. Ekonomia* No. 245 (2012): 352–353.

Moszyński, M. "Koncepcje ładu stanowionego Waltera Euckena i ładu spontanicznego Friedricha Augusta von Hayeka – próba analizy porównawczej." *Acta Universitatis Nicolai Copernici. Ekonomia* 43, No. 2 (2012): 121–134.

Moszyński, M. *Niemiecki model Społecznej Gospodarki Rynkowej – perspektywa rynku pracy*. Toruń: WN UMK, 2016.

Moszyński, M. "Ordoliberalism and the Macroeconomic Policy in the Face of the Euro Crisis." *Equilibrium. Quarterly Journal of Economics and Economic Policy* 10, No. 4 (2015): 41–58.

Moszyński, M. "Ordoliberalizm a dylematy współczesnej polityki makroekonomicznej." *Biuletyn Polskiego Towarzystwa Ekonomicznego* No. 2 (81) (2018): 45–55.

Moszyński, M. "Problemy teorii i polityki konkurencji w myśli ordoliberalnej." *Ekonomia i Prawo* 12, No. 2 (2013): 221–232.

Moszyński, M., Pysz, P. "Koncepcje polityki kształtowania ładu gospodarczego a reguły fiskalne w Republice Federalnej Niemiec." *Optimum. Studia Ekonomiczne* No. 4 (76) (2015): 72–84.

Moszyński, M. "Transformacja systemowa wschodnich Niemiec w perspektywie 'cudu gospodarczego' Ludwiga Erharda." In *Ordoliberalizm i społeczna gospodarka rynkowa wobec wyzwań współczesności*, eds. P. Pysz, E. Mączyńska, 219–238. Warszawa: PTE, 2013.

Moszyński, M. "Wybrane reguły fiskalne w Szwajcarii i Republice Federalnej Niemiec – droga ku zrównoważonym finansom publicznym?" *Acta Universitatis Nicolai Copernici. Nauki Humanistyczno-Społeczne. Ekonomia* 40, No. 391 (2009): 113–130.

Moszyński, M. "Zjednoczenie Niemiec – dwie dekady konwergencji." *Ekonomia i Prawo* 7 (2011): 253–268.

Möller, M. "An Empirical Study of the Limits and Perspectives of Institutional Transfers." Working paper, Zentrum für Interdisziplinäre Wirtschaftsforschung, No. 2 (2012), 1–26.

Mróz, M. *Prawo do broni w Polsce i Europie. Posiadanie broni strzeleckiej przez osoby fizyczne w ustawodawstwie wybranych państw Unii Europejskiej.* Warszawa: Wydawnictwo Sejmowe, 2011.

Muczyński, M. "Znaczenie instytucji nieformalnych w gospodarce rynkowej." In *Ekonomia – polityka – etyka,* Vol. II, ed. A. F. Bocian, 96–103. Białystok: Wydawnictwo UwB, 2005.

Müller, J.-W. *Constitutional Patriotism.* Princeton: Princeton University Press, 2007.

Müller-Armack, A. *Genealogie der Sozialen Marktwirtschaft. Frühschriften und weiterführende Konzepte.* Bern–Stuttgart: Haupt, 1974.

Müller-Armack, A. *Religion und Wirtschaft. Geistesgeschichtliche Hintergründe unserer europäischen Lebensform.* Stuttgart: W. Kohlhammer Verlag, 1959.

Müller-Armack, A. *Studien zur sozialen Marktwirtschaft.* Köln: Institut für Wirtschaftspolitik an der Universität Köln, 1960.

Müller-Armack, A. *Wirtschafts- und Finanzpolitik im Zeichen der sozialen Marktwirtschaft. Festgabe für Franz Etzel.* Stuttgart: Seewald, 1967.

Müller-Armack, A. *Wirtschaftsordnung und Wirtschaftspolitik. Studien und Konzepte zur sozialen Marktwirtschaft und zur europäischen Integration.* Freiburg: Verlag Rombach, 1966.

Münzel, F. "Die Rolle des Rechtes in der Deutschen Marktwirtschaft." In *Elemente der Sozialen Marktwirtschaft. Wirtschaftliche und rechtliche Rahmenbedingungen – Transformationsmöglichkeiten,* eds. K. Fasbender, M. Holthus, E. Thiel, 103–136. Hamburg: Verlag Weltarchiv GmbH, 1991.

Myant, M., Fleischer, F., Hornschild, K., Vintrová, R., Zeman, K., Souček, Z. *Successful Transformations? The Creation of Market Economies in Eastern Germany and the Czech Republic.* Cheltenham–Brookfield: Edward Elgar, 1996.

Negro, F. *Das Eigentum. Geschichte und Zukunft. Versuch eines Überblicks.* München–Berlin: C. H. Beck, 1963.

Nelson, R. R., Sampat, B. N. "Making Sense of Institutions as a Factor Shaping Economic Performance." *Journal of Economic Behavior and Organization* 44, No. 1 (2001): 31–54.

Nelson, R. R. "What Enables Rapid Economic Progress: What Are the Needed Institutions?" *Research Policy* 37, No. 1 (2008): 1–11.

Neumann, M., ed. *Ansprüche, Eigentums- und Verfügungsrechte.* Berlin: Duncker & Humblot, 1984.

"Niemcy – opodatkowanie w Niemczech." http://gia-polska.pl/praktyczne-wskazowki/niemcy-opodatkowanie-w-niemczech/.

Nimtz, K., Fels, G., eds. *Demokratie und Marktwirtschaft – ein Kuppelprodukt?* Köln: informedia-Stiftung, Gemeinnützige Stiftung für Gesellschaftswissenschaften und Publizistik, 1989.

Niskanen, W. A. "Conditions Affecting the Survivial of Constitutional Rules." *Constitutional Political Economy* 1, No. 2 (1990): 53–62.

Nizioł, K. "Analiza pojęć 'wydatków publicznych,' 'wydatków budżetu państwa' oraz 'rozchodów publicznych' na gruncie ustawy o finansach publicznych." *Studia Lubuskie* 7 (2011): 325–339.

North, D. C. "Economic Performance Through Time." *The American Economic Review* 84, No. 3 (1994): 359–368.

North, D. C. "Institutions." *Journal of Economic Perspectives* 5, No. 1 (1991): 97–112.

North, D. C. *Institutions, Institutional Change and Economic Performance.* Cambridge–New York: Cambridge University Press, 2009.

North, D. C. "Pojmowanie zmian ekonomicznych i wzrostu gospodarczego." In *Globalizacja, marginalizacja, rozwój,* ed. G. Kołodko, 137–152. Warszawa: Wydawnictwo WSPiZ im. Leona Koźmińskiego, 2003.

North, D. C., Summerhill, W., Weingast, B. R. "Order, Disorder, and Economic Change: Latin America versus North America." In *Governing for Prosperity,* eds. B. Dueno de Mequita, H. L. Root, 17–58. New Haven–London: Yale University Press, 2000.

North, D. C., Weingast, B. R. "Constitutions and Commitment: The Evolution of Institutions Governing Public Choice in seventeenth-Century England." *The Journal of Economic History* 49, No. 4 (1989): 803–832.

North, D. C. *Zrozumieć przemiany gospodarcze.* Warszawa: Oficyna a Wolters Kluwer Business, 2014.

Nuss, B. *Das Faust Syndrom. Ein Versuch über die Mentalität der Deutschen.* Bonn–Berlin: Bouvier, 1993.

Offe, C. *Drogi transformacji. Doświadczenia wschodnioeuropejskie i wschodnioniemieckie.* Warszawa–Kraków: WN PWN, 1999.

Olendzki, K. "Historiografia dziejów gospodarczych." In *Informator metodologiczny do ćwiczeń z historii gospodarczej,* ed. W. Morawski, 55–72. Warszawa: SGH, 2000.

Olewińska, M. *Federalizm w Unii Europejskiej i w Niemczech. Modele i powiązania.* Kraków: Konrad Adenauer Stiftung, TN Societas Vistulana, 2007.

Olson, M. *Power and Prosperity: Outgrowing Communist and Capitalist Dictatorships.* New York: Basic Books, 2000.

Olson, M. *The Logic of Collective Action. Public Goods and the Theory of Groups.* Cambridge: Harvard University Press, 1965.

Olzen, D. "Aktuelle zivilrechtliche Probleme des Eigentums." In *Das Eigentum. Vorträge gehalten auf der Tagung der Joachim Jungius-Gesellschaft der Wissenschaften. Hamburg am 10., 11. und 12. Dezember 1987*, ed. J. F. Baur, 103–124. Göttingen: Vandenhoeck & Ruprecht, 1989.

Opitz, G. "Enteignung und Restitution (Begründung, Durchführung, Auswirkungen)." In *Ökonomische Erfolge und Mißerfolge der deutsche Vereinigung – Eine Zwischenbilanz*, eds. G. Gutmann, U. Wagner, 59–75. Stuttgart: Gustav Fischer Verlag, 1994.

Ordeshook, P. C. "Constitutional Stability." *Constitutional Political Economy* 3, No. 2 (1992): 137–175.

Osers, J. *Zwischen Plan und Markt. Die Suche nach einer humanen Wirtschaft.* Hamburg: Verlag Weltarchiv GmbH, 1990.

Ostrom, E. "An Agenda for the Study of Institutions." *Public Choice* 48, No. 1 (1986): 3–25.

Ostrom, E. *Governing the Commons. The Evolution of Institutions for Collective Action.* Cambridge: Cambridge University Press, 1990.

Owczarczuk, M. "Atrakcyjność inwestycyjna Polski z perspektywy instytucjonalnej," *Studia Ekonomiczne* 184 (2014): 168–180.

Owsiak, S. *Finanse publiczne. Współczesne ujęcie.* Warszawa: WN PWN, 2017.

Paasch, J. M. *Classification of Real Property Rights – A Comparative Study of Real Property Rights in Germany, Ireland, the Netherlands and Sweden.* Stockholm: KTH Royal Institute of Technology, 2011.

Papier, H.-J. "Grundgesetz und Wirtschaftsordnung." In *Handbuch des Verfassungsrechts der Bundesrepublik Deutschland*, eds. E. Benda, W. Maihofer, H.-J. Vogel, 805–808. Berlin–New York: Walter de Gruyter, 1994.

Paprocki, W. "Przemiany europejskich kolei w XXI wieku." *Rynek Kolejowy* No. 2 (2006): 50–57.

Pastuszka, S. "Polityka rozwoju Wschodnich Niemiec – cele, narzędzia, efekty." *Optimum. Studia Ekonomiczne* No. 6 (84) (2016): 56–75.

Pastuszka, S., Skrzypek, J. "Regionalne zróżnicowanie poziomu PKB w Niemczech." *Modern Management Review* 23, No. 25 (2018): 191–211.

Pastuszka, S. "Zmiany w spójności gospodarczej i społecznej niemieckich landów w latach 2000–2015." *Studia Prawno-Ekonomiczne* 107 (2018): 339–357.

Pawłowski, Sz. "Solidaryzm w Konstytucji Niemiec." In *Idea solidaryzmu we współczesnym prawie konstytucyjnym. Doświadczenia polskie i międzynarodowe*, ed. A. Łabno, 294–325. Warszawa: Wydawnictwo Sejmowe, 2015.

Peichl, A., Schaefer, T. "Wie progressiv ist Deutschland? Das Steuer- und Transfersystem im europäischen Vergleich." *SOEPpapers on Multidisciplinary Panel Data Research* No. 102 (2008): 1–28.

Pejovich, S. "Karl Marx, Property Rigths School and the Process of Social Change." *Kyklos* 35, No. 3 (1982): 383–397.

Pejovich, S. *The Economics of Property Rights: Towards a Theory of Comparative Systems*. Dordrecht: Kluwer Academic Publishers, 1990.

Pejovich, S. "The Effects of the Interaction of Formal and Informal Institutions on Social Stability and Economic Development." *Journal of Markets & Morality* 2, No. 2 (1999): 164–181.

Pejovich, S. "Toward a General Theory of Property Rights." *Zeitschrift für Nationalökonomie* 31, No. 1–2 (1971): 141–155.

Persson, T., Tabellini, G. *The Economic Effects of Constitutions*. Cambridge: The MIT Press, 2005.

Peters, H.-R. *Politische Ökonomie des Marxismus. Anspruch und Wirklichkeit.* Göttingen: Vandenhoeck & Ruprecht, 1980.

Petz, B. "Przekształcenia własnościowe w krajach Europy Środkowej." *Informacja. Kancelaria Sejmu. Biuro Studiów i Ekspertyz. Wydział Analiz Ekonomicznych i Społecznych* No. 185 (1994): 1–9.

Piątek, D., Szarzec, K., Pilc, M. "Economic Freedom, Democracy and Economic Growth: A Causal Investigation in Transition Countries." *Post-Communist Economies* 25, No. 3 (2013): 267–288.

Piątkowski, W. *Wokół idei ekonomicznych*. Łódź: author's own publishing, 2017.

Pieczewski, A. "Przegląd publicystyki naukowej amerykańskiego Stowarzyszenia Historii Gospodarczej ('The Economic History Association')." In *Przegląd badań nad historią gospodarczą w XXI wieku*, eds. R. Matera, A. Pieczewski, 213–224. Łódź: Wydawnictwo UŁ, 2011.

Pieczewski, A. *Samodzierżawie a rozwój gospodarczy Królestwa Polskiego w ujęciu Jana Gottlieba Blocha*. Łódź: Wydawnictwo UŁ, 2019.

Pierenkemper, T. *Unternehmensgeschichte. Eine Einführung in ihre Methoden und Ergebnisse*. Stuttgart: Franz Steiner Verlag, 2000.

Piketty, T. *Kapitał w XXI wieku*. Warszawa: Wydawnictwo Krytyki Politycznej, 2015.

Pipes, R. *Własność a wolność*. Warszawa: Warszawskie Wydawnictwo Literackie Muza S.A., 2000.

Pitlik, H., *Politische Ökonomie des Föderalismus. Föderative Kompetenzverteilung im Lichte der konstitutionellen Ökonomik*. Frankfurt am Main: Peter Lang, 1997.

Plumpe, W., *German Economic and Business History in the 19th and 20th Centuries*. London: Palgrave Macmillan, 2016.

Pohl, H. "Öffentliche und private Wirtschaft." In *Deutsche Wiedervereinigung. Die Rechtseinheit. Arbeitskreis Staats- und Verfassungsrecht*, Vol. II: *Zur Wiederherstellung der inneren Einheit*,

Part 2: *Rundfunkrecht – Stasi-Akten – Wiedergutmachung – Öffentliche und Private Wirtschaft*, ed. K. Stern, 133–148. Köln: Carl Heymanns Verlag KG, 1992.

Polster, W., Voy, K. "Die Entfaltung der Industriewirtschafts – Zum Strukturwandel von Wirtschaft und Erwerbsarbeit in der Industriegesellschaft." In *Marktwirtschafts und politische Regulierung. Beiträge zur Wirtschafts- und Gesellschaftsgeschichte der Bundesrepublik Deutschland (1949–1989)*, Vol. 1, eds. K. Voy, W. Polster, C. Thomasberger, 25–85. Marburg: Metropolis-Verlag, 1991.

Polzin, M. "Constitutional Identity, Unconstitutional Amendments and the Idea of Constituent Power: The Development of the Doctrine of Constitutional Identity in German Constitutional Law." *International Journal of Constitutional Law* 14, No. 2 (2016): 411–438.

Pomorski, J. *Paradygmat "New Economic History." Studium z teorii rozwoju nauki historycznej*. Lublin: Wydawnictwo UMCS, 1995.

Posner, R. A. *The Economic Analysis of Law*. Boston–Toronto: Little, Brown, 1972.

Posner, R. "The Constitution as an Economic Document." *George Washington Law Review* 56, No. 1 (1987): 4–38.

Priddat, B. P. "Historische Methode und moderne Ökonomie. Über das Methodische in der 'Historischen Schule' und das Historische in der 'Neuen Institutionenökonomie'." In *Wirtschaftsgeschichte als Kulturgeschichte. Dimensionen eines Perspektivenwechseln*, eds. H. Berghoff, J. Vogel, 99–116. Frankfurt–New York: Campus Verlag, 2004.

Priddat B. P. "Ökonomie und Geschichte. Zur Theorie der Institutionen bei D. C. North." In *Neuorientierungen in der ökonomischen Theorie*, eds. E. K. Seifert, B. P. Priddat, 205–239. Marburg: Metropolis, 1995.

Prütting, H., Wegen, G., Weinreich, G. *Bürgerliches Gesetzbuch. Kommentar*. Köln: Luchterhand Verlag, Wolters Kluwer Deutschland, 2018.

Pryor, F. L. *A Guidebook to the Comparative Study of Economic Systems*. Englewood Cliffs: Prentice-Hall, Inc., 1985.

Przestalski, A. "Własnościowe aspekty partycypacji pracowniczej." *Uniwersyteckie Czasopismo Socjologiczne* No. 8 (2013): 16–31.

Przeworski, A. *Democracy and the Market. Political and Economic Reforms in Eastern Europe and Latin America*. Cambridge: Cambridge University Press, 1991.

Przeworski, A., Limongi, F. "Political Regimes and Economic Growth." *Journal of Economic Perspectives* 7, No. 3 (1993): 51–69.

Przybysz, M. "Pierwsza i druga 'reforma federalizmu' w Republice Federalnej Niemiec – zmiany Ustawy Zasadniczej z 2006 i 2009 r. w odniesieniu do kompetencji prawodawczych i stosunków finansowych Związku i krajów." *Przegląd Prawa Konstytucyjnego* No. 1 (35) (2017): 137–154.

Pszczółkowski, T. G. *Ordoliberalizm. Społeczno-polityczna i gospodarcza doktryna neoliberalizmu w RFN*. Warszawa–Kraków: PWN, 1990.

Pysz, P., Grabska, A., Moszyński, M., eds. *Ład gospodarczy a współczesna ekonomia.* Warszawa: WN PWN, 2014.

Pysz, P., Grabska, A., Moszyński, M., eds. *Stanowione i spontaniczne elementy ładu gospodarczego w procesie transformacji – dryf ładu czy jego doskonalenie?* Warszawa: PTE, 2014.

Pysz, P., Jurczuk, A., Moszyński, M. "Economics and History: Synthesis, Disintegration and Reintegration." *OIKONOMOS: Journal of Social Market Economy* No. 2 (8) (2017): 6–17.

Pysz, P., Jurczuk, A., Moszyński, M. "Ordoliberalizm a dynamika społeczno-gospodarcza." *Optimum. Economic Studies* No. 2 (96) (2019): 3–17.

Pysz, P. *Społeczna gospodarka rynkowa. Ordoliberalna koncepcja polityki gospodarczej.* Warszawa: WN PWN, 2008.

Quint, P. E. *The Imperfect Union. Constitutional Structures of German Unification.* Princeton: Princeton University Press, 1997.

Radandt, H. et al., eds. *Handbuch Wirtschaftsgeschichte*, Vol. 1. Berlin: Institut für Wirtschaftsgeschichte der Akademie der Wissenschaften der DDR, VEB Deutscher Verlag der Wissenschaften, 1981.

Radwański, Z., Olejniczak, A. *Prawo cywilne – część ogólna.* Warszawa: Wydawnictwo C. H. Beck, 2017.

Raff, D. *A History of Germany. From the Medieval Empire to the Present.* Oxford: Berg Publishers, 1988.

Ragnitz, J. "Angleichung der Lebensverhältnisse in Ostdeutschland: Eine regional differenzierte Analyse." *ifo Dresden berichtet* 16, No. 4 (2009): 28–38.

Ratajczak, M. "Instytucjonalizm – wzbogacenie czy alternatywa ekonomii głównego nurtu?" In *Ład instytucjonalny w gospodarce*, Vol. I, eds. B. Polszakiewicz, J. Boehlke, 57–72. Toruń: Wydawnictwo UMK, 2005.

Raulet, G. *Filozofia niemiecka po 1945.* Warszawa: Oficyna Naukowa, 2013.

Razjer, M. *Strategie dywersyfikacji przedsiębiorstw.* Warszawa: PWE, 2001.

Richter, R. *Institutionen ökonomisch analysiert. Zur jüngeren Entwicklung auf einem Gebiet der Wirtschaftstheorie.* Tübingen: J. C. B. Mohr (Paul Siebeck), 1994.

Rodes, J. E. *Germany: a History.* New York: Holt, Rinehart and Winston, 1964.

Roemer, J. E. *Free to Lose. An Introduction to Marxist Economic Philosophy.* Cambridge: Harvard University Press, 1988.

Rohrschneider, R. "Cultural Transmission Versus Perceptions of the Economy: The Sources of Political Elites' Economic Values in the United Germany." *Comparative Political Studies* 29, No. 1 (1996): 78–104.

Rohrschneider, R. *Learning Democracy. Democratic and Economic Values in Unified Germany.* Oxford: Oxford University Press, 1999.

Röhl, K.-H., Speicher, P. von *Ostdeutschland 20 Jahre nach dem Mauerfall. Ist die Investitionsförderung Triebfeder von Industriewachstum und regionaler Entwicklung?* Köln: Deutscher Instituts-Verlag, 2009.

Röpke, J. "Handlungsrechte und wirtschaftliche Entwicklung." In *Property Rights und ökonomische Theorie*, ed. A. Schüller, 111–144. München: Verlag Franz Vahlen, 1983.

Röpke, W. *Civitas Humana. Grundfragen der Gesellschafts- und Wirtschaftsreform.* Erlenbach ZH: Rentsch, 1944.

Röpke, W. *Die Gesellschaftskrisis der Gegenwart.* Erlenbach ZH: Rentsch, 1942.

Röpke, W. *Die Lehre von der Wirtschaft.* Erlenbach ZH: Rentsch, 1946.

Röpke, W. *Internationale Ordnung.* Erlenbach ZH: Rentsch, 1945.

Röpke, W. *Jenseits von Angebot und Nachfrage.* Erlenbach ZH: Rentsch, 1958.

Röpke, W. *Maß und Mitte.* Erlenbach ZH: Rentsch, 1950.

Rosenfeld, M. T. W., Franz, P., Heimpold, G. "Economic 'Clusters' in East Germany: Evidence on the Location and Characteristics of Spatially Concentrated Industries." *Post-Communist Economies* 19, No. 1 (2007): 73–93.

Roszkowski, W. *Gospodraka. Wzrost i upadek systemu nakazowo-rozdzielczego.* Warszawa: WN PWN, 2008.

Rozek, J. *Die Unterscheidung von Eigentumsbindung und Enteignung. Eine Bestandsaufnahme zur dogmatischen Struktur des Art. 14 GG nach 15 Jahren "Naßauskiesung."* Tübingen: Mohr Siebeck, 1998.

Rudolf, S., ed. *Nowa ekonomia instytucjonalna wobec współczesnych problemów gospodarczych.* Kielce: Wydawnictwo WSEPiNM im. prof. Edwarda Lipińskiego w Kielcach, 2014.

Rudolf, S., ed. *Nowa ekonomia instytucjonalna. Aspekty teoretyczne i praktyczne.* Kielce: Wydawnictwo WSEiA im. prof. Edwarda Lipińskiego w Kielcach, 2005.

Rudolf, S., ed. *Nowa ekonomia instytucjonalna. Teoria i zastosowania.* Kielce: Wydawnictwo WSEiP im. prof. Edwarda Lipińskiego w Kielcach, 2009.

Rudolph, K. *Die Bindungen des Eigentums. Eine rechtsvergleichende Studie.* Tübingen: Mohr Siebeck, 1960.

Runowski, H. "Rolnictwo ekologiczne – rozwój czy regres?" *Roczniki Nauk Rolniczych. Seria G* 96, No. 4 (2009): 182–193.

Rutherford, M. *Institutions in Economics. The Old and the New Institutionalism.* Cambridge: Cambridge University Press, 1999.

Rutkowski, J. *Historia gospodarcza Polski*, Vol. I. Poznań: Księgarnia Akademicka, 1947.

Rüstow, A. *Das Versagen des Wirtschaftsliberalismus als religionsgeschichtliches Problem.* Heidelberg: Verlag Helmut Küpper, 1950.

Rüstow, A. *Die Kehrseite des Wirtschaftswunders.* Hamburg: Hamburg Furche Verlag, 1961.

Ryan, A. *Property.* Milton Keynes: Open University Press, 1987.

Sabel, Ch. F. "Constitutional Orders: Trust Building and Response to Change." In *Contemporary Capitalism. The Embeddedness of Institutions,* eds. J. R. Hollingsworth, R. Boyer, 154–188. Cambridge: Cambridge University Press, 1998.

Sachs, M., ed. *Grundgesetz. Kommentar.* München: C. H. Beck, 2018.

Samuels, W. J. "Interrelations between Legal and Economic Processes." In *Law and Economics: An Institutional Perspective,* eds. W. J. Samuels, A. A. Schmid, 95–110. Boston: Martinus Nijhoff Publishing, 1981.

Sauerland, D. *Föderalismus zwischen Freiheit und Effizienz. Der Beitrag der ökonomischen Theorie zur Gestaltung dezentralisierter politischer Systeme.* Berlin: Duncker & Humblot, 1997.

Sawczuk, J. *Vertragsgemeinschaft 1989/1990. Wzlot i upadek idei konfederacji dwu państw niemieckich.* Poznań: Wydawnictwo WSB w Poznaniu, 2013.

Schäfer, H.-B., Ott, C. *Lehrbuch der ökonomischen Analyse des Zivilrechts.* Berlin–Heidelberg: Springer, 2005.

Schlatter, R. *Private Property. The History of an Idea.* New Brunswick–New Jersey: Rytgers University Press, 1951.

Schleifstein, J. *Einführung in das Studium von Marx, Engels und Lenin.* München: Verlag C. H. Beck, 1972.

Schmidt, K., ed. *Beiträge zu ökonomischen Problemen des Föderalismus.* Berlin: Duncker & Humblot, 1987.

Schmidt, K.-D. "Requirements for Successful Privatization – Lessons from the Treuhandanstalt's Approach." *Kiel Working Paper* No. 696 (1995): 1–26.

Schmidt, K.-D., Siegmund, U. "Strategien der Privatisierung." In *Treuhandanstalt. Das Unmögliche wagen,* eds. W. Fischer, H. Hax, H. K. Schneider, 211–240. Berlin: Akademie Verlag, 1993.

Schmieding, H. "West Germany's Economic Reforms of 1948: The Lessons for Central and Eastern Europe Today." In *Towards a Market Economy in Central and Eastern Europe,* ed. H. Giersch, 23–53. Berlin–Heidelberg: Springer-Verlag, 1991.

Schnabel, C. "Structural Adjustment and Privatization of the East German Economy." In *Economic Aspects of German Unification. National and International Perspectives,* ed. P. J. J. Welfens, 231–255. Berlin–Heidelberg: Springer-Verlag, 1992.

Schneider, J. *Einigkeit, Recht und Freiheit. 25 Jahre deutsche Wiedervereinigung (1990–2015). Eine ordnungstheoretische Analyse.* Stuttgart: Franz Steiner Verlag, 2017.

Schnitzer, M. *East and West Germany: A Comparative Economic Analysis.* New York: Praeger Publishers, 1972.

Scholz, R., Lieser-Triebnigg, E. "Grundgesetz und Wirtschaftsordnung in der Bundesrepublik Deutschland." In *Materialien zum Bericht zur Lage der Nation im geteilten Deutschland 1987*, 26–32. Bonn: Bundesministerium für innerdeutsche Beziehungen, 1987.

Schumann, J. "Wirtschaftliche Anreizwirkungen der Eigentumsordnung." In *Die Bedeutung der Eigentumsordnung für das Funktionieren einer Volkswirtschaft*, ed. J. Schumann, 1–20. Bad Honnef: Bock und Herchen Verlag, 1991.

Schumann, J., ed. *Die Bedeutung der Eigentumsordnung für das Funktionieren einer Volkswirtschaft.* Bad Honnef: Bock und Herchen Verlag, 1991.

Schumann, J., ed. *Probleme der Regulierung in den Volkswirtschaften Polens und der Bundesrepublik Deutschland.* Bad Honnef: Bock und Herchen Verlag, 1987.

Schüller, A., ed. *Property Rights und ökonomische Theorie.* München: Verlag Franz Vahlen, 1983.

Schuttenbach, L. von, Ganter, R. *Sektor małych i średnich przedsiębiorstw w Republice Federalnej Niemiec.* Warszawa: PAB-Font, 2000.

Screpanti, E. *The Fundamental Institutions of Capitalism.* London–New York: Routledge, 2001.

Scully, G. W. *Constitutional Environments and Economic Growth.* Princeton: Princeton University Press, 1992.

Scully, G. W. "The Institutional Framework and Economic Development." *Journal of Political Economy* 96, No. 3 (1988): 652–662.

Seitz, H. "Fiscal Policy, Deficits and Politics of Subnational Governments: The Case of the German Laender." *Public Choice* 102, No. 3–4 (2000): 183–218.

Seligson, D., McCants, A. E. C. "Coevolving Institutions and the Paradox of Informal Constraints." *Journal of Institutional Economics* 17, No. 3 (2021): 359–378.

Sherman, H. *Radical Political Economy. Capitalism and Socialism from a Marxist-Humanist Perspective.* New York–London: Basic Books, Inc., Publishers, 1972.

Shingleton, A. B., Ahrens, V., Ries, P. "Property Rights in Eastern Germany: An Overview of the Amended Property Law." *Georgia Journal of International and Comparative Law* 21 (1991): 345–357.

Siermann, C. L. J. *Politics, Institutions and the Economic Performance of Nations.* Cheltenham–Northampton: Edward Elgar, 1998.

Sinn, G., Sinn, H.-W. *Jumpstart: The Economic Unification of Germany.* Cambridge: MIT Press, 1992.

Sinn, H.-W. "Macroeconomic Aspects of German Unification." In *Economic Aspects of German Unification. National and International Perspectives*, ed. P. J. J. Welfens, 79–133. Berlin–Heidelberg: Springer-Verlag, 1992.

Sirojć, Z., ed. *Zarys historii gospodarczej. Od czasów najdawniejszych do najnowszych.* Warszawa: Wyższa Szkoła Działalności Gospodarczej, 2003.

Skodlarski, J. *Historia gospodarcza.* Warszawa: WN PWN, 2014.

Skodlarski, J. "O potrzebie rozważań metodologicznych." In *Historia gospodarcza i historia myśli ekonomicznej a teoria ekonomii. Problemy metodologiczne*, ed. J. Skodlarski, 7–10. Łódź: Wydawnictwo UŁ, 2008.

Skodlarski, J. "Stosunek judaizmu, chrześcijaństwa i islamu do działalności gospodarczej." In *Rola Kościołów w życiu gospodarczym ziem polskich*, eds. K. Kowalski, R. Matera, A. Pieczewski, 15–27. Łódź: Wydawnictwo UŁ, 2017.

Skodlarski, J. *Religia a gospodarka. Judaizm – chrześcijaństwo – islam.* Łódź: Wydawnictwo UŁ, 2020.

Skodlarski, J. *Zarys historii gospodarczej Polski.* Warszawa: WN PWN, 2005.

Skodlarski, J. "Związki historii gospodarczej z teorią ekonomii." In *Historia gospodarcza i historia myśli ekonomicznej a teoria ekonomii. Problemy metodologiczne*, ed. J. Skodlarski, 46–54. Łódź: Wydawnictwo UŁ, 2008.

Smith, A. *Badania nad naturą i przyczynami bogactwa narodów*, Vol. 1–2. Warszawa: WN PWN, 2007.

Smith, V. *Racjonalność w ekonomii.* Warszawa: Oficyna a Wolters Kluwer Business, 2013.

Smith-Morris, M., ed. *Welt Wirtschaft in Zahlen.* Düsseldorf: Wirtschaftswoche, The Economist Books, 1991.

Smyser, W. R. *The Economy of United Germany. Colossus at the Crossroads.* New York: St. Martin's Press, 1992.

Snower, D. J., Merkl, Ch. "The Caring Hand that Cripples: The East German Labor Market after Reunification." *American Economic Review* 96, No. 2 (2006): 375–382.

Sobczyk, M. *Statystyka.* Warszawa: WN PWN, 2007.

Sobiech-Grabka, K., Wallusch, J., Woźniak-Jęchorek, B. "Ekonomia instytucjonalna." In *Współczesne teorie ekonomiczne*, ed. M. Ratajczak, 131–158. Poznań: Wydawnictwo UE w Poznaniu, 2012.

Sombart, W. "Economic Theory and Economic History." *The Economic History Review* 2, No. 1 (1929): 1–19.

Southern, D. "Restitution or Compensation: The Open Property Question." *German Politics* 2, No. 3 (1993): 436–449.

Southern, D. B. "Restitution or Compensation: The Land Question in East Germany." *International & Comparative Law Quarterly* 42, No. 3 (1993): 690–697.

Sørensen, P. B. "The German Business Tax Reform of 2000: A General Equilibrium Analysis." *German Economic Review* 3, No. 4 (2002): 347–378.

Spangenberg, S. *The Institutionalised Transformation of the East German Economy.* Heidelberg–New York: Physica-Verlag. A Springer-Verlag Company, 1998.

Stabryła, A. *Podstawy zarządzania firmą. Modele, metody, praktyka.* Warszawa: WN PWN, 1995.

Stabryła, A. "Przedmiot i zakres nauki organizacji i zarządzania." In *Organizacja i zarządzanie. Zarys problematyki*, eds. A. Stabryła, J. Trzcieniecki, 11–39. Warszawa: PWN, 1986.

Stachowiak, K. *Instytucjonalne uwarunkowania bezpośrednich inwestycji zagranicznych w Polsce.* Poznań: Bogucki Wydawnictwo Naukowe, 2007.

Stack, H. M. "The 'Colonization' of East Germany?: A Comparative Analysis of German Privatization." *Duke Law Journal* 46 (1997): 1211–1253.

Stammen, T. "Das zentrale Regierungssystem." In *DDR. Das politische, wirtschaftliche und soziale System*, eds. H. Rausch, T. Stammen, 255–281. München: Bayerische Landeszentrale für politische Bildungsarbeit, 1984.

Stammen, T. "Zur Verfassungsentwicklung." In *DDR. Das politische, wirtschaftliche und soziale System*, eds. H. Rausch, T. Stammen, 204–216. München: Bayerische Landeszentrale für politische Bildungsarbeit, 1984.

Staniek, Z. *Ekonomia instytucjonalna. Dlaczego instytucje są ważne.* Warszawa: Wydawnictwo Difin, 2017.

Stankiewicz, W. *Ekonomika instytucjonalna. Narodziny i rozwój.* Warszawa: Wydawnictwo BBS PWSBiA, 2004.

Stankiewicz, W. *Ekonomika instytucjonalna. Zarys wykładu.* Warszawa: Wydawnictwo AON, 2014.

Stankiewicz, W. *Historia myśli ekonomicznej.* Warszawa: PWE, 2007.

Stawicka, M. K. "Czynniki warunkujące wybór miejsca lokowania bezpośrednich inwestycji zagranicznych w Unii Europejskiej – studium komparatystyczne lat 2005 i 2011." *Zarządzanie i Finanse* 1, No. 2 (2013): 315–329.

Stearns, M. L., Zywicki, T. J., Miceli, T. J. *Law and Economics: Private and Public.* St. Paul: West Academic Publishing, 2018.

Steeger, H., ed. *Planung der Volkswirtschaft in der DDR.* Berlin: Verlag die Wirtschaft, 1970.

Steffani, W. "Zum Selbstverständnis der Bundesrepublik Deutschland – Verfassungs – und verwaltungsrechtliche Grundlagen." In *Elemente der Sozialen Marktwirtschaft. Wirtschaftliche und rechtliche Rahmenbedingungen – Transformationsmöglichkeiten*, eds. K. Fasbender, M. Holthus, E. Thiel, 37–59. Hamburg: Verlag Weltarchiv GmbH, 1991.

Stern, K., ed. *Deutsche Wiedervereinigung. Die Rechtseinheit. Arbeitskreis Staats- und Verfassungsrecht*, Vol. I: *Eigentum – Neue Verfassung – Finanzverfassung.* Köln: Carl Heymanns Verlag KG, 1991.

Stern, K., ed. *Deutsche Wiedervereinigung. Die Rechtseinheit. Arbeitskreis Staats- und Verfassungsrecht*, Vol. III: *Zur Reform des Grundgesetzes.* Köln: Carl Heymanns Verlag KG, 1993.

Sternberg, R., Litzenberger, T. "Regional Clusters in Germany – Their Geography and Their Relevance for Entrepreneurial Activities." *European Planning Studies* 12, No. 6 (2004): 767–791.

Steuern von A bis Z. Berlin: Bundesministerium der Finanzen, 2018.

Stiglitz, J. E. "Formal and Informal Institutions." In *Social Capital. A Multifaceted Perspective*, eds. P. Dasgupta, I. Serageldin, 59–68. Washington: The World Bank, 2000.

Stobiecki, R. *Historia pod nadzorem. Spory o nowy model historii w Polsce (II połowa lat czterdziestych – początek lat pięćdziesiątych).* Łódź: Wydawnictwo UŁ, 1993.

Stobiecki, R. *Historiografia PRL. Ani dobra, ani mądra, ani piękna... ale skomplikowana. Studia i szkice.* Warszawa: Wydawnictwo Trio, 2007.

Stobiecki, R. *Historiografia PRL. Zamiast podręcznika.* Łódź: Wydawnictwo UŁ, 2020.

Stobiecki, R. *Historycy polscy wobec wyzwań XX wieku.* Poznań: Wydawnictwo Nauka i Innowacje, 2014.

Stobiecki, R. "Między kontynuacją a dyskontynuacją." In *Humanistyka polska w latach 1945–1990*, eds. U. Jakubowska, J. Myśliński, 127–155. Warszawa: Instytut Badań Literackich PAN, 2006.

Stokes, R. G. "Technology and the West German 'Wirtschaftswunder'." *Technology and Culture* 32, No. 1 (1991): 1–22.

Stradowski, M. A. *Międzynarodowe aspekty zjednoczenia Niemiec.* Toruń: Wydawnictwo Adam Marszałek, 2010.

Strzeszewski, Cz. *Własność: zagadnienie społeczno-moralne.* Warszawa: Ośrodek Dokumentacji i Studiów Społecznych, 1981.

Stützel, W. et al., eds. *Grundtexte zur Sozialen Martkwirtschaft. Zeugnisse aus zweihundert Jahren ordnungspolitischer Diskussion.* Stuttgart–New York: Ludwig-Erhard-Stiftung e. V. Bonn, Gustav Fischer Verlag, 1981.

Suwalski, A. *Własność i jej przekształcenie.* Konin: PWSZ, 2014.

Svensson, J. "Investment, Property Rights and Political Instability: Theory and Evidence." *European Economic Review* 42, No. 7 (1998): 1317–1341.

Swadźba, S. "Przyczyny i skutki kryzysu pierwszej dekady XXI wieku." In *Europa XX–XXI wieku. Społeczno-polityczne konsekwencje kryzysów*, eds. M. Gruszczyk, L. Krzyżanowski, M. Skrzypek, 299–308. Katowice: Wydawnictwo UŚ, 2017.

Szacka, B. *Wprowadzenie do socjologii.* Warszawa: Oficyna Naukowa, 2008.

Szacki, J. *Historia myśli socjologicznej.* Warszawa: WN PWN, 2002.

Szlachta, B. "O problemie wolności (dwie uwagi prawnika badającego historię myśli politycznej)." In *Kapitalizm po polsku. Państwo – prawo – gospodarka*, ed. M. Szułdrzyński, 35–46. Kraków: Ośrodek Myśli Politycznej, 2003.

Szpak, J. *Historia gospodarcza powszechna.* Warszawa: PWE, 2007.

Sztompka, P. *Kapitał społeczny. Teoria przestrzeni międzyludzkiej.* Kraków: Wydawnictwo Znak, 2016.

Sztompka, P. *Socjologia. Analiza społeczeństwa.* Kraków: Wydawnictwo Znak, 2010.

Ścibiorska-Kowalczyk, I. "Kultura ekonomiczna w Niemczech na przykładzie Euroregionu Nysa." *Pogranicze. Polish Borderlands Studies* 5, No. 2 (2017): 135–157.

Śliwa, R., Waląg, P., Tabor, S. "Ewolucja struktur produkcji i zatrudnienia w gospodarkach rynkowych. Wnioski dla Polski." *Prace Komisji Geografii Przemysłu Polskiego Towarzystwa Geograficznego* No. 30 (3) (2016): 45–58.

Šik, O. *Der Dritte Weg. Die marxistisch-leninistische Theorie und die modern Industriegesellschaft.* Hamburg: Hoffmann und Campe, 1972.

Šik, O. *Ein Wirtschaftssystem der Zukunft.* Berlin: Springer-Verlag, 1985.

Tarnowska A. "Nota recenzyjna." Review of *Ustawa Zasadnicza w praktyce Republiki Federalnej Niemiec (1949–1989)*, by D. Janicka. *Przegląd Prawa Konstytucyjnego* No. 2–3 (2010): 325–328.

Tettinger, P. J. "Öffentliche und private Wirtschaft in den neuen Bundesländern." In *Deutsche Wiedervereinigung. Die Rechtseinheit. Arbeitskreis Staats- und Verfassungsrecht*, Vol. II: *Zur Wiederherstellung der inneren Einheit*, Part 2: *Rundfunkrecht – Stasi-Akten – Wiedergutmachung – Öffentliche und Private Wirtschaft*, ed. K. Stern, 149–166. Köln: Carl Heymanns Verlag KG, 1992.

Thanner, B. "Wie kann die Bundesrepublik die Reformen in Osteuropa unterstützen?" In *Von der Planwirtschaft zur Marktwirtschaft – Chancen und Risiken für Ost und West*, eds. K. H. Oppenländer, M. Queisser, 321–333. München: Ifo-Institut für Wirtschaftsforschung, 1990.

Theil, W. "Eigentum und Verpflichtung. Einige juristische Aspekte." In *Verpflichtungsökonomik. Eigentum, Freiheit und Haftung in der Geldwirtschaft*, ed. H.-J. Stadermann, 175–200. Marburg: Metropolis Verlag, 2001.

Tietz, B. *Optionen für Deutschland. Szenariem und Handlungsalternativen für Wirtschaft und Gesellschaft. Ein Handbuch für Entscheidungsträger.* Landsberg/Lech: Verlag Moderne Industrie, 1990.

Timmermann, H., ed. *Wirtschaftsordnungen im Dialog. Bundesrepublik Deutschland und DDR.* Saarbrücken–Scheidt: Dadder, 1989.

Tischner, J. *Etyka solidarności oraz Homo sovieticus.* Kraków: Wydawnictwo Znak, 2018.

Tischner, J. *Nieszczęsny dar wolności.* Kraków: Wydawnictwo Znak, 2015.

Tkaczyński, J. W. *Prawo ustrojowe Niemiec.* Kraków: Wydawnictwo UJ, 2015.

Tokarczyk, R. *Komparatystyka prawnicza.* Warszawa: Wolters Kluwer Polska, 2008.

Tolliday, S. "Enterprise and State in the West German Wirtschaftswunder: Volkswagen and the Automobile Industry, 1939–1962." *The Business History Review* 69, No. 3 (1995): 273–350.

Tomaszewski, J. *Europa Środkowo-Wschodnia 1944–1968. Powstanie, ewolucja i kryzys realnego socjalizmu.* Warszawa: Wydawnictwa UW, 1992.

Topolski, J. "Historia gospodarcza a teoria ekonomii." *Kwartalnik Historyczny* No. 1 (1964): 85–89.

Topolski, J. *Metodologia historii.* Warszawa: PWN, 1973.

Topolski, J. *Od Achillesa do Béatrice de Planissolles. Zarys historii historiografii.* Warszawa: Oficyna Wydawnicza Rytm, 1998.

Topolski, J., ed. J. Rutkowski, *Wieś europejska późnego feudalizmu (XVI–XVIII w.).* Warszawa: PIW, 1986.

Topolski, J., ed. J. Rutkowski, *Wokół teorii ustroju feudalnego.* Warszawa: PIW, 1982.

Torstensson, J. "Property Rights and Economic Growth: An Empirical Study." *Kyklos* 47, No. 2 (1994): 231–247.

Trecker, M. *Neue Unternehmer braucht das Land. Die Genese des ostdeustchen Mittelstands nach der Wiedervereinigung.* Berlin: C. H. Links Verlag, 2022.

"Treuhandgesetz und Treuhandanstalt." https://deutsche-einheit-1990.de/ministerien/ministerium-fuer-wirtschaft/treuhandgesetz-und-treuhandanstalt/.

Trommsdorff, G. "Identitätsprozesse in kulturellen Kontext und im sozialen Wandel." In *Transformationsprozesse in Deutschland,* ed. H. Sahner, 116–148. Opladen: Leske + Budrich, 1995.

Truger, A., Jacoby, W. "Tax Reforms and 'Modell Deutschland': Lessons from Four Years of Red-Green Tax Policy." In *Germany at Fifty-Five. Berlin ist nicht Bonn?,* ed. J. Sperling, 386–410. Manchester–New York: Manchester University Press, 2004.

Tuchtfeldt, E. "The Transformation of Economic Systems: The Germany Example." In *The Economics of German Unification,* eds. A. G. Ghanssy, W. Schäfer, 18–25. London–New York: Routledge, 1993.

Tucker-Mohl, J. *Property Rights and Transitional Justice: Restitution in Hungary and East Germany.* Cambridge: MIT Open Course Ware, 2005.

Tullock, G. "The Welfare Costs of Tariffs, Monopolies, and Theft." *Economic Inquiry* 5, No. 3 (1967): 224–232.

Tyszkiewicz, J., Czapiewski, E. *Historia powszechna. Wiek XX.* Warszawa: WN PWN, 2010.

Ulen, T. S. "Foreword." In M. L. Stearns, T. J. Zywicki, T. J. Miceli, *Law and Economics: Private and Public,* V–VIII. St. Paul: West Academic Publishing, 2018.

Vanssay, X. de, Spindler, Z. A. "Freedom and Growth: Do Constitutions Matter?" *Public Choice* 78, No. 3–4 (1994): 359–372.

Veblen, T. *Teoria klasy próżniaczej.* Warszawa: PWN, 1971.

Vogell, Ch. "Privateigentum, Manager und Property Rights." In *Die Bedeutung der Eigentumsordnung für das Funktionieren einer Volkswirtschaft*, ed. J. Schumann, 43–56. Bad Honnef: Bock und Herchen Verlag, 1991.

Voigt, S. "Constitutional Economics and the Law." In *The Oxford Handbook of Law and Economics*, Vol. I: *Methodology and Concepts*, ed. Fr. Parisi. New York: Oxford University Press, 2017. https://books.google.pl/books?hl=pl&lr=&id=XTHADgAAQBAJ&oi=fnd&pg=PT243&dq=Constitutional+Economics+and+the+Law&ots=NLgSw2liHU&sig=HMBBpaghe0EWWapD0YhpeG4_qKM&redir_esc=y#v=onepage&q=Constitutional%20Economics%20and%20the%20Law&f=false.

Voigt, S. *Constitutional Economics. A Primer.* New York: Cambridge University Press, 2020.

Voigt, S. "Constitutional Political Economy." In *The Encyclopedia of Public Choice*, eds. C. K. Rowley, F. Schneider, 436–440. Boston: Springer, 2004.

Voigt, S. "Contracting for Catastrophe: Legitimizing Emergency Constitutions by Drawing on Social Contract Theory." *Res Publica* 28 (2022): 149–172.

Voigt, S. "Das Forschungsprogramm der Positiven Konstitutionenökonomik." In *Unsere Konstitution in gutter Form und Verfassung?*, eds. G. Grözinger, S. Panther, 279–319. Marburg: Metropolis, 1998.

Voigt, S. "Die konstitutionelle Ökonomik als Herausforderung für die Theorie der Wirtschaftspolitik – zugleich eine Skizze zur Weiterentwicklung einer ökonomischen Theorie der Verfassung." In *James Buchanans konstitutionelle Ökonomik*, eds. I. Pies, M. Leschke, 157–183. Tübingen: Mohr, 1996.

Voigt, S., ed. *Constitutional Political Economy*, Vol. I–II. Cheltenham–Northampton: An Elgar Reference Collection, 2003.

Voigt, S. "Empirical Constitutional Economics: Onward and Upward?" *Journal of Economic Behavior & Organization* 80, No. 2 (2011): 319–330.

Voigt, S. *Explaining Constitutional Change. A Positive Economics Approach.* Cheltenham–Northampton: Edward Elgar, 1999.

Voigt, S., Gutmann J. "Challenges in Estimating the Effects of Constitutional Design on Public Policy." In *The Oxford Handbook of Public Choice*, Vol. 2, eds. R. D. Congleton, B. Grofman, S. Voigt, 438–450. New York: Oxford University Press, 2019.

Voigt, S. "How (Not) to Measure Institutions." *Journal of Institutional Economics* 9, No. 1 (2013): 1–26.

Voigt, S. "Implicit Constitutional Change – Changing the Meaning of the Constitution Without Changing the Text of the Document." *European Journal of Law and Economics* 7, No. 3 (1999): 197–224.

Voigt, S. "Mind the Gap: Analyzing the Divergence Between Constitutional Text and Constitutional Reality." *International Journal of Constitutional Law* 19, No. 5 (2021): 1778–1809.

Voigt, S., Park S.-M. "Die Bedeutung von Werten und Normen für langfristige wirtschaftliche Entwicklung." In *Vom Sozialismus zur Marktwirtschaft. Wandlungsprozesse, Ergebnisse und Perspektiven*, eds. K. von Delhaes, W. Quaisser, K. Ziemer, 183–218. München: Olzog, 2009.

Voigt, S. "Positive Constitutional Economics II – a Survey of Recent Developments." *Public Choice* 146 (2011): 205–256.

Voigt, S. "Positive Constitutional Economics: A Survey" In *Constitutional Political Economy in a Public Choice Perspective*, ed. Ch. K. Rowley, 11–53. Drodrecht: Springer, 1997.

Voigt, S. "Veilonomics: On the Use and Utility of Veils in Constitutional Political Economy." In *Behind a Veil of Ignorance? Power and Uncertainty in Constitutional Design*, eds. L. M. Imbeau, S. Jacob, 9–33. Heidelberg: Springer, 2015.

Voigt, S., Wagener, H. J., eds. *Constitutions, Markets and Law. Recent Experiences in Transition Economies.* Cheltenham–Northampton: Edward Elgar, 2002.

Wagener, H.-J., ed. *Demokratisierung der Wirtschaft. Möglichkeiten und Grenzen im Kapitalismus.* Frankfurt–New York: Campus Verlag, 1980.

Wagschal, U. "Deutschlands Steuerstaat und die vier Welten der Besteuerung." In *Wohlfahrtsstaatliche Politik. Institutionen, politischer Prozess und Leistungsprofil*, ed. M. G. Schmidt, 125–142. Opdalen: Leske + Budrich, 2001.

Wagschal, U. "Entwicklung, Determinanten und Vergleich der Staatsfinanzen." In *Regieren in der Bundesrepublik Deutschland. Innen- und Außenpolitik seit 1949*, eds. M. G. Schmidt, R. Zohlnhöfer, 57–85. Wiesbaden: VS Verlag für Sozialwissenschaften, 2006.

Waldner, W. "Private Property and the Transformation Process." In *East Germany's Economic Development since Unification. Domestic and Global Aspects*, eds. J. Hölscher, A. Hochberg, 92–106. Basingstoke–London: Macmillan Press, 1998.

Walter, R. *Einführung in die Wirtschafts- und Sozialgeschichte.* Paderborn: Ferdinand Schöningh, 1994.

Waterkamp, R. *Herrschaftssysteme und Industriegesselschaft: BRD und DDR.* Stuttgart: Verlag W. Kohlhammer, 1972.

Wächter, G. H. "Privatization in East Germany: Success or Failure? Questions from a Transactional Perspective." In *Democracy, Market Economy, and the Law. Legal, Economic, and Political Problems of Transition to Democracy*, eds. W. F. Ebke, D. F. Vagts, 245–258. Heidelberg: Verlag Recht und Wirtschaft GmbH, 1995.

Weber, M. "'Obiektywność' poznania w naukach społecznych." In *Problemy socjologii wiedzy*, eds. A. Chmielecki et al., 45–100. Warszawa: PWN, 1985.

Weber, M. *The Protestant Ethic and the Spirit of Capitalism.* New York: Charles Scribner's Sons, 1958.

Weber, M. *Wirtschaftsgeschichte.* München–Leipzig: Verlag von Duncker & Humblot, 1923.

Weede, E. "Eigentum und Freiheit als Determinanten der wirtschaftlichen Entwicklung." In *Neuer Institutionalismus. Zur soziologischen Erklärung von Organisation, Moral und Vertrauen,* eds. A. Maurer, M. Schmid, 87–106. Frankfurt–New York: Campus Verlag, 2002.

Wehler, H.-U., ed. *Geschichte und Ökonomie.* Köln: Athenäum, 1985.

Weilepp, M. "Das System der rechtlichen Regelungen der Wirtschafts- und Sozialpolitik." In *Elemente der Sozialen Marktwirtschaft. Wirtschaftliche und rechtliche Rahmenbedingungen – Transformationsmöglichkeiten,* eds. K. Fasbender, M. Holthus, E. Thiel, 61–76. Hamburg: Verlag Weltarchiv GmbH, 1991.

Weinberger, O. "Teoria konstytucji w świetle pozytywizmu instytucjonalnego." *Ruch Prawniczy, Ekonomiczny i Socjologiczny* 55, No. 4 (1993): 1–18.

Weingast, B. R. "The Economic Role of Political Institutions: Market-Preserving Federalism and Economic Development." *Journal of Law, Economics, & Organization* 11, No. 1 (1995): 1–31.

Welker, A. M. "Privatisierung und Restitution. Zivilrechtliche Probleme bei der Rückübereignung in den neuen Bundesländern." PhD diss., Frankfurt am Main: Fakultät der Rechtswissenschaft der Johann Wolfgang Goethe-Universität, 1999.

Wendt, R. "Der Finanzausgleich im föderalen System der Bundesrepublik Deutschland." In *Handbuch Föderalismus – Föderalismus als demokratische Rechtsordnung und Rechtskultur in Deutschland, Europa und der Welt,* Vol. II: *Probleme, Reformen, Perspektiven des deutschen Föderalismus,* ed. I. Härtel, 389–423. Berlin–Heidelberg: Springer-Verlag, 2012.

Węc, J. J. "Niemcy." In *Wielka historia świata,* Vol. 12: *Od drugiej wojny światowej do XXI wieku,* ed. W. Rojek, 94–108. Kraków–Warszawa: Oficyna Wydawnicza Fogra, Świat Książki, 2006.

Wielhorski, W. *Ustrój agrarny Z.S.S.R.* Londyn: Instytut Bliskiego i Środkowego Wschodu "Reduta," 1949.

Wieling, H. J. *Sachenrecht.* Berlin–Heidelberg: Springer, 2007.

Wilczynski, J. *The Economics of Socialism. Principles Governing the Operation of the Centrally Planned Economies under the New System.* London: George Allen and Unwin, 1982.

Wiles, P. "Capitalist Triumphalism in the Eastern European Transition." In *The Transformation of the Communist Economies. Against the Mainstream,* eds. H.-J. Chang, P. Nolan, 46–77. New York: St. Martin's Press, 1995.

Wilhelm, J. *Sachenrecht.* Berlin–New York: De Gruyter, 2010.

Wilkin, J. *Instytucjonalne i kulturowe podstawy gospodarowania. Humanistyczna perspektywa ekonomii.* Warszawa: WN Scholar, 2016.

Wilkin, J. "Pogoń za rentą przy pomocy mechanizmów politycznych." In *Teoria wyboru publicznego. Wstęp do ekonomicznej analizy polityki i funkcjonowania sfery publicznej*, red. J. Wilkin, 204–219. Warszawa: WN Scholar, 2005.

Wilkin, J., ed. *Teoria wyboru publicznego. Główne nurty i zastosowania.* Warszawa: WN Scholar, 2012.

Wilkin, J., ed. *Teoria wyboru publicznego. Wstęp do ekonomicznej analizy polityki i funkcjonowania sfery publicznej.* Warszawa: WN Scholar, 2005.

Willgerodt, H. "Wiedereinsetzung der Alteigentümer (Reprivatisierung)." In *Treuhandanstalt. Das Unmögliche wagen*, eds. W. Fischer, H. Hax, H. K. Schneider, 241–262. Berlin: Akademie Verlag, 1993.

Williamson, C. R. "Informal Institutions Rule: Institutional Arrangements and Economic Performance." *Public Choice* 139 (2009): 371–387.

Williamson, O. E. *Ekonomiczne instytucje kapitalizmu. Firmy, rynki, relacje kontraktowe.* Warszawa: WN PWN, 1998.

Williamson, O. E. "The New Institutional Economics: Taking Stock, Looking Ahead." *Journal of Economic Literature* 38, No. 3 (2000): 595–613.

Wittfogel, K. A. *Die natürlichen Ursachen der Wirtschaftsgeschichte.* Rotdruck 1970. Reprint of the original edition: Tübingen: Archiv für Sozialwissenschaft und Sozialpolitik, 1932.

Włudyka, T. *Ordoliberalizm i społeczna gospodarka rynkowa w Niemczech.* Warszawa: Lex a Wolters Kluwer business, 2013.

Wojnarski, D. *Powszechna historia gospodarcza.* Warszawa: Wydawnictwo Poltext, 2004.

Workowski, A. "Etyczne i moralne aspekty posiadania – w oparciu o różne tradycje filozoficzne." In *Własność to odpowiedzialność – wiedza, praktyka, doświadczenie*, ed. B. Rogatko, 31–47. Warszawa-Kraków: Europejski Instytut Nieruchomości, 2009.

Wójtowicz, K. "Otwarcie systemu konstytucyjnego Niemiec na sprawy jedności Europy." *Przegląd Sejmowy* No. 6 (95) (2009): 125–136.

Wrocławskie Studia Erazmiańskie/Studia Erasmiana Wratislaviensia 3 (2009): *Własność – idea, instytucje, ochrona*, eds. M. Sadowski, P. Szymaniec.

Wu, W., Davis, O. A. "The Two Freedoms, Economic Growth and Development: An Empirical Study." *Public Choice* 100, No. 1–2 (1999): 39–64.

Wysokińska, Z., Witkowska, J. *Integracja europejska. Rozwój rynków.* Warszawa: WN PWN, 2002.

Wysokińska, Z., Witkowska, J. *Zrównoważony rozwój. Wybrane aspekty makro- i mikroekonomiczne.* Łódź: Wydawnictwo UŁ, 2016.

Zagóra-Jonszta, U. "Ekonomia klasyczna wobec kategorii własności." *Studia Ekonomiczne* No. 54 (2008): 23–38.

Zagóra-Jonszta, U. "Własność w ujęciu wybranych kierunków myśli ekonomicznej." *Ekonomia i Prawo* 3, No. 1 (2007): 39–59.

Zagóra-Jonszta, U., ed. *Dokonania współczesnej myśli ekonomicznej. Ekonomia instytucjonalna – teoria i praktyka.* Katowice: Wydawnictwo Akademii Ekonomicznej w Katowicach, 2006.

Zagóra-Jonszta, U., ed. *Kategoria własności w ujęciu wybranych kierunków myśli ekonomicznej.* Warszawa: Wydawnictwo WNT, 2015.

Zalesko, M. "Prawa własności filarem rozwoju gospodarczego." *Ekonomia* No. 4 (25) (2013): 92–102.

Zawilska-Florczuk, M., Ciechanowicz, A. *Jeden kraj, dwa społeczeństwa? Niemcy 20 lat po zjednoczeniu.* Warszawa: OSW, 2011.

Zbroińska, B., Gierałka, A. "Obciążenia podatkowe w Polsce i w Niemczech." *Ekonomika i Organizacja Przedsiębiorstwa* No. 1 (2007): 23–29.

Zerres, T. *Bürgerliches Recht. Eine Einführung in das Zivilrecht und die Grundzüge des Zivilprozessrecht.* Heidelberg: Springer, 2010.

Ziegelmayer, V. "Państwo socjalne w Niemczech: zmiana systemu?" In *Państwo socjalne w Europie. Historia – rozwój – perspektywy*, eds. K. Kraus, T. Geisen, K. Piątek, 93–130. Toruń: WN UMK, 2008.

Zieleniewski, J. *Organizacja i zarządzanie.* Warszawa: PWN, 1979.

Zirk-Sadowski, M. *Wprowadzenie do filozofii prawa.* Warszawa: Wolters Kluwer Polska, 2011.

Zwass, A. *The Council for Mutual Economic Assistance. The Thorny Path from Political to Economic Integration.* Armonk–New York: M. E. Sharpe, 1989.

Żurawicki, S., ed. *Historia myśli ekonomicznej.* Wrocław: Ossolineum, 1979.

LIST OF TABLES, FIGURES, AND DIAGRAMS

INDEX OF NAMES

T

Polish Studies in Economics

Edited by Ryszard Kokoszczyński

Vol. 1 Wojciech Grabowski: Employee Stock Options, Payout Policy, and Stock Returns. Shareholders and Option Holders in Large U.S. Technology Corporations. 2012.

Vol. 2 Jan Jakub Michałek / Michał Brzozowski / Andrzej Cieślik (eds.): The Relationship between Human Development, Exports and Foreign Direct Investments in Emerging Europe. 2013.

Vol. 3 Tomasz Żylicz: The Economics of International Environmental Cooperation. 2015.

Vol. 4 Juliusz Jabłecki / Ryszard Kokoszczyński / Paweł Sakowski / Robert Ślepaczuk / Piotr Wójcik: Volatility as an Asset Class. Obvious Benefits and Hidden Risks. 2015.

Vol. 5 Janusz Kudła / Konrad Walczyk / Robert Kruszewski / Katarzyna Kopczewska / Agata Kocia: Modeling Fiscal Policy in the European Union. 2015.

Vol. 6 Andrzej Cieślik / Jan Jakub Michałek (eds.): Liberalization of Transportation Services in the EU: the Polish Perspective. 2015.

Vol. 7 Katarzyna Metelska-Szaniawska: Economic Effects of Post-Socialist Constitutions 25 Years from the Outset of Transition. The Constitutional Political Economy Approach. 2016.

Vol. 8 Elżbieta Czarny / Andżelika Kuźnar / Jerzy Menkes (eds.): The Impact of the Transatlantic Trade and Investment Partnership on International Cooperation. 2017.

Vol. 9 Adam Czarnecki: Going Local? Linking and Integrating Second-Home Owners with the Community's Economy. A Comparative Study between Finnish and Polish Second-Home Owners. 2017.

Vol. 10 Adam Biela (ed.): European Questionnaire for Job Analysis (EQJA). 2018.

Vol. 11 Gabriela Grotkowska: Public-Sector Wage Premium in Poland. 2018.

Vol. 12 Piotr Dybka: What Determines International Competitiveness of the Economy? Evidence from Bayesian Model Averaging. 2022.

Vol. 13 Damian Bębnowski: The Importance of Constitutional Rules and Property Rights. The German Economy in 1990–2015. 2022.

www.peterlang.com

www.ingramcontent.com/pod-product-compliance
Ingram Content Group UK Ltd.
Pitfield, Milton Keynes, MK11 3LW, UK
UKHW041824100926
8556IPUK00002B/12

9 783631 877531